Weimar Intellectuals
and the Threat of Modernity

Weimar Intellectuals and the Threat of Modernity

DAGMAR BARNOUW

Indiana University Press
Bloomington and Indianapolis

This book was brought to publication with the assistance of a grant from the John Simon Guggenheim Memorial Foundation.

Manufactured in the United States of America

Library of Congress Cataloging-in-Publication Data

Barnouw, Dagmar.
  Weimar intellectuals and the threat of modernity.

  Includes index.
  1. Germany—Intellectual life—20th century.
2. Ideology. 3. Civilization, Modern—20th century.
I. Title.
DD239.B37 1988   830'.9'355   87-45246
ISBN 0-253-36427-2

1 2 3 4 5   92 91 90 89 88

Contents

To Jeff and to Edgar Bowers

ACKNOWLEDGMENTS

For their support of the research and writing of this book I thank the Guggenheim Foundation and Brown University. I have had much kind and competent help from the secretaries of the German Department at Brown University, from the staff at the Brown University Library, the München Institut für Zeitgeschichte, the New York Public Library, and the Hoover Institution at Stanford. And from my cheerfully critical husband.

INTRODUCTION

I.

The experience of modernity between the two great European world wars was interpreted by German intellectuals as a cultural crisis. The first part of this study, a case history of intellectual positions during the Weimar period, attempts to trace the development of such interpretation. It gives a tentative general account of how certain ideas or idea clusters emerged, how they fueled important intellectual strategies and affiliations, how they fit or clashed with the different intellectual temperaments and interests which had developed in specific socio-psychological contexts, and how the (often unreflected) processes of modification connected with the little understood dynamics of the life-world were responsible both for the simultaneous existence, that is, conflict, of many distinct ideologies *and* the sense of a distinct Weimar *Zeitgeist*.

This first part is meant to establish a context for the discussion in parts two and three of selected texts by seven authors who have articulated their cultural criticism in the medium of the novel or the essay. I will analyze in these texts the mutual dependency of a perceived crisis of culture and the experienced anxiety of cultural meaning as it was translated into narrative and conceptual strategies. My decision to discuss the question of Weimar intellectuals and Weimar culture in close readings of literary texts, including the essay, has been motivated by several related considerations. As a literary historian interested in the cultural transmission of ideas, I have not been entirely happy with the ways in which historians writing about intellectual and cultural phenomena have drawn on literary texts without risking extensive critical involvement with them. It is not so much a problem of neglecting questions of textual complexity or of fictionality but rather of how such questions are conceived and posed. The substantial literary texts of the period tend to be very much aware of the confusing wealth of contemporary intellectual issues provoked by rapid social and cultural change and of the challenges, inherent in this situation, to develop adequate narrative and conceptual strategies. The proliferation and polarization of ideas as ideologies between the two wars stimulated a new interest in the essayistic novel as "novel of ideas" or "philosophical novel." This is a European phenomenon, but it is particularly striking in Germany. There was a feeling not only that the intellectual excitement and perplexity of the time could and should not be neglected by High Literature, but that the essayistic novel and the literary essay could and would be a good medium to contain it by posing, more rigorously, more profoundly, the question of cultural meaning.

In these literary texts perspectives on cultural phenomena, though influenced by contemporary ideological positions, are explicitly filtered through a distinct intellectual temperament and a self-consciously individual probing of contemporary (natural) language as cultural artifact. For the intellectual historian this means a particularly problematic point of observation. Seeking to gain access to a past reality as social and cultural construct of which he is *and* is no longer a part, he cannot see, much less articulate it in its totality, and yet he has to reflect his partial reconstruction of it in its fragmentedness and partiality. A confrontation with the at once more complete and more subjectively selective construction of reality in contemporary literary texts may serve as a useful corrective to his more objectively comprehensive and less complete reconstruction of past intellectual issues and events. It may be difficult for the intellectual historian to integrate into his differently focused discourse, with a sufficient degree of fairness, the literary text's individuality and ambiguity in (and as a result of) looking at an ideologically charged, conflicted, and confusing contemporary world. But the attempt may result in a troubled yet potentially useful place from which to state observations on the formation and interplay of intellectual positions in their cultural context.

2.

Toward the end of the Weimar period, in 1929, Karl Mannheim saw it as

> imperative in the present transitional period to make use of the intellectual twilight which dominates our epoch and in which all values and points of view appear in their genuine relativity. We must realize once and for all that the meanings which make up our world are simply an historically determined and continuously developing structure in which man develops, and are in no sense absolute.

The intellectuals, Mannheim warns, have to be ready to seize the moment in history when "all things which concern man and the structure and elements of history itself are suddenly revealed to us in a new light." They have to be ready to "become masters of the situation" because this new vision of things in flux might disappear and a static, uniform, inflexible world might reassert itself. In Mannheim's view, the intellectuals need to be prepared for the challenge rather than the threat posed by a modern world in flux, and that includes a readiness to consider, without anxiety of cultural meaning, the presence, in this modern world, of many different ideologies: "Knowledge, as seen in the light of the total conception of ideology, is by no means an illusory experience, for ideology in its relational concept is not at all identical with illusion."[1]

The very lively contemporary discussion of Mannheim's theses presented in *Ideology and Utopia* focused, as he had anticipated, on his proposals for a "non-evaluative insight into history,"[2] that is, on the perceived problem of relativism as the loss of a center of cultural meaning and value from which to look at and speak about social phenomena in their historical context.[3] Such a debate is a culturally important fact. The sociologically, philosophically more interesting reservations[4] had to do with Mannheim's ideal of a "total conception of ideology" and the connected problem of defining criteria for judging ideologies to be, temporarily, "adequate for comprehending the actual world" or to be so no longer (*Seinsadäquatheit* and *Seinsindadäquatheit*).[5]

Mannheim's view of the role of the intellectuals in this context was arguably part of his challenging them to be open to the promises of modernity. As an "unanchored, *relatively* classless stratum . . . , to use Alfred Weber's terminology, the 'socially unattached intelligentsia' *(freischwebende Intelligenz)*"[6] is in a better position than any other group to put into perspective (the other's) false consciousness. Intellectuals are both admonished and reassured in their investigations of false consciousness with its "ideological and utopian distortions,"[7] and their attempts at maintaining an ideological "elasticity," that is, an "experimental outlook, unceasingly sensitive to the dynamic nature of society and to its wholeness."[8]

I am not stressing here Mannheim's desire to find "the road to the sought-for comprehension of the whole,"[9] a metaphysical foundation behind the dynamic comprehensive perspective on all the particular fixed ideologies. This question will be dealt with in part one in the context of a discussion of intellectual responses to ideologies which includes Mannheim's.[10] Here I am concerned with his challenge to the intellectuals not to surrender the position of critical self-awareness regarding their ability to understand social and cultural phenomena,[11] to monitor individualist tendencies and appreciate the fact that men, living in groups, act and think with and against one another.[12] When he states in the first sentence of *Ideology and Utopia*, "This book is concerned with the problem of how men actually think," he has in mind an analysis of the social collectivity of thought. And even though he removes the intelligentsia from such troubled and inevitable rootedness, declaring their position to be the most progressive one, actually less historically and socially conditioned and motivated than the positions of all other groups, he undermines the consistency of his argument[13] rather than his challenge to his contemporaries, notwithstanding the fact that it could not be met.

Ideology and Utopia is important for its diagnostic rather than its prognostic and therapeutic suggestions. Moreover, dealing, in 1929, with very troubling and difficult symptoms, its diagnosis is both perplexed[14] and passionately engaged. If the projected solutions seem too utopian, they are so in the sense in which Mannheim understood utopian thought to be culturally indispensable, namely, as motivating the gradual approximation of utopia toward reality. Utopian thought to him means the process of thinking the present (in)formed by the past into the future rather than the chiliastic merging of past and future so characteristic of Weimar utopianism and

symptomatic of the "darkness" of the time which despaired of *and* demanded a culture-centering concept of absolute truth. To Mannheim, both
the manifest contemporary plurality of thought and—too optimistically—a
general recognition of "the existence of collective-unconscious motivations"
ought to contribute to the debunking of a concept like absolute truth.[15]
Intellectual activities as "the epistemological, the psychological, and the
sociological ways of stating problems" will have to go on without its consolations.[16] Especially the intellectual will have to (and will be able to) refrain
from the "flight into a supra-temporal logic" asserting a pure and unified
truth independent of unconscious motivations;[17] otherwise, he is responsible
for ideological and utopian distortions of reality.

The single most useful provocation to Mannheim's contemporaries
could have been his insistence, in the richly detailed and generally accessible
argumentation of *Ideology and Utopia,* that truth is particular and, more
important, that it is dynamic. He does assign the intellectuals, at least by
implication, a fallaciously absolute sociological place—and this is indeed one
of the great shortcomings of his argument. But he emphatically does not
assign them a position from which to speak with the authority of truth; nor
does he expect them to formulate a systematic critique of ideologies; this is
precluded by the elastic, relational concept of truth as of ideology.[18]

3.

In its firm sociological relationism and historicism influenced by Simmel and
Weber, *Ideology and Utopia* addresses many of the most important issues of
the twenties, a period of heretofore unseen ideological polarization and
utopianist self-delusion.[19] It was, above all, Mannheim's recognition, as a
contemporary, of the disintegration of a new and therefore threatening ideological pluralism into a polarization so intense that it caused the socially
and culturally destructive desire for making total one particular ideology
which would then bring about cultural redemption. The experience of a
decay, a crisis, the (apocalyptic) end of German (High) culture produced
distorted views of the social construct of reality, and it was triggered by the
trauma of modernity in postwar Germany. In assigning the sociologically
most progressive position to the *freischwebend* intellectuals, Mannheim,
aware of their ideologies and utopias, also implored them to review their
thinking.

This, under the circumstances which will be discussed in part one, was
highly unrealistic—quite apart from the always very difficult question of the
dynamics of intellectual influence. Mannheim's argument was introduced
here because his sociological discourse proved to be capable of accommodating the experience of modernity to a degree rarely, if at all, found in contemporary fictional discourse, notwithstanding a number of serious fallacies in
Mannheim's conclusions and formal modernisms in a number of the texts

under consideration. The socioepistemological potential specific to fictional discourse has been largely inactive in these formally sophisticated and complicated texts, which are now part of a canon of High Culture, and the reason for this is to be sought in the largely unexamined ideologies and utopias of their authors in particular and of Weimar intellectuals in general. The fictional mode allows literally the presentation of reality as construct: to paraphrase Sidney, the poet does not lie because he does not affirm a specific reality or truth, he presents a nonassertive model. In the context of a culturally problematic experience of modern pluralism and relativism, he is in the envious position to present a plurality of judgments and values, modes of cognition and consciousness without having to strive for Mannheim's ideal of a "total conception of ideology." It is possible, in fictional discourse, to present experience as conflicted, contradictory, fragmented, temporary, indeed contemporary, and yet be conceptually and structurally consistent— especially in that intriguing Weimar hybrid, the essayistic novel or the literary essay. The total context of ideological perspectives can be, as it were, bracketed, as fictional discourse is less grounded in the situations of the life-world, even if the text-world clearly refers to them. The reader, guided by textual strategies, can negotiate the connection without immediately risking a distorted perspective. This is not to say that the text-world is richer or more meaningful than the life-world—it can be, depending on the text and the reader. But it is arguable that fictional discourse, by its very nature, is pluralistic and relativistic, therefore multivalent,[20] that it grants a certain freedom of interpretative choice to author and reader who share a life-world (which will have to be retrieved as fully as possible by the professional reader as intellectual historian if he is to understand the meaning of such choice; and he has to be aware of the near unavoidable circularity of reading text-world into life-world into text-world—in addition, that is, to his own ideological fixations).

4.

In the case of the novel of ideas and the essay, such interpretative elasticity is in certain ways checked, because the cultural context as complex of contemporary intellectual issues asserts itself as complex of references, including cultural values, which have to be taken into consideration in a more controlled manner. The author of fictional discourse is responsible for constituting the text-world and for mapping it. In the case of the novel of ideas and the essay, such mapping is more self-consciously focused on conceptual strategies which also control important narrative decisions. If intelligible narrative strategies seem to contradict such control, if the authorial (or narrative) voice seems to suggest the full elasticity, the nonassertive mode of fictional discourse, then such a gesture releasing the reader becomes itself an interpretative challenge to the intellectual historian. He will have to ask why the references to contemporary intellectual issues have been obscured in the textual system; that is, he will have to question closely the function of narrative strategies in the production of textual and, in some cases, intertextual meanings.[21] The novel of ideas is still a literary text and shares in the mode of fictionality as I described it above. However, the author is ostensibly trying to integrate conceptual and narrative strategies in ways which are responsible to the meanings of concepts in epistemological and cultural terms. This also means guiding the reader's activities toward such responsibility.

Putting these questions to literary texts, one has to be aware of the ambiguities and ambivalences specific to literary discourse which are a result of its interpretative elasticity. However, this can be to the intellectual historian's advantage. Analyzing them in their relation to the formation, in the text, of ideological fictions, he can see more and different aspects of the cultural significance of these fictions, which is more diffuse and (therefore) more instructive than their stated meanings.[22]

I consider the texts analyzed in this study symptomatic for Weimar intellectual culture also because they do not use the ambiguities inherent in fictionality to support conceptual complexity; but rather to undermine it. I am interested, then, not only in the entrenched ideological readings of Weimar culture which resulted in limiting self-protective fictions to be set against the political and cultural disorder of the time but also in the fact and manner of their presence in the contemporary literary discourse. The structurally open and flexible modern novel of ideas, the multifaceted modern essay with its self-consciously personal voice seem to reflect a mobile questioning intelligence. The developing forms of mixed discourse in the integration of novel and essay seem to be meant to accommodate the presentation of a world expanding and in flux, to explore the potentially exhilarating plurality and variety of modern experience. But they did so very rarely. An anachronistic ideal of German High Culture, in which meaning was centered and secured, confirmed the writers of these texts in their prescriptive rather than experimental, essayistic attitudes toward their contemporary reality. They entrusted their anxiety of meaning and their desire for cultural redemption to literary discourse in the unquestioned, unruptured tradition of High Culture as center of value.

And yet, even if the fictional mode is used in these texts to keep at bay rather than to confront a contemporary reality, even if their ideological and utopian fictions sell short the potential of fictionality, it is impossible to suppress the ambiguities, the hesitations, reservations, contradictions inherent in its relativism and perspectivism. No attentive reader prepared to take seriously a text's literariness can ignore them, and they are the stuff of a shadowy but culturally important alternate history. I did not choose these texts to arrive at yet another indictment of Weimar intellectuals, to demand of them, from hindsight, that they should have seen and interpreted their world differently. Reading them closely, I understood how they could not *and* that they might have done so.

5.

The chapters which make up parts two and three of this study explore different aspects of intellectual conflicts central to the Weimar period, and they are meant to fit themselves into an evolving argument. They are so diverse in perspective and pace, in response to the diversity of the literary texts they investigate, that the argument as a whole may seem to move too slowly or too erratically at times. Nevertheless, I believe that such responsiveness will prove useful.

The first chapter on Rathenau is probably the most immediately accessible on its own terms but not in its relation to the chapters to follow. I have read here an author's cultural criticism *and* his political acts. And while it is true that in Rathenau the conflicts and contradictions central to Weimar culture appear in such extraordinary useful clarity precisely because he combined, to a rare degree, action and reflection, it is also true that reading a person's acts will influence the way in which one reads his texts. Musil (chap. 2) based his protagonist Arnheim, the man with qualities, on the politician and the writer Rathenau. While I am less critical of Rathenau than Musil, my own reading of his texts has certainly been influenced, however subtly, by Musil's brilliantly merciless analyses of Rathenau's indeed instructively flawed reaction to the experience of modernity.

The chapter on Musil, the cultural critic as observer, links Rathenau with Thomas Mann (chap. 3), both of them centrally preoccupied with representing and defending German High Culture. These two writers, both enormously successful, saw their contemporary culture as their personal responsibility and sought to recreate it in their own image, which had been formed by nineteenth-century High Culture. Their particularly literal fascination with cultural fictions seems profoundly anachronistic in hindsight—especially in the context of Rathenau's admirably progressive rational politics in the early twenties; it did not seem so to most of their contemporaries. But this was, of course, an anachronism very common to Weimar culture in general and one of the reasons for its fragility.

The relative unity of the Rathenau and Thomas Mann chapters is partly due to the relative conceptual simplicity of their texts. The chapters on Musil and Benjamin (chap. 4), which examine their very different cultural critiques, do not achieve the same consistency and closure because they have to account for much more complex, occasionally difficult texts. Similarly focused on a German High Cultural tradition to support his own threatened cultural identity, Benjamin's acts of literary-critical recreation were more complicated and opaque, openly contradictory, and more literally directed toward cultural redemption. The difficulties which I encountered trying to locate the principal conceptual conflicts in his work are caused by his particular literary strategies which severely limit accessibility of his texts, and they will be reflected in my critical discussion of his arguments. In Musil's case I move slowly for the opposite reason. Close readings of parts of *The Man without Qualities* are meant to draw attention to conceptual and narrative strategies responsible for his admirably clear fictional presentation of a complex relational modern reality.

The Austrian Musil participated actively in Weimar intellectual culture, as did the Austrian Broch. Their reactions to the experience of modernity were fundamentally and instructively different. Musil, who had written a number of essays on the difficult experience of modernity in postwar Germany, explored in *The Man without Qualities* the Austrian genius for self-deception in fictions of redeeming historical continuity. The analogy to Weimar Germany's powerful (High) cultural conservatism is explicit throughout the text. The novel, functionally essayistic, presents a helpful model for a critique of this, if not in Mannheim's sense, total ideology which encompassed the whole spectrum of intellectual-political affiliations and profoundly influenced all the texts discussed here—with the partial exception of Döblin's. Ernst Jünger's cultural *and* political conservatism (chap. 5), which Benjamin misunderstood in important ways, has a strong echo in Broch's position (chap. 6). Both exhibit a peculiarly aggressive cultural pessimism which calls for redemption through the reinstitution of true community in total rejection of their contemporary modern mass society. Differences between them have to do with attitudes toward technology and the precise nature of true community. I could have usefully discussed together the militant German nationalist and the Austrian-Jewish intellectual with, at times, internationalist sympathies. Instead I chose to bring Broch together with Döblin in this last chapter because I wanted to compare the ways in which they related narrative strategies, above all perspective, to the problem of cultural and individual redemption. Through the elaborately perspectivistic narration of *The Sleepwalkers,* Broch moves his protagonist firmly toward personal and, by proxy, cultural redemption. The utopian fiction of true community as central value asserts itself against narrated social and psychological ambiguities. Through a similarly complex but much more fragmented narration Döblin permits the protagonist of *Berlin Alexanderplatz* a much greater share of the conflicts and confusions of experience. He submits him as an individual to the dangerous dynamics of modern urban life. More, he refrains from solving in the conceptual grid of the novel the general basic dualism between isolation (collectivity) and community, perdition and salvation, accident and redemption. It is supported and articulated in narration to the very end. Even if Döblin finally cannot bear to have his protagonist end his life unredeemed, he does permit him a kind of experience which holds only the possibility of redemption, not its anticipation—a distinction which Benjamin, in his review of the novel, characteristically cannot help fudging. And when it comes it will be, and still precariously so, the protagonist's only. But for Döblin, too, in spite of his very serious attempts in his best novel and several essays of the period, it was still difficult to question rigorously the desire for redemption. He, too, was too much a part of his contemporary intellectual culture still in transition to a less troubled experience of modernity, which would include a more balanced open attitude toward the varieties of cultural meaning.

Part One

Tempted by Distance

Intellectuals and the Grey Republic

1. POLITICS

The current interest in what we now call, with considerable ambivalent fascination, the Weimar period is motivated in part by the passing of more than half a century which enables us to retrieve and articulate events believed lost in the turmoil of Hitler's Thousand Years. More important, though, it is provoked by a contemporary experience of cultural and political crisis which can easily be directed from the last decades of this turbulent century to the extreme political constellations and violent social upheavals characteristic of Germany between the two wars. There is a sense of similarity and affinity with regard to the troubling implications of a modern technocratic mass democracy both increasingly complex as a socioeconomic system and diffuse as a context for political action and cultural identity.

The Weimar Republic, born out of the civil war of the aborted 1918–19 revolution, ended on January 30, 1933, when Hitler "seized" power. Constituted in Weimar as a progressive parliamentary democracy, it had in its last very difficult years become a presidial democracy, that is, in the view of many, a first stage toward dictatorship. Weimar's last *Reichspräsident,* Hindenburg, ancient and venerated, would have liked to appoint on that January 30 a government based on a parliamentary majority exclusive of Hitler's Nationalsozialistische Deutsche Arbeiter Partei (NSDAP). This prototypical Junker loathed what he had been elected to do: rule by decree against extremist onslaughts on the state. His democratic scruples were in part responsible for the fact that since 1930 the state of party politics in Germany had been such that exclusion of extremist parties was impossible. It is the genesis of this situation which is commonly understood to be the most important reason for the political failure of the republic.[1]

From its inception the Weimar Republic had had difficulties regarding the acceptability of parliamentarianism. The electorate's tolerance for conflict and talent for compromise were uncommonly low. The two capabilities are, of course, interconnected, and their mutually reinforced weakness would seriously threaten the success of any parliamentary system. There are many social, cultural, and historical reasons for Germany's spectacular shortcomings in this respect, and they have been researched, described, analyzed, and speculated about in great detail.[2] But though it is true that it was not easy to find sincere, stable, *and* flexible democrats in the military, the bureaucracy, and the judiciary, it is not true, even with respect to these groups, that Germany was, as has often been said, overwhelmingly a republic without republicans.[3] There were many republicans, in many different social and professional groups—with the stunning exception of the intellectuals. In their great majority they were indifferent or hostile to the state which, in spite of its disturbed internal and, at times, almost impossibly strained external situation, had very real democratic potential. Weimar culture in the more narrow sense of the arts, literature, philosophy, theology, political theory, and historiography was very much removed from the daily realities of Weimar's social and political life.[4] This distance, caused by a strangely powerful, seemingly all-pervasive feeling of cultural crisis,[5] may have added to the intellectual mobility and artistic glamour of the period. It also supported a remarkable lack of realism, a curiously eager rejection of the complexity of experience. Many of the intellectual statements on the continuing crisis of Weimar thus seem evasive and anemic in spite of their formal sophistication and conceptual intricacy.

The intellectuals' sense of crisis interfered with attempts at testing the various intellectual and artistic constructs against the shared life-world of a twentieth-century mass society beset by internal political struggle, strong pressures in foreign politics, and rapid developments in technology—that is, by open conflict of interests in all areas of social organization. Fragmentation and mechanization were seen as dangerous threats to cultural cohesiveness and meaningfulness, and they were easily connected with the "Grey Republic" which was so hard to identify with. It is not only the fictions created by intellectuals on the right and the left which point to the fear of and intolerance for the experience of fragmentation and mechanization. There are also the statements by intellectuals who are considered to have been supportive of democracy. Karl Jaspers in his 1931 sketch of the mentality of the period, *Die geistige Situation der Zeit,* praises Rathenau's 1912 *Zur Kritik der Zeit* as one of the most widely discussed "mirrors of our world" for its still highly valid "penetrating analysis of the mechanization of our life."[6] As will be shown in the first chapter of this study, Rathenau's text presents an emotionally charged total rejection of contemporary cultural developments rather than a rationally accessible analysis of certain difficult aspects. Jasper's *Die geistige Situation der Zeit,* notwithstanding the fact that his existential philosophy generally promotes freedom, democracy, and pluralism, defines the existential feeling of the period as an *"awareness of danger and loss,* as the awareness of radical crisis."[7] As Jaspers saw it, the most threatening symptoms were technology and the machine ("Apparat") as conditions for the existence of the masses, the rule of the masses, and the tension between the technical organization of the masses and the world of human existence, which was therefore profoundly ruptured.[8]

Then there is the liberal historian Friedrich Meinecke, who encouraged his students to give the republic a chance: "If we cannot have what we would love, let us love what we have"[9]—an ambivalently reasonable statement, especially in view of the fact that Meinecke, together with men like the sociologist Max Weber and the political scientist Hugo Preuss, had been a prominent founding member of the Deutsche Demokratische Partei (DDP), which was largely responsible for formulating the Weimar Constitution and above all interested in achieving a long-lasting reconciliation between the bourgeoisie and the working class.[10] His 1924 *Idee der Staatsraison in der neueren Geschichte* shows the considerable changes in attitude Meinecke had undergone since his 1908 *Weltbürgertum und Nationalstaat,* which idealized the birth of Bismarck's Prussia. But in spite of his sincere liberalism and his support for the republic, he continued to be deeply uneasy about a state that was incessantly and painfully involved in negotiating conflicts of interests. Instinctively he preferred to see politics as the concerns of a culturally and politically unified *Volksstaat*. In that he did not differ all that much from Moeller van den Bruck's radically conservative concept of the state developed in his 1923 *Das Dritte Reich* that seemed so much more successful in satisfying the longings of the young radical students who were not interested in rational historical-political discourse of the kind Meinecke had to offer.[11]

Thomas Mann had become quite rapidly Germany's most celebrated democratic intellectual after his dramatic conversion to the cause of the republic in the early twenties, following his intensely conservative nationalistic 1918 *Betrachtungen eines Unpolitischen* (Reflections of a nonpolitical man). His intellectual temperament required harmony with and representation of his cultural environment, rather than strife and opposition. But his retreat to the *nunc stans* and hermetic alchemical pedagogy of the highly successful *Magic Mountain* (1924) unmistakably left behind the sociopolitical turmoil and cultural uncertainties of the Weimar Republic. He, too, admonished audiences—students on the right, workers on the left—to love what they had gotten even if it was not what they had wanted, unconcerned with the nature of their explosive confused yearnings. There was also Martin Buber, whose philosophy of dialogue in the 1923 *Ich und Du* communicated ethical and pedagogical impulses which were of undeniable value to a developing democratic community. But he firmly restricted questions of freedom and justice to the relations between individuals, preventing them explicitly from extending to the area of interaction between the individual and the state. The state, the Weimar Republic, was gravely threatened, Buber saw, by the irrationalism of mass movements. But for him salvation was only to be found in the individual, not in political organization seeking to balance the rational and irrational energies of the human mind.[12]

The intellectuals' deep-rooted sense of a cultural crisis could not be assuaged by a vaguely positive view of the republic's political future. Even declared republicans did not envision a viable Weimar culture, and as for the intellectuals on the right and the left: they saw the task of constructing a cultural environment as outright adversary, involving repeated acts of protest against Weimar politics and its social structures. This, of course, has been true for many historical periods and locations, but it was true for Weimar to a very extreme degree. The reasons for this situation will have to be sought in the social and cultural history of intellectual positions in Germany.

2. POWER

Who or what (exactly) is an intellectual? An intellectual, said Maurice Barrès, perhaps the first to attempt a definition of this slippery species, is an artist or an academic who, notwithstanding his total lack of political power, projects and proposes social ideals.[13] The nationalist Barrès was reacting angrily to the 1898 manifesto signed by 102 "intellectuals" protesting the assaults on the truth in the Dreyfus case committed by militarism, clericalism, and anti-Semitism. Barrès's anger was ill informed: the protestors were by no means exclusively academics and artists; they came from various professions and occupational situations,[14] and they did not reject the obligations of national loyalty. It was, they argued, precisely such loyalty to the nation as a whole that had caused them to oppose the web of particular lies, based on particular interests and endangering a concept of truth that should be supported by a civilized nation. Politically powerless the intellectuals projected social ideals against the status quo upheld by the powerful, insisting on their personal perspective as the source and legitimation of such critical authority. Yet, Barrès's definition, commonly understood as defamation of the intellectuals, points to certain problematic aspects of the intellectuals' position and function in society: their attitude toward power and the ways in which this attitude informs their perspective on a social reality.

In his 1975 study of power, *Macht*, Niklas Luhmann rejects Alvin Gouldner's much-acclaimed critique of Talcott Parsons's power theory[15] as treating power too much as a symbolically generalized medium of social relations, that is, identifying power too easily and closely with legitimate "established power," the exercise of power as the normal state of affairs. In view of the brutality and selfishness of the powerful, Parsons's view of power is dismissed by Gouldner as astonishingly unrealistic and misleading. "This astonishment on the part of a sociologist," comments Luhmann,

> is itself astonishing to sociologists, even more so because it is formulated in the framework of a sociology of sociology. Of course, it is indisputable that sociology can and should concern itself with the phenomena of the brutal and selfish exercise of power. Such an interest, however, should not grow into a prejudiced view concerning social reality built into concepts and theories.
>
> The real achievement of Parsons's theory was to replace the prejudices of sociology as a science of crisis and opposition with a relatively autonomous conceptual architectonic (one thus open in its turn to criticism). However one judges the adequacy of this analytical apparatus, it is indisputable that the institutionalization of enforceable legitimate power is a phenomenon of greater social import, in comparison with brutality and selfishness. Everyday social life is determined to a much greater extent by recourse to normalized power, i.e., legal power, than by the brutal and selfish exercise of power. . . . Intervention by legitimate force is more considerable; one simply cannot think it away without disrupting and transforming almost all normal social life. Brutality and selfishness are phenomena which are compatible with many social conditions so long as they do not undermine the dominance of institutionalized power. Such an argument, of course, does not justify any single brutal act, and, moreover, does not justify tolerating or accepting it, as one knows from the history of religion and of the distribution of welfare. But this kind of accounting problem is really secondary—both historically and theoretically. It presumes the introduction of a

binary schematism to differentiate debit from credit, or right from wrong, or conformity from non-conformity.[16]

Treating power as "symbolically generalized communication medium" and placing analyses of power "in the context of the larger society in this way,"[17] enables the sociologist, as Luhmann sees it, to gain a more realistic perspective *(theoria)* on the ever "larger, more complex and more strongly differentiated social systems. In order to bridge a greater degree of differentiation, these systems develop more highly generalized and, at the same time, more highly specialized communication media and coordinate with these media the societally more significant part-systems."[18]

Luhmann's sociological functionalism continues to be controversial, particularly his insistence on the reduction of complexity as the most important performance of (social) systems. Following Max Weber, he does emphasize that social systems are those "constituted and operating through the communication of meaning *(Sinn),*" but he does not share Weber's concern with the subjectivity of meaning; that is, he does not define meaning by means of the subject but rather defines the subject by means of meaning. He is not, then, concerned so much with what makes meaning possible as with what meaning makes possible.[19]

Luhmann's emphasis on the reduction of complexity is a response to the challenges posed by the evolutionary complexity of social systems. In contrast to the German intellectual tradition of a specifically critical attitude toward modernity, he stresses the evolutionary superiority of abstractness over concreteness, artificiality over naturalness, mobility and uncertainty over stability and certainty. Preoccupation with values insofar as they support too exclusively a critique of modern society is rejected, as values, in Luhmann's view, constitute only crudely selective devices for reducing complexity, suitable for premodern stages of social development. As any evolutionary development, social evolution tends inevitably to greater complexity. It is useless to lament it, harmful to ignore it; the task is, rather, to devise a reduction of this complexity through evolving subsystems which are constantly growing in number, sophistication, and differentiation.

Luhmann is a sociologist who writes in the last third of the twentieth century, which has witnessed a particularly accelerated proliferation of social subsystems, generalization and specialization of communication, concentration but also distribution of power. It has also witnessed brutality and selfishness, a misuse of power on a scale heretofore unexperienced and therefore unforeseen. Weimar intellectuals wrote in the first third of the twentieth century when many symptoms of accelerated social evolution were clearly visible, but not—at least not to the same degree—specific forms of the concentration of power and its enormous potential for misuse. There is a dangerous temptation to read Weimar texts too much from the perspective of the failure of that most confusedly complex system, the Weimar Republic, and with the hindsight of half a century which has accumulated detailed information about the rule of a barbarous but by no means premodern regime as successful in its use of systemic complexity and diversity as in its elimination of human complexity and plurality. If one gives in to this temptation, one might ask too much and too little of these texts.

Luhmann's inversion of the relation between the subject and meaning is overstated, and his concept of sociological functionalism is overly technical, tending, occasionally, to invocation rather than analysis of complexity. But his approach to the phenomenon of power—developed, no doubt, in reaction to certain traditions in German social thought with its strong philosophical tendencies—is very useful in our context, as it clarifies important intellectual preoccupations which proved to be detrimental to a more pragmatic, realistic perspective on modernity.[20] Values like community, freedom, emancipation, justice, and equality assumed very different properties within different sets of cultural-political priorities. But they were invariably defined against an existing contemporary social reality, which was unstable, torn by conflict of interests, changing, open-ended, and their source was the intellectual's authority based on subjective meaning. The intellectual right mourned the loss of a central, all-embracing system of values; the intellectual left regained and programmed it into a more or less distant future; the liberal center hovered uneasily between both poles. But in each case there was an individual choice concerning a general set of values, and insistence on the unique importance of that choice tended to remove questions of values from discussion, compromise, or consensus. This has been particularly true for the German tradition since the turn of the century where intellectual self-consciousness had been centered so much in a stance against establishment power.

Arguing against, rather than merely analyzing, the status quo—that is, arguing against the contemporary state of (social) affairs—intellectuals have traditionally assumed a position distinct from that state of affairs and have claimed such distinctness and distance as clarification of their social perception, as substance of their lack of self-interest and of their social responsibility. They have seen themselves engaged in the responsibly critical articulation of issues related to contemporary sociopolitical problems. In the act of articulation they have claimed authority for the selection and formulation of those issues and addressing an ill- or misinformed silent majority which enables the powerful to (mis)use power, they have accepted the responsibility for these less-than-adult masses. The intellectual has seen himself meeting the obligation to articulate the truth about the other, that is, more often than not, the passive (lack of information, interest, involvement) or active (using power) distortion of truth for which the other is responsible. This implies an obligation on the part of the other to listen: the intellectual is expected to speak and he expects to be heard.

Both expectations have their source and support in the intellectual community rather than society at large. The silence of intellectuals is easily overheard outside the intellectual community, though it is judged to be betrayal inside this community. When Karl Kraus wrote in *Die Fackel,* "zu

Hitler fällt mir nichts ein" (what can you say about Hitler), and then proceeded to say nothing, because language was inadequate to the monstrous,
the highly influential investigative journalist and philosopher of language was
violently attacked by many intellectuals for his silence as well as for drawing
attention to it.[21] Significantly, in the summer of 1983, French intellectuals
found themselves accused of desertion because of their silence regarding the
Socialist Mitterand government. The accusation was made by intellectual
members of this government who considered themselves both part of and,
temporarily, outside of the intellectual community and who felt betrayed by
its silent majority. They could not move the intellectuals to address themselves to specific mainly economic difficulties confronting the Mitterand
government, much less to grant these problems the dignity of "a historic
moment." There is, of course, the old utopian dream of the philosopher-king,
now merged, like a vaguely benevolent deistic principle, with a classless
society at the end of time. But the intellectual left in France could not be
tempted.

   Asked for the reasons for their silence, a few of them spoke: intellectuals, they said, are supposed to be critical of the government in power, not
supportive—does this government want our criticism? If a leftist government
is criticized—does this not suggest that the intellectual critic speaks from a
position on the right? Mitterand's government is mainly plagued by economic
difficulties—a matter for the specialized expert rather than the generalist
intellectual. However, the main argument against verbal participation in the
leftist government pointed to the fact that the left, in power, had become
doctrinaire, embracing their own status quo, removed from the intellectual
left. It seems that the intellectual left can analyze the political reality of
power only from a distance; they are, in fact, not too much, but too little
removed from the left in power; it is their proximity that leads to silence.

3. WAR AND REVOLUTION

In a similar situation German intellectuals might have been less hesitant to
speak, that is, to speak critically. In Germany intellectuals and politicians
have traditionally been engaged in confrontation rather than communication:
when the Social Democratic Chancellor Helmut Schmidt boasted in 1975
that all intellectuals had been banned from participation in his cabinet, he
echoed August Bebel's warning at the 1903 Dresden meeting of the Social
Democratic party to beware of the intellectuals. German intellectuals on the
left and right have been more intensely, more unambiguously antibourgeois
and antiliberal than their French counterparts[22]—not to mention the situation in England;[23] on the left they have also been more antinationalist. The
ninety-three academics and artists who signed the appeal "An die Kulturwelt" in October 1914, pledging their support to the monarch and the war
effort in defense of German Culture which was, in their eyes, so profoundly
threatened by Western Civilization, were too established in their culture to

indulge in projections of a different, better, ideal alternative.[24] They affirmed and identified, where the intellectuals who had signed the Dreyfus manifesto had articulated a critical distance. Consequently they were accused of being corrupted by power and of criminal warmongering by the group of intellectuals associated with the lively, influential, leftist and pacifist, artistically innovative journal *Die Aktion*.[25] The *Die Aktion* group, in turn, felt secure in their total rejection of sociopolitical power which they equated much too simply with violence and aggression. Their dogmatically internationalist, antiestablishment position prevented them from considering the motivations of these supporters of the "ideas of 1914"[26] as well as the multivalent reality of power as "a relational world unto itself, with its own tensions, its own values, its own structure, equipping it to negotiate on equal terms with other conceptual worlds."[27]

The history of the group of writers around *Die Aktion* during World War I could be read as part of a case history of many Weimar intellectuals—on the left *and* the right—tracing, that is, their particular vulnerability to ideology, not as an instrument of power, but as a fiction enabling its constructor to disregard social reality and the complexity of power and to deny the implications of an elite status. The sincerity and consistency of their pacifist stance was and is impressive, but as the war went on and the great majority of those who had signed the 1914 appeal retreated into a neutral survival mode of (intellectual) existence or became opposed to the war, the pacifists around *Die Aktion* became increasingly sectarian and antirealistic. Where they had, in the beginning, tried to maintain a community of imaginatively critical individuals, a group that could accommodate conflict, they increasingly perceived themselves as members of a congregation,[28] willing to be catechized, ready to excommunicate everyone who had committed a "sin against the spirit," that is, the *Geist* of the *Aktion* as defined by the charismatic editor Franz Pfemfert. To be involved in pacifist activities was meaningful in that it was a preparation for the world to come, the New World of the New Man characterized by *Geist, Bewegung* (motion), *Aktivität*.

The patron saint of this intellectual activism was Heinrich Mann whose 1910 essay "Geist und Tat" calling for a spiritualization of politics was originally published in Alfred Kerr's journal *Pan* but quickly became a manifesto for the contributors to *Aktion*, reaffirming them in their total rejection of Wilhelminian society and politics. Whereas the argument in this essay was rather cloudily abstract, Mann's 1915 essay on Zola—one of his most widely read and most influential pieces which was to become the focus of his brother Thomas's attack on *Zivilisationsliteraten* in his 1918 *Betrachtungen eines Unpolitischen*—drew on French intellectual and social history in its construction of the ideal counterimage intellectual hero slaying the dragon of corrupt power. The essay was published in René Schickele's *Die Weissen Blätter*, a journal much less ideologically committed, much more cosmopolitan than *Die Aktion*.[29] But it evaluated much too positively the achievements of French democracy, disregarding the sociopolitical stagnation of the Third Republic and projecting unrealistically an idealized convergence of the people and the intellectuals.[30]

It was the wishful projection of the innate good sense of the people to take the intellectuals' point that made the Dreyfus case such an attractive foundation-myth for a tradition of the intellectuals' unshakable stance against power *and* claim to be heard—if not by those who controlled power, then by those who generally condoned such control. This myth was reinforced by a growing cult of the masses among Marxist intellectuals who were not active in organized labor, for instance, the members of the *Aktionsgemeinde*. "This Marxist cult of the 'masses,'" writes the Belgian socialist Henry de Man in his 1926 *Psychology of Socialism*,

> is the expression of a tendency of certain intellectuals towards the "projection" of their own aspirations (born of their own impatience, and of a reaction against impotence of a social stratum to which they belong) upon a great X, which at any rate has the advantage for them—of being an unknown quantity. . . . What the Marxists dream of getting from the masses is really a new leadership; their cult of the masses is another form of hero worship. The unknown masses are imaginatively endowed with all the heroic lineaments which are not discoverable in the organized workers and their leaders.[31]

Henry de Man had his Marxist faith shaken "to its foundations" through his wartime experience as a Belgian volunteer. Ardent antimilitarist and internationalist, he felt it his duty to take up arms against Germany. He was as disillusioned at the collapse of the International as at the instinctive nationalism of even socialist members of the working class and estranged from many of his former Marxist associates who joined the Bolshevik camp. From a position of economic determinism he moved "to the standpoint of a philosophy wherein the main significance is allotted to the individual human being as subject to psychological reactions."[32] The result of this changed perspective was a highly interesting and useful study of workers' reactions to their working conditions that developed out of his teaching at the Frankfurt "Akademie der Arbeit" in the midtwenties: *Der Kampf um die Arbeitsfreude* (The fight about dedication to work) based on the reports of seventy-eight industrial and office workers.[33]

It is significant that de Man's decision to ask "who exactly are the masses, and what do workers actually think or feel about their work?" was triggered by his experiences in wartime which forced him to look at rather than look away from a sociopsychological reality. *Die Aktion* had started out as an important forum for *junge Literatur* around 1910. The century was young and hopes for cultural renewal centered on the young, on their self-presentation in lyric poetry and the arts. Pfemfert's generosity toward individual artistic achievement, his intellectual curiosity and excitability had contributed largely to the appeal and success of his journal. But in contrast to the Belgian intellectual de Man, he and his followers were led by their war experience to stress the prophetic authority rather than the communicative potential of poetry, to celebrate the New Man rising out of the apocalypse of the war rather than coax the old familiar one struggling to survive it. More and more the messianic yearnings of these intellectuals separated them from "the people" to whom they wanted to explain the meaning of the apocalypse and to whom they looked for cultural meaning. The result was a strangely ambiguous concept of the sociocultural role of the intellectual: speaking for the people, the masses, they relied on the authority of their autonomous abstract idealizing construct of "the masses" *and* on having been given a mission—to speak the truth for and about the masses—by this, their own, construct. The political opportunities inherent in such ambiguity are considerable and have been exploited by shrewd political leaders, but the intellectuals were neither intent on nor equipped for such exploitation. They argued, rather, in the good faith of their own unexamined motivations.

Beginning April 17, 1915, Pfemfert published a column entitled "Ich schneide die Zeit aus"—newspaper clippings which exposed the social hypocrisy, lies, and stupidities that make up the militant mentality without which no war could or would be fought. Those documents must have shown him the vulnerability of men and women whose social behavior had been distorted grotesquely by the moral inversion caused by the fact that "there was a war on." They came from a seemingly inexhaustible supply of bloodthirsty children's literature, religious sermons celebrating national purification through blood and pain, and hideously heroic poetry written by mothers who professed themselves eager to sacrifice their sons on the altar of the fatherland. But Pfemfert was not so much saddened by human frailty as in despair over human depravity; both went unexplained. His stated aim was to document social corruption on a metaphysical scale and declare his distance to it. The November 1918 issue of *Die Aktion* affirmed the journal's achievement: "We, however, can hold our heads high before mankind. A people of seventy million—and one single small weekly represented, in August of 1914, the position of unconditional antimilitarism, humanity, conscience!"[34] The *Aktionsgemeinde* had proved to be totally incorruptible. The group's view of itself as the chosen people, radically different from the corrupted, sinful world around it, supported the missionary certainty with regard to the Coming of the New Man.

In the introduction to his documentation of a world in the state of moral chaos Pfemfert asserted that his answers to the questions posed by the contemporary situation had preceded them: he had known what was coming, had judged it, and nothing would make him change his mind.[35] In publishing clippings from the time he would, silent himself, make the period speak for itself, that is, against itself. Affirming his own silence was among other things a shrewd move against the censor, but the selection of material was, of course, a very eloquent commentary. The questions posed by this society of which he wanted no part reflected situations much more ambiguous, complex, contradictory, and torn by warring interests than Pfemfert was ready or able to see, and so his answers were premature and simplistic to the point of being detrimental to developing a concept of a better social order. More important, they prevented the planning and carrying out of strategies needed to bring about a situation in which one could think concretely of a new order.

What Pfemfert cut out and preserved during those war years is often terrifying—not the least his clippings from the official Social Democratic paper *Vorwärts* which Pfemfert liked to call "blutbesudelt" (spattered with blood).[36] The tribal aggressiveness and wishful rhetoric characteristic of the *Vorwärts* style were especially disturbing during the first two years of the war and easy targets for Pfemfert. Yet, the editorial policies of *Vorwärts* reflected a host of extremely difficult, entangled problems with which the Social Democrats had had to come to terms since the first Morocco Crisis in 1905. The party's voting record on the question of war credits could indeed have suggested opportunistic collaboration with the bourgeoisie—a view taken by Pfemfert and other intellectuals of the nonorganized left. But there were numerous specific and powerful pressures on the party executive, especially during those hectic days in July 1914. Since 1905 the impatience with parliamentary tactics had grown. Kautsky's attempts to strengthen a "Marxist center" against the "rebel's impatience" in the left wing and the "statesman's impatience" in the right wing of the party were very timely in 1910,[37] but they were increasingly difficult to carry through in the crisis to come. By 1912 the radicals worked against the party's advocacy of international armament limitations, concentrating on the fight against German nationalism and militarism and invoking, for support, the innate good judgment of the masses. Such a strategy of revolutionary isolation[38] added greatly to the difficulties of the party executive which saw itself caught between the radicals' call for mass strikes and their growing mistrust in the party and, on the other hand, a growing antilabor sentiment, beginning with the 1912 Ruhr strike. Worst of all, the great majority of the workers seemed dangerously indifferent.

At the last general congress of a united Social Democratic party in Jena in 1913, left-center and radicals voted against the military tax bill, right-center and right wing voted for it, persuaded by the—as it turned out—correct revisionist argument that the workers would be burdened with even worse taxation should the bill not be passed. Equally correct was Luxemburg's warning that voting *en bloc* for the bill meant voting for war credits in case of a war. There was a real dilemma, and the majority of the party had not collaborated blindly with the bourgeoisie. In 1914, the July 25 manifesto against the war was made possible partly by the absence from Berlin of several party leaders, especially Scheidemann (whom Pfemfert hated most passionately) and Ebert; the executive under Hugo Haase's leadership had interpreted the majority mood as opposed to the war and called for a mass demonstration. The second manifesto of July 30, when war seemed unavoidable, was arguably compromised by weakness and fear. And yet, many of those fears were only too understandable. Even an observer like Pfemfert might have been expected not to reject them as simple chauvinism and cowardice but to make some attempts at appreciating the threats, to the party leaders, of a state of siege, the effects of the precarious promises made by the government not to arrest them, if they "behaved themselves," their fear of the party contributing to a German defeat, of losing the support of the majority of the workers who at this point seemed to identify strongly with the fate of the nation. And then there was—inaccessible to Pfemfert, but very real and shared by the majority of the party—the need to belong to a larger community, that is, to participate in the temporarily overwhelming experience of falling sociopolitical barriers,[39] the desire to contribute to the *Burgfriede* which the emperor had proclaimed, asking for a cessation of party strife while the *Burg* (castle) Germany was attacked on all sides.

The *Burgfriede* was short, though not entirely an illusion. More important, it had very serious consequences for the party in terms of strengthening its reformist course and discipline. This development, however, was by no means a homogeneous process. The radicals under the leadership of Karl Liebknecht immediately went to work on constructing an opposition to the war credits. Even *Vorwärts* became a problem to the party executive because of its frequently oppositionist stand. There were minority petitions against the government's annexation politics, early calls to negotiate for peace *(Verständigungsfriede)*, e.g., the June 1915 document drafted by Bernstein, Haase, and Kautsky; there were radical and left-center votes against war credits. Also, perhaps most spectacularly and certainly most importantly in terms of later intellectual attitudes toward a sociopolitical reality, the leadership of the radicals and the left-center worked mainly in opposition to the executive *and* to each other from 1915 on.

The revolutionary isolation from reality, so characteristic for many politically concerned and involved intellectuals during the war, carried over to Weimar intellectuals on the right and the left. It found different outlets, as radical politics on the left were discouraged by the growing influence of the organized Communist party under the direction of the Soviet Union and on the right were too primitive to attract intellectuals. Politics, for the intellectuals, became literary politics—in a wide sense. But this, too, had been true for the immediate prewar period and part of the war period.

Pfemfert's *Aktion* had continued to be a forum for "junge Literatur," supporting lyric poetry as the most significant medium for statements on a social reality during wartime. By 1916, his concept of what was meaningful poetry was changing. That year his friend and contributor Ferdinand Hardekopf, today only remembered as the masterful translator of André Gide but a poet much admired by the avant-garde around 1910,[40] left Germany, unable to tolerate any longer the increasingly militaristic climate. In Zürich he joined Dada's literary activism for a while and then stopped writing altogether. In order to compose his formally sophisticated, intricate frontal attacks on the Wilhelminian bourgeoisie he needed the position of the outsider, the position, that is, of the uncompromising intellectual critic of his society. His eventual withdrawal had been prefigured in his texts—a fact appreciated by his friend Ludwig Rubiner who was unambiguously a member of the *Aktionsgemeinde,* highly important to Pfemfert as a comrade in arms and much more directly a political man than Hardekopf.

In a 1916 essay on Hardekopf, "Das Paradies in Verzweiflung" (Paradise in despair),[41] a review of what he considered to be excellent poetry written by a close personal and political friend whose integrity he greatly admired, he pointed to the unsolvable conflicts inherent in Hardekopf's position of unconditional alienation. Agreeing with Hardekopf's well-wrought rejection of a world created by (other) men, he also understood, much more clearly than Pfemfert, for example, or, later, many intellectuals during the Weimar period, the fragility of a creative minority with a highly selective awareness of sociopolitical issues and an intensely individualistic social conscience. Rubiner was able to analyze the problematic relationship between the independent, original, insightful, highly talented individual and the group as he was aware of the complicated psychological interplay of needs, desires, projections, fantasies.[42] Pfemfert, who stands here for many intellectuals hoping and working, in one way or the other, for radical change, was either unable to perceive such interplay or did not wish to deal with it. He never questioned his own intellectual authority, nor did he measure its source: namely, his claim to be in possession of the truth about the other and therefore called upon to speak, for him, against a social reality constituted by and shared with his contemporaries. It was this reliance on the subjective authority of the intellectual and of his mission that continued to inform the intellectuals' fictions between the two wars.

From the end of 1916 on, the majority of lyric texts published in *Die Aktion* show a cosmic indefiniteness, an extension, then fragmentation of perception, a growing numbness of imagery, refusing to register any but the most violent sensory stimuli. The syntax is shattered in the characteristic style of "Hochexpressionismus." These poems seek to articulate the experience of insufferable pain—often they were written in the trenches—and the desperately needed, aggressive hope for the Coming of the New Man. By the end of 1917 Pfemfert had come to doubt altogether the social usefulness or function of literature produced by a small minority of specifically talented individuals. But doubting so totally the significance of the individual voice he relied, again, entirely on his individual subjective authority. In the December 15, 1917, issue he published an essay by Franz Blei on the relations between social class and literary taste. Blei, an influential, imaginative, and generous man of letters and critic, who had helped many young writers, argued that the *Volk's* literary tastes were conservative and that the production and appreciation of literature in the more narrow sense would not survive without the educated taste to be found in the educated ruling classes. The proletariat, for their own good, would have to be willing to draw on the intellectual, creative resources of the defeated class. Pfemfert, in a postscript, countered this skeptical view: "It cannot be my task to talk down to the proletariat and presume to teach them. Rather, the proletariat has shown infinite kindness in sending us intellectuals a short way ahead."[43]

When Lenin later used his version of this vanguard theory for very obvious political reasons, Pfemfert was adamantly opposed to this cynical realpolitik—as were Rosa Luxemburg and Karl Liebknecht, all of them hopeful believers in the innate goodness and spontaneous common sense of the proletariat as a platonic idea. Especially in difficult times, such abstractions can be (mis)perceived as a considerable source of strength. When sociopolitical questions become so fraught with conflict of interest and ambiguity of interpretation, it seems natural to fabricate and formulate an authority which preserves and transcends the individual's knowledge. This can be achieved by deferring to a total perspective which clearly demarcates the all-encompassing camps of good and bad and entails a mission. It is precisely such deference that can be most easily distorted, obscuring, often irreversibly, the view of the richness of and undermining the tolerance for the ambivalence of the contemporary life-world.

One of the most impressively clear parables for this process can be found in the Swedish writer Sven Delblanc's 1980 novel *Speranza*[44] which traces the development of a young idealistic Swedish intellectual of the eighteenth century. The young count Putbus finds himself, by a combination of accident and incompetence, aboard a slave ship bound for the West Indies. He is slow to grasp the situation, but by and by the stench emanating from the ship's belly, where the blacks are held in unspeakable captivity, and his sexual craving for a negress combine to undermine his ability, achieved through the civilizing influences of education, to negotiate bondage through social intercourse. Enslaved by his desire for the black woman he totally enslaves her in acts of terrible intimacy and ends up believing the stated mission of the ship *Speranza*—to be instrumental in the transmission of the subhuman blacks to a better life.

As the situation on board grows more and more desperate, the concept of a better life becomes literally enshrouded in passage through death and Putbus becomes an expert killer in the service of the captain's authority based on the ship's mission. This process rewinds, as it were, civilization as the learned tolerance for human plurality and diversity. Putbus's arguments in support of his actions are curiously close to statements coming from young activists on the extreme right discussed later in the chapter on Walter Rathenau. But while the dynamics of ideology during the Weimar period translated more easily into physical aggression—or its verbal celebration— on the nationalist right than on the internationalist left, they were structurally similar on both sides of the political spectrum and they developed rapidly during the Great War.

In the November 17, 1917, issue Pfemfert asked for contributions to an anthology, *Jüngste Aktive Lyrik,* warning prospective contributors that it was activism rather than "mere" literature he was looking for. He was unwilling to take a chance on the ambiguity of poetry which might suggest the ambiguity of experience. Pfemfert wanted the lines drawn clearly: poetry was to be written exclusively in the mission of preaching the Coming of the New Man

and the Revolution which would, finally, annihilate the ambiguity of civilization. In 1924 he declared the death of literature altogether. His journal had
become frantically sectarian, one of the many "isms" supported by the
authority of a particular and total mission that fed the factional battle raging
on the left. The sense for reality had shrunk to a degree which seems fantastic
from hindsight. When Ernst Toller,[45] one of the intellectual leaders of the
short-lived 1919 Munich *sovjet*, had shown himself sufficiently sensible not
to resist "to the end" the Free Corps[46] sent in by the Social Democratic
government in an ill-considered effort to halt political radicalization and
chaos, but was put on trial for high treason anyway, Pfemfert attacked him
viciously from his extreme left position that supported "pure" political
action. Toller had tried desperately to avoid senseless carnage—Pfemfert
called him an "ambitious, politically naive mama's boy," "a coward totally
lacking in dignity."[47]

"True democracy" as "rule of the workers" had been the radicals'
demand set against attempts to organize elections for a national assembly
representing a wide spectrum of political interests.[48] The assembly which
finally took place in Weimar in 1919 elected the Social Democrat Friedrich
Ebert as its first president and symbol of compromise. After the 1917 Gotha
schism which had consolidated the left in its opposition to center and right,
the leadership of the (old) Social Democratic party had become more narrowly reformist in a highly volatile situation. But where they had mistrusted
too firmly the people's ability to make decisions in their own best interest, the
left had been cherishing unrealistic hopes with respect to their instant
wisdom. Both had failed to give serious thought to questions of organization
in case of a revolution. Consequently mass action, mass strikes, though more
or less spontaneous in character as the left had hoped and predicted, did not
bring about the revolution but a civil war ending in the "Grey Republic" of
Weimar.

The holding operation carried out by a provisional Social Democratic
government in the interim between the collapse of the monarchy and the
beginning of the Weimar Republic could not but attract strongly negative
sentiments from the left and the right: The party was accused both of
destroying "true democracy" by dissolving the workers' councils *(sovjets)*
and of betraying all national political and cultural values by trying to negotiate with the victorious Allies. The *sovjets* did indeed present democracy in
its purest form, but as they were not supported by any centralizing authority,
the dual problem of individual political ambition in quest for authority *and*
individual desire to surrender to the old reconstituted authority of a parliamentary system could not be dealt with. The intellectuals who were actively
involved in those councils,[49] but also those who observed them with hopeful
sympathy, tended to neglect the reality of power in political interaction. It
was a curious if—in the German Kantian tradition—familiar case of pretending that man as a political being would leave behind his sociopsychological

reality, that he would be free of needs, desires, and especially of self-interests.

The consequences of such intellectual political autism proved to be disastrous for the left insofar as it wished to remain independent of Moscow. The Independent Socialist party (USPD), the most considerable of the many left-wing factions, had by 1920 become completely disheartened by the failure of the revolution, that is, of the many local revolutions, for lack of a centralized resistance to the Social Democratic government's militant suppression of the *sovjets*. In June 1920 they sent a delegation to Russia to negotiate an affiliation with the Third International. The twenty-one conditions imposed by Lenin, however, were profoundly alien to the group of German Marxists who saw themselves as the left-wing of the temporarily corrupted Social Democratic party, that is, as the true heirs to a German social-democratic tradition. *Die Aktion* supported the Independents, and Pfemfert wrote on October 30, 1920: "We are engaged in violent battle against the plague of the German workers' movement, opportunism, and who attacks us from the rear—none other than Lenin."[50] But he insisted that political salvation could only be found in the "dictatorship of *sovjets.*" Their obvious failure to govern responsibly and democratically would "somehow" be reversed through the development of the New Man who had also "somehow" preceded the institution of the workers' councils. And it is this pattern of circular wishful thinking, operative on many different levels of sophistication, which is important for our context. The concept of the New (social, cultural, political) Order depending on the coming of and at the same time enabling the development of the New Man, who has been cleansed of all selfishness in the fires of the war and the revolution, is the product of autonomous creation, of a poetic act. In this sense it does indeed replace literature which had, in the German tradition, been charged with transcending a socially constructed reality—namely, the pervasive interconnected energies of self-interest, self-preservation, and power.

4. CULTURE AND INTELLECTUAL PERSONALITY

Individual intellectual temperament and cultural environment interlock in ways both obvious and evasively subtle. Clichés have abounded in the case of the German academic establishment but not in the case of the German intellectual, though he has been as intimately tied to his cultural social environment in the act of opposing it as has the academic in the act of affirming it. If the case history of Weimar intellectuals benefits from including consideration of their war experience, it will also benefit from a brief look at other European intellectuals' wartime perceptions of their social function. Bertrand Russell's intellectual temperament, for instance, may have been similar to Pfemfert's, yet his ideas of sociopolitical interaction were, at the time, considerably more flexible and realistic. As one of the most prominent and active members of the *No Conscription Fellowship* which had been formed against the 1916 *Universal Conscription Bill for Compulsory National Service,* he was jailed for his political agitation in May 1918 and, while in prison, read parts of Lytton Strachey's *Eminent Victorians:* "It caused me to laugh so loud," he wrote to a friend, "that the officer came to my cell, saying that prison is a place of punishment." Strachey thought it "a great honor that my book should made the author of *Principia Mathematica* laugh aloud in Brixton Gaol."[51]

Strachey was enjoying his first real literary success: the book "might be described as the first book of the 'twenties,'" wrote Cyril Connolly. "It struck the note of ridicule which the whole war-weary generation wanted to hear, using the weapon of Bayle, Voltaire and Gibbon on the creators of the Red Cross and the Public School System. It appeared to the post-war young people like the light at the end of a tunnel."[52] They were able to see into the darkness of the unquestioned Victorian virtues of piety (Cardinal Manning), progressive education and the ideal of the Christian Gentleman (Dr. Thomas Arnold), practical humanity (Florence Nightingale) and unshakable courage (General Gordon). Strachey described the most illustrious exponents of those virtues, in fact, national saints, uncovering patterns underlying the confusing wealth of biographical data which suggested a link to the gusto with which the Great War had been fought by the British. He felt free to interpret such figures as cultural constructs as he was comfortable with his position as "an inquisitive and somewhat mischievous observer from across the frontier."[53] This frontier had been erected by considerable fastidious intelligence and social sophistication, but he consciously used a distorting perspective in order to expose certain phenomena and make them accessible to rational examination. In hindsight he was certainly right about his Victorians though by no means fair: he suppressed Florence Nightingale's redeeming sense of humor, he reduced the exceedingly consistent Dr. Arnold too rigorously to the position expressed by the declaration: "My love for any place, or person, or institution, is exactly the measure of my desire to reform them."[54] Besides, he made Arnold's legs too short, slipped the brandy bottle under the inexorable General Gordon's bible, and exaggerated the emotional coldness of the piously intriguing Cardinal Manning. Yet, granted that he took all those liberties, he did manage to uncover certain important regularities underlying enmeshed clusters of problems in a manner both highly amusing and useful. An educated middle-class English reading audience was above all grateful to him. He made a whole war-weary generation laugh as they saw more clearly their own gullability in the all-too-human cracks and frailties of their cultural icons in whose defense they had fought the Great War.

Strachey despised cant. He was a declared staunch antibourgeois like so many German intellectuals. He was also a keen observer of social behavior and a psychological pragmatist to whom it seemed more interesting to understand a social reality than to draw up prescriptions for it. So he tried to understand, too, the ambiguities and psychological conflicts marking Russell's unerring, unconditional fight against the British war effort. Bertie, he wrote to Vanessa Bell on April 17, 1916,

> has been here for the week-end. He is working day and night with the N.C.F. and is at last perfectly happy—gloating over all the horrors and the moral lessons of the situation. The tales he tells make one's blood run cold; but certainly the N.C.F. people do sound a remarkable lot—Britannia's One Hope I firmly believe—all so bright and cheery, he says, with pink cheeks and blithe young voice—oh, mon dieu! mon dieu! The worst of it is that I don't see how they can make themselves effective unless a large number of them do go through actual martyrdom: and even then what is there to make the governing classes climb down? It is all most dark in every direction.[55]

Strachey spoke from the position of the cultural and social insider: the Stracheys, like the Huxleys, Darwins, and Stephens, had been a formidable source of Victorian virtues and achievements as well as educated upper-class high-mindedness and unwillingness to climb down from their comfortable elevated position. He was also deeply upset about the waste of the war and had sought support from Russell, all his subtly ironical reservations notwithstanding. Russell, on the other hand, did not at all act blindly into that darkness. His activism was politically successful to an extent and, above all, it was flexible. By the end of 1917 he had resolved to wait for the end of the war and then get involved seriously working for a lasting peace. But he also derived, as Strachey observed shrewdly, deep psychological gratification from political activism, that is, from acting in isolation with a small group of dedicated intelligent individuals who accepted his authority without questioning it.

When in the summer of 1917, at Russell's urging and with his help, Siegfried Sassoon drew up "A Soldier's Declaration" to be read in Parliament as a statement against the British war effort, his friend Robert Graves tried to talk him out of making a martyr of himself senselessly. Russell had thought that such a statement coming from an officer who had proved himself in the trenches might be very effective. Graves, however, was not that hopeful and, besides, thought such a gesture inadequate to the real dilemma of the war. Both Sassoon's *Memoirs of George Sherston* and Graves's *Goodbye to All That* share a binary structure of them/us—"they" being first the enemy on the other side of the trenches and then, with growing insight into the economic, cultural, and social mechanism propelling the war effort, the British civilians who profiteered emotionally as well as financially. Graves especially was deeply skeptical about man's social intelligence, and the continuation of the war seemed to him "merely a sacrifice of the idealistic younger generation to the stupidity and self-protective alarm of the older."[56] Yet Russell, who opposed the war unconditionally, was seen by him as a doctrinaire, although a courageous one.[57] Like many British intellectuals and poets opposing the war, Graves went back to the trenches mainly to protect the men under his command from the "grosser indignities of the military system."[58] For Sassoon, too, going back to his men was the only way of making peace with himself.

Sassoon never finished with the war experience. The remarkable *Memoirs of George Sherston* describe his own development from a self-centered but eager soldier to the young man who writes, with much inner turmoil and fear, "A Soldier's Declaration." The story is told in the first person, but Sherston, who does not write poetry like Sassoon, is shown as only on his way to becoming an intellectual. Sassoon's achievement is based on careful consideration of the intellectual's position and his developing subtle reservations. He shows the gradual process of Sherston's education, and very importantly, its largely accidental nature. Sherston's kindness and shrewdness regarding his own and others' limitations are gained at great cost. Sassoon makes it abundantly clear that pretty much everyone, that is, "sensible people with an aptitude for experience,"[59] would have come to the same conclusions about the war as Sassoon/Sherston in 1916, and that it still took Russell's prompting and Sassoon's confused courage to act on these conclusions.

Sassoon's antiwar poems collected in the 1918 volume *Counter Attack* are terrifying in a very quiet way: sparing use of metaphors, an economically focused irony, a compassionate cynicism. These poems, as well as the *Memoirs,* convey a sense of physical intimacy, an urgent awareness of the reality of the human body, its beauty, its vulnerability, and the finality of its destruction. Sassoon could not conceive Man, only a great number of very different men. He did not hope for the "New Man" at the end of the war, but for sufficient space and peace to understand what had happened to the old one. Reconstructing a world in which many wrong choices had been made by many different people in very different social roles, he was able to tolerate the social complexity of the act of choosing, insisting on individual responsibility for the choice. Profoundly disturbed and changed by his experience of the war, Sassoon had managed to understand partly rather than reject totally a modern industrial society of those aggressive and possessive behavioral patterns he was—like Pfemfert—painfully aware and to which he nevertheless belonged—a situation which Pfemfert could not accept.

5. TRANSCENDENCE: THE INTELLIGENTSIA

In the German cultural tradition it has been particularly difficult for the intellectual to consider, with some degree of negotiable detachment, the complexity, much less the ambiguity, of social choice and responsibility and of political power. The dignity of the intellectual's position has been understood as directly proportional to his stated distance from power, and this distance has translated into sociopolitical activism of the uncompromising,

confrontational kind as well as into fictions confronting rather than elucidating a social reality. Toward the end of the war, factionalism in the intellectual
camps was frequently based on the contrast between the merely rational-
analytical and the spiritual-activist positions.[60] The antibourgeois intellectual
even became the contemptible contrast figure to the antibourgeois radical.
The intricate connection between an analytical understanding of a situation
and a decision to act within it was seen as timid inability to create. Creation
was privileged over conceptualization in a way which dangerously simplified
the issues. The intellectual found himself attacked, from all sides—the bourgeois conservative, the antibourgeois radical—as *déraciné*, destructively
analytical, merely rational, and such attacks made him even more wary of
dealing analytically with the phenomenon of power. It is a situation that
would survive the 1918–19 civil war and aborted revolution, with the added
problem of right-wing intellectual and organized radicalism.

When Karl Mannheim published his *Ideologie und Utopie*[61] in 1929,
party politics had again become as confrontational as in the immediate
postwar period. Mannheim argued that the intellectual in his *freischwebend*
(free-floating) position between parties would be able to see the particularism
of all parties and consequently assume a mediating function. The "socially
unattached intelligentsia," an "unanchored, *relatively* classless stratum"
would be able to achieve "an experimental outlook, unceasingly sensitive to
the dynamic nature of society and to its wholeness."[62] Mannheim's term,
borrowed from Alfred Weber,[63] has become a household word, used to
accuse, excuse, and praise a position (allegedly) capable of transcending the
muddled politics of (self)interest. Mannheim's "essayistic,"[64] frequently
somewhat opaque mode of argumentation contributed to the ease with which
the term was taken and used out of context to either point out yet another
aspect of cultural decline or project yet another utopian hope. But Mannheim's concern with a clear view of fragmentation and particularism as the
necessary step toward a clear view and concept of the whole contemporary
culture reflects both a symptomatic preoccupation with (lost and regained)
wholeness and, given the sociopolitical situation and the widespread sense of
cultural crisis in the late twenties, a rather sane reaction to that preoccupation. It is true that Mannheim asked too much of the "new discipline of the
Sociology of Knowledge," hoping it would be capable of attempting to
transcend the fragmentary nature of all knowledge which is characteristic of
modernity. He was still, with this concept, most interested in integration of
different contemporary points of view, in wholeness rather than plurality. He
did take diversity seriously, but only as a stepping stone, and his stated goal
"to investigate not how thinking appears in textbooks on logic, but how it
really functions in public life and in politics as an instrument of collective
action"[65] still relied on the position of an investigator whose perspective
grants him a complete and total overview of all these functions. On the one
hand, Mannheim's concept of a theory of knowledge as "an attempt to take
account of the rootedness of knowledge in the social texture"[66] was in the

pragmatist tradition suppressed in nineteenth-century German thought by the Kantian and Hegelian influence. On the other hand, his desire to grasp and account for the whole of that social texture was motivated by and supportive of idealist impulses.

Mannheim did not see the situation in terms of a cultural crisis, stressing repeatedly that "to see more clearly the confusion into which our social and intellectual life has fallen represents an enrichment rather than a loss. . . . The most promising aspect of the present situation . . . is that we can never be satisfied with narrow perspectives, but will constantly seek to understand and interpret particular insights from an ever more inclusive context."[67] In that sense the intellectual who consciously broadens his perspective could be the most important contributor to "scientific politics," but this implies that his knowledge transcends the common rootedness in a social texture and that he is liberated from the otherwise fundamentally particular and partisan nature of all political knowledge and action. How can an intellectual position so rigorously above the common social texture and political knowledge be useful in their analysis, and, even more important, how can it be achieved? These are questions with which Mannheim did not concern himself.

He defined ideology quite realistically as based on the "explicit and methodically recognized" distrust of man toward man and on conscious attempts to discover "the source of [the other's] untruthfulness in a social factor."[68] Precisely such mistrust and rejection of the other's particularism as "untruthfulness" was responsible for much of the violent factionalism of the Weimar period. Mannheim's attempt to "discover a position from which a total perspective would be possible" and his view of the intellectual as "playing the part of watchman in what would otherwise be a pitch-black night"[69] might have seemed attractive to intellectuals caught in the adversarial sociopolitical confusion of Weimar's last years. But they were not given much concrete help: the way out of their predicament is to rely on unconscious tendencies "towards a dynamic synthesis" and a firm sense of what constitutes an "intellectual life."[70] Somehow and magically the urgent demand for "broad dynamic mediation" will be sufficient to provide it: "To-day more than ever it is expected of such a dynamic middle group that it will strive to create a forum outside the party schools in which the perspective of and the interest in the whole is safeguarded."[71] But such expectation proved to be utopian in the sense of utterly unrealistic.

Now, Mannheim argued that only such a total perspective was realistic in terms of being adequate to a complex social reality by transcending ideological and utopian thinking. But as the reality of modern fragmentation of experience and knowledge was undeniable, such transcending total perspective assumed distinctly metaphysical properties. Without it, he reasoned, ideological thinking, which "obscures the real condition of society both to itself and to others and thereby stabilizes it," *and* utopian thinking, favored by certain oppressed groups which are "intellectually so strongly interested in the destruction of a given condition of society that they unwittingly see only those elements in the situation which tend to negate it,"[72] prevented a diagnosis of existing social conditions.

This is a realistic observation, yet ideological and utopian thinking as Mannheim defined it had been encouraged precisely by the search for total perspectives. Diagnosis had been dispensed with because of the prevailing cultural crisis. A great variety of particular, partisan perspectives claimed totality—as prognoses or, rather, fictions. For many intellectuals *freischwebend* did indeed mean the choice to avoid identification with organized party politics. It did not, however, mean reflection on the sociocultural assumptions underlying the different political positions. Most of the intellectual fictions directed at Weimar reality were based on eclectic acceptance and large-scale rejection of such assumptions. What Mannheim intended to be a flexible negotiable intellectual distance which would facilitate comprehensiveness and clarity of perspective—it is an entirely different question whether such position is feasible at all, whether it was feasible under Weimar conditions— was, in fact, rigid and exclusive. Ideological and utopian self-sufficiency promoted intellectual fictions which increased rather than lit up the darkness of Weimar.

6. FALSE CONSCIOUSNESS: THE BOURGEOISIE

This is true to a degree even in the case of one of the most celebrated and in many ways highly effective indictments of Wilhelminianism as responsible for the war and, by implication, for the difficulties faced by Weimar democracy—Heinrich Mann's 1918 novel *Der Untertan*. Like Strachey's *Eminent Victorians, Der Untertan* was very successful with educated contemporary audiences and is fully accessible today—not as social history but as a model with which to approach historically certain aspects of cultural experience. Where Strachey debunked the self-conscious self-serving renunciation of self-interest, Heinrich Mann delivered a biting satirical attack on the corruption of self-interest by political impotence. His brilliant portrait of the *Untertan,* his majesty's slave and clone—a more complex, much more sophisticated portrait of the "authoritarian personality" half a century before its sociological invention[73]—is awesome in its anticipation of the forces that were to undermine the Weimar Republic: the vulnerability to the seductive, self-destroying discipline of ideology on the right and the left. But the novel's militantly antibourgeois stance and its gestures of total rejection anticipate, too, the positions of distance resulting in fictions that were to limit so severely Weimar intellectuals' perceptions of their modern world.

Kurt Tucholsky who admired the novel very much saw its achievement in setting up a complete "herbarium of German man":

> Here he is, true to life, in his compulsion to obey and to give orders, in his brutality and religiosity, in his idolatry of success and his miserable total cow-

ardness. Unfortunately it is true: that was German man; he who differed had no
voice, could not make himself heard, was called traitor and, by the Emperor's
order, forced to leave the Fatherland.[74]

Tucholsky, one of the sharpest, shrewdest, and funniest writers in the history
of German journalism was, like Heinrich Mann, ardently antibourgeois, and
his journalism was confrontational.[75] But his use of colloquial language in the
construction of different "types" representing socially flawed behavior was
comical rather than grotesque and less rigorously rejecting and distancing
than Heinrich Mann's *Untertan* Diederich, constructed from a collage of
mindlessly and opportunistically aggressive speech acts.

Diederich is too bad to be true; his case history is too consistently, too
brilliantly a pathogenesis of impotence and power. His jargon of obedience
and reverence—like Tucholsky Heinrich Mann knew how revealing clichés
are and he used them superbly for effect—is condensed from Wilhelm's II
notoriously aggressive speeches which instantly transposed every issue,
every question into the context of a battle field. The emperor's well-known
tendency to give all his utterances the ritual emphasis of performative speech
acts[76] was rooted in certain psychological difficulties that had developed in
childhood and young adulthood through considerable pressures brought to
bear on a person particularly ill equipped to deal with authority. His insistence to be heard and obeyed, whatever he said in whatever situation on
whatever issue, was based on a particular lack of trust in himself in his world.
The louder he spoke, the less he expected and the more he demanded to be
heard. Speaking and implementation for him had become identical; having
been given too many orders when training for the role of the ruler, he could
not speak but in the form of an order. It was precisely the origin, development, and consequences of this relation between weakness and "unshakable" strength, between the need to lean on others to gain a sense of self *and*
to dominate them totally, that interested Heinrich Mann. The source of such
volatile, conflicted self-consciousness is the late-nineteenth-century authoritarian German family looking for ideal symbolic representation to the
royal family, and the most impressive achievement of the novel is indeed the
tracing of Diederich's authoritarian personality to the specific and to us often
grotesque pressures of the Wilhelminian patriarchic family. Diederich the boy
is accessible and credible in his whining, clinging, cringing, cunning, and
bullying, but Diederich the successful businessman is so hateful that he
assumes the proportions of an allegory. His author's intentions—to present in
all his ridiculous ugliness "the German man," that is, the German bourgeois—are quite clear. But a reader who does not share Mann's perspective
of distance will have difficulty with these authorial intentions and the resulting narrative strategy. The narrative perspective is responsible for highly
illuminating insights into modes of self-presentation in social roles and political speech,[77] but it is also responsible for submerging these insights in the
starkness of the contemptuous composite caricature of "the German man."

The caricature makes clever use of certain physical traits: e.g., pink-pigletish texture and rotund pomposity so inflated that it seems close to explosion but is revealed again and again as safely foam-rubberish in substance and dangerous only in its mindless indestructability. It is satisfying as a virtuoso choreography of hatred, but it lacks the gradual, cumulative subversiveness of Tucholsky's comical common sense and Strachey's ironical ambivalence. Diederich is seen by an outsider and his grotesqueness is appealing to outsiders who see themselves as invulnerable to the temptations of, that is, the reality of, power.

Tucholsky did admire Heinrich Mann's general intellectual position and his specific novelistic achievements—he did not live to read Mann's most intelligent convincing novel about power, *Henri Quatre,* written in French exile. He committed suicide in early 1936 when he realized how completely his mode of fighting against misunderstanding and misuse of power had failed.[78] The differences are temperamental; that is, the development of an individual intellectual temperament is also, of course, very much a cultural phenomenon. And in that respect Kurt Tucholsky is closer to Heinrich Mann than to Lytton Strachey. Such comparative measuring of intellectual and cultural closeness or difference is problematic, and I do it here only to bring into somewhat sharper focus certain elusive aspects of intellectual history.

Strachey followed *Eminent Victorians* with *Queen Victoria.* Published in 1921 it was as well received critically though not at all as commercially successful.[79] Strachey's mother, the eccentric, agnostic, highly intelligent, and quite mid-Victorian Lady Jane, had written to him on January 3, 1919, in response to his plans for a new book.

> I don't fancy much your taking up Queen Victoria to deal with. She no doubt lays herself open to drastic treatment which is one reason why I think it better left alone. She could not help being stupid, but she did try to do her duty, and considering the period she began in, her upbringing, her early associations, and her position, this was a difficult matter and highly to her credit. She has won a place in public affection and a reputation in our history which it would be highly unpopular, and, I think, not quite fair to attempt to bring down.[80]

These are very shrewd reservations, but Strachey was not at all interested in denying the queen this place. He was, rather, intent on showing how such a place is reached, how precarious it can be (and had been) for a time, how secure in the end, and how incredible and predictable was the process of consolidating power. He presented and analyzed a battle of wills in which she won because she, the queen, was limited in intelligence and imagination. She served as the concrete expression of the desire of a self-consciously progressive dynamic society to neutralize explosive interpersonal power-relations by accepting so literally their symbolic representation. Roger Fry commented perceptively: "You are so kind and so unsparing. It seems to me more nearly a true perspective than anyone's yet found."[81]

Strachey was kind *and* unsparing because he understood the form of Victoria-worship as a participator, not just an onlooker. At stake was the uncovering of the foundation of a whole period: the vitality and naiveté of power in the ruling class and the growing acquiescense of the ruled in their respective identification with the empire. He portrays Victoria not as an allegory but, with admirable psychological shrewdness and tact, as an individual: her strong physical instincts, her possessive love for her family, her ridiculous worship of *her* Albert, her total lack of self-distance, her unerring predilection for banalities and clichés, her superbly silly certainty that it was she who was most suited, indeed created for the role of roles—to be the Queen of England. The achievement of this novelistic book-length essay is the matching of this mediocre, petty, sentimental woman with the worship focused on her by a nation so dynamic and expansive in industry and aggressive in foreign policy. Shifting perspectives subtly and skillfully, exploiting narrative strategies of access to subjective consciousness, he manages empathy with her and her environment. He is fascinated and frightened by the force of such mediocrity and its consequences for sociopolitical decisions. As a homosexual intellectual member of the Bloomsbury group he was abourgeois rather than antibourgeois. Able to appreciate the relational nature of power, he was less interested in attacking and rejecting a status quo than in understanding the process through which, again and again, it reestablishes itself. He wrote in an intellectual and cultural tradition shaped by Hobbes's analysis of power as based in the social imagination of the ruled and the ruler[82] and by Hume's analysis of mental operations as rooted in motivations fueled by sociopsychological experience.[83]

In presenting Diederich's unavoidable rise through his increasingly aggressive speech acts, Heinrich Mann came close to such an understanding of power. But though he was very much a bourgeois by personal background and, to an extent, lifestyle, he hated the bourgeois with a passion that proved detrimental to the clarity and accessibility of his perspective. He knew that he was no outsider himself, but this did not keep him from assuming this position as essayist and novelist. In a 1910 essay, "Voltaire-Goethe," much beloved by the *Aktionsgemeinde,* he celebrated freedom as the "menadic dance of reason" of which "absolute man" will be capable.[84] But in a 1905 essay on Flaubert and George Sand, he argued soberly and convincingly that no outsider can write successful, that is, accessible satire, because satire, in order to be truthful, requires the experience of hatred *and* community.

7. CULTURAL UTOPIAS

Mann did not always follow his own insight, though it was precisely the experience of Weimar's difficulties that helped to season his hatred with understanding.[85] Weimar was much less a Grey Republic to him than to other contemporary intellectuals. Confronted with a very volatile political situation, with profound but haphazard changes in social life, with rapid and insufficiently understood developments in science and technology, with parliamentary mass democracy and technocracy, they maintained a perspective of distance which made it difficult for them to see their world in a way which could be communicated meaningfully to a diverse group of readers. Audiences became as factional as writers. In that respect the cultural reflected the political situation though the two were quite separate otherwise. Ideologies abounded on the right and left as constructs of a utopian whole based on blatantly particular partisan truths. Those "eutopias"[86] had the great advantage that their relation to contemporary concerns did not need to be stringent. They seemed manageable by virtue of being projected, suggesting a sorely missed sense of control, and they were, in important ways, quite similar on the right and the left.

In his ambivalent attitude toward global technology and mass communication the Marxist Benjamin was quite close to Heidegger's dichotomy between *das Man* (mere public opinion) and the uniquely meaningful rootedness of the self. The Frankfurt School's concept of "critical reason" is deeply embedded in and indebted to a conservative German cultural tradition, though its denunciation of "instrumental reason" is meant to suggest dissociation from such tradition.[87] Its arguments seem, in part, perfectly reconcilable with Hermann Broch's culturally and politically conservative gnosticism and with Ernst Jünger's and Gottfried Benn's heroic nihilism and radical conservatism. Alfred Döblin shows, in some of his texts, an intelligent informed interest in the concrete dynamics of power relations and political action and great sympathy for the 1918–19 revolution. In his emphasis on the political actor's quest for personal redemption—especially Rosa Luxemburg in *November 1918*[88]—he is quite similar to Broch who abhorred the revolution with its attendant phenomenon of mass action. Brecht, the allegedly pragmatic Marxist, was as fascinated by the colorful images of Taylorism as was Ernst Jünger. His presentation of the social implications of science in *Galileo* is questionable precisely because his protagonist is a heroic tinkerer rather than one of the first modern scientists who would of course respond to his seventeenth-century cultural and political environment, but in ways insufficiently understood by the twentieth-century dramatist for whom history is bunk.

I have pointed out before that Weimar intellectuals in their great majority showed a peculiar vulnerability to ideology and utopianism. The wartime conflict between radical and organized socialist politics[89] had developed in two main directions: politically radical intellectuals on the left and the right became absorbed into highly organized extremist party politics, the Communist party (KPD) and the National Socialist party (NSDAP), or they radically distanced themselves (more or less) from all existing forms of political life. To work, as an intellectual, for the KPD or the NSDAP meant the surrender of all critical distance. Speaking for the party, the intellectual communicated the threats and promises of power without participating in, without understanding power. Most of the Communist writers were destroyed in Stalin's purges after often narrow escapes from insufficiently understood Hitlerism.[90] This study focuses on the second group, which includes Marxists like Adorno, Horkheimer, Bloch, and, in spite of their flirtation with the Communist party, Brecht and Benjamin. All of them, with the exception of Benjamin, went into exile in the United States; Benjamin went to France where he tried to construct a personal Marxist reality under Brecht's reluctant tutelage.[91] He killed himself after trying unsuccessfully to cross the border to Spain on his way to America. It also includes on the right not only writers like Hermann Broch, who went into exile in the United States, and Ernst Jünger, but also Martin Heidegger and Gottfried Benn whose short lived infatuation with Nazism might be seen as characteristic of their innocence regarding power rather than as opportunistic attempts at embracing it.[92]

Their distance from a sociopolitical reality did not, however, make the intellectuals—whether on the right, on the left, or in the center—*freischwebend* in Mannheim's sense. Though their fictions were constructed precisely to avoid coping with the confusing, disturbing contemporary conflicts of interests, they presented a partial and partisan truth as, in each case, the comprehensive and only truth. Proclaiming a cultural crisis of unforeseen dimensions and the devaluation of social to eschatological time, they did not see the need or the possibility of bringing together different fragmented views to gain a more comprehensive, truer perspective. They both lamented fragmentation and declared it inevitable, withdrawing to so many particular individual truths about fragmentation, mechanization, and accelerated sociocultural change. The highly eclectic idiosyncratic Marxisms of Bloch, Benjamin, and Adorno do not differ in that respect from the various ethics and aesthetics of cultural catastrophe presented by Heidegger, Ernst Jünger, Gottfried Benn, and Thomas Mann. All of them were mountain dwellers with the exclusive and rigid perspective (*theoria*) of spatial and temporal distance from the valley of contemporary muddle. When Benjamin attacked Tucholsky's journalism as "cozy despair" ("gemütliche Verzweiflung") he was pointing to the more serious, significant substance of his own cultural despair. But the real and important difference between the two writers lies in the fact that Tucholsky was infinitely better informed about the state of affairs that was indeed sufficient cause for despair. He could not share a perspective of distance which supported theories of cultural crisis denouncing self-interest, self-preservation, causality, and functionality and celebrating instead the values of true community, complete communication, participation, and emancipation. He knew himself and his contemporaries too well.

8. CULTURAL IDEOLOGIES

The fictions of polarity so characteristic of the period—we (I)/they—not here/ but there—not now/but then—were rooted in such theories. For the most part they were developed in the mixed mode of discourse which became prevalent during the period between the two wars in Germany: the philosophical, political, historical essay and the essayistic novel or drama of ideas. Yet there is, in these fictions, little of the archessayist Montaigne's experimental modesty and skeptical openness, but instead much epiphany of totality and truth.[93] Fictions have a long tradition as cultural tools in the always needed, always renewed attempt to clarify and sort out the clashes, defeats, and victories of different interests. When Aristotle argued against Plato's epistemological and cultural-ethical reservations regarding tragedy, he stressed precisely its closeness to moral philosophy and ethics: they all share in the investigation of human action. Tragedy relying on fiction *(poiesis)* is presented as counterpart to equity in ethics and law.[94] Negotiating between general cultural propositions and particular circumstances, fictions in this sense are based on an interplay of sameness and diversity. But the ideological fictions that flourished between the two wars were interested in prescription for rather than investigation of human action and thus too easily and too aggressively dismissive of a shared experience and a concern for rationality and meaning in communication.

Insistence on the individual intellectual's need and right to speak seemed to preclude reflection on the motivations and intentions in speaking. With few exceptions, these fictions were both self-consciously idiosyncratic and assertive in the assumption that an increasingly unfamiliar, complex world could be completely unlocked by their particular key. Lack of tolerance for the open conflict of interests, which is, after all, essential to modern democracy, led to an obsession with the need for control. The intellectual right demanded that the conflict of interests be contained in the "higher" collective of the *Volksstaat* which was also a *Machtstaat;* the left wanted it neutralized in a fully communicated, ideally balanced interplay of unalienated community; and the liberal center simply claimed the uniquely mediating properties of national cultural values while proclaiming them profoundly, critically threatened. All these eutopian positions were connected by the desire to avoid conflict by setting up elaborately constructed control-systems rather than by the attempt to question the efficacy of such constructs and negotiate the conflict. On the whole, Weimar fictions as prescriptive rather than explorative models were surprisingly self-limiting given the rapid developments in science and technology with their far-reaching implications for sociopolitical conflict and power. They encouraged withdrawal from a contemporary social reality because they helped to go on seeing it as a battlefield which had retained the overly stark, explosive demarcations of, above all, the oversimplifications of, war.

The reasons for this widespread failure of the intellectuals to cope intelligibly with the phenomenon of modernity are located in the German cultural and political tradition, that is, in the ways in which this tradition informed the experience of World War I.[95] For many intellectuals on the left there was the added difficulty of the Jewish experience. The intellectual members of this small, highly educated and articulate, precariously assimilated minority tended to be contemptuous of the powerful mechanisms upholding and reestablishing the status quo and largely unaware of the diverse reality of the majority.

This is not to say, of course, that the problems posed by Weimar eluded all German-Gentile and especially all German-Jewish intellectuals. But in their great majority the serious, substantial, intellectually demanding statements about that period in transition are characteristically flawed. It is an Austrian writer, Robert Musil, whose essays and essayistic novel *Der Mann ohne Eigenschaften (The Man without Qualities)*, tentative, explorative fictional models, differ from his contemporaries' fictions in the degree and kind of acknowledgment of the challenges posed by the twentieth century. Trained as an engineer, mathematician, philosopher, and experimental psychologist, he discussed critically in his essays and novels questions of perception and motivation, of social identity, verbal conventions and communication, consciousness of self and other. In his attempt to merge different modes of discourse in order to establish a more comprehensive and sharper perspective on his contemporary world, he went beyond a clear distinction between the rational properties of common sense and scientific activities. It was precisely this step which enabled him to tell a story which takes seriously the principle of accident and disorder in human affairs and contains it in an arrangement that makes sense.[96]

Unencumbered by the tradition of German idealism and independent of the Vienna Circle's too rigid reaction to that tradition—the Frankfurt School's passionate rejection of instrumental reason is yet another reaction to that reaction[97]—Musil was willing to articulate experimentally that which (allegedly) can be said with certainty as well as that which (allegedly) cannot be said at all.[98] This mixed approach to sociocultural experience and communication proved appropriate for a period of more and more firmly established technological and scientific priorities and correspondingly increasing attempts to control these priorities through ideological fictions—attempts which were often interesting or provocative, but largely futile. Musil's perspective of distance was more flexible, more varied, more self-conscious and self-critical. It was, above all, open to negotiation and compromise, because it was interested in the phenomenon of the social life. For him people were like other people, and they were, at the same time, astonishingly, exhilaratingly diverse. In the German cultural tradition dominated by the ideal of the successful *Bildungsroman* as entelechy, few writers have been able or willing to give up claims to the unique creative intellectual self which animates their protagonists and narrates their essays. This self is set against an amorphous collective, which is either damned for not living up to the intellectual's expectations or venerated as the means for his salvation. It seems to have been most difficult to gain a sense of the essential sameness and difference of individuals in a pluralistic culture, because daily social intercourse has been judged as needing redemption before it has ever been examined with any degree of informed critical curiosity and sympathy.

The men and women who contributed to the intellectual life of the Grey

Republic found themselves confronted repeatedly with extremely difficult, nearly impossible choices. Hannah Arendt, who came intellectually of age during the Weimar Republic, gave her collection of essays on Weimar intellectuals, such as Rosa Luxemburg, Bert Brecht, Walter Benjamin, and Hermann Broch, the title *Men in Dark Times*. However, such darkness was interpreted and acted into in different ways; there was space for a great variety of intellectual response and sociopolitical direction. It was not totally impenetrable, nor was it metaphysically fated. The intellectuals contributed to the darkness through many erroneous choices that need to be analyzed. We are their heirs, their historiographers. Our perspective on them is shaped by the distance of hindsight and relative safety, and such distance must not go unquestioned. Fairness in this case means imaginative critical empathy with the difficulties faced by these intellectuals, but also awareness of mistakes made, of symptomatically flawed judgments regarding the intellectual's function and responsibility in a modern mass society. It is impossible not to judge such judgments, but it is also impossible to hold them responsible for the collapse of Weimar. The writers who will be given a close reading here had at most a very indirect influence on sociopolitical developments. It is mainly their response to such developments that is accessible to the intellectual historian who is aware of the elusiveness of interplay between literary imagination and social reality.

In the twentieth-century intellectuals have sought to anchor their claim to responsible articulation of contemporary sociopolitical concerns in perspectives of distance, above all, distance to power. It is significant that one of the rare discussions of the structural properties of responsible intellectual speech-arts is found in Hannah Arendt's concept of meaningful political speech and action. As Heidegger's student she had been deeply influenced by his sense of a cultural crisis. Yet her biography, written during the 1930s, of the nineteenth-century Jewish intellectual Rahel Varnhagen is a socially shrewd, psychologically subtle analysis of the damage done by exclusion. For both young Jewesses exclusion had been a primary experience, and it informed Arendt's postwar involvement in the conflicts of Israel's politics of exclusion culminating in her lucid presentation of the Eichmann trial.[99] Living in the United States—for her neither exile nor diaspora—she came to view critically Heidegger's *Zeitferne* (temporal distance) which supported the dichotomy between *das Man* (mere public opinion) and the authenticity of the self. Much of his thought she considered flawed by "the old hostility of the philosopher against the polis."[100] Her political philosophy is centered in responsible speech-acts which would presuppose the speaker's intention to speak to others in order to be understood and which would be meaningful if this intention were realized. It is true that the act of speaking responsibly is limited, in her concept, to a small, exclusive group: men speaking in the *agora* whose (economic) interests do not enter their speech-acts, as they are taken care of, away from the public sphere, by women and slaves at home. What concerns us here, however, is her insistence on communication that is concretely related to community (even if it is a limited one): speech is an act that intends to be responsive and needs an answer; it is meaningful only as a political act.

In her highly idiosyncratic stimulating study of the American Revolution, *On Revolution* (1963), Arendt divides the general category of intellectuals into a small group of *"hommes des lettres,"* among whom she counts for instance the theoreticians of the French Revolution, and the large rapidly growing group of "intellectuals" who work for the expanding bureaucracies in government, industry, and the business of culture. They operate in the social sphere, which for Arendt means a sphere endangered by misunderstanding and compromise. Intellectual positions in this sphere are flawed by ambivalence and ambiguity—Arendt's mistrust of the social sphere is notorious and limits the usefulness of her political philosophy. The first group, for her the true intellectuals, has withdrawn from the social realm, asking nothing but the liberty to prepare for a future public realm where political speech will be truly possible and where the individual, distinguishing himself by speaking among other speakers, can escape the dangers of obscurity and misunderstanding.

For the Jewish intellectual Arendt these dangers were all too real and they prompted her to define the intellectual's responsibility as the attempt to bridge distances rather than establish them: speaking to the other expects, intends, and provokes an answer. It is true that the *polis* is Arendt's redemptive eutopia. In its purity and exclusiveness it is still close to Weimar fictions, but in its emphasis on speaking as and for an answer it is not. The aftermath of Weimar's failure taught Arendt the need to share a world by speaking in it and about it to the other. There is a certain irony in the fact that a rather narrow version of her concept of a completed meaningful speech-act became influential—via Habermas—in West German neo-Marxist utopianism which was so exuberant in the late sixties and early seventies. Fictions of organic community versus stratified, systemic society, of full political participation, emancipation, and cultural wholeness versus fragmentation, alienation, and mechanization, of completely expressive language versus the ambiguous discourse of power, of redemption versus the principle of accident had survived what was called "the German catastrophe" and proved to be too powerful to be open to consistent, rational questioning. These fictions have also shaped positions of cultural conservatism, privileging aesthetic and religious concerns. They have not disturbed the growing economic technocratic internationalism, and they have not lent themselves much to concrete political exploitation. In her relative sociopolitical stability the Federal Republic is essentially different from the Weimar Republic, but her intellectuals' continuing perspective of distance and inclination to speak for but not to the other have not shown much change. It is this continuity which supports significantly the contemporary sense of a cultural crisis.

Part Two

The Problem of Experience

ONE

The Threatened Self

Walter Rathenau and the
Politics of Wholeness

I.

Walter Rathenau, the German minister for foreign affairs, was murdered in the late morning of June 24, 1922, by a small group of young nationalist (*völkisch*) opponents to his reparation politics. They were the 24-year-old law student and former naval officer Erwin Kern, the 26-year-old mechanical engineer and former army officer Hermann Fischer, and the 21-year-old student Ernst-Werner Techow, all from solidly middle-class families, all of them members of the clandestine Organization Consul and ex-members of the notorious Free Corps Ehrhardt Brigade, now dissolved.[1] Much later Techow, who drove the car from which the shots were fired and the only one to survive the assassination,[2] explained the motivations of the assassins:

> The younger generation was striving for something new, hardly dreamed of. They smelled the morning air. They gathered in themselves an energy charged with the myth of the Prussian-German past, the pressure of the present, and the expectation of an unknown future. In the face of derision, against a world of foes, they gathered round a flag which they thrust into the future and in which they firmly believed.[3]

The significance, for the assassins, of the act of killing a man who had, in his successful Genoa negotiations with England and France earlier that year, taken the first important step toward regaining for Germany the status of a European power, is the reality of that act itself: rejuvenating in its energy and unifying thrust. Acting, the assassins asserted their beleaguered "us" against an overpowering "them"—a world hostile to the true essence of Germany. What counted was the act, *die Tat*.

In 1933 when, after his release from prison, he wrote those lines, Techow saw himself as a National Socialist, but he explicitly predated the history of the Third Reich beyond Hitler's putsch in November 1923. There had been groups of activist youths all across Germany, he points out, ready for reckless and relentless paramilitary engagement in their desire to make a breach in the hated "Novembersystem," the parliamentary democracy of the Weimar Republic. They were driven by their dreams of a new Germany and saw themselves as forerunners, "the lost troop of the new nationalism for which they wanted to prepare the way." Techow stresses the function of his account of the Rathenau assassination as being helpful in understanding the nature of nationalistic activism. Celebrating the murderers' extraordinary *Tat*, he explains its higher justification—it is, indeed, not a case of "common murderers."[4]

The activism was directed against bourgeois liberalism. During the chaotic months of the 1918–19 civil war, Techow had joined, for a brief time, the Marine Brigade Ehrhardt because, in contrast to other frequently reactionary (monarchistic) Free Corps groups, it was motivated by a revolutionary belief in action against the declining decayed bourgeoisie. Rathenau is seen as oscillating between Marxism and capitalism, monarchism and republicanism, driven to embrace such extremes and exploit the ensuing sociopolitical chaos by means of the unbridgeable schism between his race *(Blut)* and his German nationality.[5] But Techow's concept of activism as crystallized in the Rathenau assassination is not so much informed by anti-Semitism as by the desire for a violent and final thrust against the exponent and symbol of bourgeois liberalism: the man who had, out of chaos, solidified into a "system" everything the activist shock troops had been fighting against. "Between him and us," Techow says, "there was no trace of understanding left, only the act"—of murder.[6] Rathenau's death had to be the fatal blow to the hateful "system" as he was

> the only one who could have been successful in reviving, for a time a system sentenced to death. Fischer and Kern . . . were driven by their conscience, and they were sustained by the German *mythos*. They had dedicated themselves to the service of a new time; they were men cut off, scattered on a lost mission, but absolutely certain that what they were striving for so passionately now would one day be reality.[7]

The juxtaposition of misunderstood, isolated, and persecuted now but recognized, justified, and glorified in the future is the stuff of legend and hagiography. The formation of identity is presented as a forging procedure that ends in something gloriously impenetrable and definite, sainted dead heroes. Leaping from the projection of the act, fueled by its very passion, to the perfection of the act in the firing of the shots meant the instantaneous realization of the assassins' "German *mythos*"—if only for a moment. It was preserved in the squat large stone block crowned by a steel helmet that Hitler had erected over the graves of Erwin Kern and Hermann Fischer in the cemetery of Burg Saaleck where the two, at the end of their flight, had barricaded themselves against the police. Kern was shot on July 17, 1922, and Fischer committed suicide by the side of his dead friend. The inscription on the stone is a quote from the early nineteenth-century nationalist poet Ernst Moritz Arndt: "Do what you have to do/Win or Die/And let God decide."[8]

Techow's account is written in the adolescent actionist style of *völkisch* and Nazi publications but by no means as crude as most of those texts and clearly trying to appeal to a broad and fairly educated audience. Celebrating the death of his comrades, he quotes from Ernst Jünger's widely read *Der Kampf als inneres Erlebnis* (1922) (The battle as inner experience), a book that shaped the war experience into a shining exemplary model of significant terror for *völkisch* youth:

> To die for a conviction is the highest achievement. It is testimony, act, fulfill-ment, faith, love, hope, and goal; it is perfection in this imperfect world and absolute consummation. . . . Even dying entrenched in obvious error means having achieved the utmost. . . . Illusion and world are one and the same and he who died for an error is still a hero.[9]

Jünger exploited the carnage of the war in the both violent and precious imagery of his essays and autobiographical fictions written during the Wei-mar Republic.[10] His interest, highly stylized, in the new, modern industrial experience, his dangerously simplistic concept of the worker as ascetic warrior in addition to his peculiar mixture of Schopenhauerian detachment and nationalist heroics made him attractive to the National Socialist govern-ment in its eager search for representatives of the new Nazi culture. He was also perceived to be too elitist for their purposes, and he saw them as dull brutes. His nationalist journalism during the late twenties was too vacuous to be really influential with *völkisch* youth, but the idea and the occasionally stunning images of the ultimate act, which Jünger had prepared as a kind of existential extract from the battlefield, and above all his interpretation of accidental death as unique personal fate, as self-perfection through self-sacrifice, did draw them. Reality, in this perspective, is not the difficult complex world formed by and between people, emerging, developing, and always changing. It is, rather, the heroic moment of the meaningful act which is removed from temporal and spatial definitions and limitations, an explo-sion of epic dimensions, irreduceable to social experience.

There are several accounts of what Kern, the leader of the small group of assassins, said to his comrades about the meaning of the act for themselves and for the hostile world against which the act was directed. In Techow's story Kern speaks at the end of the day on which the murder took place; in Ernst von Salomon's 1930 version, *Die Geächteten* (The outlawed), more dramatically, just minutes before the assassination. Salomon's narrative sounds more self-consciously staged; he was, besides, only indirectly in-volved in the actual assassination, though very active in *völkisch* groups. But the Kern remembered is in essence the same, and there is the same reaction to his exhortations. Asked what they should agree on saying when caught, what should be their message to that hostile world, Kern states emphatically that anything will do. They could, for instance, condemn the fact that

Rathenau had gotten his ministerial position by blackmail, that he had married his sister to the Jewish Bolshevik Karl Radek, that he had negotiated the Rapallo treaty with the Soviet Union, that his appeasement politics were criminally wrong, that he had been supporting the stealthy advance of bolshevism, that he, according to his own statements, was one of the Three Hundred Elders of Zion: " 'they won't understand us in any case.' Kern's face hardened when, seething with wrath, he blurted out: 'Nobody will understand us and they will all shrink away from us as if we were common murderers.' "[11]

In Salomon's narration, Kern instructs his comrades to blame everything on him and under no circumstances tell the truth because it would not be understood; give some silly reasons—he enumerates the same accusations mentioned in Techow's account: They alone will be accessible to the unenlightened, hostile majority.[12] In both cases, Kern, the motivating force behind the act of murder, is portrayed as manly, upright, and totally responsible to his ideals and his comrades. He is in possession of some higher truth which he nurtures and guards unto death. The accusations used by the right to incriminate Rathenau are recognized as fabrications, even nonsense.[13] Kern's higher truth is the knowledge that they have been called upon to destroy the system which still upholds, in spite of all the chaos brought about by the revolution, the crumbling, infamous old order. Their acts would prepare a way for the true fate of the German people which, of course, has nothing to do with the people's happiness and everything to do with its greatness, that is, its rejuvenation in radical change. Rathenau supports the system which is supported by and supports the world of the fathers. The new leaders, the hope of *völkisch* youth, will transcend the old generational-cultural conflict. They will be neither fathers nor sons, but vehicles or voices of fate. First, however, there has to be separation between that which has been condemned to fall and that which carries the promise of the future: "The blood of this man must divide irreconcilably what has to be divided eternally."[14]

These are not, as some historians have judged, merely hollow phrases. They are sentiments true to the image that Kern thought to form and project of himself as one who has been called upon to see, protect, and defend unto death the true essence of Germanness. And in this the blue-eyed, blond, handsome young German with the "healthy open face, an officer's face, as we call it,"[15] was exactly that kind of young man most trusted by Rathenau and curiously close to him emotionally.

In despair over Germany's destruction Rathenau had, in 1918, appealed to German youth:

> Be blessed in your hard and inexorable nature. . . . Be blessed with consuming love which shall strike you like fire and purge you and our country of the dross of today and yesterday, and rise like the smoke of sacrifice to the throne of him who blesses. Plunge into the struggle for the soul of our people![16]

"Knallt ab den Walther Rathenau/Die gottverdammte Judensau" ("Shoot down Walter Rathenau, the goddamned dirty Jew"). The nasty jingle shouted by Free Corps groups was expressive, too, of an aggressive hatred of the "dross of today and tomorrow," of the need for sacrifice and for that inexorable hardness, and of the addiction to radical means of purification, like fire.

Rathenau, shrewd realpolitiker and neoromantic metaphysician, religious fatalist and consummate diplomat, suffered deeply from the hostility and isolation caused by the misunderstanding of both his political pragmatism and his devotion to German culture. Striving to purify his—as he saw it—complex and conflict-ridden nature in the higher service of a truer Germany, he felt challenged, to the point of exhaustion, by the sociopolitical environment in which he had to operate during the early years of the republic. The conflicts he thought so uniquely his own were actually symptomatic of the period: World War I had exacerbated rather than changed a culturally deep-rooted inability to connect different spheres of experience. Rathenau's impressive skills in dealing with questions of technological-industrial development—he had been, before and during the war, an engineer and a powerful industrialist—and his demonstrated shrewdness and flexibility in the field of foreign politics indicate an ability to appreciate, on various levels, the complex systems that constitute modern mass societies. But his high seriousness in questions of "the soul," that is, his cultural identity, speaks of a vacuous and monolithic insistence on individual uniqueness and a personal fate transcending to the higher reality of a true (German) community.

It is not so much that such insistence is anachronistic or that the interest in systems and the skill in understanding and controlling them is modern—twentieth versus nineteenth century, so to speak. It is, rather, the way in which the two are combined and reinforce each other which is highly problematic and characteristic of Rathenau's attitude in particular and the Weimar period in general. In almost all of his writing—and Rathenau had a prolific and successful career as a cultural essayist in addition to all his other achievements—he confounds what he had separated painstakingly first into the two mutually exclusive spheres of business, propelled by greed, corruption, and the conflict of interests, and of beauty, disinterested and paradisiacally pacified. As a result he ends up with deeply flawed social constructs, especially so in the utopian projections that he took refuge in during the last two years of the war. For the intellectual historian of the Weimar period, Rathenau is a most instructive exponent of the neat specialization in the sciences, in technology, in the professions, which thrived on the general cultural obfuscation and made the young republic highly vulnerable to exploitation by leaders of political movements who were aware of its sociopolitical potential, almost its need, for domination.

The split between intellectual capabilities and achievements on the one side and emotional energies and needs on the other narrowed and distorted the personal perspective to a degree which proved socially harmful. Rathenau, indulging his metaphysical longings in such a self-absorbed way, was unable to appreciate the shape these feelings assume in other people: their stupendous surface variety and the sameness of their explosive force. So he was both profoundly hurt by the hostility encountered by his politics of appeasement or fulfillment *and* accepted the danger to his person as fated and fateful.[17] Fulfillment—of Germany's obligations to the Allies—and appeasement—of the Allies' uneasiness about Germany's sincerity regarding the issue of reparations—meant for Rathenau a step-by-step process of negotiation and bargaining during which the concrete form and content of the reparations would be or could be changed continuously. He did not understand how the idea of appeasement, removed from the reality of gradual change through compromise and hardened into a slogan, could attract so powerfully the fathers' hostility engendered by anxiety about radical change and the sons' rage at its abortion, which had both coalesced into an angry sense of the betrayal of all national cultural values. But he also did not believe that his own position, so very misunderstood and, in the extremely volatile political situation, highly dangerous, could or would make death by assassination more probable. *His* death could not possibly be accidental.

In Genoa Rathenau had experienced difficult, anxious, exhausting, and yet exhilarating days: he had succeeded in convincing some of the Allies through shrewd, tenacious, and lucky negotiations[18] that Germany's adopted policy of fulfillment was in good faith, that she could indeed be trusted in her decision to meet her obligations. He had thereby averted the grave danger of a successful separatist movement in the Rhineland and prepared for the first stage of Germany's slow emergence from internal chaos and international isolation. About a month before he was killed, he wrote from Genoa to his closest friend:

> I often think and it is my greatest comfort: What a wretched sort of life is that which merely runs its even course untroubled! The wonderful thing is that all true sorrow is beautiful. Only the stupidly awry and the arbitrarily distorted is ugly. In our life everything has been Law; thus were the facts and their predestined course. Nothing has been in vain, nothing can now be thought away or given up.
> And if you honestly reflect you will find that even what seemed to be Chance was really Necessity. And is Chance going to have his own way now? My life has run too far along its course for that to be possible.
> Now at last I am free of my fellow men. Not in the sense that I could ever be indifferent to them. On the contrary, the freer I am, the nearer and dearer—despite all—they are to me, and I joyfully recognize that I exist for them, not they for me.[19]

The man to receive this affirmation of belief in a unique personal fate and in self-fulfillment through self-sacrifice for a higher good, the German people, was the *völkisch* publicist and teacher Wilhelm Schwaner. His journal *Der Volkserzieher* (Educator of the people) had welcomed, in 1914, the outbreak of the *Deutscher Krieg* (German war) as a *Gottesgeschenk* (divine gift), and the *Feldbriefpost der Volkserzieher* (military post), sent to the trenches after the subscribers to *Volkserzieher,* encouraged them "to live in faithfulness, to fight spiting death, to die laughing."[20] Rathenau supported the *Feldbriefpost* financially. He was attracted erotically to the author of a *Germanenbibel* (1904) (Bible for young Teutons), an anthology of Christian and Germanic mythological texts, and admired, if not Schwaner's racist theories, his work with blond, blue-eyed young men in the youth movement, in *Wandervogel,* and in *völkisch* groups. Schwaner was no anti-Semite, though he insisted, much to Rathenau's chagrin, on the significance of racial differences. His *Volkserzieher,* meant for a readership of teachers, was very conservative in cultural concerns but did not express hostility toward Jews, and he did not work with openly anti-Semitic *völkisch* groups.

The intense, emotionally exalted friendship between the two middle-aged men began with a letter Schwaner wrote to Rathenau on December 3, 1913, after he had read his 1912 *Zur Kritik der Zeit* (Criticism of the age). He had been connecting the Jews with Germany's difficulties, Schwaner wrote, but reading Rathenau had convinced him that the "dark Jew has redeemed the blue-blond Teuton," and he ended: "Let me shake your hand. We are brothers on the road to mankind, to God's mankind."[21] "God's mankind" would have to be blond and blue-eyed—at least in its spirit of truth, simplicity, wholeness, faith, natural harmony, and stability. Rathenau scholars have been both reluctant to state clearly the nature of this friendship and explicit in their surprised dismay that this highly sophisticated cosmopolitan powerful man could indulge in a stickily sentimental correspondence, evocative of two Wilhelminian schoolboys, with an obviously limited sectarian.[22] The love letters suggest, indeed, the emotional needs of adolescence fed by feelings of isolation and threatened identity. They are written out of a profound sense of a "we" posed against a "they" of a hostile world in need of deliverance into its own true and beautiful essence. Schwaner introduced Rathenau to the leaders of youth movement groups and thought this experience very significant for his friend. It is entirely possible that Erwin Kern, the "blue-blond Teuton" and representative of the Prussian type whose attraction Rathenau had always felt so keenly, participated with him in the *Rundgespräche* (roundtable talks), as the emotionally charged discussions of the importance of German youth for Germany's (truer, better) fate were called in Schwaner's circles.[23]

To be blond and blue-eyed was a culturally significant concept rather than physical reality. It went with an athletic body exposed to sun, mountain air, and sea water and braced by the self-discipline of sports and the challenge of nonurban environments. Images of this physique suggested a possibly victorious, certainly heroic role in the unusually bitter generational-cultural conflict as it had developed in the first decade of the century. But it is precisely because of their relative abstractness that they could become so powerful and, finally, so horribly exploited. They had been intended as a means to unification rather than separation, meant to swell the "we" of the young—which included, for instance, the young Jew Walter Benjamin who was very active in the youth movement—against the "they" of the fathers. And in their ideal abstractness they promoted a diffuse eroticism soothing to adolescent anxieties about constant if gradual physical change. The explosive combination of intense hope for the radically new and equally intense fear of the new as (just) unfamiliar, so typical for the precarious stage of adolescence, was both preserved and temporarily defused in the images which approximated the ideal German type.

Attempts to deal with the experience of World War I drew on this cluster of images, but they did not create it. Here, too, the value and usefulness of the images lies in their abstractness, that is, their potential of transcendence: against the wholesale physical destruction of technologically advanced warfare is posed, as a kind of resurrection, the higher truth and beauty of the young male body, its archangel-like invulnerability negating the terrifying fragility of real human bodies. Ernst Jünger's early texts provide good examples, especially the one that spoke to Techow:

> The spirit of the battle of ammunition [*Materialschlacht*] and of trench warfare where the battle raged, more relentless, wilder, more brutal than ever before, produced men the like of whom the world had not seen before. This was a totally new race, energy incarnate and charged with the most intense momentum. Lithe, lean, sinewy bodies, expressive faces, eyes, under the helmet, petrified in a thousand terrors. They overcame, natures of steel they, attuned to battle in its most hideous form.

George L. Mosse, dealing with the question of the Jews and the German war experience in his study of *Masses and Man: Nationalist and Fascist Perception of Reality*, quotes from this passage:

> Ernst Jünger once more summed up this stereotype in all its mixture of brutality and beauty, so common in Germany. "This was a totally new race, all energy . . . slim, lithe and muscular body, finely chiseled faces . . . These were men who overcame, natures of steel, ready for any struggle however ghastly," and Jünger thought that such struggle was a permanent condition of life. The foils of this hero were the philistines, the bourgeois and the liberals, the "retail merchant and the glove-makers" as Jünger characterized them. It was the Jewish stereotype that became the foil of this manly ideal. For like the new race of which Jünger spoke, the Jewish stereotype had over a century of history behind it and was quite ready for use. Werner Sombart's contrast between merchants and heroes (*Händler und Helden*, 1915) projected the opprobrium of the antiheroic upon the English enemy, but it was easily transferred back to the Jew. It is not necessary to cite further proof that the Jew was excluded from this heroic ideal.[24]

Mosse neatly sorts out the stereotypes, but he presents them, I think, too much from hindsight, that is, as too concrete and too impermeable. His translation of the Jünger passage prettifies and fills in the starkly outlined body-shapes and erases the surrealistic gloss of the battle scene. These shapes are more than stereotypical heroic images of handsome blond and blue-eyed German youths. They are apocalyptic figures, intended to be terrible beyond beauty; that they strike us, reading this passage more than half a century later, as dangerous *kitsch,* is another matter. A contemporary nationalist reader like Rathenau's assassin Techow would have been responsive to the transcending terror of the scene and the figures—and so would Rathenau. Rather than seeing the Jew "excluded from this heroic ideal," he would have understood the scene depicted as an appeal, to Gentiles and Jews alike, to stand by Germany in her extreme need brought on, as he saw it, by rapidly increasing mechanization in all spheres of life and an unforeseen, radically new, totally inhuman technology of warfare. When he met Schwaner he had been using images of the "blue-blond Teuton" for over a decade, and for both the nationalist Gentile and the nationalist Jew these images suggested a potential of inclusion rather than the reality of exclusion.

2 .

It was not, of course, for intellectual achievement that Rathenau admired the Nordic type: "When has a man of the blond type of the Nordic Gods ever achieved greatness in the world of art and thought?" he asks in one of his "aphorisms."[25] But this, in a (to us perhaps) paradoxical perspective which is by no means exhausted with the label "Jewish self-hatred," is seen as a profound tragedy rather than as a mere shortcoming, lack, or flaw:

> The epitome of the history of the world, of the history of mankind, is the history of the Aryan race. . . . In overflowing fertility it sends wave upon wave into the southern world. Each migration becomes a conquest, each conquest a source of character and civilization. But with the increasing population of the world the waves of the dark peoples flow ever nearer. The circle of mankind grows narrower. At last a triumph for the south: an oriental religion takes possession of the northerns lands. They defend themselves by preserving the ancient ethic of courage. And finally the worst danger of all: industrial civilization gains control of the world, and with it arises the power of fear, of brains and of cunning, embodied in democracy and capital. . . .[26]

Rathenau published this in 1902, at the beginning of his career as engineer, industrialist, prolific cultural philosopher and, finally, internationally admired politician. But the attraction and fascination, the stylization, the significant image of the Other, to whom he felt so close, never changed for him. Prussian physique, Prussian eighteenth-century architecture, Prussian landscape represented for him an ideally restrained, sparse, essential, nobly vulnerable strength of feeling with which he identified. The "dark," "oriental," "cunning" type, the "Furchtmensch" (man of fear) or "Zweckmensch" (man of purpose) as he was to call him in his major metaphysical treatise, the 1913 *Zur Mechanik des Geistes: oder vom Reich der Seele* (On the mechanism of the mind; or, concerning the realm of the soul), continued to be the arch-etypical opponent of the Nordic actionist "Mutmensch" (man of courage), the ideal self-projection of his young murderers. On the eve of World War I he wrote a poem commemorating the 1813 Prussian War of Liberation:

> Blond und stahlblau Korn und Lüfte
> Himmelsaugen heiliger Seen
> Dunkler Kiefern Waldesgrüfte
> Blasser Dünen Schaumeswehen . . .
>
> Musste sich der Mensch verschliessen
> Dass das Herz umpanzert bliebe,
> Endlich darf es überfliessen
> Land, mein Land, du meine Liebe.
>
> Blond and steel-blue grain and air
> Heavenly eyes of holy lakes
> Forest vaults of dark firs
> Foamy drifting of pale dunes . . .
>
> Man has had to close himself off
> That his heart remained armored,
> Finally it may overflow
> Land, my land, you, my Love.[27]

The title of the poem is "Die Stimme der Sehnsucht" (The voice of yearning), and Rathenau's intellectual as well as emotional choices were indeed pro-foundly informed by such yearning. It made his metaphysics a runny mixture of highly eclectic Christian and Judaic concepts, his mysticism bland and dilettantish, yet compulsive. A critic summing up Rathenau's achievement shortly after his death, commented astutely on the large majority of his many books:

> These books, in spite of their wide circulation in a period avid for metaphysics, have not exercised the slightest influence; there is not a trace to be found of real effect on the older or younger generation of really front-rank intellectuals. Today they already seem to be in the same class as the poems, architecture, and music of crowned heads: works of a superior, educated dilettante of somewhat uncertain taste, who has no idea of what has been done before him or around him, without critical awareness of what he owes to others, of what is a new discovery and what is just a new formulation.[28]

This is certainly true with regard to Rathenau's intellectual position within a rich, complex, and conflict-ridden tradition which he simplified and distorted in order to appropriate it for self-presentation and self-articulation. Writing within a lively discussion of the problematic aspects of modern mass so-cieties, for instance, Tönnies's and Max Weber's *Gemeinschaft-Gesellschaft* (community-society) theme or theses of anomie and alienation built on Marx and Durkheim, he presented his insights as his own, as original constructs in the manner of an early industrial enterprise or a work of art.

Rathenau saw his role as analyzing and rejecting historical developments he thought destructive to true European culture: a (desirable) Germanic domination slowly undermined, in the course of the last centuries, by the dominated. This shifting of old power structures, accompanied by profound economic changes, growing populations, mechanization of all aspects of sociopolitical life, results, as he points out in the 1912 *Zur Kritik der Zeit* (Criticism of the age), in a "de-Germanization" *(Entgermanisierung)*. The experience of the war made him even more urgently aware of the need to balance this critical perspective on European cultural developments by more hopeful projections into a socio-political future. His 1917 *Von kommenden Dingen (In Days to Come,* 1921)—he thought it "the most revolutionary book that has appeared for many years"[29]—calls for a new and true German socialism which will be achieved through the inner progress of the soul, that is, in mankind's ascension toward freedom and self-determination in a general responsibility of the self and to the self in the economical, moral, and legal sphere. The economic solution is state socialism, a leveling and equalizing redistribution of income which will neutralize class conflict and realize the full potential of intellectual *(geistige)* and economic forces. Contemporary man wants to have and appear *(haben und scheinen);* future man wants to produce and to be *(schaffen und sein).* The source of evil in man is fear which has been intensified by mechanization's creating greed for the new, for money, for power *(Neugier, Geldgier, Herrschsucht). Furchtmensch* and *Zweckmensch* are symptomatic of and responsible for the ills of the time. The future has no room for them.

In Days to Come speaks about the war with deep ambivalence, about the future with unquestioned, indeed messianic hope. When the war came, as he had predicted, Rathenau was wringing his hands in despair. Now, in 1916, he remembers the summer-colored gaiety, the aggressive and innocent exuberance of the people of Berlin responding to the outbreak of the war. He participated, he says, in the pride of sacrifice and strength, but the frenzy seemed to him to celebrate death, fated and terrible.[30] Rathenau saw immediately, explains his friend and biographer Kessler,

> what practically no one else did—the stupendous world machine which was being set in motion against Germany. He knew its inexhaustible sources of power, against which those of Germany were small and strictly limited; he realized the inadequacy of our political leadership, to whose importance in war people were blindly indifferent; he saw the fragile nature of the political structure in which the storm had overtaken us, and the insufficiency of our armament.[31]

Kessler's perspective on Rathenau is well-balanced though on the whole very sympathetic, but he does not, I think, claim too much. The prolific and enthusiastic reaction to the war among the liberal and academic establishment is a familiar—to us astounding and yet, in the context of the cultural situation, quite accessible—phenomenon. Moved by "die Ideen von 1914," ninety-three academics and artists had signed, in October 1914, an appeal, "An die Kulturwelt" (To the cultivated world), expressing their support for their monarch and his government in their fight for German culture, which they perceived to be threatened by Western civilization. By 1916 the great majority of the signers had withdrawn to an ambivalent or negative position toward the German war effort—with the exception of Thomas Mann whose 1918 *Betrachtungen eines Unpolitischen* (Reflections of a nonpolitical man) were constructed around the dichotomous contrast between a profound, if troubled German culture and a shallow, if well-functioning Western civilization.

It is important to keep in mind, however, that learned chauvinism was a European rather than exclusively German affair. It had been traditionally the philosopher's task to argue, in the service of the nation, that the respective war was a just one and had, beyond its national meaning, the universal meaning of the struggle for the salvation and rejuvenation of the world.[32] For the German context, philosophers like Rudolf Eucken and his student Max Scheler provide instructive examples. Eucken's *Die weltgeschichtliche Bedeutung des deutschen Geistes* (The world-historical significance of the German spirit), published in 1914, is particularly striking in its neoidealist-nationalist stance.[33] Eucken had begun his highly successful career in philosophy as a solid and thoughtful Aristotelian but had developed a spiritual existentialism in the years preceding the war which attracted a large following. He became a prolific, widely read writer—in 1908 he was awarded the Nobel prize in literature, rare for philosophers (Bergson got it in 1927) and the only one so far for a German philosopher. Trying to compensate for a deeply felt lack of spiritual identity with his time and for the decline of the German soul in the dross of superficially successful dailiness, he embraced the outbreak of the war as a breakthrough *(Durchbruch)*, as liberation of the soul from the domination of mere intellect, stressing the greatness and dignity of the sacrifice of the individual for the people, who will regain moral health through the experience of the war. These are conventional idealistic sentiments. Neoidealistic is Eucken's thesis of the war as a worldwide challenge and proof of the strength and vitality of German inwardness *(Innerlichkeit)*.

Equally representative in terms of sentiment, but much more subtle and skillful in the presentation of his argument and more enduringly influential with regard to an antipragmatist ideology among German intellectuals on the right and the left between the wars, is his student Max Scheler. In his 1914 *Der Genius des Krieges und der deutsche Krieg* (The genius of war and the German war), Scheler, who had attracted attention with his 1913 *Der Formalismus in der Ethik und die materiale Wertethik* (Formalism in ethics and the material ethics of value), bases his arguments on a dualism of spirit and life, rejecting vitalist and mechanist positions. His concept of spirit *(Geist)* differs from Eucken's and Rathenau's soul in its insistence on an "Ideen-denken" (intellectual intuition or intuitive thought) of essences and arche-types. Human spirit rises above the (merely) organic, especially the German spirit, and it is not, as is Rathenau's soul, all-inclusive. Scheler argues against the concept of an "Allgemeinmenschliches" (the generally human) and for the historically evolutionary specific race. He rejects the "ridiculous, ar-rogant idolatry of Teutonism,"[34] renouncing the goal of a unified worldview: the Indian spirit, for instance, presupposes structures and forms of intuition and thought completely different from the European. But within the struc-tural unity of the European spirit, the German spirit has a special mission, because it is alive in a German youth purified, by the fire of the war, of capitalism, that is, the calculating, mechanized world of their fathers. Here Scheler is close to Rathenau. Scheler speaks of a "holy" war only with respect to the Russian enemy, and then in terms of the task of the preserva-tion of the spirit of European culture.[35] The main enemy is England, and it is the differences between Germany and England on which he bases his binary construct of cultural affirmation. He warns Germany of territorial greed vis-à-vis France and Belgium.[36] For him the war goals are on a higher level than mere gains in territory or power as they concern the German cultural mis-sion.

Scheler's political vision seems to be that of a reconstituted balance of power in Europe, and here his suggestions are quite mild, compared with many other statements coming from the academic community at that time. However, in the last part of the book, "Zur Psychologie des englischen Ethos und des cant" (On the psychology of English ethos and cant), complete with a "Kategorientafel des englischen Denkens" (Table of categories concerning English thought),[37] Scheler presents a complete rejection of English culture, as subtly argued as it is intellectually obfuscating. In contrast to the, in this respect, quite innocent, straightforward Rathenau, Scheler is a cultural es-sayist of great skill, sophistication, and devious subtlety. He has a remarkable wealth of concrete information at his disposal and an uncanny ability to suggest shrewd observation where he, in fact, maintains a perspective of unexamined prejudice. The cultural mission of the German spirit is then based on the "fact" that English culture is undermined by cant: *our* German culture for *them* is (mere) comfort, the warrior is the robber, thought is calculation, truth is fact, a worldview based on search for truth is a self-interested (pragmatic) worldview, reason is economy, causation is habit, scientific method is inductionism, concept is economy of perception, character is stubbornness, the good is the useful, promise is contractual binding, loyalty is keeping a contract, morality is legality, nobility is old wealth, love is solidarity of interest, world is environment, community is society, emotion is sentimentality, European community is balance of power in Europe—and so on. Case by case, item by item, Scheler points out the cultural inferiority of that civilized nation so totally under the leveling influ-ence of mere, shallow, reductionist pragmatist and empiricist thought. Germany's cultural mission in 1914 emerges clearly and much more powerfully than in Eucken's direct exhortations.

Rathenau was much more ambivalent about the role of the war concerning German culture. While he started to organize the distribution of supplies and the production of weapons—he called his highly effective work in the Prussian Ministry of War "intellectual work" *(Gedankenarbeit)* as if to make it less concrete—Rathenau believed, as he does in 1916 and at the end of the war, in "honorable, God-sent salvation," but not in the "full happiness of peace" *(volles Friedensglück)*. His reasons for this transcend social, political, or military contingencies: Germany does not have the right to determine the fate of the world—nor does any other nation have that right—because the Germans have not learned to determine their own fate, as they have not achieved the will to be responsible to themselves as to others. This war is an end, not a beginning. And though Rathenau, in 1916, makes himself believe in its happy outcome, he is afraid of what will follow. There has to be, there will be new life, but it can only come about by an awakening of the soul.[38]

Who will be able to experience such awakening? Rathenau is certain of its coming as an epiphany, but he sees his own generation as one of "transition, afflicted, destined to fertilize, not worthy of harvesting."[39] His own contribution to the fertilization is his "Transzendentalpolitik" as outlined in *In Days to Come:* the presentation of a coherent world view, based on the essence *(Wesen)* and becoming *(Werden)* of the soul,[40] which Rathenau clearly means to have the dignity of "harvesting." The present soulless state of the world is caused by mechanization, the "amalgamation of the whole world into one compulsory association, into one continuous net of production and world trade."[41] In the stranglehold of mechanization and the machinations of international finance the soul withers, and it is particularly mechanization that has to be dealt with forcefully. Rathenau's suggested solution is the creation of a *Volksstaat,* which would overcome mechanization as well as the ensuing atomization and division.

> Every one of the changes that we have demanded on moral, social, and economic grounds will strengthen the powers and completeness of the state. The state will become the moving center of all economic life. Whatever society does will be done through the state and for the sake of the state. It will dispose of the powers and the means of its members with greater freedom than the old territorial potentates; the greater part of the economic surplus will accrue to it; all the well-being of the country will be incorporated in the state. There will be an end to socioeconomic stratification, and consequently the state will assume all the powers now wielded by the dominant classes. The spiritual forces under its control will be multiplied. . . . The state in which the popular will has thus been embodied and made manifest cannot be a class state. . . . We are faced with the demand for a People's State.[42]

Such *Volksstaat* is the answer to and justification of Rathenau's fervent belief in the coming of a new unified system of values, bringing with it a new sense

of wholeness into an intellectualized, mechanized world where absolute
values have been destroyed and all true commitments have been dissolved.[43]
It will be "the second, extended, and earthly immortal self of man, the
incarnation of the moral and active collective will."[44] In it is centered the
hope for Germany's political future which is independent of institutions and
above all a question of character: "What we need is independence, the feeling
of nobility [Adelsgefühl], lordliness [Herrenhaftigkeit], the will to responsibility, generosity [Grossmut], liberation [Freisein] from a spirit of superiority or inferiority, of pettiness and envy."[45] What we need is the old spirit of
the blond, blue-eyed Prussian aristocrat, a Spartan dedication to the state.[46]
This spirit will embrace the soul, which does not claim temporal happiness,
power, or honors, and share in its capacity for the solitude of renunciation
and the bliss of sacrifice.[47] But it will be found only, if at all, among Germany's youth—as Rathenau hoped, in despair, when faced with the imminent
collapse of Germany in 1918:

> To you, Germany's youth, I address myself. To my contemporaries I have but
> little more to say. I have poured out my heart before them; my faith and vision,
> my troth and my troubles, I have displayed before their souls. Many have read
> my writings: the scholars to smile at them, the practical to mock at them, and
> the interested parties to grow indignant and rejoice in their own virtue. If warm
> voices have reached me, they have come from the lonely and the young and from
> those who neither grow old nor die.[48]

But the youth of Germany, sharing, to an extent, Rathenau's vision, sharing
his longings, his troubles and anxieties, did not, of course, share his extraordinary talents, his both absolute and shrewdly practical dedication to
the moral mission of the reconstitution of a truer, better Germany.

3.

Rathenau had many of the qualities admired and rewarded by his age: he was,
after all, a competent engineer and industrialist on a grand scale, a bit of an
economist, a prolific cultural essayist, and finally—and most seriously from
our perspective—a statesman who had shrewdness and vision. Yet he lacked,
conspicuously, a balance between what he perceived as the mere intellectual
capabilities, the "mechanics of the mind,"[49] and what he celebrated and
nurtured reverently with uninhibited eloquence, the life-center rooted in the
emotion, the soul. Emil Ludwig in his perceptive essay on Rathenau criticizes him for projecting, with the "gigantic searchlight of his egocentric
spirit," the "image of his inner fate on his century."[50] He was entitled to do
so, argues his biographer Count Harry Kessler, "because his fate and the fate
of the world were curiously alike, and he was thus led to realize more vividly
than most people what must happen unless the conflict between the two
tendencies which rend the modern world ends in the victory of the spirit."[51]
If mechanization defeats the spirit and imprisons the soul, if mankind

chooses its overgrown body over its soul, it will meet with an unthinkable fate. Hence, says Kessler, "the pathos of his writings."⁵² But though it is certainly true that Rathenau's perspective on the world seemed highly appropriate to many of his contemporaries and instructively symptomatic to the historian of the period, it is also true that what he—and Kessler with him—saw as his fate and the fate of the world signified an eclectic if culturally conditioned interpretation of the German and European problem in the first decades of the twentieth century.

For Rathenau reality meant the ultimately elusive battleground of external higher forces, distinct from the mere environment controlled by the mechanics of the mind. His rejection of the intellect directed by motivation, goal oriented, bound by self-interest and self-preservation shows an autocratic lack of concern for the world of the other to whom he wants to dedicate his life, his self. The intentions informing his arguments in *Criticism of the Age* (1912), *The Mechanism of the Mind* (1913), and *In Days to Come* (1917) could be understood as revolutionary: in these books he wanted to outline the new humane social, industrial, political world order which might prepare the way for the "realm of the soul," where competitive, fear-ridden, self-interested motivations of self-preservation were no longer needed. But his arguments, though often plausible in detail, were ultimately exhortatory and visionary rather than discursive, and they were quite often logically inaccessible. The fact that *In Days to Come* was something of a commercial success, selling sixty-five thousand copies in the first year, says more about a large educated audience's fears and hopes in and for their old world than about the reasonableness or desirability, let alone the feasibility of the projected new world. The majority of Rathenau's readers were not, one may assume, among Germany's youth on the left or the right; his readers were their despairing parents. And while his messianism as well as his predilection for a paradisiacal innocence of social intercourse could be found in both groups, they were also unmistakably his, rooted in his personal background and development.

Rathenau was born in 1867 in Berlin into what was then a middle-class Jewish family. His father, later an internationally important industrialist, was at that time a mildly successful engineer and businessman and member of the Berlin orthodox Jewish community. His mother had come from a cultivated Jewish middle-class family in Berlin, admiring of, interested in romantic intellectuals and artists. For the young Rathenau, Goethe was a saint in the religious hierarchy of art and, like Rembrandt, Bach, and Shakespeare, one of the "evangelists of German culture." His own quite considerable achievements as an industrial engineer had always seemed small to him in comparison to the performances of professional writers and musicians. This reflects a thoroughly German concept of culture, especially as it enabled the competent engineer and industrialist to appropriate Goethe's greatness to focus his own identity. In terms of his familiarity with the socioeconomic sphere, his awareness of the concrete rapid changes in industry and violent ruptures in sociopolitical conventions, Rathenau differed drastically from the large majority of his intellectual contemporaries. But in terms of his understanding the social cultural conflicts tearing at the troubled young century— soul vs. mind, organic life vs. mechanization, community vs. society, rebirth vs. death—he was indeed clóse to the prevalent contemporary intellectual preoccupation with dichotomies. And it was this closeness which enabled him to claim and sustain his distance from the concrete contemporary social world which, in turn, supported his never diminished sense of a unique and uniquely meaningful personal fate nurtured in the unique culture of Germany.

Culture in the more narrow sense of the arts and literature, and here especially Prussian culture, was for Rathenau the most satisfying, the most complete access to personal identity, its lawful development and unthreatened meaning. When he met, still young but already successful, an old lady who remembered the 1840s, whose mother had been the model for Schubert's "Schöne Müllerin," who had heard Tieck read and seen Fanny Elsler dance, he remarked: "To me it is something rare and strange that I, the little electrical engineer, should actually touch with my fingers the magic ring of the Romantics."[53] In an essay on the occasion of Max Liebermann's seventieth birthday in 1917, Rathenau's portrait of the important painter, his father's cousin, shows clearly his identification with this eminent Prussian artist. It is very important to him that Liebermann and he share an ancestor, one of the early Prussian industrial magnates under Friedrich Wilhelm III— he starts the essay stating the connection: "His grandfather, whose life-size portrait painted by an unknown master is hung in his study, is my greatgrandfather."[54] And he goes on to point out that Liebermann's highly controlled art in its cool sparseness, its muted colors and restrained lines shows discreet richness, self-confident nobility, occasional greatness, even monumentality. The painter's antisentimental attitude is sustained by passion rather than skepticism, the "blood of emotions" glowing through the "cover of objectivity."[55]

> Men of will, of passion and sensuality, subjected to the pressures of external and internal battles, do not spend themselves [verschäumen] in unconscious and unmeasured instinctive creation. Rather, they produce in themselves the highest, even demonic individuality, the strength of perpetual youth, of change and regeneration in their self-created domain.[56]

None of the periods in Liebermann's work is one of youth or of age; they are all organically whole and mature; they all unfold within the circle of one personality, physiognomy, and signature. It is only mastery that grows, that renews itself and transcends.[57]

This is precisely the way in which Rathenau strove to see and to form himself, especially in the many letters which he wrote with great care and consideration for his own and his correspondents' need for self-presentation. There is little spontaneity, no playfulness, no humor in these letters; the early ones seem as firmly adult as the later ones. The work (of art) is the self nurtured in (national) culture; selfhood, a task, can become a work of (national) art. And through the experience of the Great War, the vulnerability of Germany, of German culture, finally her near-destruction which he could not prevent, Rathenau came to see self-mastery in self-conscious service, the work of the self as its immersion in a collective other, a meaningful national community sustained by a cultural tradition. Ferdinand Tönnies's 1887 *Gemeinschaft und Gesellschaft* (Community and society) had become widely read, discussed, and overinterpreted in its second edition in 1912. Tönnies, accordingly, had warned readers in the prefaces to later editions to avoid simplifying and thereby distorting the distinction as a nostalgic attempt to resurrect an older more meaningful form of social organization. He does not, he asserts, deny the "true facts" of progress, enlightenment, of liberal developments and civilization, distancing himself from a romantic glorification of the past.[58] But Rathenau, as did so many of his intellectual contemporaries, viewed progress and civilization with deeply ambivalent feelings, uneasy about the rapidly changing organizational forms and priorities in a modern mass society, unable to accept, as largely irreducible, the very concrete manifold tensions between the needs and desires of the individual and his obligations to the collective whole.

Arguing against suicide in a letter to a friend in May 1919, a period when he was deeply depressed about the state of Germany and the frustration of his attempts to be of service to her, Rathenau writes:

> Since I have ceased to take myself and my existence so seriously, simply because it does not belong to me and ought, rather, offer its services to the community, something has changed in my relation to men. Perhaps, too, because war has aged me so rapidly. I feel that I ought to serve everyone and as I cannot serve anyone truly, I try to serve all.[59]

Self-mastery could not balance the experience of a self perceived as too split, too complex, too precarious, and too precious to serve anyone in particular. Such self needed to serve all—that is, it needed to embrace all in order to escape being limited by anyone. The realm of the soul was so important to Rathenau because, all-expansive, all-inclusive, it could transcend the limiting borders of intellectual differentiation. The intellectual processes in the Buddha differ from those of Plato, Rathenau writes to a friend in 1914; yet, in the realm of the soul both are congruent. This is true, too, for the relation between different races. The Teuton and the Papuan alike, he argues, are descended from ancestors very much below them on the ladder of evolution. But such differences—between the Papuan and the Teuton, between them and their ancestors—are meaningful only in the realm of the intellect. They are dissolved in the realm of the soul: "How much more free it is, the world of the soul!"[60] It may still be described by attributes associated with the Germanic type, but, borderless, timeless, it is accessible, in principle, to every human being. Merging, embracing, to become one, to be part of a larger whole had always been Rathenau's deeper and ever more urgent desire, articulated in his prolific and often vacuous writing, but also in concrete, highly effective industrial planning and administration in the service of Germany. He had been building up her defenses during the war, and after the war he was building up her ability to coexist, that is, to survive whole—by learning to be sufficiently flexible socially and economically—within the European political complex of national conflict and power.

It is hard to say how central or traumatic an experience exclusion had been for the Jew Rathenau. It had not driven him to seek assimilation by conversion to a majority religion. His construct of the tragic, marvelous, superior, vulnerable Aryan race could be understood as a fiction which, in stressing a protective attitude toward the Other, protects the threatened Jewish self. To call such fiction an instance of Jewish self-hatred would not be very helpful. Rathenau's responses to the pressures of minority existence were self-consciously individualistic *and* determined by the socio-psychological structures and energies of the group he was part of. They reflected the situation of culturally assimilated, educated Jews within the German nation.

After studies in Strasbourg and Berlin—mathematics and physical science with Helmholtz, chemistry with August Wilhelm von Hofmann, philosophy with Dilthey—Rathenau graduated with a dissertation on light absorption by metals in 1889 and then went into the field of electrochemistry which was just in its beginnings. In 1893 he took over the management of the Elektrochemische Werke in Bitterfeld, an industrial town in the Prussian province of Saxony, where he lead a very busy, rather dreary life, determined to overcome a host of financial, administrative, and technical difficulties. When he left in 1900, the firm had become successful and he had acquired, through hard work and isolation, a sense of self-reliance, of uniqueness, of service, of a meaningful social existence seen entirely in his terms, constructed through his images, nurtured by his needs, aggrandized by his conflicts. His father Emil Rathenau had founded, in 1883, the Deutsche Edison-Gesellschaft für angewandte Elektrizität (German Edison company for applied electricity) which later became the A.E.G. (General Electric Company). Emil Rathenau's influence on German and world industry was decisive. He made mass production possible in one of the most important branches of modern industry by rationalizing production and distribution and by developing new forms of cooperation between banks and industrial concerns. Emil Rathenau "remains the most typically representative figure of German and Continental industry, because he embodied with the greatest intensity and singleness of purpose the two basic tendencies which distinguish modern big business from earlier forms of industry: the immediate utilization of every technical innovation for mass consumption, and the immediate absorption of every new source of capital for the increase of production."[61]

Walter's relationship with this extraordinarily strong and successful father was expectedly difficult, though he became much closer to him after the early death of his brother, whom both had loved very much as a more relaxed extension of their own highly compressed personal identities and a link to the outside social world. Rathenau admired in his father a creative simplicity, the talent to go directly to the core of complicated matters, an instinctive sense of purpose and direction in intellectually difficult terrain. He also understood that his father, all his experience and capabilities notwithstanding, had become caught in the momentum of the industrial build-up. He was under its control as much as he was in control, or even more so. Emil Rathenau's decisions on methods of production and distribution and on finance had made him an immensely rich man—whatever he touched seemed to turn into money—but production seemed, more and more, to become the self-propagating goal of financial conveyor belts going round and round. Much of Rathenau's deep ambivalence about industrial technological progress and fear of increasing mechanization can be traced to his sharing the experiences of a powerful industrial magnate who was his father, sufficiently similar to identify with him, sufficiently different to assume the perspective of distance.

For Rathenau's reader such perspective meant both clarification and distortion, and the two aspects complemented and reaffirmed each other in often tortuous and obtuse, sometimes remarkably illuminating, shrewd arguments. Jewishness—the community's, the family's, his father's, his own—played an important role in the way in which he understood, shaped, and used distance. His earliest published essay, "Höre Israel!" (Hear O Israel!) starts with the sentence: "I will confess from the outset that I am a Jew."[62] His biographer and friend Count Harry Kessler, who worked with him politically after the war, reads it as a "bitter and fateful sentence, like the opening theme of a tragic symphony. For Rathenau's Judaism was his ruin."[63] Kessler who had always seen Europe as his cultural home—his family belonged to the European nobility, he was completely at ease in several European languages and intimately familiar with European literature and art—had the poise of the cultural insider but shared Rathenau's intense yearning love for German culture and German landscape. He is, not the least for this reason, a very perceptive interpreter of Rathenau, though too discreet about his homosexuality, too accepting of an alleged fateful dualism in his psychological make-up, too ready to grant his Judaism an inexorably tragic dimension, and therefore too little interested in an analysis of his obsession with organic wholeness, with strength and purity as (paradisiacal) end products of a process of coming together, assimilating, merging.

Rathenau had, on the whole, a rather balanced and realistic view of the social political situation of German Jewry, but never overcame a deep sense of the alienness of Eastern Jewry. Where he related negative tendencies in modern mass societies to images of (Eastern) Jewish life, it seems that his self-conscious position outside an unstoppable, "merciless" motion of mechanization through technological progress was as much informed by his Judaism as his Judaism was informed by his embracing the position of the outsider. If he accepted his Judaism as fateful, his fate was still highly individual. As his emotional and intellectual center lay securely in a German idealist tradition sufficiently thinned out and smoothed down to provide a focus of identification for the educated German middle classes, he could acquiesce in that familiar German phenomenon of significant individuality as the inevitable step to higher community, of avoiding, that is, the messy and politically divided realm of social intercourse. In "Hear O Israel!" he advises his reader to

> wander through the Tiergartenstrasse at 12 o'clock on a Berlin Sunday morning, or else look into the foyer of a theatre in the evening. Strange sight! There in the midst of German life is an alien and isolated race of men. Loud and self-conscious in their dress, hot-blooded and restless in their manner. An Asiatic horde on the sandy plains of Prussia. . . . Forming among themselves a close corporation, rigorously shut off from the rest of the world. Thus they live half-willingly in their invisible ghetto, not a living limb of the people, but an alien organism in its body. . . .[64] Yet I know, that there are some among you who are pained and shamed by being strangers and half-citizens in the land, and who long to escape from the stifling ghetto into the pure air of the German woods and hills. It is to you alone that I speak.[65]

He was thirty years old when he wrote these lines. No matter how successful, how widely published he became, these images of division, if somewhat muted, somewhat more ambivalent, were to stay with him, and so was the gestural appeal to the reader: one outsider to another, but outsiders who by virtue of their perspective of distance on their "own" group were straining to overcome the status of stranger in the encompassing group that was the true (future) Germany. In all his texts he would appeal to some deeper instinctive understanding and sympathy, some bond between speaking voice and listener, some secret, almost intimate agreement. There had to be higher meaning in being an outsider, and such higher meaning, he realized, could be communicated only by the assertion that it be shared and by the promise that such sharing would result in a true German community.

The 1901 "Physiology of Business" has many witty and shrewd observations on the business world which read like instructions given today, almost a century later, by an intelligently cynical manager to young aspiring colleagues, but he speaks at the same time from a position outside that sphere of mere self-interest and survival, a position that insists on true cooperation and communality:

> People who fit successfully into an organization are always Germans or Anglo-Saxons. Of all forms of racial superiority this seems to me the most important. Jews are never officials. Even if it is on the most insignificant scale they are employers and business people on their own responsibility.

Jews, that is, cannot sustain or nurture a community.

> The Future. I see the rulers of the future and their children. Horrible people with huge skulls and burning eyes, men who sit perpetually, sit and count, calculate and advise. Every word an act, every look a judgment, every thought directed to that "which is." Perhaps they will be somewhat more cultured than their brothers of today, probably less healthy.[66]

Against the dark suffocating world of purpose, calculation, desire, and compulsion, the world of his father, he was to project in his later books the realm of the soul, free of desire, of will, of purpose, associating the images of light, space, motion, air—German landscape and the blond, blue-eyed Germanic type with its long elegantly narrow head and tall slim mobile body.[67] It is important, however, to keep in mind that his repulsion by things as they were and his ambivalence, at the very least, about the world of industry and high finance were not exhausted in such images and appeals: already in the "Physiology of Business" he tried to find practical solutions on a large scale which he summed up in the concept of "euplutism," requiring measures like graduated income tax; heavy duties on inherited wealth, dowries, and settlements; taxation of capital unproductively employed, especially of foreign loans; diminution of arbitrary monopolies by the right to nationalize mines, transports, and urban land; abolition of monopolies where government contracts are concerned; state control of combines, cartels, and trusts.[68]

The experience of the war had intensified Rathenau's desire to rethink existing socioeconomic structures. Much of the established intellectuals', the mandarins', enthusiasm for the "genius of the war" had been nourished and funneled by a vision of national unity—the emperor's *Burgfrieden,* the temporary but very powerful illusion of a falling of all class barriers, was the most public expression of that vision—including the somewhat magical disappearance of self-centered, calculating, divisive capitalist interests. The neo-Kantian philosopher Paul Natorp, for instance, saw in the *Zwangswirtschaft* (controlled economy) instituted by the government at the beginning of the war a welcome development toward a "German nationalization."[69] But Rathenau who had been involved in governmental economic planning wanted much more. In his *In Days to Come* (1917) and *New Economy* (1918) he projected a classless society without proletariat where hereditary oppression and privileged ruling castes would be abolished. The more visionary *In Days to Come* was dedicated to the memory of his father, who had died in 1915; and the peculiar mixture of transcendent will, free soul, and industrial-managerial know-how is indeed indicative of his closeness *and* distance to the world and the achievement of this unselfconsciously active figure of a Wilhelminian industrial baron. Commenting on the text, Kessler praises Rathenau's "sincerity" in questions of the soul, but he also claims his right to be heard on the basis of his "accurate knowledge": "A great organizer of industry speaks on the revolution of industrial organization; that alone entitles him to be listened to with respect."[70]

Arnold Brecht, a high civil servant in the Reichsministerium from 1921 to 1927 who from 1933 to 1954 taught at the New School of Social Research, commemorated the twenty-fifth anniversary of Rathenau's assassination with an essay *Walther Rathenau und das deutsche Volk* in which he stresses the central importance that Rathenau's concept of the soul had for all his work: "It remains deeply moving that he, a leader of German industry in the twentieth century and an eminent intellectual, did not hesitate to confess publicly that the source for all our difficulties [*Übel*] was to be found in our contempt for the soul." Arnold Brecht had known Rathenau personally from 1920 on and had been impressed, he writes, by the true personality shining through the remnant of a shell of intellectuality: "He had become what he had striven to be."[71]

It is significant that these two political contemporaries stress the sincerity of Rathenau's attempt to bridge very different modes of understanding and insight, but also that they do not try to evaluate the viability of such an attempt though it is the center of Rathenau's sense of identity as well as the source of the problematic aspects of his work. He was a highly competent industrialist in his contemporary economic context; his projections for radical socioeconomic change were both too vague conceptually and too eclectically detailed and prescriptive. He was a utopist in the old static meaning of the concept; the better place was exclusively designed by him, and it was exclusive, since entering it required a leap of faith.

Who would have wanted to enter that future other world? It is constructed on a specifically German dichotomy of culture and civilization so central to the culturally powerful concept of antipragmatism which has been termed, in its late nineteenth- and early twentieth-century versions, "cultural despair" or "cultural pessimism"—misleading terms, because the despair or pessimism does not refer to culture as a whole as much as to certain disquieting aspects of cultural developments which are called civilization.[72] (Conspicuous) consumption, e.g., is for Rathenau lamentably civilized, detracting from higher values. In his utopia, therefore, he wants to regulate and restrict consumption by an extensive system of taxation. The occupation of space (parks, houses, stables, garages), domestic service, luxury items, horses, carriages, motors, illumination, costly furniture, rank, title—all this will be taxed to make it (almost) prohibitive.[73] The furthest possible equalization of property means, to Rathenau, the removal of obstacles to the free unfolding of the soul. The desire for gain would then be replaced by true ambition and the joy in creation—in the case of the worker as well as the industrialist managing a large concern.

In *The New Economy* Rathenau seems less concerned about the general change of heart or freeing of the soul than about specific changes in organization. His model amounts to a highly planned economy, a sort of state monopoly capitalism with great insistence on the state's power and authority.

> The division of labour according to groups can no more be left to the free play of
> forces than the internal technical reform of individual factories; this task, like the

others, can only be accomplished by a comprehensive reorganization of industry. For good intentions alone, unless they go hand in hand with supreme authority, are helpless in the face of the arbitrary splitting up of markets.[74]

This seems to contradict the free play of substantive ambition and joyful creativity envisioned in the previous book. But his experience with Germany's wartime economy, a situation of extreme shortages of resources, transport, and labor and extreme need for speedy production and distribution, had led him to see as totally obsolete the "old and absolute right" of "everyone who can afford it to employ the labour resources of the nation for his personal comfort and show, or for any supposedly industrial purpose he thinks fit." The deciding factor must be, from now on, in a very concrete sense the needs of the community,[75] and he views them as "objective, scientifically demonstrable, and verifiable requirements."[76]

The value of the new economic order depends, then, exclusively on the success of its service to the community. Rathenau projects the basic economic organization as two complementary kinds of association or unions:

> Let us imagine that all factories of the same kind, whether industrial, commerical, or mechanical, are coordinated, say all cotton spinning mills, all iron rope factories, all joiners' work, all wholesale dealers in goods, all in separate units; imagine further that each of these associations is coordinated with the other businesses connected with it, and thus that the whole of the cotton industry, the iron industry, the timber industry, and the linen industry are amalgamated in separate groups. The first of these organizations we may call functional unions, the second industrial unions. . . . Associations of this type already exist in large numbers and in every field, but they serve only private interests, not industry in general. Functional and industrial unions would be corporations recognized and supervised by the state, enjoying extensive rights of their own.[77]

The "functional unions" or occupational associations are indeed, as Rathenau points out, the more important of the two,[78] and he describes them very much in terms of an organism, of the body: they create the economic unit, providing it with "unified force and life, eyes, ears, sense, will and responsibility."[79] And, anticipating the objection that a structure of such associations might bring back the rigidity of the old guild system, he asserts, explicitly now, its organic properties: it is "a community of production, in which all the members are organically bound up with one another, to right and left, above and below, in which they are welded into a living unity, possessed of a common vision, judgment, and will—in fact, not a confederation, but an organism."[80]

In *In Days to Come* Rathenau had evoked and postulated the "new capitalistic forms [that] will replace private enterprise, when the superfluities of individual wealth have disappeared owing to the diffusion of a general and equalized wellbeing":[81] they amount to the celebration of the state in its capacity as collective familial banker, incorporating all the well-being of the country, physically (economically) and spiritually, the state as living organism, a *Volksstaat*.[82] Rathenau's insistence on community, on the common good, on the popular will is the insistence on inclusion. His concept of democracy—in spite of his supporting the parliamentary system as the best means for the selection of politicians—is that of a fully and directly communal experience,[83] and he is more interested in its essence than in its possible form. There will be no class division in German, only German citizens, Jews among them.

To Schwaner he wrote in 1916,

> I have and I know no other blood than German blood, no other race, no other people than the German. If one drives me off my German soil I remain German and nothing will be changed. . . . My ancestors and I have found nourishment on German soil and in German spirit and we have repaid our, the German, people in whatever ways we could. . . . I am convinced that religion, language, history, and culture are of much greater importance than physiological issues of blood mixture and will offset them. I believe in the divine soul in every human spirit carrying it to a level where the material becomes dust. I believe in a divinity toward whom we are all striving.[84]

On a quite vicious instance of nationalist anti-Semitism—a young *völkisch* lieutenant had complained to Schwaner about the Jew Rathenau's work for Germany's war effort as "a shame and a scandal" and Rathenau had been told by Schwaner—he comments that "Christ would not have understood that."[85] And pointing out Schwaner's occasional distinction between "my people" and "your people," he asserts,

> My people are the Germans, and nobody else. The Jews, for me, are a German race, like the Saxons, the Bavarians, or the Wends. You will smile now, as you know all the racial doctrines. This science is of no interest to me. Science says this today and another thing tomorrow. It has nothing to say about feeling and idea, ideal and transcendence. I don't ask whether the Jews are Hittites or the Saxons Mongoloids; I don't ask whether Christ, Goethe, or Beethoven were blond; for me the question of belonging to a people or nation is decided by qualities of the heart, mind, character, and soul. And here I place the Jews somewhere between the Saxons and the Swabians; they are less close to me than Brandenburgers and Holsteiners, and perhaps somewhat closer than Silesians and Lorrainers. I am speaking, of course, only of German Jews; Eastern Jews are for me, as for any other German, Russians, Poles, Galicians; Western Jews Spaniards or Frenchmen. Anti-Semitism and particularism are about the same to me; I think a Bavarian running down Prussians really seems more unpleasant to me than his attacking Jews.[86]

And this was probably literally true. Rathenau agrees that fate controls great events, for instance the development of a true German national unity, a *Volksstaat;* but, in objection to the simple-minded, religiously nationalist Schwaner, he distinguishes between a general human sphere subject to such preordained course and a political sphere where decisive responsible action is possible and of the utmost importance.[87]

4.

Being Jewish must have made Rathenau more sensitive to the always troubled position of the imaginatively, intelligently active individual in the group, but he did not accept it as determining his fate. The dignity of fate only came with the "highest sphere" of human existence,[88] which transcended such classifications and divisions. To be Jewish meant to be challenged in unique ways; it made the issue of individuality more poignant, more self-conscious, more meaningful. Kessler remembers Rathenau's entry, after his return from isolation in Bitterfeld, exile as it were, into Berlin court society.

> Anyone who met him then will remember a slim and very tall young man, who startled one by the abnormal shape of his head, which looked more negroid than European. Deep-set eyes, cold, fawn-coloured and slow; measured movements; a deep voice; and a bland address—these formed the somewhat unexpected, and, as it were, artificial, setting for a dazzling display of intellect.
>
> In Court Society, where everybody knew everybody, his intrusion seemed strange at first. But once one had noticed him, it was impossible to forget his appearance and the peculiar impression he made: an impression of massive strength and at the same time of a certain weakness, perhaps, for all one knew, of a too tender skin. He was fascinating and somewhat mysterious. . . . Never for a moment did he forget, or allow others to forget, that he was a Jew; he seemed to want people to feel that he was proud of his race, that it made him a distinguished foreigner who had a right to special courtesies and to pass through doors closed to others. He contemplated the great ladies, and the young nobles of the Horse Guards, as though they belonged to another planet. Herbert von Hindenburg's novel *Crinett*, which had just appeared, and which gave an unfriendly but authentic picture of this world, Rathenau studied like a Baedeker. "Important material for getting at the ideas of the Prussian nobility," he sets down in his diary.[89]

This is seen through an insider's perspective—an insider, however, who is aware of his position and his perspective, aware, too, of the ways in which power and privilege are accessible to the outsider and will, if not diffuse, then certainly redefine the dividing line: The outsider becomes fascinating and mysterious; he is admitted to the exclusive group on his own terms; his uniqueness, his individuality is unchallenged; his isolation is of the higher, significant kind. It might, indeed, be compared to that of the artist—writers, composers, sculptors, painters now move in court society and older members of the court fondly reminisce about famous artists they knew when they were young—for instance, the old lady who told Rathenau about Schubert and Tieck.[90]

To Rathenau, then, Jewishness reinforced his sense of a highly valued personal uniqueness, but when he discussed the sociopolitical situation of

German Jewry he showed an impressively lucid, shrewd understanding of the problems of minority existence and prejudice. In his 1911 *Staat und Judentum: Eine Polemik* (The state and the Jews: A polemic), taking issue with a Christian proponent of a large scale Jewish conversion, he argues that the contemporary cultivated German Jew is less religious than, for instance, a Catholic and that the sense of division goes back to a very old racial antipathy which has changed on the part of the Jews during the last two or three generations, giving way to the full appreciation of a nation to which they owe the most valuable part of their cultural tradition. Christian German reservations, on the other hand, seem to him to have remained the same or decreased very slightly, having increased till the 1880s in reaction to the growing number of Jews and to their wealth, influence, competitiveness, self-confidence, and self-presentation. As long as the state accepts and justifies such antipathies and as long as certain racial peculiarities set apart the Jewish German and make him suspect to the Christian German that situation will not change.[91]

Rathenau does not think that conversion to Christianity would further the cause of Jewish assimilation. He declares the conversion concept underlying Prussian-German policies regarding Jews antiquated, wrong, inefficient, and immoral. Antiquated, because all civilized Western nations have changed in this respect without suffering any negative consequences; wrong, because measures intended against a race are actually directed against a religious community; inefficient, because an obvious Jewishness *(Verjudung)* one wishes to control is replaced by latent "Jewish" characteristics encouraged through a negative selection (he has in mind conversion motivated only by considerations of career opportunities and profit) and because a large conservative minority loyal to the state is driven into opposition; immoral, because conversion is rewarded, and large numbers of citizens who have only followed their conscience and their convictions are illegally disadvantaged in academic, military, and judicial careers. Again and again Rathenau stresses the conservative attitude of the Jewish minority, their support for the state and for national cultural traditions in addition to their importance for German industry, especially at a time of rapid industrial build-up. He expresses his conviction that, together with political and social inequality, "instinctive" animosity against the Jewish German will finally disappear.[92]

In his polemic with a member of the Prussian nobility concerning the role of Jewish citizens in Prussian government—here, too, the tone and substance of the argument is conciliatory—Rathenau points out that the existence of the Jews is predicated on the strictest conservatism known in history and that in England, France, Italy, and the United States Jews are the elements most supportive of the state. He agrees whole-heartedly that intelligence is valuable only in connection with ethical attitudes and denies the existence of a specifically "Jewish spirit" *(jüdischer Geist)* among the cultivated German Jewry, referring his opponent to the unquestionably constructive role played by baptized Jews in the Prussian judiciary, government, and army. There is one argument he does think valid: the Prussian state is a creation of the Prussian nobility, which explicitly and, to a degree, understandably, does not want to share its administration with another group. He does admit the conflict of interest, pointing out, however, that the task of administration has changed over the last one hundred years with the acceleration of technological development in industry and warfare. As always, he emphasizes that the state needs the Jews, that national loyalty and cooperation will benefit all the different but equal groups united in a healthy and powerful Prussian Germany.[93]

The threat to Germany posed by the war, her decline, and finally her near collapse proved to be an intense personal strain on Rathenau, resulting in some puzzling, even paradoxical decisions which would haunt him in his last years. He had known the *Generalquartiermeister—de facto* commander-in-chief—Erich Ludendorff since 1915 and had been at first impressed by his elasticity and quick comprehension. "I felt," he said in his essay "Schicksalsspiel" (The game of fate), published in the *Berliner Tageblatt* (November 23, 1919), "he was the man to lead us, if not to victory, at least to an honorable peace. . . .I was one of those who did everything in their power to smooth his path to the Supreme Command."[94] And indeed he did. In a letter to Ludendorff on September 16, 1916, he even supported the deportation to Germany of 700,000 Belgian workers to help the Hindenburg industrial program. As his stated war aims were international reconciliation and European economic unification and as he identified so strongly with these aims, such support seems almost self-destructive. It has to be approached in the context of his intense German-Prussian loyalties.

These loyalties, shared by most of his liberal contemporaries, certainly by the whole mandarin caste, were substantially based on fears associated with the idea of Germany's external weakness, but they were intensified in his case by his particularly needy love for the meaningful community of a German *Volkstaat*. He differs from most of the mandarins in the protective, anxious quality and in the urgency of his feelings of responsibility for a community that is both precious and very fragile. He differs, too, in the clarity of his perspective on the developments leading to the war which he feared from the beginning would destroy it. To his friend Fanny Kunstler he had written, in the fall of 1914, about the quiet beauty of autumnal Germany, bleeding from all her veins, and about his painful inability to help her:

> We must win, we must! And yet we have no pure, no eternal claim to victory.
> This exquisite genuine people does not have any clear sense of freedom. It loves authority, it desires to be governed, it gives itself and wants to obey. In the total context of historical development [*im Sinne der ewigen Geschichte*] this half virtue is an offense. We are governed by a caste, competent, self-confident, but without initiative. It worked as long as this caste was not ashamed of its backwardness. Now it wants to be modern, destroys the old yet does not bring about the new, makes the world our enemy, makes us weak externally, and suddenly attacks at a moment not chosen by us.[95]

By the spring of 1917 he had become critical of Ludendorff, telling him bluntly that England would not be defeated by German submarines shortly. In July he discussed with Ludendorff at headquarters "the small effect on English commerce, the illusory method of reckoning the total tonnage, the defensive measures, and above all the possibility of America's building more tonnage than we sank."[96] Ludendorff, the modern technocrat, as he liked to see himself, was typically unimpressed by logical argumentation and reasonable concepts of risk. In February 1917 Rathenau had described the new submarine warfare as an experiment that, like jumping across an abyss, had to be one hundred percent successful to be at all successful. "But this 100 percent includes an unknown economical factor and a psychological factor which has never been appreciated correctly here." He is afraid, he concludes, that the consequences of submarine warfare will be a prolongation of the war.[97]

It was his desire to protect and heal as much of Germany as quickly as possible, and decidedly not a wish to prolong the war, which made Rathenau publish, on October 7, 1918, in the *Vossische Zeitung,* the notorious call for a *levée en masse*. Ludendorff's precipitant request for an armistice he rejected as an extraordinarily ill-considered declaration of bankruptcy which not only ruined Germany but did great harm to all of Europe, because it destroyed, as he saw very clearly, the hopes for a reasonable peace:

> Let all who feel the call present themselves; there will be enough elderly men to be found who are yet sound, full of patriotic fervour, and ready to help their tired brothers at the front with all their powers of body and soul. Secondly, all the "Field-greys" whom one sees to-day in our towns, at the stations, and on the railways, must return to the front, however hard it may be for many of them to have their well-earned leave cut short. Lastly, all men capable of bearing arms must be combed out of the offices, the guardrooms and depots, in East and West, at the bases and at home. What use have we today for Armies of Occupation and Russian Expeditions? Yet at this moment we have hardly half of the total available troops on the Western Front. Our front is worn out; restore it, and we shall be offered different terms. It is peace we want, not war—but not a peace of surrender.[98]

Prince Max von Baden, chancellor of the new People's Government who had reluctantly agreed to the armistice proposal, asked the Supreme Command on October 8 whether, in their judgment, adequate reinforcement could be provided by the *levée en masse* as recommended by Rathenau, but Ludendorff rejected the proposal as creating a dangerous disturbance.

Rathenau had overestimated the people's desire to go on giving of themselves and, if not their need for authority, certainly their willingness to obey blindly in a situation which seemed entirely hopeless to them. So he was hated by the revolutionary masses as a reactionary wanting to prolong the war, while he had, in fact, been attacking many aspects of the governing system for years. The year 1919 was especially hard for him. Feeling painfully isolated, he poured out his frustration in many letters, protesting that he had worked for radical change through his books, especially *In Days to Come*. He thought powerful interest groups had been made nervous by his writing and were now organizing to fight him: "One did not have to wait for the effect. When the revolution came everybody agreed they wanted to get rid of me. There was no need for a pretext on the right; on the left one just used my well-known article of October 7."[99]

Rathenau had indeed put himself between various interest and power groups. It was not this fact, however, that made him particularly vulnerable to violent aggression from the right which, as he had said, did not need any pretexts. As to the left, he was not so much wary of their fanaticism and radicalism as of their sterile, doctrinaire fractionalism,[100] and he rejected, as economically antiquated and stifling, the orthodoxy of Marxism.[101] Yet, as he had little understanding for the social existence of the self, both his and others', disregarding questions of self-interest, self-preservation, and motivation, his own writing, its unsystematic essayistic flow and vacuity notwithstanding, was as prescriptive in terms of sociopolitical thought and action as any other contemporary doctrine.

But in the case of the reparations negotiations which occupied him exclusively from 1920 to his death, Rathenau was able to *act*—shrewdly, with circumspection and with imaginative patience, flexibility, tenacity. These acts were the outcome of decisions made within an almost impossibly confused, confusing, contradictory complex of sociopolitical claims and alliances, and they dealt with a dizzying force of particulars. Rathenau, however, was guided by their substance, the goal of a Germany made whole—through negotiated fulfillment of her obligations—and a viable member of a pacified Europe. In December 1918 he wrote two open letters to the victors, one to "All Who Are Not Blinded by Hate," and one to Woodrow Wilson's influential friend Colonel House. To Germany's European creditors he projects a dismal picture of the defeated country's future: "The German spirit which has sung and thought for the world will be a thing of the past, and a people still young and strong today, and created by God for life, will exist only in the state of living death." To Wilson he appealed through a friend to consider the issue of punishment and justice: "Never before has the fate of a healthy and unbroken, gifted and industrious people been dependent on one single decision of a group of men. Suppose that a hundred years hence the thriving towns of Germany are deserted and in ruins, its trade and industry destroyed, the German spirit in science and art dead, and German men and women in their millions torn and driven from their homes—will the verdict of history and of God then be that this people have been treated justly, and that the three men responsible for this devastation have done justice?"[102]

It is the German people he is pleading for in his anxiety that they not be deprived of a potential rebirth which alone would result in true community. In the 1918 *To the Youth of Germany (An Deutschlands Jugend)* he had characterized the war as the symptom of a new beginning of mankind; new men will appear who are centered in the realm of the soul, who will be neither self-seeking nor seeking for riches or power and therefore able to sustain a new order: "Do not forget: even if we could establish a German Earthly Paradise to-day, we should not have these men to administer it. . . . Look around you at these parliaments, these offices, these academies—everywhere. . . . And once again I lose heart and ask: Where are the men?"[103] Kessler remembers Rathenau saying that the future—but not the present—belongs to bolshevism: "We have not got the men for so thoroughly complex a system; it demands a far finer and higher talent for organization than we can show. . . . And several times he repeated: 'not yet.' "[104] The answer, for him, lay in Germany's youth. It was for them that he tried to negotiate a livable peace when a new order might develop, but Man, the personal potential, was the primary consideration; the new order would follow.

Rathenau saw, however, also the weaknesses, the dangers in the idolatry and rhetoric of German youth. In May 1919 he wrote to Heinrich von Gleichen-Russwurm, the conservative journalist and politican, rejecting politely the offer to join a group of young people gathered around him. Gleichen-Russwurm had warned Rathenau that the serious dedicated among Germany's youth did not entirely trust him, the highly skilled and successful overpowering speaker and writer. His personality was too strong and held too much fascination to be above suspicion. Rathenau grants that the young will see mainly the bankruptcy of the older generation; that they question authority, as the old Germany had believed too strongly in it and thus been destroyed. They do, however, he argues, have a need for leaders, and there is no leadership without authority. It was not the belief in authority itself that had proved harmful, but the belief in the wrong kind of authority. What he says about Bismarck's authority—people believed in him because he was successful, not because he was spiritually right ("nicht, weil er ein Geist war, sondern weil er die Sache gemacht hatte")—seems to point to his familiar and sterile grid of a dichotomy between the realm of purpose and goal, of measurable success and applied instrumental reason, and the realm of the soul where untainted truth can be found. So, too, does his insistence on the impossibility of creating spiritual values in a social context with democratic procedures. And yet, Rathenau is right in his complaint that the concepts *democratic* and *social* as used by the young are frequently based on a concept of truth that is both impossibly pure and idiosyncratic. All this commotion of authenticity and individuality will result, he predicts, in gray uniformity—as indeed it did. The "youth of dialectics," as he sees it, will then be followed by a "youth of pragmatics" open to authority. For authority, like experience, can be communicated, and so can truth which does not have to be new to be significant: "Who is the great statesman? He who recognizes in the contemporary complex of ideas those which are essential, right, and feasible."[105] Such a statesman will be able to establish a meaningful direction of events in what seems, in the spring of 1919, anarchic oscillation and total chaos.

Rathenau expected to be involved substantially and officially in the task of reconstruction, but in the beginning he suffered several severe setbacks. His Democratic People's League, meeting for the first time on November 16, 1919, was not meant to be (just) another party, as he wished, above all, for solidarity and unity in the new Germany, abhorring what he considered excessive parliamentary fractionalism. The league's only resolution was a demand for prompt convocation of the National Assembly. But in his "Appeal to the German People" he outlined his aims in greater detail, based on the proposals in *In Days to Come* and *The New Economy*. He addressed himself to all Germans not part of the Workers' and Soldiers' Councils or the "self-constituted" groups that made the revolution. For him the true revolutionary aims, which he sees now threatened and in need of protection, are unification, democratic freedom, the end of privilege and class barriers, nationalization of industry where suitable, right to work and education, a simpler life, that is, a life of truer, more natural (cultural) values.[106]

The league dissolved itself very soon and Rathenau turned to Friedrich Naumann's German Democratic Party (Deutsche Demokratische Partei) whose leadership included Max Weber and Hugo Preuss and which saw its task, above all, in mediation between the bourgeosie and the workers, supporting strongly a policy of international understanding.[107] His candidacy for a seat in the National Assembly was frustrated by local anti-Semitism (Oberlausitz area), he was removed from the Commission for the Socialization of German Industry—a field where neither his considerable expertise nor his willingness to be open to change could be doubted—because of the violent resistance to him by the left-wing Independent Socialists.[108] He was, strangely, hurt even more by an incident at the second session of the National Assembly in Weimar when, during nominations for the presidency of the new republic, his name was proposed by cable: "On behalf of many Germans abroad I propose as President of Germany the name—respected both at home and abroad by friend and foe alike—of Walther Rathenau. (Much merriment) May he be our leader. Eugen Müller, Stockholm. (Much merriment on the Right.")[109] Rathenau's perspective on this rather harmless incident is significant: there had been, for instance, "much merriment" on the left when Hindenburg's name was proposed. As his complaints in the 1919 *Apologie* show quite clearly, he took the ridicule very seriously, that is, personally, protesting both the impropriety of having his name brought into proximity with the "solemn proceedings" of the election and of the lack of respect for a man "of recognized intellectual standing."[110] Both the election to this office—the highest in the sense of nonpartisan representation and unifying symbolic presentation—and the divisive rejection of his person were of a profound importance to him that indicates very strong reservations regarding the role of convention, compromise, accommodation, and consensus in a parliamentary democracy.

Kessler comments that Rathenau, as a result of these incidents, "came to regard the National Assembly and indeed parliamentary government in general in a thoroughly unsympathetic frame of mind,"[111] and it is certainly true that he took them extraordinarily seriously. There are also misunderstandings, distortions of his ideas on industrial reorganization by the Social Democratic Minister of National Economy Rudolph Wissell which infuriated Rathenau and against which he wrote his last substantial book, *Die neue Gesellschaft* (1919) (The new society), a dystopian projection of the kind of socialization he abhorred, namely a totally state-controlled industrial system in which, after the disappearance of the proletariat, everybody was extremely poor and powerless.

But Rathenau had, apart from these (to him) serious irritations, a much more basic aversion to the give and take of parliamentary democracy ruled by the open play of chance and self-interest, the group's and the individual's. Significantly, it was the friendship with Joseph Wirth, the new minister of finance after the Kapp putsch, German chancellor from 1921 to 1923, and editor of the well-balanced, fair liberal weekly *Deutsche Republik,* which sustained Rathenau's rising political influence from the spring of 1920 on. The relationship was characterized by the two men's complementary talents, but above all by mutual trust, intellectual and emotional intimacy, and the sense of a substance of shared significant authority in the service of Germany.

The reparations negotiations provided Rathenau with a context for self-presentation and self-articulation which was indeed ideal—if for a short, difficult, and hectic time. For once the tension between his German and his Jewish personae, which had never been allowed to relax, may have been useful to a degree as it granted him a perspective of distance both on himself and the, in hindsight, fantastic, impossible mess of pressures, claims, anxieties, and rage surrounding the negotiations. His achievement was to see the politics of fulfillment as the challenge of a complicated gradual process rather than an imminent solid disaster. So he looked for the central point from which to unravel the complex of difficulties, insisting that reparations be seen not as an embarrassing or impossible or insulting obligation but rather as the keystone of German policy and thereby a process of German achievement which, juxtaposed to the war, would be viewed, centuries later, as the greatest German creation. Focus on the reconstruction of northern France and Belgium would enable Germany to regulate her relations with France, improve the terms of the peace treaty, modify and mitigate the reparations payments, achieve beneficial effects on Germany's internal affairs, and above all regain Germany's moral position.

Rathenau had communicated these thoughts in July 1919 to Matthias Erzberger, then minister of finance and later assassinated in August 1921 by two radical nationalists, former officers.[112] He was to adhere to precisely this concept of fulfillment as one of reconstruction, that is, an actively positive achievement. He bargained shrewdly using detailed economic arguments as well as general psychological pressures like Germany's dismal situation and his own intellectual and moral stature and integrity. But, bargaining in very concrete terms[113] and using his personal appeal to manipulate others—as any experienced, skilled negotiator would—he saw himself as an impersonal, inviolable, and fated instrument devoted exclusively to the service of Germany who, fulfilling the task of reconstruction with complete spiritual dedication, would achieve her own reconstruction, her own wholeness. Such a concept of wholeness presupposed Germany's inclusion within a European community and her own inclusive completeness in which class barriers would dissolve and minorities truly assimilate.

At the meeting of the Allies' Supreme Council in Cannes in early January 1922—a meeting held in preparation for the pan-European economic conference in Genoa planned for late spring—Rathenau did not accept an offer from the Reparations Commission to settle for a certain fixed amount though he was under pressure by the threatened fall of the relatively sympathetic Cabinet Briand. The feared news came when he was in the middle of a speech on economic hardships and impracticalities concerning the reparations claims. On the invitation of Lloyd George he proceeded, stressing again Germany's willingness, in spite of her difficulties, to fulfill her obligations to the very limits of her capacity, her desire to cooperate, together with the Western powers and Russia, in the reconstruction of Europe. The passed-over offer was made again in March by the Reparations Commission, in spite of Poincaré's open hostility to Germany. But, most important, Rathenau had made a considerable step forward in projecting convincingly another, new Germany, determined to remain peaceful and sincerely trying to fulfill her obligations and responsibilities. On this he built in his negotiations with the Russians in Rapallo and with England and France in Genoa, which regained for Germany the status of an important European power and signified the beginning of her slow, and all too short, rise out of sociopolitical chaos. His concluding words at the last plenary session in Genoa were a quote from Petrarch: "Io vo gridando: Pace, Pace, Pace!" and the response of his audience was an ovation—for the man, for his achievement, for the sentiment expressed as skillfully as it was sincere, for the hope of a new pacified Europe.

Rathenau was murdered shortly afterward. He knew about the imminent danger of political murder and included the deadly threat in the "Law" of his life about which he reflected in his last letter from Genoa to Schwaner.[114] Kessler remarks that the verse from Petrarch "summed up in a symbol" Rathenau's life work.[115] And so it did in a way. One should stress, once more, that Rathenau did not just call for peace, but very concretely, very effectively acted for it. And that it was this work for which he was murdered. But this poignant juxtaposition of the great European of Genoa and the "Judensau" of the German extreme right is instructive not so much for the violence done to the victim by the destructive forces of a split, chaotic Germany as for Rathenau's specific all-consuming preoccupation with Germany's German wholeness and with his role in protecting and recreating it.

TWO

Ulrich, a Life

Robert Musil and the
Experiment of the Real

I.

In a 1914 review of Rathenau's *The Mechanism of the Mind* (1913), "An-merkungen zu einer Metapsychik,"[1] Robert Musil reflected on the philosophi-zing of a man who was an eminently successful industrialist and widely read popularizer of dogmatic idealism, apparently excelling both in the *vita activa* and the *vita contemplativa*. This phenomenon, then, suggested that the profound and common split between life and thought, mind and soul could indeed be overcome, if in rare heroic moments by heroic individuals, and Musil, though ironically uncovering some of the questionable implications of such artful managing of this gulf, was intrigued. He thought that Rathenau had failed to deal intelligibly with an important contemporary issue, his hazy mysticism and pseudosystematics discrediting his attempt to chart and de-scribe areas of experience threatened by a growing intellectualization and fragmentation of modern life. It was not an allegedly modern negative at-titude toward the "realm of the soul" that interested Musil, but, rather, finding ways to speak about this elusive and immediately, urgently present dimension of human experience. One of his major criticisms is that Rathenau is as emphatic as he is inarticulate in his assertions of the importance and meaningfulness of this dimension of experience, substituting a rational dis-cursive mysticism for concrete descriptions of a complex emotional-intellec-tual state. To Musil, such a shift is typical of systematic attempts at describing and evaluating extrarational mental states. The spiritual and emo-tional substance evaporates under such clumsily applied pressure and the reader is left, in Rathenau's case, with metaphysics as a "heraldic speculation hanging the disembodied skin of experience on the stars."[2] He points out the lack in the German tradition of successful attempts to write systematically and imaginatively about the process of living, with the notable exception of Nietzsche: "In our culture artistic and scientific thought do not touch. The problem of mediation between the two remains unresolved."[3]

Such mediation was the focus for all of Musil's texts, beginning with his

first novel, *Die Verwirrungen des Zöglings Törless* (1906) (*Young Torless*). As
he was fully aware of the complexity of the process of experience, Musil's
response, in sharp contrast to Rathenau, was to acknowledge the methodological relevance of the *modus tollens* for the study of experience. He
understood his writing as a contribution to *Erfahrungswissenschaft* (experiential science),[4] intent on integrating—and thereby modifying—scientific
modes of thought into literary discourse so that human potential in experience could be more fully and more precisely articulated. He was decidedly
not interested in a dialectic of opposite modes of thought to be reconciled on
the obligatory "higher level" of a higher truth, because most natural sciences
as part of *Erfahrungswissenschaft* consider degrees of probability rather than
a fixed point of truth. Musil was not, as some critics contend, a *poeta doctus*
moving effortlessly "from mathematics to mysticism"—what they mean is
from computation to lyric evocation of emotions.[5] As he saw it, it is not a
question of opposites, but of shifting proportions.

Yet, truth has been a persistent cultural beacon. Pascal in his much
quoted *pensée* on skepticism stated the confusion, still with us, that seems
inherent to any consistent attempt at understanding and articulating the
whole range of human behavior:

> Qui démêlera cet embrouillement? La nature confond les pyrrhoniens et la
> raison confond les dogmatiques. Que deviendriez-vous donc, ô hommes qui
> cherchez quelle est votre véritable condition par votre raison naturelle? Vous ne
> pouvez fuir une de ces sectes, ni subsister dans aucune (no. 434).

> Who will unravel this tangle? Nature confutes the skeptics, and reason confutes
> the dogmatists. What then will you become, O men! who try to find out by
> natural reason what is your true condition? You cannot avoid one of these sects,
> nor adhere to one of them.

Consequently Pascal admonished reason to humble itself, calling out to his
reader: "Ecoutez Dieu!"—Rathenau did indeed write in a long tradition of
the suspicion of reason. The scientist Pascal was content with probabilities;[6]
the moralist was passionately concerned with the truth and restless with the
uncertainties inherent in human understanding.

It is this split which Musil analyzed critically in the Rathenau essay as
the most formidable obstacle to the development of an *Erfahrungswissenschaft*. Drafting the introduction to a volume of essays with the
working title "Versuche einen anderen Menschen zu finden" (Attempts at
finding alternate man),[7] he copied David Hume's introductory remarks to the
1739 *Treatise of Human Nature Being an Attempt to Introduce the Experimental Method of Reasoning into Moral Subjects*:

> Disputes [on moral subjects] are multiplied, as if everything was uncertain; and
> these disputes are managed with the greatest warmth, as if everything was
> certain. Amidst all this bustle 'tis not reason which carries the prize but elo-

quence; and no man needs ever despair of proselytes to the most extravagant
hypothesis, who has art enough to represent it in any favorable colors.[8]

To Musil these remarks seemed curiously contemporary in the 1920s. In his
comments he emphasized two aspects of what Hume had seen as problematic in discourses on "moral subjects" (in the broad eighteenth-century
sense): the mode of communication and the philosophical tradition of dealing
with moral and epistemological questions in the pure realm of abstraction
where it was possible to pretend that "everything was certain."[9] Both aspects
are interdependent. To insist on the relevance of daily experience, that is, a
shared life-world, for philosophical inquiry means to insist on the need to
proceed with the greatest possible degree of caution and precision from a
position of sophisticated falsificationism. Writing on questions of human
knowledge and behavior, an author cannot profitably abstract an "objective
truth" from his and his readers subjectivity.

On another occasion Hume criticized Diogenes and Pascal for having
located their static moral principles outside of "ordinary conduct" and
consequently having experimented with their lives in a vacuum.[10] Like Musil
he refused to separate reasoning from daily experience. Where Musil was
attacked by contemporary professional readers in Germany for not removing
his novel *Der Mann ohne Eigenschaften (1930, 1932) (The man without
qualities)*, which brought an experimental mode of thought to the exploration
of social behavior, identity, and knowledge, into the self-sufficient protected
realm of art;[11] that is, for being too intellectually rigorous for a novelist,
Hume had been attacked in England for not settling in the pure sphere of
philosophy, for being too literary.[12] In Germany his influence was almost
completely neutralized by the Kantian and then the Hegelian tradition.

Nietzsche was one of the very few German thinkers to appreciate
Hume's specific clarity and brightness, but he, too, then leveled Hume's
psychologically informed epistemology to a mere "Glaube an das Subjekt"
(belief in total subjectivity), unable, it seems, to grasp Hume's concept of the
subject as constituted in social interactions of the most varied kind. It was
precisely this concept which made Hume define philosophy as nothing but
"the reflections of common life, methodized and corrected."[13] Ernst Mach,
probably the single most important influence on Musil's intellectual development,[14] dedicated one of his best known studies, *Erkenntnis und Irrtum*
(1905) *(Knowledge and Error)*, to Hume, drawing attention to intellectual
affinities and stating that his own philosophy was "nothing but a scientific
methodology and epistemological psychology," *Erkenntnispsychology*. It is
not only issues and arguments in Musil's sociopsychological essays of the
twenties that reflect such rootedness in the real: much of the complex subtle
and striking imagery in his major work, *The Man without Qualities*, can be
shown as developed from responses to the shared stimuli of daily experiences
and their meanings.[15]

For Musil, literary discourse is not to be removed from the author's and reader's life-world. His concept of essayism—essay concerning an intellectual attitude rather than genre or form—implies the writer's responsibility to the world which informs strategies of writing. In an essay fragment, "On the Essay," written in the early twenties[16] Musil defines the peculiar difficulties and advantages of the essayist dealing with questions of social behavior in terms of cultural significance: he will strive for the strictest, that is, most adequate precision where a concept of pure scientific precision is meaningless. The essay appears as a medium most suitable for contributions to a science of human nature, that is, a cultural science, as it does not attempt complete solutions *(Totallösungen)* but settles for a series of partial solutions. The analysis presented by it, however, is intended to be accessible and verifiable in its references to the author's and the reader's experience. Musil remarks in this context that Rathenau provides an example for the essayist's degeneration into a philosophical dilettante,[17] pointing to the need for certainty and wholeness that prevented Rathenau from appreciating the meaning of such referentiality.

The essay does seek an order to make communication possible: lack of any systematic approach at all where the subject of inquiry is human nature as a cultural phenomenon "causes men to write poetry and live like pigs,"[18] Musil notes. But attempts at establishing an order are meaningful and useful only if they accommodate the continuous motion of essayistic reflection which includes feelings, desires, intentions—in Musil's words, "the second dimension of thought."[19]

This is a difficult proposition and has been the cause for much misunderstanding. In his important 1922 essay "Helpless Europe" Musil points out the lack of balance between the rational and irrational faculties of the human mind and the "instinctive" preference of synthesis to analysis: "It is not that we have too much reason and too little soul; rather, we don't apply enough reason in problems concerning the soul."[20] The cultural consequences could be—and indeed they were to be—disastrous. Here as in his other essays dealing with a host of problems besetting the Weimar Republic, Musil rejects prematurely arrested social constellations as well as prescribed forms of perceiving self and other. Don't deceive yourself, rely on your perception, your experience, be open to the force and fire of pragmatism and positivism as attitudes toward living, he admonishes his readers in "Helpless Europe." And he reminds them of the "furor" of the seventeenth-century return to a positive interest in evidence, to intellectual sobriety, to the testimony of reason and the senses. If there is a cultural crisis to be distilled out of all that cultural confusion—though Musil did not think in terms of crisis, rather in terms of potential and perplexity—it has to do with a deeply flawed concept of experience. The fact frequently mentioned as a symptom of Weimar's cultural crisis, that there is, at present, no (systematic) philosophy cannot, Musil argues, be understood as failure of the times to produce it—a sort of lack in spiritual strength or focus. Rather, the period discourages philosophical constructs which do not fit the concerns of a contemporary cultural reality.[21] Heidegger's *Sein und Zeit* (1927), anticipating the turn to a "new inwardness" around 1930,[22] proved Musil's point—now the case for a cultural crisis could be stated more persuasively. Musil did point to long-range shifts in the understanding of the cultural function of philosophy when he recommended to his readers in "Helpless Europe" Wolfgang Köhler's "essay in natural philosophy" *Die physikalischen Gestalten in Ruhe und im stationären Zustand* (1920) (*Gestalt Psychology*, 1929) which suggested to him possibilities of finding solutions for age-old metaphysical problems in the empirical sciences *(Tatsachenwissenschaften).*[23]

Musil had made the commitment to literary discourse after taking a degree in engineering (1901), at the Technical University at Brünn, graduate studies in mathematics, physics, and philosophy (1903–1908) at Berlin University where he wrote a doctoral dissertation on Ernst Mach's work in physics and psychology[24] with the philosopher Carl Stumpf, an admirer of Husserl and critic of Mach. He had done research in experimental psychology at Berlin University (1906–1908), inventing an instrument to test color perception, the *Musilsche Variationskreisel* (Musil's variational cylinder), but he declined offers for further research positions, deciding against an academic career. When he critically reviewed Oswald Spengler's best-seller in the essay "Geist und Erfahrung. Anmerkungen für Leser, welche dem Untergang des Abendlandes entronnen sind" (1921) (Mind and experience. Notes for readers who have come through the decline of the West),[25] he satirized the arbitrary arrangements of concepts reflecting Spengler's determination not to have his flights of fancy dragged down by evidence. Yet he also pointed out that Spengler, in his rejection of contemporary culture, had indeed seen the problem of diverging mental faculties. Musil agreed that the element of intuition in thought processes is highly important and needs to be analyzed, but he disagreed emphatically with Spengler's hostility toward reason, judging harmful his further polarization of rationalism and irrationalism and his overwhelming need to find meaning and hold on to it—even if it was that of cultural despair. Spengler's *Decline of the West* owed its spectacular success to precisely these attitudes: there were a great many readers who preferred "the truth" of an inevitable decline to skeptical, informed discourse about complex sociopsychological cultural issues. Reason, Musil pointed out dryly, really has nothing to recommend itself but the fact that it works—hardly grounds for wanting to do without it.[26] It is certainly not the human capacity that should be suspected, but, rather, the ends to which it is used. Spengler's and his audience's reluctance to pose rigorous questions demanding documentation and proof seemed to Musil symptomatic of the contemporary intellectual difficulties under investigation. The process of experience informing and being informed by human relations as cultural constructs is as complex as it is conflicted and contradictory. Success lies with writers who appear to lighten the burden instead of making it an even heavier responsibility.

Given Musil's intellectual temperament, such responsibility was unavoidable for the writer; it was only the medium that might be questioned. In the fragment "On the Essay" Musil tried out ways of defining this changeling discourse: the essay gets its "Form"—mode of discourse—from science, he says; its "Materie" from art. The order it seeks is based on connections between thoughts—logical—and its source is found in observable facts— scientific. It may be, however, that neither the facts nor the established connections are generally observable because of an always specific individual consciousness directing observation and connection.[27] In a 1918 essay on the epistemology of writing, "Skizze der Erkenntnis des Dichter" (Sketch of poetic cognition),[28] the writer is assigned the "nichtratioïd" mode of cognition, the exploration of "inner man"; the "ratioïd" mode is defined as that of the (natural) sciences, and psychology is counted among them.[29] (Musil was to change his view of the potential scope and role of psychology in the area of research that might lead to more coherent, systematic statements on emotions and motivations.)[30] More important for our immediate context is the assertion—it is emphasized by italics in the text—that it is *the structure of the world"* which assigns a specific responsibility to the writer, not "the structure of his particular talents."[31] *Ratioïd* and *nichtratioïd* are clumsy, overstated working hypotheses meant to bring more clarity to a rather obscure area of inquiry. In Musil's writing *praxis* the exploration of "inner man" did not move independently of the "outer" world shared with others. In fact, there are no distinct "inner" or "outer" worlds.

The war experience—Musil served in the Austrian army—meant an expansion of the self toward the world by which both self and world become larger, stranger, and less manageable with respect to a unified fictional construct. And it is in the texts of the postwar period that one can observe the development of that curiously right merging of the concrete and the abstract—one of the best informed students of his work speaks of his "cogito sensible," "cogito corporel"[32]—which is the substance of his prose style. In their stunningly fitting images these texts make permeable or collapse the barriers between science, philosophy, and literature; the extraordinary care given to verbal flexibility and precision supports the interaction of different modes of discourse.[33] In the essays they emerge in the voice of the author; in the novel they are carefully orchestrated in a great variety of speech-acts or conversations between politicians, industrialists, diplomats, generals, scientists, educators, artists, writers, and philosophers which constitute an encyclopedic presentation of Viennese society as a model of the modern world. The writer's responsibility, for Musil, is to describe what a person living consciously in that confusing, perturbing exhilarating time *can* do and to examine the implication of possible choices. As they are also the writer's, his evaluation is part of the analysis, yet his purpose would be defeated if the "can" were to be misunderstood as a "should." He observes and judges as a participator, and his fictional construct of social reality depends on this mobile particular perspective on the general.

Such perspective has been an issue much discussed in twentieth-century social science. In his seminal essay " 'Objectivity' in Social Science and Social Policy" written in 1904 on the occasion of his assuming, together with Werner Sombart and Edgar Jaffé, the editorship of the *Archiv für Sozialwissenschaften und Sozialpolitik,* Max Weber deals with the relationship between evaluative, normative positions and empirical knowledge. For Weber it is precisely the science dimension of sociology as "cultural science"[34] or *Wirklichkeitswissenschaft* (empirical science of concrete reality)[35] which assigns the task and responsibility of choosing to the (individual) reader of a sociological text engaged in a rational exploration of the values and ideals on which choice is based. "An empirical science cannot tell anyone what he *should* do—but rather what he *can* do—and under certain circumstances—what he wishes to do."[36]

Weber's concern about the influence of unacknowledged or not explicitly admitted (individual) value judgments on "scientific arguments" in cultural science is only one of the issues discussed in the essay which actually poses the question of a specific mediated objectivity more broadly, sharing, to a degree, Musil's concerns. The differences, however, are more instructive than the affinities. In Weber's distinction social science is charged with the analysis of facts, and social policy with the statement of ideals. And though both will be found in the journal, they will be kept apart: scientific freedom demands that it be made clear to the reader and, most important, to the social scientist as writer "at which point the scientific investigator becomes silent and the evaluating and acting person begins to speak."[37] The investigator is allowed to bring his own clear-cut ideals to the discussion— "an attitude of moral indifference has no connection with scientific 'objectivity,' " Weber states explicitly[38]—but they ought not merge with the scientific argument.

Such clean separation is problematic. Musil for one would not have thought such a pure concept of "scientific" possible or desirable in social science; perhaps even more important, he would not have removed from analysis the investigator's personal sphere of values. In Weber's scheme personal values (ideals, desires, motivations) are mentioned only insofar as they taint scientific discourse. Yet, scientific analysis of a culture cannot contribute anything to its meaning:

> The fate of an epoch which has eaten of the tree of knowledge is that it must know that we cannot learn the *meaning* of the world from the results of its analysis, be it ever so perfect; it must rather be in a position to create this meaning itself. It must recognize that general views of the world and the universe can never be products of increasing empirical knowledge, and that the highest ideals which move us most forcefully, are always formed only in the struggle with other ideals which are just as sacred to others as ours are to us.[39]

In the meaningless infinity of the world process, culture for Weber is a finite segment "on which *human beings* confer meaning and significance"[40]—he underlines "human beings" to stress the secular dignity of culture. Still, cultural science, to him, seems to be a post-Fall product and (therefore?) separated from the affirmation of cultural meaning which is walled in by particularity and largely inaccessible. Intent on marking the boundaries of the young science of sociology Weber did not consistently question the concept of scientificity which is itself an (unexamined) cultural value. Self-awareness and self-presentation of the social sciences have suffered from such lack of questioning, weakening the imaginative interplay of subjective and objective, particular and general, personal and sociocultural aspects of experience and knowledge.[41]

Musil was very much aware of this situation and its implications for his cultural essayism, and he stated the issues subtly and succinctly in a review of G. J. Allesch's *Wege zur Kunstbetrachtung* (1921) (Ways of viewing art). Visual art in the twentieth century is a highly personal, particular cultural product in terms of meaning and significance, and it is interesting that Musil should have used this occasion to state his views on the interpretation of cultural meaning in general. He had known Allesch since 1906 when they were both working in the Berlin Institute for Experimental Psychology and had, in fact, developed the *Variationskreisel* to aid his friend in his experiments. Allesch had continued in an academic career in psychology, concentrating his research—in contrast to Köhler—on subjective variability in *Gestalt* formation.[42]

Musil begins the review with the observation that books on art are in most cases either elegantly suggestive *(geistreich)* or very learned—seldom both. The book under review is and deserves the reader's attention as a successful attempt to create an order which is both lively, responsive, and enduring. Allesch's achievement is to help his reader understand the genesis of the impression made by a work of art *(Bildeindruck)* by sorting out perception of color, line, plane, and space *Gestalten* and separating them from arbitrary emotional associations without, however, neglecting consideration of their emotional effect *(Gefühlswirkung)*. The *Bildteile* (parts of the pictures) as constituents of the total impression are generally verifiable units of perception, and the *Bildeindruck* is built up by them "psychologically, that is *in reality.*"[43] Allesch, too, works with analogies both vague and ambiguous, using, for instance, concepts like tension, activity, softness, and emptiness as referents to the expressive values of lines, colors, planes, and spaces. But he also shows how these values are articulated by the relation and combination of the units of perception and that their status is one of rather fragile potentiality. In this area the interdependent process of perception and cognition cannot be seen as entirely clear and certain; its outcome has to be located on the level of a comparatively high self-balancing probability.[44]

In Musil's view such perception/cognition process is a kind of "optimal misunderstanding" with a remaining soft core which at any time might support an entirely new conception. Like people, art can only be misunderstood in sympathetic or hostile ways which will change historically.[45] This suggests that the work of art is open to infinite processes of perception/ cognition arrested in a wide variety of interpretations. But as art is the work of men and viewed by men and as human beings historically have shown limited potential for differentiation there will, in reality, not be more than a few possible interpretations which, moreover, can probably be shown to be different aspects of a comprehensive concept. In spite of the difficulties associated with the question "what is historical reality?" concerning human knowledge and action there are definite distinctions between more and less reliable methods in approaching it. For Musil inquiry into cultural achievement and cultural values has to be informed by the willingness to negotiate imaginatively and circumspectly between what can be said with a high degree of general validity and therefore certainty and what has to be acknowledged as particular perception and value. Such negotiation will be differently focused in texts intended as contributions to social science in a narrow (technical) sense and in essays intended to communicate with a general educated audience about shared contemporary cultural concerns. But the question of effectiveness remains—it is also one of intellectual temperament—and Musil answered it for himself by choosing the medium of the essay and the essayistic novel of ideas.

In their insistence on a plurality of value-positions Weber and Musil show the influence of Nietzsche. But in contrast to Musil, Weber looked at that plurality from the position of his buttressed self; he did not move within it. Certain tensions and inconsistencies in his methodological texts have their source in this perspective. Musil remarked early on the disturbing and exhilarating aspects of Nietzsche's suggestive, "conceding" way of speaking to his readers—"jene einräumende Art."[46] The Nietzsche of *Gay Science*, suggesting possibilities and combinations, gives space—the literal translation of *einräumen*—to the young Musil to find his own way in the alluringly and confusedly charted area of cultural values. Musil tried to puzzle out the merits of such "cerebral fantasies," but he also pointed to the reader's difficulties in forming value judgments, that is, in making choices when engaged in this open mode of discourse. He saw, then, at the beginning of his writing career, the central advantages and problems of a discourse of possibility which he was to develop most fully in the twenties and thirties in *The Man without Qualities*.

Nietzsche's influence was affirmed and modified by Ernst Mach whose 1906 *Populärwissenschaftliche Vorlesungen* (Lectures on science for the layman) established for Musil the importance of bringing scientific methods to the analysis of sensations *(Empfindungen)*,[47] emotions, and motivations. His 1908 dissertation on Mach was a sympathetically critical discussion of Mach's mathematical empiricism and of the epistemological implications of Mach's scientific sensualism and functionalism which were to inform Musil's concept of essayism.[48] Nietzsche had made devastating fun of the "fantastic ego" nurtured by the individualism of nineteenth-century European culture, but Mach had set to work to dismantle it soberly. The ego cannot be salvaged, "das Ich ist unrettbar": the notorious sentence in the 1886 *Die Analyse der Empfindungen und das Verhältnis des Physischen zum Psychischen (The Analysis of Sensations)* provoked many hostile reactions by humanist thinkers,[49] but its implications as Mach saw them were, in fact, convincingly humane. Gaining insight that emphasis on a firmly established ego is meaningless—Mach points out the very common experience of ego variability during the course of one's life—will lead to a renunciation of personal immortality and a freer and more serene world view which excludes both contempt and rejection of the other and exaggerated self-esteem.[50] In the 1905 *Erkenntnis and Irrtum (Knowledge and Error)* Mach had defined object and ego as similarly provisional fictions: "Ding und Ich sind provisorische *Fiktionen* gleicher Art" (The object and the "I" are provisional fictions of the same kind),[51] namely, symbols for clusters of sensations which do not exist outside of our thought processes.[52]

For Mach, and for Musil, this concept of ego as a useful mental construct or fiction meant neither the deplorable loss of an original organic wholeness—an ideal inadequate to the complexity of the human mind in any case—nor the threat of social atomization and subjective fragmentation of the world. It meant, rather, a model which was useful in epistemological psychology, the study of human knowledge which includes emotions and motivations.

The function of the ego-fiction is to facilitate and sustain connections. In the introduction to the planned essay collection "Attempts at Finding Alternate Man," mentioned above, Musil reflects on the narrating voice or consciousness that provides the direction for the essay: not a scholar, not a fictional character, not, in this case, a poet: there is only a personal ego-connection involved in grouping thoughts in response to the object of inquiry ("persönlicher Ich-Zusammenhang").[53] The protagonist of these thoughts has a fictional identity only insofar as it is useful in the process of articulation. The reader is asked to imagine an engineer who brings his trial-and-error method to the exploration of epistemological problems and moral systems as cultural constructs. It is, then, a personal mode of thinking that structures the essay, not a particular person. But the personal mode provides an important resistance to a misguided concept of objectivity in the realm of social and epistemological psychology, the realm of *Erfahrungswissenschaft*. The reason for the contemporary moral confusion given in "Helpless Europe" is the fact that we do not really involve ourselves consciously in our cultural activities: *"wir denken und handeln nicht über unser Ich"* (We do not think or act through the medium of the "I").[54] Musil means the temporary shifting ego-construct which focuses thoughts and actions so that they can be questioned meaningfully. And existing *Erfahrungswissenschaften* like psychology or sociology did not seem helpful to Musil in regard to this problem of more or less automatic action and thought—"going with the times"—which had become more urgent in twentieth-century technocratic mass societies. The study of cultural concerns, achievements, and values has to be informed by the question "how are we to live?" Social policy has to be part of social science and vice versa, and it is the essayistic discourse of possibility which encourages such interaction and interreflection.

Musil's novel adapted itself to his essayism supported by the extraordinary scope and tenacity of his intellectual curiosity. In the year of his death, 1942, he wrote to a friend that he would not be finished with *The Man without Qualities* for a long time yet.[55] He had been working on it for twenty years—or for forty years, if one takes *Young Torless,* the novellas, dramas, and essays as earlier stages or fragments of the novel. It ended when the mind engaged in exploring the activity of minds was stopped in its own activity. It was not the only lengthy and weighty novel of ideas or philosophical novel published in Weimar Germany: there were Thomas Mann's *Magic Mountain* in the midtwenties and Hermann Broch's *The Sleepwalkers* at the end of the Weimar Republic.

Like *The Man without Qualities* these novels brought together various kinds of discourses from a large number of different contemporary contexts of social class, political sympathies, cultural values, intellectual interests, and information. But they differed greatly in the way in which the original contextuality of the individual discourse is treated in the "interdiscursive"[56] text of the novel. The unique problems and achievements of *The Man without Qualities* have to do with the very high degree to which it retains and integrates such contextuality. Ulrich, the protagonist, is a "protagonist of thought," probably the most rigorously intellectual novel character in world literature. *The Magic Mountain* was admired by professional readers and large general audiences for presenting—in the shape of a good story—so many learned descriptions of physiological processes, psychoanalytic concepts, and philosophical positions, all of them coexisting neatly in the rarified atmosphere of the Swiss Alps or the Work of Art. Musil built up the interdiscursive text of the novel from his very broad *and* specialized reading in many areas of contemporary inquiry into various aspects of mental activities and cultural constructs.[57] Thomas Mann selected his reading according to the dualistic schematism which prestructures his text and the allegorically distinct shapes of his characters which were then filled in with excerpts from handbooks in medicine, music, philosophy.[58] Broch did not subject cultural analysis to the "higher level" of artistic organization. He set his "polyhistorical" novel against the conventional and modern novel as art, expecting it, in fact, to end all novels in its sweeping embrace of the contemporary world of confusion and crisis. But his insistence on reestablishing a hierarchy of religio-cultural values and moving his fictional world inexorably toward redemption leveled and negated the declared modern multiperspectivity and narrative relativity.[59] Where *The Magic Mountain* leaves the reader with ironical assertions of ambiguity and confusion, *The Sleepwalkers,* notwithstanding instances of shrewd cultural criticism, embraces a simplistic message of cultural despair and salvation.

Musil was critical of both novels. In the case of Thomas Mann he focused his critique on Mann's relationship with his readers.[60] Many diary entries deal with Thomas Mann's extraordinary success:[61] "Ull-steinisierung";[62] "Grosschriftsteller," wholesale writer, the patrician merchant as supersalesman in the area of culture—Musil used the term also for the Rathenau-figure, Dr. Arnheim, in *The Man without Qualities*[63]—"sunny writers," "applied poetry," "optimism in poetry,"[64] the writer who reaffirms his readers' prejudices[65] and becomes the center of a congregation. What he misses in *Magic Mountain* is the challenge of cultural and epistemological imagination. Mann, he notes, mistakes a doctrinaire position in a cultural tradition for intellectuality.[66] Broch, whose *Sleepwalkers* is less easily accessible than *Magic Mountain* and never became a commercial success,[67] irritated the reader Musil because "he made suspect the philosophical novel": Is a novel of ideas considered flawed if the presented ideas and reflections are confused and inconsistent, he asks. How important is failure in this respect to the question of the success or failure of the novel as a whole? A novel is considered unsatisfactory if there are formal flaws; why is there no excuse for formal flaws in contrast to intellectual flaws?[68]

Musil was very much aware of the difficulties his novel presented to the reader expecting "a novel," traditional or modern. His diaries are filled with reflections on the essayistic overgrowth in *The Man without Qualities* and on the implications for his relationship with his readers. It is important to him to be understood according to his intentions: the speech act—to use this model metaphorically for the novel as a whole here—has to be controlled to a high degree by the author as speaker in order to be successful, and a story can be a very effective control-instrument. Musil reassures himself that he can tell stories—and indeed he can.[69] *The Man without Qualities* is a web of story fragments which in the first volume assert themselves successfully among the slower essayistic passages.[70] These occasionally take over in the second volume and in the posthumously published parts, and they are problematic in a novel because they do not stay with the reader even if he stays with them.[71] Musil did not solve the problem; his novel has seemed to many readers too diffuse, confusing, badly constructed, meandering, a series of excursions.

Musil had chosen the essay-novel, half-convinced that theoretical-essayistic discourse was more responsive, more adequate to contemporary concerns.[72] But the choice did not provoke him to the recklessness of formally completing a novel of ideas, which means finally letting go of one's ideas.[73] He needed to write the novel as a "kind of biography of my ideas,"[74] because these ideas could not be developed sufficiently unambiguously within the stricter textuality of the story, and his main concern is the clarity and accessibility of his thought to the reader for whom the novel as speech-act has to establish meaning and significance. The essay as genre, on the other hand, is ultimately too fragmentary and too closed, as writing for Musil means tracing the entangled lines of the lives of ideas with passionate patience and precision. In his descriptions of his narrative method he speaks of fusing strategies of biography and essay to establish a *Gestalt*—in the figure of the protagonist—for guiding the developing clusters of ideas.[75] This protagonist is fluid; in the earlier stages of the novel Musil had considered first person narration but rejected it for its too clearly defined narrative voice. His aim is a merging of the author and his creature into a functionally unstable *Gestalt*.[76] There is no distinct narrating consciousness delegated by the author to keep the process of narration at a distance and provide for the reader the possibility of an escape into the peculiarly restful suspense of ambiguity. "I narrate," Musil asserts. "This I, however, is not a fictional person, but a novelist. An informed, disappointed, bitter man. I tell the story of my friend," the protagonist Ulrich, and of his friends.[77]

In telling this story the novelist is an observer, reflective, not active, unable, he points out, to gain a completely clear view of Ulrich's and the other characters' activities. Yet, he sees himself as part of this group and participates in their experiences. Presenting them to the reader, he makes sense of their experiences; still, they are living their own lives and resist his control, even if their lives are lives of their author's ideas. Like every biographer Musil learns that no life is fully accessible to the form of its description: "the story of this novel," Musil notes in 1932, "is that the story which it was supposed to tell is not told."[78] In the early twenties he had considered starting the novel with posing the question: "how does the writer know the fate of his characters?"[79] He does not, as he himself undergoes changes in the process of tracing their lives which will then reflect unexpected, unpredictable aspects of the authorial self. Accordingly, the first part of the first volume, "A Sort of Introduction," is not an introduction to the novel as story, but as exploration of the ways in which a life does not submit itself to narration, that is, an introduction for the readers into the process of reading this biography of Musil's ideas.

Musil's characters are based on himself and on people he knew, directly or through their work—generals and industrialists as well as philosophers and poets—who had become part of his experience in his contemporary world. He retains their reality, that is, their social individuality, to a high degree, most strikingly in the figure of Rathenau-Arnheim, the man with qualities, contrasting and complementing Ulrich's open self. They come together in a narration which acknowledges their fragmentary existence, presenting those parts which are accessible to the author and which he wants to communicate to the reader for the sake of the characters and of their readers, because they all are in this together. "People demand," Musil said in one of several testaments he wrote to himself about the novel he could not finish, "that Ulrich should do something. But my business is the meaning of the act."[80] Meaning is the meeting place of the general and the particular, of self and other, text and reader. As there are different ways of meeting there will be different shades of meaning, but not, if the author can help it, ambiguities. Musil meant the text to be sturdy and resist misreading; that is, he meant to control as much as possible the meaning of the acts and ideas presented in the narration. Their significance is the business of the careful determined reader who can mine *The Man without Qualities* like a minutely documented life whose fragmentariness is respected by him and the author as biographer.

Conflict and contradiction are self-evident aspects of any life as process of orientation in a world largely unpredictable and graphically accidental in its beginning and end. Epic and dramatic literary forms have been developed to counteract such accidentality—also where, in a modern inversion, they seem to echo it. *The Man without Qualities* is a modern novel as it concerns the experience of modernity and allows such experience to inform the ways in which it is presented: it does not reflect any self-consciously modern interest in formal experimentation.[81] The novel against which Musil defined his writing, Thomas Mann's *Magic Mountain,* was in form a nineteenth-century novel, but it was also in Musil's term "zeitbürtig"—of its time though not adequate to contemporary problems—and a quintessentially German enterprise in its affirmation of key cultural clichés. Conflict and contradiction are formally controlled, thereby neutralized, themes here, and accidentality is transcended. The reader who is persuaded by Mann's formidable narrative skills into agreeing with this kind of control will accept transference of conflict to a higher level which relieves him of taking sides. This issue was of central importance to the cultural psychology of the Weimar period and will be dealt with more extensively in the next chapter. A reader of *The Man without Qualities* does not have these options. He comes away with the contradictions and conflicts unresolved, the confusion intact, but intelligibly analyzed; he is free to take sides. He will also be free to see the racy intelligence and shrewdness characteristic of the social satire in the first volume or the slower encircling precision of the analyses of feelings in the second volume as the more satisfying achievement—or he may understand them as complementary, as Musil intended them to be. Musil wrote so that he would be read according to his intentions, but he was fully aware of the uncharted areas in the lives of his ideas. The course taken by a life can be presented in narration as long as it is understood as a functional *Gestalt,* a fiction among other fictions. All the author can do is to insist on clarity in respect to the meaning of the fiction: he has to release its significance by alerting the reader to its particular and partial truth.

Struggling with this problem Musil found himself resorting to ironical discourse. Moving through the many versions of the novel's first two hundred pages he discovered irony as the mode of narration which fit his intellectual temperament[82] and looking back on the first two volumes in 1938, an exile in Switzerland without any audience to speak of, he judged the first volume to be by far the most accessible because of its predominantly ironical mode. Irony balances the eager and passionate intellect and negotiates distances between world and self in the case of a writer and a "protagonist of his ideas" who lack a strong sense of belonging or not belonging anywhere.[83] In this context Musil reflected on the difficult *and* stimulating aspects of his existence as a sort of reversible emigrant, "zweiseitig Emigrierender." The cultural distance forced on him by the political situation modified his ironical perspective even more in the direction of linkage, removing the observer even further from a position of security and control of distances. Irony in this sense is also self-irony; it is "constructive" because it integrates the self into the act of constructing the other, thereby stressing the social existence of the self. Irony connects: "Es ist der Zusammenhang der Dinge, aus dem sie nackt hervorgeht" (It is the connectedness of everything from which it emerges naked).[84] Irony for Musil as novelist is sustained by hostility *and* sympathy,[85] by abdicating authorial omnipotence and omniscience, by merging with a protagonist who is not fully accessible or predictable.

Irony undermined historical hindsight. In the long drawn-out process of writing it, *The Man without Qualities* had become a historical novel; it takes place twenty-five years ago, Musil notes in 1938, as if surprised. It had been conceived as a novel about the present developed out of the past, "ein aus der Vergangenheit entwickelter Gegenwartsroman," but now he thinks the tension very strong. Yet the area of inquiry, which had always been beneath the surface, did not have to be moved any deeper.[86] What Ulrich and his author experience in Vienna in 1913 is the same failure to balance emotional and intellectual energies, to mediate between logically-empirically and emotionally directed thought—"empirischem Denken und Gefühlsdenken"[87]— that helped to bring about the collapse of the Weimar Republic. They do not, of course, know this as a fact, but rather as a connecting projection: Austrian history as a paradigm for German history and German history as a paradigm for world history, that is, the emergence of the modern world of the twentieth century.[88] It will reduce Ulrich, highly civilized and richly talented modern man, to a particle in the machinery of modern warfare and exile his author, one of the most articulate twentieth-century writers, into the absence of response. It will also liberate Ulrich into a much deeper understanding of himself in his world and provoke his author to write, as a contemporary, a stunningly useful novel-essay on experience and knowledge.

2.

There was a depression over the Atlantic. It was travelling eastwards, towards an area of high pressure over Russia, and still showed no tendency to move northwards around it. The isotherms and isotheres were fulfilling their functions. The atmospheric temperature was in proper relation to the average annual temperature, the temperature of the coldest as well as the hottest month, and the a-periodic monthly variation in temperature. The rising and setting of the sun and of the moon, the phases of the moon, Venus and Saturn's rings, and many other important phenomena, were in accordance with the forecasts in the astronomical yearbooks. The vapour in the air was at its highest tension, and the moisture in the air was at its lowest. In short, to use an expression that describes the facts pretty satisfactorily, even though it is somewhat old-fashioned: it was a fine August day in the year 1913.

Motor-cars came shooting out of the deep, narrow streets into the shallows of bright squares. Dark patches of pedestrian bustle formed into cloudy streams. Where stronger lines of speed transcended their loose-woven hurrying, they clotted up—only to trickle on all the faster then and after a few ripples regain their regular pulse-beat. Hundreds of sounds were intertwined into a coil of wiry noise, with single barbs projecting, sharp edges running along it and submerging again, and clear notes splintering off—flying and scattering. Even though the peculiar nature of this noise could not be defined, a man returning after years of absence would have known, with his eyes shut, that he was in that ancient capital and imperial city, Vienna. Cities can be recognized by their pace just as people can by their walk.[89] Opening his eyes, he would recognize it all again by the way the general movement pulsed through the streets, far sooner that he would discover it from any characteristic detail. And even if he only imagined he could do so—what does it matter? The excessive question of where one is goes back to nomadic times, when people had to be observant about feeding-grounds. It would be interesting to know why, in the matter of a red nose, for instance, one is content with the vague statement that it is red, never asking what particular shade of red it is, although this could be precisely expressed in micro-millimeters in terms of wavelengths: whereas in the case of something so infinitely more complicated, such as the town in which one happens to be, one always wants to know quite exactly what particular town it is. This distracts attention from more important things.

So no special significance should be attached to the name of the city. Like all big cities, it consisted of irregularity, change, sliding forward, not keeping in step, collisions of things and affairs, and fathomless points of silence in between, of paved ways and wilderness, of one great rhythmic throb and the perpetual discord and dislocation of all opposing rhythms, and as a whole resembled a seething, bubbling fluid in a vessel consisting of the solid material of buildings, laws, regulations, and historical traditions.

The beginning of the first chapter, "which, remarkably enough, does not get anyone anywhere," does provide the reader with part of the information expected at the beginning of a conventional novel: time and setting. The way in which it is given, however, is meant as a comment on the selective and interpretative nature of all information and thus on its relative usefulness or reliability. In one set of circumstances "a fine August day in the year 1913 in the city of Vienna" may be sufficient orientation in the process of understanding the events of that day, in another it may not. Moreover, insufficiency may be seen again as depending on situation: in one situation this information is insufficiently complete and distinct, in another it is insufficiently vague and comprehensive. Perception of place as *Gestalt* selected from a great number of possible observations has different functions in different contexts. Musil wishes to stress here that for civilized persons in twentieth-century cities such context for perception of place will differ widely. The reader presumably is such a person. He will come up with the *Gestalt* of a city he has known well "just" by listening to the noises related to certain motions in certain spaces. Such perceptions will tell him a great deal—

depending on how he understands his situation and on his skills in coping with it. It may not be necessary to set the actions of certain persons and the occurrence of certain events in a certain place which is also defined by its location on the time axis—events may take place in other settings, at other times; even the persons may be interchangeable to a degree. For the reader it is important to know that they are and that they themselves either think (or "know") that they are or reject such a notion.

> The two people who were walking up a wide, busy thoroughfare in the midst of it all were, of course, far from having such an impression. They obviously belonged to a privileged section of society, their good breeding being apparent in their clothes, their bearing and their manner of conversing. They had their initials significantly embroidered on their underclothing. And likewise—that is to say not outwardly displayed, but as it were, in the exquisite underlinen of their minds—they knew who they were and that they were in their proper place in a capital city that was also an imperial residence.

They are a particular man and a particular woman walking in Vienna on a fine August day in 1913. They fit in themselves as they fit in their surroundings, but this firm identity seems to provoke questions: their self-awareness, says their author to his reader, is not to be accepted that simply:

> Let us assume that their names were Arnheim and Ermelinde Tuzzi—but no, that would be a mistake, for Frau Tuzzi was spending this August in Bad Aussee, accompanied by her husband, and Herr Dr. Arnheim was still in Constantinople. So we are confronted with the enigma of who they were.

In this case the English translation unfortunately changes the intended meaning:

> Angenommen, sie würden Arnheim und Ermelinde Tuzzi heissen, was aber nicht stimmt, denn Frau Tuzzi befand sich im August in Begleitung ihres Gatten in Bad Aussee und Dr. Arnheim noch in Konstantinopel, so steht man vor dem Rätsel wer sie seien.[90]

If author and reader assume that the two walkers are definitely this rather than that (particular) person, Dr. Arnheim and Mrs. Tuzzi, they will be confronted with an enigma. It is not, as the English translation suggests, the puzzle of who *they* are which is of importance, but, rather, the puzzle of identity in general. If and only if author and reader accept a secure identity for these people, as they do for themselves, will there be an enigma. The puzzle relates not to the question of identity itself but to the question of perceiving identity. This distinction is important for the novel as the fictional presentation of reality. It is not that it "would be a mistake" to assume that they are who they think they are—Mrs. Tuzzi and Dr. Arnheim. They may or may not be right, and the reader will or will not learn this in time. Rather, "it does not fit" *(stimmt nicht)* in terms of the fictional reality. Mrs. Tuzzi, the wife of a high government official, can be expected to be in Bad Aussee at this time of the year; Dr. Arnheim who has many obligations and travels widely would not be in Vienna in August. This much the author constructing the world of his novel would know, that is, be able to tell his readers. Like almost everyone in almost every situation, he can know and tell something—not everything and not nothing. On a day which has all the qualities of a fine August day, in a city which for a person who knows it well has the *Gestalt* of Vienna, these two people, who think that they know exactly who they are and who may be known partially to somebody who sees them walking and remembers where he has seen them before (thus solving what for him had been an enigma), are suddenly stopped by what appears to be an accident. A man has been run over by a truck.

> A moment earlier the regularity had been broken by a sudden oblique move-ment: something had spun around, skidding sideways—the abrupt braking, as it appeared, of a heavy lorry, which was now stranded with one wheel on the edge of the pavement. In an instant, like bees round the entrance to their hive, people had collected round a little island of space in their midst.

The two people had not seen the forceful rupture of the traffic flow described for the reader in images suggesting natural force which emphasize the threatening and alluring properties of the phenomenon *accident*. A general violent motion breaks into different parts revealing the object thrown by the energy of velocity and mass like a boat lifted onto the beach by the power of waves. The accident is shown through the perspective of an observer who, in contrast to the two people approaching its scene now, has been there from the moment the truck started being pushed out of the regular flow of traffic and has seen the crowd *(Auflauf)* gathering. The German noun stresses the centripetal force of bodies and the German verb, "hatten sich angesetzt," which extends the analogy of people as bees, supports the association of a large number of small particles—the verb is used for insects gathering in large numbers—drawn toward a point effortlessly. The space around which people—like particles—crowd has great attractive power which can neutralize repulsion caused by fear. When the couple approaches the scene, the different forces keeping the crowd together have been established: the truck, the gesticulating truck driver, the lifeless body in the hole created by the crowd around it. The couple peering into the hole speak for the first time: the lady (mis)interprets a feeling of discomfort as compassion; the gentleman criticizes the long braking distances of trucks and quotes American statistics on traffic accidents, which are comforting to the lady because the extraordinary event, the accident, can now be fitted into a pattern. It is no longer an event that she has to respond to because it undercuts the even flow of normal, that is, intended events. And the prompt arrival of the ambulance which removes the disturbance by fitting it into its clean regularity affirms the gentleman's explanations. Both people have felt, spoken, and behaved according to their social roles.

The second chapter—chapters are short and focused by their titles—
"Abode of the Man without Qualities," has the reader continue along the
street of the accident, with or without the elegant couple: "Had the elegant
couple followed its course for a while longer they would have seen something
that would certainly have appealed to them." The German—"Sollte ihm das
elegante Paar noch eine Weile weiter gefolgt sein"—expresses more clearly
the author's uncertainty whether they had or had not followed the street and
his certainty that they would have been pleased by the sight because they are
that type or model of a cultured couple. His trying on names for them and
withdrawing these as premature has been done in the medium of a novel
where naming is an important act of creating and assigning identity and
withholding a name is an act of drawing attention to the author's privileged
position vis-à-vis his creature. Musil is interested in playing on narrative
conventions only insofar as it serves to stress what he understands to be the
specific epistemological possibilities of narrative fiction, that is, its "logical
status" as presentation or model of a world which supports the explorative
activity of author and reader.[91] To read his essay-novel as antifiction would
defeat his intentions and purposes.

Ulrich, whose life is to be told as fictional biography in the manner of the
essay, that is, as an experiment and exploration of contemporary intellectual
cultural issues, lives in a seventeenth-century house that has been added on
to in the eighteenth and nineteenth centuries, surrounded by a parklike
garden suggesting feudal spaciousness and ease. The reader is directed to the
house as something pleasant to look at—the elegant couple would be pleased
by the *Gestalt* of the white castlelike building as something "Niedliches,
Weisses, Schönes," (dainty, white, and beautiful)—and pleasant to look
into—when the windows were open "one could see into the gentlemanly
calm of a scholar's house where the walls were lined with books." He is then
informed that the house belongs to "the man without qualities," and he sees
him for the first time, not yet knowing his name. Standing at the window,
looking out,[92] Ulrich has been counting all the moving objects and calculating the energy spent by a normal (average) human being on a normal
(average) day in the city which, to no one's surprise, is enormous and far
exceeds the energy spent in the deeds of heroes: "indeed, the heroic exertion
appears positively minute, like a grain of sand laid, in some act of illusory
immensity, upon a mountain-top." Ulrich is pleased by this thought: as a
younger man he had had heroic inclinations, and he likes to put obstacles in
the paths of his former selves. This does not mean that he now celebrates the
beauty of industrial urban dynamics and the heroic dimension of dailiness.
His author takes over here to establish Ulrich's distance also to this contemporary view.

> Perhaps it is precisely the common man [*Spiessbürger*] who has an intuitive
> prophetic glimpse of the beginning of an immense new, collective, antlike hero-
> ism?[93] It will be called rationalized heroism and will be regarded as very

beautiful. But can we know of that today? However, at that time there were hundreds of such unanswered questions, all of the greatest importance. They were in the air; they were burning underfoot. The time was on the move. People who were not born then will find it difficult to believe, but the fact is that even then time was moving as fast as a cavalry-camel; it is not only today that it does so. But in those days no one knew what it was moving towards. Nor could anyone distinguish between what was above and what below, between what was moving forwards and what backwards.

"It doesn't matter what one does," the Man without Qualities said to himself, shrugging his shoulders. "In a tangle of forces like this it doesn't make a scrap of difference." He turned away like a man who has learned renunciation, almost indeed like a sick man who shrinks from any intensity of contact. And then, striding through his adjacent dressing room, he passed a punching ball that hung there; he gave it a blow far swifter and harder than is usual in moods of resignation or states of weakness.

Ulrich, then, is a man at odds with his time, and at odds with his own attempts at defining a position against the time. Yet he is by no means resigned or overwhelmed, and he is not without an identity. His identity is to live "without qualities," that is, without the fiction of the self as entelechy unfolding and growing according to some inner law. The self, as Ulrich has experienced, is a loose structure, eclectically cumulative in time.

His house reflects this openness and has attracted his father's disapproval. The third chapter, "Even a Man without Qualities has a Father with Qualities," is the first of the many case histories which introduce all the different people with qualities gathered in the novel. These introductions are focused on the characters' contributions to the process and progress of the novel as argument or discourse, and the reader is intended to get involved with the development of this discourse, not with the characters' activities and psychological developments. These case histories are story fragments which do not add up to a story; their function varies: they can serve as catalysts in the expansion of the discourse or as bridges between parts of the discourse. They stimulate the essayistic passages which approach the issues from different directions. Ulrich is the connecting link between the different characters and the different parts of the discourse. As he is not in search of cultural wholeness, but in search of an adequately open serious discussion of the consequences of fragmentation, connections are established tentatively.

His father, highly successful in academic and public life, is firmly rooted in his own shrewd social construct of Austrian reality. As a member of the Upper House he has been on the liberal bourgeois wing in spite of his elevation into the ranks of hereditary nobility. Ulrich is irritated by his building a smooth career on carefully cultivated patronage, that is, on his subservience, as a member of the intellectual elite, to the possessors of land, horses, and traditions. Yet he cannot but admire his father's "sincere veneration for what advances one's own interests—and this not for the sake of advancing them but in harmony with that advancement and simultaneously with it, and also on general grounds." Ulrich's semifeudal pretty white chateau is an affront to the old man's deep feelings about the values of and respect for social boundary lines, all the more important because they are not legally defined but seem fluid and are negotiable in the sense that the person who recognizes them to be in the order of things can use them to further his own interests.

Against this gently inexorable sense of reality the "sense of possibility" is posed in the fourth chapter, the first of several excursions into the "utopian idea of essayism."[94] Here the subjunctive mode of the possibilitarian's life is described as informed by a "constructive will, a conscious utopianism that does not shrink from reality, but treats it, on the contrary, as a mission and invention." The possibilitarian is defined by the absence of qualities, which makes him appear unreliable and incalculable in social intercourse. Ulrich, as the fifth chapter informs the reader, is such a possibilitarian—this is the first time his name is given. Where the preceding chapter had stressed, if somewhat ironically, the heroic potential of the sense of possibility in general, its attachment to and application by a particular person brings out the humorous aspects of the mission to invent reality.

When applying his sense of possibility to the cultural catechism centered in love for God and country, the young Ulrich had been intrigued by Austria's frequent victories and equally frequent territorial losses. This interruption of the mode of discourse suitable for catechizing had set him thinking and that, in turn, had led him to speculate in one of his history exercises that

> anyone who really loved his country should never think his own country the best. And then, in a flash that struck him as particularly beautiful, although he was more dazzled by its brilliance than able to see what was going on in the light of it, he had added to this suspect sentence a second to the effect that even God preferred to speak of his world in the subjunctive of potentiality . . . , for God makes the world and while doing so he thinks it could just as easily be some other way.

This brilliant insight almost caused him to be expelled from the elite school established for the education of the future pillars and sons of the present pillars of the state. What saved him from expulsion was his teachers' inability to agree on an interpretation of the sentence as either defamation of the fatherland or blasphemy.

Perceived from the outside Ulrich does not seem to reflect the uncertainties that accompany such questioning of established reality: a mathematician with a promising career in his early thirties, handsome, athletic, well-connected, socially at ease, his position seems highly desirable in terms of contemporary social priorities.[95] These mean, among other things, a great variety of choices. But Ulrich, at this stage, is unable to make choices. In that, he quite literally reflects his period of cultural transition. Trying to decorate his house, for instance, he is overwhelmed by the profusion and confusion of ideas about anything from doorknobs to bathroom appliances to garden sculpture and the shapes of sofa legs. His annoyance does not jell into a feeling of cultural crisis: his sense of cultural values is un-ideological, skeptical. He lets interior decorators take over when he realizes that they cannot, in spite of their promises, construct an identity for him, as their designs neutralize each other. Ulrich, however, does understand the cultural implications of the sudden dissolution of traditions and prejudices which limit choices but also support values and stability. He observes processes of re-formation which consist of rearranging fragments of the old traditions and prejudices into a new totality urgently sought by everybody around him. Having taken a year's sabbatical from his university position to explore living, the first thing he learns is the surface variety and underlying sameness of the meaning of that search.

The first nineteen chapters as "A Sort of Introduction" draw the reader into the argument suggesting how to read this essay-novel, and they comment explicitly on the interrelatedness of the many characters by tracing the general shared elements in individual perception and motivation. The specific informality of the text based on the structuring device of metamorphosis from particular to general, from essayistic passage to story fragment asserts itself from the beginning.[96] Such fluid structure undermines the synthesis of the *Zeitroman*:[97] Ulrich is in conflict with "his" time by disagreeing with the men and women apparently in tune with "their" time in their efforts to bring about a synthesis and to find wholeness.[98] His troubled relations to women have to be placed in this context. When he finally meets his sister Agathe he is ready to explore transitions between self and other and to risk alternate experiences of intimacy.[99] But at the beginning of his experimental year he sees women as strangers—fascinating, irritating, and not to be taken seriously. He is attracted by what he vaguely perceives as their femininity and they by his masculinity. The ironic sensuous tender portraits of women in their emotional and physical confusion when they attempt to make sense of the male world reflects on one level typically limited male views on women, male fantasies, and the author does not disassociate his perspective from Ulrich's. Yet these views and fantasies also serve to bring out the cultural conflicts and ambiguities implicit in femininity.[100]

World War I had been a catalyst for very significant changes in the relations between men and women, but in the novellas *Vereinigungen* (1911) (Unions) and especially in two essays written in 1912 for Franz Blei's experimental journal *Der Lose Vogel* (The sly bird),[101] "Erinnerung an eine Mode" (Remembering a fashion) and "Penthesileiade," Musil had already projected much more far-reaching shifts in the culturally established distances between the sexes. He is interested in more subtle, more complex, and differentiated erotic dynamics of difference supported, he hopes, by women's greater independence of men and by the resulting extension of self-knowledge—through the other—in both men and women. If, in their relations, personal instead of sexual differences could be at play more openly and assertively, erotic mediation between self and other might become a more enriching if less predictable process. Fashion, for instance, can reinforce dualistically static positions, but it can also undermine them: the fashion remembered by Musil is the pant-skirt worn by a live model in a Berlin shop window and attracting many viewers as "an ethical and—this is implied—a psychological object."[102] There is in Berlin, too, the institution of a yearly "Ball der Veränderten" (ball of the transformed), as Musil calls it, a dance for women only, where women wearing suits play the male role. Musil is intrigued by the power of perspective: seen as men, conventionally unattractive and older women will look very different to the male observer. He will see characteristic details which will influence his erotic response to the person after he realizes that she is a woman, because released from the normative ideals of female attractiveness most women are visually more attractive than men.[103] "Penthesileiade" reflects on the implications of women in political office, in positions of power—there had been the case of a Swedish couple as members of opposite parties in the same city council—for more sophisticated, more humanly developed erotic relations.[104]

Ulrich rejects the futile and frequently self-destructive searches for selfhood as wholeness, which neglect the potential rewards of openness toward the other in one's openness to the world constituted by self and other, but such openness as he realizes is by no means easy. It is not by accident that culturally normative male-female relationships have been unsatisfactory and persistent. His own affairs sketched in chapters 6 and 7 are both troubled in their reductive focus on sexuality and suggestive of unused emotional energies. As long as the distance between the male and female positions remains, as it were, a priori, eroticism will not develop. Ulrich changes the distance slightly because he is intrigued with his mistress Leona's old-fashioned beauty and the old-fashioned feelings of her sentimental innocent songs which she sings in third-class nightclubs. Leona as an out-of-date object of desire is less of an object or, at least, a reflected object. But this is Ulrich's—and his author's—construction as cultural comment; the woman is in no position to resist this male sophistication.

The second part, "Seinesgleichen geschieht,"[105] has Ulrich discard both mistresses and, more and more puzzled by his confused and needy self, self-ironically analyze similar confusions and needs in others. It is only in the third part (second volume), "Ins tausendjährige Reich (Die Verbrecher)" (Into the millennial Reich [the criminals]), that Ulrich is able to become close to another person in his incestuous relationship with Agathe. Such closeness is literally utopian and therefore specifically problematic and threatened: brother and sister, now social deviants, move farther and farther away from familiar places geographically and in their discourse on themselves.[106] Musil uses the ironical connecting perspective on the extremes of nearness—love between siblings—and distance—no place, no time—to show the difficulties and the seriousness of their adventure. Alternate intellectual-emotional experiences are dangerous to the cultural stability of the individual and the group:

as a concretely limited focus of utopian energy and direction utopia becomes inhumanly obsessive, defeating its own purpose. Agathe's and Ulrich's discourse on themselves, however, does explore their being in the world, and the "criminal" asocial sister-brother love is used as the first step in constructing flexible bridges between self and other which will help to understand and articulate more areas of social experience.

Agathe can be a person in this relationship because she is literally close to her brother: "I know now what you are: you are my self-love," he says to her shortly after they started living together. This does not mean fortification of the self but rather specific support for the open self, a certain tenderness, fondness for oneself which Ulrich had not experienced before and which helps him to be fond of the other. It also helps him to understand earlier flawed relationships as dependent on his own flawed self-perception.[107] His openness had made him casual about appropriation of the other, and Agathe's closeness and resistance makes him aware of this. He had acquired mistresses like Bonadea (chap. 7) who were distant and unresisting. In that case the act of acquisition is also linked to physical aggression: Ulrich is beaten up in a fight with three strangers and rescued by a beautiful woman who picks him up and drives him home. Barely revived, he cannot help explaining to her the heroically matter-of-fact battle experience; she cannot help being impressed by it. Encased in their respective maleness and femaleness he talks, she listens. But where he gives in to the temptation of fabricating an adventure out of an accident, she is overly eager to fit him into her fiction of the mysterious stranger. When he disappears into his house, switching on the lights, she decides to see him again, delighted by the sight of the low wings of a boudoirlike delicate little castle spread above a freshly shorn emerald-green lawn and the colorful rows of books covering the walls: "two weeks later Bonadea had already been his mistress for a fortnight."

Both man and woman have slid into this affair. The perspective on the accidental adventure and its expected outcome is mainly Ulrich's. He even names the woman, bewildered about the mechanisms controlling a physical fight between civilized men in a civilized city and the inevitable and boring casual relationship between a man and woman. He does not like that "blend of renunciation and foolish fondness that makes up the general attitude to life," the feeling that the world is always sliding back with one foot while it takes a step forward with the other. Yet, moved by irony and desire, he lets Bonadea continue an adventure that he himself thought closed when he reflected on the events of the previous night, sorting images and puzzling out their meanings.

"Kakania" (chap. 8) describes the state of the Austrian *kaiserlich-königliche* monarchy as institutionalized sliding in which the novel's construction of reality will take place and which is itself a curiously distinct construct or model. Musil's critical explanation of its structural properties does not underestimate its charm;[108] indeed, passages could be lifted out of their context as witness to their author's nostalgia about the good old times and the good old place, but the meaning of these charming surfaces is difficult to misunderstand if attention is given to the argument. There is first the portrait of the current cliché-ideal of a "super-American city"[109] where

> air and earth form an ant-hill veined by channels of traffic rising storey upon storey, over-ground trains, underground trains, pneumatic express mails carrying consignments of human beings, chains of motorvehicles all racing along horizontally, express lifts vertically pumping crowds from one traffic-level to another. . . . At the junction one leaps from one means of transport to another, is instantly sucked in and snatched away by the rhythm of it which makes a syncope, a little gap of twenty seconds between two roaring outbursts of speed and in these intervals in the general rhythm one hastily exchanges a few words with others. Questions and answers click into each other like clogs of a machine.

This passage is not overtly negative, though it does contain some stereotypical images of mechanized modern life. Fragmentation graphically expressed in the layout of modern cities is described with ironical amusement rather than direct disapproval: the towers to which one returns from work and amusement in the center of the city "and finds wife, family, grammophone and soul."

Kakania, "this misunderstood state that has since vanished," is different—or is it? The name evokes the great and pleasing natural diversity of its provinces, glaciers, cornfields, oceans, the image of a Slovakian village, "where smoke rose from the chimneys as from upturned nostrils, the village curled up between two little hills as though the earth had parted its lips to warm its child between them." There were cars, but not too many; there were roads, but the rapidly moving horizontal lines were streaking the countryside like ribbons of bright military twill, the paper-white arm of government holding the provinces in firm embrace. Colonies, overseas world markets were exotic concepts, in short, everything was on a lower scale. Tremendous sums were spent on the army but only to keep it firmly second-rate; the administration was famously effective, that is, barely perceptible, all the sharp points clipped. And yet, as Musil noted in 1920 in a harsh critique of Austrian culture, "this grotesque Austria is nothing but a particularly clear case of the modern world."[110] He stresses the connection between the prewar and postwar situation which the novel will have to expose, mentioning details of corruption in the various economic and political power groups and the cultural elite.

The well-ordered, stable state Kakania is the entropic product of violent social and political commotion. Even turbulent events do not seem quite real anymore. Here one was "negatively free, constantly aware of the inadequate grounds for one's own existence and lapped by the great fantasy of all that had not happened, or at least had not yet irrevocably happened, as by the foams of the oceans from which mankind arose. *Es ist passiert*, 'it just sort of happened,' people said there when other people in other places thought heaven knows what had occurred."

The opaque and powerful intimacy of the particular/personal and the general/typical which is called "the spirit of the times" is especially dense in Kakania. The Kakanian Ulrich, 32 years old in 1913, but also about as old as the twentieth century for the reader in the early 1930s—and for subsequent readers aware of the novel's date of publication and its cultural context—is very much of his time *and* in countermotion to it, both by virtue of his intellectual aggressivity and mobility. His three attempts at becoming a man of importance are traced by his author in the fondly ironical and slightly embarrassed way in which one remembers a series of former selves: from a very young dashing atavistic cavalry officer to a still very young civil engineer as man of the future to a research mathematician as embodiment of contemporary cultural potential (chap. 9–11). With each of them he had had to confront the specialist's highly controlled remoteness from life and living—very much a Kakanian experience. This remoteness has a curious effect on the individual's self-awareness and attitude toward the individuality of others. Bonadea, "The lady whose love Ulrich won after some talk about sport and mysticism," (chap. 12) is one example. The young attractive upper-middle-class matron has frighteningly delightful physical feelings which disrupt her highly controlled social persona and which she therefore tries to balance with strong mystical prejudices. She adores Ulrich's descriptions of modern athletic events—he shares this interest with his author[111]—because he describes so well their physicality and also explains their meaning, exciting and reassuring her. She is very much drawn to spectator sports where the single individual is most distinctly defined against the anonymous many when control and release are most extreme: the more intense the infinitely measurable individual effort, the more intense the reaction of the collective body of the crowd. Abstract—the measuring of split seconds—and concrete—the crowd's roar—shift in a relation of inversion and with it occurs a shift in identity.[112]

The modern conflict between the individual's absorption in large anonymous groups and his continuing need for and claim to uniqueness is also expressed by the phenomenon of a "race horse of genius" (chap. 13), which makes Ulrich more sharply aware of being a man without qualities. He understands that individuality nowadays can only be saved by the spectacular application of specific abilities and that he will have to look for appropriate ways of using his. Ulrich is concerned about individuality as "Eigenheit," that is, a sense of self sufficiently distinct from the other for motivated action; he is not concerned about uniqueness as expressing fundamental differences between self and other. In his friends Clarisse and Walter, however, *Eigenheit* means quest for uniqueness as genius (chap. 13). A Nietzsche disciple—Ulrich had given her a set of Nietzsche's works as a wedding gift—she believes directly *(schnurstracks)* in genius. She and Walter, too, are with *and* against the times. But where the mathematician Ulrich uses his talents, which are favored by the really important contemporary cultural priorities, to examine their meaning critically, his friends have retreated to a

Culture[113] reservation where artistic genius as absolutely, autonomously unique is allowed to survive. Far from questioning a concept like "genius," they do not understand that asserting it is very common current practice in the most diverse areas of cultural activities. Their claim of being in some ways specifically tuned to the times is largely ignored by the "real" world which accepts unquestioningly Ulrich's much questioned contemporaneity.

Ulrich's troubled intellectual and emotional position within and against his contemporary world is presented with sympathy by his author who has preceded him. In a 1913 essay, "Mathematical Man," Musil defended mathematics against complaints about its uselessness in human affairs, emphasizing its open adventurous approach to problems and its willingness to deal seriously with the dimension of the potential and recommending it to the student of social issues. But while the substance and thrust of this argument was not to change in his postwar essays and in the novel, the mode and tone of presentation was. Where Musil speaks, in 1913, of mathematics as a rare "luxurious courage of pure *ratio*" ("Tapferkeitsluxus der reinen Ratio, einer der wenigen, die es heute gibt"),[114] Ulrich as mathematical man, about as old as his author was in 1913, is much less emphatic, restrained by his own and his author's self-irony. Where the cultural preoccupation with genius, a religious pheomenon, is under investigation, it is more useful to dissolve intimations of heroicism in the ironical perspective on the interrelatedness of all sociocultural questions.

Clarisse and Walter in their self-centeredness do not see any relations. Their current passion is playing the piano, together and apart, experiencing the "immeasurable":

> A dimly outlined balloon filled with hot emotion was being blown up to bursting point, and from excited fingertips, from the nervous wrinkling of the foreheads and the twitchings of the bodies, ever more and more feeling radiated into the monstrous private upheaval.[115]

Ulrich does not like their music, and they are angered and fascinated by his distance. Moored in a meaningfully simple life which is supported by an undemanding safe semischolarly position in some branch of the Culture business, frequently intoxicated by the heavy Wagnerian brew, Walter has moved farther and farther away from the genius Clarisse had very deliberately married. The young couple, upper-middle-class in terms of educational background and opportunities, with their particular difficulties and desires, revolts, and concessions reflect contemporary tendencies. But it is Clarisse who has mainly formed their life together and largely in reaction to her own early experience: loathing her successful artist father and his turn-of-the-century studio world of crude if effective illusionism, she has turned against "mere appearance" in her search for authenticity and greatness, and the act of uncovering for her is simply heroic, not also ironical as it is for her hero Nietzsche. Her responses to the world are isolating and arresting; where she connects, it is to fortify an isolated fact with eclectic fragmented associations—she is to go insane eventually—unable to tolerate experience as processual and unpredictable. Walter has acquiesced in dealing with greatness metaphorically, she insists on it literally. Walter's kind of dilettantism is more common—"the intellectual life of the German nation is to a large extent based on dilettantism," Musil says in this context—but Clarisse's proves to be more (self-)destructive.

Ulrich and Walter were young at the turn of the century, a time of many conflicts and contradictions still virulent in 1913 and 1930. The difference was that cultural confusion appeared promising as well as threatening, and chapter 15, "Intellectual Revolution," a brief case history of the times in terms of its hopeful beginnings, evokes some of the promises:

> If that epoch had been analysed, some such nonsense would have come out as a square circle supposed to be made of wooden iron; but in reality all this had blended into shimmering significance. One could not help being affected by it when one was young.

Entering the world in those days, "even coming round the very first corner one felt the breath of the spirit on one's cheek." But how to understand and analyze such collective experience? Ulrich, looking back on the time when he and Walter were young men, is trying to understand their illusions then, that is, the changes now, which suggest "A mysterious disease of the times" (chap. 16). What has been lost is something imponderable, a certain tension and connection, a sense of proportion and purpose. But, then, Ulrich is looking at former selves from the position of an outsider, and this position does not change much in relation to his present self which he knows to be constantly changing, an unstable fiction. He imagines Thomas von Aquinas, busy getting all the ideas of his time arranged in the most orderly system possible, stepping out into contemporary traffic, an electric tram shooting right by him. The uncomprehending amazement of the *doctor universalis* amuses him, but then he sees a motorcyclist "shooting along the empty street, thundering up the perspective, bow-armed and bow-legged, on his face all the solemn, monstrous self-importance of a yelling baby." The meaningless aggressiveness of speed and noise is as keenly perceived by him, the twentieth-century intellectual and urban dweller, as by the visitor from the past. Ulrich is the utopian stranger and traveler, Hythloday's younger, more puzzled cousin, in his own time and space struck by the fact that so many contemporary cultural images related to technology and sport point to a sharp incongruity between tenacious moral conventions and expectations on the one hand and rapidly changing forms of social behavior on the other. This does not alienate him from his time as he knows that this kind of static distance would limit him in ways which are damaging.[116] Rather, the feeling of not being quite at home translates into a sharper awareness for the energy of potentiality in the traveler's existence. In contrast to his friend Walter, he does not relate the world to himself, but tries to relate himself to the world as much as possible.

It is this extension and direction of the self which is the core of his being and doing without qualities, and particularly disturbing to people with qualities, Walter among them. Trying to explain to Clarisse the differences between the past of "blood and wisdom," supportive of a "living creative principle," and the present of "death and logical mechanization," he suddenly bursts out: "He is a man without qualities." Ulrich, he asserts, "has no notion of the power of an unbroken soul! What Goethe calls personality, what Goethe calls mobile order—that's something he hasn't got an inkling of." And now Walter, with the incisive force of dislike, sums up Ulrich very well indeed:

> "And now just run your mind over the sort of man he is. He always knows what to do. He can gaze into a woman's eyes. He can exercize his intelligence efficiently on any given problem at any given moment. He can box. He is talented, strong-willed, unprejudiced, he has courage and he has endurance, he can go at things with a dash and he can be cool and cautious—I have no intention of examining all this in detail, let him have all these qualities! For in the end he hasn't got them at all! They have made him what he is, they have set his course for him, and yet they don't belong to him. When he is angry something in him laughs. When he is sad he is up to something. When he is moved by something, he will reject it. Every bad action will seem good to him in some connection or other. And it will always be only a possible context that will decide what he thinks of a thing.[117] Nothing is stable for him, everything is fluctuating, a part of a whole, among innumerable wholes that presumably are part of a super-whole, which, however, he does not know the slightest thing about. So every one of his answers is a part answer, every one of his feelings only a point of view, and whatever a thing is, it's only some accompanying 'way in which it is,' some addition or other, that matters to him. I don't know whether I made myself quite clear to you?" Oh yes," Clarisse said. "But I think it's very nice of him." (chap. 17)

Clarisse, then, sees Ulrich from a position exactly opposite to Walter's: he first lists qualities which are conventionally highly acceptable and which he does not question in themselves, and then he shows how they do not really "go with" Ulrich—"gehören nicht zu ihm." Clarisse starts with this situation and accepts it. The absence of qualities for her is a positive quality. Yet her acceptance of Ulrich is also based on some deeper disturbance in her which responds to Ulrich's essayism and utopianism, and Walter's hostile and lucid analysis of Ulrich is partly motivated by his wanting to protect her. His discovery of cultural despair has been very good for his own mental stability: the times are out of sorts; Europe is sick and decadent. It is for him, then, a meaningfully contemporary act to recognize and maintain an irreconcilable, irreversible distance to the times in his inwardness.[118]

Ulrich's abstaining from a value system and questioning the culturally anchored self can be misunderstood by Clarisse as encouraging the absolute autonomy of the self which she embraces. Such potential misunderstanding is just one aspect of Ulrich's specific self-consciousness, but an important one. Moosbrugger, a schizophrenic sexual murderer, fascinates both Ulrich and Clarisse with his peculiarly revealing, distorting perception of a sociocultural reality that they do and do not share with him (chap. 18). He is constructing a reality for and against himself, and such self-exclusion intrigues Ulrich, fatally attracts Clarisse, and will continue to connect them. For the judge who sentences him to death, Moosbrugger's criminal acts have their cause in him and so he has to be removed; for Moosbrugger, his so-called guilt consists of separate disconnected incidents each caused by some outside event in a world totally hostile to him which therefore has to be changed to fit the isolated self. Ulrich who is present at the trial is fascinated by the physically powerful murderer's shadowy attempts at articulating the fact and meaning of such isolation. Moosbrugger has taken over his own defense as he did not wish to plead insanity, and when the final affirmation of his isolation is given with the death sentence, he cries out: "I am satisfied, even though I must confess to you that you have condemned a madman!" This is not the effect of the shock, but rather his last attempt to make himself understood. Moosbrugger is not in his own eyes a madman, but his evident inability to communicate his way of being in their world makes him, he knows, a madman to them. This is what the judge as *their* representative should have recognized. They should have been able to understand that his view of himself and theirs of him can never match and that this mismatch is the root of his insane and criminal acts. Ulrich is puzzled by the darkness of Moosbrugger's existence with its dreamlike shifts and connections, but he understands the meaning of his isolation. He decides to work for a converted sentence; Clarisse adopts Moosbrugger as an alter ego. For Walter the man is a murderer and a madman, a symptom of the sickness of the times that could and should be eliminated.

His list of Ulrich's reactions to the world as a list of anti-qualities or obstacles to the formation of culturally healthy qualities is a fair sketch of the "free-floating" intellectual position described by Mannheim at the end of the Weimar Republic in his *Ideology and Utopia*[119] and defended in a speech given at the Sixth Convention of German Sociologists (6. Deutscher Soziologentag) in 1929, which was dominated by a heated discussion of Mannheim's thesis.

> You will probably be dissatisfied when I say to you I am neither an idealist nor a materialist, I *believe* neither in creative freedom in absolute space nor in an exclusively material condition of existence. You will say, perhaps, that not making a decision indicates a *weak character*. But I explicitly refrain from deciding on the basis of this antinomy which has been forced on me, as I am of the opinion that it is a much overstated either-or and I prefer to explore first the causes of this compulsive mode of thought [*Denkzwang*]. . . . I want to know

why contemporary thought is caught in these objectively *somehow* incorrect polarities as if by necessity. This question directs me toward the sociology of knowledge. I expect help from it in finding that synthetic vantage point [*Aufweis jenes synthetischen Punktes*] from which the compulsiveness and provisional nature of this forced alternative can be seen clearly. My provisional solution is that each of the feuding parties hypostasizes a partial aspect [of the whole truth].[120]

Walter would indeed be among those who see this position as symptomatic of modernity, a sign of character weakness; yet he would applaud the search for a synthetic vantage point and the value of each partial truth as part of a hypothetical whole. Ulrich, up to a point, shares the position of a modern intellectual as defined by Mannheim. He differs in that his vantage point is decidedly not synthetic; his insistence on partial truth is offensive, where Mannheim's is defensive. His thought is antisystemic and fragmentary by choice; where he seems intellectually arrogant to Walter he is in reality epistemologically modest. But in contrast to the great contemporary need for certainty his acknowledging uncertainty appears militant.

Such acknowledgment differs essentially from the Socratic strategy of pretending ignorance. Ulrich simply does not know anything for certain.[121] But his and his author's attempts to get a clearer view of the innumerable uncertainties that constitute our past, future, and present experience are frequently successful in stimulating dialogue and counteracting the anxiety of meaning which is the core of ideologies and leads to silence. Ulrich's and his author's unfinished stories can be told experimentally as stories of modernity as long as their fragmentary nature is read as a sign and not testified to as a symptom. This important distinction is especially clear in medical thinking.[122] Musil referred to it implicitly when he contrasted easily successful contemporary novels as the patient's narration of his symptoms against his own difficult narrative method as the physician's attempts at puzzling out and articulating the signs exhibited by the patient.[123] For him the meaning of the novel is the progressive diagnosis of the experience of modernity.

Unfinished experimental stories disturb the comforts of history.[124] As small centers of energy they may cause tectonic shifts in the historically constituted self-awareness of the West, introducing the element of risk. Mannheim's sociology of knowledge has the intellectual free utopian energy from its ideological limitations so that it can be understood as the motor of historical continuity. His concept of utopian impulses in this context is curiously close to Max Scheler's assumption of an autonomous creative spirit—Rathenau's soul—central to all true knowledge and cultural (German) history.[125] Musil's (and Ulrich's) essayistic utopianism interrupts rather than constructs historical continuity. His approach is by no means ahistorical, but any given historical development is seen as instructive, too, in terms of random selection between various possibilities, and it is this mixed perspective which continuously diverts the flow of narration as history.

In Austrian history Musil finds striking the insistence on undisturbed narration when confronted with complicated chains of events in which causal connections and accidental disruptions appear inseparable. Such narration extends into the future, and the Austrian genius for self-deception in fictions of continuity quite clearly shows important aspects of the troubled experience of modernity. For this reason Weimar Germany's powerful cultural conservatism can be satirically analyzed in the great fictitious Austrian undertaking of the *Parallelaktion* into which Ulrich is drawn by his father's interference in the last chapter of the introductory part: "An admonitory letter and an opportunity to acquire qualities. Competition between two imperial jubilees." Ulrich's father believes in (Austrian) history and some individuals' roles in it; he has recommended his currently unaffiliated son to a high government official and old patron for assistance in planning the most meaningful celebration of the Austrian Emperor's seventieth anniversary which will coincide, in 1918, with the mere thirtieth anniversary of the German Emperor. Nineteen-eighteen is to be declared the Jubilee Year of the Austrian Emperor of Peace—in parallel competition to Germany—and the planning committee of the *Parallelaktion* (collateral campaign) is constituted now in 1913. The introductory phase is completed; Ulrich, and the reader, are now drawn into the field of force of "Seinesgleichen geschieht"—the title (untranslatable) of the second part: events happen, tendencies emerge, time marches on, and it proves impossible to find out who actually is responsible for what everybody responds to as "our times" which will bring the first total European war.

3.

Ulrich finally becomes the honorary secretary of the *Parallelaktion* through an accident that leads to his arrest and questioning by the police (chap. 40). Under their interrogatory attacks on his identity he decides to use what he considers a fictional self, an officer of the prestigious *Parallelaktion,* to get himself out of a difficult situation to which his informal self-concept had contributed considerably.[126] The police, taking down his name, age, occupation, and address, file him away with the categories—tall build, fair hair, oval face, gray eyes, no distinguishing features.

> To his own way of feeling he was tall, his shoulders were broad, his chest expanded like a filled sail from the mast, and the joints of his body fastened his muscles off like small links of steel whenever he was angry or quarrelsome or, for instance, had Bonadea clinging to him. On the other hand, he was slim, lightly built, dark, and soft as a jelly fish floating in water whenever he was reading a book that moved him or was touched by a breath of that great and homeless love

whose presence in the world he had never been able to fathom. And so even at this moment he could also appreciate the statistical disenchantment of his person, and the methods of measurement and description applied to him by the police officer aroused his enthusiasm as much as might a love-poem invented by Satan. The most wonderful thing about it was that the police could not only dismantle a human being in this way so that nothing remained of him, but they would also put him together again out of these trifling components, unmistakably himself, and recognize him by them.

The self shifts continuously in relation to others; there are, for Ulrich, no items of personal information that could describe, much less define, the self at any given moment; at most they are elements of self-fiction. His self-perception is, in its own way, no less selective than the Ulrich *Gestalt* in the police file, but it expands where the latter contracts. It is a self-fiction, then, that gets him more seriously involved with the *Parallelaktion* which, as he already knows at this point, is fueled by fictions of the most various and most predictable kind. Finding Ulrich and being able to offer him the position he had just invented for himself would have been proclaimed a miracle by His Highness, the Imperial Liege-Count Leinsdorf, had he known the sequence of events making possible the successful conclusion of his search, the perfect match of the accidental and his desire. A leading Austrian patriot, a believer in the Catholic Church and the Goodness of the People, a competent, decent, occasionally shrewd administrator and the inventor of the "Emperor of Peace" motor for the *Parallelaktion,* Leinsdorf is very much a man with qualities, and he likes Ulrich, whom he has found in general reassuringly commonsensical. His qualities are largely the result of comprehensive unquestioned cultural formation, and in that they differ from the energetic and conflicted individualism and cultural religiosity of Arnheim-Rathenau or the emotionally intense, conceptually vacuous cultural identity which Ermelinda Tuzzi has constructed for herself.

This high-minded beauty, named Diotima by her distant cousin Ulrich, a friend of Leinsdorf, wife of a senior Austrian diplomat and in love with the Prussian industrialist and man of letters Arnheim, steers the *Parallelaktion* against the "soulless age dominated by mere logic and psychology" (chap. 22) by elevating Austrian true culture over Prussian mere civilization. She is searching for the really great, the redeeming idea for the 1918 celebration, and where Ulrich asks "Have you something definite in mind?" Arnheim, in love with Austrian culture in the shape of Diotima, thinks mere rationalism callous. Leinsdorf does not mind having the influential German industrialist among the pillars of Austrian culture and capital gathered in Diotima's successful salon. Her tasteful campaigning for the "idea of the non-Fractional Life" *(das unzersplitterte Sein)* is attractive to bankers, engineers, architects, lawyers, politicians, scientists, senior civil servants, established artists, and writers alike who blend harmoniously under the benign smile of Diotima as the "Integral Woman" *(die ungebrochene Frau)*. She has persuaded herself to be still in possession of "the magical radiation" *(jene Schicksalsmacht)*[127] that could envelop the intellect with the forces of life itself *(Seinskräften)*, which, to her way of thinking, the intellect was obviously in dire need of for its salvation (chap. 24).

But even if her guests are willing to suspend their pragmatic instincts temporarily under the influence of her imposing presence and knowledgeable hospitality, she is too bright not to experience some rather serious difficulties in getting the realities of daily living into harmony with the soul. Her suffering is caused by modern civilization disrupting all values with its "arrogant symbolic language of mathematical and chemical formulae, economics, experimental research," the reason for mankind's inability "to live in simple but sublime community" (chap. 24).[128] Civilization is everything with which her mind cannot easily and (therefore) does not wish to cope. In Dr. Arnheim she meets that rare individual whose mind seems to be coping very well with civilization and who prizes the soul above everything else, lamenting bleak rationalism—"mere logic and psychology"—and celebrating the simple strong beauty of life. Arnheim is, in fact, Diotima's redeeming idea: the Prussian strong personality must take over the spiritual leadership of the *Parallelaktion* (chap. 27).

Ulrich cannot but dislike Arnheim and mistrust him, but his criticism is developed in conversation with Arnheim and related to his own attempts at puzzling out the problematic aspects of contemporary experience. If he reacts to Arnheim as a "symptom" of the times he will also understand that this is too easy. Like his author in his review of Rathenau's 1913 *Mechanics of the Mind* he sees that this man, all his qualities notwithstanding, is after something that intrigues him, too. Arnheim, then, is a contrasting *and* complementary figure; it is possible, even necessary to negotiate distances and connections, as Ulrich finds out again and again. A short excursion into the complex of associations connected with the concept of water in chapter 28—"A chapter that can be skipped by anyone who has no very high opinion of thinking as an occupation"[129]—leads Ulrich, who had started out working contentedly on a mathematical problem, to exclaim that "if a man just starts thinking a bit he gets into what one might call pretty disorderly company." Arnheim's pseudomysticism is part of it and by no means the most surprising.

What Ulrich cannot endure, however, is the Arnheim pattern, Arnheim as a form of existence, as combination of mind, business, good living, wellreadness, and soul. Arnheim standing in the middle of the room in his impeccably tailored clothes, tall, erect, with the "Phoenician hardness of the master-merchant's skull": "It was this sureness that Arnheim's books also had: the world was all right as soon as Arnheim had regarded it" (chap. 44). It was all right, that is, in its lamentable lack of soul, and truth, and values, ruled by life-threatening mechanized chronological time and barren intellect, crying out for redemption—by Arnheim, Diotima, and the *Parallelaktion*.

The language games played at Diotima's gatherings are power games.

Arnheim is the man who can speak with everyone in their language, Ulrich the man who says that such speech is *about* communication and that it is motivated by the need to control. Leinsdorf, long used to power, has a specific kind of cultural intelligence which helps him see the flakiness *and* appreciate the effect of a greatness modeled on a cultural constant like Goethe and transposed to a twentieth-century "interesting personality" like Arnheim (chap. 47). Where Ulrich analyzes Arnheim's "being all in one person" and his own irritated reactions to that interesting phenomenon, Leinsdorf accepts the man and his own reservations about him. Combining different perspectives on Arnheim, Musil, if not Ulrich, who is too much involved at that point, reads him as a sign of the times and such reading proves instructive for the reader (chaps. 42–50). The composite portrait is far from being simply satirical, and it is the medium of the essay-novel rather than the essay which supports the perspicacious flexibility of Musil's cultural criticism.[130] The author as novelist does not withdraw behind the utterances of his characters; rather, he connects them ironically and shows how they contradict and complement each other. Arnheim *is* a highly accomplished, highly intelligent "interesting personality." He represents the best possibilities of the time. But he does so in a way that they cannot become reality, or, more precisely, that they are not understood as possibilities and therefore cannot become a reality worthy of the possibility.

Arnheim's fame (chap. 48) as the universal specialist, the Goethean who celebrates the mystery of the whole in a fragmented world and knows how to make the experience of fragmentation work for his purposes, is based on the needs rather than the generosity of others. His quoting poetry at board meetings seems slightly ridiculous to the other top level executives, but they do recognize that such control of different modes of discourse will be useful if the nature of international business concerns has to be explained to the artistic and intellectual or the technological elite. He is seen as "modern man" by modern men as cultural optimists and as true conservative by modern men as cultural pessimists. In gatherings of very specialized men he appears as the one who could connect different worlds and is therefore complete as a man. The effect of this on the specialists is the increasing popularity of quotes from Arnheim's books, which proved that one was moving with one's times into the unlimited possibilities of the future. It makes Arnheim himself believe ever more firmly in the Mystery of the Whole on which all greatness finally and simply rests, "and when he wrote this down he believed he had caught the supernatural by the hem of its cloak, and let as much become apparent in the text" (chap. 48; see also chap. 46).

Ulrich is fascinated by the phenomenon of Arnheim's fame, a construction of Arnheim by himself and others. Such cooperative construction is the substance of identity in any case, but in this case the kind and degree of control is very different. It is not just that fame is a special case, but that Arnheim's fame is a special case: the curious symbiosis of success and the soul. Thoroughly competent specialists who have to account for their deci-

sions cannot help admiring Arnheim's formula, because it works so well, and
being disturbed, because to them this seems so unexpected. They see themselves as realists, but in their professionalism they are idealists, and their
insistence on responsibility is arrogant in its isolationism. Musil and Ulrich
like them—the hard-headed banker Fischel, the dry, methodical diplomat
Tuzzi—because they neatly deflate the colorful bubbles of cultural despair,
but Musil, if not always Ulrich, is sharply aware of their cultural blinders.

In Fischel's case (chap. 51) the new wave of anti-Semitism should cause
him to look more closely at the success of certain cultural shifts and emerging tendencies. His wife, much better connected than he, had married him
because banking had seemed to her in, the 1890s, an essentially modern
profession, in pleasant contrast to the thrifty narrowness of her old civil
service family, and because she felt, as a liberal bourgeoise, proudly independent of the crude anti-Semitic prejudices of the lower middle classes.[131] But
the new nationalism welling up all over Europe and the attendant hostility to
Jews in general and particular "transformed her husband, so to speak in her
arms, from a respected liberalist into a member of a destructively analytical-
minded alien race." Fischel takes great pride in his own rationality, but this
makes him take others' irrationality too personally. The situation in his
family is part of a Central European case history, but it is *his* wife's alienation
and *his* daughter's Germano-Christian craze, and so he feels incredulous and
bitter rather than incredulous and superior, refusing to see his grievances in
their connection to modern developments of which his daughter wishes to be
part. As a serious man of business he makes fun, of course, of the "True
Progress-True Patriotism-True Austria" litanies of the *Parallelaktion* (chap.
35), but cannot help being impressed by the fact that Arnheim the modern
financier does not agree here with him at all. And so the rationalist Fischel
feels himself driven more and more to the desperate hope that something
would crash, explode soon, and reveal the inner hollowness of it all—not so
very differnt from the young Teutons around his daughter Gerda. Tuzzi, on
the other hand, is much less directly pressured by the fusion of soul and
business and so can modify his rationalist position profitably: he decides to
take more seriously what goes on in his wife's "at homes," that is, her power
by proxy (chap. 57).

The despairingly hopeful high seriousness of the *Parallelaktion* echoes
the vague all-pervasive uneasiness of the times. The stream of incoming
letters all filed away neatly with the magic formula of the Austrian administration "ass.," which means "awaiting further consideration" (chap. 56),
can be divided into "back to" (Belief, Austrian Baroque, Nature, Goethe,
Moral Purity, Germanic Law, Family, etc.) and "forward to" (chap. 48). The
extremes of cultural despair and cultural affirmation can be neutralized and
thereby normalized in the entropic Austrian state. But there is danger in this
absence of an order both flexible and sustaining, which comes to the surface
in a mind like Moosbrugger's. His fluid identity shares certain aspects with
Arnheim's soul and Ulrich's essays into another more intense state of intel-

lectual-emotional awareness (see chaps. 61, 62, 72). But as, in contrast to Arnheim and Ulrich, he has no or very little control, self and world are in a state of constant violent disruption, literally shaken as by earthquakes. Where Ulrich can reflect on that state and relate the personal experience of flux and change to cultural signs and the function of a cultural tradition,[132] where Arnheim uses the soul as a metaphorical cushion for his arguments to be reached for automatically,[133] Moosbrugger is literally terrified.

Perception for him is nonselective, language all-encircling, and so he is flooded with images and pushed in different directions simultaneously. Everything can be represented by everything else, as there is no consensus-based historically meaningful selection of symbolic signs, only the paranoia of disconnected meanings created by the self in isolation (chap. 59).[134] Both Ulrich and Arnheim are successful members of a cultural elite, and it is precisely their finely tuned control over their world that makes them deviants in ways which have nothing to do with the victim Moosbrugger as individual and cultural misfit. Arnheim's single-mindedness where certain emerging cultural tendencies are concerned makes him famous; Ulrich sees what is coming and does not like it but has the luxurious option of removing himself temporarily from "the times." Moosbrugger is not intended to be read as symptomatic of the times. All times have been more or less disturbed; it is a question of degree. Moosbrugger's manic-depressive schizophrenia is his; treatment is selected and administered by "his" society which has declared him a misfit from the beginning. It is, however, not so much this well-worn vicious circle in which Musil is interested, but rather the emergence of certain cultural changes on different levels of perception, interpretation, and acceptance.

The desire to order the world so it can be trusted is the most powerful and, in all its diversity, the most common human drive. It makes Arnheim and Musil write books and makes Ulrich reject writing.[135] It makes Moosbrugger dance in his cell, extending self and world, relating, smoothing out what is crumpled outside him (chap. 87),[136] it makes Clarisse pursue her mysterious powers and missions (chap. 97) and the Germano-Christian friends of Gerda talk endlessly about the purity of the soul, chaste community, true solidarity, unity, and pure spirit which cannot be found in the world of bourgeois liberalism (chap. 102).

The person who connects the different positions is Arnheim (chap. 78),[137] and he turns out to be the master teacher for General Stumm von Bordwehr, formerly Ulrich's colonel, now his friend, sympathetic to the civilian spirit and therefore sent by the army to be an observer at Diotima's *Parallelaktion* gatherings. Stumm, confused but eager to excel, first tries to learn from Ulrich, who can make sense but is hard to follow, and he really admires Arnheim's rhetorical ease even if he does not understand him. The idea of a redeeming idea is attractive to him in connection with Diotima, though in his position in the War Ministry he has had frustrating experiences concerning the influence of Austria's "unredeemed nationalities," or minorities, on the defense budget, and his first soldierly view of the word "redemption" was that "it simply belonged to that group of words on which linguistics have not yet cast adequate light, which we call 'high-falutin' " (chap. 108). In this mixed state of mind he draws up, with the ingenious help of several young officers, an extensive survey of the Central European stock of ideas with special attention to those ideas, and their originators, which had moved Europe in the last twenty-five years. After isolating the ideas-in-chief, marking the idea-supply lines to the front, noting how they are received by the fighting units, after producing intricate strategic plans, which to the layman Ulrich seem a colorful mess of crossing lines and overlapping shapes, Stumm's sense of order is by no means satisfied:

> "I have tried a lot more experiments of various kinds," the General said, and in his gay and lively eyes there was now a faint gleam of irritation or even panic, "trying to get the whole thing reduced to unity. But d' you know what it's like? Just like travelling second-class in Galicia and picking up crabs! It's the lousiest feeling of helplessness I ever knew. When you've been spending a lot of time among ideas you get an itching all over your body, and you can't get any peace even if you scratch till you bleed!" (chap. 85)

Stumm shares Arnheim's "real and most violent passion" for the ordering of the world (chap. 86); his initial impotence in an unfamiliar intellectual environment is comical but misleading. There are differences but also similarities regarding discipline and strategy. The army's insistence on order as the condition of (any) action is more direct; the giving of orders to establish this and no other order according to a preestablished strategy, which cannot accommodate feedback, is more rigid. The ironical connection between Arnheim and Stumm suggests that the same combination of accident and power is operative on the metaphorical battlefield of ideas and the literal battlefield of bodies. Both the military and the Cultural strategist deny the importance of accident which would disrupt order and thus threaten orderly action—the only kind of action that makes sense to the military—and controlled meaning—the only kind of meaning that makes sense to the Cultural strategist.

Arnheim is a modern variation on the military strategist; he projects a particularly clear connection between preideological 1913 and ideological 1930. Money, as Arnheim knows, but not yet Stumm, is the redeeming idea as the most flexible, therefore most reliable method of managing all relationships. As a contemporary observer of Weimar culture Musil describes in the figure of Arnheim a peculiarly modern sensitivity to the concrete interlocking power of money, where Simmel in his influential *Philosophy of Money* (1900)[138] had stressed apprehensively its abstracting effects as symptomatic for the modern age at the turn of the century. The Prince of Commerce is seen by Arnheim as "the synthesis of revolution and permanence, of armed power and bourgeois civilization, of reasoned audacity and honest-to-goodness knowledge, but essentially as a kind of symbolic configuration of the kind of democracy that was about to come into existence." The concept, realized in his person, supports his profound conviction of cultural unity which embraces and harmonizes all interests (chap. 86).

For Arnheim art is culture-affirming—Simmel,[139] speaking here from a position of late nineteenth-century liberalism, removes art from the tainting influence of general culture[140]—and such affirmation is essential to his utopia of cultural unity. But to be able to project such fusion he diffuses the whole area of art till it becomes synonymous with soul which can then be fused with business and technology more easily. Simmel insists on the total non-availability of art in an age where money makes everything totally available, and this insistence proved highly suggestive to the idiosyncratic Marxist aesthetics of the Frankfurt School and Walter Benjamin as well as to Brecht's single-minded attempts to outwit a cultural tradition and Ernst Jünger's heroic cultural anachronism.[141] Arnheim projects the total availability of art, albeit on a cloudy higher level, and this combination is characteristic for the social aesthetics of the art market in capitalist culture as well as for the political aesthetics of state approval in ideological culture. Arnheim like Rathenau does anticipate cultural tendencies that emerged in full force during the Weimar period, and the forceful fusion—in his desire for strength, wholeness, and harmony—of money, technology, and the soul is a very important aspect of the novel's "*Grundidee:* Krieg. Alle Linien münden in den Krieg" (The central idea: war. Everything else leads toward war) and "Seinesgleichen führt zum Krieg"—the times are moving toward war in 1913 and 1930.[142]

The persistent and quite violent need to connect is a sign of the times and most distinctly developed in the group of people who are seen to be and see themselves in the vanguard. Rathenau/Arnheim was a very expressive choice for the novelist as cultural critic precisely because of his many qualities which could be shown to refract a great variety of possible connections and their meanings. "One must move with the times" (chap. 89) and "one must move the times" in him are synonymous motivations; any doubts in this respect make him very uneasy. He thinks on one occasion with pleasure of the near future when technology will make it possible for senior executives to have their own airplanes and conduct international business from summer holiday in the Himalayas, but feels ambivalent about the young intelligentsia asserting themselves at a recent party at Diotima's. Arnheim is perfectly at home with the variety of *isms*—from technicism, accelerism, vitalism, individualism, lyricism, dramaticism, activism, futurism to socialism and nationalism—which served as catalysts of community before World War I. He is willing to grant the importance of controlled or free sensuality, emotional or intellectual synthesis, and he enjoys his enjoyment of the dynamics of contradiction: "the only thing they had definitely in common was the attack on objectivity, intellectual responsibility, and the balanced personality" (chap. 89), he remembers, almost chuckling.

These, however, are also unquestionable values in Arnheim's view, and while trying to imagine his way into the future, he also imagines himself continuing to represent these values in their true essence which the young will have to learn about. It is important to him that he cannot be taken by surprise, and so the future, which he intends to assist to be born, is imagined as more intensely, more ideocratically moving with the times. But the Great War, a watershed in some if not in all areas of cultural order and activity, adds a dimension of change to the times in flux which is the most puzzling and most inaccessible to the intellectual. Musil comments ironically on Arnheim's endeavors:

> And if Arnheim had been able to peer several years ahead, he would there and then have seen that nineteen hundred and twenty years of Christian morality, an appalling war with its millions of dead and whole murmuring forests of poetry that had cast their leafy shade over the female sense of modesty, were all not capable of warding off by a single hour the day when women's skirts and women's hair began to get shorter and all the girls of Europe, after so many centuries of taboos, for a while slipped out of their coverings, naked, like peeled bananas. There were other changes, too, that he would have seen, which he would scarcely have believed possible. And it does not matter how much of it will last or how much of it will disappear again. What is important to bear in mind is what great and probably vain exertions would have been necessary in order to bring about the revolutions in style of living along the road of intellectual development, so rich in responsibility, by way of philosophers, painters and poets, instead of by way of tailors, fashions and chance: for from this one can guess how much creative energy is generated from the surface of things, and by contrast how barren is the wilfullness of the brain. (chap. 90)

These are developments that Arnheim would not care to anticipate because they have no meaning and therefore no value. What he does anticipate in connecting all the different intellectual positions is the coming of something collective, pan-logical, back to nature, wholeness, and health, but modernized, an updated Garden of Eden under the guidance of personal greatness.

Arnheim is not anymore the Goethean *Geistesfürst* (spiritual leader) but his modern successor, the *Grosschriftsteller* or superman of letters (chaps. 95 and 96: backview and frontview). Musil's very funny satire on the dynamics of the contemporary Culture Market deals with the serious question of modern value strategies: whatever is advertised as great becomes great as it is thought great and this process crowds out doubting. Greatness agrees with the world in more than one sense. Arnheim finds delightful its ironical ambiguity which translates into such solid success when it supports the profound meanings of the whole. Ironically, he legitimizes his desire for greatness with his admiration for the ironical Heine's admiration for Napoleon, unaware both of Heine's historical political reasons and the elusive poet's unambiguous addiction to subversiveness. But in general, cultural elites have seen the charismatic obscurantism of greatness as rejuvenating promise rather than a threat. In Arnheim it is significantly linked to action, and he can thus be admired as bringing together the expectedly creative confusion of the intellectuals and the undoubtedly constructive order of General Stumm.

Stumm has learned that a stable order cannot be invented but has to be based on the authority of preexisting order. Made by the military, history is preserved by the filing system of libraries so that the military can go on making it. Ulrich agrees with Clarisse that one ought to invent history (chap. 83) by doubting the seemingly irresistible flux of the times or *seinesgleichen geschieht*. Arnheim sees himself participating significantly in making history move in its predetermined meaningful course, and Diotima is aroused by her contribution to this motion. The Germano-Christians hope for revolution of one history into another which will release redeeming energies. Tuzzi and Leinsdorf will go on administering any kind of bona fide history, even if, under the worst of circumstances, with reservations. But Stumm's concept is clearly the most far-sighted and cost-efficient, and Arnheim will make it even more so once the question of the meaning of history has been streamlined by the fact that "there is a war on."

Stumm's first excursion to the Imperial Library (chap. 100), where it is explained to him that reading the books would preclude getting them into order, as it would make impossible getting a view of the thing as a whole, teaches him an important connection between order and aggression. He looks at the perfected (civilian) system made up of millions of books, sees its "sheer entropy, *rigor mortis,* a landscape on the moon, a geometrical plague," and suddenly understands "why in the army, where we have the highest degree of order, we also have to be prepared to lay down our lives at any moment. I can't quite explain why. At a certain stage order somehow creates a demand for bloodshed." This is an extraordinary statement coming from the philosophically inclined, potbellied, short-legged general whose sympathies for the civilian spirit, though very useful to his career, have mainly been based on the difficulties he has had in the cavalry. Order, bloodshed, and history have always been synonymous in his experience. Understanding that they do have separate though intimately connected meanings will make him even more effective in making others experience their synonymy.

Stumm, then, has become familiar with and fond of libraries and will run into other library users, like Diotima, Ulrich, and Arnheim who have come to look for pictorial information about a successful Makart pageant in the 1870s (chap. 114). Leinsdorf has strongly recommended the medieval costume pageant which he remembers for its presentation of beauty, strength, wholeness, and hierarchy of values uniting all Austria in an upswell of enthusiasm. History, after all, does not change much, even if banking does—Leinsdorf is a client of Fischel's progressive bank. Arnheim does not think much of Leinsdorf's ideas, though he admires their "true conservatism." But he shows Stumm a book on medieval painting, lamenting the lost grandeur, simplicity, integrity, and cultural centeredness of the Middle Ages and declaring his admiration for "this Austrian plan to bestow an all-uniting example and a great communal idea upon the world, even if I do not think it entirely feasible." Austria in its slower development is in a position superior to Germany: "Very very few people know that real greatness has no foundation in reason. I mean, everything strong is simple." At this point Stumm realizes that he is no longer being talked at, but talked to: Arnheim wants something from him; this fact will be useful to the army and to his career.

The chapter is skillfully choreographed in the literal and figurative sense. The four people, connected and separated intellectually and emotionally, are waiting for a cab in front of the library on this sunny day in the bright new year 1914. For the observer informed by the author, Ulrich is the link between Stumm and Arnheim because he is skeptically sympathetic to some of Arnheim's ideas and understands—though he does not share it— Arnheim's anxiety of experience as a preoccupation with personal as cultural wholeness. This quality is the source of his decisiveness in questions concerning cultural value and his indecision in personal relationships, as Ulrich has been explaining to Diotima waiting in vain to be swept off her feet by the man she loves (see also chap. 101).[143] With Stumm he shares a pragmatic perception of the world informed by a professional mistrust of ideas—that this mistrust is different in kind is another matter. The redeeming idea sought by the *Parallelaktion* is attractive to Stumm only as a bounty to be placed, warrior-style, at the feet of the woman he admires. Unlike Ulrich, Arnheim has never convinced or persuaded him, but he now makes sense to him in terms of possible action, and at this point Ulrich stops making sense to him in terms of an intellectual charting of contemporary culture. Stumm is about to come into his own.

Ulrich also shares, if skeptically, Diotima's feelings about feelings, and it is his relative lack of mature intelligent irony that makes him reject rather than explore the affinities between himself and this woman to whom he is attracted and by whom he is is repelled because she is so different. Thinking her a goose only encourages her quality of pompous obscurantism, and so, finally stepping into the cab, she asserts once more that "any emotion that is not limitless is of no value."

Not much later Stumm will explain to Ulrich that despite having been promoted from mission D(iotima) to mission L(einsdorf), he has not changed just because he is different now.[144] And indeed he has not. He has developed militarily in response to the civilian environment which includes Arnheim's interest in the Galician oilfields (chap. 119). He has always known military logic—in contrast to civilian reason—to be iron, honorable, reckless, unfeeling, totally unswerving, but now, in the summer of 1914, he knows why it has to be that way. Ulrich who is just beginning to explore himself in the relationship with his sister is too preoccupied to pay full attention, that is, get involved. His criticism of Stumm's arguments is playful; he is half-impressed and half-amused by the military's shrewdness and Stumm's rise in his part of the world, and unwilling to see the connection to his own world, though his author, and the reader with him, does. Stumm, though still confiding in him, no longer takes Ulrich seriously.

Like Arnheim, Stumm now leads a life governed by a higher law and worthy of a biography which will assign meaning to beginning, middle, and end and interpret all the usual contradictions as significant conflict. Stumm's law is simpler and more inexorably unswerving than Arnheim's, and so the latter continues to be unnerved by Ulrich's probing. After Ulrich has suggested constituting the beginning of a general spiritual stocktaking to be completed by 1918 and, for that purpose, the founding of "a terrestrial secretariat for precision and the soul" *(Erdensekretariat der Genauigkeit und Seele)* (chap. 116), Arnheim offers him a position in his firm, high up and vaguely defined (chap. 121). Ulrich has been driven to this "utterly senseless" suggestion because the *Parallelaktion* has become all but completely mired in internal intellectual exhaustion and external controversy as to its exaggeratedly pro- or anti-German leanings—a very common phenomenon in Austrian politics. Arnheim is not so much impressed by Ulrich's statement, as angered that Leinsdorf defends him, because he understands that Ulrich is groping for a flexible imaginative order and will not propose to rearrange the world in a special way of his own. In an age of ideologies, Leinsdorf realizes, Ulrich is no ideologue (chap. 116). Arnheim's instinct is to tie Ulrich to himself so that Ulrich might help him assert his own identity as a great man, a man of substance who does not need perennial doubts, a man also capable of embracing beautiful and ambiguous things: "Never before, Arnheim thought, had he felt as intensely as in this moment the solidarity of Western civilization, with its wonderful network of forces and inhibitions. If Ulrich did not recognize this too, then he was nothing but an adventurer . . . " (chap. 121). Ulrich does not recognize this; he declines the position—Arnheim had hoped he would—and embarks on the adventure of incest. He will step even more clearly outside of the web of cultural forces and inhibitions celebrated and used by Arnheim, but his exile will not be irreversible.[145] Like his author, Ulrich will participate in the war, directed by Stumm and fed by Arnheim and Fischel; and at the end of the war his social imagination will have been sufficiently developed to prevent him from appealing—as did Rathenau and so many other intellectuals—to the New Man, impossibly purified in the fire of trench warfare. During the Weimar Republic he would not, I expect, retreat into fictions of the Coming of the New Man in a golden age of ideology or art. He would be a practicing cultural critic, a pragmatic, shrewd, ironical contemporary, and finally, like his author in the 1980s, one of the favorite authors of intellectuals who don't normally read novels—and still without redeeming ideas.

THREE

"Placet Experiri?"

Thomas Mann and the Charms of Entelechy

I.

The only provocative aspect of Thomas Mann's novels today is their former success. Musil was right in his prediction that they would pass with their times, being so much a part of them. However, professional readers in the Federal Republic as well as the German Democratic Republic are still reluctant to analyze critically Mann's extraordinary skills in reaffirming his *bürgerlich* audience's beliefs and prejudices, anxieties and hopes—what Lukács expectedly describes as "Mann's dialectically complex attitude to the middle class."[1] The hundredth anniversary of his birthday, 1975, was celebrated, like a Goethe year, in the high style of humanism; critics on vacation from the ordinary could not but approve of a greatness so palpable yet so poised in its tactfully ironic claims to immortality.

Acceptance of Thomas Mann as a great German writer came early in his career with the publication of *Buddenbrooks* (1901) for which he received the Nobel Prize in 1929. The painful scrupling he recorded in his diaries when he broke with the Nazi regime and left Germany in 1933 seems astonishingly self-centered, but it was consistent with his perception and presentation of himself as *the* German writer of his time, that is, since Goethe. The publication of the diaries which became accessible in 1975, twenty years after Thomas Mann's death, has been a very emotional issue in the Thomas Mann industry, because for many professional readers they contradict cruelly the beloved image of the great humanist. However, they are not so much brutally or tragically honest as emotionally and intellectually petty and disturbed. It is not that he did not love all his children, that he adored perfect young beautiful boys—young gardeners, his friends' sons, even his own eldest son when he was at that fragile impermanent stage which the boy-lover, by new infatuations, seeks to make permanent and thus invulnerable to feared change, that he was within his family extraordinarily self-centered, egotistical, unthoughtful, that he exploited his wife's loyalty and emotional strength, that he could not make up his mind to break openly with the Nazi regime because he could not bear to lose his audience and endanger his upper-class standard of living, that he was intensely worried about getting his gramophone and his cars out of Germany at a time when other intellectuals were beaten to death in the concentration camps. These attitudes can be and have been interpreted as being part of Thomas Mann's great, all-encompassing humanity.[2] It is, then, not the selfishness, which is unsettling and instructive, not the emotional coldness, not the lack of intellectual curiosity and generosity, not the particular self-protective voyeuristic homosexuality, not his reactions during the very difficult years 1933–36—especially not his hesitations then and especially not as behavior to be judged by a reader of my generation who on the whole has lived in a time of relatively amazing security and stability. It is, rather, the specific presentation of all those "all-too human" traits which establishes their very obvious relation to his essays and fiction. The relentless recording of his dailiness presents as equally significant the chair he sat in, the tomato soup he enjoyed, the sleeping pill he took, his sister's suicide, a political murder, a fallen government, the exact amount of time he took to make love to his wife so that he could sleep: this total, seemingly unselective recording is motivated by the view of his life as unquestionably and uniquely meaningful and to be saved, by the daily acts of recording, from deterioration through the influence of time and the spontaneous contact with other lives. It is not the obvious neurotic tendencies— the pronounced inability to accept a self subjected to change and mortality, an extreme need for self-control and through it control of others—it is, rather, the resulting concept of the cultural function and significance of art and of his own position as artist that is relevant and instructive to the literary and intellectual historian of the period.

Since the midthirties, he has had a devoted American readership which came to replace, to a degree, the faithful reading public he left behind in Germany.[3] His American readers do not, as a rule, have much knowledge of the German cultural tradition but many, if refined, prejudices against it. In the process of reading novels like *Magic Mountain,* the *Joseph* tetralogy, *Doctor Faustus,* these prejudices are both reaffirmed and rendered more subtle. In this country Thomas Mann's stature as the great humanist connotes "European culture" and "democracy," based on his presentation of himself as the preserver and pinnacle of a great cultural tradition, on his eloquent devotion to Franklin D. Roosevelt and his democracy, on his passionate denunciations of a perverted "bad" and evocations of a genuine "good" Germany. To these educated well-meaning American readers Mann has demonstrated *and* made palatable the familiar, somewhat ridiculous though unquestionably profound German predilection for dualistic constructs. Out of the German depths he has conjured up for his readers the specters of Schopenhauer, Nietzsche, and Wagner, of Goethe and Tolstoy, Goethe and Jung, inviting them to take sides in and help resolve, on a higher level, the conflict of will and idea, life and death, spirit and nature, spirit and art, life and art, culture and civilization, realism and idealism, paganism and Christianity, collective and individual, socialism and culture, myth and psychology.[4] Above all, however, he has tempted his readers with solidly constructed stories: to be fully effective,

Mann's unique recipe for indulging, challenging, and lecturing his readers depends on his specific mixture of nineteenth- and twentieth-century novelistic conventions and expectations. He manages to keep the story intact, for which most of us crave, while superimposing on its specific mocking sophistication the collective relevance of the typical, the mythical.

The Marxist aesthetician and musicologist Adorno provided Mann with all the information and much of the actual text for the devil's glib performance in avant-garde musicology so highly acclaimed by the professional readers of *Doctor Faustus*.[5] He also lent, if involuntarily, his expressive features to this entertaining "negative principle."[6] His intellectual relationship to Thomas Mann was not without complications, as he felt used by the famous novelist,[7] who was interested less in Adorno's ideas than in the ways in which they could be fitted into the composition of his novel.[8] Adorno on the other hand, not unlike Mann in his proprietary, eclectic dealings with ideas, was not impressed by the intellectual content of Mann's novels. He accordingly advised the reader to disregard the "official metaphysics of the artist" *(offizielle Künstlermetaphysik)*[9] and concentrate on sampling the delightful illusionist feats, the mimetic mockeries with which Mann the magician entertains his readers.[10]

Implicitly debunking, such advice is useful to a degree, but it neglects to deal with the culturally important question of the novel of ideas or philosophical novel which attracted such large audiences during the Weimar period. For Mann, ideas do not present challenges. There never is any danger that he might get absorbed in their exploration, lost on detours provoked by them. Unperturbed he removes them as static units from their contexts to weave them into the "giant carpet of his song," as he called the elaborate compositional structure of *The Magic Mountain*.[11] Their value to him is precisely their disponibility. Professional readers have been strongly inclined to confuse the importance of the ideas as they appear in the novels with Mann's articulated delight in the patterns which he has fashioned with them. They have been following Mann's elaborate instructions, offered in many essays and lectures about his work, about how to share and treasure this delight.[12] Quite clearly Mann did not perceive ideas as a shared medium of contact between members of a contemporary literary public. They were important to him as part of his successful presentation of his life's meaning as unique and uniquely representative of his time.

The success of this presentation was indeed astonishing. One example is the deep bond of sympathy between the patrician *Grosschriftsteller* and the *grossbürgerlich* Marxist critic-statesman Lukacs[13] who praised as humanist realism the ambiguous epiphanies of hope and meaning which Mann conjured up out of the stuff of negation: the celebration of life in the midst of death in the famous snow chapter of *The Magic Mountain*, the light guiding Hans Castorp stumbling over the World War I battlefield at the end of the novel, the golden cello tone in the void of hell at the end of *Doctor Faustus*.

Secure in his self-centered aesthetic Marxism, Adorno had not understood that the basis for Mann's success was precisely his readers' need to extract elevation from their pleasure, their eager willingness to mistake the purged, artfully arranged myths for meaningful statements about a messy reality, past, present, and future. The alleged philosophical sophistication of *The Magic Mountain* as intricate *Themengewebe*[14] seemed a natural refuge to a large audience of well-read, indignantly confused readers from what they thought the intellectual, aesthetic, political, and moral jungle of Weimar.[15] Author and audience refused to face as important cultural issues the contemporary problems of a rapidly developing technocracy within a highly polarized, politically volatile mass democracy. They preferred withdrawal to an intricate but static well-ordered arrangement of bits and pieces from High Culture that could be passed off as the past serving as beacon to a more safely meaningful future. The present would best be suspended in what Mann celebrated as magic *nunc stans* in the hermetically closed world of his mountain.[16] This is not to say that Mann did not live up to the intellectual's sociopolitical responsibility, which is always precarious in that it is difficult to establish, and in most situations impossible to fulfill. But it is necessary to point out that this declared great leader and *Repräsentant* of German Culture[17] worked with a narrow, highly eclectic concept of what constituted culture and of his responsibility toward a rich and diverse cultural tradition reflecting the intellectual and artistic experience of many other men and women before him. Weimar intellectuals as a group cannot be held responsible for the "German Catastrophe,"[18] but in many cases, Thomas Mann included, their understanding of their cultural function and responsibility was specifically flawed, and the intellectual historian of the period needs to ask why.

Buddenbrooks, today Mann's most satisfying text, presented a patrician *bürgerlich* existence as a more delicate, more vulnerable, therefore higher form of life than that of the rising industrial bourgeoisie. It was a mythical *Bürgerlichkeit* structured along a simplified Schopenhauerian pattern of will and idea, life and death. More than three decades later, when working on the *Joseph* novels, Mann traced the unfolding of his entelechy in its destined direction from the *bürgerlich* individual to the collective mythical sphere.[19] But his specific talent and temperament had early led him toward the mythical structurally rigid treatment of the puzzling, elusive, complex phenomenon of human behavior. Notwithstanding Lukács's emphatic claims for its masterful, fully developed realism,[20] *Buddenbrooks* did not deal with *bürgerlich* reality, much less with issues concerning the relatively young German bourgeoisie, but reflected Mann's playing an elaborate game with a carefully husbanded store of realia to produce the desired effect of turn-of-the-century naturalism.[21] However, in this early work the author's intense desire for order and meaningful structures, in which the self might be free of a passionately feared accidentality, was kept in check by the family story which balanced the individual's exaggerated need for self-definition. The conflicts had not yet been arrested in the cumulative dualism of the later works; the reader was guided with pleasant, still relatively flexible firmness through this coolly sentimental story.

When fame came there was an even more urgent need for the delicate young man of genius to find and articulate an appropriately unique cultural role. He portrayed it in *Royal Highness* (1909), the story of the "severe happiness" ("das strenge Glück") found by the fictional "real" Prince Klaus-Heinrich—the name of his eldest son—in his relationship with the exotic heiress Irma Spoelmann, based on Katia Pringsheim, the only daughter of a very wealthy cultured Munich family, whom Mann had married in 1905. The novel celebrates the union of two extraordinary young people in search of ordinariness of a special kind,[22] and it differs from *Buddenbrooks* in its stated intention to "heighten and brighten" the inherited naturalism till the novel as work of art would become symbolical and intellectual, "a transparency for ideas to shine through."[23] As in all novels after *Buddenbrooks,* the reader is asked to identify with the author's manipulations of his protagonist as prismatic reflection of his own unfolding entelechy. The author, still young, is on his way to the role of the German *Geistesfürst,* and Prince Klaus-Heinrich's extraordinary existence is directly related to the artist's. In *The Magic Mountain* it would be Hans Castorp's extraordinary role as mediating ruler which enabled him to represent his author.[24] Later, in exile, real-life rulers would be presented as artists: the stunted, distorted, perverted *(verhunzt)* artist Hitler, and the blessed, fully, beautifully realized artist Roosevelt.[25]

Royal Highness and *Magic Mountain* were separated by the trauma of World War I. Mann's reaction to the first modern technological war was a "grandiose mistake,"[26] in the 1918 *Betrachtungen eines Unpolitischen* (Reflections of a nonpolitical man). Like Rathenau, whom he respected, Thomas Mann deeply identified with Germany's defeat and felt rejected and robbed of his leading cultural role in the immediate postwar years, when the intellectual climate was polarized and cultural conservatism unambiguously, aggressively politicized.[27] He was, in those years, much more contemptuous than Rathenau of the common man and woman who had not risen to what he perceived to be the profound moral challenge of the Great War.[28] They had demonstrated their desire to be rid of the exploitative patterns of cultural-political myths rather than their need for meaning and greatness. Assessments of Mann's achievements tend to overlook that monstrously long, aggressively nationalist essay, or to explain it as tragic *and* therapeutic in terms of an alleged cathartic function in the process of maturation toward the role of the great democratic European: examples can be found in the Marxist Lukács's 1943 essay "Über Preussentum"[29] and his important 1945 study "Auf der Suche nach dem Bürger" (In search of bourgeois man),[30] as well as in the Swiss bourgeois critic Max Rychner's 1947 "Thomas Mann und die Politik."[31] Lukács, well trained in interpretative flexibility, was most forceful in pointing out that the *Betrachtungen* should be understood as a vicarious working through of a national problem, vicarious suffering for a nation traumatized by the disastrous defeat. Mann was very much impressed by this understanding for his cultural role in a large sense.[32] He explained in the 1948 *The Story of a Novel: The Genesis of Doctor Faustus*—the German version of this painstakingly detailed autohagiography is more appropriately titled *Roman eines Romans*—why he was so moved by this homage. He deeply appreciated Lukács's view of a higher law governing his artistic career and the shared belief that the fulfillment of his—as any great man's—entelechy was part of a meaningful fated historical process. Lukács, then, did not only see the connection of Mann's work with a German past but also, even more emphatically, with a German future.[33]

As Mann was so preoccupied with the time-transcending meaning of his life as a German artist, he was particularly disturbed by the meaningless, to him, chaos of the postwar years and the relatively weak echo of the *Betrachtungen*[34]—thirty years later he was to be extremely upset about critical reviews of *Doctor Faustus* in the United States.[35] In the preface of the *Betrachtungen* he stresses the "personal ethos" of the book, distancing his reflections and himself from a "social ethos." It is here, however, that he invokes the ironic position as that of mediation of contrasts and healing of conflicts. And that was to be his position after the lost war: elusive, ambiguous, elevated to a higher Cultural level.

2.

Mann had proceeded quite logically from the role of the artist as delicate Schopenhauerian stranger holding himself apart from the strife of life to that of the ironic artist mediating such strife from above, the spiritual Cultural leader of the republic.[36] In 1916 he had written to his then close friend Ernst Bertram, a radically conservative academic disciple of Stefan George, author of a Germanophile study of Nietzsche much admired by Mann:[37] "What you say about the fate of Germany is only too true. Not megalomania, merely the need to regard things in intimate terms, long ago led me to see this fate symbolized and personified in my brother and myself."[38] But this "intime Anschauung" needed affirmation from the public world. The love of the subjects for their *Geistesfürst* would assure him that they accepted his destined role of representing and symbolizing their fate.[39] The instructions he gave to a friend in late 1901 regarding his review of *Buddenbrooks*—it was to help the initially slack sales of the book[40]—would have been appropriate as well for *Magic Mountain* and *Doctor Faustus*: Grautoff was to stress music and philosophy as the *"genuinely German"* elements of the book, mention the Wagnerian leitmotif technique, admit the novel's melancholic and nihilistic aspects but emphasize its positive *humorous* perspective—humor as life-affirming perspective was to be replaced by irony, its more evasive, ambiguous relation, after the war. The main thrust of the author's advice to his reviewer is to counteract the allegation of the book's loveless nihilistic irony: the story of the decline of a *bürgerlich* family was not to be understood as a depressing account given from an uninvolved ironic position; rather, it was to be read as a poetic transfiguration and expiation of *bürgerlich* decline.[41] After the book had brought him fame, he wrote to another friend who had published a long admiring essay on the brothers Mann,[42] refuting certain attributes of the book as the friend had presented them, notably its "icy misanthropy," its "lovelessness toward everything of flesh and blood," its "destructive," "zersetzend" (corrosive) qualities.[43] He stresses, again, the book's Germanness, the presence and influence of Wagner and Schopenhauer and Fritz Reuter, a much beloved regional poet writing in *Plattdeutsch* (Low German). Repeatedly Thomas Mann asserts that this book could only have been written in Germany by a poet who loves and is loved by his people. He is deeply upset by the friend's prediction that he would, in his further career, receive "more cool respect than heartfelt affection": "It is not true that *Buddenbrooks* and *Tonio Kröger* have been foisted on the public by essays and that they are coolly appreciated. These expressions of myself are loved, believe me, and to such an extent that I might well feel disturbed."[44]

The large German reading public did not refuse him love, and the very great success of *Buddenbrooks*, which made him experience identity—on a higher level, of course—with his audience, caused him to modify Tonio Kröger's view of art as *zersetzend* of human feeling, of life itself. Critics might apply this view in their interpretations of *Buddenbrooks*, but the very reception of the book had assured him of his readers' "unzersetzt," whole, strong feelings for these expressions of himself, that is, for him, the author. Speaking about literary art means speaking about the relationship between reader and author. In the collection of notes for a planned essay on literature and the writer, which occupied him after the completion of *Royal Highness*, he distinguishes art as essentially a matter of life—"Die Kunst wesentlich eine Sache des *Lebens*"—from spirit which destroys the emotions and desires nothingness—"Der Geist, mit seiner Tendenz zur Zerstörung der Leidenschaften, will letzten Endes das reine Nichts."[45] Spirit, *Geist,* now occupies the position formerly held by art, but this shift indicates a change of terms rather than a substantial change in his perception of the structural relation between the work of art and the life-world. The old dualism is retained and with it the perceived task of control by meditation, be it through humor or irony.

In *Betrachtungen* he sides with art, profoundly melancholic humor, deeply ethical pessimism, and the monarchy as essentially German against "Latin" democracy with its *zersetzend* spirit of shallow progressivism embodied in the *Zivilisationsliterat,* notably his brother Heinrich, whose sympathies, throughout the war, had been anti-German and pro-French, that is, in Thomas's terms, against Culture.[46] He argues, in the last years of the war, against the politicization of Germany which he sees as destructive intellectualization, as undermining art and the artist's symbolic existence. His son Klaus in his autobiography *The Turning Point* has praise for the position and work of the writers rejected by Thomas as *Zivilisationsliteraten,* the intellectuals who had been working since the turn of the century for social, political, and cultural renewal and international understanding. He explains *Betrachtungen* as "but one running fight"—which it was—and Mann's bitter protest against politicization as indicative of his "new political interest"— which it was not.[47] Politics in the generally accepted sense of the term has nothing to do with Mann's position in *Betrachtungen* based on his "personal ethos." He is, and continues to be, exclusively interested in the politics of Culture, that is, a culture of his own definition, represented, symbolized by him. Like the kaiser, he feels forced into exile, into leaving a Germany of his own making, and *Betrachtungen* voices his protest: victory of the Entente means victory of shallow Western literature over complex, profound German poetry; democratization of Germany is synonymous with her "Politisierung," "Literarisierung," "Intellektualisierung," "Radikalisierung," that is, her de-Germanization. As he states emphatically at the end of "Der Zivilisationsliterat" (chap. 3), he will have no part of such destructive nonsense.[48]

Critics have remarked on the shrill aggressive tone of that chapter, if not on its highly confused and confusing conceptual strategies. Rathenau, Thomas Mann notes in his diary on October 9, 1918, is said to be very upset: "soll sich über den 'Civilisationsliteraten' sehr empört haben."[49] But Mann, though slightly apprehensive, does not give in. He feels betrayed by his Germany siding with the *Zivilisationsliterat* in the search for a new Germany within a European community, and this sense of betrayal is intensified and muddled by his belief that the spiritual conflicts of Europe are fought in the soul of Germany which he symbolizes as *the* German writer. These conflicts determine the destined path of German *Bildungsgeschichte.* It was precisely as great Germans that Schopenhauer, Wagner, and Nietzsche were great Europeans. He admits an increasing intellectualization of his work from *Buddenbrooks* via *Tonio Kröger, Fiorenza* to *Royal Highness*—curiously, he does not mention the 1912 *Death in Venice*—but in the situation of the total war, of a Germany beleaguered from all sides, he had done his duty as German writer in defending a German spiritual *Bürgertum* which, in contrast to the European bourgeoisie, upholds the separation of philosophy from politics, of metaphysical from social life. Working on the chapter "Bürgerlichkeit," where he develops this argument, he wrote to his friend Paul Amann, the Austrian philologist and cultural historian: "The great Germans who were the shapers of my nature all adhered to that separation: Schopenhauer most decidedly of all; Wagner in spite of '48—he hated politics . . . and above all Nietzsche, too, who with profound accuracy called himself the 'last antipolitical German.' . . . I called that separation 'Protestant.' . . . We can never settle the problem of political freedom if we do not see it deep beneath metaphysical freedom."[50]

German *Bürgerlichkeit* (chap. 5), spiritual and Protestant, had produced as its finest blossom the *bürgerlich* artist as moralist, himself. Art, he says, is for him the ethical expression of his life—it is life that is of primary importance. With respect to the heroic existence of *Leistungsethiker* like Wagner, Friedrich der Grosse, his own Aschenbach, however, he seems to be arguing that their ethics are located in their inexorable dedication to their work at the expense of life; but then, their work is their life, and life is their art, and their work is art. Chapter 5 with all its confusing crisscross rhetoric mainly repeats the accusation made already in chapter 3 and again in chapter 6, "Gegen Recht und Wahrheit" (Against justice and truth): the *Zivilisationsliterat,* his brother in more than one sense, has betrayed the embattled camp of spiritual Germany in the hour of her greatest need which is also the hour of his, *the* German artist's, greatest despair.

In early 1918 Thomas wrote in answer to Heinrich's offer of peace that he could not forgive him the "truly French spitefulness, slanders and slurs of his brilliant piece of hackwork," the Zola essay, and that Heinrich's desire for a *rapprochement* "demonstrates the frivolity of a man who has 'sought to embrace the world.' "[51] The title of chapter 6 is a quote from this 1915 essay which had been published in the Alsatian Schickele's *Weissen Blättern,* a journal dedicated to international understanding.[52] It was Heinrich, Thomas argues, who committed crimes against "Recht und Wahrheit." This chapter written in late 1916, when the nationalist battlelines were drawn more sharply on all sides, is a veritable firework of invectives,[53] most of them untranslatable in their largely irrational verbal exuberance: Thomas is mortally afraid of the coming anarchistic democracy, the rule of the masses in politics and art and, at the same time, bitterly resentful of Heinrich's role as symbol in representing this development. Isolated and apprehensive about a future which does not seem to conform to the "destined pattern" of his life, "the character of [his] destiny, of [his] role on this earth,"[54] he calls Liebknecht and Luxemburg "those raving idiots" (*blöde Berserker),* "nothing but politicians," "wild socialists",[55] and gratefully notes in his diary all the positive reactions to *Betrachtungen,* including Frau Förster-Nietzsche's and his own.[56] He complains about Heinrich's irresponsible attitude toward German Culture—he had given a speech at a meeting of the Munich *sovjet*—and the untenable situation that such a person is honored as a "leading personality."[57] The satirical poet Sternheim is nothing but "vermin" *(Geschmeiss)* because he has publicly made fun of Goethe, even of such Ur-German an epic as "Hermann und Dorothea."[58]

In those years immediately following the war Mann felt very fragile in his role as German Cultural leader and symbol; that he earned more than M 100,000 in 1919, as he records "with pleasure"[59]—it was to be M 300,000 in 1921—was not sufficient consolation. "Let the tragedy of our brotherhood unfold," he had written to Heinrich in early 1918[60] and he needed to live on the level of tragedy till the worst of chaos had subsided and he was able to resume his destined role.

3.

In July 1921 Mann expressed his interest in a new one-volume-format edition of *Betrachtungen*. He was happily absorbed in work on a lecture, "Goethe and Tolstoy," and on *Magic Mountain:* "A wealth of thoughts on education, the importance of enthusiasm, love, dedication. Read in *Wilhelm Meister's Travels.* Astounded at the truly Goethean aura of the *Magic Mountain.* The lecture will in this sense be an appropriate, full-fledged counterpart to the novel."[61] It was also the *summa* of Mann's self-perception at that time. He celebrated Tolstoy and, above all, Goethe as integral parts of his own entelechy,[62] searching for a "midpoint" from which the still disturbing Weimar disorder could be neutralized into meaningful order. Neither a "German fascism" nor Tolstoy's "pedagogic bolshevism" could provide such midpoint.

> No, on the contrary, it is the time for us to lay all possible stress upon our great humane inheritance and to cultivate it with all the means at our command—not only for its own sake, but in order to put visibly in the wrong the claims of Latin civilisation. And, in particular, our socialism, which has all too long allowed its spiritual life to languish in the shallows of a crude economic materialism, has no greater need than to find access to that loftier Germany which has always sought with its spirit the land of the Greeks.[63] It is today, politically speaking, our really national party; but it will not truly rise to the height of its national task until—if I may be allowed the extravagance—Karl Marx has read Friedrich Hölderlin: a consummation which, by the way, seems in a fair way to be achieved.[64]

The hour-and-a-half lecture given on September 4, 1921, in Lübeck as part of the Nordic Week celebration was enthusiastically received. Lübeck's most famous son presented himself in his new role as spiritual leader of the Weimar Republic, using effectively the familiar rhetorical combination of affirmation, admonition, challenge, and promise. Karl Marx had, of course, read Hölderlin; in his relations to a German cultural tradition he was much better informed,[65] less eclectic, less proprietary than Mann, who used isolated parts of it for the personal fiction of a Goethean aura that permeated his works and his existence. The "extravagance" was not meant to be taken literally—but it is revealing in its abstraction and reduction which enabled Mann to impose, as mediator, the synthesis toward which he and his audience instinctively strained.

In March 1934 negotiating from Zürich with the Nazi authorities to have his possessions in Munich released, he recorded in his diary the remark about his Munich house made by Gottfried Benn and quoted to him by a friend:

"Do you know Thomas Mann's house in Munich? There is truly something Goethean about it."—The fact that I was driven away from that existence is a serious flaw in the destined pattern of my life, one with which I am attempting— in vain, it appears—to come to terms, and the impossibility of setting it right and reestablishing that existence impresses itself upon me again and again, no matter how I look at it, and it gnaws at my heart.[66]

The major part of his possessions were soon released; he was to sit in his familiar chair at his familiar desk, surrounded by his art objects, his gramophone and records of nineteenth-century music, his library in houses in Zürich, in Princeton, in Los Angeles. Wherever he went he established his German Culture, the best of Germany, the good Germany. Neither Karl Marx nor Hölderlin were part of that Culture which continued to be spiritual *bürgerlich* and, as the realm of higher human existence, rigorously separate from politics.[67]

In 1921 he was slowly emerging from the isolation imposed on him by the interregnum of what had been a civil war. He resumed his position as *Geistesfürst:* "In the afternoon I 'governed,' " he noted in his diary on July 8, 1921, referring to one of the many duties of the position, like writing prefaces and introductions, consulting, deciding, affirming literary values in what was to him a spiritual patrician republic—like Lübeck—rather than the thriving business of Culture. He was always notoriously generous with his time and his evaluations, as long as his own leading position was not questioned. For a short time he had been forced to face a world too transient to sustain the precious destined pattern of his life, his greatness nurtured by Germany's Cultural greatness; and he rose, in the "Goethe and Tolstoy" lecture, to set against this experience the apotheosis of a "genuine nationalism" of "the German people in their central position as a world-bourgeoisie."[68]

The essay's highly rhetorical concluding passage with its sweeping syntheses is characteristic of Mann's predilection for the consolations of closure, but it bears a closer look: genuine nationalism as the nation's painstaking self-seeking, self-analysis, and striving *(Mühen)* for self-perfection[69] is proposed as synonymous with desire for freedom in terms reminiscent of Mann's *Mühen*[70] in the vicarious fulfilling of his life's destined pattern—vicarious for true Germanness. A cryptic reference to "the ironic doctrine that there is more of grace among those who at bottom 'can love nobody but themselves' " makes sense in the context of his elaborations on the mediating function of irony overcoming all conflict and contradiction in the realm of art and in the realm of politics, once it has been connected with art. True *bürgerlich* Germany, genuinely nationalist, will be ironically herself, ironically free and truly humane and thus in a position to mediate worldwide conflict. Irony as the "pathos of the middle,"[71] less allegorically harsh than the nineteenth-century optimism and twentieth-century eschatologism familiar to his audience, was surprisingly well received, even where the exquisitely scrupulous reservations of this "essential artistic principle"[72] would seem to create conceptual confusion rather than clarification. If irony is called upon, almost anything can be accommodated, even the highly questionable chiliastic speculations of a writer like Dimitri Merezhkovsky whom Mann admired at the time. Germany in the middle, significantly herself as a synthesis set against European fragmentation, is 'somehow' equated with a redeeming synthesis of animal, man, and god:

> The true saying of that Russian that the essence of the beast-god is as yet scarcely apprehended by man might strengthen our faith in the ironic doctrine that there is more of grace among those who at bottom "can love nobody but themselves." But well we know that there is no deciding the question which of these two lofty types is called to contribute more and better to the highly cherished idea of a perfected humanity.

The question was to be decided twenty-five years later by the creation of the German composer Adrian Leverkühn alias Doctor Faustus representing—ironically—the tragic, therefore true Germany.[73]

Irony for Thomas Mann is what *Seele* was for Rathenau (Arnheim); the term is omnipresent in his essays on cultural and political affairs and on his own work; as a structural mode it is central to all his fictional texts. The essay on Goethe and Tolstoy went through several editions, but it is difficult to say how many general readers read those rambling eighty pages with concentration and enjoyment. It has remained an important text for professional readers who have mined it for quotes indicative of Mann's moving toward a conversion to democracy in his 1922 lecture "The German Republic."[74] The legend that from then on he acted, that is, wrote and lectured from the position of a citizen accepting his being part of a conflicted democratic mass society is, however, highly misleading.

Nineteen-twenty-two, even more than 1921, was the year of reconciliations. In January he resumed contact with Heinrich who had been seriously ill. To Bertram he writes in February that he is "joyful, in fact wildly shaken with emotion," but has "no illusions about the fragility and difficulty of the revived relationship. . . . Real friendship is scarcely conceivable. The monuments of our dispute still stand—incidentally, people tell me that he has never read the *Betrachtungen*. That is good, and then again it is not; for it means that he has no idea what I have gone through. . . . He knows nothing of that, nothing of how time has forged me into a man, how I have grown in the process and even become the support and leader of others."[75] He is preoccupied, he writes, with "a new personal fulfilment of the idea of humanity—in contrast, to be sure, to the humanitarian world of Rousseau. I shall speak on that topic at the end of the month in the Frankfurt Opera House, before the performance of the *Magic Flute*. The occasion is Goethe week. . . . It is taking an official turn. The president of the Reich has promised to take part."[76] He had lectured on the German idea of humanity the previous year in Lübeck and "great honor [had been] accorded [him] during the event, as during the entire visit."[77] Now he was to speak about the same complex of ideas in the context of an official cultural self-presentation of the young republic,[78] and it was to be explicitly about this new state: "I owed my country such a manifesto at this moment," he wrote to Arthur Schnitzler announcing the publication of its printed version in the October 1922 issue of *Neue Rundschau,* a special Gerhart Hauptmann issue.[79]

In the introduction added to that version he insists that he is still the same, the author of *Betrachtungen,* denying an alleged *Sinnesänderung* (change of mind) toward a "social ethos" replacing the "personal ethos" invoked in the preface of *Betrachtungen.* The idea of humanity as it is presented in the essay "inwardly" constitutes "the linear continuation" of *Betrachtungen,* he says more directly in a letter to the French historian of German literature Felix Bertaux.[80] After all, as he points out in the introduction, thoughts are only instruments in the service of a "meaning" or "mind"—the German *Sinn* is usefully ambiguous here[81]—and such service is substantially to achieve a delicate balance of affirmation and ambiguity in the ironic freedom of the artist. The "dialectic" employed to this end is nothing but thoughts contradicting each other ("ein Widerspruch von Gedanken untereinander") in the rarified sphere of "pure spirit." The targeted audience is German youth—he gave the lecture several times—very much in need of a more positive attitude toward their republic. Mann's new role as *praeceptor Germaniae* had been clearly established in "Goethe and Tolstoy" where he emphatically connects "conceiving of his own ego as a cultural task" with the joy and dignity of a "leader and former of youth."[82] Yet this role is distinctly limited by his ironic disengagement from the impure sphere of mere politics, and the source of his irony and the lecture's tortuous rhetoric is the all-pervasive polarization of spirit and matter, Culture and politics: almost all the essays and lectures dealing with political problems in the twenties and thirties are flawed in this respect.[83]

Irony, of course, is "no laughing matter,"[84] but a smoothly serious affair. This "melancholy mockery of the not-yet, this tender hesitation of the soul"[85] has enabled Mann to keep his exquisite scruples and reservations, his essentially artistic distance from all the problems life might pose. Irony as the incapacity to understand the relation between thought and experience is central to the specific failure of a very talented novelist. To Mann, irony has simply meant subordination of a complex tradition of thought, that is, the articulated recorded experience of a great many other talented people to his, *the* German artist's entelechy. Curiously, he has had in this the support not only of large general audiences but of the great majority of professional readers whom one might have expected to be more critically aware of the meanings of tradition. The function of irony was for Mann to protect the destined significant pattern of his life presented in his work. Accordingly, his appeal to German youth to opt for democracy is largely self-referential: if he now speaks for the young state so should they—not, to be sure, to share the experience of more open political structures guiding social relations, rather, to be content with a "soziale Erotik" permeated by ironic reservations.[86]

Here as in the "Goethe and Tolstoy" lecture irony becomes synonymous with *Humanität* as

> truly the German mean, the Beautiful and Human [*das Schön-Menschliche*] of which our finest spirits have dreamed. It is the mean between esthetic isolation and undignified levelling of the individual to the general; between mysticism and ethics, between inwardness and the state [*Staatlichkeit*]; between a deathbound negation of ethical and civic values and a purely ethical philistine rationalism.[87]

As he asserts repeatedly in the course of the lecture, German youth has to grasp this beautiful humane, this ironic German midpoint—and everything will fall into place, including the growing pressures from the extreme left and, above all, the extreme right. Could he have believed his own advice? There will be no answer from the ironic German. But as he had so willingly assumed his destined role of *geistiger Führer* in a highly politicized situation, such silence was not his privilege. He was and continued to be exclusively concerned with his artistic self-presentation when dealing with the most complex urgent sociopsychological problems, and so he asked his audiences to participate in the ritual answering of questions that neither they nor he had even begun to understand. The responsibility of the intellectual concerns ideas, their relation to a shared sociopolitical, cultural experience, their articulation in this context, and it is here that Mann's intellectual and artistic performance, notwithstanding his good intentions and conscience, appears problematic.

4.

The essays celebrating the "idea of humanity" fed *The Magic Mountain*. Here irony alias mediation alias *Humanität* made its real, its most effective impact on large reading audiences, moving along a great many starkly outlined, colorful characters with remarkable narrative energy. The novel's foreword *(Vorsatz)* points succinctly to this spirited management beginning with the much quoted sentence:

> The story of Hans Castorp, which we would here set forth, not on his own account, for in him the reader will make acquaintance with a simple-minded though pleasing young man, but for the sake of the story itself, which seems to us highly worth telling—though it must needs be borne in mind, in Hans Castorp's behalf, that it is his story and not every story happens to everybody— this story, we say, belongs to the long ago: is already, so to speak, covered with historic mould, and unquestionably to be presented in the tense best suited to a narrative out of the depth of the past.

The author's relationship to his "hero"—that is, not the person, but Hans Castorp's mediating mediocrity—would be of crucial importance to the development of an understanding between the ironic author and his audience.

Since the war, such relationship with his audience had been even more necessary to him, and the mode of narration is meant to assure and control it. There is, then, at the beginning, a whimsically phrased but serious warning signal to the reader that the novel's hero and story are more the author's than might be expected. He will learn in time that the story is divorced from its (to him) most accessible source, the character's narrated consciousness. The reader's pleasure has its source in his accord *(Einklang)* with the author who, in the role of the "rounding wizard of times gone by" *(der raunende Beschwörer des Imperfekts)*, keeps the story safely submerged in the past. Lowe-Porter's translation here misses the important reference to the meaning of the act of narration: the epic mode makes possible a specific temporal perspective meant to bridge the chasm created by the shattering experience of the war. The "exaggerated pastness" of this narrative is magically joined to the "immediately before": the once-upon-a-time distance of the prewar period can be appreciated *and* overcome by the reader in the twenties, if he is willing to follow the author into the hermetic structure of the fairy tale suspended in indefinite time.[88]

The fairy tale *(Märchen)* dimension to which the third paragraph of the *Vorsatz* draws attention is indeed highly important; the English translation "legend" undermines the reference to a stage of mythmaking in which basic psychological facts are arranged in a general symbolic manner, untouched by historically definable modifications as they inform the more open structures of the legend. Mann's fictions clearly favor the pure exclusive contours of the fairy tale. He said so explicitly in the case of *Royal Highness* and the *Joseph* novels.[89] In the case of *The Magic Mountain,* he referred his readers to "that alchemical 'transmutation' " *(jene alchimistische 'Steigerung')* and "al-chemical-hermetic pedagogy" *(alchimistisch-hermetische Pädagogik)* taking place in the transtemporal *nunc stans* of the novel's hermetically sealed world.[90] Entering that closed sphere and accepting its one-dimensional symbolic structures will enable the reader, the author promises him, to follow with pleasure the transmutation of the novel's "simple but 'canny' hero" *(des schlichten aber verschmitzten Helden)*.

Hans Castorp's attributes *schlicht* and *verschmitzt* are invoked iron-ically and with leitmotif frequency, and they are central to the structural function of this puzzling bland and passive protagonist. *Schlicht* means "simple" in the sense of a socially approved *bürgerlich* virtue with the connotations "modest" and "dignified." The word's original meaning, "un-adorned," was extended to the general issue of conforming to convention-(group-) controlled social relations. Using the word in this way Mann empha-sizes the eminent suitability of his creature for any occasion and draws attention to the authorial success in molding such a smoothly functioning agent. Safeguarded by ironic "reservation" *(Vorbehalt)*, he had placed him-self into the advantageous position where he could amuse himself and the reader by gently poking fun at social arrangements without taking the risk of probing questions. Like a happy family, both author and reader were secure against the world in such play with mirroring surfaces within a largely private language. Lowe-Porter's admirably readable translations do not adequately deal with Mann's ironic use of verbal (social) conventions. But it is precisely his way of speaking within quotation marks, his ironic, self-protective refusal to take language, that is, other speakers' meanings, seriously, combined with his skillful avoidance of burdening his reader with the implications of such refusal, which accounts for his huge success with large *bürgerlich* audiences during the culturally transitional period of Weimar. *Verschmitzt* describes a cunning *and* good-natured charm, a light-handed, twinkly sort of confidence man: *schlicht* but *verschmitzt,* Hans Castorp may be bland and passive, but he is a thoroughly pleasant and very willing young man.

Not unexpectedly, the synthesis of *schlicht* and *verschmitzt* is synonymous with an "erotically most cunning irony oscillating, mediating between life and spirit," (eine höchste, erotische verschlagenste, zwischen Leben und Geist spielende *Ironie*).[91] Hans, repeatedly described as *verschlagen* (cunning), will in the course of the novel fulfill the destined pattern of his *Steigerung* and grow into his author's system of ironic mediation. He will acquire the skills of *Verbindlichkeit,* a gracious poise instrumental in bringing (literally, tying) people together, and finally will "govern" in his author's stead.[92] He learns to deal with Settembrini's high-minded democratic optimism as well as with Naphta's militant chiliastic pessimism by mediating between them in his pleasantly *verbindlich* fashion. Transcending with respectful irony the mechanical grind of their disputations, he is finally ready to take on, in the figure of Mynheer Peeperkorn, the richly inarticulate, charmingly perplexing ambiguity of "the personality." That he is able to do so, his author explains, "must be laid to a certain shrewd geniality [*verschmitzte Lebensfreundlichkeit*] native to him that found everything fish that came to his net, and not only bound to him people of the most diverse tastes and characters, but exerted enough power to bind them to each other."[93] But Hans's *verschmitzte Lebensfreundlichkeit,* his canny kindness toward life, is the result of his author's alchemical skills and narrative single-mindedness which have kept him from ever considering seriously Settembrini's offer, "placet experiri?" He is, however, allowed to acknowledge the transmutation to which he has been subjected.[94] Designed and operated by his author, he has taken his destined "spiritual way" *(den genialen Weg),*[95] leading through death to life, which means getting along with Mynheer Peeperkorn and stumbling, not yet fallen for good, over the battlefield of World War I, its terrifying darkness lit up fitfully by an unmotivated light. Unhindered by sociopsychological considerations,[96] Hans's "spiritual way" has proceeded smoothly from one neatly arranged set of ideas to the next, moving irresistibly toward the higher level of thought as befits true German humanism:[97] the ambiguous yet uplifting conclusion seemed sufficiently reassuring in this respect to author and audience alike.

Professional readers have frequently insisted that all serious German novels have had to come to terms with that German phenomenon of an Ur-novel, Goethe's *Wilhelm Meister*, the *Bildungsroman* as unfolding entelechy. The importance and continuing accessibility of that novel, however, rests in the fact Goethe did not really come to terms with either concept. Most of the best German novelists did not—certainly not Gottfried Keller, Theodor Fontane, Rilke, Kafka, Heinrich Mann, Robert Musil, or Alfred Döblin. Thomas Mann, however, did. Filling simultaneously the role of reincarnation and confidence man in a Goethe myth largely invented by himself,[98] Mann understood the ironic, essentially German enterprise of conforming to the Ur-pattern in his modernization of the *Bildungsroman* as *imitatio* and parody.[99] The mixture was effective. Hans was indeed, as Mann wrote in December 1924, "finding friends in the world. . . . Ah, well, he is a good young man; I was sorry to let him go."[100] It is in the context of the modernization of the *Bildungsroman* that he emphatically insists on the novel's humorous, *lebensfreundlich* aspects and its demonstrated good will. Hans, he admits,

> is sensuously and intellectually infatuated with death (mysticism, romanticism); but his dire love is purified, at least in moments of illumination, into an inkling of a new humanity whose germs he bears in his heart as the bayonet attack carries him along. His author, who there takes leave of him, is the same who emerged from the novel to write the manifesto "The German Republic." He is no Settembrini in his heart. But he desires to be free, reasonable and kindly in his thoughts. That is what I would like to call good will, and do not like to hear branded as hostility to life.[101]

The question, however, is not the author's desire to be free, reasonable, and of good will, but the meaning of his protagonist's experience as it is accessible to the reader. Those moments of illumination, e.g., the snow chapter, are ambiguous and ironically elusive; above all, they have no demonstrable influence on Hans. Like a "good boy" he sits down as usual to the rich Berghof meal after his life-affirming narrow escape from death in the snowstorm and promptly forgets all about it, getting on, by decree of his author, with his *Steigerung*. In the end the good young man can imitate his author to perfection in creating an atmosphere of humorous tolerance for the most diverse aspects of humanity, from soberly enthusiastic Settembrini, Peeperkorn alias the intoxicated Goethean Gerhart Hauptmann,[102] to Naphta alias Georg Lukács[103] who emerges as by far the most satisfying coherent figure in the novel. It is Naphta to whom the author, if not Hans, is clearly most attracted and to whom he therefore grants a certain degree of intellectual credibility, that is, independence from the rigidly and often coyly ironical narrative mode of the novel. Taking his Goethe *imitatio* so seriously, Mann is unable to see the fundamental difference between his attitude toward his protagonist as "good boy" and Goethe's toward Wilhelm as his "beloved likeness" *and* a "poor dog," who, unlike Hans, is allowed some untidy groping for self-knowledge and slow uncertain growth in experience.

The difference between the imitated and the imitation, the allegedly parodied and the parody is such that it precludes any viable connection, especially that of parody.

In the 1939 Princeton lecture on *The Magic Mountain* Mann tried to explain the extraordinary success of that novel with contemporary readers to an audience of young privileged Americans.[104] The educated middle-class German reader of the time, he said, could identify fully with the *schlicht* but *verschmitzt* protagonist because the specific difficulties of the postwar period had subjected him, like Hans, to suspension in a *nunc stans* of indefinite time. He, too, had undergone a "hermetic magical transformation."[105] Making the connection on the familiar higher level, he also makes irrelevant the interesting and substantial question of the novel as prewar *Epochenroman* dealing intelligibly with postwar issues. Mann does claim a dual temporal perspective in passing, but he refrains from pointing out to his young listeners that the intellectual political problems of Weimar owed their profuse growth to the unresolved, insufficiently examined problems of the prewar period. The connection did not interest Mann, because the destined meaningful coherence and pattern of his own existence which represented German Culture was significantly based on the private heroic overcoming of a traumatic public schism that, for him, separated once and for all prewar and postwar life. His novel, then, did not attempt to analyze similarities, transitions, ruptures, surfaces, and underground connections; rather, it neatly organized and, on a higher level, neutralized a number of conflicts and thus proved to be highly attractive to a large number of readers, who were glad for the vicarious destined coherence and believed they could share in its meaning which would then take care of the problems.

5.

Mann took three years to break officially with Nazi Germany. His two eldest children, Erika and Klaus, both deeply involved in antifascist activities, urged him to come to a decision and take his place among the other exiles, and he finally did with an impressive open letter to the Swiss critic Korrodi in February 1936[106] which resulted in his expatriation and the withdrawal of the honorary doctorate which had been conferred on him to his great pleasure[107] by Bonn University in 1919. Mann answered the December 1936 notification from Bonn immediately; the letter was published in *Neue Züricher Zeitung* in January 1937 and then as a pamphlet under the somewhat misleading title "Briefwechsel mit Bonn" (An exchange of letters), and it contains the following much quoted sentences:

> From the beginning of my intellectual life I had felt myself in happiest accord with the temper of my nation and at home in its intellectual traditions. I am better suited to represent those traditions than to become a martyr for them [Ich

bin weit eher zum Repräsentanten geboren als zum Märtyrer]; far more fitted to
add a little to the gaiety of the world than to foster conflict and hatred in it.
Something very wrong must have happened to make my life take so false and
unnatural a turn.[108]

To be in opposition, to be isolated from German Culture made him feel
literally like a martyr. There are many diary entries during those years about
psychosomatic symptoms related to his present position forced on him by
the events and also by his associates. There is for instance an angry outburst
on November 13, 1937, about the publicity given in the Basel *Na-
tionalzeitung* to

> my letter to the Paris Committee for Freedom and Justice in Germany in which I
> expressed myself in the strongest terms.[109] Worry about troublesome con-
> sequences. . . . At dinner discussed with Katia and Golo the possible role of
> fascism, the world's inexorable trend in that direction, the senseless sacrifices
> one makes—for whom, one does not know—poisoning one's own blood in trying
> to fight it. No more offers of help! [*Keine Vorspanndienste mehr!*] No statements
> and answers. Why arouse hatred? Freedom and serenity. One ought to claim
> one's right to them at last.[110]

He had settled in Zürich, reassembling with his rescued Munich possessions his stately Weimar existence; the initially difficult situation with his
publisher, Bermann-Fischer, which was the main reason for his hesitating to
make the break with the Nazis, had been resolved by the move of the
publishing house to Vienna and then Stockholm; his income continued to be
more than sufficient; compared to almost all the other exiles he had been
extremely fortunate, as he told himself. Reading in the diaries of these years
one cannot but be irritated by and yet convinced of the strength of his desire
to continue in the role of *Repräsentant* of German Culture which was so
natural to him and which he thought naturally his.

The same entry records the completion of a Wagner lecture he had been
asked to give at Zürich University on the occasion of a *Ring* performance:
"Finished, God be praised, the lecture 'Richard Wagner and the Ring'.
(*Beendete* in Gottes Namen den Vortrag "Richard Wagner u. der Ring des
Nibelungen"). The emphasis on having finished and the resigned "in Gottes
Namen" indicate quite clearly, much more so than suggested by the English
translation, his feelings of exhaustion and ambivalence in writing about *the*
German composer who had so profoundly shaped his nature and had now
been appropriated by the Nazi regime. It had taken a great deal of rhetorical
skill to assert both his closeness to Wagner and his distance to Nazi Germany, but he had absolved himself well by making the lecture into a statement about *his* relation to Wagner and his music, about *his* passion, *his*
absorption, *his* enchantment, finally *his* admiration as *the* artist's admiration
for that which is not himself, much too large to be himself, "yet something to

which he feels most intimately allied, most powerfully congenial—to approach which more nearly, 'to penetrate with the understanding,' to make utterly his own, his nature passionately demands."[111]

It had been in his role as *Repräsentant* of German Culture that he selected parts of that tradition "utterly his own"—the essays on Schopenhauer, Nietzsche, Wagner, Goethe, Schiller, and Fontane are bewilderingly eloquent examples—and in doing so had been accepted as representing that tradition as a whole. In the letter to Bonn University he writes about his difficulties in deciding to endanger this role and asserts that the Harvard honorary doctorate of 1935 had reassured him greatly in this respect. He quotes from the diploma that the honorary degree was conferred on "Thomas Mann, famous author, who has interpreted life to many of our fellow-citizens and *together with a very few contemporaries sustains the high dignity of German culture. . . .*"[112] Gradually his role of Cultural *Repräsentant* adjusted itself to exile, and by 1941 he could write to Karl Kerényi from Princeton that "exile has become something wholly different than in the past; it is no longer a condition of waiting oriented to a homecoming but a foretaste of a dissolution of nations and a unification of the world." He wished that Kerényi could join the transatlantic European community in his new country "which will, after all, *nolens volens,* surely assume the leadership of the world."[113]

In early 1937 he was still intensely interested in reactions to his letter to Bonn, that is, concerned about his public role as exile.[114] But increasingly he was absorbed by the *Geistesfürst* dimension of that role which transcended exile, by the pleasurable duties and privileges of "governing."[115] Since the fall of 1936 he had been working on *Lotte in Weimar (The Beloved Returns).* With the third of the Joseph novels, *Joseph in Ägypten,* published by Bermann-Fischer in Vienna in October 1936, he had not yet left his German audiences. The book, he thought, was "capable of bringing a bit of brighter cheerfulness into a country that can certainly use some cheerfulness."[116] This was hardly realistic, but he evidently needed to believe that there still was a vital link between him and his German readers. *Lotte in Weimar,* the text which reflects most directly Mann's sense of "the intimacy, not to mention the *unio mystica*" with Goethe,[117] interrupted the sequence of the *Joseph* novels. It was published in 1939 by Bermann-Fischer in Stockholm in an edition of ten thousand—*Joseph der Ernährer,* the fourth and last volume, was published in 1943 in the small edition of five thousand. Mann's real audience during those years was American, reading the translations of his works published by Knopf. It is interesting that *Lotte in Weimar* marks the transfer: the elaborately articulated "mystery of identity" with Goethe sustained him, so it appears, in his separation from first Germany and then Europe. During Mann's highly successful and enjoyable lecture tour in the United States in the spring of 1938—the opening of a Thomas Mann Library at Yale University, sold-out lectures coast-to-coast, the offer of a teaching position from Princeton University, an honorary doctorate from Columbia

University, saluting policemen in New York[118]—Hitler invaded Austria. Mann was most upset about the consequences for "European thought": "Anguish and worry thinking of my writing, wondering if there is anyone interested in reading," he noted on March 20, 1938, in the train to Salt Lake City, where he was to give a lecture at the university. "Presumably we were again fortunate in being away." (This time from Europe.) "I must trust that the characteristically fortunate quality of my life will see me through. Also the preservation of German intellectual life of my stamp will be possible one way or another, possibly by Knopf's establishing a German language publishing house."[119] He decided to leave Europe, bringing German Culture with him. There was indeed no reason to worry. *The Beloved Returns*, published by Knopf in 1940, was an American success—a few copies were smuggled into Germany—as the *Joseph* novels had been since 1935. Settling in Princeton in the fall of 1938 he was hopeful about his new life as the "present president of the spiritual Republic"[120] of Germany in the United States, and in the last days of this eventful year he read with fascination and satisfaction Hermann Rauschnings's *Die Revolution des Nihilismus*. The fiction of a good and an evil Germany was taking shape.

  Joseph the Provider, the last volume, is written explicitly against nihilism and despair. It is his most unambiguously *lebensfreundlich* work and, in its celebration of life, testimony to the good years he spent in the United States. Significantly, the beginnings of the tetralogy go back to the good stable years of the Weimar Republic. Postwar chaos had subsided; *The Magic Mountain* which had exorcised the trauma of the lost war had finally been finished and become an overwhelming success; its author was, without doubt, Germany's most famous writer, and 1925, one of those magically "round" years charged with personal and more-than-personal significance, was just the right time to start a work that would present the career of fate's favorite son. He drew attention to the lucky and meaningful chronological correspondences structuring his life and work in general and this work in particular in *Lebensabriss* (*Sketch of My Life*, 1930) and "Meine Zeit" (1950).[121] He was leaving behind the darkness of the past and of contemporary nihilism which, he said, found its perfection as a form of life in the Second World War brought about by National Socialism, that "revolution of nihilism" with its sinister beliefs in the inhuman, the earth, folk, blood, past, and death.[122] Even more than Rauschning, Mann saw National Socialism exclusively and too simply as Hitlerism, and *Joseph the Provider*, which was written in his new country, presents Joseph as anti-Hitler. He had not left behind the dualism which provides structure and energy for all his texts: *lebensfreundlich* are counteracted by *lebensfeindlich* (hostile to life) principles, and in this balance they are also profoundly, significantly, and mysteriously connected. The most curious and disturbing witness to this neoromantic dialectic is the essay "Bruder Hitler," published first in *Esquire*, March 1938, under the title "This Man Is My Brother." This "ironic joke"[123] is an ambivalent rhetorical tribute to the exceedingly interesting phenomenon Hitler, the "political medicine-man" with his "not unfounded if rather illegitimate reverence" for "the musician-artist whom, after all, Gottfried Keller called a hair-dresser and a charlatan," Richard Wagner.[124]

As in all his pieces on artists who are important to his self-perception and his artistic identity, Mann, in the Hitler essay, concentrates on his own reactions. It is with *"interest"*[125] rather than hatred that the phenomenon Hitler has to be approached, he asserts; and it is this *interest* as well as the phenomenon itself that ought not be underestimated: "For interest connotes a desire for self-discipline; it inclines to be humorous, ascetic; to acknowledge similarity, even identification with oneself; to feel a sense of solidarity." Interest is connected with irony, and so Hitler has to be approached with irony as the "native element of all creative art": "The fellow is a catastrophe. But that is no reason we should not find him interesting as a character and an event."[126] And so Mann traces the development of Hitler's rhetorical skills out of his "dreamy, obstinate arrogance" with a perceptiveness based on feelings of solidarity. But the description of Hitler's phenomenal success with his German audiences, the meteoric rise of the "one-time melancholic ne'er-do-well, simply because he has learned—for aught he knows, out of patriotism—to be a political animal," shows Mann's astonishingly self-centered naiveté. He found repellent the turbulent and bewildering politics of Weimar and kept them at a distance which was direct, unambiguous, and which had nothing to do with ironic interest. It was Hitler as a person who fascinated him, Hitler as the uniquely grand distortion, *Verhunzung,* of the artist and brilliant perpetrator of Nazi "fauler Zauber" (tainted magic),[127] as he calls it in the 1938 lecture "The Coming Victory of Democracy."

> Ah, the artist! I spoke of moral self-flagellation. For must I not, however much it hurts, regard the man as an artist-phenomenon? . . . A brother—a rather unpleasant and mortifying brother. He makes me nervous, the relationship is painful to a degree. But I will not disclaim it. For I repeat: better, more productive, more honest, more constructive than hatred is recognition, acceptance, the readiness to make oneself one with what is deserving of our hate even though we run the risk, morally speaking, of forgetting how to say no.

This, however, does not worry him; besides, the moral sphere "is really not altogether the artist's concern." Rather, he finds something soothing in the realization that in spite of all modern learning the mystery of the mind is still largely intact: "there is still absolutely no limit to the extent the unconscious can go in effective projection of itself upon reality."[128] Hitler the artist can do it as well as Thomas Mann: forcing Austria's *Anschluss,* he forced Thomas Mann's decision to leave Europe and he informed the counterimage of the politician as the good artist presented in Joseph and Roosevelt.

The Hitler essay attacks the *Verhunzung* of nationalism, myth, philosophy, irrationalism, faith, youth, revolution, and even genius, arguing that such *Verhunzung* is inevitable and necessary.[129] What, then, is the point of this "work of my pain, and hatred, and mockery?"[130] It is, it turns out, the plea to move on to conscience, which is higher than innocence, by accepting art's contempt for itself expressed in the recognition of the bond between Hitler and the artist. Such *Sündenbewusstsein*, original sin, is presented as synonymous with the higher spiritual level of real democracy in "The Coming Victory of Democracy."[131] Both essays end with familiarly uplifting conclusions—"Bruder Hitler":

> I like to think, yes, I am certain, that a future is now on the way in which art uncontrolled by mind, art as black magic, the issue of brainlessly irresponsible instinct, will be as much condemned as, in humanly frail times like ours, it is reverenced. Art, certainly, is not all sweetness and light. But neither is it all a brew of darkness, not all a freak [*blinde Ausgeburt*] of the tellurian underworld, not simply "life." More clearly and happily than ever will the artist of the future realize his mission as a white enchanter, as a winged, hermetic, moon-sib mediator [*ein beflügelt-hermetisch-mondverwandtes Mittlertum*] between spirit and life. And mediation itself is spirit.

I have quoted so extensively from this essay, because in all its strange contorted argumentation it does give a fairly clear self-presentation of Mann at the time of his emigration to the United States when the past, his life during the Weimar period, is just beginning to take shape. Hitler is black art to be left behind; he has, in fact, already been conquered in *The Magic Mountain* with the help of that "good young man," the mediator Hans Castorp. Joseph, Mann's present and future artistic incarnation, is white art, certainly as hermetic as Hans, but more "winged" and "moon-sib," utterly charming as God's confidence man. In falling to Hitler, Europe followed a destined pattern, as did Mann's entelechy when he left Europe but continued in the role of German-European Cultural leader. *Verhunzung* of all German-European Cultural values was inevitable, therefore meaningful: one last outbreak of life before it could be contained permanently in paradisaically artful balance with spirit.

6.

The figure of Joseph had its physical roots in a classmate of Mann's younger children at the Schloss Salem school, one of the perfectly beautiful adolescent boys Mann was attracted to, in this case a boy "of Spanish blood" whom he met in July 1925.[132] Its spiritual source was Mann's sense of supreme self-fulfillment in the second half of the twenties, culminating with the 1929 Nobel prize. In the 1930 *Sketch of My Life,* a highly, self-consciously structured account of his life's stages as meaningful sequence, he connects the completion of *Magic Mountain* with his appointment to a small group of electors in the newly founded literary section of the Prussian Academy of Arts and Letters. In this function he gave a speech at a formal meeting in the presence of Minister of Education Becker on November 18, 1926, where he explained the "official recognition of literature as an organ of national life" as "a logical consequence of Germany's social and national development": "It was not chance that I had been asked to speak; as perhaps no other, I had suffered in my own person, with whatever violent struggles, the compulsion of the times, which forced us out of the metaphysical and individual stage into the social. . . ."[133] When the Nobel prize was awarded once more, after seventeen long years, to a German writer, he was not unprepared: "It lay, I suppose, upon my path in life—I say this without presumption, with calm if not uninterested insight into the character of my destiny, of my role on this earth. . . ."[134] He had become intrigued with the figure of Joseph when he knew his own artistic-public life to be fully realized in Germany. He was fascinated, he wrote in retrospect, by the "idea of leaving the modern bourgeois sphere so far behind and making my narrative pierce deep, deep into the human. . . . Myth and psychology—the anti-intellectual bigots would prefer to have these two kept far apart. And yet, I thought, it might be amusing to attempt, by means of a mythical psychology, a psychology of myth."[135]

This formula was to become the main key to the *Joseph* tetralogy, to be repeated, again and again, by Mann himself and then, after him, by many professional readers. After completion of the first volume in 1930, he planned to write a Goethe book for the 1932 jubilee, a plan which was strongly supported by his publisher, but which he gave up promptly: the intimacy and *unio mystica* he desired was not to be achieved in a book about Goethe, but rather a book in which Goethe would be the protagonist, the reflection of his author Mann—*Lotte in Weimar (The Beloved Returns)*. However, Goethe's reflected presence is unmistakable in the unfolding of God's beautiful plan with his favorite charmer and magician-confidence man Joseph. *The Sketch of My Life,* which celebrates the beautiful order of Mann's life,[136] ends with the author's preparation for a voyage to Egypt and Palestine, the scene of the *Joseph* novels: "I expect to find the sky above and much of the earth beneath unchanged after three thousand five hundred years." It was indeed the descent into "the human," the collective, the mythical; and the Californian sky above Mann as he worked on the last volume of the tetralogy turned out to be as blue as the Egyptian. Psychology, however, was another matter entirely.

In the attempt to understand Mann's method in constructing the elaborate cross-reference system of the *Joseph* novels, one profits from his correspondence with the Hungarian historian of religious and mythological traditions Karl Kerényi. The translator of the correspondence, Alexander Gelley, writes in his preface that it reflects "Mann's receptivity to new facts and ideas." His own short collage of Mann's statements on that subject, quite apart from the evidence provided by the texts, however, shows quite clearly that it was not interest in new ideas, but, as Mann put it, the almost magic act of finding what at any given moment is needed by the work, a transmutation of what is found into something invented.[137] On another occasion Mann described this "montage technique" as a "ruthless process of structuring and

amalgamating factual, historical, personal, even literary data, in such a way
. . . that palpable reality was forever indistinguishably merging into perspec-
tual simulations and illusions."[138] Mann professes to be profoundly disturbed
(bestürzt) by the very force with which the technique asserts itself—he is
speaking about his most difficult novel, *Doctor Faustus.*[139] In the case of the
Joseph novels the technique was perhaps less forcefully assertive, but certainly not less ruthless in terms of abstracting ideas and images from their
original historical context in preparation for the usual structuring and weaving process.

Mann used the montage technique in *Buddenbrooks* as well as *Holy
Sinner,* in *Magic Mountain* as well as the *Joseph* novels—not to speak of a
quotation-novel like *The Beloved Returns.* Only the materials change, or,
rather, the places and periods from which they are mined, and they do so in
relation to the unfolding and filling out of the destined pattern of his entelechy. Myth and psychology, too, had been linked together before, most
clearly in Aschenbach, in Naphta. It is Mann's serenity that is new: Naphta
can be rehabilitated into Joseph. In his preface to a 1928 reading from the first
Joseph novel he speaks of the essence of myth as "timeless always-presence"
and "dreamy psychology of the self," less circumscribed than ours, more
open-ended toward the past, a paradigmatic existence following much used
mythical tracks which grants a "higher dignity" also to an evil or cursed
character like Esau.[140] Mann saw his own enormous task of telling "the
beautiful story and God-invention of Joseph and his brothers"—the last
sentence of the tetralogy—in terms of such mythical following. The first two
volumes were completed when he wrote for the first time to Kerényi on
January 27, 1934, thanking him for the offprint of his essay "Unsterblichkeit
und Appollonreligion":

> I confess that the idea of a "dark," a "wolfish" Apollo was new to me, but I
> became accustomed to it immediately. The connections between mind and death
> (afterlife), between distance and knowledge (here we would have to take account
> of another concept dear to me, that of *irony*), and the insight that the spirit of
> Apollo may be perceived in the recuperative world, recuperative from *life*—all
> this touched the roots of my intellectual existence and delighted me.[141]

The correspondence with Kerényi was to provide Mann with much that he
could use in the all-absorbing weaving of his tale, and occasionally he left
Kerényi somewhat breathless.[142] On the whole, though, Kerényi was prepared to grant that a "great entelechy such as his could not be easily
circumscribed. . . ."[143] Mann, whom he admired, had a higher right to those
materials according to the needs of his entelechy as man and artist. So
Kerényi helped him develop the "career" of his "favorite divinity," Hermes,
the god who embodied for Mann that "marvelously enticing and mysterious"
world of "correspondences,"[144] by supplying detailed information and occasional warnings. And Mann thanked him by expressing his delight in his own

easy appropriation of so much knowledge: "These are mysterious games of the spirit which prove that sympathy, to a degree, can count for scholarly knowledge."[145]

Joseph, who plays god and is god, who is Hermes and is not Hermes, follows his destined road and mediates tactfully and charmingly between above and below, spirit and instinct, death and life, the Dionysian and Apollinian principles, God and Man. As *Joseph the Provider* he learns to master his author's language, ever more elaborate, precious, and elegantly ambiguous in its solemn and festive, light and mocking play with myth and mystery, showing a Goethean disposition. Mann writes about his progress from Princeton;[146] he will soon move to the "paradisaical" climate of southern California with its Egyptian-blue sky. Critics have observed a change in the Joseph of the last volume: as the Provider he appears less narcissistic, he shows more interest in others, he is socially more active. These changes have been connected with Thomas Mann's antifascist activities in the United States and his admiration and support for Roosevelt and his New Deal.[147] The fourth volume *is* different, Joseph *is* changed, and the connection with Roosevelt is very important in this respect; but there has been little interest in asking how Mann used the connection as paradigm for Joseph's clever Keynesian economics.

By the time he has become the Provider, Joseph has drawn into his uncommonly pleasing mythical presence the paradigmatic essence of three gods, Aphrodite, Eros, and Hermes: he has become Hermaphroditos, signifying the lucky constellation of commerce, theft, and love. Mann was working on the central chapter (3) of the *Provider,* the long conversation between Joseph and young Pharaoh who is so understanding and intelligently admiring of Joseph's composite spiritual and physical beauty, when he was helped again by Kerényi in his interweaving of the moon, rogue, and intermediary motives. He thanks him for his and C. G. Jung's collaborative *Essays on a Science of Mythology: The Myth of the Divine Child and the Mysteries of Eleusis*[148] in a letter of February 18, 1941:

> That you and Jung could find a common ground, mythology linked to psychology, is a most remarkable, propitious, and in the present intellectual climate, highly characteristic achievement. . . . I have long been a passionate adherent of this combination, for actually psychology is the means whereby myth may be wrested from the hands of the Fascist obscurantists to be "transmuted" [*umfunktioniert*] for humane ends. For me this combination represents no less than the world of the future, a human community that is blessed by a spirit from above and "out of the depths that lie below."[149]

Here Mann quotes himself[150] and Ernst Bloch who had written to him on June 23, 1940: "It is clear that your powerful 'Joseph' presents the most convincing and happiest example of an *Umfunktionierung* of myth"—a formulation that Mann was to use frequently from then on in letters and essays.[151] Joseph, "so-called inspired lamb" and roguish "young middleman and moon-magician," is the perfect instrument for such *Umfunktionierung:* "Is he not wonderfully pretty and well-favored, like a god of light?" young Pharaoh asks his shrewd mother.[152] She and his author and the intended reader agree that Joseph is, and, like Hans Castorp, he is allowed to explain with his author's help why that should be so. In the course of his career which is and is not a god's career he has come to realize that

> it is an I and a single individual through whom the typical and the traditional are being fulfilled, and thereby, in my feeling the ideal of divine reason is vouchsafed to them. For the pattern and the traditional come from the depths which lie beneath and are what binds us, whereas the I is from God and is of the spirit, which is free. But what constitutes civilized life is that the binding and traditional depth shall fulfil itself in the freedom of God which belongs to the I; there is no human civilization without the one and without the other."[153]

In 1934 Mann had described his position regarding contemporary irrationalist misuse of myth to Kerényi as that of a "man of balance": "I lean left by instinct when the canoe threatens to capsize to the right, and vice versa."[154] This self-perception has been widely accepted, but it is highly misleading in terms of the idea-constructs of Mann's texts. They reflect an exclusive focus on the magically stilled center of conflict where all the battling ideas merge and dissolve into an effervescent freedom of the spirit which is preeminently the artist's—and it is here that Hitler and Roosevelt meet.

I do not, of course, wish to express any doubts regarding the sincerity of Mann's antifascist position, but the specific inadequateness of his means in this fight suggests a deep-seated inability to understand a sociopsychological phenomenon like fascism. Joseph, whose subtlety seduces young Pharaoh,[155] is presented as successful Hermes-mediator, a "statesman and businessman of sovereign cunning," but it is only in the spirit of a divine rogue's tale that his transactions can be justified morally and aesthetically, as Mann writes to Kerényi in 1941.[156] Joseph will give Pharaoh the desired "answer of peace"[157] which is deeply and functionally ambiguous: he speaks and does not speak; he is and is not a god. This divine ironic jesting will fill out the destined pattern of Joseph's entelechy in the service of the good fortunes of Egypt where politics follow the pattern of fairy tale. Like German Hans, cosmopolitan Joseph is an extraordinarily skilled manager of people, once their author has lined them all up properly. Hans may have to pay for his magically developed skills: he may or may not escape death on the battlefield. Joseph is protected from such threat by his "fundamentally *real* mythical identity," established in the early stages of his career[158] and meant to justify all deception and ambivalence on the higher level of its predestined meaningful pattern. This protection was to remain with him when he moved into the realm of statesmanship and economy, when he was grafted onto the figure of Roosevelt. Here is the description of Joseph's New Deal:

And now his harvest time had come, and he reaped as he had sown. The sowing was his tax economy during the good years; the harvest time was the distribution, a crown business of proportions never son of Re had known since the time of that god. For as it is set down, and told in song and story, "the dearth was in all lands; but in all the land of Egypt there was bread. . . ." He did this by a combination of liberality and exploitation, of government usury and fiscal measures such as had never been seen before. His mingling of severity and mildness impressed everyone, even the hardest hit, as superhuman and godlike—for the gods do behave in just this ambivalent way and one never knows whether to call it cruel or kind.[159]

In either case, Joseph's technique was divinely "witty" and *lebensfreundlich,*[160] very much like Roosevelt's whom Mann had met in person in January 1941, just before he received Kerényi and Jung's book. He used both the impressions from the visit and the book to complete the outfitting of Joseph with Hermes attributes. The "dizzying height" of his journey to Washington had been the visit to the White House, for

> the cocktail in the study while the other dinner guests had to cool their heels below. And yet we had already had early breakfast with "him!" "He" once again made a strong impression on me, or, shall I say, aroused my sympathetic interest: this mixture of craft, good-nature, self-indulgence, desire to please, and sincere faith is hard to characterize. But there is something like a blessing upon him, and I am drawn to him as the born opponent, so it seems to me, of the creature that must be toppled. . . . I felt strengthened afterward.[161]

Aristocrat and friend of the people, Roosevelt, like Joseph is the born, the blessed mediator. In the 1945 eulogy "Macht und Güte" (Power and kindness) Mann praises Roosevelt's "intuitive knowledge" of contemporary necessity *and* the "will of world-spirit." He quotes Goethe to put into the right higher perspective Roosevelt's adaptability, his political temperament, his shrewdness, and he calls on Joseph to bring out the essential genius of the man: "A Hermes nature of skillful and serenely artful mediation, he radiated perfect, bewitching aesthetic charm."[162] This man, "an artist and a *hero,*"[163] was the most powerful man on earth and the determined opponent of that profoundly evil and stupid "diabolism" to which poor Germany had fallen prey.[164]

Roosevelt and Joseph share in the "*real* mythical identity" of the chosen, the identity of man with god. Artists themselves, they follow the pattern laid out by the ultimate artist and doing so they will bring peace. The 1942 Library of Congress lecture "The Theme of the Joseph Novels" reminds the audience "that we owe the tribulations which we now have to endure, the catastrophe in which we are living to the fact that we lacked intelligence toward God [*Gottesklugheit*] to a degree which had long become criminal. . . . The word peace always has a religious ring, and what it signifies is a gift of intelligence before God [*ein Geschenk der Gottesklugkeit*]." Future generations, Mann asserts, will "win the peace," that is, they will live "in a world of happier equalization between spirit and reality."[165]

Such equalization, which is synonymous with peace which is synonymous with piety, is anticipated in Mann's fictions of ironic mediation with which he put the world around him into an order that would make sense to him in that it reaffirmed the meaning and significance of his own life and work. Roosevelt could be fitted into this work of artful ordering as easily as any other phenomenon,[166] because Mann had never asked questions of the world; he had always begun by constructing answers. Pious and ambivalent, elaborate and simple, these answers were accepted as profoundly humanistic statements. The really interesting aspect of Thomas Mann as *Grosschriftsteller* is his managing his audience with seemingly supreme self-assurance in a time of extreme intellectual confusion, of urgent questions, of revolts, of anxiety, of desperate hopes and finally resignation. The *Joseph* novels tell the story of divinely skillful management; they spell out, in inexorable detail and mythical redundancy, the recipe for becoming a *Grosschriftsteller*. Musil, who had no access to the last two *Joseph* novels nor, of course, to the diaries, would have been amused at the accuracy of his analyses. Not that such accuracy is surprising: Musil, after all, was used to test his models. Reality to him was something larger than his temporary self, and neither could be fitted into comforting or uplifting patterns. If modernity means more and better informed questions, that is, more uncertainty about the macrocosm of the world, the microcosm of the self is even more severly shaken. Against all evidence, however, Thomas Mann held onto his entelechy. In his seventy-seventh year he writes to a literary scholar who had just sent him an essay on the sources of the *Holy Sinner,* admiring its author's encyclopedic learnedness and his achievements as "universal specialist":

> In the course of a long life I have truly dwelt under many roofs, have learnt a great deal, parasitized a good deal, and am fairly justified in saying that nothing human is alien to me. Even in these times it is possible for a man to construct out of his life and work a culture, a small cosmos, in which everything is inter-related, which despite all diversity forms a complete personal whole, and which stands more or less on an equal footing with the great life-syntheses of earlier ages.[167]

He had managed to fulfill the "destined pattern" of his life as significant synthesis under indeed difficult circumstances, and irony, the instrument of self-protection and control, was the most important, most powerful tool in this enterprise: it had enabled him to turn away from a threatening reality shared with others toward a reassuring reality which was only his.

Aboard the *Nieuw Amsterdam* in September 1938, leaving Europe behind, Mann recorded his reactions to Hitler's Czechoslovakian victory: "Detachment, detachment [*abwenden*]! One must restrict oneself to his own immediate concerns and the life of the mind. I require serenity and the consciousness of my favored existence [*Bevorzugung*]. Impotent hatred must not consume me." The "ironic jest" about Hitler, his artist-brother, had been written earlier that year, but not yet appeared in German. He wondered whether Bermann-Fischer would dare to bring out the essay now, "after that wretch's triumph? It is more apropos than ever."[168] But for whom? For a reader who accepts Mann's irony as protective distancing from painful experience and who shares in the author's belief that a favored existence, like a work of art, is an *a priori* meaningful fiction.

The Czechoslovakian events signify an assault on the famous author's great entelechy: Fascism might invade the United States too and disrupt the meaningful pattern of his existence. Diary entries in 1940, before the move to California, reflect an increasing anxiety about the war as aimed at him personally, coupled with a curiously sanguine attitude toward the wholesale destruction of other lives.[169] He quotes public and private assessments of his stature in letters to his friends and records them in his diary—for instance, a young British soldier's statement that he was "not only the greatest living writer, but the greatest living man in our history."[170] Such affirmations are "wohltuend" (soothing and restoring), as is the magic suspension of conflict in the fairy tale of Joseph the chosen one, blessed from beneath and above, the statesman as artist:

> In Joseph the ego flows back from arrogant absoluteness into the collective, common; and the contrast between artistic and civic tendencies, between isolation and community, between individual and collective is fabulously neutralized [*hebt sich im Märchen auf*]—as according to our hopes and our will, it must be dissolved in the democracy of the future, the cooperation of free and divergent nations under the equalizing sceptre of justice.[171]

Thomas Mann's fictions promise the reader not just escape but spiritual freedom from the reality of conflict and change in a utopia of well-wrought permanence. The "precious superiority of art" *(köstliche Überlegenheit der Kunst)* over "mere intellectual activity," which he had praised in the chapter "Politics" of *Betrachtungen,* was never to be questioned. The source of such superiority is its "vivifying ambiguity, its profound reserve [*Unverbindlichkeit*], its spiritual *freedom.*" The artist, according to Mann, "never *takes quite seriously* the spiritual, the intellectual," which is important only in terms of its use for the artistic composition.[172] He is the first and only maker as creator of his aesthetic myth and responsible only to his entelechy, and his utopia of art is hermetically sealed and allows no language but that of its creator: utopias have traditionally been predicated on protection by walls and silence. It is for these reasons that the most elaborately and exuberantly talkative texts in German literature have little to say to readers who are suspicious of utopias, because they are more tolerant of transience, plurality, change, and uncertainty as the inevitable presupposition and product of experience.

Part Three

The Seductions of Redemption

FOUR

Marxist Creationism

Walter Benjamin and the
Authority of the Critic

I.

More than forty years after his suicide at the French-Spanish border which, trying to escape from occupied France, he was not permitted to cross, Benjamin's writings have finally been collected. The edition of the Marxist critic's *Gesammelte Schriften* is almost complete even though the Benjamin archive in East Berlin refused to cooperate with the West German editors. Benjamin shares the impact of profound cultural contradictions and conflicts—the cruel ironies of dark times—with many of his contemporaries. His individual intellectual temperament, developed in his particular German-Jewish cultural environment, made him accept a significant fatedness, calamitous constellations ruling the events and decisions that shaped his life and work. His belief in the principles of hope and redemption was a belief in their fated significant absence. Seriously ill and in despair over an unredeemable cultural crisis, he could not muster the energy necessary for survival. His texts, edited with great care and painstaking, enormously detailed commentary, have survived the crisis—though their survival, in this form, is instructively connected with our own contemporary cultural crisis.

When the publisher Suhrkamp, respected for his impeccable attention to intellectual trends, celebrated the 1982 completion of the Benjamin edition with a colloquium arranged in cooperation with the University of Frankfurt, Leo Lowenthal, a surviving member of the Frankfurt School, gave the laudation. It is entitled "The Integrity of the Intellectual"[1] and presents Benjamin as the archetypical intellectual whose absolute independence had been essentially nurtured by his voluntary, significantly self-imposed cultural exile. Lowenthal seems unaware of the possibility that his construct might provoke questions in view of Benjamin's now-established status as a Marxist writer. Referring to the *Gestalt* of Benjamin the intellectual, he declares himself uninterested in social, cultural, and psychological arguments concerning definitions of intellectual positions. All attempts to synthesize Benjamin's intellectual existence are doomed to fail whether they stress the

152

messianic, the Jewish, the Marxist, the surrealist dimension of his thought. The *Gestalt* of *the* intellectual Benjamin is only accessible to that reader who is open to the "unrelenting mournful glance," "the idiosyncratic, the unceasing searches," the "difference."[2] To Lowenthal, Benjamin is the Pariah,[3] the ragpicker, "who knows no disguise in social roles, who is stigmatized and still independent," who never takes refuge in "false consciousness, false politics, false experiments."[4] What Kafka meant for Benjamin, Benjamin means for Lowenthal: the beauty that is the unquestionable meaning and significance of failure.[5]

With his equation of intellectual integrity and exile, Lowenthal emphasizes the intellectual's act of distancing himself from his sociocultural environment. This fiction is highly important to him, because it seems to make possible and permanent his memorial to the friend which defeats the sentimental bourgeois celebration of permanence. Benjamin, now a classic German writer with a classic's edition, will not be touched by the fate of the classic German writer; he will remain in the safety of his integrity which is protected by the distance of self-imposed exile. The *Gestalt* of the intellectual as negative theologian, thinker of contradictions, and architect of the rubble pile of history carries with it immunity against even the gravest danger inherent in the status of a classic: the threat that anamnesis will be buried with the *Klassikerausgabe* (edition of the classics).

It is this paradox which is the basis for the current intellectual fascination with Walter Benjamin, celebrated by German critics as his *Aktualität*. From the distance imposed by a late twentieth-century perspective the cracks in the perfection of Benjamin's allegorical distance are obscured. The appeal of his *Aktualität* is that of the literally doomed, the failed, and the only true intellectual—attractive to late twentieth-century intellectuals in their attempts to cope with the threat of cultural failure. This threat has perhaps the greatest reality for academic literary critics—an audience that did not exist in Benjamin's Germany. There is a sense of dark times, if not in particular political then certainly in broad cultural terms, and it is reflected in the current state of literary (cultural) criticism and theory. Benjamin as professional reader practiced a curiously familiar mixed eclectic approach in his translations of conceptual sequence into imagistic immediacy,[6] and in the best of his critical pieces this metaphorical activity was ingenious and intelligently suggestive. His curiously familiar assertive claims for the autonomy of the individual literary text and the literary critic were supported by such activity: both the reader who doubts the functionality of the poetically elliptic semantics and grammar which are the substance of Benjamin's critical style and the reader who accepts them as deeply meaningful are helped along by stunning images which may or may not clarify the conceptual issues but still lure with the promise of illumination and of the presence of the marvelous. Both kinds of readers are impressed, if in different ways, by Benjamin's single-mindedness. And the question of whether his concept-images, his *Denkbilder,* are indeed "dialectic"[7] in a logically accessible sense or whether Benjamin, mesmerized by antithetical energies, just intended them to be, and then in what way, may indeed seem almost petty when one allows oneself to be open to their provocative power.

Still, the momentarily persuaded critical reader of Benjamin's texts remains permanently confronted with the problem of translating them, which concerns more than the extremely difficult mediation between an intricate, often turgid and obfuscating German and another language, e.g., English, which has no cultural safety net, as it were, for the German variation of speculative complexity. Rather, it concerns Benjamin's general inability to understand language as a socially developed tool for making sense of a world by sharing the need for such activity and its successes and failures. Though he had professionally translated from the French (Baudelaire and Proust) and written on the philosophy of translating, he continued to work with the concept of one language which had the prelapsarian properties of complete autonomy *and* accessibility. Jean Selz, collaborating with him on a French translation of *Berliner Kindheit* was disturbed by Benjamin's always profoundly sad, bewildered reaction to the fact that the fitting French equivalents he had invented were nonexistent.[8]

Benjamin judged the question of accessibility entirely from the vantage point of the (his) text, and he was the more rigorously exclusive in this perspective the more rigorously serious the respective text was in its articulated search for truth. It does not make much difference whether "truth" concerns the metaphysics of language as in the earlier texts, or his later theological variations on the theme of Marxist cultural doctrine which in some cases exhibit a misleading surface clarity. As Hannah Arendt has pointed out, Benjamin, without being a poet, *"thought poetically."*[9] Viewing metaphor as the greatest gift which enabled him to translate literally, directly, sensually the abstract into the concrete, he felt he was meeting the most profound challenge to his aphoristic talent and temperament and he experienced his deepest pleasures. When in the thirties he tried to emulate Brecht's ideologically persuasive "plumpes Denken" (coarse thinking)—one of several Brechtian fallacies in the service of ignoring the implications of an elite status—he fought his addiction to metaphor, ending up with wooden and still unclear, ambiguous texts. Attempts to connect theory and praxis were fraught with contradictions which could not be solved dialectically, at least not by an observer as attentive to his chosen guide and model and as self-absorbed as Benjamin. "There are many," he wrote in his 1935 review of Brecht's *Threepenny Novel,*

> who believe the dialectician an amateur of subtleties. So it is uncommonly useful that Brecht puts his finger on the "coarse thinking" that dialectics produces as its antithesis, includes within itself and needs. Coarse thoughts have a special place in dialectical thinking because their sole function is to direct theory toward practice. They are directives *toward* practice, not *for* it: action can, of course, be as subtle as thought. But a thought must be coarse to find its way into action.[10]

The translation further obscures the untranslatable punning juxtaposition of the two prepositions because it does not take the preceding images literally:

> Plumpe Gedanken gehören geradezu in den Haushalt des dialektischen Denkens, weil sie garnichts anderes darstellen als die Anweisung der Theorie auf die Praxis. *Auf* die Praxis, nicht *an* sie.

Coarse thoughts are part and parcel of the economy *(Haushalt)* of dialectic thought, because all they represent is the dependence of theory on, its orientation toward practice. The meaning of the pun itself is ambiguous and relies on the suggestive radiation of *Haushalt. Anweisung auf* is a technical term used in monetary transactions—writing a check against an account; *Anweisung an* means to give an order to a person. Is the relation of theory to practice then presented as enabling practice, making it active in the way in which writing a check against an account would do with money? But the result would be at least as direct and forceful as the order given to a person. The reader is left with an ambiguous if concrete simile for the allegedly unambiguous relation between theory and practice. Only the doctrinally correct general association *economy* is accessible.

The forms of "coarse thinking," as Benjamin goes on to explain, change slowly, for they have been created by the masses—and with this he has found a transition to a discussion of Brecht's use of proverbs as a "school of coarse thinking," which will enable him to engage with a good conscience in puzzling out the subtleties of language, proletarian or not. His use of simile is not in essence different from his reliance on metaphor in the earlier texts: his kind of dialectics had always relied, continued to rely on forceful disruption of contextual rules and agreements,[11] on cutting off the discrete textual unit from its complex intertextual dependency, on expecting truth to be revealed by the significant rupture of a continuum of experience and thought processes.

Such rupture reflects the exile's allegorically clear, distorted perspective; from his strictly defined distant point of observation he sees the world in radically purified outlines and with brightly lit areas of conflict. The darker the times, the stronger the need for having the perspective harden into theory. When exile is no longer an individually, significantly chosen allegory for the general intellectual condition but an imposed, therefore meaningless particular reality which threatens the intellectual's identity, the ambiguity of the images becomes more aggressive, pressing for the final, the apocalyptic rupture. This process can be traced in Benjamin's texts in the thirties, whether they are accessibly Marxist or not.

Benjamin shared with many Weimar intellectuals the view of the intellectual's identity as defined by his experience of disconnection, distance, and exile. But his distance was more distinctly, allegorically perceived, and it led him to a more eclectic fragmented vision which is central to his "thinking in images":[12] arresting contrasts and conflicts, they keep the distance alive. His position in his contemporary culture was therefore more ambiguous. Arendt, in her generous and shrewd assessment of her brilliantly confused and confusing friend, pointed to the fact that Benjamin had great erudition,

> but he was no scholar; his subject matter comprised texts and their interpreta-
> tion, but he was no philologist; he was greatly attracted not by religion but by
> theology and the theological type of interpretation for which the text itself is
> sacred, but he was no theologian and he was not particularly interested in the
> Bible; he was a born writer, but his greatest ambition was to produce a work
> consisting entirely of quotations, he was the first German to translate Proust
> (together with Franz Hessel) and St.-John Perse, and before that he had trans-
> lated Baudelaire's *Tableaux parisiens,* but he was no translator; he reviewed
> books and wrote a number of essays on living and dead writers, but he was no
> literary critic; he wrote a book about the German baroque and left behind a huge
> unfinished study of the French nineteenth century, but he was no historian,
> literary or otherwise; I shall try to show that he thought poetically; but he was
> neither a poet nor a philosopher.[13]

Benjamin wanted to be considered a literary critic—as he wrote to his friend Gershom Scholem from Paris on January 20, 1930, "C'est d'être considéré comme le premier critique de la littérature allemande" (That is to be considered as the first critic of German literature). For fifty years, he explains, literary criticism in Germany had not been considered a serious genre, and so it was necessary "la recréer comme genre."[14] Scholem in his extraordinarily clear-sighted answer translates this claim into "your pre-sumptive position as the only true critic of German literature," and takes it seriously, reminding his friend of his changing critical priorities between the poles of Judaism and Marxism. He points out that Benjamin's choices would always be mediated through personal attraction and attachment—the practic-ing scholar of Judaism, Scholem, on the one side, the practicing Marxists Lacis, Brecht, and later the Frankfurt School on the other. Given the consti-tution of his life it seemed certain that Benjamin would end up in a position other than he had intended,[15] and they ought to avoid deceiving themselves and each other with a *Privat-Apokalyptik* by acknowledging that intellec-tually they were going separate ways.[16] They were indeed—despite the ob-viously Jewish elements in texts like the essays on Kraus (1931) or on Kafka (1934 and 1938) or the "Theses on the Philosophy of History" (1940). But so were Brecht and Benjamin—despite the elaborately straightforward faithfulness to Brechtian doctrine in the pieces Benjamin wrote about the Marxist dramatist and his work.

2 .

In the person of the first and only true critic of German literature setting out to recreate a whole genre of critical discourse single-handedly, Benjamin did indeed combine all the talents and activities listed by Arendt, and they indicate a broad concept of literature—but not of culture. In the complex of cultural activities Benjamin privileges literature to a degree which seemed extraordinary even to his contemporaries.[17] His emphasis on literature, that is, on the literary text, is based on his concept of language as the totally significant, redemptive mediation between creation and creator, the profane and the sacred. And it is the critic more clearly than the poet who participates in these acts of communication. He does so from a critical position which for Benjamin needed to be redefined within the existing frame of cultural reference, which he continued to redefine and which he, nevertheless, believed to be attainable like truth. For young intellectuals of his generation Zionism and communism were accessible forms of rebellion against the status quo world of the fathers, and Benjamin was indeed quite unique in his attempts at keeping both routes open to himself and, in his vacillations, creating curious mergers and forkings. As the critical position he hoped to forge had to be one of alliance and aloofness, his plans shifted continuously. His letters to Scholem in Jerusalem concerning his strategies of starting the study of Hebrew or giving up on the idea of taking lessons, establishing himself academically or rejecting the hopeless bourgeois establishment of *Literaturwissenschaft,* joining the party or holding back[18] are disturbing in their lack of self-distance and realism. Scholem, pedantic, loyal, and remarkably perceptive, was upset about Benjamin's anarchic attitude toward other people's resources and frustrated about his ideological oscillations, but he also understood the sources of restlessness. It cost him dearly, as Arendt pointed out: "He was quite young when he adopted this radically critical attitude, probably without suspecting to what isolation and loneliness it would eventually lead him."[19]

It was this isolation that encouraged Benjamin's inclination to insist on the total autonomy of the literary text—as a sacred revealed text—and he was not to change this position in his Marxist period when he ostensibly no longer stressed the autonomy of literature. A number of essays written during the second half of the thirties seem to contradict this statement, but only at first glance. Here, too, specific conceptual conflicts and inconsistencies show up on close reading as does the continuity of Benjamin's basic concept of language and the text: the lecture "Der Autor als Produzent" (1934), "L'oeuvre d'art à l'époque de sa reproduction mécanisée," written in French for publication in the *Zeitschrift für Sozialforschung* (1936),[20] "Der Erzähler. Betrachtungen zum Werk Nikolai Lesskows" (1936),[21] "Eduard Fuchs, der Sammler und Historiker" (1937).[22] Finally, "Über einige Motive bei Baudelaire" was published in 1939 after a good deal of discussion with Adorno, who rigorously objected to what he understood to be a lack of theoretical mediation between Benjamin's astonished gaze producing the magic epiphanic rupture in the perception of the then meaningful object and his obsession, as Adorno put it, with the positivism of mere objects.[23] For the Frankfurt School Marxists these pieces presented a *Vulgärmarxismus* developed under Brecht's influence whose untheoretical "positivism" was distasteful; for Brecht they are, on the whole, highly idiosyncratic, even mystifying variations on a Marxist theme.[24] Still, when he was writing under Brecht's direct influence, Benjamin was motivated differently toward his reader, especially in cases, as Brecht observed shrewdly, where he was somewhat disengaged from the subject of his inquiry.[25]

On the surface, then, one could see a difference in degree of accessibility. Yet the distinction made in the 1921–22 essay on Goethe's novel *Wahlverwandschaften* (Selective affinities),[26] which is itself a curiously formulaic allegorical flatland of psychological conflict staged with surrealist clarity and rigid ambiguity and seems to be written for the professional reader only, was to remain central to Benjamin's concept of the relation between the critic and a reading audience. It is a clearly hierarchical distinction between the role of the critic and that of the commentator: criticism searches out the truth content of a text *(Wahrheitsgehalt)*, commentary its factual content *(Sachgehalt)*.[27] In this split between cognition and interpretation greater significance and dignity is assigned to the former and, above all, a remarkable degree of independence from and vis-à-vis the text. When speaking about the historical process of reception he does so less in terms of ongoing sociocultural change which will influence the reading of the text,[28] but rather in terms of the critic's increasingly autonomous, that is, all-powerful position: at the beginning stage of the text's curiously smooth, remote-controlled, as it were, journey through time, its truth content is intimately linked to its factual content, and it is the degree of the intimate interrelatedness which determines the significance, the importance of the text ("dass der Wahrheitsgehalt eines Werkes, je bedeutender es ist, desto unscheinbarer und inniger an seinen Sachgehalt gebunden ist").[29] In the course of the journey, though, this intimacy will be disrupted; the truth content will remain hidden, but the factual content, at first more or less easily accessible, will appear increasingly strange, adding to the critic's task of unveiling the truth now also the interpretation of the unfamiliar, astonishing elements of the text's factual content.

At this conceptually critical point of the argument Benjamin, as is his habit, introduces one of his striking similes: bending over the many-layered text, the critic like a paleographer begins his work by lifting off the uppermost layer. But though the image is arresting, the comparison does not work conceptually, because in contrast to the critic the paleographer does not have to peel off layers of his own perspective. There is for him no change in the degree of strangeness, whereas there is for the critic; and the fact and articulated degree of this change has profound implications for the position of authority claimed by the critic.[30] Benjamin assumes and accepts the critic's perspective of distance which is interrupted by sudden immediacy: it is, he says, with the abruptness of revelation that the critic, engaged in elucidation of the text's factual content, finds himself able to pose the "fundamental critical question": does the becoming visible of the text's truth content depend essentially on factual content or is it the other way around? In the more elaborate German formulation of this question: "Ob der Schein des

Wahrheitsgehaltes dem Sachverhalt oder das Leben des Sachgehaltes dem Wahrheitsgehalt zu verdanken ist."[31] With its play on the dual meaning of *Schein* as illumination/radiance and illusion the sentence may suggest that the critic, responsible for the unveiling of the text's truth, may be in danger of being limited to the level of illusion. But the following sentence—"Denn indem sie im Werk auseinandertreten,[32] entscheiden sie über seine Unsterblichkeit"—presents the disjuncture of truth and factual content as an inevitable outcome of historical processes in which the text participates *and* again states the critic's responsibility for the privileged transhistorical existence of the text: articulating this disjuncture, elucidating its significance, the critic can assure the text's immortality. And, as Benjamin then suggests (in a grammatically obscure sentence), this will mean greater power for critique: "In diesem Sinne bereitet die Geschichte der Werke ihre Kritik vor und daher vermehrt die historische Distanz deren Gewalt"—*deren* referring to *Kritik* which is made more powerful by historical distance.[33]

These are highly problematic statements in a context of very involved difficult epistemological-cultural questions and, again, Benjamin resorts to a simile. He introduces it in a manner which suggests that the simile carries its own justification independent of any attempt at conceptual clarification— "Will man, um des Gleichnisses willen, . . .": if one considers the "growing"[34] (in time) work of art (the text) a flaming pyre, then the commentator stands before it like a chemist and the critic like the alchemist. Whereas for the chemist wood and ashes are the objects of analysis, for the alchemist it is the flame itself that poses the puzzle of life: "So the critic asks after the truth whose living flame continues to burn above the heavy logs of that which is past and the light ashes of that which has been experienced."[35]

Passages like these sing—especially in their original German—and they are one of the major sources of Benjamin's appeal as alchemic critic.[36] Critical discourse then participates in poetic discourse and the question of meaning is shifted to a different level of communication: truth can be the critic's in ways in which it can be the poet's. In Benjamin's 1919 dissertation on the concept of criticism in the German romantic movement[37] it is assigned the task to "uncover the secret dispositions of the work itself, to realize its hidden intentions." In reflecting the text according to its intentions, criticism must transcend the work of art and make it absolute. For the romantic poets-philosophers-critics their activity means, above all, the method of the text's completion, and thus their assertion that "poetry can only be criticized by poetry" is nothing but logical.[38] Benjamin's embracing of this attitude does not suggest his "radical dissatisfaction with all subjectivist philosophical doctrines";[39] rather, it points to the attraction that the romantic concept of the critic's authority held for him. Like Friedrich Schlegel he liked the idea that the critic could and would use and thereby control art as a medium of reflection focused by the individual work of art, the individual text.[40] Truth will depend on the critic to show itself and be known. Reclaiming, after a century, the romantics' theory or perspective on critical activity, Benjamin seems uninterested in the reality of historical processes which had already added different dimensions to the romantics' works, critical or poetic; that is, they had brought about far-reaching changes with respect to the sociocultural role of literature and its readers, professional or general.

Benjamin was temperamentally drawn to think in terms of transcendence and transhistoricity, but it would be misleading to call this deep religious need a radical, "relentless philosophical will."[41] Consistently he poses epistemological questions in terms of redemption, particularly clearly in the "Erkenntniskritische Vorrede" (Epistemo-critical prologue) to his book on the German Baroque *Trauerspiel* (finished 1925, published 1928), which reflect, in certain ways, the influence of Franz Rosenzweig's 1921 *Stern der Erlösung (The Star of Redemption).*[42] Redemption, *Erlösung*, means literally the act of dissolving, the permeation of borders, the changing of substances which will then release whatever has been caught in them. There is in this literal meaning less the suggestion of recovery or being reclaimed, but of set free, let go, a negative thrust.[43] In the position of the first, the only true critic of German literature Benjamin did reclaim for the body of German literature certain of its properties that had been neglected. In the *Trauerspielbuch*, for instance, he created critically the significance of allegory. But redemption would also, and more important, mean the critic's favoring texts which themselves had dissolving qualities and could not be fit easily into existing genre structures. Benjamin admired Proust's texts precisely for their genre transgressions and fusions which he describes in his 1929 Proust essay:

> It has been said and rightly so that all great works of literature either found a genre or dissolve it, that they are, in one word, special cases. Among them this one is one of the most incomprehensible.[44] From its construction which all at once presents poetry, memoir, commentary, to the syntax of boundless sentences (the river Nile of language[45] which here overflows, fertilizing the expansiveness of truth) everything transcends the norm. That this great unique case of poetry also represents the greatest poetic achievement of the last decades is the first important insight confronting the reader.[46]

He started translating Proust in 1925 and had, from the beginning, felt close to his "philosophical way of considering things" *(Betrachtungsweise),* as he wrote to Scholem.[47] The essay is entitled "Zum Bilde Prousts" and attempts to contribute to the poet's portrait by means of discussion of his poetic method. Proust's *Bild*—his image and his portrait—is to the critic-viewer Benjamin the "most intense physiognomic expression found for the irresistibly increasing discrepancy of poetry and life."[48] These passages written in 1929 reflect and reaffirm by now familiar concepts: the connection between language and truth, the critic's responsibility to establish and articulate this connection revealed in moments of sudden illuminations brought on by a rupturing of the temporal and spatial continuum. Proust's total surrender to the unity of the text, the poetically created continuum as the "actus purus of remembrance itself," is accessible to Benjamin in a curious sort of immediacy. As critic of Proust's texts he participates in the poet's "passionate cult of similarity," that is, his insatiable attempts at retrieving the image that would appease his curiosity and his homesickness. He is homesick, in Benjamin's view, for a world shifted to the state of similarity—the association is "state of innocence"—in which the true surrealist face of existence can penetrate or rupture the surface of normality and show itself.[49]

The exile's homesickness (which is Benjamin's, too) is nurtured by his yearning for similarities in which distances are suspended, and (poetic) language is the locus where they converge. The 1929 essay "Der Sürrealismus," subtitled "The Last Snapshot of the European Intelligentsia," posits the "true creative" transcending of religious illumination in "profane illumination," which Benjamin describes as "a materialist, anthropological inspiration" with hashish and opium as a preparatory course[50]—a dangerous one, though, he adds, and religious illumination is stricter.[51] Profane illumination occurring in the moment of rupture reveals similarities, and it is this significant moment of revelation to which Benjamin refers when he speaks of the "dialektischer Kern" (dialectic core) of surrealism[52] or the dialectic properties of this *Trauerspielbuch*.[53] The notes on language, written down shortly before he left Germany in 1933, attempt to chart the place of convergence, the "magic aspect of language" where semantic connections extracted from the sound of sentences can release similarities with the rapidity and force of lightning. There is, he says, a profane and also magic meaning of reading: the pupil reads his primer and the astrologer reads the future in the stars.[54] Man's "mimetic talent" has enabled him to engage both in profane and magic reading, and language and writing have become the "most complete archive of sensual similarities."[55]

Writing in 1933 to Gretel Adorno about these notes which he thought very important, Benjamin relates them explicitly to the early essay "On Language in General and on the Language of Man" (1916).[56] The argument presented in this immature, highly redundant text circles around a concept of language which was to remain fundamental to Benjamin's work up to the 1940 "Theses on the Philosophy of History." Man's language, he argues here, is distinct from all other languages in his acts of naming, that is, of establishing direct significant nonarbitrary connections, of signs and the signified: *"it is in the name that man's spiritual essence communicates itself to God."*[57] For Benjamin the archphilosophical act is the Adamic naming of the world, that is, the assigning of meaning. The language of naming does not have to be tested in terms of its communicative functionality:[58] its reconstitution will enable the philosopher-poet-critic to attain the paradisaical moment of revealed similarities, illuminated correspondences.

The "Erkenntniskritische Vorrede" to the *Trauerspielbuch,* written after the analysis of the plays had been completed and handed in to the University of Frankfurt in the spring of 1925, was characterized by Benjamin as "a kind of second, I don't know if improved, stage of the earlier paper on language."

The prologue, he writes, is intended as a prolegomena for a theory of cognition *(Prolegomena zur Erkenntnistheorie)* and, as such, shows "fantastic chutzpah" *(masslose Chuzpe)*. This nice instance of intellectual self-irony is unfortunately quite isolated: Benjamin's prose, perhaps at its most tortuous, most obscure, and most ambiguous in this text, can only be paraphrased more or less sympathetically.[59] His concept of cognition is rooted in an understanding of idea as symbol and of symbol as name. The symbolic dimension is the essence of the word, but in empirical understanding this symbolic dimension is more or less hidden and the evident meaning of words is profane. The philosopher's task is to restitute, by presentation, to its position of primacy the symbolic character of the word in which the idea reaches self-communication *(Selbstverständigung)*, which is the opposite of all communication directed outward. As philosophy cannot presume to speak with the authority of revelation, such restitution can only be undertaken by going back, in remembrance, to the first, the archunderstanding.[60]

In all his serious texts, Benjamin is concerned about redeeming language from its alienating communicative function, turning it back on itself, as it were. This process is almost graphically reflected in the entwined syntax which causes the sentence to move so haltingly. Between each sentence and the reader he puts several obstacles as if attempting to create an undisturbed space for the idea in communication with itself. Benjamin had no interest in and no patience for accessible conceptual discourse. Concepts turn into images refracting hidden essences. One can detect in his argument some very general Platonic and Hegelian echoes, but there is no sense of a philosophical cultural tradition within which he might want to define his own thought and communicate with his reader. To an extent the *Trauerspielbuch* came to reflect his desire to write a book consisting entirely of quotes. In large parts the argument moves through juxtapositions of quotes which he had collected painstakingly from esoteric sources—he wrote to Scholem in May 1924 about his eccentric precision and pedantry with respect to amassing and arranging the more than six hundred quotes, reminiscent of the way in which he collected rare children's books or antique toys.[61]

The preciousness of the quotes was their disponibility. Taken out of their contexts they could be made to yield, by fission, those moments of profane illumination in which the magical properties of language were restored, the original correspondences reestablished, and the presence of meaning unquestioned—a meaning which was the critic's and his alone. Gathering these quotes out of the texts and arranging them meant to Benjamin the ability to redeem, that is, release their meanings which are the true meanings of the texts. It was precisely the fact that he was working with esoteric material which enabled him to recreate textual truth in this manner: he needed to quote extensively; there were no editions of these texts to which he could refer his (academic) reader. Rehabilitating the allegorical mode of the German baroque drama, the *Trauerspiel,* which was, at the time, the most discredited, least desirable, most obscure part of the German literary canon, he laid claim to the position of the first, the only true critic of German literature.

The forceful arbitrariness of this procedure has seldom been discussed. The fact that the book was unacceptable to German academics judging his qualifications for a university career has almost always been interpreted through Benjamin's perspective: the book's intended unacceptability seems to make the fact that it was unacceptable totally the fault of the German academic establishment, a corrupt bourgeois institution.[62] The German academic establishment was, of course, deeply troubled—though in different, much more significant and dangerous ways than those pointed to by Benjamin. The question that remains to be asked concerns the cultural meaning of Benjamin's appropriation and magical transformation of a body of literature, that is, of texts written by others in another period with very different intentions. It is the question of his indeed radical neglect of the cultural-historical alterity of texts.

In this context Benjamin's relation to Panofsky and Saxl's study of Dürer's "Melencolia I," published in the series *Studien der Bibliothek Warburg* in 1923, is instructive. Panofsky is almost never mentioned in Benjamin criticism—partly because the *Trauerspielbuch* is more often praised than read and partly because it is philosophical connections which have seemed most important to the Benjamin image. In a letter to Scholem of December 22, 1924, Benjamin, assuring the friend that he is almost done with the work, defines the achievement of the *Trauerspielbuch* as bringing to life "the organic power of the allegorical as the primordial source [*Urgrund*] of the baroque." He admits both to the "maddest mosaic technique" of the text—it consists almost entirely of quotes, he writes—and to a level of profundity perhaps unnecessary had he known more about the Latin Middle Ages, but then, of course, he would not have been able to write this kind of book. I am aware of a degree of unfairness involved in listening in, as it were, to a conversation between friends where Benjamin feels free to leave for a while the position of high intellectual seriousness and speak openly about certain familiar strategies of taking shortcuts. However, in trying to find one's way through his frequently impenetrable study, it is helpful to consider what he knows is lacking and how he justifies it.

Panofsky's analysis of Dürer's famous allegorical engraving, which Benjamin regards as "the last work of incomparably fascinating research," seemed close to his own particular interests, and so he is very disappointed when Panofsky reacts coolly to a preprint of a portion of the *Trauerspielbuch* sent to him by Hofmannsthal, who had tried to be helpful to Benjamin in establishing the desired connection with the *Warburg Kreis*.[63] Benjamin finds Panofsky's reserved attitude incomprehensible. It seems quite obvious if one compares their different approaches to the allegorical mode. Benjamin had found fascinating the presentation and analysis of the copresence of opposites in the allegorical figure of *Melancholy* reflecting the Saturn-induced *furor melancholicus* which stimulates theologians, philosophers, and poets:

"Winged, yet cowering on the ground—wreathed, yet beclouded by shadows—equipped with the tools of art and science, yet brooding in idleness, she gives the impression of a creative being reduced to despair by an awareness of insurmountable barriers which separate her from a higher realm of thought."[64]

"Melencolia I," Panofsky argues, is the "Artist's Melancholy." Benjamin was sensitive to the artist-geometrician's experience of inspiration from above and of powerlessness, made to suffer by wrestling with the very discipline he loved. Having nurtured the hope, in his earlier years, of capturing beauty by means of a ruler and compass, Dürer had come to abandon this hope shortly before he composed "Melencolia I" and some years later remarked that the "lie is in our understanding, and darkness is so firmly entrenched in our mind that even our groping will fail."[65] But where Panofsky leaves the Renaissance artist's dual nature unresolved and unredeemed, showing, rather, how the effectiveness of the composition of allegorical objects is intimately linked to the presence of suffering from "human frailty and intellectual finiteness,"[66] Benjamin is intent on rupturing the allegorical composition, isolating its components so that they can be perceived as keys to a more profound, more unmediated knowledge which he, the twentieth-century critic, will reveal.

In the long excursus on melancholy at the end of part one of the study, "*Trauerspiel* and Tragedy," which circles around Dürer's "Melencolia I," he asserts an essential connection between melancholy and allegory, presenting the princely protagonist of the *Trauerspiel* as "Paradigma des Melancholischen."[67] The locus of melancholy is the dialectic of Saturn,[68] that is, the dual properties of Saturn as heavy, cold, dry, connected with the hard material world of agriculture on the one hand, and on the other related, as the highest of the planets, to the spiritual, contemplative religious sphere. The wisdom of the melancholic is extracted from absorption (*sich versenken*) in the cold heaviness of the earth, that is, for Benjamin, concentration.[69] Melancholic concentration betrays the world for the sake of knowledge, but in doing so it rescues and redeems the dead object in contemplation, that is, in its loyalty to the object as fragment of the world of things. It is, as Benjamin says in concluding the excursus, Dürer's genius of winged melancholy that makes the crude stage of the German baroque drama come alive in allegorical language.

The dialectic core of allegory, which is of central importance to Benjamin, fuses such "coming alive" with the death of things in stiffening, hardening processes, in their becoming ruins: it is precisely the death of things which assures their eternal safety in the presence of the ruin. In the second part, "Allegory and *Trauerspiel*," Benjamin is concerned with this paradox which is the source for the power of the allegorist's melancholic gaze. When history becomes part of the setting in *Trauerspiel* it does so as script, "written on the countenance of nature in the characters of transience." The allegorical physiognomy of the nature-history, which is put on stage in the *Trauerspiel*, is present in reality in the form of the ruin. In the ruin history has physically merged into the setting.[70] But it is the allegorist and he alone who will be able to read this script and reveal its truth:

> If the object becomes allegorical under the gaze of melancholy, if melancholy causes life to flow out of it and it remains behind dead, but eternally secure, then it is exposed to the allegorist, it is unconditionally in his power. That is to say it is now quite incapable of emanating any meaning or significance of its own; such significance as it has, it acquires from the allegorist. He places it within it, and stands behind it; not in a psychological but in an ontological sense. In his hands the object becomes something different; through it he speaks of something different and for him it becomes a key to the realm of hidden knowledge; and he reveres it as the emblem of this. This is what determines the character of allegory as a form of writing. It is a schema; and as a schema it is an object of knowledge, but it is not securely possessed until it becomes a fixed schema: at one and the same time a fixed image and a fixing sign.[71]

Both sign and signified are "in the power" of the allegorist, and if his power is to be meaningful, the sign has to be meaningful—itself, as Benjamin states in this context, "an object worthy of knowledge." With the romantics, he says, allegory became self-conscious in this regard.[72] Quoting from Franz Baader's *Über den Einfluss der Zeichen der Gedanken auf deren Erzeugung und Gestaltung* (On the influence of the signs (signifiers) of thought on their production and formation), Benjamin does not seem to be interested in his remarks on the symbolic-conventional consensus-based character of the sign but stresses, rather, Baader's speculation that man's ability to "pronounce" the language of signs, which, one might argue, exists already in nature, would have to come "quite simply from somewhere else."

Baader is interested in man's capacity for symbolic activity, Benjamin in the "somewhere else" which makes this "arbitrariness" meaningful: " 'From somewhere else' the allegorist then takes it [i.e., pronunciation] up, by no means avoiding that arbitrariness which is the most drastic manifestation of the power of knowledge." It is not so much that Benjamin, as admiring critics contend, has succeeded in redeeming allegory as an eminent form of signification *(Be-deutung)*, no less so than symbol,[73] but that he has assigned to the reader as writer, the critic as allegorist, an extraordinary autonomy in relation to the world of things and to the text. Where Baader speaks about the process of abstraction in symbol making—man assigns the sign to the signified both arbitrarily and by (socio-historical) convention—Benjamin has the allegorist demonstrate his arbitrariness as the "power of knowledge." But knowledge of what? Of the essence of things. The allegorist does not present the essence behind the image: he "drags the essence of what is depicted out before the image."[74] Independent of signifier and signified it exists for him and through him; it is truly "unconditionally in his power."

Dürer's allegorical engraving "Melencolia I," which Benjamin thought so important for his own understanding of allegory, balances in its composition the experience of approaching and not reaching knowledge, the dual situation of never knowing nothing and never knowing everything, which is the modern experience. Benjamin's construct of allegory is based on the premodern (or postmodern) juxtaposition of not knowing at all and knowing fully, of straining for the momentary revelation and articulation of hidden, silent, infinite knowledge. This gnostic attitude is reflected in his polarized concept of language. Scholem remembers meeting with Benjamin in Paris in 1938 and finally discussing, as Benjamin had wanted, the 1933 notes on language. The Kabbalah scholar was slightly dismayed about the extent of his friend's mysticism: Benjamin, he realized, quite literally based all language theory on God's in contrast to Man's word, notwithstanding his Marxist conviction. Benjamin's editors who in their extensive commentary rely heavily on Scholem's memoirs and want to stress Benjamin's unique philosophical achievements, correct Scholem's remarks by pointing to the complexity of Benjamin's concept of language. They quote from a letter Benjamin wrote to the liberal bourgeois Swiss critic Max Rychner on March 7, 1931, about the *Trauerspielbuch* which he had managed to get published in 1928 but which had not had much of a reception and had not gotten him into an academic career:

> Now this book most certainly was not materialist, if it was already dialectical. What I did not know at the time when I wrote it, and what became increasingly clear to me shortly afterwards, is the fact that there exists a mediation between my specific language-philosophical position and the views of dialectic materialism, even if it is a strained and problematic one.

This is the portion of the letter quoted by the editors who are interested in precisely that mediation. Benjamin continues:

> But none to the saturated state of bourgeois academia [*Wissenschaft*]. Cur hic?—not because I "profess" a materialist world view, but because I wish to direct my thinking to those subjects in which truth exists more intensely. And today this does not concern "eternal ideas" or "timeless values."[75]

However, then speaking directly about the negative reaction to the *Trauerspielbuch,* Benjamin emphasizes that his ability to distinguish his work from the "hideous waste of this official and unofficial business" of German academia was based on the fundamental metaphysical orientation ("metaphysische Grundrichtung") of his studies, and that for this he had not needed a Marxist mode of thought with which he had become acquainted only later. He distinguishes, that is, between a serious metaphysical orientation which can be linked up with dialectic materialism—he could have referred Rychner to the Hegelian dimension of Marxism—and the vacuous transcendentalism of bourgeois culture. But the problem, as both Adorno and Scholem saw quite clearly, was not the fact but the kind of Benjamin's metaphysics, what Scholem called his mysticism. When Scholem pointed out to him the conflict between his magic and materialist concepts of language, Benjamin would admit them as an area where much work was still to be done. He was presumably thinking of the texts on Baudelaire's Paris, the *Passagenwerk*— though what exists of this study is very much marked by this conflict. In his last text, the "Theses on the Philosophy of History," the materialist dimension is absorbed, again and again, by the magical through a series of alchemic transfigurations.

3·

The conflicted coexistence of the magic and the materialist in Benjamin's perspective creates irritating tensions in those texts which ostensibly attempt a Marxist interpretation of cultural phenomena or which draw self-consciously (and eclectically) on elements of Jewish tradition. There are texts, though, notably some of his portraits of cities, where he succeeds as a curiously precise *and* inventive cultural cartographer, intimate and accessible in his attempts at sharing the pleasures of suddenly locating and unlocking the hidden. In these texts the tensions of his dual perspective sometimes work *for* rather than *against* the reader. Benjamin's fascination with Marxism, which began in the early twenties, had always been a fascination with individual Marxists, that is, with his attraction to them and, accordingly, their intimate power over him. He reads and charts cities with the help of markers of significant personal relationships, and in a similar fashion he tries to find his way into the confusing unstable construct of a complex social doctrine. He became involved with Asja Lacis, "the Bolschevist Latvian from Riga, an actress and director, a Christian," as he introduces her in a letter to Scholem of June 13, 1924, while writing the *Trauerspielbuch* on Capri; a month later he mentions her as "one of the most remarkable women I have met"[76]—she was to become one of the three most important women in his life. In the June letter he also mentions Lukacs's 1923 *Geschechte und Klassenbewusstsein (History and Class Consciousness)* which Ernst Bloch had reviewed recently and which looked important to Benjamin: "Of course, I cannot read it now"[77]—because he is hard at work on the *Trauerspielbuch*. In September he still has not read the book but has had talks about it with Bloch, who has in the meantime been on the island. He is interested in the grounding of theory in praxis and can see, he writes, how in Lukacs's argument such grounding contains a "hard philosophical core."[78] There is a fairly clear subtext to this letter which deals with Benjamin's important personal experience of concrete, timely communism *(aktueller Kommunismus)* in the person of Lacis, and "eminent Communist."[79] Lukacs's emphatic connection of eschatological history with the proletariat[80] is suggestive to Benjamin in his own search for redemption of alienated language. But even if he were to argue from a Hegelian position against Lukacs's argument,[81] he writes, he would be able to see communism as an attitude of commitment in a different light from now on.

The difficult relationship with Asja Lacis, whose intellectual curiosity and capacity was considerably exaggerated by Benjamin,[82] was of profound importance to him though it did not cause the turn in his mode of thinking which some critics assume—here I agree with his biographer Werner Fuld.[83] I disagree, however, with Fuld's emphasis on Lukacs's influence on Benjamin's thinking.

As Fuld sees it, Benjamin must have read Lukacs on Capri during that summer of 1924—Benjamin quite clearly says that he had not.[84] The reception of Marxist thought through the medium of Lukacs would clearly have taken place on a level different from that of conversations with Lacis in whom Benjamin appreciated also the good listener. Lacis was not a theoretically talented intellectual—but neither was Benjamin. It is arguable that he never worked his way with any degree of concentration through the pieces collected in *History and Class Consciousness,* which were written in clumsy, simplistic German, and were presumptive, abstract, and redundant in their argumentation. Notwithstanding all their obvious shortcomings, these texts did establish Lukacs as an important theoretician of Marxism, and this fact was known and important to Benjamin. Benjamin, on the other hand, could be an extraordinarily good cultural essayist, but never in those texts where he overstrains his small talent for theory.

Benjamin's interest in Marxism as a concrete attitude toward the troubled contemporary world developed at a time when he experienced dramatic changes in his upper-middle-class background because of serious difficulties with his parents who had suffered severely from the inflation. The situation was made worse by the bankruptcy of his publisher and the failure of his attempts at establishing himself in an academic career. A letter to Scholem in May 1925 is instructive in this respect: if he does not find a satisfactory situation soon, he will concentrate more on Marxist politics and the party with the hope of getting to Moscow fairly soon, at least temporarily. Sooner or later he will take this step in any case as the horizon of his work has changed, although he foresees great conflict between this course and studying Hebrew. He does not know how to arrive at a decision, but feels that he has to make the experiment of getting involved in both experiences in order to gain the totality of an intellectual horizon at which he can only guess now.[85]

The clearly admitted defeat was personal; it concerned his difficult relationship with Asja Lacis. It was, of course, intimately connected with conflicts and contradictions inherent in both protagonists' intellectual-political experiences and expectations. In the essay which Benjamin published about his stay in Moscow he worked with a particularly constrained perspective which is, in some ways, peculiarly effective, though it is hard to judge how far he controlled his intentions. What he saw of Moscow in December 1926 and January 1927 was what Lacis showed him or what he thought she withheld from him and what he, therefore, had to search out himself against specific odds, which, whether he realized it or not, informed his way of looking at what he found.

He had looked at a city with her before, in September of 1924, and he and Lacis together wrote about what they had seen.[86] The piece on Naples is probably the most light-hearted of Benjamin's texts. He already knew the city well and looked at it, this time, with a perspective protected by his comparative happiness. He finds himself released, for once, from the need to relate what can be seen directly, that is, too exclusively, to the preoccupations of the (one) observer. Naples is perceived and presented convincingly as a strange city, but in the sense of different rather than alien. Itself the source of its people's "rich barbarism," it is contained securely in the lap of the Catholic church which, through the confessional, controls the considerable sexual and criminal energies at play among the volatile people of Naples.[87] It is a city that eludes the traveler as tourist: "Here the churches cannot be found, the starred sculpture always stands in the locked wing of the museum, and the word 'mannerism' warns against the work of the native painters."[88]

There is a whole dimension of the hidden in Naples, yet it is not the solidity, but the porosity of walls that hides. That porosity, for once, is not burdened with the observer's significance; its meaning remains with the images of permeated walls, curtained but often invisible door openings, interpenetrated spaces: "Porosity results not only from the indolence of the Southern artisan, but also, above all, from the passion for improvisation, which demands that space and opportunity be at any price preserved."[89] Opportunity to use space for presentation of action—all of Naples as a popular stage—is predicated on such openness: nothing is closed, concluded, finished; construction and destruction of buildings merge. The city is not only the stage for improvization; it itself reflects the open-endedness and fragmentariness of human affairs, and the viewer records instances of such reflection. There are, to be sure, a few signaling efforts to endow the position of the viewer, Benjamin's perspective, with a special significance. For instance, he distinguishes his penetrating perception from the shallow one of the bourgeois tourist: "Fantastic reports by travellers have touched up the city. In reality it is gray: a gray-red or ocher, a gray-white. And entirely gray against sky and sea. It is this, not least, that disheartens the tourist (Bürger). For anyone who is blind to form sees little here."[90] Benjamin and his intended reader, of course, have the required sight.

But, on the whole, there is the admission in this essay that it suffices to see the forms and let them be, that is, attempt to understand their meaning in the context of the city but refrain from appropriating their significance. This restraint may very well reflect the influence of Lacis—not so much her particular intelligence and sensibility,[91] but the acknowledged presence of another observer and narrating consciousness. The joint authorship, even if it concerned only a piece of journalism, suggests the extension of an intimacy of experience from which the reader can profit. There are by far fewer ideological assumptions at work in this text—whether they concern the cultural preeminence of language, the importance of texts, of the critic's position, of reading, of establishing particular (in this case Marxist) significances. Experience is allowed to remain fragmentary; even more, it is allowed to channel energy into history which is then neither fictitiously continuous nor ruptured. The city itself embodies the recurring bursts of presented activities, the erratic flow of history: "What is enacted on the staircases is a high school of stage management. The stairs, never entirely exposed, but still not enclosed in the gloomy box of a Northern house, come shooting out of the houses in fragments, make an angular turn, and disappear, only to burst out again."[92] Walking by stalls which offer leavings from restaurants, boiled cat skulls, and fish shells, by vendors selling cigarette butts for a fixed price, the observer, moved by the brilliant *(strahlende)* music, circulates through the streets together with joyful mobile things like toys and ice cream. Porosity and motion complement each other. Music penetrates the distinction between weekdays and Sundays, trade becomes a game of chance and a festive occasion, the private and communal merge in the motion of people bursting out of houses into front yards and streets, even sleep comes in fragments and is not the solid protected nightly stretch of Northern sleep: "Here, too, there is interpenetration of day and night, noise and peace, outer light and inner darkness, street and home."[93]

The overriding interest in extracting sets of opposites which can then be fused together does limit the perspective of the observer to an extent, but his structuring activity does not impose itself too forcefully on the observed surface of the city which remains, for the reader, pleasantly accessible, richly detailed, and colorful. And the concluding passage, significantly, presents as acceptable the inaccessibility of a social intercourse in which the observer as outsider cannot participate. For once, the otherness of the moment lived by others in another place is observed without regret, without longing, without fear, and without illusions created by the intrusion of the self. For once, Benjamin is not in search of the meaning of selfhood to be sought and found in any and every place. Here he is literally *interested* in the otherness of a place which he has seen so often before and now, being there, sees again. It is not a question of seeing differently, shocked by profane illumination; it is a question, rather, of seeing precisely, with curiosity and concentration— sufficiently so as to be able to share the view by talking about it. It is not what it could mean that is of importance here, but that it can be seen. In Naples, Benjamin is the traveler in the other place which he tries to understand for its own sake, that is, for the pleasure of understanding:

> The language of gestures here goes further than anywhere else in Italy. The conversation is impenetrable to anyone from outside. Ears, nose, eyes, breast, and shoulders are signaling stations activated by the fingers. These configurations return in their fastidiously specialized eroticism. Helping gestures and

impatient touches attract the stranger's attention through a regularity that excludes chance.[94]

He describes here a language of gestures *(Gebärdensprache)* that supplements and supports language as language-game rather than as naming. The observer as outsider accepts it as a language which he cannot understand, from which he cannot translate, which he cannot measure against its own paradisaically pure abstraction. It exists and therefore it is important to perceive it and share the perception.

"Naples" is a light-hearted but not a slight text; its peculiar accessibility is related to the experience of the city's alterity: Benjamin did not, as he did with the other cities (Moscow, Berlin, Paris), read Naples like a (verbal) text and, in the act of reading, appropriate it. Peter Demetz's introduction to the pieces collected in *Reflections* sends the bemused English-speaking reader on his way suggesting that perhaps the "best way to approach Benjamin's writings would be to imitate his willingness to keep the sensibilities open to the sober and profane illuminations that come to people who quietly and attentively walk through the astonishing streets of a foreign city." This is in many ways a good piece of advice. In his *Städtebilder,* with the exception of the essay on Naples, Benjamin does indeed explicitly search out the shock of (profane) illumination and is fascinated by the experience of amazement, reading cities like texts and charting texts like cities.

In "Naples" he does not seek that shock; his openness is both more concentrated and less directed, and it deals less with the astonishing properties of the other than with the endlessly, continuously fascinating otherness itself. Benjamin did not exploit the experience of "the alienated and the alien,"[95] because Naples is different rather than alien. The viewer's perspective brings into clear focus the otherness of the viewed, but it is not alienated. "Naples" is the only one of the *Städtebilder* in which the viewer's perspective is not so self-conscious as to create that tension between the familiar and the alien—in the shorthand of critics: the familiar becoming alien/the alien becoming familiar—which in reality detracts from the otherness of the other. In his Moscow essay Benjamin was to appropriate the spaces, sounds, shapes, and colors for his own intellectual and emotional purposes, even if the charm of the piece depends, to a degree, on the articulated recognition that the city resists him. He was to map Berlin in the process of recreating his childhood, and he was to rearrange Paris so that those correspondences which were of significance to him could surface in supernatural clarity. In the Naples essay he is not interested in digging toward layers of profounder meaning, and so the fiction of "Naples itself" can present itself to the reader for pleasurable consideration—as it were, without obligations.

One might argue that the ease of this essay is due, in part, to the fact that in the case of Naples no rupturing the familiar was needed, no attempt to arrest the distance of the distant in an image "out of the reach of the devouring force of familiarity."[96] (And it is certainly true that Benjamin has always been overly anxious about such devouring force.) He knows Naples and it still remains calmly unfamiliar. But this is the result of his perspective. In contrast to the Moscow essay Benjamin does not try here to establish a significance of the unfamiliar itself and thus does not introduce the rupturing paradoxical tension between distance and closeness. Naples remains accessibly unfamiliar because the meanings of the surface, of what can be seen, are accepted as sufficient. Great care is taken in the articulation of these meanings which include, for instance, the dimension of the hidden. Yet they stop with the city; they are not lifted out of, abstracted from the maze of its houses and streets. For once, Benjamin is content to be the outsider and use the advantages of this position, that is, the ability to grant both the object of observation and his reader an illuminating degree of otherness and of independence.

"Naples" is an exception, only rarely does Benjamin—as reader of texts as well as of a cultural reality—permit himself such openness and flexibility of perspective.[97] When he reviewed, shortly after the book's publication, Werner Hegemann's 1930 *Das steinerne Berlin. Geschichte der grössten Mietskasernenstadt der Welt,* he brought to this study of rapid urban growth a perspective which is instructively rigid. Hegemann, a well-known architect, architectural critic, and urban historian who was also familiar with urban architecture in the United States (*Amerikanische Architektur und Stadtbaukunst,* 1925), presented a wealth of information about Berlin's tenements, making his critical views accessible to any but the most reactionary reader. Benjamin in his review essay, published in *Frankfurter Zeitung* under the title "Ein Jakobiner von heute,"[98] professes to be highly impressed by the informational value and the organizational intelligence of the book which has, he asserts, succeeded in "correcting" pragmatic historiography. However, Hegemann, his undeniable achievement notwithstanding, has not contributed to the "revolution" *(Umwälzung)* of pragmatic historiography which has been accomplished by historical materialism. Though Hegemann has correctly considered and traced the connections between the means of production and power, his "incorruptibly critical" mind remains arrested in the "pragmatic" dimension: it is the dialectical gaze only which can penetrate to the core of history. His book, then, just misses "that absolute perfection" which not only makes the "fate of the book independent of its subject," but, moreover, makes it the "fate of its subject."[99]

"Pragmatic" for Benjamin, as for Adorno and Horkheimer, is an all-comprehensive concept charged with intensely negative (in the sense of "nasty") power.[100] "Pragmatic," to say it colloquially, is the pits, profoundly shallow. Benjamin as reader of Hegemann reacts to the absence of the astonished, penetrating, rupturing gaze which causes the absence of the text's sacred dimension, its absolute perfection. Historiography for Benjamin is the setting down of truth rather than the search for truth or, more honestly, for probability. Now, ironically, his concept of historiography is entirely pragmatic in the accepted sense: it concerns history as the historian's purposeful construct in pursuit of a truth—be it the greatness of the ruler or the pure power of ideology—which precedes evidence supported by critical consensus and which remains independent of such evidence. What Benjamin asks of Hegemann as urban historian is as curious as it is consistent with his intellectual temperament: a perspective that will allow the historian to see beauty in the most profound disfigurement ("Ist es aber unbillig, dem Historiker jenen Blick in das Antlitz der Dinge zuzumuten, der Schönheit noch in der tiefsten Entstellung sieht?").[101] Hegemann, recording the inhuman spaces of substandard tenement housing, was clearly not able to afford this astonished gaze resulting in the shock of profane illumination. He was interested, above all, in sharing his detailed documentation of sociocultural inequity with his reader as a contemporary. Benjamin's insistence on the paradoxical fusion of concrete sociocultural disfigurement and transcendent beauty reflects nothing if not the extreme, the unredeemed distance of the critic from his own culture. Significantly, it will be redeemed only in the momentary shock of profane illumination which is the critic's—and only his. It may be arguable that there is room for both Hegemann's and Benjamin's perspectives on a city. Perhaps. But Benjamin's idiosyncratic, distorted reading of Hegemann's intentions points very clearly to the more questionable aspects of his charting of Moscow, Berlin, and finally, Paris.

"More quickly than Moscow itself, one gets to know Berlin through Moscow" ("Schneller als Moskau selber lernt man Berlin von Moskau aus sehen").[102] It is unfortunate that the English version of this important first sentence is so misleadingly and, moreover, unnecessarily free. It was, for Benjamin, never a question of *knowing* a city, but always a question of significant perspective. One learns to *see* Berlin more quickly—the *Gestalt* of Berlin, its meaning—from the perspective of Moscow:

> For someone returning home from Russia the city seems freshly washed. There is no dirt, but no snow, either. The streets seem in reality as desolately clean and swept as in the drawings of Grosz. And how true to life his types are has become more obvious. What is true of the image of the city and its people applies also to the intellectual situation: a new perspective of this is the most undoubted gain from a stay in Russia.

The traveler-observer, then, will judge events at home from the point of view of Russian events. Moreover, the observer, aware of this direction of his perspective, will gain a clearer view of his place of origin, and it is *therefore* that a stay in Moscow becomes so precise a touchstone for the foreigner: "It obliges everyone to choose his standpoint. Admittedly, the only real guarantee of correct understanding is to have chosen your position before you came. In Russia, above all, you can only see if you have already decided."[103] "Seeing correctly" *(die rechte Einsicht)* is anchored in a perspective which is independent of what can be seen, of the evidence.[104] This is, of course, an important ideological point, but it seems curious that Benjamin presents it so emphatically, and presently it becomes clear that *die rechte Einsicht* is not, after all, congruous with an ideologically correct political position but rather with a concept of truth transcending such position. It is not a question of a better reality, a better direction, but rather a question of which reality will become inwardly convergent with truth:

> which truth is inwardly preparing itself to converge with the real? Only he who clearly answers these questions is "objective." Not toward his contemporaries (which is unimportant) but toward events [Zeitgeschehen] (which is decisive). Only he who, by decision, has made his dialectical peace with the world can grasp the concrete. But someone who wishes to decide "on the basis of facts" (an Hand der Fakten] will find no basis in the facts [dem werden diese Fakten ihre Hand nicht bieten].[105]

The "dialectical peace" with the world supports the astonished glance of the observer, and thus, from the beginning, the city unfolds as a private yet strangely accessible adventure. The adventure starts with the arrival at the station. Kiosks, arc lamps, buildings "crystallize" into unique configurations which "disperse" rapidly as soon as the traveler armed with very little Russian, seeks words to help him find his way. The German zerstieben,[106] "disperse," is used for light airborne particles like snowflakes, and what the traveler sees everywhere and immediately, of course, is snow, which both absorbs and projects, "the dirty snow that has already installed itself and the clean snow slowly moving up behind. The instant one arrives, the childhood stage begins. On the thick sheet of ice on the streets walking has to be relearned. The jungle of houses is so impenetrable that only brilliance strikes the eye."[107] It is the snow that provides the true perspective for the traveler: the astonished glance, the glance of childhood, the illuminating glance is provoked by snow, hiding and exposing, and by extreme, exotic, adulthood-transcending cold. The most suggestive images for sensations, the most striking descriptions of shapes, colors, motion of objects are extracted from the exorbitant masses of snow and the surrealistically solid cold.

There is the picture of caravans of sleighs gliding rapidly through the streets, close to the sidewalk; the passengers, on the same level with the pedestrians, brush the passersby with their sleeves:

> Where Europeans, on their rapid journeys, enjoy superiority, dominance over the masses, the Muscovite in the little sleigh is closely mingled with people and things. If he has a box, a child, or a basket to take with him—for all this the sleigh is the cheapest means of transport—he is truly wedged into the street bustle. No condescending gaze: a tender, swift brushing along stones, people and horses. You feel like a child gliding through the house on its little chair.[108]

The snow which makes this magical gliding possible, and with it Alice-in-Wonderland crossings, also brings to life the extraordinary colors which give objects their real existence. There are (Christmas)tree decorations sold in the street, the glass balls, yellow and red, glinting in the sun: "it was like an enchanted apple basket in which red and yellow are divided among different fruit."[109] It is the childlike glance, helped by the snow, that sees the color as indistinguishable from the (still) magic object, the toy. Benjamin starts with the observation that the colors "do their utmost against the white,"[110] his appreciation of the intense visual stimulation and entertainment:

> The smallest colored rag glows out of doors. Picture books lie in the snow; Chinese sell artfully made paper fans and still more frequently, paper kites in the form of exotic deep sea fish. Day in, day out, children's festivals are provided for. There are men with baskets full of wooden toys, carts and spades; the carts are yellow and red, yellow or red the children's shovels. All these carved wooden utensils are more simply and solidly made than in Germany, their peasant origin being clearly visible. One morning, at the side of the road stand tiny houses that have never been seen before, each with shining windows and a fence around the front garden: wooden toys from the Vladimir government. That is to say, a new consignment of goods has arrived. Serious, sober utensils become audacious in street trading. A basket seller with all kinds of brightly colored wares, such as can be bought everywhere in Capri, two-handled baskets with plain square patterns, carries at the end of his pole glazed-paper cages with glazed-paper birds inside them. But a real parrot, too, a white ara can sometimes be seen.[111]

Benjamin is fascinated by clearly marked crossings: from the hidden to the visible, from the cold shapeless white of the piled-up snow to the sharply contoured, warmly colored objects standing out against it, from shape to color, from color to shape, from the solid to the fragile, even fluid, from the large to the small, the small to the large. Could not those tiny houses be real houses, suddenly emerging from underneath the snow by the side of the road, appearing to the passerby like toy houses, so small and quaint; but could not that passerby magically *and* matter-of-factly enter a real toy house? His noting the presence of the South in the North, too, points to his focus on the permeability of objects in their configurations. The act of "seeing correctly" which Benjamin invoked in the introductory passage is not directed toward the city of Moscow as in general terms an unquestionably significant Communist experiment, but toward Moscow as a place rich in private significances. He sees with a perspective that enables him to resume, continue, and explore the child's openness to rich excitements of transformation. Significantly, the diary he kept while in Moscow records in detail his intense desire for the toys he sees on display, for toys hidden in places difficult of access, his finding them, his buying them till they fill his large suitcase.[112]

For Benjamin, the magic of Moscow is in its objects. It is the profusion of objects in "the wild variety of the street trade" that reminds him of the South. Happily absorbed, he enumerates the objects sprawling on the open street "as if it were not twenty-five degrees below zero but high Neapolitan summer." The difference, it strikes him, is in the silence. The sellers address the passersby with "measured if not whispered words in which there is something of the humility of beggars."[113] Street trading is partly illegal. Benjamin states this fact but does not seem to be interested in the paradoxical situation, given the number and variety of objects for sale. Similarly, talking about the aggressive, quite barbarous hordes of war orphans ganging up on the lonely pedestrian—foreigners are warned against them—and describing the centers established for them, he notes the difficulties involved in managing those wild, tough, street-wise, mistrustful children: "Politics [stressing the appeal of the collective] in the organization of crowds of such children, is not tendentious, but as natural a subject, as obvious a visual aid, as the toy shop or dollhouse for middle-class children."[114]

For whom are all the toys intended that fill the streets of Moscow and feed the traveler's consuming greed? The considerable charm of Benjamin's essay rests precisely in the superimposition of the middle-class child's toy-trained sensibility on the highly perceptive, articulate adult writer.

Occasionally Benjamin remembers the obligations to his official perspective. He is pleased to see how the Russian "proletariat has really begun to take possession of bourgeois culture, whereas on such occasions in our country they have the appearance of planning a burglary."[115] Proletarian children visit the toy museum with its free puppet show; the adults look at bourgeois genre painting at the Tretiakov museum. And here Benjamin makes a curiously inconsequential but telling observation:

> Here the proletarian finds subjects from the history of his movement: *A Conspirator Surprised by the Police, The Return from Exile in Siberia, The Poor Governess Enters Service in a Rich Merchant's House*. And the fact that such scenes are still painted entirely in the spirit of bourgeois art not only does no harm—it actually brings them closer to this public. For education in art (as Proust explains very well from time to time) is not best promoted by the contemplation of "masterpieces." Rather, the child or the proletarian who is educating himself rightly acknowledges very different works as masterpieces from those selected by the collector. Such pictures have for him a very transitory but solid meaning, and a strict criterion is necessary only with regard to the topical works that relate to him, his work and his class.[116]

Do these stricter criteria apply, then, to the distinction between bourgeois genre painting and time-and-class-transcending masterpieces after all? Do such masterpieces by virtue of having transcended time and class restrictions negate the bourgeois sensibility which might be detrimental in questions of class doctrine? And how does the observer know what meaning individual pictures have for the viewers he views from a considerable acknowledged distance? We are not told. Benjamin is much more interested in recording impressions for a later leisurely fitting into configurations of his specific sensibility than in understanding what is going on.[117]

He sees beggars and admires with some envy their survival skills which entail a very detailed knowledge of Moscow topography, noting that nobody ever gives them anything. Why are they still there in comparatively large numbers and picturesque poses? The strongest foundation for begging, the bad social conscience, has gone: "Beyond this it appears as an expression of the unchanging wretchedness of these beggars; perhaps, too, it is only the result of judicious organization that, of all the institutions of Moscow, they alone are dependable, remaining unchanged in their place while everything around them shifts."[118]

But this is whimsy out of *Alice in Wonderland,* presenting the beggars as acting out a paradoxically consistent and elusive strategy devised by a playful if somewhat Kafkaesque authority which is the source of energy for *remonte,* the experimental shaking up of Russia. Gide in his report on his journey to the USSR insists that the reader see that this immense country is, as it were, in labor: "one feels that one is contemplating the parturition of the future." His report is really an attempt to document how this process of giving birth to a new society is perceived, experienced by the participants, whom he observes closely and to whom, whenever it is possible, he talks.[119] Benjamin does not talk to people; when he observes them at all they appear caught in the careful composition of an old photograph or moving jerkily with large gestures, as in a silent movie. Their gestures, their motions are motivated by the perspective of the unquestioning observer who finds what he is looking for. This perspective does have its charms; in contrast, Gide's critical, questioning, self-questioning report is rather lifelessly informative about certain observed aspects of the experimental lives which he witnessed. Benjamin, interested above all in his reading of the city, tries to transmit the sense of shifting foundations, receding demarcations, of lives in flux, which surprise, that is, enchant, the onlooker with their constant kaleidoscopic changes. The focus, then, is not on the people of Moscow caught in, moving along with the changes, but on the observer's perception of their motion:

> Each thought, each day, each life lies here as on a laboratory table. And as if it were a metal from which an unknown substance is by every means to be extracted, it must endure experimentation to the point of exhaustion. No organism, no organization can escape this process. Employees in their factories, offices in buildings, pieces of furniture in the apartments are rearranged, transferred, and shoved about. New ceremonies for christening and marriage are presented in the clubs as at research institutes. Regulations are changed from day to day, but streetcar stops migrate, too, shops turn into restaurants and a few weeks later into offices.[120]

It is the impact of the dissolving forces of change, the permutations of spaces, objects, and functions which delight Benjamin and which he tries to articulate. Now and then he remembers his obligation to see from the position of one who "has already decided." Talking about the abolition of the private life by bolshevism and the lack of living space in Moscow, he mentions that many families share an apartment and describes the living arrangements:

> Indoors one only camps, and usually the scanty inventory is only a residue of petit-bourgeois possessions that have a far more depressing effect, because the room is so sparsely furnished. An essential feature of the petit-bourgeois inte-

rior, however, was completeness: pictures must cover the walls, cushions the sofa, covers the cushions, ornaments fill the mantlepiece, colored glass the windows. (Such petit-bourgeois rooms are battlefields over which the attack of commodity capital has advanced victoriously; nothing human can flourish there again.) Of all that, only a part here or there has been indiscriminately preserved. Weekly the furniture in the bare rooms is rearranged—that is the only luxury indulged in with them, and at the same time a radical means of expelling "coziness," along with the melancholy with which it is paid for from the house. People can bear to exist in it, because they are estranged from it by their way of life. Their dwelling place is the office, the club, the street.[121]

The observer's perspective creates considerable ambiguities. Who is depressed by the residue of petit bourgeois possessions, whose sensibilities are offended? Hardly the people's who put the objects into the rooms. Why is the furniture habitually rearranged? Do the inhabitants of these rooms consciously want to expel bourgeois coziness and melancholy? Are they estranged from these rooms because they are so inadequate or because they prefer the clubs? Do they prefer the clubs because their rooms are so inadequate? Are the rooms so inadequate, because their energy is directed to public life and they prefer clubs?

Benjamin does not know about the people of Moscow because he is not sufficiently interested to look at them. He views the rooms in which they live remarking on their (on the whole) antibourgeois bareness and barrenness; he establishes the negative contrast with the archetypical petit bourgeois interior. It is this contrast which is the stated responsibility of the European visitor to the USSR, and occasionally Benjamin refers himself to his statement at the beginning of his essay. The contrast is meant to reveal: in this case the act of revealing is literally an act of drawing off covers—off walls, off windows, off floors, off furniture. Once they have been removed the merging process, the crossings and transitions become possible; that is, he can see them. The Moscow essay works in part because Benjamin gives in smoothly to a perspective which searches out private significances. He permits himself to read the city as a text for which he is responsible and to which he brings his concept of reading and of the text. There is an Adamic perspective on objects: naming them makes them appear in significant configurations. The magic gaze is quite effortless;[122] transformation happens without the shock of a rupture. In this sense of seeing a world rearrange itself with magic ease under the astonished gaze of the observer, Moscow does have paradisaical properties, and they are sometimes shared with the reader in the precise perceptions and images which speak directly and happily:

> The intoxicating warmth that overcomes the guest on entering these taverns, on drinking the hot tea and enjoying the sharp *zakuska,* is Moscow's most secret winter lust. Therefore no one knows the city who has not known it in the snow. . . . In Moscow, life in winter is richer by a dimension. Space literally changes according to whether it is hot or cold. People live on the street as if in a

frosty chamber of mirrors,[123] each pause to think is unbelievably difficult. It needs half a day's resolution even to mail an already addressed letter, and despite the severe cold it is a feat of willpower to go into a shop and buy something. Yet when you have finally found a restaurant, no matter what is put on the table—vodka (which is here spiced with herbs), cakes, or a cup or tea—warmth makes the passing time itself an intoxicant. It flows into the weary guest like honey.[124]

Again and again Benjamin pushes aside the many concrete difficulties which control daily life in Moscow and which he describes in detail in his diary. Then he feels at peace in the city's strangeness, and literally savoring the moment, its shape, color, taste, smell, he takes care to share what he experiences with his reader. Writing for Buber's journal *Die Kreatur,* he could afford to leave those moments personal, that is, unstrained by "theory"—a luxury that he could not afford when writing on Baudelaire in Paris for the Frankfurters' *Zeitschrift für Sozialforschung.* Trying to appropriate the meaning of Moscow—he had, after all, gone there to find his decision to go justified—Benjamin realized his defeat but refrained from elevating it to a significant failure. Lacis was just recovering from a nervous breakdown, seemed lost and hostile politically, intellectually, emotionally, also petulant, endlessly demanding and rejecting. The diary documents in painful detail his always futile, always renewed attempts at understanding her and coming close to her. She consistently and irrationally denies him access to herself, to Marxism, and to Moscow. The diary records very few moments of peace, and they are entirely private,[125] poignant for the professional reader observing Benjamin's life, but not communicable in the sense in which he shares the strangeness of Moscow with his readers in the essay he wrote for publication. On his way to the station, leaving Lacis and Moscow, he sits in the sleigh crying, on his lap a large suitcase filled with the many objects he collected. He did not see Moscow again, but in his essay he reconstructed his seeing the city at certain moments when, through magic configurations of objects, he kept her strangeness intact.

He eventually divorced his wife because of Lacis, with whom he lived in 1929 and 1930 when she came to Berlin and Frankfurt, but he did not join the party. Their relationship remained troubled, and Brecht replaced her as Benjamin's mentor in applied Marxism. When Benjamin wrote to Buber about the Moscow essay for *Kreatur* in February 1927, only a few weeks after his return, he characteristically fudged the issue of theory. He is still, he writes, at work on the essay, but one thing he can promise Buber already: namely, the absence of theory in his description. He hopes thus to be able to let the *Kreatürliches* speak—the human dimension unmediated by theory—but he expresses skepticism regarding his ability to understand fully "this very new disturbing [*befremdende*] language" which he found in Russia; he wants to present Moscow at this moment when "everything factual is already theory." His abstention from theory, then, does not seem to mean the absence of the important (to him) theoretical dimension after all, though he is ambiguous about the meaning of this dimension. He is surprisingly clear, however, about the fluidity of the situation: Moscow suggests a possible success as well as a possible failure of the revolution to the observer and will not have a future which conforms to official (rosy) descriptions, a *program-matische Zukunftsmalerei.*[126]

The Moscow essay, if not the Moscow diary, tries to understand the city's new strange language to the point where it can be translated, where Moscow can indeed be read like a text according to the critic's perspective and intentions. They do, however, shift quite noticeably in those passages where aspects of the USSR as an exemplary social experiment are brought in as a sort of counterweight to the personal magical gaze. The interpretation of Moscow as text is and remains ambiguous, and this ambiguity is not based on or fed by the critic's specific openness to Moscow's as yet unrealized potential as is suggested in the letter to Buber. Rather, it is based on the critic's inability to define his intellectual-emotional position in his contemporary cultural (German) context which he had defined as cultural crisis.

Benjamin read the shapes, colors, sounds, tastes of Moscow as richly strange because he could relate them to the texts of other cities. Where he seriously thought Moscow's language to be "very new" to the point of being "disturbing"—the German *befremdend* means strange in the sense of repelling rather than attracting—he tried to neutralize its alienness by supplying bits and pieces of correct, i.e., accepted, expected superstructure. But the success of the essay depends on the interpreter's sure focus on the literalness of hidden and revealed insights in snowbound, cold-encircled Moscow. In this perspective intensely distinct objects (shape, size, color) become so because they have been redeemed from the state of being hidden; their meaning is their distinctness. And the reader can enjoy this distinctness, taking the redemption for granted.

In the early thirties when the cultural crisis had caught up with the intellectuals and exile was imposed externally rather than self-imposed, Benjamin began to explore himself in his Berlin past. The first version of this exploration, "Berliner Chronik,"[127] was probably begun on Ibiza in the summer of 1932, and he continued to work on the text, rearranging and enlarging it, all through the thirties. He published parts of what he called *Berlin Childhood* but tried for years to have it appear in book form. The earlier version is the more interesting, engaging text, less carefully arranged, also less static, more intimate in its restlessness and fragmentedness. It charts more clearly the process of getting lost in the maze that the city could or should become. There will be need for a map only if there is need to find one's way. Only if the self is experienced in time will there be the effort of digging through its and the city's layers; only if the self experiences expansion will there be interest in marking boundaries. The later smoother vision is less determined in this respect because it presents the child-self's shorter excursions in the more simply reconstructed city. It may be that Benjamin arranged the smoothed-out sketches in that rather mannered fashion because it seemed to reconstruct the past more reassuringly. In 1938 he wrote about the difficulties of finding a publisher for the book, which he acknowledged was hard to place but which, he thought, would probably appeal strongly to many German exiles in search of their past.[128] "Berliner Chronik" is more involved with the significance of the search itself which is a series of detours.

> I have long, indeed for years, played with the idea of setting out the sphere of life—bios—graphically on a map. First I envisioned an ordinary map, but now I would incline to a general staff's map of a city center. . . . I have evolved a system of signs, and on the grey background of such maps they would make a colorful show if I clearly marked in the houses of my friends and girl friends, the assembly hall of various collectives, from the "debating chambers" of the Youth Movement to the gathering places of the Communist youth, the hotel and brothel rooms that I knew for one night, the decisive benches in the Tiergarten, the ways to different schools and the graves that I saw filled, the sights of prestigious cafes whose long-forgotten names daily crossed our lips. . . .[129]

Mapping and reading a map are important activities for Benjamin in search of himself in the city, but he did not set out *bios* graphically on a map, and the markers he mentions would have merged immediately. For he is really looking for a specific kind of losing himself as part of the search—as one loses oneself in a nonsymbolic, natural environment:

> Then, signboards and street names, passers-by, roofs, kiosks or bars must speak to the wanderer like cracking twigs under his feet in the forest, like the startling call of a bittern in the distance, like the sudden stillness of a clearing with a lily standing erect at its center. Paris taught me this art of straying. . . .[130]

It is the art of reading signs according to their unmediated significance; there is no convention and no arbitrariness. Proust's "deadly game" is invoked[131] to warn the self not to play too easily with related possibilities, with correspondences, but the dunes of the Baltic landscape have appeared to the former self "like a *fata morgana* here on Chausseestrasse, supported only by the yellow, sandy colors of the station building and the boundless horizon opening in my imagination behind its walls."[132]

The marked boundaries are social in the sense of class distinctions[133] and impede the self's Adamic straying, whether Benjamin realized this or not. This impediment was to present problems in the texts on Paris, where he employs a system of socioeconomic demarcations hoping it would support the magic immediacy of the signified, the object, which concretely merges with its sign. And the many quotes, that is, quoted observations made by other viewers of the city of Paris, which make up the bulk of what survived of the *Passagenwerk,* are like so many concrete particles which build up the city as a mosaic—as the study of the German baroque drama had been built up of quotes in "the maddest mosaic technique."

What in the Paris texts appears, or, rather, in mosaic fashion is intended to appear, connected is left seemingly disjointed in "Berlin Chronicle."

There are apparently contradictory strategies of getting lost in the city: Parisian straying as seeking out correspondences is juxtaposed with digging up the city for mementos of the past: "the images, severed from all earlier associations, that stand—like precious fragments or torsos in a collector's gallery—in the prosaic rooms of our later understanding." It is not so much the completeness of one's findings that counts in the work of memory, but "this dark joy of the place of the finding itself,"[134] which is both repeated and disconnected: ever-new places, ever-deeper layers. These disconnected places and layers are significant because they are found and interpreted by the finder. Are these acts of finding, then, in juxtaposition to the straying openness to correspondences? Actually in both cases the perspective is significantly isolating: lifting the precious memory image from its past context, focusing on a particular correspondence in a complex cultural texture.

4.

Benjamin's search for the self or its significant fragments was mapped onto cities which he read as texts and onto the texts of other writers. Karl Kraus and Franz Kafka are the most direct examples, and, to an extent, Leskov, on whom he tried some of the questions of the writer's social identity which he had taken over from Brecht. The piece on Kraus, written in four installments for *Frankfurter Zeitung* in 1931, "enraged" as well as "impressed" Scholem;[135] he had very much admired the earlier short piece on Kraus which had appeared in the 1928 *Einbahnstrasse* (One-way street) and what he says about it in his memoirs of their friendship is quite revealing: "The wonderful prose piece about Karl Kraus, 'Kriegerdenkmal' [War memorial] he [Benjamin] read with an almost Georgian solemnity in an inimitably raised voice.[136] It made a profound impression on me, and to this day I regard it as one of the most beautiful pages he wrote."

Reading the 1931 text, he is irritated by "the downright fantastic discrepancy between the true method and the method presented by the terminology." Everything becomes "lame because the insights of the metaphysician about the language of the bourgeois—*in fact even about the language of capitalism—in an artificial and therefore all too transparent manner* are identified with those of materialism about the economic dialectics of society *(so much so that they seem to derive from each other!)*"[137] It is true that Scholem is disturbed also by Benjamin's approach to the Jewish aspects of Kraus's writing. Ten years earlier he had, in the company of Benjamin and Ernst Lewy, speculated about a specifically Jewish fascination with the phenomenon of language and linked Kraus's style to that of the great medieval Hebrew halakhists. Benjamin had asked him repeatedly to write down his thoughts on that connection, but the historian Scholem did not think he knew enough to do so. Later he was to resist Benjamin's eclectic appropriation of certain aspects of the Jewish tradition to be used in the construction of his Kafka (self-)image.[138] But more than that, he seems irritated by the curious opaqueness and righteousness of Benjamin's argument when he assigns a cultural position to Kraus's critique of corrupt language. A passage like the following can serve as an example for Benjamin's procedure; the context is a general discussion of empty language, cant *(die Phrase):*

> Or, as Kraus says so splendidly and succinctly: "It ought to tell us something about technology that, unable to coin new platitudes, it leaves the spirit of mankind in the state of being unable to do without the old ones.[139] In this duality of a changed life dragging on in unchanged forms, the world's ills grow and prosper." In these words Kraus deftly tied the knot binding technology to the empty phrase. True, its untying would have to follow a different pattern, journalism being clearly seen as the expression of the changed function of language in the world of high capitalism. The empty phrase of the kind so relentlessly pursued by Kraus is the label that makes a thought marketable, the way flowery language, as ornament, gives it value for the connoisseur. But for this very reason the liberation of language has become identical with that of the empty phrase—its transformation from reproduction to productive instrument. *Die Fackel* itself contains models of this, even if not the theory: its formulas are of the kind that tie up, never that untie. The combination of biblical grandiloquence with stiff-necked fixation on the indecencies of Viennese life—that is its way of approaching phenomena.[140]

Is, then, the language critique of *Die Fackel* insufficient in, for example, the manner of Hegemann's critical study of Berlin's tenements? It seems so, reading the quoted passage. But Benjamin goes on to praise just that "biblical grandiloquence," assimilating his own style to Kraus's and clearly warming to the task of showing how right Kraus's method of extending his cross-examination of language to the dead in their graves, his total indictment of Viennese bourgeoisie had been. With the outbreak of the war Kraus had arrived at the true, the earliest subject of his prophetic perspective: In the fall of 1914 "he called this subject by its name in the speech 'In This Great Age,' with which all the demons that had populated this possessed man passed into the herd of the swine who were his contemporaries."[141]

The essay on Kraus is not, as is the indeed impressive short piece in *Einbahnstrasse,* centered on Kraus; its central energy comes from the play of Benjamin's sensibility. The critic's perspective is, of course, always and importantly informed by his intellectual temperament and by his concept of self-presentation in language; it is a question of degree. Benjamin describes Kraus's approach in images which appear curiously self-sufficient and independent of his subject of inquiry. Quoting a long passage from "In This Great Age," he comments on its last sentence, "Let him who has something to say step forward and be silent!"

> It is the same with everything Kraus wrote: a silence turned inside out, a silence whose black cape is caught by the storm of events making it billow, turning its garish lining outward. Notwithstanding the abundance of its causes, each of

them seems to break on him, surprising him, with the fierce suddenness of a gust of wind.[142]

In spite of some interspersed statements of reservation regarding the ultimate cultural significance of Kraus's position Benjamin is essentially uncritical of Kraus as critic of language. The second part of the essay which is entitled "Demons"—the first part has the title *Allmensch,* suggesting a symbiosis of everyman and cosmic elements—begins with the shrewd observation, "It is deeply rooted in Kraus' nature, and it is the stigma of every debate concerning him, that all apologetic arguments miss their mark."[143] He is right in arguing against certifying Kraus as an ethical personality. But his own celebration of Kraus's demons needs to be questioned. The *Einbahnstrasse* text, too, had been constructed around a highly stylized concept-image of Kraus's grandiose archaic mode of existence: the Chinese idol in an ancient armor, wearing a fierce grin.[144] Now he states explicitly that "the dark background from which his image detaches itself is not informed by his contemporaries, but is the primeval world or the world of the demon. The light of the first day falls on him—thus he emerges from this darkness."[145] The viewer has to adjust his sight to this dark world, to the first light; otherwise, he will only see parts of the figure in spite of the furious attempts made by Kraus to be seen:

> For, as in the fairy tale, the demon in Kraus has made vanity the expression of his being. The demon's solitude, too, is felt by him who gesticulates wildly on the hidden hill: "Thank God nobody knows my name is Rumpelstiltskin." Just as this dancing demon is never still, in Kraus eccentric reflection is in continuous uproar.[146]

Rumpelstiltskin, like the little hunchback, *das bucklichte Männlein* from *Berliner Kindheit,*[147] is a figure from Benjamin's private mythology. In Kraus he sees the demons of his own eccentricity and of his own "idiosyncrasy as the highest critical organ."[148] And Kraus's conflation of divine justice and language, "the genuinely Jewish somersault by which he tries to break the spell of the demon," has been Benjamin's somersault too. Where Kraus accuses the substance of the law, where he charges "the betrayal of justice of law,"[149] Benjamin measures all texts against the first text, which is the garden of innocence mapped in redeemed language. Here there is no arbitrary division between sign and signified and consequently no ongoing change; here Adamic language is safe from language use. It is in this preoccupation with the singularity, purity, and immediacy of (German) language that the only true[150] cultural critic Kraus and the only true literary critic Benjamin become curiously congruent. Notwithstanding the few gestures to Kraus's bourgeois limitations, Benjamin is centrally uncritical of the great journalist's absolutist attitude toward social discourse, that is, toward the plurality and pluralism of language games. Yet, it was precisely this attitude which many of Kraus's admirers found disturbing.[151] To Benjamin "sanctification of the name" is the essence of Kraus's concept of language, and he admires "its

Jewish certainty." And though Kraus was not as directly preoccupied with naming, Benjamin's image of Kraus in those passages where he speaks about the sources of his belief in language is accurate because it is congenial.

In his portrait of Kraus Benjamin fitted certain properties into kaleidoscopically shifting constellations—the great surface variety of Kraus's preoccupations and activities—and yet it is anchored in a concept of language very close to his own. Kafka, too, he approaches in a curiously unmediated manner; in both cases the constructedness of the emerging figure, the distinctness of the individual parts in the sequence of rearrangements is not caused by the critic's informed reflected distance but rather by a process of partial identification. All critical activity involves some charting of physical and intellectual phenomena in search of the self. It is, however, particularly intense and single-minded in Benjamin, and the peculiar effectiveness and flawedness of his performance as critic is arguably related to this intensity. Kafka resisted him more than Kraus, because his situation in the (literary) tradition is more ambiguous than Kraus's and because Benjamin tried to understand and use it in more specific terms.

The Kafka essay published in *Jüdische Rundschau* in December 1934 had been a long time in the making. In June 1931, Benjamin, contemplating a review of a posthumously published Kafka text, *Beim Bau der Chinesischen Mauer,* asked Scholem for "hints" on his thoughts on Kafka, and Scholem advised him to begin his inquiry with the Book of Job, "or at least with the possibility of divine judgment which I regard as the sole subject of Kafka's production. . . ." He points out the affinity of Kafka's language to the language of the Last Judgment and stresses the importance of the canonical form:

> It would be an enigma to me how you as a critic would go about saying something about this man's world without placing the *Lehre* (teaching), called *Gesetz* (law) in Kafka's work, at the center. I suppose this is what the moral reflection—if it were possible (and this is the hypothesis of presumptuousness!)—of a halakhist who attempted a linguistic paraphrase of a divine judgment would have to be like. Here, for once, a world is expressed in which redemption cannot be anticipated—go and explain this to the goyim! I believe that at this point your critique will become just as esoteric as its subject; the light of revelation never burned as unmercifully as it does here. This is the theological secret of perfect prose. The overwhelming statement that the Last Judgment is, rather, a martial law was made, unless I am mistaken, by Kafka himself.[152]

The Kafka essay published three years later reflects the influence of Brecht and of Scholem, and the resulting tension is uneasily contained in the complicated fragile structure of the essay. There are other indications of subliminal conflicts which threaten the coherence and accessibility of the argument. Werner Kraft whom Benjamin had asked to read the essay in 1934—he did not make any changes for the publication in *Jüdische*

Rundschau, but collected readers' responses, Scholem's included, in a folder marked "For a *Kafka* Revision"—expressed serious reservations regarding the essay's intelligibility.[153] He refers to Brecht's physical and metaphorical vicinity to Benjamin who was at the time visiting him in Denmark, suggesting that Brecht ought to be able to show him in a new light the problem of intelligibility, *Verständlichkeit.* This would mean, for Kraft, cutting all similes *(Gleichnisse)*—he mentions specifically the Potemkin story which serves as an introduction. He wants the leading ideas developed more clearly, especially the swamp-world of Kafka's characters, the complex of "gestus" and "gestic behavior," and of forgetting, the demonic aspects of the little hunchback in relation to Kafka's world. These composite concepts are thought-images, *Denkbilder,* and therefore more sensually suggestive than rationally elucidating. Kraft who had written on Kafka and was interested in clarification of complex cultural issues was not persuaded by this peculiarly Benjaminian approach, though his detailed comments are on the whole sensitive and shrewd. He wants Benjamin to help the reader find his way in the dense text more easily, that is, to try to state his objectives in a way which tells the reader exactly what he can expect: "damit der Leser sofort weiss, *was* er hier zu erwarten hat. . . ." This, of course, had never been Benjamin's authorial intention, not in the explicitly Marxist texts where he ostensibly tried to be clear but above all not in a text so fraught with personal tension and significance as the Kafka essay.

Kraft, Scholem, and Adorno approve of Benjamin's focus on the theatrical element in Kafka, specifically his discussion of the Nature Theater of Oklahoma in *America,* but whereas Kraft and Adorno accept the introduction of gestus—Adorno does state his reservations regarding the connection to Chinese theater, which clearly reflects Brecht's influence[154]—Scholem, with rather uncharacteristic emphasis, rejects the intimations of gestus and gestic as "completely incomprehensible" for any reader not entirely familiar with all the ramifications of Benjamin's work. He pleads with the friend to understand that such degree of condensation and abbreviation could only be highly irritating.[155] It is true that Benjamin's usage of gestus and gestic seems to be motivated by references to sources which are largely inaccessible to the reader. Where he mentions them at all, they seem to be introduced into his argument in a curiously arbitrary way. The very important but unmentioned source is Brecht;[156] explicit references to Franz Rosenzweig's *Star of Redemption* seem improvised. Quoting him with respect to the lack of individuality in Chinese spiritual life, "What distinguishes a Chinese is something quite different from character: a very elemental purity of feeling," Benjamin makes the connection to gestus by simply stating: "this purity of feeling may be a particularly sensitive measurement of gestic behavior; the Nature Theater of Oklahoma in any case harks back to the Chinese theater. One of the most significant functions of this theater is to dissolve happenings into their gestic components."[157] It is indeed odd that Benjamin chose Rosenzweig, who was for him closely (if vaguely) linked to Jewish theology, to introduce the Chinese association pointing to Brecht.[158] Revising the essay in 1935, he cuts the connection between Nature Theater and the gestus of epic theater. Following the last word of the Rosenzweig quote, "feeling," he inserts:

> Oklahoma appeals to this purity of feeling. The name "Nature Theater" conceals a double meaning. Its hidden meaning is: in this theater people appear according to their nature. Their acting talent of which one should think first is of no importance. . . . And here we remember those most playful of Kafka's characters, who do not wish to represent respectability in bourgeois society and for whom there is infinite hope. They are the assistants. We all are like them, not more than they, in the Nature Theater: assistants of a play tied, by Kafka, to a process of decision in a curious and rather vague manner. After all, it takes place at a race track. There is much that suggests that this play is about redemption.[159]

While the link between Brecht and Kafka is weakened,[160] Kafka's world theater appears in a more hopeful light. The insert combines short passages taken out of two different contexts in the earlier version and changes their meaning dramatically. In one of them Benjamin had characterized applicants to the Nature Theater of Oklahoma as having to meet only the expectation that they *play* themselves (my emphasis), because it is impossible "that they could in all seriousness *be* [Benjamin's emphasis] what they claim to be."[161] For Kafka's characters, as Benjamin sees it here, this theater is the last refuge which does not preclude that it is redemption, as redemption is the last way out for the person whose path is entirely blocked. The change, then, collapses the dichotomy between *play* and *be* and defuses the paradox of being lost *and* being redeemed. The second passage is a quote from a conversation between Brod and Kafka where Kafka, asked about the reality of hope, answers with a smile: "Oh, plenty of hope, an infinite amount of hope—but not for us."[162]

Hope and hopelessness, redemption and failure appear smoothly connected in the revision. There is infinite hope for the assistants and we are like them; redemption, Scholem's warnings notwithstanding, can be anticipated. The figure of Kafka continued to be important to Benjamin as it presented to him an image of modern cultural crisis which was allegorically distinct and shifted with different perspectives. In the revisions of the essay in 1935 he is trying to develop the possibility of a fusion which might accommodate more hopeful cultural energies. This attempt is reflected in other texts of the period—perhaps the most widely known and discussed today is "The Work of Art in the Age of Mechanical Reproduction," published in the Frankfurt Institute's *Zeitschrift für Sozialforschung* in 1936.[163] At first glance this essay seems resonant with Brechtian themes in its strongly affirmative interpretation of technologically induced changes in the arts and their cultural meanings. Benjamin introduces his famous concept-image of "aura" as the unique presence of the work of art emanating from its basis in ritual, but he does so only to announce its demise. The destruction of the aura by the mechanical reproducibility of art is viewed positively as the emancipation of the work of art, "for the first time in world history," from its "parasitical dependence on ritual."[164] This loss of the aura signifies removal of the work of art from its all too firm embeddedness in a cultural tradition and thus affords the viewer a perspective which reveals the contemporary relevance of the work of art as affirmation of the politically most advanced class.

Adorno reacted strongly to the "very sublimated remnant of certain Brechtian motifs" in a long letter of March 1936. (Brecht, in a diary entry, reacted to the sublimation.)[165] He stresses his own interest in the liquidation of art and the disappearance of aura. The loss of the auratic element, however, he connects not so much with mechanical reproducibility but with inherent autonomous formal laws of art, pointing to the "technicity" of avant-garde art. Significantly, he minds most (and credits to Brecht's influence) Benjamin's assigning a magical aura also to the autonomous avant-garde work of art which in this view assumes the counterrevolutionary properties of bourgeois art. He warns Benjamin not to politicize art in a (Brechtian) way which destroys its truly progressive dialectically transcending potential. His privileging film is dangerous, Adorno writes, because its progressive components are largely illusory.[166]

Brecht's presence in the essay, so feared by Adorno, is in fact rather diffuse. Benjamin, if one reads him attentively, is much more ambivalent about the direct politicization of art and much more ambiguous about the inevitable and desirable loss of aura than his assertive gestures toward materialism may lead one to expect. Consider the following statement:

> The technique of reproduction detaches the reproduced object from the domain of tradition. By making many reproductions it substitutes a plurality of copies for unique existence. And in permitting the reproduction to meet the beholder or listener in his own particular situation, it reactivates the object reproduced. These two processes lead to a tremendous shattering of tradition which is the obverse of the contemporary crisis and renewal of mankind. Both processes are intimately connected with the contemporary mass movements. Their most powerful agent is the film. Its social significance particularly in its most positive form, is inconceivable without its destructive, cathartic aspect, that is, the liquidation of the traditional value of cultural heritage.[167]

Benjamin is not centrally interested in affirmation of politically and culturally progressive new art forms like film—though there are those statements which provoked Adorno: "Mechanical reproduction of art changes the reaction of the masses toward art. The reactionary attitude toward a Picasso painting changes into the progressive reaction toward a Chaplin movie."[168] What really fascinates him is the shattering and destruction, the catharsis and revelation, and most of all the appearance of the magical *Ding-an-sich:* the paradoxical reactivation, by reproduction, of the object itself. The essay's line of argument is erratic and fragmented, its fifteen short parts are not logically connected. Images, similes, verbal gestures create a mood, an ambience, in which the doctrinal statements (printed in italics like the one quoted above) stand out as foreign bodies. A passage in the first version of the essay explicitly links the smashing *(Zertrümmerung)* of the aura and the subsequent peeling the object out of its husk to the now possible perception of similarities *(Sinn für das Gleichartige in der Welt)*, which has little to do with a new collectivity. The smashing of the aura suggests, rather, the shock of the profane illumination of correspondences.[169] The aura is indeed not lost in its destruction but transformed, transcended.[170]

The redemption of the auratic element is transformed to yet another level of ambiguity in the 1939 *Zeitschrift für Sozialforschung* essay "On Some Motifs in Baudelaire." Adorno had rejected its first version "The Paris of the Second Empire in Baudelaire" in 1938 because he had found it lacking in theoretical interpretation of the magically perceived objects.[171] In the version of 1939 the threatened aura is presented as a complex of highly important and valuable human experiences associated with ritual, community, and tradition and destroyed by modern society. Speaking about Baudelaire's ambivalent feelings about photography as both a threat to his sensibility and an important modern phenomenon, Benjamin quotes Valéry on the inexhaustible hold on us of the work of art and comments: "the painting we look at reflects back at us that of which our eyes will never have their fill. What it contains that fulfills the original desire would be the very same stuff on which the desire continuously feeds." A photograph, in contrast, would feed the hungry, would still and deaden the desire, and the "crisis of artistic reproduction" is precisely this satiation in which "the beautiful has no place." The decline of the aura, then, is unambiguously presented as impoverishment, and the loss of beauty is a potent metaphor for the loss of humanity in the modern world:

> What was inevitably felt to be inhuman, one might even say deadly, in daguerreotype was the prolonged looking into the camera, since the camera records our likeness without returning our gaze. But looking at someone carries the implicit expectation that our look will be returned by the object of our gaze. Where this expectation is met . . . there is an experience of the aura to the fullest extent. . . . Experience of the aura thus rests on the transposition of a response common in human relationships to the relationship between the inanimate or natural object and man. The person we look at or who feels he is being looked at, looks at us in turn. To perceive the aura of an object we look at means to invest it with the ability to look at us in return.[172]

In his best texts, especially his *Städtebilder,* Benjamin had always done just that. The profound and central ambiguity of all his texts, including the hermetically opaque pre-Marxist critical work, is caused by the difficulties he encountered when he had to mediate conceptually between moments of auratic perception, when he had to construct fragile meanings out of contradictory evidence instead of having it revealed, with magical directness, as truth. On the simplest, most accessible level the ambiguity concerns his attitude toward the emancipatory energies of art, and here the essay "Work of Art in the Age of Mechanical Reproduction" is the most obviously troubled text.

The figure of Baudelaire through whom, as his alter ego, he reads Paris, enables him to invoke redemption of beauty, tradition, and community in failure. The moment of auratic perception will be lost, but its meaning has been recognized and thereby redeemed. This is the more complex and more disturbing dimension of Benjamin's ambiguity. His juxtaposition of Marxist assertions and messianic intimations, of loss and redemption of aura, tradition, beauty, community and of a new progressive collectivity supported by the destruction of aura, of unstilled desire creatively connecting and of isolating barren satiation is only a symptom. One of his more circumspect critics warns of appropriating this or that Benjamin for this or that (ideological) position by pointing to his "radical" cultivation of an ambivalence "which makes of his work so explosive a mixture, eluding even the most sophisticated attempts at synthesis."[173] But in trying to understand Benjamin's cultural position and significance one has to go beyond the statement of ambiguity or ambivalence and see how they are firmly anchored in his anticipation of redemption or, in the last text, the "Theses on the Philosophy of History," in his despair of it.

Benjamin came back to his reflections on Kafka in connection with Brod's Kafka biography. The proposed essay was not written, but it is contained partly in a long letter to Scholem on June 12, 1938.[174] He quickly passes from his harsh critique of Brod's approach, in which he finds too much psychological familiarity preventing him from getting to the "basic aspects of Kafka's existence," to his own thoughts on them. One of his criticisms, however, is important for his new Kafka image: Kafka—and Brod did not deal with this fact—"was evidently not willing to be responsible to posterity for a work the greatness of which he was well aware of."[175]

The two extreme foci of Kafka's work are for Benjamin the experience of mystical tradition and the experience of the modern city dweller, which he connects with modern science.[176] Both aspects of his work interconnect: "What is actually and in every literal sense wildly incredible in Kafka is that this most recent world of experience was conveyed to him precisely by this mystical tradition." There had to be an appeal to the forces of this tradition if Kafka was to be confronted with his modern reality, which is an advanced technological warfare. Kafka's world, "frequently of such playfulness and interlaced with angels," is a world uniquely complementary to his modern era which has introduced the mass destruction of men, and in that, it is closely related to Klee's.

> His gestures of terror are given scope by the marvelous *margin* which the catastrophe will not grant us. But his experience was based solely on the tradition to which Kafka surrendered; there was no far-sightedness or "prophetic vision." Kafka listened to tradition, and he who listens hard does not hear.[177]

The connection with Klee is highly important here. Benjamin had bought Klee's watercolor *Angelus Novus* in 1921,[178] and though he later bought another of Klee's paintings, the *Angelus* was his most treasured possession, a concrete and allegorical focus, for twenty years, of his meditations and reflections on his troubled intellectual existence; certainly a picture that returned his gaze without ever satiating him. The description of the Kafka figure with his large gestures of terror—"margin" does not fully translate the German *Spielraum,* literally the protected space in which a play can unfold— is the description of the Klee painting, as is the figure of the angel of history in "Theses on the Philosophy of History." The tradition is sick to death; only indistinct sounds reach the listener who has to strain to hear. The consistency of truth has been lost, and it was, writes Benjamin, Kafka's real genius that he sacrificed truth for the sake of clinging to the "transmissibility" of the tradition in his parables, that is, to its "haggadic element" which then does not submit easily to doctrine or Halakah. It is this attitude that makes him profoundly vulnerable, and Benjamin regrets the apologetic character of the earlier Kafka essay which had not accounted for the fact that "to do justice to the figure of Kafka in its purity and its peculiar beauty one must never lose sight of one thing: it is the purity and beauty of a failure."[179]

In his answer of November 1938 Scholem sensibly qualified Benjamin's thought-image of failure which is indeed based on the concrete image of Klee's *Angelus Novus.* There is no need, he writes, to be so shattered and amazed by this failure as it is inherent to Kafka's intentions as a writer: he articulated what he wanted to say, he did what he wanted to do, namely, comment on the tradition. Why, then, speak of failure?[180] Because, for Benjamin, experiencing the loss of the consistency of truth could only be borne as the beauty of failure. In 1940 when the world had never looked darker to him, he returned to the angel's large gestures of terror.

> A Klee painting named "Angelus Novus" shows an angel looking as though he is about to move away from something he is fixedly contemplating. His eyes are staring, his mouth is open, his wings are spread. This is how one pictures the angel of history. His face is turned toward the past. Where we perceive chains of events, he sees one single catastrophe which keeps piling wreckage upon wreckage and hurls it in front of his feet. The angel would like to stay, awaken the dead and make whole what has been smashed. But a storm is blowing from Paradise; it has got caught in his wings with such violence that the angel can no longer close them. This storm irresistibly propels him into the future to which his back is turned, while the pile of debris before him grows skyward. This storm is what we call progress.

The ninth of the "Theses on the Philosophy of History"[181] is the center around which the other seventeen theses are loosely arranged. The angel is a powerful allegory for that sadness of empathy with which, as thesis seven states, historical materialism has broken. It may very well have done so, but Benjamin has not. The historical materialist in thesis seven may successfully "brush history against the grain" in the effort of gaining access to the genuine historical images, which have been suppressed by the victorious; after all, thesis seven bears a Brechtian motto. But Benjamin is much more eloquent in his empathy with other historians' despair over grasping and holding that genuine image while it flares up for a brief moment. If we really look at this angel of history we see that he, unseeing, listening intently for the message he carries, is not a historical materialist. However, if we look at the historical materialist as he is described in thesis seventeen, we recognize the influence of the angel:

> Thinking involves not only the flow of thoughts, but their arrest as well. Where thinking suddenly stops in a configuration pregnant with tensions, it gives that configuration a shock, by which it crystallizes into a monad. A historical materialist approaches a historical subject only where he encounters it as a monad. In this structure he recognizes the sign of a Messianic cessation of happening, or, put differently, a revolutionary chance in the fight for the repressed past.

The historian's concern then is not the past of the oppressed, but the repressed past *(die unterdrückte Vergangenheit)*; its contemplation will be rewarded with the shock of profane illumination which will reveal the past in its totality so that he can grasp it—it "crystallizes into a monad"—if only for a moment. When he argued with Brecht over the contemporary relevance of Kafka's work in the midthirties and the discussion turned to the story "The Next Village" which Brecht liked because of its anti-individualist concept of uninterrupted, collectively extensive lived time, Benjamin countered with his own interpretation which stressed remembrance as "the true measure of life." Remembrance needs the interruption of lived time, the "Messianic cessation of happening"; it singles out the moments in which (the individual) life is revealed as meaningful. Retrospectively, remembrance

> traverses life with the speed of lightning. As quickly as one turns back a few pages, it has gone back from the next village to the point where the rider decided to take off. He whose life has turned into writing, like old people's, likes to read this writing only backward. Only so does he meet himself, and only so—in flight from the present—can his life be understood.[182]

The angel of history is the allegorical focus for the historian who reflects, above all, on his position in a profoundly threatened cultural tradition. Appendix A to the "Theses" distinguishes "historicism," that is, for Benjamin, linear historiography, diachronic and causal, from the kind of historiography to which he referred as "materialist" in the "Theses." Its practitioner "stops telling the sequence of events like the beads of a rosary. Instead, he grasps the constellation which his own era has formed with a definite earlier one. Thus he establishes a conception of the present as the "time of the now" [*Jetztzeit*], which is shot through with chips of Messianic time.

These "chips of Messianic time" make possible the historian's "flight from the present" leading to revelation. He will be able to grasp and articulate connections in a constellation which is meaningful. History and language are meaningful by virtue of their having been created, and redemption of their meaning is the most important challenge to the historian and critic and the basis of his authority.

There is a curious surface similarity between Benjamin's thought-image of the "chips of Messianic time" *(Splitter)* and a passage in a letter written from the trenches by Franz Rosenzweig in February 1917 which Benjamin might have read in the 1935 edition of his letters.[183] Rosenzweig speaks of " 'sparks' *(Funken)* of a *Messianic* 'today' " scattered through normal "today" in the context of discussing two kinds of Zionism; and he locates the conflict central to contemporary Jewry in the "equation between the today that only intends to be a bridge to tomorrow and the other today which is the springboard to eternity. . . . No day has written on its forehead whether it is this or that today. 'One can never tell.' By no means of small importance. They help us continue with life in time."

The contrast between the meaning and function of messianic intermittence in each case echoes that between Benjamin's language *for* revelation and Rosenzweig's language *as* revelation.[184] For Benjamin the "chips of Messianic time" disrupt today and the possibility of infinite hope prepares for such redeeming rupture: it might *happen* any day. For Rosenzweig " 'sparks' of a *Messianic* 'today' " connect one day as a unit of lived time with the other *and* with eternity: it *might* happen any day; one cannot tell but has to live and live well with this uncertainty. Benjamin could not bear the present as such uncertainty, that is, the possibility of a continued unfulfilled, unredeemed search for meaning.[185] His desire to be the first and only true critic of German literature, to remake, in an act of remembrance as second creation, the meaning of a German cultural-literary tradition had its source in this anxiety.

FIVE

The Magic Spaces of Terror

Ernst Jünger and the Aesthetics
of Authenticity

I.

For most of his long writing career Ernst Jünger has successfully maintained
the image of the controversial, significant outsider. Actually, since the late
twenties when books about the Great War became popular he has had loyal
middle-class reading audiences,[1] sharing them, to a degree, with Thomas
Mann. There have been recent prestigious prizes, like the Frankfurt Goethe
Prize; there is the curious fact of his current popularity, shared with Heidegger and Nietzsche, among French intellectuals. There is also his astonishingly productive longevity: in 1985 he published, at the age of ninety,
his first and well-received detective novel[2] set in the late nineteenth-century
Paris *demimonde* and constructed on the reliable aesthetic-didactic pattern
Jünger has used for all his texts: in this case the aesthetic interest of the crime
and the moral message revealed with reconstruction and resolution, the
exposing of a decadent society. There has been no change, in almost seven
decades, in Jünger's emphasis on the ethics of construction: he has been
celebrating the unredeemed state of the world because fictions as acts of
construction can authoritatively assume the promise of redemption and
define its meaning. The most detailed, sophisticated, centrally uncritical
study of Jünger's early works which are highly important to all his subsequent texts has the promising title *Die Ästhetik des Schreckens* (The aesthetics of terror).[3] But its author, Bohrer, privileges the aesthetic dimension to
the point where he feels justified to claim a development for Jünger, at least in
"human" (psychological) terms,[4] which did not take place. The thesis of
Bohrer's study is the socially and politically subversive, "deconstructing"
power and effect of Jünger's aesthetic constructs, which requires stressing
Jünger's importance as a significantly contemporary writer,[5] that is, changing
and developing in accordance with and in response to German sociopolitical
developments. Such changes would become noticeable with the 1939 *Auf den
Marmorklippen (On the Marble Cliffs)* and emerge fully after the collapse of
the Reich in 1945. But the nature of his work during the twenties and thirties,

including the *Marble Cliffs*, contradicts sharply notions of substantial change and significant contemporaneity, that is, of sociopsychological maturation. And so does, if not that clearly, his production after World War II.

The source of Jünger's writing is remembrance, as it is for many of the radically antibourgeois intellectuals caught in the particularly distinct and bitter generational conflict—Benjamin, for instance. Both share the inability to let go of the personally significant moment and are then tempted to present it in terms of cultural meaning. There are certain recognizable aesthetic variations in the sequence of texts on the war experience, starting with the 1920 *In Stahlgewittern (Storms of Steel)*,[6] but the core remains the same: the appeal to the significance and authenticity of his experience in the archetypical primordial landscape of trench warfare which he likened to Africa, the "incomparable school of war."[7] He would always feel profoundly obliged to this school, not because he had learned to survive its horrors, hardened and strengthened, but because he was taught to look at the horrors from the outside as into magic spaces,[8] which reaffirmed his sense of a unique and uniquely meaningful self untouched by the raging forces of the *Materialschlachten* (material warfare) of the first modern technological war.

Jünger joined the army in 1914 at the age of nineteen after a very short episode in the Foreign Legion[9] from which his rather strict and reserved father had competently rescued him. He was eighteen when he ran away from his upper-middle-class home, but all his (literary) life he has insisted that he had immersed himself totally in his great adventure at the age of sixteen, to better celebrate the heroic spontaneity and vulnerability of youth. The concept and image of generational conflict was to remain important to him: he presented himself explicitly as the spokesman of the "glorious youth" of the fatherland threatened by the Weimar *System* when he was almost forty. His first experiences at the front were clinically traumatic; he ran away in shock. It is this anti-act and anti-decision of running away from the responsibility of a (completely inexperienced) young officer in charge of men much older and much more experienced than he which has formed his views, that is, his literary constructs of social reality. They stress the significant act and decision, the natural order, which supports elites and hierarchies, as stable as it is distinct with an allegorical gloss. After repeated attempts to describe, in a mixture of memoir and diary, the great battles of the war[10] he presented their deeper meaning in the 1929 *Das abenteuerliche Herz* (The adventurous heart), an essayistic diary in which he created the self as authentic *persona* through images pregnant with meaning. The archetypical "fiery dream-landscapes of war" are here reentered and their lasting validity for the conscious state of modern urban life is stressed: "We move across glassy floors and continuously dreams ascend toward us, embracing our cities like stony islands, penetrating into their coldest districts. Nothing is real and yet everything is the expression of reality."[11] Dreams, we are told again and again, reach deep; they touch the essences. All his protagonists are variations on the self in the role of observer, diarist, and historian, priding themselves on their skills in tracing, tracking down the secret meaning, the reality behind, underneath, beyond: "It is my secret pride that I ferreted out, behind the mathematics of the battles, the magnificent dream into which life plunged when light had become too boring.[12]

All these dreams are acts of remembrance focused on the remembered decisive act committed at the right, the significant moment. In Benjamin's texts the act of remembrance, notwithstanding the narrator's rupturing gaze, tends to absorb the remembered act, event, or object in a motion which mimics the flow of time but which is also balanced in the elusive appealing transtemporality of the text. Jünger, with his mesmerized staring at the remembered act as the decisive therefore significant moment, freezes the flow of time and experience. This is the source of the often noticed stasis of his texts, the curiously even, lacquered, or glassy surface of narration, which moves from one set of images to the next following the many sententious signposts of meaning.[13] There is one important change clearly recognizable in the 1939 *Auf den Marmorklippen:* the observer who remembers does so as a nonparticipant, as a viewer of the acts of others. But it is still a series of disconnected, uniquely significant acts even if, as is the case with texts written after World War II, the observer is a historian who is in a position to view the past "directly" with a science-fiction-like instrument.[14] Remembered, the unique perfection and meaning of the act is left intact. The historian as observer collects those acts and presents them to the reader as the precious moments of unviolated significance.

Already in the texts of the early twenties the past is always the observer's who has appropriated it in the fascinated fixed stare which he himself remembers as the significant moment of observation.[15] In the war diaries this fixed stare on the terrible is really the substance of the self-conscious construct of experience. Beginning with the 1929 *Das abenteuerliche Herz* the act of viewing merges with the act of remembering, and the self is placed not only outside the event (if not the significant act) but also outside the viewing of the event. The self, then, becomes more and more clearly the consciousness viewing a (the) consciousness in the act of viewing. The interesting aspect of such increasing artificialization or emphasis on the constructedness of perspective for our context is that it does not dissolve the significant moment or subvert the decisive act but rather affirms moment and act. The writer's obvious preoccupation with the meaning and significance of the terrible in the texts of the twenties and thirties cannot simply be abstracted into the category of the aesthetic, which is then assigned a specific sociopsychological energy entirely removed from the writer's concrete experience in a concrete social context.[16]

Jünger's identity was shaped irreversibly in extreme situations which temporarily distorted or, in Jünger's view, transcended normal experience of space and time. The position of the officer as omnipotent feudal lord was stamped on the man-child as rigid pose; appeals to *Haltung,* the deportment worthy of a true man, with associations of unyielding (self-)righteous strength, are central to all his texts. He was never to question or reflect critically the fantastically literal wartime connection between a command given and the threat of death, the terrible unmediatedness of power. The preposterous school of war had done him incomparable psychological damage. Its impact on his writing is of great interest to the historian of the period as it points out so clearly the problems of this generation of young Germans who resisted the hated *System* of Weimar, retreating to the illusionary community of *Frontgeist,* the blood fraternities of the trenches. Jünger's texts in the twenties made much of this community, even if he did not, in most of them, resolve the conflict with the individual.

It seems curious that evocations of *Frontgeist* in the trenches could have been so effective given the reality of a rather rigid hierarchy supported by privilege which Jünger describes quite clearly. But his readers, by the mid-twenties, were mostly former officers[17] or were identified with this *Haltung.* His striking inability to consider the vulnerability and fragmentariness of human life was supported by the privilege of survival—there are several incidents where "his" men take great risks and pay with their lives to get him out of danger—and reaffirmed by the adolescent's belief that some (strong) individuals' lives were (much) more valuable than others' and that valuable lives were uniquely meaningful. No death relating to such a life, therefore, could be accidental or meaningless. Death is presented in terms of the survivor as the great life-enhancing force[18] and, more abstracted and stylized in the texts written after World War II, as "Lord of the world" and "the ultimate reality."[19]

The heroic whole survivors of World War I were of course hugely outnumbered by the dead and mutilated—a fact that had to be taken into account by appeals to the memory of the war experience as source of energy for future heroic acts in the interest of a time-transcending glory of the fatherland. Jünger became more aware of it and he made certain telling revisions during the twenties and early thirties for the different editions of *In Stahlgewittern.*[20] The original version of 1920 ends with the description of his reaction to the award of the *Pour le merite* in 1918, an extraordinarily high decoration for a young officer. He is in hospital with wounds which, though serious, did not mutilate or leave other permanent damage. (All his wounds are lovingly described throughout the text, whereas the most gruesome mutilations suffered by his men are dealt with matter-of-factly.) Counting all the wounds he received, he comments:

In the course of this war where the attacks had been concentrated on space rather than individual men [he is referring to modern material warfare, the *Materialschlacht*] I had nevertheless managed to have eleven of those shots directed at me personally. Therefore I rightfully attached the "Golden Decoration for Wounds Received in Battle" which I had recently been awarded to my uniform. This decoration is, in my eyes, of equal value to the cross of blue rays of the Pour le merite, the highest German decoration.[21]

The 1929 English translation is instructively different here. There still is the counting of wounds, but he leads up to it with a passage about "that internationality of the heart that every decent man and educated soldier ought to uphold," and among the "decent men" he can now count his own batman, who had shown extraordinary loyalty to him, following him to the hospital.[22] Significantly, he removed the statement about the unique fated meaning of his wounds. But on the whole his concept of material warfare remained profoundly anachronistic. His declared fascination with the technological aspects of the war does not prevent him from reaffirming the difference, in value, of human life: the batman's loyalty serves to underscore the value of the young officer's life as does the death of another common soldier when carrying him to safety.

This view of the war and of his role in it was largely that of the German officer caste, but Jünger brought to it a perspective which produced stunningly literal images of chaos and order, the elite and the masses, trenchscape and inviolate inner space, whole and broken bodies, elemental and technological forces. It is the directness of these images, mistaken for the authenticity of the narrator's experience, which reinforced the peculiar dangerous politico-religious gnostic nationalism of many of Jünger's contemporaries, for instance, the Rathenau assassin Techow. In this context the conclusion of the "diary" in the English translation is instructive:

> And so, strange as it may sound, I learned from this very four years' schooling in force and in all the fantastic extravagance of material warfare that life has no depth of meaning except where it is pledged for an ideal and that there are ideals in comparison with which the life of an individual and even of a people has not weight. And though the aim for which I fought as an individual, as an atom in the whole body of the army, was not to be achieved, though material force cast us, apparently to the earth, yet we learned once and for all to stand for a cause and if necessary to fall as befitted men.
>
> Hardened as scarcely another generation ever was in fire and flame, we could go into life as though from the anvil; into friendship, love, politics, professions, into all that destiny had in store. It is not every generation that is so favored.[23]

Jünger goes on to reassure his British audience that the *Reichswehr* (truncated postwar army) battles are over. Given the cultural importance of the German army before the war and of its dispersion after the war, this seems a message of some significance. Jünger, because of his high decoration, had been taken over by the *Reichswehr*, and he had, after serving several years avoiding all involvement with the Free Corps, resigned in 1923 in order to concentrate on his literary career and his zoological studies. He had not shared, then, the feeling of total impotence experienced by the majority of officers when their war and their army was lost and their feudal identity was torn off with their epaulettes by rebelling soldiers who pushed them from the

Middle Ages into the twentieth century. In hindsight the severity of their predicament seems as impressive as the inadequacy of their reactions, and both contribute to their being attracted to Jünger's texts in the twenties and early thirties. And Jünger does not end with this brief evocation of possible peaceful coexistence but with an opaque yet unmistakable threat. He sees in the dim light of the future

> the tumult of fresh battles [and] we—by this I mean the youth of this land who are capable of enthusiasm for an ideal—will not shrink from them.

> We stand in memory of the dead who are holy to us, and we believe ourselves entrusted with the true and spiritual welfare of our people. We stand for what will be and what has been. Though force without and barbarity within conglomerate in somber clouds, yet so long as the blade of a sword will strike a spark in the night may it be said: Germany lives and Germany will never go under![24]

Much of this rhetorical swell can be attributed to the sentiments of closure, but it does bear closer inspection. There are the images of natural and archaic cultural force. There is a total affirmation of the past which, in rational terms, means denial of important aspects of Germany's sociopolitical responsibilities. There is the time-transcending millennial vista in accord with the concept of a Third Imperium, but also the reference to "barbaric" forces within as well as the threatening powers on the outside. This is, in short, a collection of images and associations which conjures up much of the national sentiment responsible for the success of the extreme right, and it does so in terms and in a context which reveals its source and the power of its self-deception.

In his introduction to the translation the British writer Ralph Hale Mottram, author of the antiwar trilogy *The Spanish Farm 1914–1918* (1924–26), stresses the authenticity of the diary, especially the loyalty and dedication of the young fighter for whom he expresses respect. But he also points out the man-child's delight in physical prowess, his need to affirm his (German) manhood. The English reader, he was sure, would not be provoked by this adolescent boastful attitude as he knows the outcome—the inevitably lost war:

> He [Jünger] was nearly as good a specimen as ever worshipped Mars, and to what did he come?—to that inescapable doom that brings to meet violence precisely such resistance as shall cancel and annul it. On this point the strength and the finality of the testimony cannot be missed. It is to hope the book will be widely read.[25]

But while it is not very useful to speak, from the outside, of Germany's defeat in these terms, it is misleading to neglect that they had neither been perceived that way by many Germans, nor had they been accepted. The violence of the first "authentic" version of 1920, amended with nationalist prophecies and exhortations in the 1924 edition,[26] which then appeared, too, in the English translation, is both unselfconscious and deliberately shaped by the writer's desire to present an irresistible ideal of German manhood. Culturally defined, this ideal is also very much personal. The more pragmatic 1924 revision was motivated by his decision to embark on a literary career and his intention to focus on a specific audience which at this time was militaristic in traditional terms and culturally conservative. The third edition from 1934, published by the Nationalsocialist Hanseatische Verlagsanstalt, went back to the first edition, presumably because the hopes for a glorious German future expressed pedagogically in the second version had now been fulfilled. (Goebbels had read the second version and recorded in his diary in 1926 that he found it "a brilliant, highly significant book.")[27] But by that time Jünger had withdrawn from cultural politics and politicized culture into the eclectic cultural stylizations of the self in the different versions of the *Aben-teuerliches Herz*. The introduction to the 1934 edition is remarkably bland.

Mottram did not, as he thought, respond to the direct, authentic record-ing of a young German officer's war experience—Jünger had never written such a record. But what Mottram read had also been self-consciously re-structured: first, in the midtwenties, for a German nationalist militarist audience and then, in the late twenties, for an English audience. And he seems to have missed, if not the attempts at rationalizing in fairly general terms the experience of a disastrous defeat, then the implications of the frequent juxtapositions between the "cold light of reason" and the deeper, warmer wisdom of the blood,[28] and of references to the mystical presence of the dead and their claims to fresh blood[29]—claims forcefully presented in Hitler's political speeches.

Amended and unamended, the classic war diary was at first slow to find larger audiences,[30] and the additions of correct militaristic right-wing senti-ments are not really instructive. What is instructive is the ongoing process of cultural self-stylization in Jünger's texts written during the twenties. He had become associated with appreciating the technological aspects of modern warfare, the fearsome novelty of the *Materialschlacht*. But his double fas-cination with the modern (technological) and archaic (organic) dimensions of warfare does not result in a balance of ambivalence: the deeper, wider, infinite, magical wisdom of death, blood, and dreams penetrates all experi-ence including the seemingly made to order nationalist sentiments.[31]

2.

In the second half of the twenties Jünger becomes increasingly preoccupied with the *Unbehaustheit* (homelessness) of German youth with which he, no longer all that young, identifies. Lost and vulnerable, this youth has to seek protection under the roofs built by their parents before the war, be it for shelter, profession, politics, or morals. They do not so much remember that they had been bored to death before the outbreak of the Great War as that the parents' generation was to be held accountable for the defeat. The task of this young generation is to reinterpret the defeat into victory on a higher level. Jünger sees "a secret mathematics of the last war" reflected in the lost position of German youth: "he who has lost the most seems to have gained the most. All men and all things in this period are pushing toward a magic point zero. To pass it means to be exposed to the flame of a new life; to have passed it means to be part of the flame."[32]

Das abenteuerliche Herz contains many passages like this: they work with suggestive images and associations rather than discursive cultural analysis. Jünger has been criticized by professional readers for his nihilistic glorification of war, especially after World War II,[33] but rarely for his stylized mysticism and radical irrationalism.[34] The first sentence of his 1930 essay "Die totale Mobilmachung" (Total mobilization) states bluntly that "the heroic spirit resists seeking the image of war in a battle that can be determined by human action."[35] The heroic spirit, then, had been seeking his images of war in the grandiose and typical phenomena of primordial nature: thunderstorms, hurricanes, tidal waves, earthquakes, volcanic eruptions. True, the extreme political right used his images, but this does not make Jünger a protofascist. He sought cultural meaning in the experience of material warfare, and not so unexpectedly it turned out to be metaphysical. His political interests were as vague as his military knowledge was sketchy. But he had been confirmed a hero by the highest authority in the land, and he never stopped drawing on the personal fated authenticity of his experience as the source for his cultural authority, beginning with the 1920 edition of *In Stahlgewittern* where the narrating voice seems stately and weighty beyond the author's years. Concrete political events were obscured for him by the same mysterious veil which threw into sharper relief his own heroic position—even more so after, as he saw it, the fated, inevitable ascendancy of Hitler:

> When I close my eyes I sometimes see a dark landscape with stones, cliffs, mountains at the brink of infinity. In the background, on the shore of a black ocean, I recognize myself, a tiny figure, as if drawn with a piece of chalk. This is my outpost, right next to nothingness—down there at the abyss I am fighting for myself.[36]

This is how he presents himself in the autobiographical notes written during World War II, *Strahlungen* (Radiation). This catastrophe, too, had served to support his entelechy, his lonely heroic fight for meaning.

Singled out by fate, fate had come to him in the shape of war. Under the mysterious force of the exploding shell, a terror transcending human experience, his men crouch, he stands upright, observing. He does not seek credit for his cool courageous behavior, because his *Haltung* comes, like the explosions tearing the bodies of others apart, from the unimaginable beyond. The materials of material warfare are made by evil gods who are totally admirable, because they protect his wholeness, his heraldic self magically erect in the magic spaces of terror. The introduction added to the 1924 revision of *In Stahlgewittern* draws the reader's attention specifically to the magic quality of terror: "As time went on, it grew more and more dangerous to lift a corner of the veil that fell like a magic hood over the specter that was at once so near and so fatally far off." And it is life itself, heightened by the deadly terror of trench warfare, that can be heard "speaking out of the confidence of its savage and visionary heart." His men, of course, cannot really appreciate the true splendor of the terror, yet their leader knows intuitively that their true yearnings go beyond mere peace: "Time only strengthened my conviction that it was a good and strenuous life, and that the war, for all its destructiveness, was an incomparable schooling of the heart."[37]

In addition to the second revised edition of *In Stahlgewittern* (1924) Jünger's publisher Mittler, specializing in texts of military interest, brought out *Das Wäldchen 125 (Copse 125)* in 1925. Jünger had radically restructured his material by concentrating on the battles of the summer of 1918 and by emphasizing the diary form and thus the authenticity of the experience. The changes in the descriptions of battles are substantial and clearly meant to stress energizing ideals in the service of the war effort. This is stated in the introduction to the first 1925 edition which was cut in the 1935 second revised edition but retained in the 1930 English translation. These ideals, echoing the key concepts of cultural conservatism, are linked with the "immortal deeds" of the dead which provide an "eternal fount of strength" for him and his generation, which is one of heroes. The war naturally dwarfed the individual; dying for smaller and smaller scraps of land is absolutely justified and totally meaningful, for "the shaping of a world still hidden in the future" was bound up with them.[38] *Copse 125* focuses on the spiritual dimensions of war: material warfare is "not a material matter."[39] The humblest soldier's sacrifice of self for the fatherland is of historic importance which only the future will reveal.

The 1925 text is interspersed with reflective passages on the necessity of being prepared for war.[40] Such preparedness calls for technological modernization but above all for *Kampfmoral* or *Kampfelan*. Battle is a phenomenon on the level not of a material process but of the "highest decision."[41] There are frequent references to the distinction between mere dying (*sterben*) and being killed in action *(fallen)*.[42] Invoking a noninstrumental *(zweckfreier)*[43] heroism he calls for a nationalist war propaganda, a national art including film in the "teutonic style."[44] Like Rathenau, he both argues against the "soulless and numerical notion of material superiority" and is convinced of the decisive importance of the machine in battle. At the same time his ambivalence toward the machine, especially the plane, is unbalanced toward a celebration of its magical properties to which the young heroic pilots whom he particularly admires respond naturally: flying a plane is an act of magically taming natural forces. In the later revised version he kept a passage which describes a group of young pilots who still have in their blood the lighthearted century-old spirit of cavalry, their daring acts a fiery marriage of the spirit of the old knighthood and the cold precision of modern forms of labor.[45]

It is this juxtaposition and magical symbiosis which intrigues him and which he elaborates in all his later texts. In *Abenteuerliches Herz* he describes the "lonely and darkly heroic image" of a machine at work, moving like a panther, "soporific and terribly exciting at the same time," provoking the "very modern feeling" of unappeasable rage which in its dangerous games with matter will—it is hoped—destroy bourgeois values. This observation leads him into a long passage about pilots whose company he has always been seeking because among them he has found the highest measure of race possible in our time, a higher species of workers and soldiers *(ein gesteigertes Arbeiter- und Soldatentum)* minted in good metal, with a well functioning intellect and yet not without a certain aristocratic generosity and lightness of being. These pilots are not so much admirable because of their nerves of steel but because of their peculiar sensibility in their symbiosis with the machine drawing on a mysterious "metaphysical power." It is this sensibility which signifies the superior health and resilience of this elite bearing up magnificently under pressures which will break the common life—here he refers to historical materialism and social Darwinism.[46]

Jünger used some of the properties assigned here and in *Copse 125* to the heroic fighter pilots for his 1932 *Der Arbeiter* (The worker), the stylized compactly abstract figure of the worker, metaphysical and soldierly, straight out of the war diaries. This treatise did not, of course, deal in any empirical fashion with the problem of nationalism and the workers, Goebbel's concern,[47] but continued Jünger's familiar search for meaning in the experience of war and his finding the higher meaning of war in all cultural phenomena if subjected to his radically conservative perspective. The changes have to do with emphasis. In the 1925 edition of *Copse 125* he is occasionally naively imitative of the bruitism and vulgar vitalism of Italian futurism and fascism: "nothing pleases me more than seeing the bullets of a machine-gun plastering the target in front of me," he claims, and he attacks pacifism as being untrue to life because it cannot understand the life-enhancing intoxicating power of victory even in death.[48] In the later version the emphasis is more consistently on the mysterious power of death itself revealed in images of cavelike openings, of the motion of wind and time, in shadowy memories and dreams within dreams.[49] But though the crudely circular arguments for Germany's naturally fated ascendancy[50] and threats to the people responsible for her defeat are cut in the second version, a general cultural nationalism remained a strong undercurrent in this as in all his texts: the survivors are the truly deserving, the metaphysically fittest, the unquestioned elite.

3.

While this change in emphasis can be traced quite clearly in the revisions of texts made in the late twenties and early thirties when Jünger was in the process of withdrawing from the lowlands of an extremely difficult and conflicted sociopolitical reality to the elevated vantage point of higher, more essential meaning, there was a period of journalistic activity between 1925 and 1928 when he was involved directly with militarist interests. Some of his structural decisions regarding his material can be clearly linked with the groups and journals for which he was writing, but certain narrative preoccupations had developed from earlier texts. To begin with, the 1925 *Feuer und Blut* (Fire and blood), published not by Mittler but by the more aggressively nationalist Stahlhelm Verlag, narrows the focus on one offensive in March of 1918 between Arras and La Fere. The intention is to provide a "microscopic cross section" through a "great" battle and thus even fuller access to "the meaning of our time," namely, "eine grosse gemeinsame Kampffront" (a great common shared battlefront). This text more than any other—with the exception of the journalistic pieces written during these three years—diffuses the dichotomy between the unique heroic individual and the large anonymous group which underlies all of Jünger's texts. Here individual and folk merge euphorically in the great flow of becoming and decline. Fate is embodied in these grand natural cycles, and war is now justified by invoking the creative powers of earth itself which can be directed, even controlled, by the heroic folk.

As this particular emphasis on linkage between fate, the creative powers of the earth, and the heroic folk was relatively short-lived in Jünger's work, it would not merit attention in our context were it not for the fact that it stimulated a remarkable narrative emphasis on the battle as fantastically effective theater, a grand performance of supernature. This focus on the act of looking itself as meaningful and fully revealing is new and was to become important for all of Jünger's later texts. Curiously, it is in this context of explicit desire for the submersion of the individual in the heroic folk that he uses so clearly the distancing narrative strategy of self-conscious looking. It seems that the authenticity of experience supported by remembrance, in detail, of the "great" battle is now seen as enhanced rather than diminished by clearly recognizable staging.

Jünger's troop has been hit by a powerful shell while resting in a large shell-hole. The choice of the resting place has been especially unfortunate also because they are carrying a large quantity of machine gun ammunition. He himself watches the disaster from a smaller crater at the edge of the big one. Here is the description used in the 1920 and 1924 editions and the English translation of *In Stahlgewittern:*

> I picked myself up half-unconscious. The machine-gun ammunition in the large shell-hole, set alight by the explosion was burning with an intense pink glow. It illumined the rising fumes of the shellburst, in which there writhed a

heap of black bodies and the shadowy forms of the survivors, who were rushing from the scene in all directions. At the same time rose a multitudinous tumult of pain and cries for help.

I will make no secret of it that after a moment's blank horror I took to my heels like the rest and ran aimlessly into the night. It was not till I had fallen head over heels into a small shell-hole that I understood what had happened. Only to see and hear no more! Only to get away, far away, and creep into a hole! And yet the other voice was heard: "You are the company commander, man!"[51]

It is instructive that Jünger did not introduce the theatrical imagery he had used in the 1925 *Feuer und Blut* into the revisions of *In Stahlgewittern* for the translation into English. The reason could be that this version attempts to stress the good relationship between the young lieutenant and his men, that is, his sensitivity to their needs.[52] These images were added to the 1934 edition of *In Stahlgewittern* and retained, in a more stylized, more distancing form, in the last revisions made for the editions of the collected works in the sixties.

Feuer und Blut does not, as do the earlier texts, merely imply the arenalike setting of the big shell-hole; it brings it out fully. The reader is carefully moved toward the observation of the climactic performance by being made to look first at troop movements in preparation for the expected battle as grandiose sinister spectacle. He is made aware of great restlessness, the roar of motors, wheels, hooves, and shown the "triumphal parade of a deadly will in which is revealed the terrible depth of power," silent and irresistible, suggesting "only *one* motion and *one* will."[53] The shell-burst itself is observed by the narrator from the little "niche" or "alcove" above the large yawning hole into which he is looking "as if into a horrible arena." The reader participates in the spectacle through its narrated effect on the observer; the dreamlike, ghostlike brightness which paralyzes his will, the image that is etched into his brain: "death, crouching on the shell, has flung himself into the midst of life." Filled, along its walls, with fleeing shadows, and, at its bottom, with a dark revolving mass of the badly wounded and dying, the crater is a Dantean inferno. Bodies writhe like reptiles in a boiling lake lit up magically by the piercing supranatural pink light of the burning machine-gun ammunition. There is an eternity of two seconds before the onset of the "terrible many-voiced scream of the wounded" finally realizing what has happened, and it is this inhuman, superhuman "scream from the abyss" that makes him run. When he turns back, it is not because of his responsibility—the role of the individual (the officer) is consistently diffused in *Feuer und Blut*—but because of the elemental power of the scream likened to that of fire: "das Geschrei flackert höher und eindringlicher auf."[54] The terror is entirely visual.

The 1934 version of *In Stahlgewittern* with its much shorter description of the shelling incident stresses clearly the theatrical setting: the narrator looks into the huge magically lit crater as if from a "balcony," mesmerized by the fleeing shadows, writhing bodies, and terrible screams. There is no reference to Dante. The crater as huge, smoking, red-hot kettle speaks for itself as a "hellish dream image" tearing open, for a second, "the utmost abyss of pain," which becomes, in the last revision, "the utmost abyss of terror."[55]

The imagery in *Feuer und Blut* associating "dark blood" with the instinctive forces of the earth and "bright fire" with the controlling will[56] has its source in an irrationalism more radical than can be found in any other Jünger text. The narrative emphasis on *looking* at the grandiose spectacle of man-made *Materialschlacht* does have a distancing effect, but it is also motivated by the attempt to draw the reader closer to the observer of terrible destruction and thereby to the incomparable natural grandeur condensed in the most magnificently frightening elemental force, fire. Theatrical imagery will be an important device in later texts, but it will exclude the reader. When, in reaction to the ascendancy of the National Socialist faction on the right, Jünger returned from his excursion into the metaphysics of community to the metaphysics of the heroic individual, which he was never to leave again, he was intent on presenting himself as the great outsider who had charted, but never succumbed to, the magic and the lure of the abyss of pain and terror. Looking and observing have become acts of distancing; the narrator as observer is shown in a position of ultimate rigid *Haltung*[57] when staring at the magic terror of the *Materialschlacht,* arrested in a distance from the observed as well as the self.

Emphasis on staring, *Starren,* as magically frozen fascinated attention, is found in the revisions after 1934 and understood by critical readers to signify the cold remoteness of the narrator in the pose of the superwarrior as the nihilistic connoisseur of terror. However, these passages can also be read differently,[58] and it is mainly in the diaries of World War II, collected in *Strahlungen,* that one encounters the most offensive examples of the *poseur.* Even here the issue is not really the cold rapture of the connoisseur of destruction: Jünger on the roof of the Hotel Raphael in 1944 Paris, toasting, with a glass of Burgundy, the grandiose darkly beautiful spectacle of a British air raid on the city, which he presumably loved deeply and which he had come to know intimately as an officer in the German occupational forces. He does not forget to mention that a perfect strawberry floats in the glowing liquid red of the wine while the same glorious color—of life in a higher sense, to be sure—flows over sky and buildings.[59] But he was not so much gloating over the sinister beauty of destruction, as hovering above it in a heraldic pose. It is this pose of cold fastidiously polished distance which has made many of his male readers respond with adoring approval or with intense dislike. To a critical female reader, bemused by all this maleness, the curiously rigid, conceptually banal high-seriousness, the outright *kitschy* sententiousness permeating all his "mature" texts of the last forty-five years may seem more disturbing than his obvious posing—because they point to the profound arrest of a talented writer's cultural imagination.

4.

What Jünger wrote during the Weimar period did not help his contemporary readers to view critically the conflicts of their time. To the historian of the period, however, his often stunning lack of cultural imagination and intelligence can indeed be useful. He did not look at his contemporaries, only at himself, but, extrapolating from a highly stylized self-fiction, he provoked a number of cultural resonances with his peculiar mix of radical cultural conservatism and isolated instances of modernism. From hindsight it almost seems too clear, too simple to be effective: machines appear all too predictably in images of panthers and noble horses, cool mathematical calculation is metaphorically superimposed on hot pulsating bodies of flesh and iron. Blood, fire, and earth are invoked to force the modern urban masses into the mold of heroic folk. The archetype of the worker signifies the cultural gnosticism of antibourgeois anticalculation, antimechanization, and antirationalism embodied in blood and race, both völkisch and aristocratic.

His stylized self-fictions could be presented most naturally in the peculiar blend of diary, report, and recollection which he developed during the twenties. There are few novellike texts in Jünger's oeuvre and only one in the Weimar period, the 1923 fragment *Sturm* (Storm), which was published in sixteen installments in the widely read and respectable *Hannoversche Kurier* without finding a sizable echo and therefore was not published in book form.[60] The lack of echo is instructive, as the clearly autobiographical novel both reaffirms and questions the higher vitality and beauty and the meaningful fate of young men killed in battle. The protagonists feel secure in their physical and mental superiority vis-à-vis the mediocre world of their fathers, but they also feel free to question the meaning of all that dying, and they are remarkably hostile to (the uses of) technology. The central ambiguity of the (third-person) narrating position did not attract an audience; the enthusiastic nobly barbaric warrior and the questioning young intellectual could not be brought together successfully, and Jünger was not to try it again. He gave his warriors (himself) superior mental powers and, starting in the late twenties, self-consciously exquisite eclectic props of high culture, but never intellectual curiosity or ambiguity. They were a small elite of the initiated; there was no need to be curious.

Jünger's contributions to a number of militarist journals in the midtwenties show his willingness to conform to their stated goals of rebuilding German militarism, that is, a certain variety of perspective and emphasis depending on the journal for which they had been intended. The most pragmatically militarist pieces published in the midtwenties in *Die Standarte* (The ensign)[61] were appreciated as support for that journal's efforts to build a *Frontkameradschaft* (buddy system) of young men in order to work up a potential reservoir of soldiers for the very top-heavy *Reichswehr*.[62] But the whole rather broad spectrum of the right was reflected in the journals to which Jünger contributed: from the bourgeois, vaguely *völkisch Grenzboten*

(Messenger across the border) and *Volkswart* (Guard of the people), Diederich's elitist *Die Tat* (The act), the Herrenclub's[63] *Das Gewissen* (The conscience) to the aggressively *völkisch Das Deutsche Volkstum* edited by the Christian anti-Semitic nationalist Wilhelm Stapel.[64] Though Jünger continued to contribute to these journals throughout the twenties—as late as 1929 he wrote "Die Geburt des Nationalismus aus dem Kriege" for *Deutsches Volkstum*—his heroic narcissistic individualism with its cultural eclecticism and autism was increasingly perceived to impede rather than further *völkisch* strategies which, by the midtwenties, began to focus on the "virtues" of the masses, that is, the anxieties and desires of the lower middle classes, the silent majority. These virtues were linked to the familiar values of stability, family, home, which flatly contradicted Jünger's existential adventurism and decisionism and which he therefore despised.

While his exclusive *Frontkaempferhaltung* (heroic pose of the front-line fighter) and his formulaic appeals to *Frontgeist* were seen by the journals as liabilities, Jünger saw their increasing *Verbürgerlichung* as yet another aspect of inevitable cultural decline. After a series of short-lived editorial adventures with journals financed by the former Free Corps leader Kapitän Ehrhardt, *Arminius* and *Der Vormarsch* (The advance), he decided to concentrate on what he perceived as his specific mission: a heroic individualism which was informed and supported by a radical cultural nationalist conservatism sufficiently eclectic to admit some French influences.

The break was clearly marked by the texts collected in the 1929 *Das abenteuerliche Herz* published in book form by the Berlin Frundsberg Verlag, successor to Mittler. They had been preprinted in seventeen installments by Hugenberg's conservative *Der Tag* (The day) beginning in October 1928, and some of them had appeared as early as February 1927, placed in Ehrhardt's *Arminius* and *Vormarsch,* and in *Widerstand* (Resistance) which was edited by Jünger's National Bolshevist friend Ernst Niekisch. These were written against accusations of political irresponsibility made by the group around *Stahlhelm* (Helmet of steel), which was steering a course of strict legality away from the extremism of the National Socialists. But it is significant that they as well as the more radical Ehrhardt supporters found troublesome Jünger's vague unrealistic predictions of Germany's future glory coming from a position which was radically conservative in literary rather than political terms. Helmut Franke who contributed to *Arminius* and, like Jünger, thought the *Legalitätskurs* of *Stahlhelm* bourgeois and therefore unproductive, bitterly complained in an article of November 14, 1926, "Die Tragödie der Frontsoldaten," that their "geistige Führer," among them Ernst Jünger, had shown themselves unable to make concrete political suggestions. And Jünger was not to change. His three "Briefe eines Nationalisten" (Letters of a nationalist), first published in February and March 1927, warn emphatically of the danger of giving in to the banality of everyday reason, admonishing the reader to remain open to the magic of the great childhood figures Robinson Crusoe, Old Shatterhead, the Count of Monte Cristo, and

Don Quixote.[65] He remembers how these great unique individualists in their stance against mechanization, calculation, and fragmentation had inspired him at the age of sixteen (!) to run away to the Foreign Legion and the challenge of the primeval African landscape.[66]

Throughout these texts Jünger appeals to the higher meaning of blood, muscles, and senses in the service of German honor and glory. A piece, "Betrachtungen" (Reflections), in *Widerstand* (January 1928), which he uses for the conclusion of *Abenteuerliches Herz*, significantly invokes the poet's unique responsibility to preserve the total vision of battle expressive of the higher reality of the soul and thereby the poet's superiority over men whose vision is partial. Here, too, the preeminence of youth is stressed: he presents his ideal of nobility in the image of a very young soldier, a fragile heroic man-child stumbling into his certain death under the burden of a huge ammunition box. In the observer's fictionalizing perspective he can be certain of the supreme significance of his sacrifice for the purity of German Culture.[67] A passage entitled "Aus meinem Skizzenbuch" states that the enormous effort of winning the next war will only be justified if the Germans can be taught to give up all of Stendhal's work for a single Hölderlin or Novalis poem or a short Hamann passage. This seems to contradict the frequent favorable if highly eclectic references to French cultural history throughout *Das abenteuerliche Herz*. But Jünger is above all interested in teaching his readers the importance of cultural meaning based on a hierarchy of value, which is rigidly exclusive in terms of ranking yet flexibly inclusive in terms of personal preference.

The three writers mentioned are profoundly German in that they represent so distinctly the profundity of German Culture—Heine, for instance, would not do here at all. Jünger argues that the "magical point zero" can only be crossed by those truly initiated persons who recognize "our own" German (rather than European) heritage as an absolute cultural measure[68]—the motto for both book versions of *Abenteuerliches Herz* was a quote from Hamann suggesting a mystical (German) unity between mind and world. It might seem curious that he would think such celebration of High Culture suitable for publication in the militarist-nationalist *Vormarsch* where it appeared on July 2, 1928, after his resignation from the editorship.[69] But Hölderlin and Novalis had been misused to support cultural nationalism in World War I and were to be adopted for Nazi reconstruction of German Culture. In the context of the entire book the cultural jingoism of a passage like this is diffused by others celebrating certain French authors—for instance, the grandiosely wicked *(verrucht)* de Sade whose diabolical solitary profundity makes him, in Jünger's eyes, a much more readable author than Rousseau.[70]

On the whole, Jünger's self-presentation in *Abenteuerliches Herz* draws less on spiritual-cultural Germanness in a narrow sense than on the substance of certain "spirits of the highest order" *(Geister erster Ordnung)* or "leading spirits of breeding" *(führende Geister von Rasse)*. These are infinitely superior to "mere intellects" *(Intelligenzen)* because, in contrast to modern calculating specialists, they possess the key to all knowledge which is magical. This elite in the purest sense includes de Sade as well as Paracelsus, Augustin as well as Hölderlin, Pascal as well as Hamann, the Abbé Galiani (an eighteenth-century free-thinking economist) as well as Swedenborg, Roger the Norman as well as King Murat, and, in addition, all the warriors, adventurers, the wild drinkers of life and dark aristocrats of dream. They all possess what Jünger admonishes his readers to seek: the *abenteuerliche Herz* synonymous with an antibourgeois *Haltung* par excellence. For these leading *Geister* among whom he dwells, wave, cloud, and flame are the key to all form, intoxication, and sleep, and death the key to all experience.[71] There is no real, authentic experience outside this elite group. Nothing seems more distasteful and self-defeating to Jünger than intellect without breeding *(Verstand, der keine Rasse hat)*, a *Bohemeverstand*, degenerate *(entartet)* in its journalistic irony. Breeding as spiritual form is needed for fertilization of mere intellect. And the noble hunt *(hohe Jagd*—one of Jünger's favorite images) of an intellect thus fertilized yields the only authentic intellectual booty which can then be thrown to the mob of the intellectuals as technicians and dried-up scholars.[72]

Many such images expressing Jünger's value system, which culminated in the heroically gnostic *Haltung,* had echoes in fascist rhetoric and Jünger's usefulness in this respect seems quite obvious. However, his relentless emphasis on the uniquely meaningful self in the center of a cultural universe of his own making made him seem a less reliable ally to the extreme right. It was responsible, too, for the strongly idiosyncratic, private dimension of all his texts which would undermine the subversive potential read into them by a critic like Bohrer. He translates Adorno's "negativity of art" into wickedness *(Bösartigkeit)* as the central element of art, warning Jünger's reader not to remove it from Jünger's texts in interpretation. Professing to be disturbed by the harmlessness of the German literary tradition—no de Sade, no Celine!— he argues that it drove Jünger to the aesthetic celebration of existential terror. He judges Jünger to be less experienced in literary but more experienced in political terror than the European literary avant-garde. This is a highly questionable assumption, especially as he extrapolates from it Jünger's "desperate attempt" to reject all political solutions as merely "rational," replacing them with "fantastic constructions." These, in Bohrer's view, represent Jünger's naive but sincere endeavor to achieve a genuine "reflection of crisis" from a postenlightenment position which realizes the profound reality of terror. "It is true that Jünger's ambitious attempt was a failure; but it places him into that tiny group of daringly esoteric authors willing to take great risks whose epistemological concept of literature distinguished them from the mass of entertaining good novels which do not contribute anything to knowledge."[73]

The general reader would be hard-pressed to find such contribution in any text written by Jünger over a period of five decades. It would be even more difficult to ascribe to Jünger any concrete political experience, for instance, of fascist terror during the late twenties and early thirties. His explicitly political statements were as conceptually vague as they were irrational, and they were made outside of the tightly controlled fictions of his "fantastic constructions." More important, the centrality of terror, *Schrecken,* as an all-embracing aesthetic-existential category was introduced into the earlier texts after the fact by an author who compulsively revised, obsessed with the fact and significance of his entelechy.[74]

Jünger has never been a esoteric author; his writing has always been clear and simple and disturbing precisely for its lack of reflected reservation in addressing the most complex contemporary issues. His understanding of the modern world has been muddled, but his attitude toward it, his *Haltung,* has been one of manly simplicity and directness. Bohrer's ascribing to Jünger an "Ambivalenz zwischen archaischer Rückwendung und moderner Diagnostik" (ambivalence concerning the retreat to an archaic existence and modern diagnosis)[75] assumes an analytical potential which cannot be documented. Existential archaism is an important component in the experience of modernity, but it is as pervasive in Jünger's texts as it is unreflected, notwithstanding all the distancing references to mathematics and microscopes in *Abenteuerliches Herz.*[76]

Jünger has never allowed the experience of terror to be real; it was magically veiled in the earlier versions of his self-presentation and later became an aesthetic abstraction. The "abyss of pain" in the 1934 rendering of the climactic battle scene by no means implied the viewer's surrender to the experience of pain—the lost war, the lost battle, the slain, the wounded—and the later change to "abyss of terror"[77] separated the viewer even further from the viewed. It is the pain and the terror of others to be viewed with *Haltung.* There are recorded dream fragments dealing with terror or horror *(Entsetzen)* in both book versions of *Das abenteuerliche Herz*[78] where the observer narrates his fascination with the overpowering violating quality of terror experienced by others. There are skillfully executed Poe-like settings which are quite effective. But the reader is given lectures about the art of imagining violation by terror rather than images demonstrating such violation. There is no attempt to imitate Poe's technique of reproducing the experience of terror by narrative immersion. Moreover, the darkly decorative character of these settings is highly self-conscious: torture takes place in geometrical arrangements of black and blood color highlighted by images of confinement, silence, and metaphysical pain.[79] The observer as narrator repeatedly draws attention to the narrated dreamlike quality of these slow-moving sequences, but they have nothing in common with the erratic shifts and patterns of real dreams; rather, *dreamlike* refers to the observer's protected viewpoint. Ostensibly recalling one of his dreams, he is looking at mere images, which cannot really touch him, even if he proclaims them to be more real or of a higher reality than that of the common life-world. There is a certain degree of awareness regarding the staged abstract effect of this distancing perspective.

One of his favorites in the Napoli aquarium is a small exquisite kind of octopus which shows him every morning "how to die in beauty—to use a popular phrase of art nouveau."[80] Whether he records scenes observed in the Great War, in dreams, or in the aquarium, he always uses the figurative or literal glass walls which shield him to the extent that he can reconstruct chaos, pain, and terror in patterns of fantastic decorative stable orderliness.

Pain, we are told in the introductory passage to the 1934 essay "Der Schmerz" (Pain), is among those "great and immutable measures which prove the value of man." "Tell me your relation to pain and I will tell you who you are." The heraldic dignity of pain as metaphysical *Haltung* is central to the texts of the thirties: from the 1930 "Die totale Mobilmachung," the 1932 *Der Arbeiter,* to the 1939 *On the Marble Cliffs.* Removed from its physiological and psychological reality, pain for Jünger becomes the "key" which will open both the innermost recesses of the self and the dynamics of the social world. "Approaching the point where a person shows himself equal or superior to pain, one gains access to the sources of his power and to the secret of his domination." The desire to unlock this secret of how to gain and sustain control of self and then, inevitably (and less significantly), others always had been and continued to be the focus of Jünger's writing. There has been no change in substance, only in emphasis. Notwithstanding Jünger's preoccupation with control, domination, and hierarchical order, his perspective on the complex sociopsychological phenomenon of power has been as uninformed, vague, and simplistic as that of the most unworldly instinctual pacifist.

5.

By the early thirties Jünger's audience had become larger, more diffuse, more bourgeois, and, with few exceptions,[81] seemed to see no need to respond to the reasons behind this uncompromising author's *Haltung. Der Arbeiter,* published in two editions in 1932, found a lively critical echo on the right and the center. With *Das Abenteuerliche Herz* and his 1930 anthology *Krieg und Krieger,* Jünger had established himself as an intriguingly provocative "national revolutionary" intimating elements of National Bolshevism and representative of heroic nihilism which would destroy bourgeois individualism. *Krieg und Krieger* (War and warrior) was also reviewed on the liberal left by Klaus Mann who read the collection as prime example of "Kriegs-Sadismus" and, more ideologically, by Walter Benjamin who analyzed it as "Theories of German Fascism."[82] Benjamin's review is particularly instructive in its refusal to appreciate the antibourgeois stance of the contributors to the volume. It is true that their and their bourgeois readers' concept of antiindividualism was very muddled, but Benjamin was not concerned with this issue. He himself argued from a rigorously antibourgeois position, but he could not acknowledge it in the texts coming from the other end of the political spectrum. Thus he simply blames the separation between the technological and the spiritual aspects of the war, which is indeed typical for the right, on the whole of "bourgeois society" which, he says, "cannot help but resolutely exclude technology's right of codetermination in the social order. Any future war will also be a slave revolt of technology."[83] It is true that dealing intelligently with technocracy was a central problem for the bourgeois Republic of Weimar and has continued to be so for all technologically advanced mass societies. Neither his laying blame summarily nor his projecting a future war indicated any concrete interest on Benjamin's part in understanding the dangerously confused sociopolitical situation in which these texts had been written and had found a positive echo.

The contributions to the anthology, especially Jünger's, share much rhetoric with (Italian) fascism, but the "boyish rapture" of their cult of war pointed out rightly by Benjamin, their adolescent self-stylization as warrior, cannot be understood if seen as "nothing other than an uninhibited translation of the (bourgeois) principle of *l'art pour l'art* to war itself."[84] They certainly do not encourage a "theory of fascism." The writers are searching for personal meaning by adopting a heroic *Haltung* against the hated *System* of Weimar and the very awkwardness of their love for war, which Benjamin nicely ridicules in well chosen quotes, also undermines his argument. Above all, he does not appreciate the fact that cultural needs of which he does not approve may nevertheless be sufficiently concrete to be taken seriously—for instance, the writers' need to reconstruct their own lost youth in the cultic celebration of the lost war. Benjamin at first seems to be willing to consider the cultural trauma of the lost war, but he soon gets caught up in his own ingenious verbal play with the meanings of losing and winning:

> What does it mean to win or lose a war? How striking the double meaning is in both words: The first, manifest meaning certainly refers to the outcome of the war, but the second meaning—which creates the peculiar hollow space, the sounding board in these words—refers to the totality of the war and suggests how the war's outcome also alters the enduring significance it holds for us. This meaning says, so to speak, the winner keeps the war in hand, it leaves the hand of the loser; it says the winner conquers the war for himself, makes it his own property, the loser no longer possesses it and must live without it. And he must live not only without the war per se but without every one of its slightest ups and downs, every subtlest one of its chess moves, every one of its remotest actions. To win or lose a war reaches so deeply, if we follow the language, into the fabric of our existence that our whole lives become that much poorer or richer. And since we have lost one of the greatest wars in world history, one which involved the whole material and spiritual substance of a people, one can assess the significance of this loss.[85]

Yet he seems to be unable to do that. Clearly warming up to the task of paraphrasing the meaning of the loss of this war, he completely neglects to apply it to the texts under consideration. Their writers, he says, "continued to celebrate the cult of war when there was no longer any real enemy." Had not he himself tried to make it clear that the winner's appropriation of the whole war experience fed the continued confrontation? Losing "one of the greatest wars in world history" could mean for some, for many, not to be done with the winner who continued to be seen as (and occasionally continued to behave like) the "real enemy." Benjamin not only refused to take seriously such experience, but he also proclaimed its particularly disturbing articulation in Jünger's anthology as simply synonymous with the experience and the reaction of all of "bourgeois society."

> They complied with the desires of the bourgeoisie, which longed for the decline of the West, the way a schoolboy longs for an inkblot in place of his wrong answer. They spread decline, preached decline wherever they went. Not even for a moment were they capable of holding up to view—instead of doggedly holding onto—what had been lost. They were always the first and the bitterest to oppose coming to one's senses. They ignored the great opportunity of the loser—which the Russians had taken advantage of—to shift the fight to another sphere until the moment had passed and the nations of Europe had sunk to being partners in trade agreements again.[86]

The elaborate stylization of the warrior in these texts was a reaction to the experience of a loss which Benjamin himself had understood to be of the highest cultural significance.[87] It was not, to be sure, a reaction one would have hoped for; but it certainly was not responsible for the comparatively sane bourgeois normalization of trade agreements. Nor could Russia be held up as a viable alternative at this point, if only for the reason, important to Benjamin's argument, that her cultural politics had caused the unambiguous rejection rather than critical examination ("held up to view") of the past. In Germany, where the war had been lost in very different terms, the attitude toward the past was one of profound and destructive ambivalence, and it was shared by intellectuals across the political spectrum. The sons, looking toward a glorious future, be it a nationalist or Marxist utopia, rejected the bourgeois world of the fathers whom they saw as responsible for "the war" *and* for its loss. The fathers, remembering a better past, could not come to terms with the sons' world established after the loss of the war for which they refused to take any blame. Neither understood that this particular war had been the primary problem, not "the war," nor its loss, and that the present had emerged from the past as their shared responsibility. If they collaborated in the collapse of Weimar they did so unwittingly, in different ways and for different reasons.

Significantly, Benjamin's own ambivalence toward the past emerges quite clearly in this context. As an important stage of his argument he introduces his admired dead friend Florens Christian Rang[88] "whose biography better exemplifies the German than whole hordes of these desperate characters. . . ." First he refers to Rang's sensible denunciation of a particular spiritual tendency to throw away life in the moment of intoxication attracted by the idea of gaining an eternal halo around a short-lived sacrifice.

But then he seeks to demonstrate Rang's authentic, radical Germanness with the following quote which, he says, "may sound familiar to those around Jünger":

> Two hundred officers, prepared to die, would have sufficed to suppress the revolution in Berlin—as in all other places; but no one was to be found. No doubt many of them would have liked to come to the rescue, but in reality—not actuality—nobody quite wanted to begin, to put himself forward as the leader, or to proceed individually. They preferred to have their epaulets ripped off in the streets.[89]

This observation made by Rang in the early twenties is repeated by Benjamin at a time when he could have been much better informed about the socialization of the German officer during World War I. The orderly chaos of trench warfare with its rigid hierarchy supported by the literal imminence of death had been based on the simultaneity of sharply defined absolute power over many individuals and absolute accountability to a few individuals and the amorphous nation. It left the officers, especially the young ones, totally impotent when faced with and submerged into the disorderly chaos of the revolution. Their reaction to the destruction of their individuality and manliness—their rank marked on their epaulets—was the cultic celebration of war and the warrior. It was not useful to call the hollowness of their heroic stance cowardice. Their unwillingness to act in this situation was caused by their highly conditioned willingness to die in another. It is hard to say, of course, how many of Jünger's contributors or readers were still in need of coming to terms with this experience or how concrete and sincere such need might have been. But to discuss these issues critically also involves trying to see them in sociopsychological terms.

In their majority, the contributors were an unpleasant lot: there were the aggressive nationalists Erich Guenther and von Schramm singled out in Benjamin's review; there was the intelligent and cynical Ernst von Salomon who had been on the fringes of the group responsible for Rathenau's assassination;[90] but there was also Ernst Jünger's more mellow, rather harmless younger brother Friedrich Georg. His contribution had provided the title for the anthology and echoed, if somewhat toned down, statements about the effect of the Great War on the future made by Ernst in his 1922 *Der Kampf als inneres Erlebnis* (The battle as inner experience)—a text quoted by some young *völkisch* terrorists as justification for their acts.[91]

In the case of Friedrich Georg, Benjamin simply disapproved; he reacts quite differently to the striking images of Ernst's "total mobilization" or Salomon's "landscape of the front," in spite of his dismissing them as typical for all war-glorifying literature on the right. Ernst Jünger and Ernst von Salomon are clearly much more talented than the rest, and Benjamin responds to the energy and force of their personal images of war. It is when he speaks of them that he wanders into the mindscape of his then recently published *Trauerspielbuch.* Ostensibly he is attacking the perversions of

German feeling for nature and of German idealism to be found in the nationalist militarist texts under consideration. But the real enemy is technology, and he is more interested in allegorical images of its fearful power
than in a rational analysis of its problematic social implications:

> Etching the landscape with flaming banners and trenches, technology wanted to
> recreate the heroic features of German Idealism. It went astray. What it consid-
> ered heroic were the features of Hippocrates, the features of death. Deeply
> imbued with its own depravity, technology gave shape to the apocalyptic face of
> nature and reduced nature to silence—even though this technology had the
> power to give nature its voice. Instead of using and illuminating the secrets of
> nature via a technology mediated by the human scheme of things, the new
> nationalists' metaphysical abstraction of war signifies nothing other than a
> mystical and unmediated application of technology to solve the mystery of an
> idealistically perceived nature.[92]

Benjamin speaks here from the position of an unexamined shared radical
cultural conservatism; what he describes as "their" perspective on the
modern world is largely his own. Like so many of their intellectual contemporaries across the political spectrum, both Benjamin and Jünger were
suspicious of mere, shallow technology. Both, too, had arrested the "secrets"
of an abstracted nature in magically inviolate images, which they intended to
stem, to neutralize the uncontrollable cultural changes of modernity. Wild
geese flying over a battlefield which he crosses safely and comfortably in a
plane after the war assure Jünger of the ultimate tameness of technology. The
unique significant image as transtemporal magic constellation—gazed at,
stared at—is in Jünger's as well as Benjamin's view a powerful comment on
the banal temporality of technological systems. For both writers the secrets
of nature are mysteries to be suddenly unveiled rather than gradually solved
and understood. And remembrance of such revealing moments is important
to both of them for its power to rupture the intolerably unselfconscious flow
of time. It is this rupture which creates magic spaces around significant
objects or acts and thereby protects their meaning and illuminates their
significance against the temporality of technology. Jünger and Benjamin are
similarly motivated by the need for such protection and illumination, though
Benjamin's language is, on the whole, a more flexible sophisticated instrument in the attempts to balance a deeply ambivalent concept of contemporaneity.[93]

Both Benjamin's and Jünger's concepts of fascism were as idiosyncratic
as they were self-protective. Directed by his interest in establishing an aesthetics of fascism which would allow him to control the disturbingly complex
phenomenon, Benjamin stylizes all the contributors to the volume as members of the "caste of dependable fascist class warriors," having passed
through the predictable stages of the World War I volunteer and the postwar
mercenary. They support the former bourgeois, now fascist, ruling class
which "bears the Sphinx-like countenance of the producer who very soon

promises to be sole consumer of his commodities. Sphynx-like in appearance, the fascists' nation thus takes its place as a new economic mystery alongside the old."[94] But in German fascist rhetoric which was so attractive to the masses—a fact which Jünger acknowledged contemptuously and Benjamin explained away—nature-images quite clearly reflect anticapitalist energies: it is the dark secret *and* the shallowness of capitalist machinations, of calculation and mechanization that has to be destroyed and with it the Sphynx-like *and* ignoble features of the Weimar *System*. In Hitler's and Goebbel's speeches the dark mysterious powers of earth and blood are tamed by the bright blond-blue-eyedness of the German family. The *Systemzeit*—their favorite term for the Weimar period—combining the shallow temporality of technological civilization and the transtemporal stage of the twilight of the gods is overcome by the meaningful time of the *Volk*, guaranteed to last for a thousand years through the community of millions. The existentially solitary pose of the heroic warrior intimating wishful omnipotence did not appeal to the fascist masses unless it was viewed as significantly serving community. But Jünger's warriors had long since left behind consideration of the reality of fascism and so had Benjamin. The difference was that they had done so explicitly and he by implication.

6.

The wave of war books published in 1928 and 1929 included Remarque's fantastically successful antiwar novel *All Quiet on the Western Front* as well as texts stressing the positive aspects of war by nationalist writers like Werner Beumelburg, Wilhelm Michael, and Franz Schauwecker which had much smaller but still considerable audiences.[95] They all related the significance of the war experience directly to the buddy system sustaining the common soldier in the trenches. *Kameradschaft* and *Schützengrabengeist* (spirit of the trenches) were important instead of Jünger's abstractly hovering *Frontgeist* because they stressed the humanity of workers in wartime, that is, before they (presumably) had come under the influence of the Moscow-controlled German Communist party.

Notwithstanding his militaristic anthologizing activities in the late twenties and early thirties, Jünger was writing now for an educated largely apolitical bourgeois elite. His elaborately constructed concept-image of *Der Arbeiter* has nothing in common with the various Nationalist and National Socialist attempts to deal concretely with the issue of nationalism in the working classes. Nor does his extremely vague concept of foreign politics seem in any way influenced by the arguments of his National Bolshevist friend Ernst Niekisch, who rightly attacked the Social Democrats for never having considered seriously the interrelation of nationalism and foreign politics before 1914 in his 1925 *Grundfragen deutscher Aussenpolitik* (Essential questions of German foreign policy).[96] As editor of *Widerstand* Niekisch wanted to inform his readers on the concrete details of their social exploitation by the *System* and of Germany's political weakness. He judges harshly both the control by Moscow of the German Communist party unable to develop its own character and direction and the "wicked and crazy" treatment of the USSR at Brest-Litovsk, and praises Rathenau's negotiations at Rapallo. It would have been in the interest of revolutionary Germany to gain Russia's friendship and her support against the Versailles powers. For Niekisch the social revolution can only be successful if it is reflected in worldwide political goals. The general thrust of his argument is expansionist, but there are shrewd observations on geopolitical and sociopolitical realities and a well-taken critique of the intellectuals' (right or left) self-centered, self-absorbed lack of interest in them. Perhaps most important in this context is Niekisch's insistence that the German workers will only become the real power in the state in terms of instigating and carrying through real social change if perceived as the most reliable organ of national self-preservation.[97] Notwithstanding his critique, Niekisch did believe in the cultural mission of a better-informed intellectual elite, especially in the late twenties when the dangers of Hitlerism could be seen more clearly.

Niekisch's 1932 *Hitler—ein deutsches Verhängnis* (Hitler—a German catastrophe), published the same year as Jünger's *Der Arbeiter,* is as aggressively nationalist as it is shrewd in its analysis of the reasons for Hitler's resistible rise. He rightly stresses the messianic aspects of National Socialism, its escapism, its belief in and promise of miracles and therefore its determination to literally eradicate those who resisted the miraculous victory of the party, that is, questioned its ability to come through with the promised miracles. Hitler as the fascist pope celebrates the miracle of German redemption—a lamentable perversion, in Niekisch's eyes, of the goodwill and dedication of so many young people in Hitler's organizations SA and SS.[98] For Niekisch Hitler is the bourgeois carried to the absurd, the ultimate in Wilhelminian Byzantinism, dilettantism, political swindle—bourgeois, that is, in sociocultural rather than political-economical terms. Hitler, after all, emphasized and exploited the generational conflict between the bourgeois world of the "have" fathers and the socialist world of the "have-not" sons, at the same time attacking bolshevist nationalization of property. Niekisch was to see more clearly after the war and to modify his nationalism considerably.[99] Many of his observations in the twenties and thirties, however, if not pretty or admirable in sentiment, were quite realistic. He understood what losing the war meant in concrete terms for those, too, who had not been determined warriors but the frightened, bewildered common soldiers described by Remarque, workers mobilized for what, in the end, seemed a total war. Jünger, who had never looked at contemporary sociopolitical reality with any degree of unprejudiced concentration, who had been secure and content with his own images and constructs, was not to undergo such a change. His nationalism remained what it always had been, an aggressive sociocultural elitism with clearly enunciated metabiological racist accents.

Significantly, the Hitler-figure in the 1939 *Marble Cliffs* is a feudal lord gone wrong, and the worker in *Der Arbeiter* a loyal vassal.

The modern surface of this 1932 text is deceptive. The worker is a noble fantastic monster in a constructivist *Planlandschaft* (technologically planned landscape), the *totaler Raum* (total space) as the result of significantly victorious futuristic technology. In this text particularly, Jünger indulged his predilection for superhuman dimensions. The worker appears as total *Gestalt*[100] and heroically anonymous under his mask in his planetary moonscape setting, evocative of primeval Africa and trenchscape. The figures and settings of Lang's *Metropolis* come to mind, too; there is, however, the important distinction that Jünger's worker has magically retained a heroic individuality within his heroic anonymity. This quintessentially German robot is easily as mindless as Asimov's, but so much more determined, decisive, authentic. Jünger has programmed his creature firmly as the modern version of the *Abenteurer* (adventurer) in search of the unknown. Much adolescent posing from *Das abenteuerliche Herz* has been carried over into *Der Arbeiter,* though critics have, on the whole, either praised the text's "heroic nihilism" or condemned it for its militaristic totalitarianist tendencies.[101] But Jünger's praising his worker's total devotion to the total state is sentimentalist rather than nihilistic. Though there often is a psychological connection between these two positions, the assumption of a radical nihilism has been made too easily in attempts to define a uniform fascist mentality of the text. Consider the devotion asked of the worker as soldier in the battles of the future. The treatise ends with a celebration of renunciation—a familiar phenomenon in German culture: "The real contest is about the discovery of a new and unknown world, a discovery more ruinous and consequential than the discovery of America. It is only with profound emotion that one can look at man occupied, in the midst of zones of chaos, with the tempering of weapons and hearts, prepared to renounce the escape of happiness."

Higher happiness is promised as reward for such heroic renunciation. This is to be expected, but the promised higher level is transhuman in a peculiarly literal sense. Jünger's projection of future men in a future total technoscape as so many pillars of a future total state results in an arbitrary prefabricated myth of technology rather than informed, responsible extrapolation. Yet, like much bad science fiction, it is instructive because it reflects, in surrealistic clarity, the important cultural conflicts of the period. For once (and not for better), there is no mystic veil, no introspective hesitation. Kurt Hiller, brilliant, controversial, and often shooting from the hip, included Jünger in the group of intellectuals whom he called "Linke Leute von rechts" (Left guys from the right) in a 1932 article in *Weltbühne*. His demonstration of the crossing over or merging of positions on the left and the right, not just among the anonymous masses but also among the intellectuals, did not make him popular with either camp. He had succinctly named unresolved problems of leadership and community in an increasingly technocratic mass society struggling with what was seen as the imposition of democracy.[102] Jünger, in contrast, had consistently translated these problems into evocative patterns of images: the new community of the solitary heroic warrior or worker as source for the new unity of ecstasy and asceticism, untamed instinctive force and cool computation, "fire and ice." In this community the worker as soldier can assume his *Gestalt* which will enable him to discover his fate in the significance of (self-)sacrifice to and for community. This *Gestalt* is trans- or metaphysical in its immutability, that is, protected from the ravages of temporality. The wholeness of such *Gestalt* is the wholeness of the leader who, containing the whole, i.e., of community, is entitled to claim it.[103] Jünger's relating heroic community and heroic leadership was abstract and glaringly circular, but the problems associated with these shadowy concept-images were real and contemporary.

Read closely, *Der Arbeiter* reveals that Jünger was less interested in the heroic community of *Arbeitswelt* (work-world) as totally planned technoscape than in the transindividual inviolable *Gestalt* of the worker as soldier, suspended unchanging in the magic spaces of pain and terror. Understandably, his contemporary readers had concentrated mainly on the projection of *Arbeitswelt*. Its indestructable constructs of steel and stone could be read as appropriately modern version and promise of the *Unzerreissbarkeit* of communal ties established by the power of blood, earth, roots, and the old-new promise of a millennial *Reich*.[104] All these concept-images suggest that the individual is once and for all contained in these ties and that it is precisely this transtemporality which constitutes their cultural significance. Heidegger's notorious 1933 inaugural speech stresses, above all, the transtemporal magnificence of the *Aufbruch* (the rising), that is, the departure from the present as redemption of the greatness of the past in the glory of the future: "We will our people to fulfill its historic mission. We will ourselves. For the young and the youngest force and spirit [*Kraft*] of the people reaching beyond us has already decided so."[105] The people's essence is its historic mission, that is, the people's willing this mission *and* accepting it as fated, fulfilling itself and being fulfilled.

The crude archaistic verbal magic of this willed nonsense does not differ in kind from Jünger's formulaic fictions during the late twenties and early thirties which, in hindsight, seemed much less offensive to many readers.[106] The allegedly functionalist planetary *Arbeitswelt* of the glorious future projected by Jünger does not present the phenomenon of power as a modern complex system of interrelations but as springing forth spontaneously from the old heroically simple sources of social-psychic energy: belief, loyalty, (self-)discipline, (self-)sacrifice. Giving itself, the self gains authenticity; the worker under his mask signifying his willed *and* fated surrender to the heroic collective is the true heroic individual establishing true community. In the chapter "Die Kunst als Gestaltung der Arbeitswelt" (Art giving form to the work-world) Jünger argues that the present is unable to be productive in the spirit of the old symbols which are *Abbilder* (reflected images) of a force

whose *Urbild* (original image) and *Gestalt* has vanished. He senses great
striving in the present toward these *Urbilder,* but all such activity is doomed
to be *museal.* We have to learn to see our existence in terms of a new and
original, primeval relationship *(Urverhältnis)* whose substance has not yet
found expression in appearance *(in der Erscheinung).* "The question is
whether we are not already in possession of a freedom which we yet have to
learn how to use and which, at the same time, is perfectly obvious and
accessible. Here a critical position is no longer valid, for the insights, on
which we have to rely, are of a different kind."[107]

    Urbilder and *Urverhaeltnisse,* then, connect an authentic past with an
authentic future thereby overshadowing the present completely. In *Das abenteuerliche Herz,* happiness *(Glück)* was characterized as the state of being
one with the magical logic of *Urverhaeltnisse* which meaningfully relates the
individual and the cosmos. In *Der Arbeiter* higher realization of self through
self-sacrifice is synonymous with renunciation of happiness *(Glücksverzicht).*
Yet, in the authentic spaces where pain and terror are the only and absolute
measure of the rank of man, all possible contradictions are resolved in higher
syntheses. The worker is not asked to renounce oneness with the magical
logic of *Urverhältnisse* in general, but only in its individual form. The utopia
of the future *Arbeitswelt* appears to differ from the utopian spaces of the
adventurous heart because of its seemingly exclusive emphasis on community. But the self's sacrifice for community signifies self-preservation on a
higher level.[108]

7.

On the Marble Cliffs was published in 1939 when Hitler's version of *Arbeitswelt* had been established with the help of a similarly circular bio-
metaphysics of the community of the chosen. This political reality may have
caused Jünger to become more ambivalent about participation in community
and more reticent about self-sacrifice. The fiction of the narrating self as
participating observer, developed through the twenties and modified in the
early thirties, becomes central again, but is more ambiguous than in *Abenteuerliches Herz,* and more subtle. The narrator as observer still draws on the
authority of his personal memory, yet he is no longer so obsessively concerned with the meanings of the concrete decisive act. He has been allowed
to relax somewhat in the relative freedom of his fictional status. The wars in
which he participated in the past were fought according to elaborate rules
defined by technologies which seem both archaic and futuristic. Emphasis
on the formal nature of the game of war as elegant orderliness of extreme
experiences is supported by the text's self-conscious fictionality. It is responsible for its notorious coldness and remoteness, the stylized haughtiness of
its "beautiful" account of brutal totally destructive power.

    In his 1919 *Politische Romantik,* Carl Schmitt discusses romantic uto-
pian imagery which was to pervade, as if by some peculiar *Zeitgeist* affinity

and pollination, much of the cultural critique on the left and the right during the Weimar period. The "romantic subject," stressing the potential rather than the real, is particularly open to the mysterious, the fantastic, the distant as the truly familiar, the miraculous and protean. Negating the here and now as the experience of mere temporality, the romantic subject, expansive and self-sufficient, negates the concrete, that is, the social dimension of action. The merging of past and future in a mystic landscape of the mind produces (concept-)images of an abstract formulaic beauty and Schmitt responds to them. Pointing out that neither religious nor moral nor political decisions are possible in the realm of the aesthetic, he also seems to think regrettable the tainting of beautiful heraldic *Haltung* by the muddled substance of decision and act. This may be the reason for his liking Jünger's rather predictable and redundant fictions of *Haltung* though they clearly prevented any accessible, coherent discussion of the phenomenon of political power, the main object of Schmitt's problematic but often provocatively realistic political analyses in the twenties.[109] He thought the cold smooth static beauty of the friend's prose arresting and did not, presumably, expect much social intelligence in the texts of a poet:

> You all know the wild grief that besets us when we remember times of happiness. How far beyond recall they are, and we are severed from them by something more pitiless than leagues and miles. In the afterlight, too, the images stand out more enticing than before; we think of them as we do of the body of a dead loved one who rests deep in the earth, and who now, in his enhanced and spiritual splendour is like a mirage of the desert before which we must tremble. And constantly in our thirst-haunted dreams we grope for the past in its every detail, in its every line and fold. Then it cannot but seem to us as if we had not had our fill of love and life; yet no regret brings back what has been let slip. Would that this mood might be a lesson to us for each moment of our happiness.
>
> Sweeter still becomes the memory of our years by moon and sun when their end has been in the abyss of fear. Only then do we realize that for us mortals even this is great goodfortune—to live our lives in our little communities under a peaceful roof, with pleasing discourse and with loving greeting at morning and night. Alas! Always too late do we grasp that, if it offered no more than this, our horn of plenty brimmed with riches.[110]

The literal preoccupation with memory as the mindscape of the past, which is characteristic for Jünger, is reinforced here by the peculiar narrative combination of stunning visual imagery and vacuous sententiousness. This combination can be found, too, in his earlier texts, but it emerged more clearly with *On the Marble Cliffs,* probably because the balancing effort had become more self-conscious in this relatively new situation of enforced rather than "freely" elected cultural isolation. (As Jünger was contemptuous of post–World War II developments which he saw exclusively in terms of the decline of elites, he retained the narrative stance of *Marble Cliffs.*) The text's stasis or rigidity, depending on the reader's perspective, is the result of the narrator-protagonist's combined expansive visual sensitivity and his dull narrow high-mindedness. The combination might seem improbable in general, but in Jünger it appears curiously fitting, if irritating and frequently boring. More important in our context, it allows him to preserve the fictitious purity of *Haltung* through cultural remoteness, claiming it, at the same time, as significant vantage point for cultural critique. The reader is confronted with sharply outlined brilliantly colored surfaces of political violence in heroic landscapes, which Steiner aptly refers to as the result of "hard enamelling."[111] But the cultural orientation is as eclectic and vague as are the geographical locations and the politics.

The narrator speaks to the reader from a presumably shared vantage point of having survived the catastrophe, Hitler's seizure of power. His position toward his cultural-political crisis is one of seemingly deliberate inertia; moreover, his way of speaking suggests that he expects his reader to accept it and share it as an important component of *Haltung*. It is the "abyss of fear," the catastrophe itself that makes the memories "sweeter." Seen from the viewer's balcony at the edge of the huge mine crater, the deadly arena of the Great Battle, time past becomes meaningful: "So it is that I think back to the times when we lived on the Great Marina—it is memory alone that evokes their charm."

Many of the human and mythical animal figures to appear in *Marble Cliffs* are recorded in *Abenteuerliches Herz*, especially in the second version of 1938. Frequently, key images go back to the battle scenes reconstructed in the war memoirs of the twenties. The connection is sometimes quite direct, sometimes subterranean. Effects of staging and orchestrating become increasingly noticeable, but the substance of repressed panic is preserved in all the textual variations: the immense effort of controlling fear and terror had become inextricable from the self constituted in remembrance.

Snakes, so important to the plot and setting of *Marble Cliffs*, appear repeatedly in both versions of *Abenteuerliches Herz* where they are clearly linked to the "greater" reality of dream and terror. One of the novel's main characters, the Chief Ranger (*Oberförster*), constructed as a Hitlerian allegory of brutal power, is introduced here with attributes of mythical natural force in the relatively harmless shape of a cranky warlock who laughs through a large wooden cuckoo flute and talks like a (minor) romantic poet about his blue snakes in a hieroglyphic language which is magically shared by the narrator.[112] Jünger worked on the second version of *Abenteuerliches Herz* while composing *Marble Cliffs*, and the changes and additions he made are instructive because they stress a more coherent fictionality of the past in general and a more diffuse space and time of "concrete" remembered events. They also suggest, more clearly than the first version nine years earlier, a tentative, decorative despair. This is most obvious in yet another version of the Great Battle—this time the German side had done the destroying:

> All of a sudden, in its most significant crescendo, the enraged roar of the battle changed to silence. With the destruction of the enemy, the law of action had been

fulfilled and at the same time abrogated; and for a short time the battle hill looked like an anthill whose revolt had been frozen under the curse of sense-lessness. Everybody stood very still—like the spectator at the end of the display of giant fire works, but also as an actor guilty of terrible deeds.

The theater images in this passage are then moved into the realms of dream and insanity, and these are described as states of being which may hold the promise of the "stunning solution of a much contemplated puzzle." The world may just be a giant asylum for the mad and that madness may just be maliciously controlled and directed to limit man's role to that of an extra. The hyperaction of battle leaves the actor passive, like the spectator, but it also draws the spectator to the position of the guilty participator. In that the narrative perspective extends beyond the fascinated stare at the monstrous in the earlier versions, though the concept of guilt is as abstract as the carefully staged "terrible deeds": "Perhaps the world had put on too many baubles, the red and yellow colors of fire; now, as an after-image, its shoddy black scaffolding showed all too clearly. Above it, however, as if brushed on lightly, there was the touch of serenity similar to that which, in waking up, accom-panied memories of confused dreams."[113] This sketch is entitled "An-schaulicher Skeptizismus"—concrete in contrast to the allegedly less dangerous skepticism of the philosophers. But, then, Jünger's attitude here as in *Marble Cliffs* is anything but skeptical in the shared sense of the term. The balance of ambivalence is carefully maintained on the "higher" aesthetic level so that it can comfortably support a certain amount of cultural despair. Fate is no longer unambiguously realized by the warrior as its agent. But the willed submersion of the narrator-protagonist in the flow of fated events is accompanied by all-pervasive images of fire and blood, that is, images of the primeval battle, which in their distinct connectedness form a forceful and disturbing subtext.

Jünger has been unable to leave the *Urbilder* of World War I and to relinquish control to other voices temporarily. It is only when he himself narrates that the calming familiarity of the most terrible and painful scenes can be asserted in remembrance. In *Marble Cliffs* this familiarity with the terrible has become a kind of mystic and gentle affinity; the narrator as spectator seems to have literally absorbed the great conflagration which he watches—and describes—from the protected distant height of the cliffs:

> Not a sound mounted up to me, as if all space were devoid of air; the spectacle unfolded in terrible silence. Below me I could hear neither the children weeping, nor the mothers wailing, nor the war-cry of the clans nor the bellowing of the cattle in their byres. Of all the terrors of destruction, only the shimmering golden light of the flames rose up to the Marble Cliffs. So distant worlds flared up to delight our eyes in the beauty of their ruin.
>
> Nor did I hear the cry which issued from my mouth. Only deep within me, as if I myself were engulfed in flames, did I hear the crackling of this blazing world. And it was only this gentle crackling that came to my ear as the palaces

fell in ruins and from the harbour store-houses the corns-sacks flew high into the air to scatter their glowing contents. Splitting the earth, the powder magazine at the Cock Gate blew up.[114]

The world which should have been his, and his responsibility, had he not willfully distanced himself, explodes, sinking "without a sound into the raging flames." His fascination is that of the connoisseur—even while scrambling to gain the temporary safety of the cliffs he notices the particular beauties of general destruction around him—*and* that of the young shell-shocked soldier. When the Chief Ranger's hounds catch up with him on the cliffs he can neither stir nor cry out, moving in a trance. He is magically rescued from the lead hound in a sequence of dream images: his elflike illegitimate son Eric has roused the huge snakes on the cliff and they, in a dance of *art nouveau* splendor, gently send the terrifying dogs to their terrible deaths. The narrator and his brother Otho (based on Friedrich Georg) have time to celebrate their departure from their beloved *Hermitage* on the cliffs with a libation of old wine in beautiful goblets which they break on the hearthstone, leaving behind years of peaceful living and fulfilling labor, the collection of a large herbarium.

They take with them only the magic mirror of the magician-scientist Nigromontanus, a figure who will reappear in several major postwar texts. In a scent amphora they carry the head of a young prince who had failed in his valiant attempts to fight the forces of darkness and who evokes the noble image of the boy-soldier stumbling to his death under the burden of the ammunition casket. Looking back at their house, already remote observers, they see it self-igniting as if by magic. The flame springing up was in color "like the tiny flame in the lamp of Nigromontanus—a deep dark blue— and its tip was jagged like the cup of gentian." Their house and their work destroyed, there still is the consolation of fatedness: Nothing can be brought to completion on this earth and "what lives eternally in us does not lie in our works. This we perceived in the flames, and yet there was joy in their radiance."[115]

Protected by magic the brothers easily succeed in their escape. Behind them the Marble Cliffs rise gleaming out of the lowland mists, before them opens their friends' great hall and they "passed through the wide open door as if into the haven of our father's house."

The reader is dismissed with these sentences. The brothers leave behind the real blood and fire forced by the Chief Ranger (alias Hitler) on Germany. Their traumata, never acknowledged, have been magically healed. Self-immersed in remembrance, the narrator does not see the meaning of the events he recounts—not their roots in a past which was also his, not their consequences for a future from which he has already removed himself. This is not a narrator who always knows something, but never everything, and whose understanding changes with time. It is, rather, a narrator who has always known certain things deeply and others not at all and who cannot allow his knowledge to change. *On the Marble Cliffs* found many responsive readers in the educated middle classes, though it is difficult to guess whether (or why) they found it an effective indictment of Hitlerism. Its fairy tale atmosphere of suspended time and ritualistic sequence of acts would speak against it, though not, of course, against its attraction which lies in the coolly beautiful evocation of fated terror and its higher meaning.

Some of the text's archaism does correspond to the regime's cultural politics, and some passages can be read as an open if mild critique of such tendencies.[116] On the whole, Jünger is too much absorbed in the aesthetics of his construct, especially in the arrangements of bits and pieces of archetypical landscape—the Marina, the Campagna, Alta Plana, and the Forests—with their carefully listed flora and fauna including the human: fishermen, peasants, herdsmen, hunters, tribal warriors, ascetic warrior intellectuals, and the forest-dwelling subhuman riffraff with their mythical dogs. Weapons and tools are archaic with a touch of science fantasy; culture is organic (even where it is technological), and politics is tribal.

Descriptions of the warring tribes may have played on certain similarities to political figures on the extreme right in the thirties—Göring, for instance. Jünger is most intrigued with his creation of an intellectual warrior caste, the Mauretanians, with whom the brothers had at one time been associated. They, too, courted the Ranger and were courted by him. His world is pagan and savage, in contrast to the paganism and syncretism of theirs: the Marina with its highly civilized Latin echoes or the nobly simple culture of feudal Alta Plana. The forest is dominated by barbarous idols in animal shape demanding sacrifices unworthy of man—for instance, the unspeakable acts carried out by a goblin-torturer, which have been read as a critical reference to Nazi practices of torture.

The Mauretanians are utopian technicians,[117] bearing "the unmistakable stamp of nihilism in its later stages" with their cold "rootless intelligence" and their proclivity for the "pleasures of mimed sensuality." They do and do not answer to the epithet *zersetzend* (corrosive), omnipresent in Nazi attacks on the intellectuals. The Mauretanian Braquemart resembles Goebbels physically, but not intellectually, at least not in any intelligible useful sense. The narration stresses both his negative attributes—creation has died in his heart and he has reconstructed it like a mechanism—and the positive effects of his *Haltung,* further enobled by a "subtle air of suffering," a sickness of heart under his professional rigidity and remoteness. The dark brutal forces, he knows, cannot be combated successfully, but he will die fighting them.

Such portrait of the heroic solitary intellectual is informed by Jünger's need for fanciful self-stylization rather than by any cultural reality. Yet this elaborate pose is as instructive a cultural image as was the earlier one of the heroically individualistic nationalist young officer. The Mauretanian may be a technocrat and therefore suspect to a degree, but in his own way he is authentic. Even the Ranger shares in such authenticity, be it one of fear, pain, and terror. Like many of his contemporaries, the narrator, above all, adores authenticity. This is the main reason why *On the Marble Cliffs* fails conspicuously as a political fable. It is also by no means clear that this autobiographical fiction had been intended as an accessible political statement. But given the situation in 1939, one would assume that the author expected his readers to approach the text in these terms.

Braquemart, the intellectual technocrat, loses the fight for possession of the Marina: where the Ranger wants to people it with beasts, he wants to construct a rigidly hierarchical society of lords and slaves. Jünger stated later that in constructing the figure of Braquemart he had been interested in the combination of misanthropy, atheism, and great technical intelligence which he thought typical for the time and which included a Heydrich as well as a Goebbels, Hitler's supporters as well as his opponents.[118] In a diary entry of April 2, 1946, he remembers his position during the Nazi period as that of a precise observer of a complicated game, icily passionate in his curiosity about the end. He especially prides himself on the cool dispassionate recording of violent acts and events and on his finely honed talent for appreciating them in aesthetic-intellectual terms which are "profound" precisely because they acknowledge the sufferings of others only by transcending them.

Jünger has always liked to express admiration for great technological intelligence, but he has never shown his authorial or narratorial self to be technologically or scientifically informed—not, that is, in terms of modern scientific thought and technological development. *On the Marble Cliffs* reflects a distinctly premodern concept of science: the brothers collect and catalogue plants according to the schemata designed by "the masters." Accumulating, spreading out, they imitate a created order to which they bring no questions. Braquemart the technician has attempted to create and has failed; they, reverently, "draw nourishment from created things, and herein lies the power of science."[119]

Stripped of images and action and actors, this conceptual dichotomy seems too transparent and primitive to find an echo with readers. Yet it was central to the cultural conflict of the Weimar period and is very much with us today. It is, on the one hand, the suspicion that science with its cold mechanical probing will disturb the created, given, therefore humanly meaningful order of things, and, on the other hand, the fascination by the inexorable motion of the scientific, technocratic spirit of the time, borne on the wave of "it's coming." The assumption that no order is given in the sense of original creation and that all order is humanly meaningful precisely because it is constituted culturally in processes of human questioning and probing has seemed an intolerable encroachment on human dignity engaged in the search for higher, that is, culture-transcending meaning. And Jünger has posed the question of human dignity with an irritating stunningly literal insistence on man's highest rank in the universal order of things and on some men's highest rank in the universal order of men.

This insistence on a static hierarchy of value controlling all aspects of the life-world did reflect contemporary anxieties but prevented Jünger from producing any useful social analysis. And this was not to change; he has never observed; he has always arranged, ranked, passed judgment. It is true, his naive enduring anti-Americanism[120] has not kept him from being intrigued by various aspects of technology, but he has been uninterested in their concrete sociopolitical implications and unable to understand the complex dynamics governing the development of technocracy. When he described the position and power games of the Chief Ranger exclusively in terms of their atavistic properties, he completely neglected the perhaps most important aspect of the Nazis' political success: the simultaneous assertion of national-individual meaning as nurtured and preserved by the (reinterpreted) past and promise of such meaning as continued and enhanced in a victorious future. Victory synonymous with higher meaning would be achieved by the profound and disciplined German genius putting advanced technology in the service of the glorious survival of the naturally (unquestionably) superior people.

Hitler had negligible technical intelligence, but he understood extremely well certain dynamics of mass technocracy. With his palpably modern love for cars, highways, and planes he demonstrated the taming of potentially dangerous technological forces which would now be prepared to serve the German everyman as *Volksgenosse*,[121] that is, the individual German as member of the body of the *Volk*. In the late twenties and early thirties the deep pleasures of blood and soil and rich promises of technology did not cancel each other out but rather combined to redirect Weimar technocracy so that it would support a brutal atavistic totalitarian regime. Science as questioning of physical processes was firmly anchored in the unquestioning acceptance of created social order. The Nazi regime was radical in its reassertion of a status quo in all fields of cultural activity with the exception of science and technology because these were tied to the survival of the *Volk* most literally.

Jünger never understood Hitlerism, neither its temporary appeal, nor its enduring catastrophic potential. In that, of course, he was not alone among German intellectuals. What set him apart from Marxist and liberal intellectuals is the radical concreteness of his cultural conservatism, derived from an unusually intense need for self-preservation. For Jünger the trauma of the survivor did not so much entail the issue of the survivor's guilt but of his inviolateness. The trauma is central to modern experience, and much of Jünger's power to attract as well as repel is related to his particular preoccupation with the survivor as the authentic person who unchanging, unaffected, towers about the flux and disorder of social reality.

The survivor is the true aristocrat who has passed through pain and fire. Increasingly he becomes static, fixed in his position of literal superiority: higher,[122] purer, more remote from life and more in tune with its essence of truth, a neo-idealist aesthetic phenomenon. The brothers' reverent description of Pater Lampros provides a good example:

We often discussed this over our fire of wine-cuttings in the Hermitage, for in times of threat such personalities tower above the weak herd. Sometimes we asked ourselves if to him ruin seemed already too far advanced for cure, or whether modesty and pride[123] prevented him from joining in party strife with word or deed. But Brother Otho best summed up the situation by saying that, for such natures as his, destruction had no terrors, and that they were so constituted as to pass into the fiery furnace as if through the portals of their father's house. Of us all, perhaps he alone, deep in his dreams behind the cloister walls, was in complete contact with reality.[124]

Of a higher nature, that is. Leaving behind the life lived in the static order of the Hermitage to be received, in the end, into "the haven of our father's house," they see Pater Lampros in front of his burning church, the huge window behind him like the "mouth of a furnace." The moment of his death is the moment of transformation to a higher form of being and of initiation, for the brothers, to a secret symbolism which unlocks meaning. The noble beauty of his death flows out of his terrifying power and, suitably, his and the brothers' world collapses around him, is left behind.

The direct association of Pater Lampros with fire reflects Jünger's preoccupation with fire as *Urbild* for rites of passage. The "old master" Nigromontanus had bestowed on the brothers a mirror with the property of intensifying the rays of the sun into flames. "Things set aflame by such ardor passed into incorruptibility" as the purest distillation of their essence, and the realms that lie behind destruction are magic spaces: the master called them "the haven of annihilation and we resolved to seek it when the hour of ruin had come."[125] The rites of passage do not lead to adult responsibility and intelligent risk, but, rather, into the haven of paradisaical permanence and literal meaning, that is, of the redeemed "higher" childhood of the prelapsarian state.

Images of the magic mirror's power echo images of fire and blood celebrating the more real, more true experience of the warrior in the magic moments and spaces of battle. With *On the Marble Cliffs* Jünger had finally found the permanently safe higher realm of authentic existence behind the destruction of the familiar life-world. The young soldier's pathological preoccupation with survival, the result of a severe trauma which had never been acknowledged and never been attended to, had been redeemed magically in the truer life behind the fire, the truer inviolable self after the passage of self-sacrifice. In our context, Jünger's dialectics of fire and blood is only the most literal and savage form of the contemporary German preoccupation with cultural redemption. He differs substantially from other Weimar intellectuals because of his total physical immersion in the war and his self-transcending performance and pose as warrior, but he shares in their cultural conservatism, even if his is more literal and more radical. This attitude caused the infusion of an incomplete past with a paradisaically complete future and burdened culturally useful acts of remembrance with culturally destructive projections of redemption. Like many other Weimar intellectuals across the political spectrum,[126] Jünger was unable to question contemporary culture rationally. Caught, as they were, in the vicious circle of concrete rejection and abstract hope, the conceptual muddle preventing any serious attempts at mediation appears more obviously self-defeating in his case. His fictions seem more rigid, more dysfunctionally static, and more exclusively self-centered. But, caught in this way, they all do share in the peculiar anxiety of cultural meaning which was (and has been) symptomatic of the failure to examine critically, as contemporaries, the experience of modernity.

SIX

Redemptive Narration

Hermann Broch, Alfred Döblin, and the Metaphysics of Community

I.

A recent evaluation of the significant contemporaneity of Broch's work culminates in the assertion that his "humanistic comprehensive vision leading to a synthesis" *(humanistische Zusammenschau zu einer Synthese)* gives new life to scientific, philosophical, and sociological ideas by inspiring them, in a very literal sense, with higher meaning.[1] Hermann Broch, who himself made precisely those claims for his novels and essays, has been hailed by professional readers as *the* poeta doctus, poet *and* mathematician, logician, politician, scientist, essayist, whose mystic-poetic vision achieves the precision of a mathematical formula.[2] This heady combination—Rathenau's identification with a composite Einstein-George comes to mind—is a well-known symptom of the cultural conflict central to Weimar period. That critics still think it possible to appeal to it points to the uneasy cultural position of the humanities in the last decades of this century. Such appeals enable critics today, as they enabled Broch half a century ago, to embrace scientificity as the modern cultural priority *and* transcend it, thereby neutralizing its intellectually and socially disturbing aspects.

Broch has not been taken seriously as philosopher, political scientist, sociologist, or mathematician by professional readers outside the humanist scholarly community of literary historians and critics. His best-known work, the trilogy *Die Schlafwandler* (1930–32) *(The Sleepwalkers)*[3] is a novel of ideas explicitly intended to address the totality of the conflicts and complexities of the modern world. Like Musil's *Man without Qualities*, André Gide's *Faux-Monnayeurs*, Aldous Huxley's *Point Counter Point*, all published within six years of each other, *The Sleepwalkers* touches on the most important clusters of sociopsychological and sociophilosophical questions confronting intellectuals between the two world wars. But Broch emphatically placed his novel as "polyhistorischer Roman," outside the group of contemporary philosophical novels. His novel, he wrote, again and again, to his friends, to his publisher Brody, to his excellent translator Willa Muir, was

uniquely innovative, original in its development of a new novelistic concept
and form intended "to integrate those areas of philosophy which address
themselves to metaphysical needs but, according to the current state of
science, *Wissenschaft,* must be acknowledged to be unscientific or, quoting
Wittgenstein, 'mystical.' "

It is precisely this integration and its dimension of totality which Broch
defines as the specifically *wissenschaftliche* dimension of his *polyhistorischer Roman.*[4] It is true that Broch's concept of *wissenschaftlich* is
very much informed by the broader German and French understanding of the
term—*Geisteswissenschaften, sciences humaines.* But the intellectually curious industrialist and trained engineer, who was interested in many different
fields of inquiry and approached them with the dilettante's engaging eagerness and not infrequent conceptual confusions, had the "hard sciences" in
mind, too, when he reassured his publisher that not only was the time ripe for
a polyhistorical novel like his—it was calling for it. No other philosophical
novel had been able to solve the problems posed by such attempt at such
total integration. Joyce, Gide, Mann, and Musil could be seen as forerunners
of the polyhistorical novel, Broch concedes, but not more than that. Besides,
they severely "trivialize" the attempt itself.

Significantly, in making this serious accusation, Broch uses the term
verkitschen—to make inauthentic, trivial—which signifies an important aspect of the thrust of his radical cultural conservatism and which, like many of
his key concepts, is never defined in any logically accessible manner.[5] The
only definition his correspondents, and, by extension, his professional readers are given is that his novelistic "methodology" differs profoundly and
significantly from that of all other serious contemporary fiction. The novel,
Broch argues in a much-quoted letter to Brody,[6] is poetry; poetry is concerned with the deepest primeval forces *(Ur-Motiventien der Seele). Poly-
historismus* in the novel cannot therefore be established through "the
horrible institution" of sophisticated polite conversation or through scientist-
protagonists. No other novelist, he maintains, has gone beyond the decorative introduction of bits and pieces of science into their narration. From
this indictment he exempts, to a degree, Musil and Joyce: "Musil's method"
is granted some degree of "legitimacy" presumably because Broch was
sensitive to a specific conceptual stringency in Musil's literary discourse.
Besides, Musil was recognized as a highly intelligent, demanding writer by
critics who mattered to Broch. Joyce had become increasingly important for
Broch's self-presentation since Brody's Rhein Verlag had brought out a
translation of *Ulysses* in 1927. It was not, however, a matter of intellectual
stimulation and of learning from Joyce's narrative innovations but rather the
phenomenon of Joyce as *the* modern writer against which Broch needed to
define his own achievement which also meant to him the challenge of superseding Joyce.

Broch wanted to develop the novel into a medium capable of solving the
contemporary, modern conflict between the intellectual-scientific and the

emotional-creative tendencies and energies of the mind. His concept of the cultural conflict, however, and his narrative strategies contributed to rather than deflected its virulence. In his 1936 essay "James Joyce und die Gegenwart," which is essentially a statement about his own uniquely contemporary polyhistorical novel, he assigns to poetry the "ethical task" of raising itself to a higher sphere of knowledge, *Erkenntnis*. The *wissenschaftlich* dimension is established through the linkage and integration of the rational and irrational components in the agents and the action of the novel. Five years earlier he had written to Willa Muir about the "risk" *(Wagnis)* of a "vital science" *(lebendige Wissenschaft)* in the novel, with which only he and Joyce had succeeded. And to Daisy Brody he had pointed out, at the same time, the unique scale of *The Sleepwalkers,* covering the "totally irrational" in the story of the Salvation Army girl and the "complete rationality of the theoretical," by which he means his "theory" of the disintegration of value.[7] This theory, however, is derived from a radically conservative, largely irrational, metaphysical position of cultural despair which he shared, even in details of blood and soil imagery and rhetorical appeal, with the extreme right: modern urban men and women are like sleepwalkers, caught in profoundly inauthentic lives, in desperate need of redemption and finally somehow redeemed. This does not, of course, make the upper-middle-class Austrian Jew Broch, who loved the Austrian mountains for their authenticity and set his most ambitious novel in several German industrial cities, a protofascist. But it does, once again, bring into sharp focus the similarity of cultural concerns and conflicts underlying a wide spectrum of political and intellectual affiliations.

When Broch wrote the Joyce essay, *The Sleepwalkers* had achieved critical if not commercial success, and he wanted to draw on Joyce's authority when explaining the "formal" aspects of the (his) new integrative narration. So he describes the technique of simultaneity in *Ulysses* as intended representation of "a totality of life and man" from "the deepest irrational stratum up to his most rational thought"—precisely his own goal in *The Sleepwalkers*. The Joyce esssay also introduced the concept of the "Erzähler als Idee" (narrator as an idea), which, following Broch's wishes, has become a much used term in Broch criticism. Broch projects a vaguely associative analogy between the process of his narration and the theory of relativity which is then used to support his claim to a specific scientificity characteristic of the specifically integrative "methodology" of his novel. He includes "ideal observer" and an "ideal act of observation" into the novel as "field of observation," which, he says, results in the unity of the subject of representation, i.e., the *Erzähler als Idee,* and the object of representation *(Darstellungssubjekt und-objekt).* He then substitutes the medium of representation *(Darstellungsmedium),* i.e., language, for the subject of representation *(Darstellungssubjekt),* a juggling act which enables him to present Joyce's (and his own) method as "unity in which one grows naturally out of the other," because, in its totality, it is subject to the novel's *Architektonik.*[8]

By means of his *Architektonik* the "act of observation in itself" *(Sehakt an sich)* is objectified, that is, the author as narrator has been eased out of the novel, be it Joyce or Broch.

This highly speculative reshuffling of narrative positions does not do much for *Ulysses;* it is positively harmful, because misleading, in the case of *Sleepwalkers.* Here the author as narrator is effectively present in all three parts of the novel, always clearly recognizable by his specific position of cultural pessimism and his general emphatic missionary impulses: he exhibits a compulsive need to ensure, again and again, that his characters as well as his readers get and "swallow" the authorial messages most heavily concentrated in the essayistic and lyric inserts of the third part.[9] And yet, it is particularly this part for which Broch claims virtual narrative independence of the author. This independence is realized, he says, through the text's *Architektonik.* But actually it is those inserts with their explicit authorial messages which constitute most clearly the structuring components.

Poetry, Broch says in a 1933 lecture on the world view of the novel ("Das Weltbild des Romans"), is the impatient desire to know—the much quoted "Ungeduld der Erkenntnis."[10] Precisely this precipitous desire for instantaneous knowledge and solution of the most difficult, the most entangled cultural problems, which originated in his intellectual temperament and was intensified by the darkness of the times, made him such a forceful meddler in his own texts and undermined his considerable narrative talent. He seemed to recognize the connection, but only much later, in exile, and he never associated it with the perfect (to him) achievement of *The Sleepwalkers.* After the war, trying to rework the fragment of a religious novel which he had left in 1936 as a curiously ambiguous description of mass seduction, he wrote to his concerned friend and skeptical publisher Brody about his difficulties: what a pity the *Bergroman* could not sustain the "geniale philosophische Salat-Methode" (ingenious philosophical salad) of *The Sleepwalkers.*[11] He understood that his fascination with earth and mother cults and his hope for finding redemption in the cultural innocence and integrity of the peasant had to be directly integrated into the narration of life in a mountain village. He knew that he had to resist the temptation to remain the omniscient metacultural stranger as narrator who had moved his lower gentry *(Sleepwalkers,* 1: *Pasenow)* and lower-middle-class *(Sleepwalkers,* 2 and 3: *Esch, Huguenau)* characters like puppets toward redemption and salvation, at his own speed and without encountering any obstacles.

Broch's extremely idiosyncratic idea of *Wissenschaftlichkeit* based on his indeed impatient desire to know, is largely responsible for the considerable conceptual confusion of the trilogy which bothers even critics admiring of the "higher humanity" of the novel.[12] He saw himself literally as the potential founder of a totally new all-embracing science founded on a (his) new logic and extending to the human, social, and natural sciences; characteristically, he was much more careful with such assertions of a "total science" when communicating with his fellow Princetonians Einstein, an admirer of the *Death of Virgil,* or the mathematician Weyl.[13] He calls, especially in exile in the United States, for a strict scientificity of political and sociological discourse which seems curiously out of place when held against his nebulous project of a "new science" of his largely opaque political and mass-psychological texts.

Broch's reaction to the theory of relativity was exactly what scientists had warned against: he lamented the loss of a Center of Meaning. He purportedly shared with contemporary physicists the acceptance of the theory of relativity as advancing scientific inquiry. But, notwithstanding his many claims to the contrary, he did not allow this scientific theory to influence the way in which he chose and posed philosophical questions in the novel, not even in a figurative sense. A multiplicity of viewpoints and the function of time as the fourth dimension[14] are frequently mentioned in his own and his critics' descriptions of his integrative structural strategies in *Sleepwalkers.* However, they are not put to use to help the reader gain multiple access to the concepts which centrally and exclusively preoccupy the author. His theory of *Wertzerfall,* of a total disintegration of value, derived from a radically conservative concept of culture as stabilizing, centering, meaning-producing, precedes all the questions the novel might pose and arrests all possible processes of knowledge for the reader.

Broch neglected to consider that what was new in the history of physics was by no means new in the history of philosophy and literature, where, apart from philosophical dogma and literary didactics, it had not seemed advisable or feasible to assume that man could be posited as a fixed point on a cultural coordinate system. Significantly, then, the theory of relativity, which views the object not in terms of its absolute authentic *(an sich)* existence, but in terms of its being constituted in relation to points of observation, signifies for Broch the introduction, into philosophy, of mere opinion and subjectivity. He does not see any need to demonstrate the validity of this analogy, but proceeds to assert, emphatically, the need to liberate philosophy from such inauthenticity by reintroducing theology, even theological dogma, or radicalizing the subject to the point where it assumes the absolute authority of poetry, "das Dichterische als Instanz."[15] At the same time such absolute authority has to be supported, in his view, by a rigorous concept of scientificity, *Wissenschaftlichkeit,* to be realized in and through the *polyhistorischer Roman.* Mathematics, the only really scientific discipline in his eyes—he audited university courses in mathematics, did some work on his own, and believed his mathematical notes to be a valuable contribution to basic research in the natural sciences and mathematics[16]—provides a "natural," much used metaphor for the allegedly scientific dimension of the novel. But poetry, producing an "immediate ethical effect,"[17] clearly remains the transcending force, making possible the desired unmediated access to knowledge which even mathematics fails to do.

In exile in the forties, Broch's attitude to poetry as fiction became more ambivalent. He substituted his work in epistemology and mass psychology—

that is, his highly idiosyncratic versions of these fields of inquiry—for what he had come to consider "mere narration." However, he retained his claim of unmediated transcending insight and value for his integrative "methodology" in the social sciences and continued to appeal to the redeeming force of poetry.[18] But the shift is clear. Numerous general references to mathematics as the only truly rigorous, real science now strongly suggested its culturally redeeming value. Marx had supplanted Joyce as the high point of cultural achievement, and Broch set out to supersede Marx in developing his all–embracing *and* rigorously scientific "new science."[19]

Broch's curiously competitive view of cultural priorities was motivated by the desire for a metaphysics which contemporary philosophy did not meet, *and* by the modern intellectual's concern about the growing cultural preeminence of the sciences. His concept of *Wissenschaftlichkeit* was purportedly influenced by the Vienna Circle. He had occasionally audited lectures and was in the habit of presenting his connection with the circle as a highly important formative component in his intellectual development. In his 1942 "Autobiographie als Arbeitsprogramm" (Autobiography as a work program) Broch explained the consequences of the "rule of positivism" for a confused young generation who experienced individual fragmentation and relativism of value as a truthful mirror of cultural-political conflict which had exploded in the Great War and had nowhere to go with their metaphysical needs and yearnings and ethical impulses. He was very much of that generation, but he also thought that "it was necessary to apply strictly critical methods, that is, those of critical positivism, in the area of the idealist position to thus be able to preserve the idealist origin of all philosophizing and yet proceed with that rigor and directness which philosophy needs if it wants to fulfill its eternal ambition, namely, to be a science."[20]

Broch had always held onto this mechanical abstract concept of, as it were, arch-mediation: the application of a dose of rationalism to irrationalist positions, polishing a discourse essentially based on *a priori* assumptions with a bit of scientific rigor.[21] The result was a deep seated conceptual confusion in his nonfictional texts written in exile which he was—for this reason?—unable to finish.[22] An exception was the 1949 essay *Hofmannsthal und seine Zeit* (Hofmannsthal and his times) where his cultural critique was usefully contained by the subject of his inquiry.

2.

In the year 1888 Herr von Pasenow was seventy, and there were people who felt an extraordinary and inexplicable repulsion when they saw him coming towards them in the streets of Berlin, indeed, who in their dislike of him actually maintained that he must be an evil old man.

This beginning of *The Sleepwalkers* has often been used to support Broch's description of his narrative strategies in parts one and two: a multiperspective narration made possible by the *Erzähler als Idee* position of the narrator who functions like the *physikalische Person* in the field of observation. The author attempts, by shifting points of observation, to have a diffuse narrative consciousness become more aware of the protagonists' shifting states of consciousness. A learning process, then, is said to go on in the narrating consciousness, and the reader can participate in it. By setting up, from the very beginning, an elaborate steering system, however, the author controls the points of observation rigorously. He works with a program which he does not wish to have upset by any unforeseen development in his characters which the "narrator as idea" might perceive. To equate this narrator metaphorically with *die physikalische Person* in the field of observation is misleading not only because the theory of relativity works with multiple recordings of data and not with observing real or ideal "persons" but also because the narrator's observations are prerecorded—by the author. Whenever Broch tried to relate scientific thought processes to narrative strategies he did so in a loosely associative manner which says a great deal about his own *idées fixes* regarding certain, admittedly very important, cultural issues but very little about his actual narrative procedures.

The fallacies in Broch's self-commentaries bring into sharp focus his lack of interest in getting to know the other's consciousness by imagining what it is like to be the other. His considerable narrative talent was flawed by precisely this lack of interest: it prevented him from ever fully realizing the difficulties, challenges, and rewards inherent in the attempt to imagine the other in narration and exploit the possibility of reflection on this process provided by the novel of ideas. It seemed easy to him, too easy, to tell "Gschichtl" (little stories)[23] as he called it. He was not interested in what he could do with stories as negotiable, temporary fragmentary models of sociopsychological experience. He was intent, rather, on getting to truth and meaning beyond such experience and so took seriously neither the story nor experience nor the connection between them. The purportedly *wissenschaftlich* dimension of *The Sleepwalkers,* supported by the claim to have bridged successfully the (neatly split-up) rational and irrational components of the human mind, moves this supernovel beyond mere stories which would present a social reality shared with others. Human experience and the experience of the merely human seemed too miserable to be taken seriously. Man, Broch insists, has to be confronted with the Ur-fact that he has been created in the image of God and such confrontation cannot but result in the existential devaluation of all modern men. In their "empirical wretchedness" *(empirische Erbärmlichkeit)* which taints all their thoughts, feelings, and actions, they are, every one of them, totally disoriented, sleepwalkers, desperately in need of redemption. Only the archetypically human man, the peasant, has transcended such wretchedness to a level of authentic being.[24]

The reader of *The Sleepwalkers* is pushed inexorably to recognize, acknowledge, and transcend this contemptible human reality. If he tries to break away from the author's control, he will be unable to make sense of the novel. The men mentioned in the first sentence, suggesting an additional, differentiating perspective, do not appear again, instead the narrating voice is used to make sure the reader views the hateful old man in the appropriately meaningful context of all-pervasive cultural sleepwalking. The narrative perspective is then momentarily placed in the crowd through which old Pasenow passes; a deluded young man is mentioned, who possibly contemplates an aggressive act against the old man, and this shadowy one then analyzes with loving hate the old man's way of walking, a visually intriguing *Gestalt* description of Broch's strong-willed and difficult industrialist father who had not approved of his son's intellectual aspirations. But when this one starts to sum up his intense dislike for this miserable specimen of mere humanity, he is immediately supplanted by the narrating voice:

> but the horrible and disgusting thing was that he was a three-legged pacer, a tripod that had set itself in motion. And it was horrible, too, to realize that this three-legged purposiveness of the man's walk must be as deceptive as its undeviating rapidity: that it was directed towards nothing at all.

This directive given to the reader at the end of the second page will be repeated over and over again throughout the novel: man with his shallow instrumental rationality which causes his profound existential disorientation, *Dahindämmern,* cannot but march directly into nonbeing, nonmeaning. Again and again the flux of narration is halted to make sure the reader is not lagging behind in his lesson in higher knowledge.

The Pasenows are gentry. Not unlike Rathenau, Broch had a distinct predilection for a mythical nonurban, nonbourgeois (Prussian) landed aristocracy, but being Austrian and, compared to Rathenau, a small industrialist finding happiness vacationing in the Austrian mountains, his ideal of humanity was the individualist *Bergbauer,* the peasant working a small and difficult plot in the mountains which forced him to use comparatively archaic methods of farming. The reader is shown the disintegration of the Pasenows' feudal world, not because it is an anachronism in 1888—as is Broch's *Bergbauer* in the 1930s—but because the Pasenows, as their author's creatures, are intent on elevating "earthly things into the realm of the absolute" *(Irdisches zu Absolutem),* so that they have to be punished. This explanation, as obscure as it is essential for the narrative direction, is tentatively put into the mouth of the intellectual Bertrand, the most elusive figure of the whole trilogy, and yet the most important one for the reader who expects the novel to make sense: "This is what Bertrand might have said."[25]

In the second part, *Esch oder die Anarchie,* Bertrand is only present in and through the minds of other characters. In the last part, *Huguenau oder die Sachlichkeit,* he appears reincarnated in Dr. Bertrand Müller, a sort of everyman intellectual that Broch finds useful for his narrative and ideological purposes in spite of his strongly expressed contempt for the intellectual as protagonist in the modern novel of ideas.

Bertrand, largely a shadow, is the structurally most important character. Broch had originally planned, he wrote Brody in June 1930, to use his name as the title for the whole novel. Some months earlier he had explained the role of Bertrand to H. G. Meyer, a competent sensible editor known for his successful launchings of difficult authors—Heinrich Mann, for instance. Meyer who was now working for Brody's Rhein Verlag habitually cautioned Broch with respect to his compulsively high-minded didacticism vis-à-vis his readers which expressed itself so clearly in the descriptions he wrote of his book for use by the publisher in the advertising campaign for the novel. Bertrand, Broch had written, is "the passive main protagonist of the whole novel, typical 'rational man,' in many ways precursor of the positivist [*sachlich*], but not value-neutral, rather value-negating, ethical and structural counter pole to the sin of being unawakened [*Sünde des Unerweckten*] and destroyed by the sin of the rational [*Sünde des Rationalen*]."[26]

This is how he saw the Bertrand figure before he had reworked the third part, *Huguenau,* that is, before he had inserted the essayistic chapters on *Wertzerfall* which are authored by Dr. Bertrand Müller. The Bertrand figure would then represent the lament of the loss of a meaningful cultural center. Yet, in the first two parts where he is seen through the shifting perspectives of young Joachim Pasenow and the bookkeeper Esch who are, in turn, linked by their obsessive search for redemption, Bertrand could be said to represent the value-negating position assigned to him in the earlier letter by his author. He is used to help in the articulation of the yearnings and anxieties of the two protagonists, yet as Broch self-consciously tries here to do without the figure of the intellectual, it is often impossible to distinguish between the narrating voice and Bertrand. In addition, this voice often corrects or mitigates Joachim's sexually paranoid perspective on Bertrand. In *Esch* all the comments are given by the narrating voice, as Bertrand, by the author's fiat, is outside or beyond Esch's fictional reality. Bertrand's final transcendence in part two results in an even greater emotional ambiguity and conceptual confusion. The reasons for his metaremoval from the fictional scene are left unclear; the petty bourgeois Esch is, after all, not less articulate than the simple *Landjunker* Joachim Pasenow, nor are his yearnings in important ways different.

Esch is in many respects an interesting figure; the experience of running, reluctantly, the family business before he turned to full-time writing with *The Sleepwalkers* may have helped Broch to develop his talent for seeing and presenting the *Gestalt* of an individual figure. This talent served him well with characters from his own class and background, but also with characters from the expanding *and* stratified middle-class world of the clerks, which became increasingly important in cultural and political terms during the Weimar period. But he could never refrain from overburdening his often visually clear, well-drawn protagonists with deeper meanings which diffused them and confused his readers.[27] Where Musil used the fusion of the character's narrated monologue and authorial comment in his attempts to help the reader see more clearly the genesis of culturally significant psycho-logical states, Broch used such fusion in constructing an increasingly elabo-rate ambiguity.

Esch's need for redemption seems to be more urgent than Joachim's, though, in part two, less consistent; this will change in part three. For Joachim, Bertrand is both attractive and repulsive in a metasexual way. He combines for him the androgynous properties of an angel and of an effemi-nate actor. It is the narrating voice which emphasizes, for the reader, this recurrent linkage of contrasting associations and its deeper meaning. For Esch Bertrand is many more, and more different, things. But, then, his identity is secured by his balancing bookkeeping, which extends to matters of the soul, whereas Joachim's is sustained only by the stark meaning of his uniform.

In the case of Esch's reaction, too, the association *actor* is important, but the concepts and images of dream, sleepwalking, death, and redemption are now linked to Bertrand in an increasingly dominant manner. Esch's courting of Mutter Hentjen, the elderly unattractive widow of an innkeeper, which signifies his search for *the* mother, and his eagerness to sacrifice himself so he could be redeemed, connects Mutter Hentjen and Bertrand, of whom he is suspicious but to whom he also looks up as to someone from a higher sphere. Then there is a link between the vaudeville actress Ilona, whom Esch associates with redemption, and Bertrand. All the images and associations clustered around the concept of redemption are both highly controlled and redundant. They are neither psychologically nor socially credible or instructive as they are not intelligibly related to a character Esch whom the reader could come to know and understand gradually. In spite of a certain number of well-chosen visual details—for instance, Mutter Hentjen's pub, her clothes and gestures, the gait of a crippled union organizer—Esch in his world remains opaque under the pressure of his author's relentlessly repetitive lamentations over the total disintegration of value which tran-scends all concrete cultural concerns.

At the end of part two the reader is sent on to *Huguenau* with Esch's statement that "here on earth we have all to go our ways on crutches." This will be literally true for the disintegrating world of part three, the last two years of the Great War. There seems to be no possible fulfillment for man in his miserable social reality. Yet, all along Esch's consciousness has been consistently controlled by his author's gnosticism distributed by the nar-rative voice. The sentence preceding Esch's statement is instructive in this context:

> When presently they [Esch and Mutter Hentjen] got married, and the business was knocked down for an absurdly low price, these were stations on their symbolical road, yet at the same time stations on the road leading them nearer to the lofty and eternal, which, if Esch had not been a Freethinker, he might even have called the divine.

If the reader agrees with this gnostic thrust he can find his way through the novel by holding fast to the narrating voice, and it will not make much difference whether it fuses with certain characters or not. If, however, he is uncertain or critical, he will get lost in the interweaving of voices, which is characteristic of part two, and the *Architektonik* or "counterpoint" structure of part three, which even a generous and sympathetic reviewer like Hesse called an unnecessary "Zerschnitzelung" (chopping up).[28] Broch's puzzled professional readers have constructed heroically elaborate interpretations in the attempt to make sense of the "symphonic" or "architectonic" structure of part three and, if possible, understand Broch's position regarding the question of cultural redemption.[29]

The *Anarchie* of Esch's world in part two has become the *Sachlichkeit* (matter-of-factness) of Huguenau's world in part three. Bertrand had earlier been characterized as *sachlich,*[30] which would make him the precursor of the ruthless *sachlich, wertfrei* (value neutral) opportunist Huguenau who at the end of the trilogy murders Esch. On the one hand, this would not fit at all the fact of Dr. Bertrand Müller's authorship of *Wertzerfallstheorie* and his purification if not redemption. On the other hand, Huguenau's criminal act is assigned a higher (and highly ambiguous) meaning. He approaches Esch "with a few feline tango-like leaps," and runs the bayonet into his angular back; Esch falls on his face without making a sound:

> Huguenau felt grateful to him—all was well now! He crouched down and looked into the sidewards-turned face with its unshaven stubble of hair. When he failed to find in it the jeering expression he had feared he was satisfied and clapped the dead man benevolently, almost tenderly, on the shoulder. All was well. (p. 614)

Is there, then, redemption for the killer and the victim? The epilogue, "Disintegration of Values," which troubled the sensible reader and publisher Brody, concludes with the resounding "Pauline consolation":

> from our bitterest and profoundest darkness the cry of succour comes to the helpless, there sounds the voice that binds all that has been to all that is to come, that binds our loneliness to all other lonelinesses. And it is not the voice of dread and doom; it falters in the silence of the Logos and yet is borne on by it, raised high over the clamour of the non-existent; it is the voice of man of the tribes of men, the voice of comfort and hope and immediate love: "Do thyself no harm! For we are all here!"

Pasenow, now a middle-aged officer, Esch, and Huguenau have been received, it seems, into the ultimate, the most meaningful community; they have been saved.

Brody had recommended a slight silver cloud in the horizon for a conclusion of the novel; trilogies especially, he wrote, ought not to end in desolation. But he could not see how Broch could possibly justify a good ending for *Huguenau.*[31] One cannot but agree with him, even though Broch

had stressed in the epilogue that Huguenau had forgotten the murder immediately and that this sleepwalker, caught in the "commercial system," could
not help himself, could not be held responsible.

> For the irrational in man has an affinity with the irrational in the world; and
> although the uncertainty in the world is, so to speak, a rational uncertainty,
> often, indeed, merely an economic uncertainty, yet it springs from the irra-
> tionality of the super-rational, from an independent reason that strives towards
> infinity in every province of human activity, and so, reaching the super-rational
> limits of its infinity, overthrows itself and becomes irrational, passing beyond
> comprehension. (p. 640)

There is indeed no intelligible connection between the two quoted passages,
and the messages they contain are not logically accessible. Like Thomas
Mann, Broch was addicted to the consolations of closure which helped to
mitigate the picture of a chaotic self-destructing world. But in Broch's text
the anxiety of meaning is not ironically diffused, and the conflicting positions
are not as neatly—nor as safely—separated. Cultural redemption is a more
urgent issue for the German-Jewish intellectual Broch. The religio-gnostic
dimension of the trilogy which was both intensified and expanded in his next
fictional text, the 1936 novel-fragment *Bergroman,* has its source in Broch's
attitude toward knowledge, his *Ungeduld der Erkenntnis* (impatience for
knowledge), which was not directed toward a world of which something can
and might be known, but toward a world which will reveal its meaning totally
and, to the seeker, instantaneously.

Broch had an outline of *The Sleepwalkers* sent to Musil in early 1930. In
a diary entry in January 1930, Musil acknowledges similarities in their
interests and intentions. After reading the novel, however, he is much more
critical: Broch, he notes, makes the philosophical novel suspect. "Is a novel
of ideas [*Gedankenroman*] mistaken if its ideas are wrong? And at what point
does it become so? Is a *Gedankenroman* a bad novel if it is formally flawed?
But why are readers so unwilling to excuse formal flaws?"[32]—in contrast,
that is, to flawed thought and conceptual confusion. Musil, whom many
critics have considered to be too intelligent to be a real artist, did not
appreciate the fact that the novel as work of fictional art had, at least for the
last two hundred years, been quite aggressive and successful in setting its
own rules regarding truth statements. Sentences on reality are not only not to
be questioned as rigorously in a fictional context, but they are to be given a
special benefit of doubt in order to realize certain useful aspects of fictionality—for instance, the uses of perspective. But even more important,
especially since the early nineteenth century, they have been protected by the
art status of the literary text: the concept of consensus has been much more
diffuse if it concerned statements as parts of an artistic structure.[33] With the
philosophical novel, however, the implications of fictionality have to be
restated, and Musil's misgivings ought to be seriously considered.

Broch's cloudy gnosticism is allowed to infuse a purportedly philosophical discourse on cultural issues, the *Wertzerfallstheorie,* because this discourse is considered part of the artistic *Architektonik* of part three of *Sleepwalkers.* The novel's "contrapuntal" structure results in a continuous reshuffling of intellectual positions intended to realize the stated goal of the *polyhistorische Roman,* which is the mediation of rational and irrational components. As Broch never really clarifies what he means by rational or irrational,[34] the process of mediation moves back and forth erratically preventing an intelligible development of the characters in their world. Where *Magic Mountain* simplifies the conceptual arrangements to a glossy surface clarity overlying a deep ambiguity of cultural value, *Sleepwalkers* produces a teeming conceptual confusion overlying a radical pessimism concerning cultural value.

It is this conceptual confusion in its connection with cultural motivation and value which Musil thought detrimental to the concept and potential of *Gedankenroman.* When Sidney, almost half a millennium ago, asserted the nonassertive mode of poetic discourse, he emphasized a specific status of truth in fiction: The poet does not lie because he does not affirm, that is, he does not expect the reader of his fictional statements to agree or disagree as he would in the case of nonfictional statements. The poet's license in constructing is met by the reader's license in considering the construct, which means that, ideally, both poet and reader are liberated from doctrine. Now, in a novel like *Magic Mountain,* the reader is bound by the doctrine of a higher truth of the work of art transcending the truth-status of statements on cultural value and suspending the reader's license to consider them critically. In *The Sleepwalkers,* the reader is bound by the doctrine of a cultural *Wertzerfall* of cosmic proportions transcending mere social experience which is presented in the form of a work of fictional art, but this form, especially in part three, is determined by doctrine.

Broch's novel of ideas raises interesting epistemological questions, because its ideas—a gnostic hodgepodge of highly simplified neo-idealist concepts interspersed with vague if emphatically stated references to the novel's "scientific," "positivist" dimension—dominate the flux of narration to the point of undermining its fictional status. In Mann's case, form is meaning, transcending and self-protective; in Broch's case, meaning is transcendence, and its self-evidence is reflected in the novel's "architectonic" or "symphonic" form. Broch was firmly convinced that he had written the "best German novel of the last twenty years," and he believed the blurb he sent to Brody to be a truthful description of his achievement: *The Sleepwalkers* as *polyhistorischer Roman* represented a completely new type of novel, in fact a "turning point in the history of the novel":

> With its completely original philosophy of history and poetic vision, with its scientific and visionary precision, the novel has reached a significantly elevated

vantage point from which the poet can read our time, pointing the way into the future.[35]

The high-mindedness of this passage is essentially untranslatable—in more than one sense. Broch made some ironical gestures in the accompanying letter to the friend, but he also reasserted his belief in the effectiveness of such statement for advertising his book to (what had to be) an educated audience. After all, he used similar language and reasoning in almost all his texts, fictional or essayistic.[36] Visionary heights are plentiful and they unerringly point away from what to his mind was a totally disintegrated urban culture toward redemption through immersion in authentic (rural) community.

In the 1943 essay fragment on mass psychology "Geschichtsgesetz und Willensfreiheit" (Historical law and free will) Broch, claiming to work with a scientific model, states bluntly that a theory of history can only work if it is assumed that the mass of men, mass-man, cannot but be a mass of *Dämmerwesen*, disoriented, not quite conscious beings, without a will, dreaming, sleepwalking. Having accepted this first thesis because it is so overwhelmingly supported by a contemporary social reality, the theoretically inclined historian can then proceed to "produce" a mass of *Dämmerwesen*— for the sake of supporting the thesis with which he had started his argument. If taken together, the fragments "Autobiographie als Arbeitsprogramm" (Autobiography as a work program) and "Geschichtsgesetz und Willensfreiheit" present over three hundred pages of circular reasoning that historical laws require *Dahindämmern* (living in a state of disorientation), sleepwalking and thus the absence of (disruptive) will, because there would be no controlling regularities otherwise, and that sleepwalking is the prevailing state of men according to historical law.[37] Broch never stopped to ask what such *Dahindämmern* might mean concretely. Bertrand Müller's *Wertzerfallstheorie* is lyrical gnostic lamentation, Esch becomes a neurotic mystic in his obsessive yearning for redemption, Huguenau fulfills a "higher" law in committing a criminal act which intimates mystic community. Apart from the "unconsciously-conscious, unknowingly-knowing" wise peasant, Broch's man is blithely subjected to regularly occurring bloody instances of a historically given *Zerrissenheitswahn*, a fated state of extreme fragmentation, disorientation, and delusion.[38]

Broch finds the proof for his "firmly established theories of inhumanity" in the corrupt power of the Catholic church (*papale Verrottung*) as well as in fascism or bolshevism. They have their source in man's inability to live up to his responsibility grounded in his having been created in the image of God, his *Gottesebenbildlichkeit*. Modern urban man in his "god-forsaken stupidity"[39]—here the notoriously generous and charming Broch is curiously inexorable in his attitude and extraordinarily aggressive in his indictments— cannot ever acquire the organically grown wisdom of the peasant. His *Dämmern* is as fated as his "witty selfish inability to know," his "promiscuous knowledge" and "erkenntnislose Erkenntnisvermessenheit" (hubris of knowledge devoid of knowledge), his "Physiognomie- und Ichlosigkeit." Such mechanical shuffling of prefixes and suffixes, of terms and concepts is characteristic for Broch's "mass psychological" texts. The resultant effect of dysfunctional redundance and the opaque argumentation are even more irritating than the recurrent verbose celebrations of an agrarian idyl.

Broch had experienced urban crowds in 1918; he had disliked the experience intensely, and from then on he had condemned urban life as totally destructive of community and urban man as totally inauthentic. The 1918 crowd was described as nothing but a "Massenaggregat" of "mouths, noses, beards, potbellies" clamoring for freedom, but harboring an idea of freedom which seemed, to the thirty-two-year-old observer Broch, so "filthy," so much oriented toward mere "shallow enjoyment of freedom that it makes one want to vomit." Against this glaring immaturity of the street crowd Broch posits a concept of politics as "a pure ethical challenge" (reine sittliche Forderung) with which the filthy masses will have to be confronted, though they will only taint the pure ideal.⁴⁰ He sees the only solution for this dilemma in a dictatorship, as he explains in the 1919 essay "Konstitutionelle Diktatur als demokratisches Rätesystem" (Constitutional dictatorship as a democratic system of councils). Any healthy state is dictatorial, he claims here—in American exile he was to call for a "totalitarian democracy"—and democracy is only possible if and when "the political state has been totally penetrated by the apolitical idea."⁴¹ This is not pseudo-Hobbesean realism à la Carl Schmitt, who, though problematic, is incomparably more intelligent and more circumspect. This is homemade neo-idealism à la Broch who for decades tried to fulfill what he thought was *his* ethical task: to solve, by poetic fiat, be it in the medium of the novel or the essay, the problems of a technocratic mass society which he instinctively abhorred and of which he knew very little.

Echoing the *deus ex machina* Pauline consolation at the end of *The Sleepwalkers*, Broch planned a grand finale for "Geschichtsgesetz und Willensfreiheit": Even urban man in his "ravaged and ravaging" (wüstes und verwüstendes) Dämmern can find hope against all hope in "genuine prophecy" and "genuine poetry," that is, in its "never ending ethical plea to participate in truth, which means, at the same time and for all time, true humanity and with it the regaining of the human face."⁴²

Like Benjamin and Ernst Jünger, Broch thought poetically against his contemporary culture, though he searched for and claimed redemption through his fictions in more literally gnostic ways than they. With Benjamin he shared the desire to achieve self-realization through fulfilling, that is, transcending, a German cultural tradition. With Jünger he shared a number of key concepts and images reflecting a position of radical cultural conservatism and an all-pervasive sententious didacticism. All three wrote out of a general sense of profound cultural inauthenticity and loss of meaning which could be reversed only by the epiphanic shock of redemption.

3.

Broch used the theory of relativity metaphorically in his attempts at constructing a modern composite perspective on the modern fragmented,
alienating experience of collectivity, but he did so out of a deeper and finally
decisive need for a transcending totality as meaningful community. Alfred
Döblin in his 1929 novel *Berlin Alexanderplatz,* too, is interested in this need,
but on the whole more in its symptoms and etiology than its ontology.
Trained in internal medicine and psychiatry,[43] he had a psychiatric practice
in working-class East Berlin, the area around Alexanderplatz, and he could
not but observe the sociopsychological and physiological interdependencies
causing his patients' mental and emotional disturbances. Moreover, the concept of a coherently, significantly developing self, of unique and always
distinct personhood, had always been problematic to him. This is not to say
that he, like Musil, was intellectually unable to give serious consideration to
such concept. He was, in fact, strongly drawn to religious affirmation of the
self through its linkage with divinity, but his very considerable intellectual
curiosity about the world around him and his medical training and experience
served, for the first and more productive part of his literary career, as forces
countering that seductive pull.

    As a young student of medicine in Berlin, Döblin had been influenced by
Fritz Mauthner's critical observations, in his 1901–1902 *Beiträge zu einer
Kritik der Sprache* (Contributions to a critique of language), on the social
uses of verbal reification in support of exploitable fictions of self in relation to
the other. His interest in explorative rather than determinate approaches to
the (re)construction of thought processes had informed the narrative strategies of his early novel *Der schwarze Vorhang* (1902–1903) (The black cur-
tain). The novel was a failure, but it reflected its young author's awareness of
the processual nature of consciousness and language and of the negative
force held and exercised by words whose meaning has been arrested for the
sake of smoother socialization. Significantly, Döblin gave it the heady subtitle *Roman von den Worten und Zufällen* (A novel about words and accidents). Like Broch and, more subtly and rationally, Musil, and like most
young intellectuals of his generation, Döblin was fascinated by the challenge
of bridging empirical and metaempirical modes of experience: attempting to
say in fiction what "cannot be said" in reality. Mauthner's declared "agnostic
mysticism" in its asystematic aphoristic form suggested to him a similarity of
interest and purpose. He asked Mauthner whether he might send him the
manuscript of the novel, stating that perhaps the critic of language usage
might be interested in a text whose subject is the "conflict between the
perceived illusory nature of a word—love—and the seductive attraction it
holds for the compulsively metaphysical protagonist."[44] Döblin, at this
point, saw only his distance from his protagonist; the reader who follows his
development sees also considerable affinities.

    On one level *Der schwarze Vorhang* is very much a young man's novel:

caught in a sexual conflict of pathological intensity, the Dostoevskian-Nietzschean protagonist kills the woman he desires. But this conflict is also used to bring out the solitariness and disconnectedness of the individual in his social group and its medium, language. At this point only individuals, accidental, disconnected, and solitary, have reality for Döblin. Attempting to present them, he developed the stylistic principle of a montage of shifting perspectives which he was to perfect in *Berlin Alexanderplatz* where the protagonists are the city and the modern "Kollektivwesen Mensch."[45] Already in this early text he uses, in simpler form, the techniques so characteristic of *Alexanderplatz:* breaking, splitting open the protagonist's self, immersing the author and the narrating voice in this process of dissolving the self as a centered consciousness and accessible set of values.

The reality of the disconnected and accidental in individual development experienced, on a daily basis, by the medical student and physician, confirmed the concept of an erratically processual self and supported narrative strategies which would be able to articulate such self. Where *Vorhang* stresses the solitariness of the protagonist, *Alexanderplatz* stresses the new collectivity of the modern metropolis, the modern form of association and socialization. However, the protagonist Franz Biberkopf is in many ways as disconnected, chaotic, and threatened as the young protagonist of *Vorhang*. His finding sociopsychological stability in the new collectivity is, in the end, the result of the author's fiat rather than of his creature's development. The distinct achievement of *Alexanderplatz* is precisely the attempt at penetrating, or at least suggesting an analysis of, the sociocultural meanings of language usage and at presenting the changing self through verbal reactions and interactions. In this his best novel Döblin succeeded to a high degree in establishing a multidimensional mobile narrative position which would leave the reader with the impression of an anonymous energy responsible for the grouping of concepts and images rather than of a particular narrating voice. And yet the author explicitly wanted to be more present in this novel than he had thought desirable in previous novels, and he is.

A multiperspective view on the protagonist's thoughts and actions and on sequences of events is worked out by a composing intelligence which is by no means central, that is, endlessly interfering like the Jamesian narrator watching jealously over each unfurling sentence. On one level the protagonist's progress toward redemption is presented clearly and inexorably: partly by summarizing comments preceding each chapter or "book," which tell the reader how to fit the broadly and brilliantly narrated chaos into the narrow road toward (unexpected) salvation; partly through the control of images clustering around the themes of sacrifice, death, and rebirth. On another level—and here lies the enduring importance of the novel—the text manages to create the sensation of being constantly on the move, in the process of organization, deorganization, reorganization. Both protagonists, the city and the petty bourgeois criminal Biberkopf, are constructed, disassembled, and reconstructed before the eyes of the reader.

There is no emphasis placed on the loss of a center of cultural meaning. Such loss seems to be taken for granted quite calmly, and its implications are explored rather than lamented. The onomatopoeic mimetic rendering of the rapid and surprising flux of life in a modern metropolis is remarkably uninhibited, over long stretches, by a concurrent or countercurrent subtext of individualist mysticism which seems to contradict Döblin's remarkable social experience and psychological perceptiveness. This subtext emerges in full force only in the last chapter of the novel, but it does cause its central ambiguity and conflictedness. Intellectually irritating, this "inevitable dualism," as Döblin used to call it, is nevertheless instructive in view of the increasingly polarized and violent mass politics and the precarious role of the individual during the last years of the Weimar Republic. The process of Biberkopf's sociopsychological disintegration is narrated in images and concepts of mental illnesses familiar to the physician,[46] and its catalyst is the homosexual psychopath Reinhold. Yet even where they become so intense and self-threatening as to suggest a mystic annihilation of the self—admittedly a fascination for Döblin—they still present, for the most part, an accessible reading of the signs of Weimar's illness.

Like Rathenau, Benjamin, and Broch, Döblin was Jewish, but he grew up in a situation much less stable and privileged than theirs. The family experienced a very concrete downward mobility when the father left them to build a new life with a much younger woman. The five children were taken out of high school; the mother, from a solid middle-class family, had to work to support them; and they had, finally, to leave the "paradise," Stettin, on the Baltic where Döblin had spent the first ten years of his life and survive in Berlin on the uncle's charity. Döblin gave several accounts of this early trauma of being abandoned, excluded, and uprooted. His 1928 "Erster Rückblick" (First retrospect) introduces the fifty-year-old Döblin reminiscing in a café at Alexanderplatz, at home and happily immersed in the energetic fluctuating rhythms of the metropolis which he has known for forty years. He is fascinated and absorbed by the complexity and conflictedness of urban life which, as he perceives it, not only allows for but demands a plurality of perspectives on human behavior, and so he narrates his father's deserting the family from different perspectives: from his own perspective of the small boy whose world was shattered and from that of his father, the many-talented dilettante, who had always allowed others to make important decisions for him—what wife to marry, what profession to choose—and who now, in middle life, caught in the web of necessities and obligations, does not see any other way out but that of deception and desertion. He escapes into the illusion of a new life. The composite perspective on the father as middle-aged philanderer is realistic, ironic, even sarcastic, but also sympathetic. And so is his presentation of the mother: handsome, a good catch, not very bright, a victim of the father's weakness and of her own strong and unfounded convictions about the safety of bourgeois marriage and loyalties.

Döblin tells the story three times. However, the effect is not primarily one of enabling the reader to share, with the narrator, different viewpoints associated with different characters and to accumulate information, but rather of having the reader follow the narrator moving around and toward the object of investigation, which is the ambiguity of guilt. The only certain aspect of this situation is the victimization of the children by the parents' troubled relationship together and apart. But even the state of the victim can assume different aspects in narration: here he is, forty years later, richly experienced, familiar with men's and women's lives and their stories, able to see and narrate human dilemmas and traumas sympathetically and shrewdly, even if they have been in significant ways part of his own experience.[47]

Such narration of changes of self in changing environments does not suggest that there had not been traumatic incisions as intimations of the irrevocable and final. It is precisely the finality of the rupture and the finality of the father's futile attempts to make it a bridge to a new life which, together, had hurt and aged the child and made the man more vulnerable. But it is much too simplistic and therefore misleading to suggest, as some critics do, that the trauma of the father's desertion dominated Döblin's intellectual-emotional development to the point where all his texts document his need to escape social conflict by transcending rather than reflecting it and his *kleinbürgerlich* (petty bourgeois) inclination toward aggressivity and the aesthetics of shock and terror. They read Döblin quite simply as a case study in the cultural malaise of the petty bourgeoisie,[48] notwithstanding occasional gestures to the undeniable achievement of *Alexanderplatz Berlin*.

This is not to suggest that critical readings of Döblin are not welcome. He is a very uneven and frequently uncontrolled writer and has been particularly admired—and particularly with the Berlin novel—by artists who temperamentally share his spontaneous and undisciplined creativity. Günter Grass refers to him as his teacher in the title essay of a 1968 essay collection; Fassbinder took fifteen film hours to recreate, as an homage, the expansive chaos of *Alexanderplatz*. It is not only the lack of structural control and the often automatic, compulsive production of language which is problematic, but also a lack of control over certain intellectual and psychological preoccupations. They became more pronounced in exile, especially the intense yearnings for meaning and redemption. But they are clearly present in *Alexanderplatz*, irritating and frustrating precisely the reader who admires the author's remarkable perceptiveness where the dynamics of contemporary sociopsychological conflict are concerned.

After the success of the book he was often asked to comment on its place in his oeuvre; Döblin would point out his conversion, in the late twenties, to the close observation of contemporary reality. However, this turn had not been abrupt, but long in coming. His first major text, *Die drei Spruzünge des Wang-lun* (The three leaps of Wang-lun), was published in 1915 but had been completed in 1913, the year of Döblin's critique of futurism in his open letter to Marinetti.[49] The novel, as Döblin describes it almost ten years later, had been written in eight months, which included the time taken up by the

considerable preliminary gathering of information about a social movement
and its charismatic leader in China around 1800. Narration literally "poured
out of him"—riding the elevated train in Berlin, on night duty at the emer-
gency station, between two consultations, while getting ready to make a
house call.[50]

Some of the reasons for this literary "dam break" are to be found in his
medical career. He had been working as an intern in psychiatry and internal
medicine after the completion of his 1905 dissertation on disturbed memory
function in Korsakoff psychosis, that is, cases of compensation, with fantastic verbal inventions, for extensive memory loss caused by alcoholism.
Döblin understood memory as an organic and organically based process and
tried to analyze memory disturbances as a multifactor syndrome genesis—an
approach that was original and advanced at the time, precisely because it was
specifically cautious and perceptive regarding the interdependencies of mind
and body. During those intern years, he published a considerable number of
medical research papers and became increasingly intrigued by puzzles posed
in internal medicine by the complexity of the interconnectedness of organs
and the complexity of the effects of medication on them. His research, in
fact, became increasingly focused on highly specific connections and less
speculative, and it was this concrete and specific focus which he found
intellectually stimulating. Deciding to get married in 1910, he had to leave, for
financial reasons, a work situation in which he had been happy. Private
practice, which meant much resented divorce from medical research, did not
agree with him, especially in the beginning, and writing the novel helped to
counteract very real professional frustrations, especially, too, as the financial
situation of a *Kassenarzt* (physician working for fixed insurance fees) in the
Alexanderplatz area was by no means rosy.

It is significant that Döblin's notoriously boundless energy and curiosity,
previously absorbed by demanding and highly satisfying medical research,
was now redirected to the fictional analysis of sociopsychological conflict.
The autobiographical sketch he drew of these years which he spent, in part,
as a military physician, is really a list of titles, the writing of fiction taking the
place of living.[51] In the 1913 *Wang-lun,* the 1914 *Wadzeks Kampf mit der
Dampfturbine* (published in 1918) (Wadzek's battle with the steam turbine),
and the 1920 *Wallenstein,* Döblin was above all interested in showing a great
number of major and minor characters in their relation to each other and to
their cultural objects and spaces. In *Wang-lun* and *Wallenstein* he creates
mass scenes which combine an allegorical clarity with expressionist urgency.
He is fascinated by terror, that is, in terms of its primordial social importance
and its narrative presentation.

In contrast to Jünger he is not interested in terror as an aesthetic
phenomenon; in contrast to Broch he does not transform it into metaphysics.
Both novels are directly responsive to contemporary cultural problems of the
greatest importance. The messianic figure of *Wang-lun* reflects the messianic
hopes of contemporary revolutionary intellectuals for a better world to be

brought about by the ultimate cleansing process of revolutionary fire. *Wallenstein* reflects the experience of the Great War. Both novels lack a specifically psychological dimension. There is, in these narrative presentations of social upheaval on a grand scale, a curiously ethological reserve: the narrator does not interfere, his presence is restricted to observation. Speaking about his authorial connection with the texts, he points to the fact that he is incapable of expressing himself other than through the distancing device of fiction: "Also via China and Heiliges Römisches Reich" (So via China and the Holy Roman Empire).[52]

4.

The reason for such reserve is Döblin's concept of *Naturalismus* in fiction, which was to change between *Wallenstein* and *Berlin Alexanderplatz*. In his 1913 open letter to Marinetti, "Futuristische Worttechnik" (Futuristic verbal technique), Döblin had attacked Marinetti's 1909 novel *Mafarka le futuriste* for its pure formal mechanical exercises in shuffling words and syntax fragments though he did recognize the "futuristic" novel's cultural contribution in its willingness to take the risk of moving forward. However, complaining about the self-referentiality of the novel which resulted in its prescriptive verbal abstractionism and its lack of structural direction, he contrasted futurism with what he called *Döblinismus*.[53] By that he meant a (his) willingness to look at the complexity of the real and to resist the temptations of a self-indulgent, self-absorbed "writerly" prose with its neat reductionist arrangements of rich confusions.

His 1913 "Berliner Program," in which he addressed authors of fiction and their critics, recommends *Naturalismus*—or, by implication, *Döblinismus*—against the contemporary established "lifeless realism" based on an attitude of psychologism. To his mind, such psychologism achieves nothing but a rationalist reductionist presentation of motivations and conflicts, that is, speculative, "scholastic" fictions:

> One ought to learn from psychiatry, the only science with a holistic approach to the human being; it has long since recognized the naiveté of psychology and limits itself to the careful noting of processes, movements—shrugging off ontological questions which go beyond observation.[54]

Yet there is an explicit qualitative difference between fictional (epic) and scientific precision—as there is an acknowledged difference between the poet *(Dichter)* and the physician Döblin.

At this stage, Döblin's suggestions about how fictional prose might achieve adequate precision in its responsiveness to a complex dynamic sociopsychological reality are rather reminiscent of futurist prose and so is his celebration of a depersonation of the author *(Entselbstung, Entäusserung des Autors)* as the articulated courage to develop a "kinetic fantasy":[55]

clearly, he wants to share in the élan of the new movement. But here, too, his demand to pay attention to a shared reality of the life-world and his expressed *(Döblinist)* willingness to submit poetic language to the test of experience create a useful critical distance.[56]

In the 1919 essay "Reform des Romans" on the occasion of reviewing Otto Flake's self-consciously modernist *Stadt des Hirns* (City of the brain) Döblin argues against a contemporary modern insistence on the need to explode *(zersprengt)* the form of the traditional novel. His argument strikes the reader in the 1980s as curiously contemporary: such explosion is promised to result in modernist features which are really quite indistinguishable from the so-called postmodernist properties of randomness, indeterminacy, heterogeneity, dispersion, pluralism, multiplicity. Sensibly, Döblin points to the production of modernist novels in the eighteenth and the nineteenth centuries (and postmodernist critics might do well, today, to recognize the fact that postmodernism in fiction is frequently identical with modernism since the turn of the century). But the point of his argument is not to call for a better informed, more balanced historical perspective on the phenomenon of the modern novel. Rather, he proposes to question the justification for such explosive force in general: which novels really need it or can make meaningful use of it? It is again the attempt to define a position against abstractionism and theorizing in the novel. The novel is presentational and representational; it is *about* something as concrete as a shared life-world, about experience, about thoughts and emotions, the more, and the more varied, the better. In presenting a fictional world, the novel can represent multiple aspects of a life-world which is shared by different readers to different degrees. Döblin does not distinguish between the presenting and the representing properties of fiction, and his argumentation, as in all of his essays, is rather loose and frequently erratic, even opaque. But the main thrust is usually quite clear: he thinks it important to attack modern tendencies to make the novel (epic) an ethics or aesthetics, which produce the "god-awful novel jargon"[57] with its self-conscious mixing of reflective and narrative passages in the forceful and futile attempt to integrate art and science. The high-minded intention to retrieve, for the novel, "the power of thought"[58] does not do anything for the novel unless it includes a consistent willingness to take seriously the problem of its fictional representation.

Art has its own referential resources. Döblin shrewdly points out that the modern novel has developed, quite unnecessarily, a bad conscience in reaction to the powerful modern cultural preeminence of science and has started to aim at an impossible integrative totality. This bad conscience distinguishes to a degree the modern novel around 1920 from the modern novel around 1910. Döblin mentions *Mafarka* again, implying a changed situation, but the problem of a self-centered, self-referential formalism, be it that of an exploded form, has remained. The 1924 essay "Der Geist des naturalistischen Zeitalters" (The spirit of the naturalistic period) is a plea to perceive the accelerated changes of the present as an understandable reaction against the tenacious past: culture has too long been associated with High Culture, frequently a narrow-minded humanism. The (naturally) modern "naturalistic impulse" surfaces in the shape of rapidly developing, powerful technology precisely because *geist,* associated with High Culture, has been very conservative and unwilling to consider change. Clearly, the cultural achievement of the twentieth century is scientific, technological; the mental-spiritual *(geistige)* realm of human activities thrives because of the contributions of science, not in spite of it. Parts of this essay seem to be echoing Musil's arguments. Döblin sees quite clearly the fallacies of the cultural malaise, pointing out, in considerable detail, the intellectual implications of many "merely" scientific technological achievements. A Gothic cathedral is not more significant culturally than the invention and development of the dynamo machine or the laboratory synthesis of fruit sugar; it is irrational to attribute enormous importance to a column by Phidias and take the subway for granted: "It is going to be like that: the starry heavens above me and the rails underneath me."[59]

This seems a sensible argument against the German preoccupation with (*a priori* significant) Culture versus (mere, shallow) Civilization. But the mediation suggested by Döblin, in contrast to Musil, is too simplistic; moreover, he proceeds to undermine it himself in the second part of the essay. His description of modern urban life with its functioning collectivism and fruitful differentiation seems at first to support the positive aspects of the influences of technology on modern urban man and woman. They are bright, active, healthily rational, and their enemy is the antirationalist, the humanist of the old school. Moral as well as intellectual *(geistige)* values have been changing very slowly, too slowly, but they are changing: "Man as collective being presents the superior kind of man."[60] The energy and vitality of modern cities is self-evident as a phenomenon and an evolutionary fact. Cities are the "adequate incarnation" for "the new naturalistic spirit" and they are as uniformly expressive of their modernity as were, in their time, the *castella* established by Rome.

Curiously, it is here that the argument begins to change direction. Döblin is still moving toward the sentence I quoted above, which seems to express a positive view of *Kollektivwesen Mensch*—if only because that presents a (necessary) stage in the evolutionary process. But he then proceeds to compare the will to power of the "technisch-naturalistisch" force established in trade and industry to the *ecclesia militans* of the Middle Ages.[61] And once he has begun to concentrate on the issue of force and power, mentioning Soviet Russia, he becomes more and more interested in the emergence of a counterforce. When he speaks about the conservatism of the *Geistigen*—he is referring to the intellectuals in the service of High Culture, the artists—he is by no means unambiguously critical: "It is essentially in the nature of the *Geistigen* to perceive and receive little, to knead through, work through, and digest the old issues and not do much with the new ones."

On the one hand he points out the slowness, the "denseness" of the artists: "The majority of artists and friends of the arts today think, and this is understandable, in terms of 1800 or 1600. Nineteen-hundred will emerge only in 2100." The new movements in literature and the arts had to concentrate, at first, on shock effects in order to draw attention to this discrepancy. But even they were slow to change: "formally liberated they still celebrated the old subjects like the moon, canaries, nightingales."[62] In transitional periods cultural countercurrents are especially powerful. Döblin mentions racism and Zionism with their antiurban tendencies, whereas the urban centers of cultural energy attract movement away from the country. But he does not discuss the tensions resulting from the meeting of these counterforces and their exploitation in cultural politics on the right. He points to the simultaneously effective dynamic poles of the cultural spectrum and suggests that they might be absorbed by the mystical as the boundary concept (*Grenzbegriff*) of science. Here he invokes again the authority of Fritz Mauthner's "godless mysticism,"[63] drawing attention to a new religious current which is asserting itself against the mock materialism of the technical age. He sees, in addition, a thrust toward the mystical and the occult which looks to science for justification. The cities and their inhabitants reflect all these tendencies, and yet they all participate in the specifically modern urban tempo which is defined by technology. In this situation collectivity increasingly becomes an ethical factor: "And this period which does not recognize a god governing the world from the Great Beyond, will see that the essence of this world is, on a grand scale, social and neighborly—much more so than was the case in the humanist past."[64] This, Döblin argues, is one of the most important consequences of the naturalist age: What will become of our world when it really starts rotating around the sun instead of god? The intellectual (*geistige*) consequences of Copernicus's insight have not yet been fully realized. It will not be done by the sciences passionately absorbed in learning nature's secrets, because this learning process is just the first stage; the more advanced stage is mystery: "It is the great *geistig* task of this age to feel the mystery and articulate it in its own way."

This concluding sentence leaves the reader with a powerfully disruptive conflict which has not only not been resolved—this, after all, is not to be expected—but which has been stated ambivalently. The new "naturalist" collectivity seems to be a phenomenon which Döblin views positively, even optimistically. But it also seems dependent on realizing the social consequences of a modified secular anthropocentricity which for Döblin is a *geistig* rather than a scientific task, and, moreover, the *geistig* dimension is conflated with the mystical.

The essay was published in December 1924 in *Neue Rundschau* just after Döblin had come back from a four week trip to Poland financed by his publisher Fischer. This trip proved to be very important to Döblin's gradually, erratically changing view of the human condition. Visiting cities like Wilno (Vilnius), Lublin, Lemberg (Lvov), and Lodz, he learned to appreciate, for the first time, the Jewish experience of cultural energy and unity and of political fragmentation. He identified, to a degree and temporarily, with the realized Jewish unity and understood the conflict but from a certain distance. The much more profound, the essential reality of Poland he found in Krakow where he experienced, also for the first time, an almost orgastic surrender of selfhood and gained, he thought, the sense of a possible deeper, an all-encompassing, whole meaning of (his) life in Polish Catholicism.[65]

Döblin had become more interested in Jewish topics and problems[66] since the occurrence of anti-Semitic disturbances in his neighborhood in late 1923, but rejected a Zionist offer to visit Palestine. In March 1924 he gave a lecture on "Zionismus und westliche Kultur" and in August reviewed Yiddish fiction which he admired for its spontaneity and openness and its both relaxed and compelling oral mode. There are also receipts from the Preussische Staatsbibliothek found among his papers which point to his reading in preparation for the trip to Poland books on Jewish theology and specifically on the cabbalah.[67] In the Poland book he described his attempt to see the rabbi of Gura Kalwarja, member of a famous Hassidic rabbinic dynasty going back to the "Gerer Rebbe" Isaak Meir Alter. He had been impressed by the charismatic power of this spiritual leader *(geistlicher Fürst)* and intrigued by the marvelous, fantastic stories told about him. He was, however, not allowed to see the rabbi and he noted: "Could I, could anybody go back to this stage?" Still, he was clearly fascinated by that mysteriously alien world, remarking on the sixth century *Sepher Jesirah,* the first systematic presentation of Jewish mysticism, that it did indeed reflect another species of man, but "how silly not to listen to it, to trust in the wisdom of a short-lived period like ours." He was later received by another *geistlicher Fürst,* the Strickow Rebbe in Lodz, and he commented on the conversation: "a wonderful talk, a perfect restorative and comfort."[68]

Both the Jewish and the Catholic experience went into the making of *Berlin Alexanderplatz,* but the hope for redemption and meaning set against personal and cultural chaos and death which he found in the crucified Christ was stronger and went deeper, leading to his conversion to Catholicism in 1941 in Los Angeles. It is this hope that caused the "dualism" of the novel which Döblin found inescapable but also, in contrast to most of his admiring critics, not really disturbing, though he did admit, as if to pacify them, that the last part was indeed somewhat problematic. In a much quoted letter to the literary historian Julius Petersen he suggests heaven as the really fitting setting for a conclusion: "another soul saved, well, that was not possible. Still, I had to blow the trumpets in the end whether it was psychologically credible or not. As I see it so far: the dualism cannot be resolved [*ist nicht aufzuheben*]."[69] He refers his reader to his 1927 mystic verse epic set in India, *Manas,*[70] which prefigured Biberkopf but mediated the dualism through the device of mythical rebirth—precisely what Biberkopf's somewhat premature metapsychological rebirth did not achieve. More important, Döblin suggested a link between *Berlin Alexanderplatz* and the 1927 philosophical essay *Das Ich über der Natur* in the preface to a 1932 lecture where he stresses the fact that establishing a *geistig* foundation preceded all his larger epic works. It is in the nature of epic composition, however, that the position from which it starts is gradually superseded in the process of narration, and the epic work (novel) that had begun with a certainty ends with a question.[71] Where the essay represented the world as the conflict between two Gods, oscillating between construction *(Aufbau)* and destruction *(Zerfall)*, the novel, engaging the reader in the process, presents these two modes simultaneously. There is (bourgeois) order and there is chaos (criminality), but one cannot be real without the other. Franz Biberkopf, having left prison, is shown in his very serious attempts to lead a respectable life. But he and his author realize that he cannot do it; again and again he is beaten down in the effort.

This, of course, does not really say anything about the *geistig* foundation of the novel. But it does point to Döblin's view of the process of narration which is at its most erratic, hectic, colorful, spontaneous, "oral," flexible, mobile, scintillating, and confusing in the fictional presentation of Berlin. Döblin had subdued his visionary and fantastic (if not his mystical) impulses in *Berlin Alexanderplatz* and had focused on the world around him: the novel documents how, living among them, he perceived his fellow men.[72] His long suffering publisher Fischer hoping for a commercial success after a series of difficult novels, epics, and essays which had been commercial disasters, had not thought the title *Berlin Alexanderplatz* effective, though he very much approved of a novel about Berlin, the modern metropolis. "That's just a subway station," he demurred, asking Döblin to add the subtitle "the story of Franz Biberkopf."[73] Döblin, who wanted to stress the preeminence of the urban life-world, followed the suggestion and subtly undermined it: His subtitle *Die Geschichte* vom *Franz Biberkopf* deemphasizes, to an extent, the importance of the single individual protagonist and stresses the *story* told in a language echoing the rhythms of Berlin.[74] Yet, as many critics have remarked, the novel ultimately emphasizes more the fictional story of Biberkopf than the fictional presentation of a metropolis. And though the deassembling and reassembling energies of modern urban life are reflected in the skillfully recorded rhythms of Berlin, the conceptual substance of the novel's dualist direction has not been fully integrated into the process of narration but has been allowed to form undissolvable obstacles of conflict: collectivity against community, the individual against mass society, social and personal responsibility against redemption, accidentality against fate.

5.

The transport worker Franz Biberkopf is released from prison where he had spent four years for manslaughter—the killing of his girlfriend with an egg-beater in a fit of rage. Entering the city which seems changed, uncertain of his identity because he has not participated in the change of an environment on which he has had and will have to depend, he promises to be good, but finds that he cannot keep his promise. He tries to find honest suitable work but ends up with a gang of burglars; he tries to become and stay whole and strong but loses an arm and never really regains emotional stability; he tries to be worthy of the great love and loyalty of a young woman but ends up working as her pimp; he loves her for her devotion, her common sense, her lovely freshness, her innocence, but stays entangled in a latently homoerotic relationship with a pathological killer who will murder her. He knows and befriends many different people and is loved by many, especially women, for his warm spontaneity and rough generosity but cannot learn to understand their emotions or his or to respond to them in any reliably controlled way. It is not, then, the Brechtian emphasis on the fact that "this old world of ours ain't built that way" in the first Threepenny-Finale on the "Uncertainty of Human Circumstance," which had been so successful with liberal-bourgeois audiences in Berlin the same year which saw the successful prepublication of *Berlin Alexanderplatz* in the respected bourgeois newspaper *Frankfurter Zeitung*. It is, rather, the problem of the individual, a part of the group, who is responsible for his acts and reactions, and Franz is too slow to acknowledge this responsibility. He is punished cruelly for his willingness to accept the accidentality of his acts and their results for others and blame the results for himself on fate. His author has delegated a narrating voice to inform the readers of the inevitability of this punishment and to reaffirm, throughout the novel, this moral message. But this punishment is also meant to initiate the rebirth of Franz into Franz Karl Biberkopf, a new man, who is not strong but weak, not active but passive, not impulsive but cautious, and who knows once and for all that "it is also nicer and better to be with others. Then I feel and I know everything twice as well. A ship cannot lie in safety without a big anchor, and a man cannot exist without many other men. The true and the false I will know better now."[75] The question remains: what kind of true and false, and what kind of man? The new Franz, much reduced in vitality, curiosity, and (destructive) energy who is able to fit himself into a group only after having undergone what amounts to a lobotomy?

Walter Benjamin reviewed the novel for *Gesellschaft*, and he found a way to transcend the novel's dualism by treating it as indicative of both a "crisis of the novel" and, with its "radical-epic tendencies," the overcoming of this crisis.[76] He sees the "epic" quality of the novel in its innovative and highly successful presentation of spoken language, the "rhythms of Berlin." In contrast to the lonely silent writer as novelist, the epic writer Döblin pulls his reader into an oral situation: never before has the reader been thus drenched to the bone by the foaming surf of real, spoken language.[77] And it is indeed arguable that he has not. The witty skepticism and exuberantly inventive realism of Berlin speech with its irreverent, richly associative mixture of dialect and slang, its mocking ritualisms and debunking idioms had never been captured like this before. Berlin has for a long time been known as a curiously verbal city, both reserved and accommodating, with its many bars where coming together in speech easily and spontaneously has been a way of experiencing a fragmentary temporary community in the flux of collectivity. Notwithstanding all his troubles, the old Franz had not been as alone on Alexanderplatz as his author makes him think after his rebirth, or at least not always: "Now at last he is assistant door-man in a medium-sized factory. He is no longer alone on Alexanderplatz. There are people to the right, and people to the left of him, some walk in front of him, others behind him."[78] But the really important difference between Franz I and Franz II is that he no longer talks with them as he had done before—openly, sloppily, shrewdly, searchingly, trustingly, and always at the risk of misunderstanding and being misunderstood.[79]

Benjamin is rightly impressed by the thoroughness and skill that went into the recording of the voices of Berlin in a seemingly chaotic montage of everything audible in the city, including the shouting of newspaper headlines and political slogans, popular advertisements, songs sung in the streets, the noises of people in motion and of machines. He praises Döblin, the epic medium or "megaphone" for his recording and arranging activities, managing to integrate biblical verses as well as statistics relating to the daily existence of a metropolitan population in the late twenties. In this he is as perceptive and appreciative a reader as Döblin could have hoped for. But he neglects to deal with the issue of Franz's redemption and rebirth, that is, with the conflict between collectivity and community. He does not, for instance, relate the story of Franz Biberkopf—he speaks of Franz's being cured (*Kur an* Franz) as if it were a medical, i.e., localized, affair and not part of a complex sociopsychological development—to what he perceives as the "radical epic" dimension of the novel.

Biberkopf, for Benjamin, is just one of the particles that make up the fast chaotic life of Alexanderplatz. Also, he does not, as does Döblin, draw attention to the shifting, occasionally submerging dividers between the world of the criminal and that of the bourgeois. Franz's development from criminal to petty bourgeois "only describes," he says, "a heroic metamorphosis of bourgeois consciousness." But Döblin, a long-time cultural-political activist on the left who, in contrast to Benjamin,[80] actually lived for decades as a neighbor of the petty bourgeois and the criminal and talked to them in bars and in his consulting room, was not interested in such neatly packaged transformations. His intention is not to expose a petty bourgeois consciousness but to evoke the rich and complex variety of habits, desires, frustrations, expectations, and moral shortcuts linked with the primary need for some physical and emotional security and comfort which is fulfilled or thwarted by people living together and making the best or worst of it.

Benjamin clearly admired the breadth of Döblin's perspective on the lively chaos of Alexanderplatz and the surety of his descriptions, but he did not understand how the many near futile attempts at carving out some tiny segments of order were an important part of that chaos. Too intent on an indictment of the petty bourgeois, he sees Franz's giving up his "hunger for fate"—and he is the rare reviewer to single out this crucial issue—and his final contentment with a mininum of spiritual and material security as the essential precondition for the negative metamorphosis of bourgeois consciousness. This, clearly, was not Döblin's intention. His protagonist's hunger for fate was very much his concern, and much of the novel's conceptual and structural difficulties have their source here—as do many successful passages presenting Franz's disturbed needy searching in powerful images of illness: individual and social dissociation, fragmentation, paranoia, disorientation. But he neither prejudges this need nor does he explore its social implications consistently. His analysis is fragmentary and by no means fully satisfying, but it is not reductionist.

What we learn about Franz in the course of the novel suggests that he might have emerged from the passage through death in a less diminished form. We are told by the narrating voice, which repeatedly admonishes Franz, that he has to learn to recognize the passive, reactionary substance of his strength, its illusionary quality which has been responsible for his destructive acts. He has to learn to recognize and acknowledge his guilt.[81] But he has also been given this strength by his author who is responsible both for arranging the gift, installing the narrating voice, and designing the course of Franz's life. He is a particularly threatening man with his violent temper and great physical power, but he also displays emotional sensitivity and curiosity about the world around him. He is easily attracted and attractive, attentive in his observations,[82] but slow to relate them to his emotions or to clarify them in thought. A man who has no difficulty talking but who is inarticulate.

He is, we are finally told in the preface to the sixth book or chapter, no ordinary man:

> he is an ordinary man only in the sense that we can clearly understand him and sometimes say: step by step, we might have gone the same way, experienced the very things he experienced. I have promised, unusual though it be, not to keep quiet about this story. It is the ghastly truth, this thing I have reported, how Franz Biberkopf left his home suspecting nothing, participated against his will in a burglary, and was thrown in front of an auto. He is lying beneath the wheels: he had doubtless made the most honest efforts to go his orderly, decent, and legitimate way. But isn't this enough to justify despair, what sense can we find in this impudent, loathsome, miserable nonsense, what lying sense can be injected into it so as to construct therewith perhaps some sort of destiny for Franz Biberkopf? I say: there is no reason to despair. I know something, perhaps many others who read this already discern something. A slow revelation is here in progress, you will experience it as Franz experienced it, and then everything will become clear.

The first instruction, preceding the first book, how to read Franz's story, mentions "this thing" which "crashes against our man" three times. Scrambling up again and again, he finally gives up, and it is then that "his eyes are forcefully opened":

He is most distinctly given to understand how it all came about. To wit, through himself, that's obvious, through his scheme of life, which looked like nothing on earth, but now suddenly looks entirely different, not simple and almost entirely self-evident, but prideful and impudent, cowardly withal and full of weakness. This awful thing which was his life acquires a meaning. Franz Biberkopf has been given a radical cure. At last we see our man back on Alexanderplatz, greatly changed and battered, but, nevertheless, bent straight again.

To listen to this and to meditate on it, will be of benefit to many who, like this Franz Biberkopf, ask more of life than a piece of bread and butter.

If Benjamin constructs an inexorable development of petty bourgeois consciousness out of the materials of Franz's life, he can invoke the authority of these instructions to support his fiction. But they are superimposed on the much more ambiguous, ambivalent conflicted presentation of Franz's power-ful and erratic hunger for fate and the fateful accidents which shape it and contain it. *Berlin Alexanderplatz,* Benjamin argues, is the "utmost, giddy, last, most extreme stage of the old bourgeois *Bildungsroman,*"[83] that is, a dialectic synthesis which presumably negates and preserves *(aufhebt)* and therefore (somehow) reconciles the antithesis between the new collectivity (Alexanderplatz) and the old individual hungering for fate and a meaningful community (Franz Biberkopf).

Still, Benjamin did try to find meaning in the novel's "dualism," and he did understand and accept Döblin's acceptance of his protagonist's neediness. He did not, however, perceive the irony of the fact that this novel, which is most consistently concerned with and most convincingly articulate about the modern experience of collectivity, is also, in the explicit authorial instructions, direct narrative interferences and structuring strategies, con-sistently and urgently concerned with redemption. After the war Döblin said that the central theme of *Berlin Alexanderplatz* was sacrifice, referring to the novel's rich textural strands of biblical images and scenes, especially Isaac and Job, to the haunting realistic slaughterhouse images, to the recurrent verses from a familiar folksong about Death the Reaper.[84] But even here, speaking from a position of hindsight, from the experience of personal and cultural chaos which had led to his 1941 conversion, he still echoes the old conflict:

> The *good* man Franz Biberkopf with the claims he made on life, resists being broken till he dies. But he had to be broken, he had to give himself up, not just externally. Of course, I myself did not know how. The facts come rushing against you, but mere rigidity does not help.[85]

It is still the problem of Franz's active resistance and his forced, passive acceptance which Döblin both admits and glosses over. He did not have, he wrote in retrospect, any particular subject matter in mind for the novel:

but I was surrounded by the great Berlin and I knew the individual Berliner, and so I started writing, as always, without a plan, without directions, I did not construct a plot; the line was: the fate, the moves of a man who had so far been a failure. I could rely on the language, the spoken language of Berlin, it inspired me, and the fates that I had observed and in which I had participated, and my own fate guaranteed my un-impeded momentum.[86]

Franz had to change because Berlin did not: punished, he had to make a sacrifice of himself and was redeemed.[87] Looking back at the novel, Döblin juxtaposes the strong steady rhythms of Berlin with the erratic precarious course of Franz's life. And the city is indeed overpowering; its beat is all-pervasive, it underlies all the surface chaos. Döblin himself in the act of presenting the city did not escape its seduction, and the importance of his novel is intimately connected to his surrender. But when he speaks about the novel after the war he focuses on Franz's and his own change rather than their surrender to the shape and beat of cultural and political chaos at the end of the Weimar Republic, when the masses are marching.[88]

The novel is quite clear about the fact of surrender—the images and sounds of the finale leave no room for ambiguity; it is not clear about the meaning of surrender. Frustrated in his search for Reinhold who had implicated him in the murder of Mieze, Franz becomes temporarily insane, that is, ready to be processed for rebirth. His intense relationship with Reinhold has been curiously inarticulate,[89] but Reinhold's role as catalyst in Franz's fate has been worked out quite clearly. He caused the loss of Franz's arm, resenting his strength and relative wholeness; he murdered Franz's girl because of his pride in her devotion to him and her determination to keep him whole. Yet the question of Reinhold's guilt is never posed; it is only Franz who has to be brought to acknowledge his guilt. The world of Alexanderplatz resists such clear questioning; it also resists being judged or sentenced. It simply keeps moving. The borderlines between criminal and bourgeois arrangements are easily crossed, can easily be overlooked; so can the distinctions between emotional or sexual loyalty and promiscuity, between hetero- and homosexual attractions. Attachments fluctuate, linking several partners simultaneously. Mieze, devoted to Franz, is strongly drawn to Eva, his former girlfriend who still loves Franz, gives Mieze advice on how to handle him, and, with her enthusiastic encouragement, plans to have a child by him. If Mieze had not also been attracted to Reinhold, there would not have been an occasion for the murder. Reinhold's compulsive need to destroy her is triggered by Franz's need to demonstrate to him Mieze's unquestioned and unquestionable loyalty and his violent anger when this need is frustrated.[90]

It is not, however, the new morality with its smudged demarcations between good and bad, the expanded conventions, the profound shifts in all established social structures, sexual and political, which cause Franz's restlessness. He has arranged himself quite comfortably with the new collectivity. And his going under is after all not so much linked with his periodically erupting hunger for fate and meaning as with his specific volatile temperament and his inability to acknowledge, much less to question, his motivations. Franz broods about the inequities of his world, but he is also curious about it, occasionally delighted by it, and at home in it. Like his author he takes easily to Alexanderplatz with all its strange and naturally different people—and his author has given him a good eye for their differences. He likes the orthodox Jew with his weirdly sane stories which help him to overcome his anxiety in reentering chaotic fast moving, fast talking Berlin. He is intrigued by gays and their problems. His interests and fascinations are realistically fragmentary and temporary; his attention span is short. The Jew's stories are about the interdependencies of individual and group energies and about the importance of recognizing social roles as the basis for power games. "So we can go on talking," says the storyteller. "A lot can still be learned from other people."[91] But where he has done precisely that and constructed his stories against chaos, Franz will be only momentarily calmed by them and will not be able to use them.

Franz, as his author has made him, does not and cannot learn, and yet he is punished for his inability. When he is finally forced to learn, the experience is overpowering, total, and final, while his life had been processual, erratic, and fragmented: learning is no less than rebirth. The narration of Franz's life on Alexanderplatz is quite clear about its accidentality which is characteristic of urban modernity. Social pathology and psychology work without a cultural hierarchy of values. The characters moving in and out of Franz's story are granted uncharted areas of emotions and motivations; if they present case histories, these are not meant to be complete. Stories are analytical tools rather than synthetic solutions. As long as the reader is just periodically reassured by an all too self-assured narrating voice that Franz's life will take a certain meaningful course, he can stay within the flux of skillfully narrated fragmentary accidental urban life without too much effort. This, however, changes at the end of book eight when the narrating voice promises ominously that "we are nearing the point where everything will become clear."[92] Franz, finally broken down, is taken to the insane asylum and, through the passage of mental illness or death of the old person, delivered into Franz II.

Franz's condition, diagnosed as catatonic stupor for want of a better description, does not indicate the treatment attempted by some of the younger physicians: talking to him and inflicting electroshock to shake him up existentially and make him speak. The Head Doctor says: "They'll soon believe that paralysis is a psychic condition and that spirochetes are nothing but lice that happen to be in the brain. The soul, the soul—it's simply sentimental modern gush. Medicine soaring on the wings of Song."[93] The younger doctors are silently contemptuous of their older pragmatic superiors, and Döblin, in contrast to his younger psychiatrist self, seems to be with them. Franz's soul, though not accessible to them, is forced to listen: "Franz

Biberkopf hears Death, this Death, hears him slowly singing, singing like a stutterer, repeating himself over and over again like a saw cutting through wood."[94] The figure of Death is used to force upon Franz the recognition that he has to change completely by reversing an excessive need for self-preservation and unquestioned strength. Images of transformation—Death hacking him to pieces with his hatchet, a loaf being put into the oven—accompany the shadows rising from his past: Reinhold whom he still protects and who taunts him about his strength, Ida whom he killed, Mieze whom he almost killed and who was killed by Reinhold. To Reinhold, Franz admits that he is no longer strong; Mieze makes him weep not about life but about *his* life which all along has been his responsibility.[95] With this recognition of his guilt the old Franz dies and his rebirth begins—a process underscored by the life-affirming ecstatic chanting of victorious Death and the exit of the defeated "Whore of Babylon" who seems to represent certain aspects of modern sinfully irresponsible life in the metropolis.

The process, as any birth, is violent and is linked to the self-sacrifices made to Napoleon by French soldiers and, a century later, to the fatherland by German soldiers. Death makes the connection and affirms it: "Death folds his cloak and sings: Oh yes, oh yes, oh yes." The meanings of these references and associations are not entirely clear, but there seems to be an emphasis on the communal force of the sacrifice. Death's affirmation is accompanied by the steady powerful beat of marching:

> Marching, marching. We march to war, with iron tread, a hundred minstrels march ahead. Red of morning, red of night, shines on us death's early light. One hundred minstrels beat the drum, drumm, brumm, drumm, if we can't walk straight, we'll walk crooked, by gum, drumm, brumm, drumm.[96]

The new Franz Biberkopf is back in Berlin, letting Eva take care of him and fending off all demands: "Nope, I can't do nothing now." He is calm and seems contented. After a visit to the cemetery—he thinks: once a year is enough—Eva and he sit quietly and companionably in a pastry shop, "thinking backward and forward, eating honey-cake and devil-cake with whipped cream"[97] to the memory of Mieze who could not get enough of them. Franz's rebirth into Franz Karl is completed. However, the message about his socialization is confused. Where he had been spontaneous, he now seems to be cautious but mainly in a self-protective way: an attitude that Death had sought to break down. Where he had been impulsive and aggressive, he is now slow and circumspect but, evidently, still open to the seductions of an illusionary kind of community potentially strong enough to whip even his new dull reasonableness into a frenzy. His author withdraws him from the swirling exhilarating chaos of Alexanderplatz and its language. Words are too dangerous, motion too life-threatening. He is made to watch, from his door, the parades organized by the right and left in their attempt to drain and regulate disorder in the interest of a particular power. Watching, he repeats to himself his lesson: stay out of it, do not simply revere fate but take a good look at it! Yet a voice interrupts this implanted lesson: "Keep awake, eyes front, attention, a thousand belong together, and he who won't watch out, is fit to flay and flout. The drums roll behind him. We tramp to war with iron tread, a hundred ministrels march ahead, red of night and red of day, death-wards leads the way."

This very clearly echoes the passage above and with it allusions to soldiers' meaningful sacifices. Is the marching beat of the parades then a threat, a promise? The immediately following concluding passage, set apart by the print type, is a curious, darkly suggestive invocation of an old world crumbling and a new world in the throes of rebirth which is accompanied by the steady sound of marching and the irregular rhythms of battle. These could be the sounds of a new war which will easily drown out the newly found small voice of social reason.

What, then, is it Döblin wanted to say about Franz Biberkopf and his society? His self-ironical reference to the uplifting grand finale is in character with his notorious informality, but though the need for the consolations of closure is quite real and has to be taken seriously, the grand finale itself, in contrast, for instance, to Broch's, is confusingly ambiguous. The last book (9) has many passages which reflect an almost automatic verbal energy and self-intoxicating language. There is much evidence in Döblin's oeuvre of such letting go which occasionally results in trite or sentimental verbosity. Still, the recurring allusions to sounds of war do provide some structure, and they are intended to conclude this magnificently chaotic conflicted novel in some way meaningfully.[98] The discrepancy between the social intelligence and shrewd generosity characteristic of the authorial attitude toward Franz I in books one through eight and the righteous unimaginative and ambivalent handling of Franz II in book nine is particularly disturbing in view of the obscurity of that meaning. Döblin seems to have set aside at the end his pragmatic clear-headed view of the inhabitants of Alexanderplatz and with it his intimate hard-earned knowledge of their precarious potential and their deeper vulnerabilities.[99]

In the 1931 book-length essay *Wissen und Verändern* (Knowledge and changing) Döblin tried to sort out the contemporary intellectual profusion of cultural and political options and the difficulties of making choices and of action. The essay had its source in an open letter written to a student who had asked for ideological orientation, and Döblin began by asking his young correspondent why was he so disturbed by the current proliferation of doctrines and truths. The appeal to him to provide an answer for the young to many troubling questions had pointed to the well-known fact of his fairness and of his intense dislike of dogmas.[100] Döblin's answer was that the questions had to be rethought, particularly those of alliance. He proposed the intellectuals should take a position not yet occupied by either the right or the left, namely, "the arch-communist position of human individual freedom, of

spontaneous solidarity and association between people." Socialism needed
to be restituted as a pure, *geistig* force independent of political programs.[101]

While this is familiar liberal abstractionism, much of the essay's fragmentary argumentation, circling around the problems rather than confronting them systematically, is quite pragmatic and sometimes refreshingly
shrewd. Döblin is above all concerned about the political polarization—he
had himself experienced it painfully in the self-destructive cultural politics of
writers' organizations.[102] The concept of class struggle seems to him a
(dangerous) tool used in power politics rather than a useful perspective on
current social reality. He suggests speaking about the situation in terms of the
group interests of *Grossbürgertum* and *Kleinbürgertum* rather than bourgeoisie and proletariat, because doing so would acknowledge underlying
similar interests—for better or worse:

> The victory of the petty bourgeois who call themselves proletarians is just one
> stage in the battle, it does not really lead away from the old bourgeois world with
> its categories of war, violence and submission. The result will be, at the very
> best, neo-bourgeois state capitalism.[103]

Döblin remarked on developments in Soviet Russia, pointing out that
there was no existing revolutionary alternative to the contemporary political
stalemate in Germany. He asked the young intellectuals to look at the history
of Marxism from the position of a critical observer of the current German
political situation in order to make them understand that, while they should
be allied with the workers, their position was not at the side of the workers'
leaders.[104]

The "human" or "archcommunist" position will be informed by the new
naturalistisch way of thought which will be the basis for the development of
naturally social man: *Entfaltung des natürlichen gesellschaftlichen Menschen.*[105] The main characteristic of this new man, the tentatively presented
model for the young intellectuals addressed by Döblin, is an unbiased
asynthetic openness to the shared life-world which is their responsibility.[106]
With all his utopist appeals to a *geistig* position of pure socialism, Döblin
manages to resist the temptations of synthesis, of a finally meaningful whole.
Consistent with his pleas for a pluralistic empiricist perspective on sociopolitical phenomena is his suggestion to his correspondent and his friends
to reflect critically on their uninformed view of what they have been calling
Moloch Masse. It is not only the ruling classes, including liberal bourgeois
intellectuals, who have demonstrated a harmful blind spot with regard to the
existence and behavior of the crowd but also the theoreticians of the workers'
movement. The urban masses are a quintessentially modern phenomenon, a
highly important and little understood product of technological-industrial
and economical-political developments. What Döblin says in this context
about the urban masses with their dull gullibility and apathetic confusion,
their surface contentment and their tormented rebelliousness against the

pressures and demands coming at them from all sides,[107] points to the Berlin novel. His friend Brecht left the shifty, marvelously treacherous world of the *Threepenny Opera* and its mock redemption for the predictable and safely redeeming answers of the party. But Döblin, during these last years of the Weimar Republic, continued to look at the world around him with the same curious mixture of intelligent skepticism and muddled hopefulness which had informed the Berlin novel. Perhaps it is precisely this mixed attitude, irritating and provoking though it may be in its ambiguity and ambivalence, which enabled him to produce one of the most useful, truthful documentations of that difficult period. Obsessed with meaning, it preceded and foreshadowed events which were to question profoundly the meanings of human culture.

Epilogue

"That Certain Grey Veil of West German Boredom"

The German intellectual tradition so profoundly informed by utopian hopes and ideological certainties survived the rupture of "the German Catastrophe,"[1] reemerging fully in the early sixties. A symbiosis between the intellectuals' attacks on the status quo and the attacks on the intellectuals by the majority supportive of the status quo is a familiar feature of any highly developed democratic mass society, and national-cultural differences in this respect are a question of degree. In the West German situation of considerable social and political stability, the intellectuals as the distinct minority have been particularly eager, as were Weimar intellectuals, to accept such distinctness as distinction. They have continued in the assumption that speaking against a silent majority means literally speaking for it. The articulate minority has again felt entrusted with the responsibility of speaking the truth about the other for (the higher good of) the other and has considered it the other's responsibility to listen and to understand the intellectual's position of negation as one of (higher) affirmation. The intellectuals' battle has continued to be with the culture of the masses—notwithstanding their embracing certain select aspects of popular culture in the late seventies and eighties—and with established power as system. The result has been the continued reluctance to integrate into their discourse the intention to be fully understood. The clear distinction between high and low culture has survived; in order to be meaningful, intellectual discourse, be it in the mode of the essay or of the novel, has to be difficult to penetrate. Communication has been a perceived problem and the single most important focus for ever expansive utopias.

Jürgen Habermas, in a 1967 lecture delivered in New York to an American audience curious about the student protest movement in the Federal Republic, declared to be impressed above all by the fact that the conflict between the students and the rigid academic institutions had crossed the boundaries of the academic community. Radical students had become the backbone of the extraparliamentary opposition (APO) seeking to transform the whole social and political life of the Federal Republic. Looking back at the past decade from this vantage point, Habermas remarked on the growing political isolation of intellectuals on the left: the increasingly conservative reactions of the Social Democratic Party (SPD) which had resulted, as he sees it, in the decision to distance itself from its young left wing, the strongest political group among the students (SDS), now perceived to be too radical for mainstream Social Democrats.

Habermas explained the students' position in terms which are strongly reminiscent of Marcuse's arguments in *Eros and Civilization* (1955) and, more simply, in *One-Dimensional Man* (1964):

> They do not understand why the institutionalized struggle for existence, the discipline of alienated labor, or the eradication of sensuality and esthetic gratification should be perpetuated—why, in short, the mode of life of an economy of poverty is preserved under conditions of a possible economy of abundance. On the basis of a fundamental lack of sympathy with the senseless reproduction of now superfluous virtues and sacrifices, the rising generation has developed a particular sensitivity to the untruth of prevailing legitimations. Outrage against the double standards of the older generation's morality is, of course, repeated in every generation. But today protest is directed towards a society that has lent the emancipatory ideals of the 18th century the force of constitutional norms and has accumulated the potential for their realization—while it has not abolished hunger in the world of potential abundance, while it has widened the gap between industrial and developing nations, exporting misery and military violence along with mass hygiene.

For the German students this is the symbolic meaning of the American intervention in the Vietnamese civil war. Their world view has been "shaped by the impression that social institutions have coalesced into a relatively closed, conflict-free and self-regulating, yet violent apparatus" which can be opposed only "by uncorrupted individuals on the margins of the apparatus. Whoever assumes a function within it, however unimportant, becomes integrated and neutralized."[2] The students' protest as the great "instinctual refusal" of repressive rationality and complexity[3] must mobilize for the sake of mobilization itself, "going beyond the legitimate rules of the game."[4] Speaking of this "relatively small, very active minority whose attitude is . . . symptomatic of a trend," Habermas embraces their rejuvenating vital new actionism and anarchism borrowed from Mao and Castro, though he does note that their field of operations is urban and that there are certain dangers, recognized, he thinks, by the students themselves, of being diverted into "an easily consolable hippie subculture" or into fruitless acts of violence.[5]

Significantly, Habermas does not mention here important cultural problems inherent in this situation: The future intellectual elite of a technologically highly developed democratic mass society has been caught up in a near total revolt against rationality, the performance principle, functionalism, alienation, manipulation, etc.,[6] that is, against the apparatus, the system. In comparison the young intellectuals' utopian hopes for the Coming of the New Man after World War I seem almost realistic, taking into consid-

eration their different sociohistorical experience. Arguably, it was the conceptual confusion and obscurantism, the ideological polarization, the
utopianist single-mindedness which isolated the young left intellectuals in
the late sixties rather than the growing conservatism of the Social Democrats, growing also in response to the Great Refusal. The students looked at
what should have been or become their world from too great a distance,
claiming too exclusively the guilt of the fathers instead of analyzing their own
troubled sense of responsibility, and their perspective was obscured by this
peculiarly one-sided generational conflict. This obscurity may very well have
helped them to fit themselves so comfortably into "the system" once it had
reasserted itself (and they had themselves become fathers) and to embrace
the aesthetic consolations of "post-modernism," including the work of Ernst
Jünger.

Habermas argued that the students needed to engage in provocation
"beyond the legitimate rules of the game" in order to be heard. His social
philosophy has seemed to articulate most convincingly the intellectual's
position in postwar Germany, because he has been able, through all his
changes in focus and method of argumentation, to speak, as a cultural critic,
from a place clearly marked by his concern for communication as the
unrestrained exchange of ideas among fully emancipated, fully participating
subjects. From the early *Strukturwandel der Öffentlichkeit* to the recent
Theorie des kommunikativen Handelns, Habermas has held up such communication as a counterprojection to the status quo. But his Marcusean
interpretation of the students' revolt as "negation of the performance principle" emerging "not against but *with* the progress of conscious rationality,"[7]
that is, as the dialectically inevitable consequence of the increasingly complex system, implies a curiously broad and vague concept of communication.
He never asks whether or in what sense the students' forceful even violent
insistence on being heard could have been or become part of a communicative action. Whether it might not have precluded any intention to speak
understandably of the end of the revolt and the beginning of a common effort
of reconstruction. Habermas seems interested above all in the emergence of a
clear position on the left which he does not want to be fudged by compromise
and negotiation. He accepts the students' interpretation of the status quo as
catastrophic and welcomes the chiliastic vision of profound cultural rupture.
For him, the communicative dimension of the students' provocations is
located in the release of utopian energies.

In 1968, on the occasion of Marcuse's seventieth birthday, Habermas
was unambiguous in his praise for the "celebrated teacher of the New Left"
who never taught in Germany and whose enormous influence on a whole
student generation in West Germany rested with his books *Eros and Civilization* and *One-Dimensional Man*.[8] The fact that the cultural critique developed in these texts was directed against a mass culture in the United
States, which was deeply alien to Marcuse and which he frequently misunderstood on very basic levels, did not seem to disturb Habermas, nor did the

German students' unquestioning application of these texts. Marcuse's vision of the return of the "repressed harmony of sensuousness and reason—the eternal protest against the organization of life by the logic of domination, the critique of the performance principle,"[9] is reminiscent of Weimar attempts at instant transcendence of (mere) reason in the utopian realms of the soul. It was apparently acceptable to Habermas as an adequate reaction to the problems posed by a contemporary technocracy and so was Marcuse's hope for a nonrepressive sublimation: "Reactivation of polymorphous and narcissistic sexuality ceases to be a threat to culture and can itself lead to culture building if the organism exists not as an instrument of alienated labor but as a subject of self-realization. . . ."[10]

Arguably, Marcuse's concept of "self-realization" as becoming the whole individual "in union with the genus and with the 'archaic' past," sustained by the imagination "against the world of the antagonistic *principium individuationis,*"[11] may have seemed informed too much by Jungian depths and silences to appeal to Habermas in his search for the good place, where unrestrained communication between sovereign, historically articulated individuals is possible. Habermas's utopian projection of communication has been influenced by Arendt's model of the Periclean *polis,* as she developed it in *The Human Condition,* and does not extend, as does Marcuse's, into the prehistoric and prerational. But where Marcuse, contradicting his own argument, distances himself from Jung as obscurantist and reactionary,[12] Habermas, in his attempt to lift the grey veil of contemporary West German boredom, calls on allies who have strong affinities to the pre-/posthistorical and pre-/postrational.[13]

On the occasion of the thirtieth birthday of the Federal Republic in 1979, Habermas sent a letter to approximately fifty writers, critics, and social scientists asking them to contribute to volume 1000 of *edition suhrkamp,* which he gave the title *Stichworte zur "geistigen Situation der Zeit,"* their assessment of the "spiritual situation of the age." He is referring here to Karl Jaspers's 1931 *Die geistige Situation der Zeit* published as volume 1000 of the popular Göschen collection. I briefly discussed in part one Jaspers's diagnosis of a profound (High) cultural rather than political crisis of the age and his lamentation of a loss of cultural value and meaning. Habermas, in this letter, does not state, much less analyze, Jasper's argument, but he points to the beginnings of *edition suhrkamp* in the early sixties as a literary series with philosophical relevance. He lists Adorno, Beckett, Benjamin, Bloch, Brecht, Enzensberger, Frisch, Grass, Szondie, Walser, Weiss, and Wittgenstein among the early authors, later Barthes, Chomsky, Foucault, Laing, Lévi-Strauss, Marcuse, Mitscherlich, and younger social scientists "who located themselves in this tradition." Habermas sums up the series' program as representative of intellectual tendencies dominant in postwar Germany:

> I refer to the resolute affiliation with the Enlightenment, humanism, bourgeois radical thought, and with the esthetic and political avantgarde of the 19th

century. If there ever was anything (in Germany, that is) to the slogan "The spirit stands on the left," then it was during those years when, despite the massive social restauration, the memory of nazism, the tradition with which it had broken had kept alive—and by an intellectual left that could place its stamp on the cultural milieu with a certain conviction that it had been entrusted with this task.

All this, however, is over.[14]

The left is reacting "meekly" to a New Right, Habermas complains; and the New Right has constituted and defined itself through educational policy, philosophy, and the social sciences rather than through literature and art. In this situation it seems "meaningful to test . . . our ability to react—that is to determine the state today of an intellectual left which into the seventies had, as we say, 'made' the cultural life in Germany." He asks of the potential contributors that they let themselves be stimulated by Jaspers's text "into taking a position with regard to our own situation." They will have to combine the following three attributes: "those whose identity was formed only after the end of the war; those who have exercised a certain intellectual influence in the Federal Republic of Germany; and those who stand committed to the traditions against which a German regime established itself in 1933."[15]

Habermas focuses this letter, which became part of the preface to the collection, on issues which support the intellectual view of a cultural continuity between the Weimar Republic and the Federal Republic—up to the *Wende,* that is, the turn taken by political and cultural events after the New Right came to power. He appeals to this continuity directly in the last sentence I quoted, but the implicit, indirect connections established throughout the letter and the rest of the preface are much more instructive. The letter stresses both the cultural importance of High Literature and the intellectual *dominance* of the position articulated by the texts published in *edition suhrkamp:* the intellectual left was in a position to place its "stamp" on the cultural environment; it "made" the cultural life; it was able to sustain the conviction that "it had been entrusted" with this task.

Such benevolent domination is legitimatized by the left's "resolute affiliation with the Enlightenment"—a curious assertion in view of the highly idiosyncratic inverted concept of the Enlightenment at the center of the Frankfurt School's cultural critique and Habermas's enduring indebtedness to its radical neoromanticism. It is true, he revised somewhat his appraisal of Adorno-Horkheimer's total (and almost totally uninformed) rejection of American mass culture in their *Dialectic of Enlightenment:* where in 1963 he had praised them unreservedly, he states reservations in 1982. But what he criticizes now is the aggressivity and rigidity of their style rather than the ahistorical eclecticism and conceptual confusion of their argumentation.[16]

Like Jaspers, Habermas laments the fact of not a political but a cultural crisis: the loss of the position of dominance, in the culture of a mass democracy and technocracy, of the intellectual left carrying on the tradition of High Culture. It is the loss of the, as he sees it, culturally formative imagination which has opposed the reality principle and fueled the utopian vision of radical authenticity and meaningful centeredness. Significantly, he stresses the rejection of the artistic imagination by the New Right in its attempts at self-presentation: he is concerned less about the neoconservatives' undoing the political and social achievements of the Federal Republic than about their diffusion of a meaningful (High) cultural continuity.

In the introduction to the published collection Habermas is noticeably diffident about the contributions which, he says, contain few surprises. He seems disappointed that neither the shift in ideological currents (*Tendenzwende*) nor the ecological crisis, both most important to the seventies, have been discussed in any detail: "The one is more or less ignored; the other is respected, but without acknowledgment of its epochal significance. In short, the reader is confronted with unpolemical essays, with honest, unpolished and unguarded reflections. They may not draw one into the fray, but at least they provide a forum for discussion."[17]

The contributors to *Stichworte* come from a broad professional spectrum: literary historians and critics, social and political historians, theologians, philosophers, sociologists, political scientists, writers, jurists, and a prominent politician. Dealing intelligently and intelligibly with a great variety of problems characteristic of a highly developed mass democracy, they appear to Habermas merely sensible. There are a few exceptions, singled out for praise by him, for instance, a woman theologian's lamentations about the existential threats of consumerism which she sees poignantly expressed by, of all things, jeans: "Thou Shalt Have No Other Jeans before Me" is the title of her contribution, which does not even distinguish between jeans as a reasonably priced comfortable long-lasting useful commodity and designer jeans as overpriced and overadvertised status symbol. Not to mention her obliviousness to the emergence of asexist baggy chic in connection with the conformist individualism of the punk movement and its gesture of *weg damii,* that is, the spiky garish Great Refusal of the late seventies and eighties. In her myopic view everybody wears jeans, and all wearers of all jeans are preoccupied with consumption which she judges to be "graceless" in the ontological sense, that is, life-denying. Arguably, it has been precisely the threat of aconsumerism among many young wearers of jeans which has spurred designer jeans advertising to its greatest creative (if not moral) efforts. For Habermas, however, this simply uninformed piece is an "impressive" description of the consumerist redefinition of personal life spheres.

On the whole the contributors are well informed in their balanced analysis of contemporary mass society as system, which Habermas wants more clearly and strongly rejected as bringing about "a *devastation of the communicative capacities of the life-world.*"[18] All the developments associated with this system: "instrumentalization of the professional life," "competition and performance pressures," "monetarization of services, relations and life's stages," consumerism, legal regulation *(Verrechtlichung)* of private spheres of action, "and above all the political-administrative incorporation of school, family, education, and cultural reproduction in general"—all these developments point to "a new problem zone that has arisen on the borders separating system and life-world."[19]

"System" is obviously a bogey, and "life-world" is its positive counterpart. Furthermore, Habermas simply poses a separation between them, unaware, it seems, of the danger that this will assure, rather than control the intrusionary potential of "the system." Not unexpectedly, Habermas's list of negative aspects of modern society as system reads like a list taken directly from *Eros and Civilization* and *One-Dimensional Man*. It clearly suggests that he feels uncomfortable with cultural analyses which, like the contributions to *Stichworte,* are fragmentary, temporary, conflicted in their evaluative thrust, and open to considerations of compromise because they have been open to the irritations of actual experience. In the tradition of the German intellectual since the beginning of the twentieth century, Habermas finds it difficult to be without the consolations of closure afforded by the power of negation which transcends cultural activities or, better yet, posits a transcending culture.

It is true that Habermas has tried to move with the times, bringing to bear on his work philosophical questions from non-German cultural contexts, notably from the Anglo-Saxon tradition of the philosophy of language. But they have been dissolved quite literally in the utopia of communicative action, and his intellectual position has continued to be one of profound ambivalence where the modernity of the late seventies and eighties is concerned: I mean the broad cultural modernity which reflects the gradual integration, however difficult, of scientific and technological developments into social and cultural organization. So it is, after all, not so unexpected that he seizes on the "noncontemporaneous," according to one contributor, character of contemporary West German culture, arguing that the "young-conservatives" Jünger, Heidegger, Benn, and Carl Schmitt could be seen as important cultural critics in the twenties and early thirties as well as today precisely because of their noncontemporaneity. First he describes them quite aptly as having existed "in the remnants of unraveled traditions, the uncreative commotions of a ruthlessly exploitative present and their own fanciful anticipations of a vaguely imagined past." But he thinks their "diagnostic sensitivity to the times" sharpened by their noncontemporaneity in the Weimar period well suited to the "ambiguous phenomena" of contemporary West Germany. And he expresses "a twinge of regret that the intellectual line of this generation, one not only bewitched but instructed by Nietzsche, has been broken."[20]

Habermas does not stop with this suggestive connection; he draws attention to Karl-Heinz Bohrer as the only intellectual in the Federal Republic "who has preserved, in a politically innocent and sovereign manner, something of the radicalness and neoromantic intelligence of a young-conservative." This is not in reference to Bohrer's *Stichworte* essay but to an earlier article "Germany—A Spiritual Possibility," where he called for a "return to our innately grand style of imagination, metaphysics" so that we would not remain "spiritually and psychologically colonized." Bohrer combined this battle cry with an assault on "functionalist sociology, the technocratic idea of Europe, statistics instead of esthetics, social partnership instead of politics, right as well as left, the prohibition of conflict." Habermas expresses some reservations about Bohrer's position, feeling himself to be "too much a part of the 'West German intelligentsia' Bohrer here places on trial." But this, he continues, "is the only official context in which a statement from the alternative culture such as the following appears, a statement only too true: 'Only if one dares to say I instead of referring to statistics, will perhaps that certain grey veil of West German boredom fade away.' "[21]

It is difficult to get a clear view of the place from which Bohrer speaks.[22] In his *Stichworte* essay "The Three Cultures," he sides with "Popular Culture" against the "Old Culture" and the "New Culture" of the sixties. According to him New Culture, by which he means "all experimental dissolutions of classical modernism" in literature and the "philosophy of art since Benjamin and Adorno," "has either lost its fascination or has come to approximate the Old Culture."[23] It is arguable that there never had been any useful distinction to begin with. Bohrer, however, is not interested in understanding modernity as a difficult ongoing process—his own discontent with the current cultural situation clearly echoes *Eros and Civilization* and *The Dialectic of Enlightenment*—but in disjunctions as antirationalist and therefore vitally, exorbitantly "real." Popular Culture is for him "Punk Anarchism, Terror Anarchism, and the New Cynicism";[24] it fascinates him precisely because it is not subject to the "scruples of reflection" associated with High Culture, Old or New: "Beyond the objections of cultural criticism it possesses the vitality of its own self-regenerating reality."[25] It is better than art; it is the new art. And in his voluminous study of the early works of Ernst Jünger, *Die Aesthetik des Schreckens* (1978) (The aesthetics of terror),[26] he posits admiringly a subversive force of Jünger's High Culture texts in their insistence on the role of the heroic individual in the magic expansion and dissolution of the world. Habermas and Bohrer alike appreciate Jünger's "diagnostic sensitivity to the times" in his radical rejection of that struggling precarious enterprise in modern parliamentary mass democracy, the "Grey Republic." More, they are both inclined to avail themselves now of the irrationalist energies of his work in order to make fade away "that certain grey veil of West German boredom."

NOTES

INTRODUCTION

1. Karl Mannheim, *Ideology and Utopia* (New York: Harcourt, Brace & World, Inc., 1936), pp. 85f.

2. Mannheim was careful to deflect what for many readers were the negative associations of "relativism" by substituting in this context the concept of "relationism": "This first non-evaluative insight into history does not inevitably lead to relativism, but rather to relationism" (p. 85).

3. See below Chap. 6.

4. See the essays collected in Hans-Joachim Lieber, ed., *Ideologienlehre und Wissenssoziologie Die Diskussion um das Ideologieproblem in den zwanziger Jahren* (Darmstadt: Wissenschaftliche Buchgesellschaft, 1974); see below n. 13.

5. *Ideology and Utopia*, p. 96.

6. Ibid., p. 155.

7. Ibid., pp. 96–98.

8. Ibid., p. 38 and p. 154.

9. Ibid., p. 105.

10. See below pt. 1, sec. 5; see also Lieber's instructive introduction, *Ideologienlehre*, pp. 38ff.

11. See "The Problem of the Intelligentsia: An Enquiry into Its Past and Present Role," a group of three "Essays on the Sociology of Culture" written in the early thirties; quoted in Kurt H. Wolff, ed., *From Karl Mannheim* (New York: Oxford University Press, 1971), p. XC.

12. *Ideology and Utopia*, pp. 3f; the part in which he makes this statement was added to the German version (1929) for the publication in English in 1936 ("Preliminary Approach to the Problem," pp. 1–54) where he stresses, from hindsight after the collapse of the Weimar Republic, the intellectuals' responsibility to be aware of distortions in their perception of a social reality; but the essays collected in the German version make such responsibility abundantly clear.

13. Contemporary reviewers have addressed this problem, notably Hans Speyer, "Soziologie oder Ideologie? Bemerkungen zur Soziologie der Intelligenz," now in Lieber, pp. 568–88; Helmuth Plessner, "Abwandlungen des Ideologiegedankens," now in Lieber, pp. 589–616; Günther Stern, "Über die sogenannte 'Seinsverbundenheit' des Bewusstseins," now in Lieber, pp. 548–67; Hannah Arendt, "Philosophie und Soziologie," now in Lieber, pp. 530–45.

14. See Mannheim, *Ideology and Utopia*, p. 42.

15. Ibid.

16. Ibid., p. 33.

17. Ibid., p. 42.

18. Mannheim, notwithstanding his Marxist interests, differs essentially in this respect from the Frankfurt School.

19. In his 1925 essay "The Problem of a Sociology of Knowledge," which marks an important stage in his development toward *Ideology and Utopia*, Mannheim, above all, distinguishes his own positions from Max Scheler's in his 1924 "Probleme einer Soziologie des Wissens." The main differences between Scheler's phenomenological and his own historicist approach—that is, his view of the duality of

being and meaning as only phenomenological, and to be mediated in an approach which would combine history, philosophy, and sociology—have to do with Mannheim's "historicizing" the unconscious, with his view of a mutual dependency between superstructure and substructure, and with his concept of social strata rather than culturally defined "epochs." All these distinctions serve to stress his attempts to show the powerful social contextuality for all intellectual activities, including philosophy, and thus to prevent the formation of destructive, because unexamined, utopian and ideological fictions.

20. See here pt. I, sec. 8, and chap. 2, sec. 2.

21. See here especially the chapters on Thomas Mann (chap. 3) and Hermann Broch (chap. 6). It is instructive that an intellectual historian like Wolf Lepenies does not seem to pose these questions to literary texts in spite of his very welcome attempts at bringing together literature, history, and sociology. See his reading of Thomas Mann's cultural-political position in *Die drei Kulturen: Soziologie zwischen Literatur und Wissenschaft* (München: Hanser, 1985), p. 31.

22. On meaning/significance see chap. 2, n. 81.

PART ONE:
TEMPTED BY DISTANCE

1. See Hagen Schulze, "Das Scheitern der Weimarer Republik als Problem der Forschung," *Weimar Selbstpreisgabe einer Demokratie Eine Bilanz heute,* ed. Karl Dietrich Erdmann and Hagen Schulze (Düsseldorf: Droste, 1980), pp. 23–41.

2. See chap. 1, n. 32, 58.

3. Schulze, in *Weimar Selbstpreisgabe einer Demokratie,* pp. 33ff.

4. See Henry Pachter, *Weimar Etudes* (New York: Columbia University Press, 1982), pp. 303ff.

5. See Alexander Schwan, "Zeitgenössische Philosophy und Theologie in ihrem Verhältnis zur Weimarer Republik," *Weimar Selbstpreisgabe einer Demokratie,* pp. 259–285; see also chap. 2.

6. Karl Jaspers, *Die geistige Situation der Zeit* (Berlin: de Gruyter, 1965), p. 15; see also Schwan, p. 273.

7. Jaspers, p. 79.

8. Jaspers, pp. 32ff: "Spannung von technischer Massenordnung und menschlicher Daseinswelt."

9. See n. 4.

10. For an analysis of the highly interesting development of the DDP during the first years of Weimar see Robert A. Pois, *The Bourgeois Democrats of Weimar Germany* (Philadelphia: American Philosophical Society, 1976); Jürgen C. Hess, *"Das ganze Deutschland soll es sein" Demokratischer Nationalismus in der Weimarer Republik am Beispiel der DDP* (Stuttgart: Klett-Cotta, 1978); Jürgen C. Hess, *Theodor Heuss vor 1933* (Stuttgart: Klett, 1973). Heuss, the first president of the Federal Republic of Germany, had been a prominent member of the DDP.

11. See chap. 1 and chap. 5; see Wolf Zuelzer, *The Nicolai Case* (Detroit: Wayne State University Press, 1982).

12. Schwan, pp. 275ff.

13. Dietz Bering, *Die Intellektuellen Geschichte eines Schimpfwortes* (Stuttgart: Klett-Cotta, 1978), p. 44.

14. Ibid., p. 38.

15. Alvin Gouldner, *The Coming Crisis of Western Sociology* (London, 1971), pp. 290ff; Talcott Parsons, *Political and Social Structure* (New York: Free Press, 1969), pp. 352–404.

16. Niklas Luhmann, *Trust and Power,* ed. Gianfranco Poggi (Chichester, N.Y.: John Wiley, 1979), pp. 117f.

17. Ibid., p. 108.

18. Ibid.

19. See Gianfranco Poggi's introduction, *Trust and Power*, pp. VII–XVII, p. XI.

20. Arthur Mitzmann, *The Iron Cage: An Historical Interpretation of Max Weber* (New York: Knopf, 1970) and *Sociology and Estrangement: Three Sociologists of Imperial Germany* (New York: Knopf, 1973).

21. There were only two issues of *Die Fackel* between December 1932 and April 1935: the October 1933 issue containing an obituary for Adolf Loos, the influential architect and close friend of Kraus, and the poem "Man frage nicht" (ending with the line: "Das Wort entschlief als jene Welt erwachte"), and the July 1934 issue (the biggest issue ever) "Warum die Fackel nicht erscheint" with the collection of anti-fascist responses to the 1933 issue, "Nachrufe auf Karl Kraus," and a plea of loyalty to the Christian Socialist government of Dollfuss, whom Kraus did not admire but thought he had to support under the circumstances. Dollfuss was assassinated by Austrian Nazis on July 25, 1934. Kraus's commentary on the attacks on his silence: "Zum grossen Thema des Aufbruchs der Hölle versagt mit leidenschaftlicher Feigheit der, dessen Werk vergebens getan war: den Teufel an die Wand zu malen."

22. See Nicole Racine, "The Clarté Movement in France, 1918–1921," *Journal of Contemporary History* 2 (1967): 195–208; René Schickele, "Die Gruppe Clarté," *Werke in Drei Bänden* (Cologne: Kiepenheuer & Witsch, 1959), vol. 3, pp. 499–513.

23. Paul Fussell, *The Great War and Modern Memory* (New York: Oxford University Press, 1975).

24. The appeal was signed by, among others, Lujo Brentano, Richard Dehmel, Rudolf Eucken, Ernst Haeckel, Gerhart Hauptmann, Max Liebermann, Friedrich Naumann, Max Planck, Max Reinhardt, Wilhelm Röntgen, Karl Vossler, Siegfried Wagner, Ulrich von Wilamowitz-Moellendorff, Wilhelm Windelband, Wilhelm Wundt. It was an established academic and artistic elite whose cultural nationalism was unquestioned though, in most cases, not aggressive.

25. Dagmar Barnouw, "Literary Politics in World War I: *Die Aktion* and the Problem of the Intellectual Revolutionary," *German Quarterly* 52 (1979): 227–247. Michael Stark, *Für und Wider den Expressionismus Die Entstehung der Intellektuellendebatte in der deutschen Literaturgeschichte* (Stuttgart: Metzler, 1982), pp. 157ff, 210ff.

26. See chap. 1, n. 32.

27. Leonard Krieger, "Power and Responsibility: The Historical Assumptions," *The Responsibility of Power: Historical Essays in Honor of Hajo Holborn*, ed. Leonard Krieger and Fritz Stern (New York: Doubleday, 1967), p. 8.

28. See Barnouw, "Literary Politics," p. 230.

29. Friedrich Bentmann, *René Schickele: Leben und Werk in Dokumenten* (Nuremberg: H. Carl, 1976).

30. See Stark, *Für und Wider*, p. 156.

31. Henry de Man, *The Psychology of Socialism* (New York: Henry Holt, 1927), trans. from the 2d edition of the German original, *Zur Psychologie des Sozialismus* (Jena: Diederichs, 1926, 1927), p. 34.

32. Ibid., pp. 12f; the title of the first chapter: "The Theory of Motives as the Central Problem of Socialism."

33. Henry de Man, *Der Kampf um die Arbeitsfreude* (Jena: Eugen Diederichs, 1927).

34. "Wir aber stehen vor der Menschheit aufrecht! . . . Ein Volk von siebzig Millionen—und ein einziges kleines Wochenblatt repräsentierte im August 1914 die unbedingte Kriegsfeindschaft, die Menschlichkeit, das Gewissen!"

35. "Meine Antworten waren, ehe sie [die Zeit] mir ihre Fragen stellte." *Aktion*, April 17, 1915, Sp. 214.

36. See *Aktion*, 1918, Sp. 521; *Aktion*, 1916, Sp. 579.

37. Carl E. Schorske, *German Social Democracy 1905–1917: The Development of the Great Schism* (New York: Wiley, 1955), p. 185, pp. 200ff.

38. Ibid., pp. 254ff.

39. Ernst Toller, one of the leaders of the 1918–19 Munich soviet, remembers the mood: "The Kaiser recognized no parties; there it was in black and white; all factions were to be united; everybody defended one mother: Germany," from *I was a German* (London: J. Lane, 1934), p. 53.

40. Dagmar Barnouw, "Avantgarde und Engagement: Ferdinand Hardekopf," *Gedenkschrift für Siegfried Sudhof,* ed. P. P. Schneider (Senat der Hansestadt Lübeck: Lübeck, 1981), pp. 58–65.

41. *Die Weißen Blätter,* vol. 3, no. 2 (1916): 97–101.

42. See also Ludwig Rubiner, "Der Kampf mit dem Engel," *Aktion,* 1917, Sp. 211ff.

43. "Nicht als 'Lehrer' habe ich das Proletariat zu begönnern und zu leiten: das *Proletariat* hat die unendliche Güte gehabt, uns ein wenig vorauszusenden!" *Aktion,* 1917, Sp. 670.

44. Sven Delblanc, *Speranza* (New York: Viking, 1983).

45. In 1917 Toller had contributed to *Aktion* one of the agitprop texts wanted by Pfemfert, "Marschlied."

46. See chap. 1, n. 1.

47. *Aktion,* 1919, Sp. 525; "das ehrgeizige, politisch ahnungslose Bürger-söhnchen, der würdelose Feigling Herr Toller." See the sensitive portrait of the older Toller in exile in the United States, haunted by the cruel ironies of political activism: Christopher Isherwood, "The Head of a Leader," *Exhumations* (New York: Simon and Schuster, 1966), pp. 125–32.

48. *Aktion,* 1918, Sp. 624, 612.

49. See the carefully researched but too rigid account of the Munich soviet in Allan Mitchell, *Revolution in Bavaria 1918–1919: The Eisner Regime and the Soviet Republic* (Princeton: Princeton University Press, 1965).

50. *Aktion,* 1920, Sp. 592: "Wir stehen im heftigsten Kampf gegen die Pest der deutschen Arbeiterbewegung, den Opportunismus—und in den Rücken fällt uns . . . Lenin."

51. Quoted in Michael Holroyd, *Lytton Strachey: A Critical Biography* (London: William Heinemann Ltd., 1967), vol. 1, p. 127 and p. 127, n. 2.

52. Holroyd, vol. 2, p. 329.

53. Ibid., p. 284.

54. Ibid., p. 304.

55. Ibid., p. 174.

56. Robert Graves, *Goodbye to All That* (1929; reprint, London: Cassells, 1957), p. 217.

57. Siegfried Sassoon, *The Complete Memoirs of George Sherston* (London, 1937), p. 511.

58. Graves, *Goodbye,* p. 206.

59. Sassoon, *George Sherston,* p. 530.

60. See Bering, *Die Intellektuellen,* "Die Geistigen," pp.82ff. One of the most prolific, visible *geistig*-activist writers was Kurt Hiller: see his manifesto "Philosophie des Ziels," Kurt Hiller, ed., *Das Ziel Aufrufe zu tätigem Geist* (Munich and Berlin, 1916) pp. 206ff. There were two more *Ziel* yearbooks: *Tätiger Geist! Zweites der Ziel-Jahrbücher* (1918), and *Das Ziel: Jahrbücher für geistige Politik* (1919). Hiller defined "die Geistigen" in his manifesto: "'Die Geistigen'—was bedeutet das? Es bedeutet (mit dreissig Buchstaben): Die, die sich verantwortlich fühlen." "Die Geistigen"—in contrast to the mere intellectuals—feel responsibility and act accordingly. Responsibility means, as Hiller goes on to explain, to be held responsible not for the past, but for the future, to live up to the experience of one's mission ("das Erlebnis

seiner Sendung tragen"), to suffer from the world meaningfully ("an der Welt fruchtbar leiden"), to be obsessed by the idea of improving the world, not the individual existence. "Die Geistigen" have no purpose but a goal ("die Zwecklosen und Zielhaften"), they are the madmen of the "ought" ("die Tollen des Soll"). In this social activism during the last years of the war and the early years of the Weimar Republic Hiller ostensibly emphasized the need to be rational. His "ratioaktiv" (his pun) strategies in support of issues like women's rights and pacifism were colorful but realistic to a degree. Yet his political concept of "geistige Politik," his philosophical definitions of the role of the intellectual were irrational and idealist in the German cultural tradition, stressing the spiritual dimension, the authenticity of experience, the utopian hope for *Gemeinschaft* (community)—rather than society—in the future, denouncing mere purpose—the Frankfurt School's "instrumental reason," Max Weber's "zweckrational"—in favor of a reason-transcending energy that would gather up and sweep a culture paralyzed by intellectualism toward a/the goal of cultural rejuvenation. This combination of cultural conservatism, vitalism, and messianism was to become increasingly, dangerously effective in the utopianism of the radical right after the war. This does not, of course, make the left activist Hiller a protofascist; it points to the pervasive sameness of an experienced cultural crisis spreading over the whole spectrum of political sympathies or affiliations. The redemptive goal, a new homogeneous world of human *Gemeinschaft,* had to transcend the rationality held responsible for the alienated, fragmented old society, the world of the *fin de siècle.* It is interesting to note here that Georg Lukács had become so attracted to Buber's *Baal Shem* and *Rabbi Nachman*—he reviewed the two books in December 1911 under the title *Jewish Mysticism*—because the "irrationalism" of Hasidism achieving *Gemeinschaft* refuted the accusations made against Jews that they, as a group, were excessively rational and therefore responsible for the mechanization and alienation of the modern world. See Lee Congdon, *The Young Lukács* (Chapel Hill and London: University of North Carolina Press, 1983), pp. 76ff.

61. References to *Ideology and Utopia,* trans. Louis Wirth and Edward Shils (London: Routledge and Kegan Paul, 1936).

62. Ibid., p. 137.

63. Ibid.

64. See ibid., p. 47. For further discussion of ambiguities in Mannheim's argumentation see chap. 2.

65. *Ideology and Utopia,* p. 1.

66. Ibid., p. 29.

67. Ibid., p. 94.

68. Ibid., p. 54.

69. Ibid., p. 144.

70. Ibid., p. 142.

71. Ibid., p. 144.

72. Ibid., p. 36.

73. See Theodor W. Adorno, Frenkel-Brunswik, Levinson, and Sanford, *The Authoritarian Personality* (1950) which measured authoritarianism by applying the famous "F-Scale"—F for fascism—that had been defined according to qualities characteristic for the lower-middle-class white American and, not unsurprisingly, found the lower-middle-class white American in general conforming to the authoritarian type.

74. Kurt Tucholsky, *Gesammelte Werke,* ed. Mary Gerold-Tucholsky and Fritz Raddatz (Reinbek: Rowohlt, 1960), vol. 1, pp. 383f.

75. Tucholsky has been unfairly accused of contributing to the fall of the Weimar Republic by writing sharply critical articles on its social-cultural life (see, e.g., Gordon A. Craig, *Germany 1866–1945,* New York: Oxford University Press, 1978) and by satirizing Jewish types in *Die Weltbühne.* (Gershom Scholem and Walter

Laqueur were especially aggressive narrow-minded critics of what they thought dangerous instances of Jewish self-hatred. See here Kurt R. Grossmann, "Deutsche Juden auf der Linken, Ihre politische Aktivität in der Weimarer Republik," in *Gegenwart im Rückblick,* ed. Herbert A. Strauss and Kurt R. Grossmann. (Heidelberg: Lothar Stiehm, 1970), pp. 86–105. Istvan Deak, *Weimar Germany's Left Wing Intellectuals* (Berkeley and Los Angeles: University of California Press, 1968).

76. Dorothy Emmet, "The Concept of Power," in *Power,* ed. John R. Champlin (New York: Atherton Press, 1971), pp. 78–103: "The fact that performatory utterances are a class of ritual utterances in which the pronouncing a form of words effects what it signifies, in a rationally defensible way, may have encouraged the survival of the idea that ritual words can be causally efficacious in effecting changes in the physical world in the magical sense, through a failure to distinguish between the performatory and causal kinds of efficacy" (p. 94). Heinrich Mann shows how the effect of the kaiser's oratorical style on his subjects *(Untertan)* as listeners or readers is supported by the desire to participate in the power of causing (magically easy) change in a complex social environment. It is, in this case, the peculiarly concrete aggressiveness of that style that suggests identification with and thereby participation in power. Nazi mass propaganda exploited this mechanism very cleverly.

77. See Dagmar Barnouw, "Heinrich Mann und die Ethologie der Macht," *Schillerjahrbuch* 21 (1977): 418–51.

78. See Tucholsky's long letter to Arnold Zweig, December 15, 1935, on the lack of realistic Jewish self-criticism with regard to specific difficulties inherent in a specifically problematical minority status. By the time the letter reached Zweig, Tucholsky had committed suicide. The letter and Zweig's answer were published in *Die neue Weltbühne,* no. 6, February 6, 1936 *(Die Weltbühne* in exile in Prague). Reprinted in Kurt Tucholsky, *Politische Briefe* (Reinbek: Rowohlt, 1969), pp. 117–23.

79. Holroyd, vol. 2, pp. 406ff.

80. Ibid., p. 346.

81. Ibid., p. 408.

82. Thomas Hobbes, *Leviathan,* pt. 1, chap. 10, "Of Power, Worth, Dignity, Honour and Worthinesse."

83. Dagmar Barnouw, "Skepticism as a Literary Mode: David Hume and Robert Musil," *Modern Language Notes* 93 (1978): 852–70.

84. Heinrich Mann, *Essays* (Hamburg: Claasen, 1960), p. 20.

85. In contrast to his brother he did not undergo an alleged conversion but struggled to remain a good republican: see chapter 3.

86. The poem introducing the first book of More's *Utopia* ends with the line "Eutopia merito sum vocanda nomine" (I deserve to be called Eutopia, the good place). The whole first book is taken up with the attempts by Hythloday, the (fictional) Utopian traveler, to demonstrate that the nowhere (Utopia) can become a good place (Eutopia) only if related to the reader/listener as a story that can be related to his social experience.

87. See, e.g., the detailed list of English (civilization: shallow, functional versus German (culture: profound, authentic) character traits in Max Scheler's 1914 *Der Genius des Krieges und der deutsche Krieg* (see below chap. 1, sec. 2).

88. See my review of her letters to Leo Jogiches, *German Quarterly* 54 (1981): 105–6.

89. See Hans-Helmuth Knütter, *Die Juden und die deutsche Linke in der Weimarer Republik 1918–1933* (Düsseldorf: Droste, 1971), pp. 14ff.

90. See my " 'Die Kommune lebt,' " *Merkur* 37 (1983): 201–6.

91. See chap. 4, sec. 4.

92. See Henry Pachter, *Weimar Etudes,* pp. 210ff.

93. More than twenty years later Adorno prescribes precisely such epiphany in his "Der Essay als Form." See the discussion of concepts of the essay in my "Literat

und Literatur: Robert Musils Beziehung zu Franz Blei," *Modern Austrian Literature* 9 (1976): 168–99.

94. See Kathy Eden, "Poetry and Equity: Aristotle's Defense of Fiction," *Traditio* 38 (1982): 17–34.

95. See chap. 1, n. 32.

96. See above n. 83.

97. See Dagmar Barnouw, " 'Beute der Pragmatisierung': Adorno und Amerika," in *Die USA and Deutschland, Wechselseitige Spiegelungen in der Literatur der Gegenwart*, ed. Wolfgang Paulsen (Bern and Munich: Francke, 1976), pp. 61–83.

98. See my "Loos, Kraus, Wittgenstein and the Problem of Authenticity," in *The Turn of the Century: German Literature and Art 1890–1915*, ed. Gerald Chapple (Bonn: Bouvier, 1981), pp. 249–73.

99. See Dagmar Barnouw, "The Secularity of Evil: Hannah Arendt and the Eichmann Controversy," *Modern Judaism* 3 (1983): 75–94.

100. Quoted in Elisabeth Young-Bruehl, *Hannah Arendt: For Love of the World* (New Haven and London: Yale University Press, 1982), p. 303.

PART TWO:
THE PROBLEM OF EXPERIENCE

I. THE THREATENED SELF

1. See Karl Rohe, *Das Reichsbanner Schwarz Rot Gold Ein Beitrag zur Geschichte und Struktur der politischen Kampfverbände zur Zeit der Weimarer Republik* (Düsseldorf: Droste, 1966); Hagen Schulze, *Freikorps und Republik 1918–1920* (Boppard/Rhine: Boldt, 1969); Hans-Joachim W. Koch, *Der deutsche Bürgerkrieg Eine Geschichte der deutschen und österreichischen Freikorps 1918–1923* (Berlin: Ullstein, 1978). For an interesting if highly fictional stylized presentation of the different kinds and degrees of violence committed by these paramilitary groups and the exploitation by the Nazis of an atmosphere of fear, see Ernst Jünger, *Auf den Marmorklippen* (Hamburg: Hanseatische Verlags-Anstalt, 1939). See also Emil J. Gumbel, *Vier Jahre politischer Mord* (Berlin: Neue Gesellschaft, 1922) and Wolf Zuelzer, *The Nicolai Case* (Detroit: Wayne State University Press, 1982). For the years 1918–22 Gumbel, professor of mathematics and well-known pacifist, documented 314 assassinations by the right as opposed to 13 by the left. Punishment for political murder committed by the right was notoriously mild.

2. See Harry Wilde, *Walther Rathenau in Selbstzeugnissen und Bilddokumenten* (Reinbek by Hamburg: Rowohlt, 1971), pp. 147ff, and Count Harry Kessler, *Walther Rathenau: His Life and Work* (New York: Howard Fertig, 1969), pp. 367ff. Kessler's very perceptive and informative biography—he knew Rathenau personally and was associated with him politically in the postwar years—was published originally in German in 1928 (Berlin and Grunewald: Hermann Klemm). All subsequent studies of Rathenau have relied heavily on Kessler, who had been able to secure the cooperation of the Rathenau family, and none has really superseded him: James Joll, "Walther Rathenau Prophet without a Cause," *Three Intellectuals in Politics* (New York: Pantheon, 1960), pp. 59–129 (helpful); Peter Berglar, *Walther Rathenau Seine Zeit Sein Werk Seine Persönlichkeit* (Bremen: Schünemann, 1970) (helpful); Ernst Schulin, *Walther Rathenau Repräsentant, Kritiker und Opfer seiner Zeit* (Göttingen: Musterschmidt, 1979) (too uncritical). For Rathenau's political activities during 1920–22 see David Felix, *Walther Rathenau and the Weimar Republic, The Politics of Reparation* (Baltimore: Johns Hopkins University Press, 1971); for reactions to the essayist Rathenau see D. G. Williamson, "Pro and Contra Rathenau: The Controversy in the German Press 1914–1918," *The Wiener Library Bulletin*, n.s., vol. 28, nos. 33–34

(1975): 32–43. Unless stated otherwise, translations into English from primary and secondary sources are mine.

3. Ernst Werner Techow, "Gemeiner Mörder?!" in *Das Rathenau-Attentat,* Serie Nationale Zeitfragen (Leipzig: Scholl, 1933), p. 20.

4. Ibid., introduction. See Ina Prowe-Isenbörger, "Schuld und Sühne Walther Rathenau," in *Deutsche Juden* (Bonn: Warnecke, 1962), pp. 159–69: she uses a story told by an American journalist (*Politics,* January 1947) who in 1940 met Techow alias Tessier, then an officer in the French Foreign Legion, together with a group of Jewish Foreign Legionnaires at the Libyan Border and was very much impressed by the man's intelligence and articulateness and his perfect French. Techow/Tessier was carrying with him the letter Rathenau's mother had written to his mother on learning that Mrs. Techow experienced much hostility during her son's trial (on the letter, see Wilde, p. 151). He showed it to Rathenau's nephew, who happened to be one of the group, stating that this letter had become the most important document in his life as it had inspired him to read Rathenau's writings during his eight years (1922–30) in prison. He had learned to see, he said, how the Nazis had distorted the Jewish question and had consequently turned against them, having fought against their evil influence and actions for eighteen years (pp. 168f). This, of course, does not agree at all with the date of his writing the account of the Rathenau assassination. The journalist describes Techow as tall and lean, with a brutal chin, intrepid gray eyes, a sonorous gentle voice suggesting a priest, and an ironically polite manner. He was, obviously, much taken with the man's complex *persona*—as it was presented and as he saw it—the combination of civilized sophistication and solitary daring activism, heroic self-reliance: Techow/Tessier, the journalist learned a year later, was involved in espionage against Hitler Germany, and, having saved single-handedly more than seven hundred Jews, was known and admired all over Marseille as a lone agent ("Ein-Mann-Kommittee," p. 169), as bold as he was effective. The story sounds too romantically contrived and edifying to be true—Joll, *Three Intellectuals,* p. 127, does not think that it has any evidence to support it—and was used by Prowe-Isenbörger for its guilt and expiation aspects. More probably Techow was killed as a German soldier, at the eastern front, but the story would have suited to perfection his activist temperament of embracing causes and need for dramatic self-presentation.

5. Techow, p. 17; pp. 21ff.

6. See the description of the assassination by an eye witness, the construction worker Krischbin in *Vossische Zeitung,* June 25, 1922, quoted by Wilde, pp. 145ff.

7. Techow, p. 24.

8. Tu was du musst/Sieg oder stirb/Und lass Gott/Die Entscheidung; a photo of the grave stone in Wilde, p. 152.

9. Quoted by Techow, pp. 124f: "Der Tod für eine Überzeugung ist das höchste Vollbringen. Er ist Bekenntnis, Tat, Erfüllung, Glaube, Liebe, Hoffnung und Ziel; er ist auf dieser unvollkommenen Welt ein Vollkommenes und die Vollendung schlechthin . . . Mag einer sterben, in einen zweifellosen Irrtum verbohrt; er hat sein Grösstes geleistet . . . Der Wahn und die Welt sind eins, und wer für einen Irrtum starb, bleibt doch ein Held." Techow leaves out some sentences in this passage which indicate, too clearly for his taste, the relative unimportance of the content (*Sache*) of a conviction—for instance, Jünger's bird's-eye perspective on two armies (German and French) locked in battle: *Der Kampf als inneres Erlebnis* (Berlin: Mittler, 1922), p. 10.

10. See below chap. 5. See Karl O. Paetel, *Ernst Jünger in Selbstzeugnissen und Bilddokumenten* (Reinbek by Hamburg: Rowohlt, 1962), pp. 59ff. Jünger was one of a small number of junior officers—another was the later Field Marshal Rommel—decorated with the *Pour le mérite* for exceptional bravery and demonstration of outstanding strategic talent in attacking the enemy. Judging from his account of his experiences in trench warfare, *In Stahlgewittern* (1920; *The Storm of Steel,* 1929) which had a large number of editions and was translated into seven languages, his

bravery was reckless with regard to his men's lives and his strategic talent not convincingly demonstrated. On this influential war diary-fiction see chap. 5, sec. 3. See also Karl Prümm, *Die Literatur des soldatischen Nationalismus (1918–1933)* (Kronberg/Taunus: Scriptor, 1974), vol. 1, p. 101. The Nazis did not trust him but, in the beginning, courted him, reprinting his early texts and allowing one printing of the 1939 *Auf den Marmorklippen,* presumably critical of Hitler's regime (see chap. 5, sec. 7). Jünger worked with and temporarily belonged to several nationalist groups. His 1932 treatise on the worker, *Der Arbeiter Herrschaft Gestalt* published by the nationalist Hanseatische Verlagsanstalt attracted Communists. The ultimate value for him was Germany as an ideal fiction, and his nationalism was so much and so exclusively integrated with the substance of his imagery that it lent itself to be appropriated by a great variety of attempts at categorization—from "soldatischer Nationalismus" (see above Prümm) to "conservative revolution" (Armin Mohler, *Die Konservative Revolution in Deutschland 1918–1932. Ein Handbuch* (Darmstadt: Wissenschaftliche Buchgesellschaft, 1972) to "conservative anarchist" (Hans-Peter Schwarz, *Der Konservative Anarchist Politik und Zeitkritik Ernst Jüngers* (Freiburg: Rombach, 1962)). See also O. E. Schüddekopf, *Linke Leute von Rechts* (Stuttgart: Kohlhammer, 1960)—this formulation, pointing to the crossing over of left and right, that is, the revolutionary momentum in some nationalist groups on the right, was coined by Kurt Hiller in his 1932 essay "Linke Leute von Rechts," in *Weltbühne* 2 August 1932.

11. Techow, p. 8: "sie verstehen uns ja doch nicht—Kerns Gesicht wurde hart als er zwischen den Zähnen hervorstiess: keiner wird uns verstehen, und alle werden sie von uns abrücken, als ob wir gemeine Mörder wären."

12. Wilde, p. 8.

13. It is interesting that the rumor of Rathenau's having married off his sister to Radek—she had, in fact, married the Gentile Fritz Andrae during the war—could have been considered to be effective political slander and therefore promoted by some groups on the right. The insinuation of miscegenation makes bolshevism a racial issue which intimates the existence of taboos, the breaking of taboos, consequently the magically strong threatening alliance between the bolshevist and German politicians. In the eyes of Rathenau's assassins these were fairy tales for the dumb masses, yet they themselves were acting out the fairy tale of the redeemer-prince fighting his way to the princess, Germany, and so was Rathenau.

14. Ernst von Salomon, *Die Geächteten* (Berlin, 1930), p. 302, 304, 307.

15. See the eye witness report, above n. 6.

16. Walther Rathenau, *An Deutschlands Jugend* (Berlin, 1918), p. 127; quoted in Joll, *Three Intellectuals in Politics,* p. 125.

17. On the various death threats and assassination plans see Wilde, pp. 142f.

18. See Felix, *The Politics of Reparation.*

19. Letter to Wilhelm Schwaner, May 17, 1922, quoted in Kessler, pp. 360f.

20. "Treu leben, todtrotzend kämpfen, lachend sterben!" See Schwaner's letter to Rathenau, August 25, 1914, extolling the popularity of *Feldbriefpost* and the courage of his young men in a curious repulsive mixture of bravado—with respect to the death of others—and eroticism: "Nun ist das lachende Sterben buchstäblich Wahrheit geworden. . . . Ich könnte diese Kerle der Reihe nach abküssen! Du, jetzt kommt *unsere* Zeit! Wohlan: ich bin gerüstet! Heil und Sieg! Dein Wilm." (Now to die laughing has literally become reality. . . . I could cover these boys with kisses, one after the other. Thou, here comes *our* time! Now then: I am prepared!) (Bundesarchiv Koblenz, Nachlass Rathenau I, partially quoted in Wilde, p. 88).

21. Schwaner's verbal coinage, heavy on compounds, managed to be both cute and heroic: "Gottmenschheit" (Bundesarchiv Koblenz, Nachlass Rathenau I, partially quoted in Wilde, p. 156).

22. Kessler, in his otherwise admirable biography, had set this trend, by being too

discreet in this respect. He had the family's cooperation regarding access to documents though there were restrictions as to their use. But he was too much inclined to stylize Rathenau's psychological conflicts into the respectably significant German-Faustian theme of the "two souls." See also Berglar, *Walther Rathenau,* p. 315.

23. See Schwaner's letter, June 14, 1918, Bundesarchiv Koblenz, Nachlass Rathenau I, quoted in Wilde, p. 92.

24. George L. Mosse, *Masses and Man: Nationalist and Fascist Perceptions of Reality* (New York: Howard Fertig, 1980), pp. 279f. Jünger, *Der Kampf,* p. 33: "Der Geist der Materialschlacht und des Grabenkampfes, der rücksichtsloser, wilder, brutaler ausgefochten wurde als je ein anderer, erzeugte Männer, wie sie bisher die Welt nie gesehen hatte. Es war eine ganz neue Rasse, verkörperte Energie und mit höchster Wucht geladen. Geschmeidige, hagere, sehnige Körper, markante Gesichter, Augen in tausend Schrecken unterm Helm versteinert. Sie waren Überwinder, Stahlnaturen, eingestellt in den Kampf in seiner grässlichsten Form."

25. Quoted in Kessler, p. 24.

26. Quoted in Kessler, pp. 36f.

27. Walter Rathenau, *Gesammelte Schriften in fünf Bänden* (Berlin: S. Fischer, 1918), vol. 1, p. 293). The translation is taken from Joll, *Three Intellectuals in Politics,* p. 61.

28. Kurt Singer, *Staat und Wirtschaft seit dem Waffenstillstand* (Jena, 1924) p. 145. The translation is taken from Joll, *Three Intellectuals,* p. 88. Rathenau's intellectual vanity, very considerable and much commented on by his contemporaries, caused him to pluck ideas out of their cultural context in a highly autocratic fashion. There are many andecdotal accounts of his tendency to sermonize, moving from one concept to the other as brilliantly as arbitrarily. When his father died, Rathenau himself made the funeral oration. The powerful industrial magnate had been, in contrast to his son, a practicing Jew, but Walter quoted widely from Moses and Jesus, managing to make uncomfortable both his Jewish relations and his Christian friends gathered for the occasion. Obsessed with the idea of an organic (vs. mechanistic) wholeness of culture, he had no sensitivity to others' perception of their cultural tradition. See also below n. 92.

29. Letter to Peter Hamm, June 23, 1919: Walther Rathenau, *Briefe* (Dresden: Carl Reissner, 1926), vol. 2, p. 160.

30. *Von kommenden Dingen* (*Gesammelte Schriften,* vol. 5), p. 235. Unless otherwise stated references are to this edition and the translations are mine.

31. Kessler, p. 177. See also Emil J. Gumbel, *Vier Jahre politischer Mord* (Berlin: Neue Gesellschaft, 1922) and Wolf Zuelzer, *The Nicolai Case* (Detroit: Wayne State University Press, 1982). See n. 1.

32. See Hermann Lübbe, *Politische Philosophie in Deutschland Studien zu ihrer Geschichte* (Basel and Stuttgart: Benno Schwabe, 1963), pt. 4, "Die philosophischen Ideen von 1914." Lübbe is extremely helpful both in reading the—to us—overexcited, extravagant statements in their cultural context and in providing a balanced perspective on western reactions, showing, e.g., that writers like Nietzsche or the Prussian historian Heinrich von Treitschke were wrongly accused as a matter of course of providing, directly and massively, the political ideology for Germany's aggressive militarism. On the other hand, Lübbe appreciates British philosophers' rejections of Nietzsche as representative of a revolt against European civilization in view of their much less strongly developed predisposition to "kulturkritische" exaltations (pp. 174ff). See also Leonard Krieger, *The German Idea of Freedom: History of a Political Tradition* (Boston: Beacon Press, 1957); Fritz Ringer, *The Decline of the German Mandarins: The Academic Community 1890–1933* (Cambridge, Mass.: Harvard University Press, 1969); Fritz Stern, *The Politics of Cultural Despair: A Study in the Rise of the German Ideology* (Berkeley: University of California Press, 1961) and "Die politischen Folgen des unpolitischen Deutschen," *Das kaiserliche Deutschland,*

Politik und Gesellschaft 1870–1918, ed. Michael Stürmer (Düsseldorf: Droste, 1970), pp. 168–86; George L. Mosse, *The Crisis of German Ideology: Intellectual Origins of the Third Reich* (New York: Grosset & Dunlap, 1964) and *Masses and Man: Nationalist and Fascist Perceptions of Reality* (New York: Howard Fertig, 1980); Hans Joachim Lieber, *Kulturkritik und Lebensphilosophie Studien zur deutschen Philosophie der Jahrhundertwende* (Darmstadt: Wissenschaftliche Buchgesellschaft, 1974); Helmuth Plessner, *Die verspätete Nation Über die Verführbarkeit des bürgerlichen Geistes* (Stuttgart: Kohlhammer, 1951); Ralf Dahrendorf, *Society and Democracy in Germany* (Garden City, NY: Doubleday, 1967); Walter Rüegg, ed., *Kulturkritik und Jugendkult* (Frankfurt: V. Klostermann, 1974); Dietz Bering, *Die Intellektuellen* (Stuttgart: Klett-Cotta, 1978).

33. See also his *Lebenserinnerungen* (Leipzig: Veit, 1921).

34. *Der Genius des Krieges und der deutsche Krieg* (Leipzig: Verlag der Weissen Bücher, 1916), pp. 269ff.

35. Ibid., pp. 338ff.

36. Ibid., pp. 342ff.

37. Ibid., pp. 354–415.

38. *Von kommenden Dingen,* p. 236.

39. Ibid., p. 237.

40. Ibid., p. 245.

41. Ibid., p. 35.

42. Ibid., p. 259; and (reference) *In Days to Come* (London: Allen and Unwin, 1921), p. 203.

43. *Von kommenden Dingen,* p. 221.

44. Ibid., pp. 273f.

45. Ibid., p. 287.

46. See *Von kommenden Dingen,* p. 106.

47. Ibid., p. 118.

48. *An Deutschlands Jugend* (1918), quoted in Kessler, pp. 249f.

49. Rathenau's 1913 *Zur Mechanik des Geistes: oder vom Reich der Seele* was the closest to him of all his books: see his letter of February 14, 1919 to Constantin Brunner (Leo Wertheimer), elitist Jewish philosopher (*Die Lehre von den Geistigen und dem Volke,* 1908), whose 1918 *Der Judenhass und die Juden* he admired (*Briefe,* vol. 2, p. 122). See also below n. 92.

50. Quoted in Kessler, p. 93.

51. Kessler, p. 93.

52. Ibid., p. 94.

53. Quoted in Kessler, p. 45.

54. Walther Rathenau, "Max Liebermann. Zum siebzigsten Jahr," *Gesammelte Schriften,* vol. 4, p. 75. On Liebermann's temperamental contradictory attitudes toward his own Jewishness, the problems of a (highly successful) Jewish painter, and anti-Semitism see Heinrich Strauss, "Judentum und deutsche Kunst (Zum Problem Max Liebermann)," *Deutsches Judentum Aufstieg und Krise,* Robert Weltsch, ed., (Stuttgart: Deutsche Verlagsanstalt, 1963), pp. 289–304.

55. Rathenau, "Max Liebermann," p. 81.

56. Ibid., p. 82.

57. Ibid., p. 83.

58. Ferdinand Tönnies, *Gemeinschaft und Gesellschaft* (4th and 5th editions, 1922), p. XL; for variations in the evolution of the juxtaposition "live organism = community vs. mechanistic, artificial construct = society" in Weimar cultural interpretation see chaps. 4–6. Tönnies's terms are descriptive rather than normative, meant to trace the transition from an agrarian to an industrial European society. Using them to define a basic dichotomy between meaningful and merely utilitarian social organization stretches or distorts Tönnies's intentions, but it is easy to understand their appeal

in the cultural situation before and between the two wars to writers on the right and the left. From the hindsight of the Nazi *Volksgemeinschaft* one is tempted to stream-line perceptions of the cultural situation and reactions to it too easily into a German ideology inevitably leading to Nazism. See Juan J. Linz, "Political Space and Fas-cism as a Late-Comer: Conditions Conducive to the Success or Failure of Fascism as Mass Movement in Inter-War Europe." *Who Were the Fascists: Social Roots of European Fascism,* ed. Stein Ugelvik Larsen, Bernt Hagtvet, Jan Petter Myklebust (Bergen and Oslo: Universitetsforlaget, 1980), pp. 153–89. Linz asks whether fascism would have been possible without World War I and thinks it doubtful that a movement of the scope of Nazism could have arisen in Germany, "even though political tenden-cies with similar characteristics would have appeared, either in a democratized German empire or in a subsequent German republic" (p. 173). "Proto-fascist" move-ments emerge in periods when the "new liberal democratic and social forces find it difficult to assert themselves in the multi-national empires threatened by conflicts of modern nationalism and in societies confronted with the demands of modern imperi-alism." Their success lies in their attempt to create a "contradictory synthesis of tradition with modernity, attacking many of the values of the Establishment and at the same time rejecting its modern challengers" (p. 174). They stress a true community of "the people" *(Volk)* against the self-interested motivations of a political class; they are strongly antielitist, but, at the same time, they argue for a new elite. Linz points out the importance of World War I in allowing these undercurrents "to emerge with force and acquire a certain degree of respectability and power." However, without the racial imperialism of anti-Semitism and the national imperialism of pan-Germanism, fas-cism in Germany "would still have been a powerful anti-democratic, anti-liberal nationalist and anti-proletarian attempt at social integration, but its effects would never have been so tragic. Without such *völkisch* undercurrents it is also doubtful whether the defeat of the fascist ideological alternative would ever have been so total" (p. 176). I don't quite agree with the last sentence: see n. 10 above. But it certainly is important to insist on the reality of conflicts of interests which have emerged with ever greater force since the turn of the century. It is not so much atomization per se, but the adversary energy of all those "atoms" that is the problem, and embracing "community" vs "(mass) society" is an understandable but self-defeating attempt at a remedy. See Bernt Hagtvet, "The Theory of Mass Society and the Collapse of the Weimar Republic: A Re-Examination," *Who Were the Fascists,* pp. 66–117, especially on the difference between atomization and divisiveness which are frequently con-nected too easily (as they are by Rathenau) or even conflated (pp. 94ff).

59. *Briefe,* vol. 2, p. 147.

60. *Briefe,* vol. 1, p. 131.

61. This evaluation is quoted in Kessler, pp. 14f; see also Hermann Brinckmeyer, *Die Rathenaus* (Munich: Wieland, 1922) who admires Emil's achievement but is skeptical of Walter's leadership qualities.

62. The essay is published in Maximilian Harden's *Zukunft,* March 6, 1897. An old friend and, during his last years, bitter enemy of Rathenau, Harden was seriously wounded in an attack on him by right-wing assassins on July 3, 1922, from which he never recovered. His political weekly *Die Zukunft* was a one man show expressive of Harden's highly idiosyncratic political sympathies and alliances—monarchist, anti-democratic, prolabor, pacifist, and anti-National Socialist.

63. Kessler, p. 36; see also Harry Graf Kessler, *Tagebücher 1918–1937* (Frankfurt: Insel Verlag, 1961), especially interesting for the years 1918–25.

64. These images are strikingly reminiscent of Nazi images of Jews as alien, hostile, aggressive elements attacking the immune system of the body of the German people and therefore to be destroyed whenever, wherever possible. Mystery of race which had singled out the Jews had made them into an evil principle and the discussion of community in terms of race had fostered physical images for the *Volk,*

its strength and its vulnerability. See George L. Mosse, *Towards the Final Solution: A History of European Racism* (New York: Howard Fertig, 1978), especially chaps. 8 and 9.

65. Quoted in Kessler, p. 36.

66. This text, too, appeared in Harden's *Zukunft*, quoted in Kessler, p. 41.

67. *Von kommenden Dingen*, p. 278.

68. Quoted in Kessler, p. 42.

69. Paul Natorp, "Der Tag der Deutschen" (1915); see also Rudolf Eucken, *Lebenserinnerungen*, pp. 104ff; Werner Sombart, *Händler und Helden. Patriotische Besinnungen* (München, 1915). All these texts are decidedly against established mere capitalist interests.

70. Kessler, pp. 191f.

71. Arnold Brecht, *Walther Rathenau und das deutsche Volk* (Munich: Nymphenburger Verlagshandlung, 1950), p. 17; see also Arnold Brecht, *Aus nächster Nähe Lebenserinnerungen eines beteiligten Beobachters 1884–1927* (Stuttgart: Deutsche Verlagsanstalt, 1966) p. 246. Brecht puts a great deal of blame on the Versailles Treaty and the Allies' reluctance to support the German democratic governments.

72. See n. 32 and 58; Thomas Mann's 1918 *Betrachtungen eines Unpolitischen* (Reflections of a nonpolitical man) is a harsh critique of "Zivilisations-Literaten" like his brother Heinrich, whose easy attraction to "shallow" rationalist French *Zivilisation*—especially in his essay on Zola—Thomas contrasted with his own "profound and painful" rootedness in the (to him) much more complex German *Kultur* and one of the most archetypically clear examples of such dichotomy.

73. *Von kommenden Dingen*, pp. 142ff.

74. *Die Neue Wirtschaft* (*Gesammelte Schriften*, vol. 5), p. 218; the translation is Kessler's (p. 208).

75. It is only then that the construction of a "Mittelwelt" (mediating world) can prepare the rise of absolute value and the growth of the realm of the soul: see *Von kommenden Dingen*, pp. 101ff.

76. *Die neue Wirtschaft*, p. 228.

77. *Die neue Wirtschaft*, p. 231 (Kessler's translation, p. 209).

78. Ibid.

79. Ibid., pp. 231f.

80. Ibid., p. 235 (Kessler's translation, p. 212).

81. *Von kommenden Dingen*, pp. 128f.

82. Ibid., pp. 216f; the *Volksstaat* is praised as a living organism enabling man to rise from animal realm to that of the spirit and finally up to the soul; it is conceived as materially unlimited ("der materiell unbeschränkte Staat": ibid., p. 115).

83. This ideal is at the root of the utopianism of so many Weimar intellectuals (see part one, sec. 7) and it has, strangely, survived Weimar and World War II. See Karl-Otto Apel, "Ist die Ethik der idealen Kommunikationsgemeinschaft eine Utopie?" *Utopie-Forschung*, ed. Wilhelm Vosskamp (Stuttgart: Metzler, 1982), vol. 1, pp. 325–55, a curious attempt to conflate the ethics of ideal communication and the utopia of the ideal community and thereby establish a philosophical (rational?) basis for both.

84. January 23, 1916, *Briefe*, vol. 1, pp. 203f.

85. August 18, 1916, *Briefe*, vol. 1, p. 219.

86. Ibid., p. 220.

87. Ibid., p. 221.

88. See ibid.

89. Kessler, pp. 43f.

90. See this chapter, sec. 3.

91. *Gesammelte Schriften*, vol. 1, pp. 185f. See also Arnold Zweig, "Die Demokratie und die Seele der Juden" in *Vom Judentum* (Leipzig, 1913). Zweig, a student of

Max Scheler and an admirer of *Der Genius des Krieges und der Deutsche Krieg* (see his emphatically positive review in *Die Schaubühne* vol. 11, no. 16 (1915): 268–71) became, through the experience of the war, a pacifist and socialist—his best known novel is the 1927 *Der Streit um den Sergeanten Grischa.* He developed strong Zionist sympathies, influenced by Martin Buber and the radical socialist and anarchist Gustav Landauer (murdered in 1919 by members of the right-wing Free Corps), and they, in turn, supported his interest in Eastern Jewry: *Das Ostjüdische Antlitz* (Berlin: Welt-Verlag, 1920). Zweig stressed organic, antiparliamentary elements in future social organization, praising Eastern Jews for their sense of community. He shares with Rathenau certain notions of an organic wholeness of the social body to be established against atomization and mechanization, but he differs sharply in the way in which he sees the social—if not the cultural—role of German Jewry.

92. Rathenau, *Gesammelte Schriften,* vol. 1, pp. 186ff. He is close here to Constantin Brunner, *Der Judenhass und die Juden* (Berlin, 1918), who sees Zionism as the most destructive consequence of racial hatred, arguing that anti-Semitism will be the less dangerous the stronger the state and the more supportive the Jews are of state and nation (pp. 116ff). In a letter of February 10, 1919, Rathenau recommends to an acquaintance the "powerful concluding chapter" of the book—Brunner praises true Christianity as the most important cultural achievement of Judaism, arguing for a deeper unity of mankind underneath surface differences—as the "only way" for spiritual Judaism ("geistiges Judentum"): *Briefe,* vol. 2, p. 120. On Jewish responses to anti-Semitism see Donald L. Niewyk, *The Jews in Weimar Germany* (Baton Rouge: Louisiana State University Press, 1980), especially chaps. 5–7.

93. *Gesammelte Schriften,* vol. 1, pp. 192ff.

94. Quoted in Kessler, p. 242; see David Calleo, *The German Problem Reconsidered: Germany and the World Order 1870 to the Present* (Cambridge: Cambridge University Press, 1978). Calleo argues against putting too much of the blame for Germany's aggressiveness on the *Junker* class, pointing out that, after all, German liberals, university professors, and the protestant clergy were among the most intransigent annexationists. He also stresses the important role of inidividuals: men like Admiral Tirpitz and Ludendorff, vulgar social Darwinists interested in the manipulation of the public, were not "radical conservatives" (like Rathenau: see also n. 10), but, rather, rootless technocrats "who in the name of progress and modernity brought the ruin that unhinged a whole society" (p. 54).

95. Letter of November 1, 1914, *Briefe,* vol. 1, pp. 171f; and December 6, 1914, to the same friend (*Briefe,* vol. 1, pp. 173f) about his plans for after the war: he will buy a house and garden on one of the mild green-blue lakes in Switzerland and live there: "I will not be able to bear the rule of incompetence and arrogance and the spiritual [*geistig*] regress necessary to excuse all the mistakes that were made." See here Norman Rich, "Die deutsche Frage und der nationalsozialistische Imperialismus: Rückblick und Ausblick," *Die deutsche Frage im 19. und 20. Jahrhundert,* ed. Josef Becker and Andreas Hillgruber (Munich: Ernst Voegel, 1983), pp. 373–92.

96. "Schicksalsspiele," quoted in Kessler, p. 244.

97. Letter of February 26, 1917, *Briefe,* vol. 1, p. 239.

98. Quoted in Kessler, p. 256. Rathenau does not seem to have seen some of the motives behind Ludendorff's decision: above all, the intention to burden the Social Democrats with the undesirable armistice and its consequences.

99. Letter to Socialist Prussian Minister A. Südekum, November 16, 1919, *Briefe,* vol. 2, p. 193.

100. Letter to Peter Hammes, June 23, 1919, *Briefe,* vol. 2, pp. 160f.

101. Letter to Wolfgang Schumann, February 11, 1919, *Briefe,* vol. 2, p. 121.

102. Quoted in Kessler, pp. 273ff.

103. Quoted in Kessler, pp. 251f.

104. Kessler, p. 252.

105. Letter to Heinrich Freiherr von Gleichen-Russwurm, May 23, 1919, *Briefe,* vol. 2, pp. 148–53.
106. The appeal is quoted in Kessler, pp. 259ff.
107. See below this section.
108. See Rathenau's letter of December 16, 1918, to future President Friedrich Ebert, then People's Commissary (*Briefe,* vol. 2, pp. 87–89); he refers to his critical attitude toward the old system and the war, his "new scientifically reasoned and based complete economic system," the popularity of his future-oriented writing, and the misunderstood purpose of his call for a *levée en masse,* repeating his opinion that it was wrong to negotiate, defenseless, for an armistice instead of negotiating, armed, for peace, that events had proved him right, and that this opinion in no way undermined his "social and democratic position."
109. Shorthand report of the Reichstag proceedings, quoted in Kessler, p. 265.
110. *Apologie,* pp. 106f.
111. Kessler, p. 266.
112. Letter of July 16, 1919, *Briefe,* vol. 2, pp. 167–71.
113. When Wirth became chancellor in May 1921, he asked Rathenau to take over the Ministry of Reconstruction. In his first speech to the Reichstag on June 2, Rathenau said: "I have entered a Cabinet of Fulfillment. We must discover some means of linking ourselves up with the world again" (quoted in Kessler, p. 305). To achieve such linkage he suggested German-French cooperation in reconstructing the devastated areas in France. Germany could thus prove her goodwill—still profoundly questioned—and her capacity for work, and she could also replace payments in gold by deliveries in kind and labor. Payment of the first billion gold marks on August 31, 1921, had made the dollar shoot up from 60 to 100 marks (the 'normal' rate had been around 4 marks)—an indication that further payments in gold would lead to a collapse of German currency. The Wiesbaden agreement of October 6 and 7, 1921, regulated direct deliveries in kind from German industry to French war victims, the industry being paid in German currency. This ingenious scheme did not work: French industrialists had found the devastated areas their most profitable market and resisted it. But it enabled Rathenau to prove several important points to the Allies: Germany's goodwill, her inability to pay in gold, the inability of the Allies to receive deliveries in kind on the suggested scale—7 billion gold marks for France within a period of 4½ years—without ruining their own trade. (In 1922 France demanded and received deliveries in kind to the value of 19 million goldmarks only). See David Felix, *Walther Rathenau and the Weimar Republic: The Politics of Reparation* (Baltimore: Johns Hopkins University Press, 1971).
114. See this chapter, sec. 1 and n. 19. Letter to Wilhelm Schwaner, May 17, 1922.
115. Kessler, p. 359.

2. ULRICH, A LIFE

1. Robert Musil, *Prosa Gesammelte Werke II,* ed. Adolf Frisé (Reinbek by Hamburg; Rowohlt, 1978), pp. 1015ff. For Rathenau's text see chap. 1, sec. 2. Musil's essays, dramas, diaries, and letters still have to be translated into English; translations from these texts are mine, references are to *Prosa Gesammelte Werke.* Quotes from *Der Mann ohne Eigenschaften (The Man without Qualities)* are taken from the translation by Eithne Wilkins and Ernst Kaiser, references are by chapter (chapters are short) to avoid confusion in the present situation of several paperback (Putnam's, Picador Books) and hardcover (Secker & Warburg) editions which are currently out of print or not easily available, and a new translation to be published by Knopf which will include the second volume of the novel. The best general introduction to Musil available in English is still Burton Pike, *Robert Musil: An Introduction to His Work*

(Ithaca, N.Y.: Cornell University Press, 1961). Of the other two book-length studies of Musil available in English, Frederick George Peters, *Robert Musil Master of the Hovering Life: A Study of the Major Fiction* (New York: Columbia University Press, 1978) is uninterested in Musil's cultural criticism *and* his achievements as a novelist, combing the texts for mystic utterances; the much more substantial David S. Luft, *Robert Musil and the Crisis of European Culture 1880–1942* (Berkeley, Los Angeles, and London: University of California Press, 1980) suffers from inexperience in reading multiperspective fictional texts in general and highly intricate aphoristic prose like Musil's in particular. He is also, as an intellectual historian of the H. Stuart Hughes School, too rigidly concerned with "generations" and neglects the difficult but central question of a balance between the individual talent and the sociocultural context in which it develops. The texts, especially the essays and *Man without Qualities*, are then mined for culturally important concepts and too little attention is given to Musil's critical discussion of these concepts in the context of the novel which does not, as Luft believes, "mediate his culture's antagonisms between intellect and feeling, truth and subjectivity, science and art" (p. 2), but rather reveals and explores the complex fallacies inherent in such antagonisms. The best introductions in German are Marie-Louise Roth, *Robert Musil Ethik and Asthetik Zum theoretischen Werk des Dichters* (Munich: List, 1972) and Helmut Arntzen, *Musil-Kommentar*, 2 vols. (Munich: Winkler, 1980 and 1982). Arntzen has extensive intelligently arranged bibliographical notes.

2. "Metaphysik als Nobilitierung und heraldische Spekulation, die die entleibte Haut des Erlebnisses an die Sterne hängt" (*Prosa*, p. 1019).

3. Ibid.: "Wir Deutschen haben—ausser dem einen grossen Versuch Nietzsches—keine Bücher über den Menschen; keine Systematiker und Organisatoren des Lebens. Künstlerisches und wissenschaftliches Denken berühren sich bei uns noch nicht. Die Fragen einer Mittelzone zwischen beiden bleiben ungelöst."

4. Lothar Schäfer, "Pascal und Descartes als methodologische Antipoden," *Philosophisches Jahrbuch der Görresgesellschaft* 81 (1974): 314–40.

5. Especially Walter Jens, *Statt einer Literaturgeschichte* (Pfullingen: Neske, 1957).

6. See n. 4.

7. Robert Musil, *Tagebücher*, ed. Adolf Frisé (Reinbek by Hamburg: Rowohlt, 1976), vol. 1, p. 663ff; see also *Tagebücher*, vol. 1, pp. 643ff.

8. David Hume, *A Treatise of Human Nature*, ed. L. A. Selby-Bigge (1888; reprint, Oxford: Clarendon Press, 1960), vol. 1, pp. 305f, quoted in *Tagebücher*, vol. 1, p. 664.

9. Ibid.

10. Appendix to the 1758 *Inquiry Concerning Human Understanding*, "A Dialogue," in *The Philosophical Works*, ed. Thomas Hill Green and Thomas Hodge Grose (London: Longman's, Green, 1886), vol. 4, p. 299.

11. See my "Skepticism as a Literary Mode: David Hume and Robert Musil," *Modern Language Notes* 93 (1978): 852–70, n. 7; see also Walter Benjamin, *Briefe*, ed. Gershom Scholem and Theodor W. Adorno (Frankfurt: Suhrkamp, 1966), vol. 2, p. 575: "ich habe diesen Autor [Musil] bei mir mit der Erkenntnis verabschiedet, dass er klüger ist als er's nötig hat."

12. See "Skepticism as a Literary Mode," pp. 853f.

13. *The Philosophical Works*, vol. 4, p. 133.

14. See below, this section; Jan Aler, "Als Zögling zwischen Maeterlinck und Mach. Robert Musils literarisch-philosophische Anfänge," *Probleme des Erzählens in der Weltliteratur*, ed. Fritz Martini (Stuttgart: Metzler, 1971), pp. 234–90.

15. See especially Jürgen C. Thöming, *Zur Rezeption von Musil- und Goethe-Texten* (Munich: Fink, 1974).

16. *Prosa*, pp. 1334–37.

17. Ibid., p. 1337.

18. Ibid.

19. Ibid.

20. *Prosa*, pp. 1075–94, p. 1092.

21. Ibid., p. 1085; see a diary entry in the thirties on the veneration of intellectual dictators ("geistige Diktatorenverehrung") before the emergence of political dictators: Stefan George, Karl Kraus, Freud, Jung, Klages, Heidegger (*Tagebücher*, vol. 1, p. 896).

22. See Helmut Lethen, *Neue Sachlichkeit 1924–1932 Studien zur Literature des "Weissen Sozialismus"* (Stuttgart: Metzler, 1970), pp. 140ff.

23. *Prosa*, p. 1085.

24. Robert Musil, *Beitrag zur Beurteilung der Lehren Machs* (Berlin and Wilmersdorf: Dissertationenverlag Carl Arnold, 1908); see n. 14 above.

25. *Prosa*, pp. 1042–59.

26. *Prosa*, p. 1055.

27. *Prosa*, p. 1335.

28. "Skizze der Erkenntnis des Dichters," *Prosa*, pp. 1025–30. Writing, for Musil, means to be engaged in the experiment (essay) of understanding the relation of self and world; in this very important sense there is no difference between the poet and the essayist, and art is not a privileged medium of understanding: see also *Tagebücher*, vol. 1, p. 652. Musil differs sharply here from writers like Thomas Mann, Adorno, Walter Benjamin, and Brecht, who privileged art, and Hermann Broch whose rejection of art proved detrimental to his later work (see chap. 6). See Hans Heinz Hahnl, "Zu Musil's Aktualität," *Musil-Forum* 7 (1981): 169–73.

29. *Prosa*, p. 1029.

30. See n. 43; see Renate von Heydebrand, *Die Reflexionen Ulrichs in Robert Musil's Roman "Der Mann ohne Eigenschaften" Ihr Zusammenhang mit dem zeitgenössischen Denken* (Münster: Verlag Aschendorf, 1966), chap. 3, 4.

31. *Prosa*, p. 1029: *"dass die Struktur der Welt und nicht die seiner Anlagen dem Dichter seine Aufgabe zuweist, dass er eine Sendung hat!"* (emphasis Musil's). The richness and variety of this *Welt* as it appears in the novel—the details seen and heard—has often been remarked on: see Edmonde Charles-Roux, "Aspects de l'austrianité de Musil," in *l'Herne Robert Musil*, ed. Marie-Louise Roth et Roberto Olmi (Paris: Editions de l'Herne, 1981), pp. 179–86.

32. Marie-Louise Roth, *Robert Musil Biographie et écriture* (Paris: Encres, 1980), pp. 30ff.

33. See Walter Moser, "Diskursexperimente im Romantext. Zu Musils *Der Mann ohne Eigenschaften*," in *Robert Musil Untersuchungen*, ed. Uwe Baur and Elisabeth Castex (Königstein/Taunus: Athenäum, 1980), pp. 170–97, pp. 178ff.

34. Max Weber, "'Objectivity' in Social Science and Social Policy," in *The Methodology of the Social Sciences*, trans. and ed. Edward A. Shils and Henry A. Finch (New York: Free Press of Glencoe, 1949), pp. 49–112, pp. 54ff.

35. Ibid., p. 73.

36. Ibid., p. 54.

37. Ibid., p. 60.

38. Ibid.

39. Ibid., p. 57; see Wolfgang Mommsen, "'Verstehen' und 'Idealtypus.' Zur Methodologie einer historischen Sozialwissenschaft," in *Max Weber, Gesellschaft, Politik und Geschichte* (Frankfurt: Suhrkamp, 1974), pp. 208–32, pp. 211ff.

40. Weber, p. 81.

41. Weber's *ideal-type* construct was meant to deal with this problem: pp. 90ff, pp. 110ff, but he was fully aware of the limited usefulness of scientific "laws" in the social sciences when faced with the "qualitative aspects of phenomena" (pp. 74ff).

42. Heydebrand, pp. 20ff, p. 232.

43. Robert Musil, *"Wege zur Kunstbetrachtung," Prosa*, pp. 1517–21, p. 1519: "Es liegt also der Wert der *Wege* gerade darin, dass die 'Bildteile,' aus denen sie den Eindruck aufbauen, wirklich solche sind, über die sich etwas Festes, für grosse Menschengruppen Gültiges sagen lässt, mit einem andern Wort, dass sie das sind, woraus sich der Bildeindruck psychologisch, d.h. in *Wirklichkeit* aufbaut" (Musil's emphasis). See also Musil's letters to Allesch about the book July 15, 1921, and December 16, 1921 (*Robert Musil Briefe 1901–1942*, ed. Adolf Frisé and Murray G. Hall (Reinbek by Hamburg: Rowohlt, 1981), vol. 1, pp. 236, 252). Allesch's contribution to *Gestaltpsychologie* was an emphasis on the subjective variability in *Gestalt* formation, whereas Wolfgang Köhler tried to exclude such variability because of the ensuing complications. Musil became increasingly interested in the subjective variations in the later stages of *Man without Qualities* where he has Ulrich trying to work out, in his conversations with his sister, more consistent, comprehensive statements on his emotions.

44. Ibid., pp. 1520f.

45. *Prosa*, p. 1520.

46. *Tagebücher*, vol. 1, pp. 19f, around 1902.

47. I do not know whether Musil made a clear distinction between sensation and perception (*Empfindung* and *Wahrnehmung*), as sensation does not normally occur without some interpretative directive elements. See however D. W. Hamlyn, *Sensation and Perception: A History of the Philosophy of Perception* (London: Routledge & Kegan Paul, 1961).

48. Stumpf, a friend of Husserl's and negative in his attitude toward Mach, wanted Musil to assume a more decisively critical position. See also Henri Arvon, "Robert Musil und der Positivismus," in *Robert Musil. Studien zu seinem Werk*, ed. Karl Dinklage (Reinbek by Hamburg: Rowohlt, 1970), pp. 200–213. John T. Blackmore, *Ernst Mach: His Work, Life and Influence* (Berkeley: University of California Press, 1972).

49. Ernst Mach, *Die Analyse der Empfindungen und das Verhältnis des Physischen zum Psychischen* (1886; reprint, Jena: G. Fischer, 1911), p. 20. Marxist critics upset about Mach's (and Musil's) skepticism with regard to the intelligibility of a so-called *objektive Aussenwelt* and *objektiver Geist* have shown themselves unable to see the useful social implications of Mach's critical experimental approach to epistemological questions which they have rejected as "subjectivist." Ernst Fischer in his essay "Das Werk Robert Musil's Versuch einer Würdigung," *Sinn und Form* 9 (1957): 851–901, deplored Mach's influence—"diese Verflüchtigung der objektiven Aussenwelt in ein Bündel subjektiver Empfindungen" (pp. 862f)—on Musil. The Frankfurt School, insisting on a dichotomy between "traditional theory" (i.e., in their definition, instrumental subjective reason) and their own "critical theory" (dialectic objective reason), have notoriously misrepresented Mach's achievement: see here Max Horkheimer, *Vernunft und Selbsterhaltung* (Frankfurt: S. Fischer, 1970), pp. 31ff.

50. *Die Analyse*, p. 20: "Das Ich ist unrettbar. Teils diese Einsicht, teils die Furcht vor derselben führen zu den absonderlichsten, pessimistischen und optimistischen, religiösen, asketischen und philosophischen Verkehrtheiten. Der einfachen Wahrheit, welche sich aus der psychologischen Perspektive ergibt, wird man sich auf die Dauer nicht verschliessen können. Man wird dann auf das Ich, welches schon während des individuellen Lebens vielfach variiert, . . . nicht mehr den hohen Wert legen. Man wird dann auf individuelle Unsterblichkeit gern verzichten und nicht auf das Nebensächliche mehr Wert legen als auf die Hauptsache. Man wird hierdurch zu einer freieren und verklärten Lebensauffassung gelangen, welche Missachtung des fremden Ich und Überschätzung des eigenen ausschliesst."

51. Ernst Mach, *Erkenntnis und Irrtum* (Leipzig, 1905), p. 13.

52. Ernst Mach, *Populärwissenschaftliche Vorlesungen* (Leipzig, 1906), p. 231.

53. *Tagebücher*, vol. 1, pp. 643f.

54. *Prosa*, p. 1092 (Musil's emphasis).

55. Letter to Klaus Pinkus, January 10, 1942, *Briefe*, vol. 1, p. 1386.

56. See n. 33.

57. The diaries are a quarry of notes, excerpts, cross-references containing many years of concentrated critical reading in the cultural sciences. Claudio Magris, "Die Odyssee des Robert Musil," *Merkur* 33 (1979): 138–48, stresses the intimate relation between the encyclopedic nature of the novel and its incompleteness; more careful and useful on the same issue is Adolf Frisé, "Unvollendet-Unvollendbar? Überlegungen zum Torso des *Mann ohne Eigenschaften*," *Musil-Forum* 6 (1980): 79–104, and Jean-Francois Peyret, "Von jenen, die auszogen, den *Mann ohne Eigenschaften* zu verstehen. Zu Musils fragwürdiger Aktualität," in *Robert Musil Untersuchungen*, pp. 31–45, pp. 34ff.

58. See chap. 3.

59. See my "Autorenstrategie und Leser im Gedankenroman. Zu Fragen von Perspektivik und Bedeutung," in *Erzählforschung 3*, ed. Wolfgang Haubrichs (Göttingen: Vandenhoeck und Ruprecht, 1978), pp. 223–55.

60. Musil's critical analysis of Thomas Mann's success has been frequently misunderstood as the deplorable envy of the less successful writer: Karl Corino, *Robert Musil-Thomas Mann. Ein Dialog* (Pfullingen: Neske, 1971).

61. See especially *Tagebücher*, vol. 1, pp. 813ff.

62. Ullstein commendably specialized in publishing "good books" for large audiences—today the association would be BBC soap operas.

63. See chapter 95 "Der Grosschriftsteller, Rückansicht" and 96 "Der Grosschriftsteller, Vorderansicht." On Rathenau-Arnheim see part 3 of this chapter.

64. *Tagebücher*, vol. 1, p. 745.

65. Ibid., p. 766. The readers couldn't agree more with the writer: "er spricht ihnen aus dem Herzen." Musil here uses a witty neologism: "zeitbürtige Romane" based on "ebenbürtig" (equal).

66. *Tagebücher*, vol. 1, p. 480.

67. In contrast to Musil, however, Broch had a publisher who was both devoted to him and intelligently critical, and his *Schlafwandler* trilogy was immediately translated into English by the excellent Edwin and Willa Muir who arguably improved the text.

68. *Tagebücher*, vol. 2, pp. 1224f. Broch, more relaxed intellectually and (therefore) more generous sent the first volume of *Man without Qualities* to his translator Willa Muir expressing reservations about the "rational" method of the novel but stressing its importance and his hope that it might find readers in England. (July 19, 1931, *Tagebücher*, vol. 2, p. 613).

69. Especially the three novellas in *Drei Frauen* (1924).

70. See Hedwig Wieczorek-Mair, "Musils Roman *Der Mann ohne Eigenschaften* in der zeitgenössischen Kritik," in *Robert Musil Untersuchungen*, pp. 10–30. She documents the difference in the reception of volume 1 and volume 2 which is more predominantly essayistic. The more difficult political-economic situation in 1932 may have added to the less enthusiastic reception of that part of the novel; the first part had been a critical success.

71. *Tagebücher*, vol. 1, p. 816; Musil reflects on his own reactions as reader of Chesterton (whom he greatly admires) and of Undset (whom he thinks a competent storyteller).

72. Ibid., p. 652.

73. *Prosa*, pp. 869f.

74. *Tagebücher*, vol. 1, p. 678: "Hauptsache: eine Art Biographie meiner Ideen," he notes in the late twenties. This note stresses the preeminence of the novel's conceptual development.

75. Ibid., p. 608.

76. Ibid., p. 643.
77. Ibid., p. 579; see also *Der Mann ohne Eigenschaften (Werke I)*, p. 1818.
78. *Mann ohne Eigenschaften*, p. 1937.
79. *Tagebücher*, vol. 1, p. 317.
80. *Mann ohne Eigenschaften*, p. 1940: "Ich habe es aber mit dem Sinn der Tat zu tun."
81. I am using here a distinction of meaning/significance taken from Gottlob Frege, "Über Sinn und Bedeutung," *Zeitschrift für Philosophie und philosophische Kritik*, N.F., 100 (1892): 25–50, well aware of its problematic aspects: there are of course evaluative-interpretative elements in system-inherent "meaning" (or sense) as no reader first establishes the meaning of a text and then allows it to assume significance; it is a question of degree, of shifting emphasis, rather than difference in kind. The distinction here is meant to help clarify Musil's emphasis on making sense.
82. *Tagebücher*, vol. 1, p. 928: "dass die mir gemässe Schreibweise die der Ironie sei."
83. Ibid., p. 973: "der sich selbst nirgends ganz hin, nirgends ganz fortgehören fühlt."
84. *Mann ohne Eigenschaften*, p. 1939; see also *Prosa*, pp. 920, 941.
85. *Tagebücher*, vol. 1, p. 973.
86. *Mann ohne Eigenschaften*, p. 1941; see also p. 1938.
87. Ibid., p. 1938.
88. *Tagebücher*, vol. 2, p. 1148.
89. Musil's texts, fiction, drama, and essays alike, but especially *Der Mann ohne Eigenschaften* in its aphoristic compression and peculiar shifting between abstract and concrete, are extremely difficult to translate. The English translations are frequently awkward and blur fine shades of meaning: "Städte lassen sich an ihrem Gang erkennen wie Menschen. Die Augen öffnend, würde er das gleich an der Art bemerken, wie die Bewegung in den Strassen schwingt, beiweitem früher als er es durch irgendwie bezeichnende Einzelheiten herausfände." *Gang* describes a person's way of walking, a highly individual composite phenomenon, and is also used to describe the pace of a place, of events, of a life. The analogy between a person and a city, suggested by the same shared noun *Gang* and extended by the verb *schwingt* is made here in the context of a comment on perception. Both the walk of a person and the motion of a city are perceived as *Gestalt* involving the same questions of selection, interpretation, margin for error, etc., and the pleasurable experience of recognition.
90. There is a great deal of narrated monologue in *The Man without Qualities* which frequently merges with the narrating voice; where the narrating voice is distinct I will refer to it as "the author" as the issue for the reader of this essay-novel is the authorial responsibility for what is said.
91. See John R. Searle, "The Logical Status of Fictional Discourse," *Expression and Meaning Studies in the Theory of Speech Acts* (Cambridge, London, and New York: Cambridge University Press, 1979), pp. 58–75.
92. Ulrich (the novel in general) has been found lacking in sensuality by critics, one example repeatedly mentioned is the fact that he frequently stands at a window, looking out without sharing views of natural objects with the reader: see Bernd-Rüdiger Hüppauf, *Von sozialer Utopie zur Mystik Zu Robert Musils der Mann ohne Eigenschaften* (Munich: Fink, 1971), pp. 33ff. It is true that the act of seeing is in most cases directly related to intellectual activity, and landscape imagery mostly has the function of clarifying emotional states. Ulrich's sensuality is both vivid and subtle, but his perception is naturally meaningfully selective and Musil, narrating the life of Ulrich as a "biography" of his own (and Ulrich's) ideas, is interested in perception as an aspect of mind. Sensuality is in the images.
93. See Georg Simmel, *The Philosophy of Money*, trans. Tom Bottomore and

David Frisby (London, Henley, and Boston: Routledge & Kegan Paul, 1978), chap. 6, esp. pp. 481ff.

94. See esp. chapters 61 and 62.

95. *Tagebücher*, vol. 1, p. 578: "Typen aus denen sich die Handlung aufbaut, müssen konstitutiv für das heutige Leben sein. Etwa: Der Schachspieler und der Mathematiker."

96. Most helpful for charting the novel is Helmut Arntzen, *Musil-Kommentar 2*, pp. 79ff. See also Peter L. Berger, "The Problem of Multiple Realities: Alfred Schutz and Robert Musil," in *Phenomenology and Social Reality: Essays in Memory of Alfred Schutz*, ed. Maurice Natanson (The Hague: Martinus Nijhoff, 1970), pp. 214–33.

97. See the interview with Oskar Maurus Fontana, April 30, 1926, *Prosa*, pp. 939–42. Asked about his sense of a cultural crisis Musil points to his satirical treatment of declines of the West and their prophets: "Urträume der Menschheit werden in unseren Tagen verwirklicht. Dass sie bei der Verwirklichung nicht mehr ganz das Gesicht der Urträume verwirklicht haben—ist das ein Malheur? Wir brauchen auch dafür eine neue Moral. Mit unserer alten kommen wir nicht aus. Mein Roman möchte Material zu einer solchen neuen Moral geben. Er ist Versuch einer Auflösung und Andeutung einer Synthese" (p. 942).

98. *Tagebücher* vol. 1, p. 579.

99. Ibid., p. 613: "Diese 'Güte' der Liebe als Schwesterlichkeit, Verwischung der Ichpolarität . . ."; see also the diary entries concerning alternate social-psychological relations in the "moralische Experimentallandschaft" of another planet: ibid., pp. 840ff.

100. Susan Brownmiller, *Femininity* (New York: Simon & Schuster, 1984). Many of her honest and shrewd observations on women's use of their femininity are illustrated in *The Man without Qualities*.

101. *Prosa*, pp. 983–84, 985–87.

102. Ibid., p. 984.

103. Ibid.

104. Ibid., p. 986.

105. "Seinesgleichen geschieht" is (almost) untranslatable. Kaiser-Wilkins' "The Like of It Now Happens" does not make much sense.

106. *Tagebücher*, vol. 1, p. 613: "Und dazu stimmt auch, dass die Vorstellung Schwester für ihn trotz aller geschlechtlichen Erlebnisse einen seltsamen Zauber behielt."

107. "Du bist meine Eigenliebe! . . . Mir hat eine richtige Eigenliebe, wie sie andere Menschen so stark besitzen, in gewissem Sinn immer gefehlt . . ." (*Mann ohne Eigenschaften*, vol. 2, chaps. 24, 25); see also vol. 1 chap. 40 ("A Man with All the Qualities but They Are a Matter of Indifference to Him"): "It's simply that I'm not fond of myself."

108. See Hans Hahnl, "Autorengespräch," *Literatur und Kritik* 149/150 (1980): 607–11.

109. Claude David, "Musil und die Stadt," ibid., pp. 518–24; on "Amerikanismus" during the Weimar period see Lethen, *Neue Sachlichkeit*, chap. 1, "Amerikanismus. Genesis und Funktion einer intellektuellen Mode"; see also the texts conveniently collected in Anton Kaes, ed., *Weimarer Republik Manifeste und Dokumente zur deutschen Literatur 1918–1933* (Stuttgart: Metzler, 1983), pt. 2, chap. 5, "Die Auseinandersetzung mit dem kulturellen Amerikanismus."

110. *Tagebücher*, vol. 1, p. 354.

111. *Prosa*, pp. 792ff; Uwe Baur, "Sport und subjektive Bewegungserfahrung bei Musil," in *Robert Musil, Untersuchungen*, pp. 99–112.

112. See my "Mind and Myth in *Masse und Macht*," *Modern Austrian Literature* 16 (1983): 65–79.

113. I will capitalize the term when referring to a self-consciously selective concept of culture.

114. *Prosa,* pp. 1004–8, p. 1006.

115. "Die Gesichter waren gefleckt, die Körper verbogen, die Köpfe hackten ruckweise auf und nieder, gespreizte Klauen schlugen in die sich auf-bäumende Tonmasse. Unermessliches geschah; eine undeutlich umgrenzte, mit heissen Empfindungen gefüllte Blase schwoll bis zum Platzen an, und von den erregten Fingerspitzen, den nervösen Runzeln der Stirn, den Zuckungen des Leibs strahlte immer neues Gefühl in den ungeheuren Privataufruhr." I am quoting the German to give an example of the skillful instructive blending of high-cultural clichés with expressive images of particular sensation and emotional states.

116. Chap. 16: " 'One can't be angry with one's own time without damage to oneself,' Ulrich felt. And indeed he was always ready to love all these manifestations of life. What he could never manage, however, was to love them unreservedly, as is required for a general sense of social well-being."

117. The German is clearer: "Immer wird für ihn erst ein möglicher Zusammenhang entscheiden, wofür er eine Sache hält."

118. On the turn toward inwardness around 1930, see above pt. 1; see Ernst Robert Curtius, *Deutscher Geist in Gefahr* (Stuttgart and Berlin, 1932), especially his attacks on Mannheim's *Ideology and Utopia;* Siegfried Kracauer, Die Angestellten (Frankfurt, 1930).

119. See above Introduction, sec. 2, and part one, sec. 5.

120. Quoted in Arnhelm Neusüss, *Utopisches Bewusstsein und freischwebende Intelligenz Zur Wissenssoziologie Karl Mannheims* (Meisenheim/Glan: Anton Hain, 1968), p. 57; Mannheim's emphasis (my translation).

121. *Prosa,* p. 920: "*Sokratisch* ist: Sich unwissend stellen. *Modern:* Unwissend sein!"

122. See "Signs and Symptoms," Lester S. King, M.D., *Medical Thinking: A Historical Preface* (Princeton: Princeton University Press, 1982), pp. 73–89, pp. 75ff. The medical dictionary definition is: "a sign is an objective symptom of disease; a symptom is a subjective sign of disease"—not very helpful. Important for our context is the emphasis on the different goals: a symptom is the patient's (coherent) construct, a sign is the stimulus for the physician's puzzle-solving activity.

123. *Tagebücher,* vol. 1, p. 862: "*Zur Krisis des Romans:* Wir sollen erzählen, wie es der Kranke dem Arzt tut. (Dann haben wir Erfolg). Warum nicht, wie Ärzte miteinander oder wenigstens wie der Arzt den Kranken aufklärt?"

124. For contemporary examples see the novels of Milan Kundera, especially *The Book of Laughter and Forgetting* (1978) (New York: Knopf, 1980) and *The Unbearable Lightness of Being* (1984) (New York: Harper & Row, 1984).

125. Max Scheler, "Cultural Sociology: Sociology of Real Factors and the Hierarchical Laws Governing the Effectiveness of Ideals and Real Factors," *Problems of a Sociology of Knowledge* (1924) (London and Boston: Routledge & Kegan Paul, 1980), pp. 33–63.

126. See n. 31, 108.

127. Diotima is a collage of some key clichés of middle-brow cultural conservatism; the German *Schicksalsmacht* is more potently obscurantist and therefore more representative than "magical radiation."

128. A good example today in a situation of an even more accelerated technology is the wave of home computers and the quite irrational pleasurable feeling of potency in joining the "new technological elite" simply by using a word processor. During the Weimar Republic, "Amerikanismus" thrived largely on the same illusion that one must not under any circumstances get left behind and that it suffices to embrace wholeheartedly (uncritically) every new trend to be in the cultural (technological) vanguard.

129. The emphasis is more subtle in German: "Ein Kapitel, das jeder überschlagen kann, der von der Beschäftigung mit Gedanken keine besondere Meinung hat."

130. Henry Pachter in the Rathenau chapter of his *Weimar Etudes* (New York: Columbia University Press, 1982), an otherwise very shrewd and fair observer, did not understand how Musil used the novel to explore important cultural issues represented by a figure like Rathenau. In this context it is a moot question whether Musil did or did not sincerely admire Rathenau's dedication to his political office.

131. See John Boyer, *Political Radicalism in Late Imperial Vienna: Origins of the Christian Socialist Movement 1848–1897*. (Chicago: University of Chicago Press, 1981).

132. See chap. 34, "A Hot Ray and Walls Grown Cold": Ulrich, walking, responds to the different historical layers of the city, from the *Stephansdom* to what was, in 1913, a provocation to many Viennese, Adolf Loos's modern house at the Michaelerplatz.

133. See chap. 86: Arnheim has recently become uncomfortably aware of a certain mechanistic element in his endeavors to combat the harmful mechanistic tendencies of his age by fusing soul and business: dictating one of his cultural essays he notices that his secretary, instead of waiting for him when he pauses for the phrase "silence of the walls" has gone ahead with "silence of the soul."

134. Chap. 59: Moosbrugger sitting in his cell, thinking: He is amused by the examining psychiatrists' interest in his calling a squirrel "perhaps a fox or a hare or a cat"—he knows a number of different regional expressions like "oak pussy" *(Eichkätzchen)* in the south, "tree-fox" *(Baumfuchs)* in the west—and in his adding fourteen plus fourteen to "about twenty-eight to forty"—who says that one has to stop at 28? In his experience everything hangs together, the face of a girl becomes a rose and has to be cut off. Unable to escape the isolating ensnarement by interconnected images and objects, Moosbrugger acts criminally: "Generally he just used all his gigantic strength to hold the world together."

135. At this stage, Ulrich emphatically rejects the idea of writing a book: to Tuzzi (chap. 91), to Gerda Fischel (chap. 103), to Arnheim (chap. 121).

136. Moosbrugger danced "until it was all outside, all out of him, clinging to the things about him, brittle and fine-spun, like a cobweb stiffened in the frost."

137. See also chaps. 95 and 96, "The Superman of Letters: Backview" and "Front-view"; see Musil's remarks on Thomas Mann as *Grosschriftsteller*, above, pt. 1 of this chapter.

138. For the influence on the young Lukacs see Lee Congdon, *The Young Lukács* (Chapel Hill and London: University of North Carolina Press, 1983), pp. 24ff.

139. Georg Simmel, *The Philosophy of Money* (London and Boston: Routledge & Kegan Paul, 1978), chap. 6, "The Style of Life," has shrewd suggestive observations on urban culture: his concept of alienation is much less mechanical than it was to become in Lukács's 1923 *History and Class Consciousness* (see especially chap. 6, pt. 3, on alterations in distance in urban life and the function of money, pp. 470ff).

140. Ibid., p. 473.

141. See below chap. 5.

142. *Mann ohne Eigenschaften*, pp. 1851, 1901; see Ernst von Salomon, *Frage-bogen* (1951) (Garden City, N.Y.: Doubleday, 1955), pp. 56ff. Salomon was sentenced to five years for his participation in the Rathenau assassination (on his 1930 *Die Geächteten*, see above chap. 1; Musil mentioned it as one of the most interesting books he had read in 1930 in the left liberal *Das Tagebuch*, Dec. 13, 1930, praising the literary talent of the author and remarking on the unformed but moving intense energy and desire of those lost young people (*Prosa*, p. 1722). Salomon finally settled down to writing film scripts for UFA and after the war wrote the voluminous *Fra-gebogen* (the questionaire that every German had to fill out after World War II for the denazification procedure) pointing out the many conflicts and contradictions beset-

ting most lives lived during this period. It is a highly personal, cynical, and intelligent book and a helpful text for students of Weimar. The group of confused young people, children really, carried out their assassinations from a messy, almost illegible list to which names were added spontaneously and crossed out in the same fashion. Kern, their leader, was very much impressed and influenced by Rathenau's "men-of-fear" and "men-of-courage" theory, which was seen as modern and, later, as fascist.

143. Musil may have read Kessler's Rathenau biography which prints letters Rathenau wrote to a woman friend and which show a hesitation and indecision reminiscent of Arnheim's feelings for Diotima.

144. *Mann ohne Eigenschaften,* posthumously published part, chap. 53, "Die Referate D und L."

145. *Mann ohne Eigenschaften,* p. 1887: "Als letztes bleibt—in Umkehrung der Reihenfolge—die [Utopie] der induktiven Gesinnung, also des wirklichen Lebens, übrig! Mit ihr schliesst das Buch."

3. "PLACET EXPERIRI?" THOMAS MANN AND THE CHARMS OF ENTELECHY

1. All references to the original texts are to Thomas Mann, *Gesammelte Werke* (Frankfurt: Fischer, 1960) 13 vols. Georg Lukács, *Essays on Thomas Mann,* trans. Stanley Mitchell (New York: Grosset & Dunlap, 1965), p. 9; see the solid if too uncritical studies by T. J. Reed, *Thomas Mann: The Uses of Tradition* (London: Oxford University Press, 1974), and Nigel Hamilton, *The Brothers Mann* (New Haven: Yale University Press, 1979); see also the official voluminous biography (imitating Thomas Mann's style) by Peter de Mendelssohn, *Der Zauberer Das Leben des deutschen Schriftstellers Thomas Mann Erster Teil 1875–1918* (Frankfurt: Fischer, 1975); the second part has not yet been published.

2. See the introductions to the six volumes so far available, edited by Peter de Mendelssohn and Inge Jens, *Tagebücher 1933–34, Tagebücher 1935–1936, Tagebücher 1918–1921, Tagebücher 1937–1939, Tagebücher 1940–1943,* and *Tagebücher 1944–46* (Frankfurt: Fischer, 1977–86). See the introduction to the English translation of a selection from the diaries, *Diaries 1918–1939,* selection and foreword by Hermann Kesten, trans. Richard and Clara Winston (New York: Harry N. Abrams, 1982). See also Hans Mayer, "Die Tagebücher," in *Thomas Mann* (Frankfurt: Suhrkamp, 1980), pp.449–87. Reference to the diaries will be made by date, and translations are mine unless the entry can be found in the English selection to which I will refer by date and page. For the years 1933–36 see also Mann's correspondence with his publisher, *Thomas Mann's Briefwechsel mit seinem Verleger Gottfried Bermann Fischer,* ed. Peter de Mendelssohn (Frankfurt: Fischer, 1973), and with his eldest son Klaus in Klaus Mann, *Briefe und Antworten,* ed. Martin Gregor-Dellin (Munich: Ellermann, 1975), vol. 1, p. 122ff.

3. See below sec. 5 of this chapter; see also the letter of October 8, 1950, to Klaus W. Jonas on the (1950) Yale Mann exhibition, *Letters of Thomas Mann 1889–1955.* Selected and translated from the German by Richard and Clara Winston (New York: Knopf, 1971), pp. 603f. Translated letters will be quoted from this edition by date and page; reference to letters in German editions will be by date, unless otherwise specified, and translations are mine. The most important selection of Mann's letters is *Thomas Mann Briefe,* 3 vols, ed. Erika Mann (Frankfurt: Fischer, 1961 on).

4. See Peter de Mendelssohn, *Der Zauberer,* pp. 790ff; see also *Mythology and Humanism: The Correspondence of Thomas Mann and Karl Kerényi,* translated and introduced by Alexander Gelley (Ithaca and London: Cornell University Press, 1975).

5. See Mann's letter to Adorno, Dec. 30, 1945, *Letters,* pp. 493–96, which he

wrote in the morning hours usually set aside for the "real" work, because it concerned the delicate matter of what Mann calls "higher copying" from "certain parts of your essays on the philosophy of music. These borrowings cry out all the more for apology since for the time being the reader cannot be made aware of them; there is no way to call his attention to them without breaking the illusion. (Perhaps a footnote: 'This comes from Adorno-Wiesengrund'? It won't do!)." See also Mann's 1949 description of the relationship in *The Story of a Novel: The Genesis of Doctor Faustus* (New York; Knopf, 1961), pp.42–48 (*Die Entstehung des Doktor Faustus. Roman eines Romans, Werke,* vol. 9, pp.245–49).

6. Goethe's Mephisto: "Ich bin der Geist, der stets verneint."

7. Adorno seems not to have been entirely satisfied with the ways in which Mann had shown his gratitude: the above mentioned letter recording their "conversation" "for posterity" (*Letters,* p. 496); the punning dedication in Adorno's copy of the novel: "dem Wirklichen Geheimen Rat" which does play nicely on Adorno's and Mann's sense for cultural hierarchy—it is a title that honored cultural achievement, Goethe, e.g., was "Geheimer Rat"—and acknowledges the real *(wirklich)* advice *(Rat)* which is kept a secret *(geheim);* the (dis)appearance of his middle name "Wiesengrund" (meadow) somewhere in the middle of the novel. Mann tried to settle the affair by taking some pages in *The Story of a Novel* (pp. 42–48) to describe the relations with Adorno. He did not, as he claims in a letter of October 15, 1951, to Jonas Lesser, write the *Story of a Novel* mainly to give Adorno credit. In this letter—he is irritated by Lesser's (uncritical, rather plodding) attempts at collating the sources for Leverkühn's musical speculations—he complains bitterly about Adorno's vanity. Adorno was vain, but so was Mann whom Adorno admired as *Geistesfürst* and from whom he expected a degree of intellectual generosity that the older, world-famous writer was not prepared to show to the still unknown, younger writer. There was a similar problem with Mann's using Schönberg's twelve-tone system and theory of harmony: see *Story of a Novel,* p. 52, and letters to Schönberg on February 17, 1948, and December 19, 1949 (*Letters,* pp. 546f, 587f), where Mann argues that (a) Schönberg's creations are "an enormously characteristic cultural phenomenon of the epoch" and "every Hottentot" nowadays knows of them and their creator, and that (b) "in a higher sense" they had become Mann's property. The problem is precisely that he wants to be able to use a rich cultural context eclectically for the sake of his own work, which he won't allow to become "just" a part of such context: his own work has to be accepted, like his life, as absolutely unique, if representing important cultural tendencies.

8. See his letter to Jonas Lesser, October 15, 1951, where he expresses his lack of interest in Adorno's *Minima Moralia* which he had placed with his publisher Fischer; see his letter of August 27, 1946, to Fischer in which he recommends the manuscript warmly and mentions that he has learned a great deal from Adorno's "musical conversations" (*Briefwechsel mit seinem Verleger,* pp. 462f).

9. Theodor A. Adorno, "Zu einem Portrait Thomas Manns," *Noten zur Literatur* (Frankfurt: Suhrkamp, 1965), vol. 3, pp. 19–29.

10. "The Magician," "der Zauberer," was the nickname Mann's children gave to their father: Klaus Mann, *The Turning Point* (New York: L. B. Fischer, 1942), p. 5.

11. Mann uses this metaphor in the 1930 *Sketch of My Life* (New York: Knopf, 1960), p. 61, ("Lebensabriss," in vol. 11, *Werke,* p. 133) and the 1939 Princeton "Introduction to *The Magic Mountain,*" ibid., p. 609.

12. The professional reader will always be a critical reader of authors' comments on their own work, but the degree of his watchfulness will vary based on his general attitude toward the author's work. There is, then, always the danger of a hermeneutic circle: I appreciate the clarity and communicative precision of Musil's texts, therefore I am inclined to take his comments on his work very much at face value; if they make sense to me—and they do mostly—this may also be connected to my general willing-

ness to accept them. In the case of Thomas Mann, I am generally suspicious because the ambiguities, the conceptual fuzziness of his fictional and essayistic texts have put me on guard. I mention these reactions here because they are not easy to control, very important, and, though obvious, seldom fully acknowledged.

13. See n. 1; see also Lee Congdon, *The Young Lukács* (Chapel Hill and London: University of North Carolina Press, 1983), a useful discussion of Lukács's intellectual roots and developments.

14. *Werke,* vol. 11, p. 611; see also n. 11; in this context Mann also uses the term *Gedankenkomposition,* composition of thoughts.

15. Mann's diaries of 1918–21 are filled with angry, even shrill reactions to a contemporary "disorder" much feared and totally rejected.

16. See sec. 4 of this chapter.

17. See Klaus Schröter, ed., *Thomas Mann im Urteil seiner Zeit Dokumente 1891–1955* (Hamburg: Christian Wegner, 1969). I will capitalize *Culture* when referring to Mann's and his audience's concept of culture.

18. See here Kurt Sontheimer, *Thomas Mann und die Deutschen* (Frankfurt: Fischer, 1965).

19. See his letter to Kerényi, February 20, 1934, in *Mythology and Humanism,* p. 37; also "The Theme of the Joseph Novels," in *Thomas Mann's Addresses Delivered at the Library of Congress 1942–1949* (Washington: Library of Congress, 1963) pp. 1–19, p. 6. See sec. 6 of this chapter.

20. Lukács, "In Search of Bourgeois Man," in *Essays on Thomas Mann,* pp. 13–46; see my "Flucht nach Utopia: Lukács and Thomas Mann," in Hans R. Vaget and Dagmar Barnouw, *Thomas Mann Studien zu Fragen der Rezeption* (Bern and Frankfurt: Ottendorfer Series Neue Folge Band 7, 1975), pp. 109–25.

21. See Mann's introduction to the 1939 American edition of *Royal Highness* (New York: Knopf), p. VII. See also Klaus Jürgen Rothenberg, *Das Problem des Realismus bei Thomas Mann* (Cologne: Kohlhammer, 1969).

22. See Peter de Mendelssohn, *Der Zauberer,* chaps. 5, 6; Katia Mann, *Unwritten Memoirs,* trans. Hunter and Hildegarde Hannum (New York: Knopf, 1975).

23. See n. 21.

24. See sec. 4 of this chapter and n. 92.

25. See secs. 5 and 6 of this chapter, and nn. 123 and 162.

26. *Thomas Mann und die Deutschen,* p. 137.

27. See especially the diary entries 1918 and 1919, e.g., December 29, 1918, *Diaries,* pp. 26f.

28. See diary, January 8, 1919.

29. *Internationale Literatur,* now in Georg Lukács, *Schriften zur Ideologie und Politik,* ed. Peter Ludz (Darmstadt: Luchterhand, 1961) *Werkauswahl II,* p. 348.

30. *Essays on Thomas Mann,* pp. 13–46.

31. *Neue Schweizer Rundschau,* December 1947.

32. See his letter to Max Rychner, December 24, 1947.

33. *The Story of a Novel,* pt. 11.

34. Almost thirty years later he wrote to Max Rychner (December 24, 1947) about his sense of futility with regard to his vicarious efforts, *Mühen,* for a nation unwilling to follow him.

35. See his letter to Alfred A. Knopf (on December 4, 1948, *Letters,* pp. 566f.) thanking him for having stood up for the book to journalists and quoting from praising comments like Lion Feuchtwanger's in the Los Angeles *Daily News:* "Most readers will agree that *Doctor Faustus* is a great book with grave things to say. It conveys insights and sensations such as can be found in no other book of the past decade."

36. Like 1918–19, the years 1933–34 were particularly difficult for Mann because this position was threatened; during this time he needed—and was particularly grateful for—reassurances: see, e.g., his diary entry for June 30, 1933, where he

quotes from a letter written to him by an American teacher of German "Dass Sie als Künstler und Mensch noch immer als Führer des geistigen Deutschtums gelten."

37. See the diary entries September 1918, *Diaries*, pp. 3ff.

38. November 25, 1916, *Letters*, pp. 81f.

39. See his letter to Heinrich, February 27, 1904, telling his brother about the party where he met his later wife. He is equally pleasantly awed by the princely atmosphere of the Pringsheim's elaborate German-Italian neo-Renaissance house and by the attentions of his admirers. Katia's family, he writes, does not at all suggest Jewishness, only Culture. Katia's beauty is exotic, her brother, informed, gracious, makes a North-German impression, "mit norddeutschen Formen."

40. *Buddenbrooks* was published in October 1901, eighteen reviews to the end of 1902, eight in 1903, ten in 1904; it was the second edition in early 1903, one volume and half the price (following the advice of the Hamburg critic Paul Raché who had reviewed the two volume edition in 1902) which made Mann famous overnight.

41. Letter to Otto Grautoff, November 26, 1901; Mann's emphasis.

42. *Leipziger Tageblatt,* March 24, 1906.

43. March 28, 1906, *Letters*, pp. 48–52; "zersetzend" was the favorite Nazi term for all art that did not conform to Nazi specifications and could therefore be destroyed.

44. *Letters,* p. 51.

45. Quoted de Mendelssohn, *Der Zauberer,* p. 792.

46. See pt. 1 and chap. 1, of this study.

47. *The Turning Point,* pp. 39–42.

48. *Werke,* vol. 12, p. 68: "es gilt, um das Lieblingswort, den Kriegs- und Jubelruf des Zivilisationsliteraten zu brauchen, die *Demokratisierung* Deutschlands, oder, um alles zusammenzufassen und auf den Generalnenner zu bringen: es gilt seine Entdeutschung . . . und an all diesem Unfug sollte ich teilhaben?"

49. Diary, October 9, 1918.

50. December 16, 1916, Thomas Mann, *Letters to Paul Amann 1915–1952* (Middletown, Conn.: Wesleyan University Press, 1960), pp. 80–82.

51. January 3, 1918, *Letters*, pp. 88–90.

52. See pt. 1 of this study.

53. See *Werke,* vol. 12, pp. 149–221; his remarks on the Dreyfus affair as a "geistreicher Zank und Stank," pp. 180ff.

54. *Sketch of My life,* p. 73; see also n. 66.

55. Diary, January 6, 1919.

56. Diary, September 16, 1918 (*Diaries,* p. 5); October 13, 1918 (*Diaries,* pp. 13f); December 17, 1918.

57. Diary, December 4, 1918.

58. March 21, 1919.

59. November 26, 1919.

60. *Letters,* p. 89.

61. July 16 and 26, 1921, *Diaries,* p. 118.

62. *Sketch of My Life,* p. 3.

63. *Werke,* vol. 9, p. 170: "jenes höhere Deutschtum, das immer 'das Land der Griechen mit der Seele' gesucht hat." Quote from Goethe's *klassisches* drama *Iphigenie* which has become integrated into nineteenth- and twentieth-century *bürgerlich* speech patterns and refers to the culturally desirable attitude toward the higher things in life.

64. "Goethe and Tolstoy," *Essays of Three Decades* (New York: Knopf, 1947), p. 173. Mann extended the lecture to the long rambling 1922 essay "Goethe und Tolstoi. Fragmente zum Problem der Humanität," in *Werke,* vol. 9, pp. 58–173.

65. See Peter Demetz, *Marx, Engels and the Poets* (Chicago: University of Chicago Press, 1967).

66. March 14, 1934, *Diaries*, p. 200.

67. See his presentation of Roosevelt, sec. 6 of this chapter.

68. *Essays of Three Decades*, p. 174.

69. *Werke*, vol. 9, p. 172: "Der Instinkt vorbehaltvoller Selbstbewahrung des welt-bürgerlich-mittleren Volkes der Deutschen ist echter Nationalismus. Denn so nennen wir die Freiheitsbegierde der Völker, ihr Mühen um sich, ihr Trachten nach Selbsterkundung und Selbstvollendung."

70. July 26, 1933, *Diaries*, pp. 167f; the English translation here is seriously misleading. Mann is trying to convince himself to accept the really very pleasant exile on the French Riviera, especially as his life had always been difficult and there is then, little reason for the sufferer to cling to accustomed conditions: "So glücklich war er (Mann the sufferer) nicht, dafür war gesorgt, und in Fällen, wo immer dafür gesorgt ist, gibt es nicht allzuviel Anhänglichkeit;" "It (Mann's existence) was not entirely happy, for it had its troubles, and wherever trouble is present one's sense of attachment is naturally mitigated." Significantly, the English version entirely leaves out the rather emphatic reference to a fated suffering: "dafür war gesorgt."

71. *Essays of Three Decades*, p. 173.

72. See ibid.

73. See sec. 4 of this chapter.

74. See Kurt Sontheimer, *Thomas Mann und die Deutschen* and his *Antidemokratisches Denken in der Weimarer Republik* (Munich: Nymphenburger Verlagshandlung, 1962), p. 396; Klaus Schröter, *Thomas Mann im Urteil seiner Zeit*, pp. 77ff.

75. February 2, 1922, *Letters*, pp. 116–18.

76. Ibid.

77. September 17, 1922, *Diaries*, pp. 119f.

78. See September 8, 1933, *Diaries*, p. 171: "When one recalls the modesty and respect ("bescheidene Ehrerbietung") with which the trade-union man Ebert approached cultural matters, one has to recognize what a dreadful course democracy has taken since those days."

79. September 4, 1922, *Letters*, pp. 118f. On Hauptmann see n. 102.

80. March 1, 1923, *Letters*, pp. 123–25; Bertaux had asked him for biographical facts for a Mann portrait in *Revue Européenne*.

81. The introduction is excluded from the English translation: "Ich habe vielleicht meine Gedanken verändert—nicht meinen Sinn. Aber Gedanken, möge das auch sophistisch klingen, sind immer nur Mittel zum Zweck, Werkzeug im Dienst eines Sinnes, und gar dem Künstler wird es viel leichter als unbewegliche Sittenwächter wissen können, sich anders denken, anders spechen zu lassen als vordem, wenn es gilt, einen bleibenden Sinn in veränderter Zeit zu behaupten." ("Von deutscher Republik," in *Werke*, vol. 11, p. 809). The artist, then, is both free to "let himself think and speak" in ways which differ from previous statements, but he does so only to assert permanent meaning and significance in times of change, that is, he has not changed his mind/meaning. The whole introduction not only sounds like but *is* sophistry—and not very skillful at that. Mann had been very disturbed by his audience's accusations that he had suddenly changed his mind, as he was not used to, in fact, could not bear to have his audience disagree with him. ("The German Republic," in *Order of the Day* (Freeport, New York: Books for Libraries Press, 1969), pp. 3–45).

82. *Essays*, p. 160.

83. The one exception is the impressive 1930 "Deutsche Ansprache," in *Werke*, vol. 11, pp. 870–90; "An Appeal to Reason," *Order of the Day*, pp. 46–68.

84. Peter Gay, *Weimar Culture: The Outsider as Insider* (New York: Harper and Row, 1970), p. 123. Gay seems to be slightly critical of *The Magic Mountain*, but only in passing. Mann is but the most extreme case against his outsider-as-insider thesis. In

different ways almost all German intellectuals of the Weimar period stylized the true (German) Culture they felt part of into a higher, better sphere outside (above) the lowland of political and social concerns. See pt. 1 of this study.

85. "diese schwermütige Neckerei des Noch-nicht, dieses innige Zögern der Seele . . ." (Werke, vol. 11, p. 170); Lowe-Porter translates: "the teasing melancholy of the not-yet, the inward hesitation of the soul . . ." (Essays, p. 173).

86. Werke, vol. 11, pp. 831ff; Order of the Day, pp. 25ff. Whitman and Hardenberg (Novalis) play an important role in this context.

87. Order of the Day, p. 45; Werke, vol. 11, p. 852.

88. See the Princeton "Introduction to The Magic Mountain," Werke, vol. 11, p. 612.

89. See the introduction to the American edition to Royal Highness, (New York: Knopf, 1939), p. VIII; Sketch of My Life, p. 36; "The Theme of the Joseph Novels," Thomas Mann's Addresses, p. 14: the English here has "fabulously neutralized" for the German "hebt sich im Märchen auf" ("Joseph und seine Brüder," in Werke, vol. 11, p. 667).

90. "Introduction to The Magic Mountain," pp. 610, 612, 616.

91. Betrachtungen, in Werke, vol. 12, p. 84.

92. See chapters entitled "Hippe," "Of the City of God," and "The Great God Dumps."

93. The Magic Mountain (Penguin, 1960), p. 580; Werke, vol. 3, p. 804. Hans even mediates between Peeperkorn and Mme. Chauchat: Magic Mountain, pp. 567ff and 600ff; Werke, vol. 3, pp. 787ff and 833ff.

94. Magic Mountain, p. 575; Werke, vol. 3, p. 796.

95. Magic Mountain, p. 596; Werke, vol. 3, p. 827.

96. See Musil's discussion of Mann's novel, above, chap. 2, sec. 1.

97. See especially Jürgen Scharfschwerdt, Thomas Mann und der deutsche Bildungsroman (Cologne and Mainz: Kohlhammer, 1967).

98. On the whole, professional readers have been eager to accept and paraphrase Mann's version of his mythical relation to Goethe: see especially Bernhard Blume, Thomas Mann und Goethe, (Bern: Francke, 1949). See Mann's letter to his youngest brother, Viktor, October 4, 1946, Letters, pp. 507f: the British prosecutor in Nuremberg quoted Goethe on the Germans, thinking it authentic when it was really from The Beloved Returns, and the British press pointed out his mistake. Asked what the truth of the matter was by the embassy in Washington, Thomas Mann replied "that I would guarantee that everything Goethe thinks and says in my novel might very well have been thought and said by him, so that in the higher sense the prosecutor had quoted correctly after all."

99. Letter to Felix Bertaux, July 23, 1924.

100. Letter to Hedwig Buller, December 24, 1924, Letters pp. 129f.

101. Letter to Josef Ponten, February 5, 1925, pp. 136–38.

102. See Mann's letter to Hauptmann, April 11, 1925, Letters, pp. 140f, apologizing for the "higher copying" of his person for the character of Peeperkorn. He has sinned against him, but the need was artistic: Hauptmann was just right for the character he was seeking, he accepted therefore what was offered to him (talking to Hauptmann over wine): "I did wrong but I was right." The needs of the work or art gave him the right to that "transmutation"—actually a vivid and perfectly recognizable caricature of the then very well known poet who "looked like Goethe in a state of intoxication" (The Turning Point, p. 66). He appeals to the all-important artistic solidarity between himself—"I have much more of the artist-child in me than is suspected by those who rattle on about my 'intellectualism' "—and Hauptmann, who forgave him gladly.

103. See Mann's letter to Max Rychner, December 24, 1947: "Lukács who is somehow sympathetic toward me [der mir irgendwie wohlwill] and evidently has not recognized himself in Naphta." The point is not so much that Mann misjudged so

blatantly his readers' perceptiveness—he always hoped he would get away with whatever higher copying he had indulged in—but rather—though there is of course a connection—that he believed so literally in the transmuting power of his art.

104. See also *Sketch of My Life*, pp. 6off.

105. *Werke*, Vol. 11, p. 612.

106. February 3, 1936, *Letters*, pp. 244ff.

107. See diary entries August 1919; see Paul Egon Hübinger, *Thomas Mann, die Universität Bonn und die Zeitgeschichte. Drei Kapitel deutscher Vergangenheit aus dem Leben des Dichters 1905–1955* (Munich: Oldenbourg, 1974).

108. "An Exchange of Letters," in *Order of the Day*, p. 107.

109. Letter to the "Europäische Konferenz für Recht und Freiheit in Deutschland" meeting in Paris, November 13–14, 1937; the conference had been arranged with Communist initiative and resulted in a shortlived "Centre International."

110. *Diaries*, p. 283: the English translation "No more offers of help" for "Keine Vorspanndienste mehr" is too free and, in fact, misleading: the German clearly transmits the sense of being pushed and used—"vorspannen" means to put a horse to a carriage and "Dienst" means service—when asked to come out with unambiguous statements.

111. "Richard Wagner and the *Ring*," in *Essays*, p. 353.

112. "Exchange of Letters," p. 106; emphasis Mann's in the original German: "Briefwechsel mit Bonn," *Werke*, vol. 12, p. 786.

113. February 18, 1941, *Mythology and Humanism*, p. 101.

114. See diary entries in January, February, and March 1937 which quote reactions. January 1: *Diaries*, p. 269; January 31: *Diaries*, p. 273; March 5: *Diaries*, p. 274.

115. See sec. 3 of this chapter.

116. Letter to Bruno Walter, August 25, 1936; see also August 23, 1936, *Diaries*, p. 263.

117. Letter to Ferdinand Lion, January 2, 1939.

118. Diary, May 19, 1938.

119. *Diaries*, pp. 295f.

120. Diary, December 28, 1938.

121. *Sketch of My Life*, p. 78; "Meine Zeit," *Werke*, vol. 11, p. 314.

122. "Meine Zeit," p. 315.

123. Letter to Bermann-Fischer, December 6, 1938, *Briefwechsel mit seinem Verleger*, pp. 194–96: "jener ironische Spass." On the publisher's misgivings regarding the inclusion of this piece in the 1938 essay collection *Achtung, Europa*, see ibid., pp. 187ff.

124. "A Brother," in *Order of the Day*, p. 156, "Bruder Hitler," *Werke*, vol. 12, p. 848.

125. Ibid., p. 154/p. 846. Mann's emphasis in the English version.

126. Ibid.

127. "The Coming Victory of Democracy," in *Order of the Day*, p. 116; "Vom kommenden Sieg der Demokratie," *Werke*, vol. 11, p. 913; the German *Verhunzung*, which is the leitmotif concept/term of the Hitler essay, is hard to translate: it is much stronger and more concretely specific than "distortion," connoting an effort or sustenance gone bad, become foul, poisonous. The essay is not about similarities that Mann and Hitler do indeed exhibit, namely their acceptance by large audiences—not necessarily different ones—as cultural leaders promising, if in different ways, spiritual renewal; whether they meant it or not is a moot question. Mann is not aware of this aspect of his stature as *Grosschriftsteller* and humanist-superman. Where he refers to such assessments of his stature—and he does so often and with pleasure in the diaries—he understands them as affirmation and "Unterstützung mythischen Spiels" of his art (March 5, 1937, *Diaries*, p. 274: "bolster the mythic game"). It is this game of the work of art and its control, which is to him the only important issue, and it is

only with respect to art that he concedes dialectic connections between a game of goodness, beauty, and light and one of evil, ugliness, and darkness.

128. *Order of the Day*, pp. 156–58; *Werke*, vol. 12, pp. 848–50.

129. *Order of the Day*, p. 160; *Werke*, vol. 12, p. 852.

130. *Briefwechsel mit seinem Verleger*, p. 195.

131. *Order of the Day*, pp. 123–25; *Werke*, vol. 11, pp. 918–20.

132. Hans Bürgin and Hans-Otto Mayer, *Thomas Mann. A Chronicle of His Life* (Birmingham: University of Alabama Press, 1969), p. 69.

133. *Sketch of My Life*, p. 65.

134. Ibid., p. 73.

135. Ibid., pp. 66–68.

136. Ibid., p. 78: "Our wedding anniversary is near at hand, brought round by a year which is a round number, like all those that have been important in my life. It was midday when I came into the world; my fifty years lay in the middle of the decades, and in the middle of a decade, halfway through it, I was married. This pleases my sense of mathematical clarity, as does also the fact that my children come and go, as it were, in rhymed couples: girl, boy, boy, girl, girl, boy. I have a feeling that I shall die, at the same age as my mother, in 1945."

137. See Mann's letter to Erich Auerbach, October 12, 1951, *Werke*, vol. 11, pp. 691–93.

138. *The Story of a Novel*, p. 32; *Werke*, vol. 11, p. 165; I am quoting from Gelley's adapted version of the translation, *Mythology and Humanism*, p. IX.

139. Ibid.

140. "Ein Wort zuvor: Mein 'Joseph und seine Brüder,' " *Werke*, vol. 11, p. 628.

141. *Mythology and Humanism*, p. 33.

142. See his answer of March 1, 1934, to Mann's letter of February 20, 1934, outlining the amazing transcultural, transhistorical "career of a god," Hermes. Most helpful on the details of Mann's creative myth-mixing is Manfred Dierks, *Studien zu Mythos und Psychologie bei Thomas Mann* (Bern: Francke, 1972 Thomas Mann Studien 2), pp. 215ff.

143. *Mythology and Humanism*, p. 18.

144. Ibid., pp. 37, 46, 48.

145. Letter of February 20, 1934; my translation, as Gelley's is in this case inaccurate. It is true, however, that the German is functionally elusive here where Mann wants to establish a relationship in which Kerényi will continue with information, advice, affirmation, *and* with his respect for the higher needs and wisdom of the creative process: "Das sind geheimnisvolle Spiele des Geistes, die beweisen, dass Sympathie für gelehrtes Wissen bis zu einem gewissen Grade aufkommen kann" ("Briefe an Karl Kerényi," *Werke*, vol. 11, p. 632). Gelley's translation (p. 38): "Such things reveal a mysterious play of the spirit and prove that sympathy for scholarly lore can, to a certain extent, arise of itself."

146. October 25, 1940, *Mythology and Humanism*, pp. 96f.

147. Klaus Schröter, "Der historische Roman," *Exil und innere Emigration*, ed. Reinhold Grimm and Jost Hermand (Frankfurt: Athenäum, 1971), p. 145.

148. New York: Bollingen Series XXII, 1949, trans. R. F. C. Hull, *Einführung in das Wesen der Mythologie* (Amsterdam and Leipzig, 1941).

149. *Mythology and Humanism*, p. 100; *Werke*, vol. 11, p. 651.

150. *Joseph the Provider* (New York: Knopf, 1944), p. 110; *Werke*, vol. 5, p. 1422.

151. See Dierks, *Studien zu Mythos und Psychologie*, p. 260.

152. *Joseph the Provider*, pp. 109, 151, 108.

153. Ibid., p. 110.

154. February 20, 1934, *Mythology and Humanism*, p. 38.

155. *Joseph the Provider*, pp. 148, 128.

156. *Mythology and Humanism*, p. 101.

157. *Joseph the Provider*, p. 111.

158. Letter to Kerényi, March 24, 1934, *Mythology and Humanism*, p. 47.

159. *Joseph the Provider*, p. 233; *Werke*, vol. 5, p. 1582.

160. Ibid., p. 235; *Werke*, vol. 5, p. 1584.

161. Letter to Agnes E. Meyer, January 24, 1941, *Letters*, pp. 353–55.

162. *Werke*, vol. 12, p. 942. See also his 1944 "Wahlrede" (election speech), *Werke*, vol. 11, p. 982: "hochentwickelt und einfach wie das Genie"; see "Coming Victory of Democracy," in *Order of the Day*, pp. 130ff, on the aristocratic attributes of "real democracy."

163. *Werke*, vol. 12, p. 943.

164. Ibid., pp. 942f.

165. *Thomas Mann's Addresses*, p. 16; *Werke*, vol. 11, pp. 668f.

166. Richard Hofstadter, *The American Political Tradition* (New York: Vintage, 1959), pp. 315–52, analyzes critically the "ambivalent ways" of Roosevelt the "Patrician as Opportunist": "the New Deal will never be understood by anyone who looks for a single thread of policy, a far-reaching, far-seeing plan. It was a series of improvisations, many adopted very suddenly, many contradictory. Such unity as it had was in political strategy, not economics" (p. 332). Roosevelt's "enlightened administration" attempted "a true concert of interests"—"something for everybody" in Hofstadter's translation (p. 334). The essential difference between Joseph governing, with his author, the fictional shadows and Roosevelt is the resistance the latter had to cope with—concrete and considerable—in his middle and mediating position: "Since Roosevelt was baited and frustrated by the right and adopted by the left, his ego was enlisted along with his sympathies in behalf of the popular point of view" (p. 338). However, his politics vis à vis the unions were not really progressive—workers called the NRA "National Run Around" (p. 336). His answer to this conflict of different powerful tendencies and energies was to concentrate his campaign on the issue of his person: "There's one issue in this campaign," he said in 1936. "It's myself, and people must be either for me or against me" (p. 336). Roosevelt was, as Thomas Mann understood quite clearly, a strong if enlightened ruler—not so unlike the Prussian Frederick the Great, another one of Mann's heroes. Wartime economy relieved him of having to cope with the sociopolitical consequences of the New Deal. It was not power that posed a problem to him, but certain aspects of the exercise of power. He was characteristically aware of the advantages in negotiating with a dictator: "Stalin is the only man I have to convince. Joe does not worry about a Congress or a Parliament. He's the whole works" (p. 348). Mann referred to American democracy habitually as "Roosevelt's democracy": the admired great individual was its creator, and it was, at its best, a composition, like a work of art.

167. Letter to Hermann Weigand, April 29, 1952, *Letters*, p. 642.

168. September 20, 1938, *Diaries*, p. 306.

169. See May 28, 1940; June 9, 1940; June 16, 1940.

170. October 3, 1940.

171. "Theme of the Joseph Novels," *Thomas Mann's Addresses*, pp. 14f; *Werke*, vol. 11, pp. 666f.

172. *Werke*, vol. 12, pp. 228f, Mann's emphasis.

PART THREE:
THE SEDUCTIONS OF REDEMPTION

4. MARXIST CREATIONISM

1. Leo Löwenthal, "The Integrity of the Intellectual: In Memory of Walter Benjamin," *The Philosophical Forum*, vol. 15, nos. 1–2 (1983–84): 146–57.

2. Ibid., p. 153.

3. See Hannah Arendt, *The Jew as Pariah* (New York: Grove Press, 1978).

4. Löwenthal, pp. 153, 151.

5. Ibid., p. 151: for a discussion of Benjamin's stylization of Kafka in these terms see sec. 4 of this chapter.

6. For examples see sec. 2 and sec. 4 of this chapter.

7. On Benjamin's usage of *dialectic* see sec. 2 and sec. 4 of this chapter.

8. Jean Selz, "Walter Benjamin à Ibiza, *"Les lettres nouvelles"* 2 (1954): 14ff. The German translation of this text is in Theodor W. Adorno, ed., *Über Walter Benjamin* (Frankfurt: Suhrkamp, 1968), pp. 45ff.

9. Hannah Arendt, "Walter Benjamin: 1892–1940," in *Men in Dark Times* (New York: Harcourt, Brace & World, 1968), pp. 156, 205.

10. Walter Benjamin, "Brecht's *Threepenny Novel*," in *Reflections,* ed. Peter Demetz (New York: Harcourt, Brace, Jovanovich, 1978), p. 199; "Brecht's Dreigroschenroman," Walter Benjamin, *Gesammelte Schriften* (hereafter *G.S.*), vol. 3, ed. Hella Tiedemann-Bartels (Frankfurt: Suhrkamp, 1972), p. 446. Benjamin's pieces on Brecht mimic his self-consciously pedagogical gestural style to an amazing degree. Such mimicry (here the expression of Brecht's intellectual-emotional influence on Benjamin) is a comparatively frequent phenomenon among critics, who are in specific ways open to language games, suggesting an imitative configurative rather than conceptually organized critical approach to the texts under consideration. Benjamin's critical activities may be more easily accessible if seen from the perspective of cultural *imitatio*—Brecht is just a particularly direct, therefore striking case.

11. He used the principle of disruption to give meaningful direction to his style and shape to his life—it made much of his writing esoteric and many of his reactions incomprehensible. See Jean Selz, p. 50; Hannah Arendt, pp. 168ff; Gershom Scholem, "Walter Benjamin und sein Engel," in his *Walter Benjamin und sein Engel* (Frankfurt: Suhrkamp, 1983), pp. 35–72; Gershom Scholem, *Walter Benjamin: The Story of a Friendship* (Philadelphia: Jewish Publication Society of America, 1981), pp. 157ff.

12. See Peter Szondi, "Benjamins Städtebilder," in *Lektüren und Lektionen* (Frankfurt: Suhrkamp, 1973), p. 146. The editors of *Gesammelte Schriften* collected the portraits of cities written between 1925 and 1929 (see sec. 3 of this chapter) under the title "Denkbilder" (*G.S.*, vol 4, p. 305).

13. Arendt, p. 156.

14. Walter Benjamin, *Briefe,* ed. Gershom Scholem and Theodor W. Adorno (Frankfurt: Suhrkamp, 1966), vol 2, p. 505.

15. *Briefe,* vol. 2, pp. 510–512.

16. Ibid., p. 511; see also Scholem, *Friendship,* p. 161.

17. See reminiscences collected in Adorno, *Über Walter Benjamin.*

18. See Benjamin to Scholem, May 1925, *Briefe,* vol. 1, pp. 381f. Scholem, *Friendship,* pp. 120ff.

19. Arendt, "Walter Benjamin," p. 188.

20. *G.S.,* vol. 1, pp. 435–508 (first and second German versions); pp. 709–39 (French translation); "The Work of Art in the Age of Mechanical Reproduction," in *Illuminations,* ed. Hannah Arendt (New York: Harcourt, Brace & World, 1968), pp. 219–53; see Benjamin's letter to Brecht's assistant Grete Steffin, March 4, 1936 (*G.S.,* vol. 1, p. 1026) discussing the possibility of having the piece published in German in the Communist Moscow-based journal *Internationale Literatur.*

21. *G.S.,* vol. 2, pp. 438–65; "The Storyteller," *Illuminations,* pp. 83–109.

22. *G.S.,* vol. 2, pp. 465–505; "Eduard Fuchs: Collector and Historian," *New German Critique* 5 (1975): 27–58.

23. *G.S.,* vol. 1, pp. 605–53; "On Some Motifs in Baudelaire," in *Illuminations,* pp. 157–96; see Adorno to Benjamin, November 10, 1938, *Briefe,* vol. 2, pp. 786f; see also the editor's comments, *G.S.,* vol. 1, pp. 1064ff.

24. See Brecht's journal entry on July 25, 1938: Berthold Brecht, *Arbeitsjournal Erster Band 1938–1942*, ed. Werner Hecht (Frankfurt: Suhrkamp, 1973), p. 16.

25. Brecht to Benjamin concerning the essay on Fuchs ca. 1937, *G.S.*, vol. 2, p. 1354.

26. Hugo von Hofmannsthal very much admired Benjamin's essay and published it in his *Neue Deutsche Beiträge* 1924 and 1925; he praised it for its extraordinary purity and sureness of thought in a fragmented tormented world (*G.S.*, vol. 1, pp. 816f).

27. "Goethes Wahlverwandtschaften," *G.S.*, vol. 1, p. 125; unless stated otherwise translations are mine.

28. See the "Epistemo-Critical Prologue" to *The Origin of German Tragic Drama*, trans. John Osborne (London: New Left Books, 1977), pp. 27ff; *Ursprung des deutschen Trauerspiels*, in *G.S.*, vol. 1, pp. 207ff.

29. *G.S.*, vol. 1, p. 125.

30. As Benjamin's concept of writing is essentially informed by the notion of a sacred text underlying all verbal utterance he does not concern himself with questions of perspective and historicity.

31. *Verdanken* here signifies a total and fundamental relation. Anson Rabinbach, "Critique and Commentary/Alchemy and Chemistry: Some Remarks on Walter Benjamin and This Special Issue," *New German Critique* 17 (1979): 3–14, sensibly paraphrases this passage to make it accessible, but he then still claims that the substance of Benjamin's appeal to his reader is something marvelous. Like most English critics who write admiringly on Benjamin, he smooths out, in his paraphrases and translations, the considerable and specific difficulties in Benjamin's language and so makes the fuzziness of his arguments more familiar. Rabinbach's translation of this sentence reads: "Is the appearance of truth indebted to the subject matter or is the life of the subject matter indebted to truth" (p. 5). However, *verdanken* here means "to owe its existence to" which changes the meaning of the sentence considerably.

32. *Auseinandertreten* merges the spatial and the temporal in a way which is typical for Benjamin and can be very effective in his pieces on cities *(Städtebilder)*. Benjamin's thought is indeed arrested in images, which makes access to his critical discourse very difficult and reading him an often frustrating experience. Anglo-American critics tend to express their impatience and frustration with Benjamin's style but seem content with the assumption that there is some higher and valid reason for its turgidity.

33. *G.S.*, vol. 1, pp. 125f.

34. Rabinbach, p. 5, has "Aging Work" to suggest the historical process.

35. *G.S.*, vol. 1, p. 126.

36. See Rabinbach, p. 5: "As a critic he is closer to the alchemist than the judge. . . ."

37. *Der Begriff der Kunstkritik in der deutschen Romantik*, in *G.S.*, vol. 1, pp. 11–122.

38. Ibid., p. 69.

39. See Richard Wolin's totally affirmative study, *Walter Benjamin: An Aesthetic of Redemption* (New York: Columbia University Press, 1982), p. 90.

40. *G.S.*, vol. 1, p. 72.

41. Wolin, p. 91, speaks of Benjamin's "relentless philosophical will to transcendence."

42. It is this emphasis on redemption that influenced much of the thought of the Frankfurt School; see George Friedman, *The Political Philosophy of the Frankfurt School* (Ithaca and London: Cornell University Press, 1981), pp. 100ff. On the influence of Franz Rosenzweig's 1921 *Star of Redemption*, see Stephané Moses, "Walter Benjamin and Franz Rosenzweig," *The Philosophical Forum*, vol. 15, nos. 1–2 (1983–84): 188–205. Rosenzweig sees the messianic moment embedded in experi-

enced dailiness, Benjamin as rupturing an experiential continuum which Rosenzweig is too realistic and psychologically astute to assume. Moses does not make this distinction sufficiently clear. He usefully shows which parts of *The Star of Redemption* Benjamin had really worked with; quotations are taken from two short passages in part one and from one thematically related passage in part two: the China passages (part one) from which Benjamin includes fragments in his 1934 Kafka essay (see sec. 4 of this chapter) and the discussion of the metaethical self and the silent hero of Greek tragedy (part one) which, together with the remarks on modern tragedy (part 2, book 3) is important for the *Origin of German Tragic Drama* (p. 191). Benjamin, then, was interested in Rosenzweig's very general and problematic cultural fictions more than in his specific seminal Jewish religious philosophy. Regarding the issue of the speechless tragic hero, he writes to Scholem in a letter of February 19, 1925, about his boundless chutzpah ("masslose Chutzpe") considering the epistemological intentions of the introduction to *Origins*, ("nicht mehr und nicht weniger als Prolegomena zur Erkenntnistheorie") and the new theory of tragedy presented here which he largely got from his friend Florens Christian Rang and from Rosenzweig. His Rosenzweig quotes, he writes, annoyed the sociologist Gottfried Salomon who supported him at Frankfurt University, and who pointed out that Rosenzweig's remarks on tragedy can be found in Hegel. This, Benjamin concedes, is not impossible, but he had not been able to look at the complete *Asthetik* and, besides, his *Trauerspielbuch* completes rather than begins an area of study for him . . . (so, there is no need to ground his conceptual strategies?) (*Briefe*, vol. 1, pp. 372f). Instead of Hegel he read Thomas Mann's *Magic Mountain* fascinated by the author's supreme formal skills ("schlechthin souveräne Mache"), ibid., p. 374.

43. On the influence of Benjamin's concept of disruption on Adorno's early *Habilitation* on Kierkegaard and his later *Negative Dialektik*, see Friedmann, p. 212.

44. "Zum Bilde," *G.S.*, vol. 1, p. 310; "The Image of Proust," in *Illuminations*, p. 203; the German *unfasslich* suggests more concretely the difficulties involved in even considering this fact.

45. Ibid.; the metaphor extends the literal meaning of *uferlos*.

46. Ibid.

47. July 1925, *Briefe*, vol. 1, p. 395.

48. "Zum Bilde Prousts," p. 311; "The Image of Proust," p. 204.

49. Ibid., p. 314, and ibid., p. 207.

50. *G.S.*, vol. 2, pp. 295–310; *Reflections*, pp. 177–92. See also the 1932 piece "Hashish in Marseilles," in *Reflections*, pp. 137–45; *G.S.*, vol. 4, pp. 409–16.

51. "Sürrealismus," in *G.S.*, vol. 2, pp. 296f, and *Reflections*, p. 179.

52. Ibid., p. 296, and ibid., p. 178.

53. See his letter to Max Rychner, March 7, 1931, *Briefe*, vol. 2, p. 523.

54. "Lehre vom Ähnlichen," *G.S.*, vol. 2, p. 205. *G.S.*, vol. 2, pp. 950ff.

55. Ibid., p. 209; Jean Selz (see n. 8) has interesting remarks on Benjamin's insistence on such direct, unmediated similarities when talking about the world around him, a kind of *pensée sauvage*.

56. Letter to Gretel Adorno, June/July 1933, *G.S.*, vol. 2, pp. 933, 952.

57. "Über Sprache überhaupt und über die Sprache des Menschen," in *G.S.*, vol. 2, p. 144; "On Language as Such and on the Language of Man," in *Reflections*, p. 318: *"in naming the mental being of man communicates itself to God"* (Benjamin's emphasis) does not retain the connotation of the German—*Im Namen teilt das geistige Wesen des Menschen sich Gott mit*—which suggests a participation of God in man's spiritual existence drawn by the act of naming.

58. See his early letter to Martin Buber in 1916, the same year in which he wrote the essay on language, *Briefe*, vol. 1, p. 127.

59. Almost all English speaking critics state their reservations or dismay regarding Benjamin's tortuous, obscurantist style, but they do not explicitly relate Ben-

jamin's contempt for conceptual accessibility, that is, language as communication, to his so-called language theory. It is true that language is a sense-making tool and communication just one of its aspects, but the emphatic denial of this very aspect does say something about Benjamin's sense-making activity. For examples see the smoothly contradictory George Steiner in his introduction to the translation of *Ursprung des deutschen Trauerspiels* (*Origins*, pp. 12ff), the somewhat better balanced though essentially uncritical articles by Charles Rosen, "The Ruins of Walter Benjamin," *New York Review of Books*, vol. 24, no. 17 (1977): 31–40, and "The Origins of Walter Benjamin," *New York Review of Books*, vol. 24, no. 18 (1977): 30–38. See also Terry Eagleton's variations on the theme of Benjamin, *Walter Benjamin or Towards a Revolutionary Criticism* (London: New Left Books, 1981), especially pt. 2.

60. *G.S.*, vol. 1, p. 216; *Origins*, p. 36. The German strikes me as nearly impenetrable.

61. *Briefe*, vol. 1, p. 339.

62. Benjamin does seem to admire certain aspects of the work of a critic (especially his expressionist adjectives) who was to become a representative of Nazi Germanistik—see his letter to Gershom Scholem on September 16, 1924, *Briefe*, vol. 1, p. 354; Hans Cornelius and Franz Schulz who had the last say on the passing of Benjamin's application for *Habilitation* told Benjamin that they did not understand a word of his book—this is usually seen as evidence for their extreme narrow-mindedness. But Scholem, well aware of Benjamin's willed failure in this regard and the very possibly extraneous esoteric quality of his style (see *Walter Benjamin-Gershom Scholem Briefwechsel, 1933–1940*, ed. Gershom Scholem [Frankfurt: Suhrkamp, 1980], p. 134), summed up the *Habilitation* fiasco with the sensible remark that "no one could have accused them of ill will in their attitude towards Benjamin" (*Walter Benjamin: The Story of a Friendship*, p. 129).

63. In a letter to Scholem of December 22, 1924 (*Briefe*, vol. 1, p. 366) Benjamin mentions that he had found Panofsky-Saxl's admirable 1923 *Dürers 'Melencolia I'* after the completion of the rough draft of the *Origins*. See Raymond Klibansky, Erwin Panofsy, and Fritz Saxl, *Saturn and Melancholy: Studies in the History of Natural Philosophy, Religion and Art* (London: Thomas Nelson, 1964); this book is based on the new, revised, enlarged second edition of *Melencolia I* which could not be published in Germany in 1939. On January 30, 1928, Benjamin mentions to Scholem Panofsky's "resentful" ("ressentimentgeladenen") letter (*Briefe*, vol. 1, p. 457).

64. Erwin Panofsky, *Albrecht Dürer* (Princeton: Princeton University Press, 1948), vol. 1, p. 168.

65. Quoted ibid., p. 171.

66. Ibid.

67. *G.S.*, vol. 1, p. 321; *Origins*, p. 142.

68. *G.S.*, vol. 1, pp. 327f; *Origins*, pp. 149f.

69. *G.S.*, vol. 1, pp. 330f; *Origins*, pp. 153f.

70. *G.S.*, vol. 1, p. 353; *Origins*, pp. 177f.

71. *G.S.*, vol. 1, p. 359; *Origins*, pp. 183f.

72. "Auch über diesen Zug kam die Allegorie mit den Romantikern zum Anfang einer Selbstbesinnung" (*G.S.*, vol. 1, p. 360); *Origins*, p. 184, tries to make sense of this unclear sentence: "The Romantics were the first to begin to become conscious of this aspect of allegory too." But this is not what the highly idiosyncratic German says.

73. See Hans Heinz Holz in his 1956 (still much quoted) celebration of Benjamin's allegorical thought, "Prismatisches Denken," *Über Walter Benjamin*, ed. Theodor W. Adorno (Frankfurt: Suhrkamp, 1968), pp. 62–110.

74. *G.S.*, vol. 1, p. 361; *Origins*, p. 185.

75. *Briefe*, vol. 2, p. 523.

76. *Briefe*, vol. 1, pp. 347, 351.

77. *Briefe*, vol. 1, p. 350.

78. *Briefe*, vol. 1, p. 355.

79. Ibid.

80. *History and Class Consciousness*, vol. 4.

81. *Briefe*, vol. 1, p. 355.

82. He expressed his doubts in his *Moskauer Tagebuch*, ed. Gary Smith (Frankfurt: Suhrkamp, 1980). On the essay he published from these notes, see below.

83. Werner Fuld, *Walter Benjamin Zwischen den Stühlen* (Munich: Hanser, 1979), pp. 157ff.

84. See Fuld, pp. 158f, and the useful essay by Bernd Witte, "Benjamin and Lukacs. Historical notes on the Relationship between their Political and Aesthetic Theories," *New German Critique* 5 (1975): 3–26.

85. *Briefe*, vol. 1, pp. 381f: "Die Totalität des dunkler oder heller von mir erahnten Horizonts kann ich nur in diesen beiden Erfahrungen gewinnen."

86. Walter Benjamin and Asja Lacis, "Neapel," *Frankfurter Zeitung*, August 19, 1925; *G.S.*, vol. 4, pp. 307–16; "Naples," *Reflections*, pp. 163–73. Adorno thought that Lacis had nothing to do with the writing of the piece as he did not like her influence on Benjamin: see *G.S.*, vol. 4, p. 987.

87. *Reflections*, p. 163; *G.S.*, vol. 4, p. 307.

88. Ibid., p. 164; ibid., p. 308.

89. Ibid., pp. 166f; ibid., p. 310.

90. *Reflections*, p. 165; *G.S.*, vol. 4, p. 309. The English *tourist* does not have the distancing connotations of *Bürger*.

91. Her own texts do not suggest a sensibility close to Benjamin's.

92. The German is rather difficult to translate here, though not, as it is so often in the "serious" texts, opaque. The translation of this passage is partly my own; I will quote the passage in German and, where it diverges, the translation in *Reflections*, which in some places distorts too much: "Eine hohe Schule der Regie ist, was auf den Treppen sich abspielt. Diese, niemals ganz freigelegt, noch weniger aber in dem dumpfen nordischen Hauskasten geschlossen, schiessen stückweise aus den Häusern heraus, machen eine eckige Wendung und verschwinden, um wieder hervorzustürzen" (*G.S.*, vol. 4, p. 310) "but still less enclosed in the gloomy box of the Nordic house, erupt fragmentarily from the buildings. . . ." (*Reflections*, p. 167).

93. *Reflections*, p. 172; *G.S.*, vol. 4, p. 315.

94. *Reflections*, p. 173; *G.S.*, vol. 4, p. 316.

95. See Peter Szondi, "Benjamins Städtebilder," in *Lektüren und Lektionen* (Frankfurt: Suhrkamp, 1973), p. 146.

96. Szondi: "Die Sprache der Bilder erlaubt, das Fremde zu verstehen, ohne dass es aufhörte, fremd zu sein; der Vergleich bringt das Entfernte nah und bannt es doch zugleich in ein Bild, welches der verzehrenden Kraft der Gewohnheit entrückt ist" (ibid.). Szondi, like many Benjamin critics, does what Benjamin does with the texts of others: he finds, for his own reasons, his own images for Benjamin's images though he shares many of Benjamin's preoccupations.

97. See his 1930 review of Ernst Jünger's collection *Krieg und Krieger* (War and warrior), in *G.S.*, vol. 3, pp. 238–50; translation in *New German Critique* 17 (1979): 120–28.

98. (A Jacobin of today), *G.S.*, vol. 3, pp. 260–65.

99. "Das Innere der Geschichte ist dem dialektischen Blick vorbehalten" (ibid., p. 263). Ibid., pp. 263f: "Unbestreitbar ist Hegemanns Buch ein Standardwerk. Man legt es aber schwerlich aus der Hand, ohne sich zu fragen, woran es liegt, dass es die schmale Spanne nicht überschreiten konnte, die es von jener letzten Vollkommenheit trennt, welche das Schicksal seines Buchs unabhängig von dem seines Gegenstands, ja, ein Schicksal dieses Gegenstands werden lässt."

100. See Dagmar Barnouw, " 'Beute der Pragmatisierung': Adorno und Amerika,"

in *Die USA und Deutschland*, ed. Wolfgang Paulsen (Bern and Munich: Francke, 1976), pp. 61-83.

101. *G.S.*, vol. 3, p. 265.

102. *Reflections*, p. 97; *G.S.*, vol. 4, p. 316. Benjamin wrote the essay on the basis of his Moscow diary for publication in Martin Buber's *Die Kreatur* (1927).

103. *Reflections*, p. 97; *G.S.*, vol. 4, p. 317. The translation first obscures and then stresses certain contradictions or obstacles in the argument: "*Darum* ist *andrerseits* ["But, equally, this is why"] der Aufenthalt für Fremde ein so sehr genauer Prüfstein. Jeden nötigt er, seinen Standpunkt zu wählen. *Im Grunde freilich* ist die einzige Gewähr der rechten Einsicht, Stellung gewählt zu haben, ehe man kommt. Sehen kann gerade in Russland nur der Entschiedene." I have underlined the phrases which are more or less flexible than their English version suggests.

104. André Gide's 1936 *Retour de l'U.R.S.S.*, in contrast, presents a good example of an ideologically predisposed and yet open-minded, open-eyed observer. Gide declared his loyalty to the USSR, in spite of certain misgivings, in a speech delivered in Red Square a few days after his arrival: "The fate of culture is bound up in our minds with the destiny of the Soviet Union. We will defend it" (*Return from the U.S.S.R.* [New York: Knopf, 1937], p. XII). After quoting himself in the introduction to his critical account of the USSR he states his growing doubts and the reasons for stating them: "I have always maintained that the wish to remain true to oneself too often carries with it a risk of insincerity; and I consider that if ever sincerity is important, it is surely when the beliefs of great masses of people are involved together with one's own" (Ibid.). He feels, he says, responsible for his readers to whom he owes a statement concerning the changes in his feelings, the increasing doubts. "There are things more important in my eyes than myself, more important than the U.S.S.R. These things are humanity, its destiny and its culture" (Ibid., p. XIII). Above all, Gide emphasizes, the observer in Russia, the reader of his observations, has to keep in mind that "the Soviet Union is 'in the making'; one cannot say it too often. And to that is due the extraordinary interest of a stay in this immense country which is now in labour; one feels that one is contemplating the parturition of the future" (Ibid.). It is, of course, true that Gide wrote about his experience almost ten years later when Stalinism had fully established itself and was beginning to penetrate many Western intellectuals' self-protective belief-constructs. Still, in our context it is important to consider his attempts at seeing as clearly, comprehensively, and fairly as possible.

105. *Reflections*, pp. 97f; *G.S.*, vol. 4, p. 317.

106. *Reflections*, pp. 98f; *G.S.*, vol. 4, p. 318.

107. Ibid., p. 99; ibid., p. 318.

108. Ibid., p. 112; ibid. p. 331.

109. Ibid., p. 113; ibid., p. 332.

110. Ibid., p. 100; ibid., p. 319.

111. Ibid., pp. 100f; ibid. pp. 319f.

112. Walter Benjamin, *Moskauer Tagebuch*, ed. Gary Smith (Frankfurt: Suhrkamp, 1980), pp. 168ff. The last sentence of the diary: "With the big suitcase on my lap, crying, I rode to the station through the darkening streets."

113. *Reflections*, p. 101; *G.S.*, vol. 4, p. 320.

114. Ibid., p. 103; ibid., p. 323.

115. Ibid., p. 104; ibid., p. 323.

116. Ibid., pp. 104f; ibid., pp. 323f.

117. Gide, on the other hand, continuously questions the moment when observed events and facts become or are used as evidence: see pp. 29ff.

118. *Reflections*, p. 106; *G.S.*, vol. 4, p. 325.

119. See n. 104; see Gide, *Return*, pp. 3f, 15f, 27f.

120. *Reflections*, p. 106; *G.S.*, vol. 4, p. 325.

121. Ibid., pp. 108f; ibid., pp. 327f. For a sober, if dry, attempt to describe this depersonalization reflected in the living arrangements see Gide, *Return*, pp. 25f.

122. *Reflections*, p. 129; *G.S.*, vol. 4, p. 347.

123. This translation is slightly misleading: "Man lebt auf der Strasse wie in einem frostigen Spiegelsaal. . . ." *Man* is more general than *people* here, and *Spiegelsaal* is a hall of mirrors, suggesting the large space and sky-high ceiling. The observation and the simile are meant to suggest a certain quality of being outside in the extreme cold but in the city.

124. *Reflections*, p. 129; *G.S.*, vol. 4, p. 347.

125. He describes Christmas Eve: after spending the afternoon in a toy museum he meets, an hour late, the friends with whom he had a date for buying provisions for the evening, they buy Russian delicacies, hectically, in an overcrowded store, also sweets and a little Christmas tree, and Benjamin, overloaded with objects, among them a large Chinese paperfish, takes everything home in a sleigh. Later the friends come, among them Asja, with a samovar. With its humming filling a Russian room, with Asja close by, with the little potted tree next to him, he had, he said, "for the first time in many years been feeling safe [*geborgen*] on Christmas Eve," *Moskauer Tagebuch*, p. 63.

126. *Briefe*, vol. 1, pp. 442f (February 23, 1927).

127. *Berliner Chronik* was edited by Scholem in 1970 (Frankfurt: Suhrkamp) from a manuscript in the Frankfurt Benjamin archive. Demetz (see his introduction, p. XVI) in his collection *Reflections* (pp. 3–60) includes this version rather than the later *Berliner Kindheit um Neunzehnhundert* (*G.S.*, vol. 1, pp. 235–304); on the arrangement of the pieces, see *G.S.*, vol. 4, pp. 964ff.

128. Letter to Karl Thieme, May 1938, *G.S.*, vol. 4, pp. 967f.

129. *Reflections*, p. 5.

130. *Reflections*, pp. 8f.

131. Ibid., p. 7.

132. Ibid., p. 10.

133. Especially the passages about the suicide of his friends who were socially concerned and died in the meeting house of the Youth Movement located in an area of old-fashioned apartment houses which were marked off from the proletarian quarters of Moabit by the Landwehr Canal. *Reflections*, pp. 18f.

134. *Reflections*, p. 26.

135. *Walter Benjamin: The Story of a Friendship*, p. 168.

136. Ibid., p. 140. "Georgian" refers to the highly stylized incantation, the way in which poetry was read in the cultic circle around the poet Stefan George.

137. *G.S.*, vol. 2, p. 1078.

138. See below, this section.

139. I am using my own translation for these lines as the translation in *Reflections* contains a serious error. The original German reads: "Oder, in grossartiger Abbreviatur bei Kraus: 'Es sollte Aufschluss über die Technik geben, dass sie zwar keine neue Phrase bilden kann, aber den Geist der Menschheit in dem Zustand belässt, die alte nicht entbehren zu können.'"

140. *Reflections*, pp. 241f; *G.S.*, vol. 2, p. 337.

141. Ibid.

142. *G.S.*, vol. 2, p. 338; the translation is mine as the translation in *Reflections* (p. 243) contains several serious errors.

143. *Reflections*, p. 250; *G.S.*, vol. 2, p. 345.

144. *G.S.*, vol. 4, p. 121.

145. *Reflections*, p. 250; *G.S.*, vol. 2, p. 345.

146. Ibid.

147. *G.S.*, vol. 4, pp. 302ff. *Das bucklichte Männlein* is a central figure in Benjamin's store of mythical self-reflections; the concluding part of *Berliner Kindheit* is

devoted to the little demon. The first part of Arendt's long essay on Benjamin is entitled "The Hunchback" (*Men in Dark Times*, p. 153).

148. *Reflections*, p. 251; *G.S.*, vol. 2, p. 346.

149. *Reflections*, p. 254; *G.S.*, vol. 2, p. 349.

150. Kraus had, for decades, written his highly influential journal *Die Fackel* single-handedly.

151. See Elias Canetti, "Karl Kraus, Schule des Widerstands," in *Das Gewissen der Worte* (Munich: Hanser, 1973), pp. 39–49. Dagmar Barnouw, "Loos, Kraus, Wittgenstein and the Problem of Authenticity," in *The Turn of the Century. German Literature and Art 1890–1915*, ed. Gerald Chapple (Bonn: Bouvier, 1981), pp. 249–73.

152. Letter of August 1, 1931, quoted in *Story of a Friendship*, pp. 169ff.

153. Letter of September 16, 1934, *G.S.*, vol. 2, pp. 1167ff. Benjamin took these responses seriously, marking and annotating them for further reference.

154. Letter to Benjamin, December 17, 1934, *G.S.*, vol. 2, p. 1177. In a short note of the previous day (ibid., p. 1173) he had written that the fact of their concurring in the "philosophical center" had never been as clear to him as in this essay.

155. Scholem to Benjamin, August 14, 1934. *Benjamin-Scholem Briefwechsel*, p. 169.

156. See his 1931 essay "Was ist das epische Theater? Eine Studie zu Brecht," *G.S.*, vol. 2, pp. 519–39; the second part, which is most relevant here (ibid., pp. 532ff), also in *Illuminations*, pp. 149–56. Scholem, of course, knew of this essay which is centered on gestic behavior, and his reaction may have been caused, in part, by the presence of Brecht in Benjamin's text. Benjamin tried to explain the function and importance of certain intellectual relationships in his life, which his friends tended to judge as somewhat obsessive, in a letter of June 1934 to Gretel Adorno (*G.S.*, vol. 2, p. 1369) where he explains Brecht's (alleged) influence on him as one instant of a recurrent constellation: "It is true that in the economy of my existence a small number of relationships play a part which enables me to maintain a viewpoint in polar opposition to my original mode of being." His closest friends have always reacted more or less vehemently against these relationships—he mentions especially Scholem in the case of Brecht—and he can only hope they will have enough trust in him to recognize with the "danger" inherent in these relationships, also their undeniable intellectual stimulation.

157. "Franz Kafka," *Illuminations*, p. 120; *G.S.*, vol. 2, p. 418.

158. See here Moses, "Walter Benjamin and Franz Rosenzweig," pp. 195f. Moses documents the arbitrariness in the inclusion of this quote—the other quote from Rosenzweig is his description of the Chinese ancestor cult (*G.S.*, vol. 2, p. 430; *Illuminations*, p. 132) which he links to Kafka's fascination with the world of ancestors. In the case of the first Rosenzweig quote, Moses tries to read its use as "a paradoxical figure of thought used to emphasize this dialectical tension [between Brecht's and Scholem's claims on B.] and at the same time hint at its possible solution" (p. 196). Yet, his essay refutes such affirmation.

159. *G.S.*, vol. 2, p. 1262. Moses's translation of this passage (pp. 196f) is in several cases inaccurate.

160. This would actually have been more true to Brecht's position as Benjamin records it in his "Conversations with Brecht," in *Reflections*, pp. 206ff, especially the entry for August 5, 1934 (pp. 208ff), where Benjamin records the "long and heated debate on my Kafka" and Brecht's charge that "it advanced Jewish fascism. It increased and propagated the obscurity surrounding this author instead of dispersing it. Whereas it was of crucial importance to clarify Kafka, that is, to formulate practicable proposals that can be derived from his stories." Brecht points out to Benjamin the "Kafkaesque irony that the man who seemed convinced of nothing more than of the invalidity of all guarantees was an insurance official. Moreover, his unrestricted pessimism is free of any tragic sense of fate."

161. *G.S.*, vol. 2, pp. 422f; my translation. A slightly misleading version in *Illuminations*, p. 124f.

162. Ibid., p. 414; *Illuminations*, p. 116.

163. For a recent analysis of the essay's contradictions and ambiguities see Jennifer Todd, "Production, Reception, Criticism: Walter Benjamin and the Problem of Meaning in Art," *The Philosophical Forum*, vol 15, nos. 1–2 (1983–84): 105–27. Todd provides a useful corrective complement to Susan Buck-Morss's two-part article "Walter Benjamin—Revolutionary Writer," *New Left Review* 128 (July–August, 1981) and 129 (September–October, 1981). Joel Snyder, "Benjamin on Reproducibility and Aura: A Reading of 'The Work of Art in the Age of its Technical Reproducibility,' " *The Philosophical Forum*, vol. 15, nos. 1–2 (1983–84): 130–45, does not deal with Benjamin's ambiguous attitude toward aura but concentrates on Benjamin's thoughts on depiction-perception, "solving" the profound contradictions in the essay by interpreting Benjamin's concluding assertion that a "politicization of art" has been achieved by communism in the following way: "Art in its new definition is the sole means by which the members of the revolutionary class can come to see themselves as shown by themselves. Through this art they can test the world, accept the real, reject the illusory. They can reproduce the world in their own image—in the image that they themselves produce" (p. 143). No matter how sincere Benjamin's interest in a politicization of art might have been, under Brecht's influence, at that time, the argument of the essay does anything but support such a neat dichotomy of real and illusory or such smooth linkage between reproduction and production. The essay has been given much attention by Marxist critics because it touches on important issues concerning the social existence of art. When Habermas, somewhat skeptical regarding Benjamin's Marxism, pointed out his ambiguous attitude toward aura, that is, his interest in its transcendence rather than destruction ("Bewusstmachende oder rettende Kritik—die Aktualität Walter Benjamin's," in *Zur Aktualität Walter Benjamins*, ed. Siegfried Unseld (Frankfurt: Suhrkamp, 1972), pp. 196ff), he stirred up a lively debate: see Philip Brewster and Carl Howard Buchner, "Language and Critique: Jürgen Habermas on Walter Benjamin," *New German Critique* 17 (1979): 15–29. See also Eugene Lunn, *Marxism and Modernism: An Historical Study of Lukács, Brecht, Benjamin and Adorno* (Berkeley: University of California Press, 1982); cautiously critical of Benjamin's "supple" Marxism (p. 150), he points out quite rightly that the "vulnerability of the essay (besides the fact that it had not caught up with Soviet realities of the 1930s) lay in his apparent insistence that all these changes were not so much potential uses as *inherent* implications of the new media" (p. 154).

164. *Illuminations*, p. 226. The translation included in *Illuminations* (pp. 219–53) is based on the second draft of the essay, *G.S.*, vol 1, p. 481.

165. Brecht: "Nothing but mysticism, and adopting an attitude against mysticism! That's the form in which materialist history has been adapted! It's god-awful" (see above n. 24); Adorno to Benjamin, March 18, 1936, *G.S.*, vol. 1, pp. 1001–6, especially, pp. 1002f.

166. Ibid., pp. 1003f; Adorno refers in this context to his discovery that the progressive elements of jazz (montage, collective) are in reality a façade for its truly reactionary properties; on his determination not to learn anything about jazz see my " 'Beute der Pragmatisierung': Adorno und Amerika," pp. 62f.

167. *Illuminations*, p. 223; *G.S.*, vol. 1, pp. 477f.

168. *Illuminations*, p. 236; *G.S.*, vol 1, p. 496.

169. *G.S.*, vol. 1, p. 440.

170. This is true even for the argument in part 15 where Brecht is on one level distinctly present in the concept of a progressive distractedness—the relaxed audience of the epic theater—of the masses before the work of art and the reactionary concentration on the work of art: But Benjamin can't resist playing with the contrasts: "A man who concentrates before a work of art is absorbed by it. . . . In contrast, the

distracted mass absorbs the work of art. This is most obvious with regard to buildings. Architecture has always represented the prototype of a work of art the reception of which is consummated by a collectivity in a state of distraction" (*Illuminations*, p. 241). Absorbing and being absorbed are curiously fused here, in spite of the materialist terms *collectivity* and *distraction*.

171. On the discussion between Adorno and Benjamin concerning the publication of this essay on Baudelaire, a part of the book project on the Paris Arcades, see *G.S.*, vol. 1, pp. 1065–1136. See also above sec. 1 of this chapter.

172. *Illuminations*, pp. 189f; *G.S.*, vol. 1, pp. 645f.

173. Lunn, p. 171.

174. Walter Benjamin, *Briefe*, vol. 2, pp. 756–64; included in *Illuminations*, pp. 141–48.

175. Ibid., p. 758; ibid., p. 142.

176. In order to support this connection he quotes a long passage from Eddington's *The Nature of the Physical World* which, however, makes the experience of the every day world by the 'scientific man' a positively mystical experience. Benjamin, without further comment, sees much of Kafka in Eddington or *vice versa*. (*Illuminations*, p. 145; *Briefe*, vol. 2, p. 761).

177. Ibid., p. 146; ibid., p. 762.

178. On Benjamin's relations with the painting see Gershom Scholem, "Walter Benjamin und sein Engel," *Walter Benjamin und sein Engel* (Frankfurt: Suhrkamp, 1983), pp. 35–72.

179. *Illuminations*, pp. 147f; *Briefe* vol. 2, pp. 763f.

180. Scholem to Benjamin, November 6–8, 1938, *Walter Benjamin–Gershom Scholem Brief-wechsel 1933–1940*, ed. Gershom Scholem (Frankfurt: Suhrkamp, 1980), pp. 285f. Scholem also points out that emphasis on the mere transmissibility of tradition is inherent in the wave motion of mystical tradition and that the anomie of the haggadic element is not specifically Kafka's problem.

181. I am quoting from the text included in *Illuminations*, pp. 255–66.

182. "Conversations with Brecht," pp. 209f.

183. Franz Rosenzweig, *Briefe*, ed. Edith Rosenzweig (Berlin: Schocken, 1935), p. 158.

184. Moses draws attention to the contrast in Benjamin's and Rosenzweig's concept of language (p. 198), but does not see such contrast in their concepts of messianic time; I disagree with his reading of Rosenzweig in this case (pp. 202f). Brecht was remarkably charitable in his evaluation of the "Theses," which he sums up along the lines of his own thinking, stressing Benjamin's critique of linear progress, especially of the social-democratic variety, and which he finds "clear and de-confusing (in spite of all the metaphorics and Judaism)." Several of the theses echo passages in the 1937 Fuchs essay which Brecht liked for its relative ("materialist") clarity (see above n. 25). He was not interested in the fact that Benjamin's "Judaisms" were as idiosyncratic as his Marxism.

In his letter to Gretel Adorno of April 1940 (*G.S.*, vol. 1, p. 1223), announcing the manuscript of the "Theses," Benjamin states that the text is not meant for publication and that it contains thoughts he had preserved and hidden ("verwahrt") for a period of twenty years, almost hidden, too, from himself. He directs her attention to thesis seventeen which, he thinks, will show her the connection with the body of his work by commenting succinctly on its method. He relates the "Theses" in general with problems of remembrance and forgetting, which, he writes, will occupy his thoughts for a long time yet.

185. Following Scholem ("Walter Benjamin und sein Engel," p. 64), the editors read the "Theses" as having been triggered by Benjamin's shocked reaction to the Hitler-Stalin pact, (*G.S.*, vol. 1, p. 1228); for a detailed discussion of this connection see Rolf Tiedemann, "Historical Materialism or Political Messianism? An Interpreta-

tion of the Theses 'On the Concept of History,'" *The Philosophical Forum*, vol. 15, nos. 1–2 (1983–84): 71–104. Tiedemann stresses on the whole a continuity between the "Theses" and much of Benjamin's earlier work, attempting to sort out the most obvious contradictions. The essay is helpful in this respect, but uncritical of Benjamin's concept of historiography and, above all, of his practice of cultural criticism. Very possibly, the act of writing down, in this form, thoughts which he had indeed articulated before in various ways and various contexts was triggered by Benjamin's disappointment over the alliance of fascism and communism (see Tiedemann, pp. 87ff; see thesis eight) but the substance of the "Theses" had undeniably been central to his concept of the historian-critic for a very long time (see n. 184).

5. THE MAGIC SPACES OF TERROR

1. See Karl O. Paetel, *Ernst Jünger in Selbstzeugnissen und Bilddokumenten* (Reinbek by Hamburg: Rowohlt, 1962), pp. 165ff. In the fifties, critics like Max Rychner, Friedrich Sieburg, Curt Hohoff, H. E. Holthusen praised him for his *Haltung* (see below). For Jünger's importance to young *volkish* readers see pt. 1 and chap. 1. Unless stated otherwise, references are to Ernst Jünger, *Sämtliche Werke* (Stuttgart: Klett-Cotta, 1978ff); translations are mine. For a general introduction in English see Gerhardt Loose, *Ernst Jünger* (New York: Twayne 1974).

2. Ernst Jünger, *Eine gefährliche Begegnung* (Stuttgart: Klett-Cotta, 1985). See the review in *Spiegel* 13 (1985): 227ff.

3. Karl-Heinz Bohrer, *Die Ästhetik des Schreckens Die pessimistische Romantik und Jüngers Frühwerk* (Muenchen: Hanser, 1978).

4. Bohrer, p. 493, on the "turn" *(Wendung)* in Jünger's development, that is, a significant incision after the *Frühwerk:* "Die Selbstkorrektur korrespondiert mit der Epoche humaner Bescheidenheit, mit dem Ende der Katastrophe als "ästhetischer Kategorie."

5. Ibid.: "Diese Wendung zeigt Jünger abermals als keinen willkürlich privaten, sondern historischen Autor."

6. On the many revisions of this text from the twenties to the sixties see sec. 3 of this chapter. References are to the English translation *The Storm of Steel: From the Diary of a German Storm-Troop Officer on the Western Front* (London: Chatto & Windus, 1929).

7. *Das abenteuerliche Herz*, first version in *Sämtliche Werke (SW)*, vol. 9 (1979), pp. 96f; see also "Author's Preface to the English Edition," *Storm of Steel*, p. XII: "Time only strengthens my conviction that it (life in the trenches) was a good and strenuous life, and that the war, for all its destructiveness, was an incomparable schooling of the heart."

8. On Jünger's use of theatrical images see sec. 3 of this chapter.

9. *Afrikanische Spiele*, in *SW*, vol. 15 (1978); *African Diversions*, tr. Stuart Hood (London: J. Lehmann, 1954).

10. See sec. 2 of this chapter.

11. *Das abenteuerliche Herz* I, in *SW*, vol. 9, p. 148.

12. Ibid.

13. On Jünger's sententious tendencies see the useful detailed analysis of his 1939 allegorical diary-novel *On the Marble Cliffs* by Hans-Jörg Schelle, *Ernst Jüngers "Marmor-Klippen" Eine kritische Interpretation* (Leiden: E. J. Brill, 1970), pp. 18ff, 69ff, 129ff.

14. See the 1949 *Heliopolis* (*SW*, vol. 16 (1980)) and the 1977 *Eumeswil* (*SW*, vol. 17 (1980)). The historian can recall past events on the "Luminar," but as there is no reflection on his perspective—he sees them "as they were"—the learning process consists of gathering and cataloguing.

15. The act and moment of observation is always charged with higher meaning, but there are certain variations in emphasis: on Jünger's arrangements of the position of the observer which becomes, as far as the visual remembrance of the great battles is concerned, increasingly one of fascinated staring, see the analysis of the evolving theater imagery in sec. 3 of this chapter; see also the study of Jünger's revisions in Ulrich Boehme, *Fassungen bei Ernst Jünger* (Meisenheim am Glan: Verlag Anton Hain, 1972), pp. 26ff. On the neutralization of the horrible in the fascinated visual attention see the usefully critical Wolfgang Kämpfer, *Ernst Jünger* (Stuttgart: Metzler, 1981), p. 43.

16. Bohrer, *Ästhetik des Schreckens,* bases his argument on an assumed subversive force, or at least potential of (Jünger's) art, but his assumptions are to a very high degree speculative and ahistorical. It is true that Jünger's aestheticism controlled his view of the world, but this meant that he attempted to control the world so that it would be his construct and entirely manageable, i.e., beautiful, meaningful, and to a very high degree unreal. Such calculated pose of remoteness cannot possibly have any concretely usefully subversive effect. See here the excellent early analysis of Jünger's aestheticism in Christian von Krockow, *Die Entscheidung Eine Untersuchung über Ernst Jünger, Carl Schmitt, Martin Heidegger* (Stuttgart: Ferdinand Enke, 1958), esp. pp. 115ff.

17. The number of officers in the Reichswehr was disproportionately high in relation to that of enlisted men; as a group they had had a disproportionately higher survival rate in World War I.

18. The life-enhancing power of death is presented in the war diaries as a profound existential mystery; see, e.g., *In Stahlgewittern,* in *SW,* vol. 1 (1978), p. 384; the passage is somewhat watered down in the English translation, *Storm of Steel,* p. 152.

19. See also Kämpfer, p. 154.

20. In a diary of March 18, 1946, Jünger noted that a page of prose examined again and again for the sake of improvement can be likened to a wound which is not allowed to form a scab. Boehme fittingly uses this unpublished passage, which Jünger had crossed out in the typescript of *Jahre der Okkupation* (Stuttgart: Klett, 1958), as a motto for his *Fassungen,* a study of Jünger's revisions. The comparison is very telling and to be taken quite concretely.

21. The causal connection is significant here: he only deserves the decoration because he has "managed" ("hatte ich es immerhin erreicht") to have those eleven shots fired at him personally ("dass elf von diesen Geschossen auf mich persönlich abgegeben wurden"): "therefore," etc. This presupposes a higher power controlled by the young officer to the extent that he has succeeded in wrestling from it affirmation of his unique existential significance as warrior.

22. *Storm of Steel,* p. 314.

23. Ibid., pp. 316f.

24. Ibid., pp. 318f.

25. *Storm of Steel,* p. VII.

26. See here Gerda Liebchen, *Ernst Jünger: Seine literarischen Arbeiten in den zwanziger Jahren* (Bonn: Bouvier, 1977), p. 292.

27. "Ein grosses glänzendes Buch," in *Das Tagebuch von Joseph Goebbels 1925/26,* ed. H. Heiber (Stuttgart, 1961), p. 849.

28. See *Storm of Steel,* p. 317.

29. See ibid., p. 141; for nationalist additions to the 1924 introduction see Liebchen, p. 31; they were cut in the bland introduction in the 1934 revised edition.

30. *In Stahlgewittern* reached large audiences only in the late twenties when the market had become favorable to books dealing with the war experience; see below n. 95.

31. Compared to nationalist writers like his friends August Winnig and Ernst Niekisch, Jünger's articulation of these sentiments is remarkably vague: see nn. 97,

98, 101, 102. Goebbels commented on the "new nationalism" of Jünger and others that the really important thing was missing, namely, "recognition of the task of the proletariat" in constructing the new Germany. This diary entry of June 30, 1926, could reflect Goebbels's reaction to a Jünger article published in *Standarte* (June 3, 1926, no. 10) "Schliesst euch zusammen" (Unite) which had called for a national unification of the extraparliamentary right on the basis of Kapitän Ehrhardt's negotiations with the *Frontsoldatenbund. Standarte,* to which Jünger contributed frequently at that time, was an offshoot of the *Bund's Stahlhelm Verlag.* The *Frontsoldatenbund* had been founded in 1919 by and for veterans of World War I, but from 1923 on also admitted young men who were not veterans but whom it hoped to educate in *Frontgeist* by publishing the literary work of the generation of *Frontsoldaten.* Jünger's first publishing house, Mittler, was more technically military in its direction and wanted Jünger to develop expertise in this field. But Jünger was not interested. In the article he is noticeably vague about details of political strategy, referring to the workers in the *Bund* as "socialist masses" and expressing his hope that they would be joined with the "nationalistische Endfront," the final nationalist battle line. The main thrust of this as of many of his articles at that time was the plea for a "true" community of "true" soldiers.

32. *Abenteuerliches Herz I, SW,* vol. 9, pp. 116f.

33. Jünger has always had reliable loyal audiences and sympathetic critics (see n. 1), but in the last decade, with the increasing cultural conservatism of the intelligentsia in the Federal Republic, the sympathetic critics have grown in number, attracted, by their own testimony, to the phenomenon of a controversial outsider who has, over a long period, preserved his integrity *(Haltung)* vis-à-vis a culture market which is said to undermine such authenticity. This fallacy is instructive to the (German) intellectual historian, because it points so clearly to the curiously anachronistic dimension of our contemporary literary culture which is reminiscent of the Weimar period. See the useful short analysis of Jünger's reception in Karl Prümm, "Vom Nationalisten zum Abendländer Zur politischen Entwicklung Ernst Jüngers," *Basis* 6 (1976): 7–29. Prümm points out rightly Jünger's consistently radical metaphysical attitude (p. 25); see also his quotes of celebratory statements on the occasion of Jünger's eightieth birthday in 1975 (pp. 7f) coming also from rather unlikely admirers like Böll, which emphasize Jünger's contributions as those of a nobly masculine erudite competent critic of the technological age who constitutes, in his person, a rich cultural memory. This view neglects to examine the nature of Jünger's largely private acts of remembrance: memory means for him collecting rare flora and (human) fauna as well as rare quotes from rare books—hardly supportive of a concept of cultural remembrance which would be adequate to the late twentieth century. There is an interesting account of a visit with Jünger by Margret Boveri, who saw Jünger quite critically—she also was unexpectedly impressed—and was struck by his rigid habit of placing every name and event that came up in conversation in some sort of scheme, chronological or otherwise. The need to categorize and reassure himself of safe memory storage seemed quite striking. (*Die Schleife Dokumente zum Weg von Ernst Jünger,* ed. Armin Mohler (Zurich: Die Arche, 1955, pp. 90–94.) See also the description of a typical Jünger working day, "Ein Tag im Leben eines modernen Schriftstellers," (ibid., pp. 115–33) which concentrates on the collections and dreams of the author and situates "modern" in the image of Jünger bending over a microscope to look at one of his beetles.

34. This is true of the criticism coming from the German Democratic Republic, e.g., Hans-Joachim Bernhard, "Die apologetische Darstellung des imperialistischen Krieges im Werk Ernst Jüngers," in *Weimarer Beiträge* (1963), pp. 321–55, esp. pp. 344ff, and Helmut Kaiser, *Mythos, Rausch und Reaktion Der Weg Gottfried Benns und Ernst Jüngers* (Berlin: Aufbau Verlag, 1962). There are very important differences between Jünger's and Benn's attitudes to a contemporary modern culture

(see below n. 126), and Kaiser, by neglecting them, does not understand the peculiar nature of Jünger's irrationalism. This is also true, to an extent, of the useful critiques by Prümm and Kämpfer.

35. This essay was part of the 1930 anthology *Krieg und Krieger,* edited by Jünger; it was reviewed extensively by Benjamin: see sec. 5 of this chapter.

36. *Strahlungen I, SW,* vol. 2 (1979), p. 359.

37. *Storm of Steel,* pp. XIf.

38. *Copse 125* (London: Chatto and Windus, 1930), p. VIII.

39. Ibid., pp. IXf. He attacks here the "typically shallow French attitude" expressed in Henri Barbusse's highly successful antiwar novel *Le feu* (1916) which stresses the material aspects of war and laments its destruction because the author has "no mind to accept the responsibilities that demand sacrifice of such corruptible treasures as life and property when a nation's greatness and its ideas are at stake. It is here, though, that the greater moral strength lies . . . " (p. IX).

40. For the 1935 revised edition of *Wäldchen 125* Jünger cut these passages and changed the structural organization which had stressed the diary properties of the text. The sections are now marked by very general indications of place, e.g., "front-line," and the attempted effect is one of a higher, more generally valid level of discourse. These changes were retained in the last revision for the first edition of the collected works in ten volumes, published in Stuttgart by Klett, 1960–65.

41. See, e.g., *Copse,* pp. 172ff; *Wäldchen* (1925), pp. 166ff. This passage stressing the spiritual truth of war was cut for the 1935 edition (see *SW,* vol. 1, p. 386).

42. See *Copse,* p. 169; *Wäldchen,* (1925), p. 162; being killed in action preserves the "link with blood, earth and feeling."

43. Here Jünger is close to the position of the Frankfurt School—they all share a metaphysical dimension of cultural thought.

44. *Copse,* p. 196; *Wäldchen* (1925), p. 189. The German artist ought to learn from the *Nibelungenlied:* "Art must become German again, just as we soldiers have only been taught by the war what Germany is."

45. *Copse,* pp. 86ff; *Wäldchen,* in *SW,* vol. 1, pp. 354ff.

46. *Abenteuerliches Herz I,* in *SW,* vol. 9, p. 155. See here also *Gläserne Bienen* (Stuttgart: Klett, 1957) (*The Glass Bees,* New York: Noonday Press, 1960). This short science fiction novel deals quite interestingly with the "lost" situation of the young officer in Weimar society, noting his anachronistic loyalties and predilections in conflict with the social-technological realities of the *Systemzeit.* There is a deus-ex-machina ending, and the young officer is allowed to remain his attractive feudal self *and* survive well in the essentially alien environment, helped by the (recurrent) figure of a magician-technocrat who has a deeper understanding of the deeper values of the young officer's substance and "breeding."

47. See above n. 31.

48. *Copse,* pp. 140, 152ff: this passage is cut in the 1935 revised edition.

49. See *SW,* vol. 1, pp. 384ff.

50. See *Copse,* pp. 172–92.

51. *Storm of Steel,* p. 245.

52. See also the passages added for the translation, e.g., *Storm,* p. 294: Relieving a badly hit trench section later in 1918 when the English are gaining ground, he gives a fairly detailed description of what in all the German versions is just referred to as "fearful injuries"—several of his men had both eyes shot out—and goes on to comment on his own behavior, that is, his speaking in his "usual tone of ironical pessimism" when helping to clean out the gruesome mess: "I felt the look of horror in the eyes of a new recruit, a seminarist, who was gazing at me. Looking along the channel of his thoughts I had a shock when I realized for the first time how callous the war had made me. One got to regarding men as mere matter." This insight, however,

did not prevent him from leaving in the English version a statement about the absolute power of the still almost adolescent commander over his men: "A man, unless his inherent worth is beyond all doubt, must have obedience drilled into him, so that his natural instincts can be curbed by the spiritual compulsion of his commander even in the most awful moments" (Storm, p. 301).

53. Feuer und Blut, in SW, I, p. 467. Like Wäldchen, Feuer und Blut had a second revised edition in 1935 and was revised again for the collected works.

54. Ibid., pp. 473f.

55. In Stahlgewittern (1934), p. 251; SW, vol. I, p. 234.

56. Feuer und Blut, in SW, vol. I, p. 508.

57. SW, vol. I, p. 245, added after the 1934 revision.

58. Ibid., p. 249. The German verb starren clearly connotes rigidity (the adjective starr means rigid): the viewer is temporarily (as if) paralyzed by the concentration of looking; the element of compulsion in starren suggests victimization which needs to be disguised by the pose.

59. Particularly this image of the coolly passionate, profoundly mystically existential, and mathematically precise observer-writer was used by the German press in their laudationes for Jünger's ninetieth birthday, even the notoriously impudent Spiegel bought this unlikely combination (see n. 2).

60. It was rediscovered after World War II and published in book form in 1963. See also Godfrey Carr, " 'The Golden Age or Nothingness': Some German Intellectuals and the Idea of Suicide," in The Weimar Dilemma Intellectuals in the Weimar Republic, ed. Anthony Phelan (Manchester: Manchester University Press, 1985), pp. 98–102.

61. Die Standarte was published first in 1925 as a supplement to Stahlhelm Verlag, from April 1926 by Frundsberg Verlag, the successor to Mittler. The editor was Jünger's friend Helmut Franke, who was much more concerned with the concrete political implications of the journal's position.

62. See Helmut Franke, Staat im Staate: Aufzeichnungen eines Militaristen (Magdeburg, 1924).

63. See here Kurt Sontheimer, "Der Tat-Kreis," in Vierteljahreshefte für Zeitgeschichte 7 (1959): 229ff, and Armin Mohler, Die konservative Revolution in Deutschland 1918–1932. Ein Handbuch (Darmstadt, 1972).

64. Das deutsche Volkstum was published by Hanseatische Verlagsanstalt Hamburg, later an important National Socialist publishing house; during the Weimar period it had been connected with the lower-middle-class nationalist Deutscher Handlungsgehilfenverband. A helpful analysis of the emerging class of the clerks, Angestellte, as opposed to civil servants, Beamte, is the literary reportage by Siegfried Kracauer, Die Angestellten: Aus dem neuesten Deutschland published in installments in the feuilleton of the Frankfurter Zeitung (Kracauer was an editor) in 1929 and in book form in 1930, now in Siegfried Kracauer, Schriften I (Frankfurt: Suhrkamp, 1971), pp. 203–304. See Wilhelm Stapel, Der christliche Staatsmann Eine Theologie des Nationalismus (Hamburg: Hanseatische Verlagsanstalt, 1932) which distinguishes between France's secular concept of the national state, and of civil rights and the German theological idea of a Reich and interprets their conflict in terms of European domination. Stapel's key concepts in this text are very similar to those appearing in Jünger's texts of the same period, especially "Die totale Mobilmachung" (1930) and Der Arbeiter published the same year as Stapel's book and with the same publishing house. Stapel worked with the concept of a "Gemeingeist eines Volkes" (Wilhelm Stapel, Die Fiktionen der Weimarer Verfassung Versuch einer Unterscheidung der formalen und der funktionalen Demokratie [Hamburg: Hanseatische Verlagsanstalt, 1928], p. 112), which was nourished by the folk's strength and suffering (Theologie, p. 269) and supported its fated right to rule through the Reich,

the fated community. As intent on establishing folkish elites and a strictly hierarchical order, Stapel was more interested in the heroic group than the heroic individual, but his nationalist concepts are as vague and irrationalist as are Jünger's. The Nazis found useful his anti-Semitism: see Wilhelm Stapel, *Die literarische Vorherrschaft der Juden in Deutschland 1918 bis 1933* (Hamburg: Hanseatische Verlagsanstalt, 1937).

65. *Abenteuerliches Herz I*, in *SW*, vol. 9, pp. 40ff, 52ff, 92ff.

66. Ibid., p. 43; *Storm of Steel*, p. X.

67. *Abenteuerliches Herz I*, in *SW*, vol. 9, pp. 174–76. Compare this to Remarque's realistic description of the role of the very young recuits in this kind of warfare: they are sent to the trenches without any training and "fall like flies." "Modern trench-warfare demands knowledge and experience; a man must have a feeling for the contours of the ground, an ear for the sound and character of the shells, must be able to decide beforehand where they will drop, how they will burst, and how to shelter from them. The young recruits of course know none of these things. They get killed simply because they can hardly tell shrapnel from high explosive. . . . Their pale turnip faces, their pitiful clenched hands, the fine courage of these poor devils, the desperate charges and attacks made by the poor brave wretches, who are so terrified that they dare not cry out loudly, but with battered chests, with torn bellies, arms and legs only whimper softly for their mothers and cease as soon as one looks at them. . . . Between five and ten recruits fall to every old hand" (*All Quiet on the Western Front* [New York: Fawcet Crest, 1984], pp. 116f.

68. *Das abenteuerliche Herz I*, in *SW*, vol. 9, pp. 135f.

69. Ibid., pp. 132ff.

70. Ibid., p. 159.

71. Ibid., pp. 68, 72, 160.

72. Ibid., p. 100. This echoes Broch's denunciation of the corrosive intelligence of faceless urban man, see chap. 6, sec. 2.

73. Bohrer, *Ästhetik*, pp. 491f.

74. See Bohrer, *Ästhetik*, pp. 173ff; see the entries in the 1938 second version of *Abenteuerliches Herz*, in *SW*, vol. 9, pp. 180ff, on the challenges and subtle delights experienced in the recasting of older texts.

75. Bohrer, *Ästhetik*, p. 492.

76. *SW*, vol. 9, pp. 33, 96. Here he explicitly compares the lab coat to the uniform, and the microscope to the gun in the service of life. After he left the army in 1923 he took university courses in biology which led to his lifelong interest in building his considerable collection of beetles. The note was written while he worked at the Napoli Aquarium.

77. See above n. 55.

78. *SW*, vol. 9, pp. 35f, 185f.

79. See *Abenteuerliches Herz*, ibid., pp. 36, 66, 76, 81, 195.

80. Ibid., pp. 96f.

81. See the list of reviews from 1920 to 1933 in Liebchen, *Ernst Jünger*, pp. 332–41.

82. Klaus Mann, *Auf der Suche nach einem Weg* (Berlin, 1931), pp. 370–73; Walter Benjamin, "Theories of German Fascism: On the Collection of Essays *War and Warriors*, edited by Ernst Jünger," *New German Critique* 17 (1979): 120–28. This review essay was originally published in *Die Gesellschaft* 7 (1930): 32–41.

83. Benjamin, ibid., p. 120.

84. Ibid., p. 122.

85. Ibid., p. 123.

86. Ibid., pp. 123f.

87. Benjamin rightly draws special attention to the language used in these pieces (pp. 125f), but he does not go on to question it with sufficient critical imagination.

88. On his importance for the theoretical underpinnings of the *Trauerspielbuch* see chap. 4, sec. 2.

89. "Theories of Fascism," p. 124.

90. See chap. 1, sec. 1.

91. On the influence of this text on the Rathenau assassins see chap. 1, sec. 1.

92. "Theories of Fascism," pp. 126f.

93. *Das abenteuerliche Herz,* the most informative text with respect to Jünger's self-concept and self-presentation, contains many images of archaic methods of attack and defense against a hostile, subhuman, shallow technology. Natural images (*SW,* vol. 9, p. 117, the gray geese) serve to extend the lived time shortened by technology; he sees a tragic coldness in the distance created between living things by technology; see also his dislike for photography (ibid., p. 118) as bestowing too much validity on the merely temporary: here he echoes certain aspects of Benjamin's ambivalent attitude toward photography.

94. "Theories of Fascism," p. 127.

95. Jünger had edited and prefaced a collection (*Der Kampf ums Reich* [Berlin: Andermann, 1929]) of pieces whose contributors had all been involved in the illegal postwar battles in the Baltikum, Upper Silesia, the Ruhr area, the revolts connected with the Kapp and Hitler putschs, and the so-called *Landvolkbewegung:* Ernst von Salomon, Gerhard Günther, Hartmut Plaas, Fritz Kloppe, Gregor and Otto Strasser. The edition of this as of two other war collections edited by Jünger in 1930 and 1931 was small. In contrast, Erich Maria Remarque's 1929 *Im Westen nichts Neues (All Quiet on the Western Front)* became famous overnight: his publisher Ullstein, then the most modern publishing house in terms of managing and advertising techniques, advertised in September 1929 (*Literarische Welt,* vol. 5, no. 39 (1929): 2) that the number of copies sold at that point was Germany: 800,000; England: 220,000; France: 275,000; U.S.: 215,000, and that the book had been translated into twenty-two languages. In 1930 the numbers according to an Ullstein advertisement were Germany: over 1,000,000; England: 360,000; France: 340,000; USSR: 440,000; Spain: 105,000; Esperanto: 2400. The war literature on the right covered a fairly broad culturally conservative spectrum—the names of the publishing houses are suggestive: Tradition, Cultura, Hamburger Bücherborn—and on the whole they sought to "rescue" the past; that is, they attempted a cultural reinterpretation of the loss of the war rather than preparation for another war. Unfortunately, such attempts prepared their audiences for Nazi rhetoric which suggested the desirability of the latter.

96. Ernst Niekisch, *Grundfragen deutscher Aussenpolitik,* in *Der deutsche Arbeiter in Politik und Wirtschaft,* no. 1 (Berlin: Verlag der Neuen Gesellschaft, 1925), p. 3. The series was meant to reach a reading audience of workers and reaffirm them in their sober, rational fight against radicalism.

97. Ibid. pp. 37ff. See also Niekisch's disagreements with Eduard Bernstein on the attitudes of the working classes in the *Entente* nations in contrast to the German working class and the importance of the Social Democratic Party's attitude toward national liberation in terms of their attempting to deal with the very serious problems of mistrust between the bourgeoisie and the workers in the area of foreign politics (pp. 34f).

98. Ernst Niekisch, *Hitler—ein deutsches Verhängnis* (Berlin: Widerstandsverlag, 1932), p. 13. Jünger, in a diary entry of March 30, 1946 (*Strahlungen, SW,* 3 (1979), pp. 610f), remembers how Niekisch had shown him his Hitler book and how he had advised him not to publish it. Niekisch, as Jünger sees it (wrongly), was no political opponent in the usual sense of the word, but "suffered more deeply on a level where there is no fear." Jünger justifies this assumption by pointing to Niekisch's fated disappearance into the prisons of Hitler shortly afterward. It is instructive that Jünger could not understand the friend's considerable political real-

ism, but needed to stylize him into an existentially more significant opponent to Hitler.

99. See Ernst Niekisch, *Das Reich der niederen Dämonen* (Hamburg: Rowohlt, 1953).

100. Many of the reviews on the right (Liebchen, pp. 338ff) stressed the *Gestalt* aspect of Jünger's concept of *the* worker as literary-ideological achievement. Siegfried Kracauer (n. 64) was one of the few critics to point out Jünger's apolitical position in his perceptively critical review "Gestaltschau oder Politik," *Frankfurter Zeitung*, October 16, 1933, pp. 1–2.

101. In his *Das Reich der niederen Dämonen* (Hamburg: Rowohlt, 1953), p. 69. Niekisch sees Jünger's "heroic nihilism" especially in "Die totale Mobilmachung" and *Der Arbeiter* as the most radical efforts made by nihilism in order to avoid to have a good look at itself (if this is indeed what he means, the German is ambiguous here): "Der radikalste Aufwand, in den sich der Nihilismus stürzt, nachdem es für ihn schon fast unvermeidlich geworden ist, sich endlich selbst ins Gesicht blicken zu müssen." This is a perceptive recognition of the purely gestural properties of Jünger's nihilism.

102. Kurt Hiller, "Linke Leute von rechts," *Die Weltbühne* 28/31 (August 2, 1932): 153–58. See also Henry Pachter on Karl Otto Paetel (who admired Jünger's *Haltung* and wrote the Rowohlt *Bildmonographie* on Jünger; see n. 1), "Requiem for a National Bolshevist," in *Weimar Etudes* (New York: Columbia University Press, 1982), pp. 246–51. He remembers meeting Paetel in the late twenties in Professor Julius Petersen's class on German romanticism at Berlin University—the same Petersen to whom Döblin had tried to explain the inescapable "dualism" of his novel about modern collectivity, *Berlin Alexanderplatz* (see chap. 5, sec. 4, n. 69). Petersen, remembers Pachter, was "a zealous nationalist who used his lectures to praise war, and Karl Otto believed in the Gothic revival as part of Germany's rebellion against the humiliating Treaty of Versailles—as a means to liberate her from Western rationalistic capitalism. I, by contrast, loved romantic poetry and would have liked to find the link between that artistic expression of human yearnings and Marxism" (p. 246). Paetel was truly one of those "linke Leute von rechts," denouncing Hitler as a petty bourgeois demagogue who had substituted anti-Semitism and anticommunism for socialism and had betrayed whatever anticapitalist tenets had been in the National Socialist program. Like Niekisch, Paetel thought that the true German revolution could only be socialist, moreover, that it could be victorious only in alliance with the Russian revolution (p. 247). Jünger was far removed from positions like this and from their degree of political realism; his crossing over is purely imagistic and cannot be seen in terms of political-social concepts. The differences between his thoughts on the problem of the worker and those of August Winnig are instructive in this respect. Winnig, coeditor with Niekisch of *Widerstand*, who, in contrast to Niekisch, continued to write in support of the Nazis though he did not join the party, was a generation older than Jünger and Niekisch and from the working class. His membership in the Social Democratic Party in the 1880s cost him his admission to the teaching profession; he became a bricklayer instead. From 1913 on he rose quickly in the SPD and from 1919 to 1920 he was Social Democratic *Oberpräsident* of East Prussia, an experience which turned him into a fervent nationalist in sympathy with the healthy natural conservatism of the East Prussian nobility whom he much preferred to the progressive capitalist haute bourgeoisie. He became involved in the illegal battles in that area and supported Kapp's activities, hoping for a revolution from the right. After the Kapp Putsch he had to resign from the SPD and the union. During the twenties he wrote prolifically in support of nationalist causes hoping to teach the SPD to take seriously the emotional force of national identity, the difficult (exploitable) dynamics of group and individual, and the importance of leadership in a mass society. See his *Das Reich als Republik* (Stuttgart: Cotta, 1928) and his *Arbeiter und Reich* (Leipzig and Berlin: Teubner, 1927). Notwithstanding his blood and earth

rhetoric, he did not stylize the worker into a heroic cardboard figure, nor did he subordinate him to the myth of the proletariat. Having made very wrong choices and formed destructive alliances, he still knew much more than intellectuals like Jünger or Benjamin about the psychological needs and conflicts of the working-class individual as part of a bewildering technocratic mass society.

103. See chap. 1 of *Der Arbeiter,* in *SW,* vol. 8 (1981).

104. See here Hans Freyer, *Pallas Athene Ethik des politischen Volkes* (Jena, 1935), pp. 121ff; see also his *Revolution von rechts* (Jena, 1931).

105. Martin Heidegger, *Die Selbstbehauptung der deutschen Universität* (Breslau, 1933), p. 22. Pachter (*Weimar Etudes,* pp. 210f) writes of the "gibberish" of Heidegger's inaugural speech and that his line-up with the Nazi government had not surprised him as he had never considered him "a meta-physician standing aloof." Drawing attention to the careful ambiguity of Heidegger's language, he also points out that he had not found "a word about Jews or race in any of Heidegger's writings" and during his short tenure as rector at Freiburg University "no anti-Semitic demonstrations were allowed at the University; nor were any books burned at Freiburg." Krockow (n. 16), in his useful analysis of Jünger's, Heidegger's, and Schmitt's decisionism, overlooks in his discussion of Heidegger's relation to Tönnies important differences in their concepts of *Gemeinschaft* (pp. 97ff).

106. Krockow's study, relatively early and on the whole well balanced, is a good case in point. He does see quite clearly the similarities in the three writers' cultural attitudes, but he is too rigid in the case of Schmitt, the political thinker, and too admiring of Jünger's detached attitude toward concrete power. This detachment is supported by the fastidious aesthetics of *Haltung*—a fact not sufficiently appreciated by Krockow—and has little to do with responsible political judgments. Jünger's ambiguous critique of Hitlerism (see sec. 7 of this chapter) was too closed and abstract in its fictionality to be of use. If anything, it allowed the reader to enjoy the fiction and refrain from questioning its (and his own) passivity.

107. *Der Arbeiter,* in *SW,* vol. 8, pp. 209f.

108. Bohrer tries to interpret Jünger as a significantly utopist writer in the sense of the Frankfurt School's significantly subversive negativity of art. In his view, Jünger disrupts the utopian plan—Bohrer naturally does not like "mere" utopianism—by breaking the taboo of (un)happiness, that is, by making *Glücksverzicht* such an important characteristic of the utopian *Arbeitswelt.* This renunciation is distinct from and of greater value than Marxist as well as fascist utopian plans (pp. 483f). Moreover, the concept-images of *Maske, planetarische Herrschaft,* and the challenge of *Glücksverzicht* suggest to Bohrer an "anti-enlightenment radicalism" which does not tend toward a fascist program but rather toward "the pessimistic introversion of modern art and literature" (p. 488). He does not explain how such introversion directed by images of a radical cultural conservatism can be "subversive."

109. Carl Schmitt, *Politische Romantik* (1919; Munich and Leipzig, 1925), pp. 21f. See also his *Politische Theologie* (1922; Munich and Leipzig, 1934); *Die Diktatur* (1921; Munich and Leipzig, 1928); *Die geistesgeschichtliche Lage des heutigen Parlamentarismus* (1923; Munich and Leipzig, 1926); *Der Begriff des Politischen* (1927; Hamburg, 1933) (*The Concept of the Political,* with Comments on Schmitt's Essay by Leo Strauss [New Brunswick, NJ: Rutgers University Press, 1976], esp. pp. 89ff, Strauss's useful critically comparative discussion of Hobbes's and Schmitt's concept of status naturalis as status belli); *Legalität und Legitimität* (Munich and Leipzig, 1932).

110. *On the Marble Cliffs* (New York: Penguin, 1983). *Auf den Marmorklippen* was completed in August 1939; the summer had been, like that of 1914, a particularly radiant one. By the spring of 1940 Jünger's publisher Klett had sold over thirty-five thousand copies before further printing was stopped by the authorities. However, Jünger was not harassed and the book was not put on the index. It was published by

John Lehmann in 1947 in the excellent translation of Stuart Hood whose "Translator's Note" points out parallels between certain characters and Nazi dignitaries, stressing the *in tyrannos* thrust of the text. George Steiner's thoughtful introduction (1970) concurs in this reading but is (rightly) more critical of the text's success as a political fable.

111. Ibid., p. 13.

112. *Abenteuerliches Herz II*, in *SW*, vol. 9, pp. 212ff.

113. Ibid., pp. 253f, p. 255. The last passage is reminiscent of the 1942 diary entry mentioned above which records the beauties of a bomb raid on Paris.

114. *Marble Cliffs*, pp. 106f.

115. Ibid., p. 111. Ernst Niekisch in his memoirs *Gewagtes Leben Begegnungen und Begebnisse* (Cologne and Berlin: Kiepenheuer & Witsch, 1958), pp. 190ff, points to the escape motif—the brothers leaving the battle—central to Jünger's work, his predilection for the persona and position of the spectator-narrator.

116. See Schelle (n. 13) for details on possible connections, especially chap. 5, "Die Mosaiksteine."

117. *Marble Cliffs*, pp. 82f; in the 1949 *Heliopolis*, a literary utopia with science fantasy features, the protagonist Lucius, a historian, political advisor, and warrior (and very much a wishful self-projection of Jünger) reflects on the self-assuredness of the Mauretanians, an order of warriors-researchers engaged in the quest for an *Urwissenschaft* (original archscience) or *Superwissenschaft;* the development of a grand synthesis of all branches of knowledge on the basis of the discovery of an *Urform*. Lucius describes the three phases of technological development in Helipolis: 1. "titanic" = rule of machines; 2. "rational" = perfect automation; 3. "magical" = automata are given life by being given *Sinn*, meaning (*SW*, vol. 16 [1980], pp. 39ff, 186). There are no descriptions of technological development in *Marble Cliffs*, not even in vague terms. At one point Braquemart comes up to the cliffs in a car (which at any rate could also belong to the young Prince with whom he is politically associated) and the image used to describe the machine's power is instructive: "a powerful car humming softly like an almost imperceptibly vibrating insect" (*Marble Cliffs*, p. 79).

118. See Schelle, pp. 36ff.

119. *Marble Cliffs*, p. 77.

120. *Abenteuerliches Herz*, in *SW*, vol. 9, p. 118.

121. Good examples for this kind of argumentation in Otto Dietrich, *Das Wirtschaftsdenken im Dritten Reich* (Munich: Zentralverlag der NSDAP, 1936), pp. 25ff, on the führer's dedication to the great and sublime task of technological and scientific progress. He will see to it that it will be subservient to the people, so that technology in the most advanced stage of creative synthesis truly serves nature again, having overcome the stage of mere control. Technology will then open nature's inexhaustible beauty and power to the *Volksgenossen* on a higher level. Dietrich was the head of the office for communication, *Reichspressewesen*.

122. Schelle has a whole chapter on Jünger's concept of *Hoheit*, highness, and the hierarchical ranking of all the figures in *Marble Cliffs* which the author and his protagonists take literally. Pater Lampros, e.g., is extremely valuable to the brothers ("von höchstem Wert") because he knows how to communicate, apart from his extensive erudition, "those supreme moments ["Augenblicke hohen Rangs"] of experience in which the true meaning of our own work runs through us like a lightning flash" (p. 60).

123. For Jünger this is very much an aristocratic combination (see p. 60).

124. *Marble Cliffs*, pp. 61f.

125. Ibid., p. 67.

126. It is important to notice the differences within the same camp as well as the similarities between ostensibly very different camps. See here the thoughtful early

study of the differences between Jünger's and Gottfried Benn's attitudes toward modern culture with its technological, scientific priorities, and achievements by Max Bense, *Ptolemäer und Mauretanier* (Cologne and Berlin: Kiepenheuer, 1950), pp. 32–34. (See also Bense's nicely ironical motto: "Widerstehe den Anfängen"—Resist the origins: since the romantic period they had been much too alluring to German intellectuals.) Benn had frequently been lumped together with Jünger, especially after the war, under the label "heroic nihilism," but unlike Jünger he had reflected on the culturally problematic lack of balance between the rational and the irrational energies of the mind. Like Heidegger, he had, in the beginning, sympathized with the Nazis' metabiological promises of national renewal. A dermatologist by training, Benn had become a well-known writer with effective expressionist-realistic poems about the accidentality and casual finiteness of human life (e.g., his texts about the cancer ward). During the Weimar period he wrote difficult short essay-fictions and lyric poetry which do and do not acknowledge the natural fragmentedness and precarious cultural significance of human existence. But in his troubled and determined searches for higher meaning he managed to preserve a remarkably firm intelligence. Bense, comparing Jünger's World War II diaries *(Strahlungen)* and Benn's intellectual-autobiographical reflections *Der Ptolemäer,* contrasts Jünger's linear and simple mental procedures with Benn's multidimensionality and complexity. Bense clearly recognizes Jünger's lack of conceptual grasp and talent for organization and his tendency, so common among essayistic writers of the Weimar period, to diffuse conceptually complex texts and merge them with his own solely for the sake of atmospheric properties which appeal to him, or the sake of their indisputable cultural rank—e.g., Pascal. There is no attempt in Jünger's texts to deal responsibly with the culturally important ideas of others, and it is this thoughtlessness in a literal sense which prevented him from approaching the question of modernity from the position of a critical contemporary.

6. REDEMPTIVE NARRATION

1. Joseph Strelka, ed., *Broch heute* (Bern and Munich: Francke, 1978), p. 19. Unless stated otherwise references are to Hermann Broch, *Massenpsychologie,* ed. Wolfgang Rothe (Zürich: Rheinverlag, 1959), vol. 9; *Essays Band I und II,* ed. Hannah Arendt (Zürich: Rheinverlag, 1955), vols. 6 and 7; *Briefe,* ed. Paul Michael Lützeler (Frankfurt: Suhrkamp, 1981), vols. 1–3 by page; by letter number to *Hermann Broch–Daniel Brody Briefwechsel 1930–1951,* ed. Bertold Hack and Marietta Kleiss *(Archiv für Geschichte des Buchwesens,* 12, 1972); translations are mine. References to *The Sleepwalkers,* trans. Willa and Edwin Muir (New York: Grosset and Dunlap, 1964).

For a detailed discussion of Broch's highly idiosyncratic uses of a German philo-sophical tradition and the negative impact of his extravagant epistemological claims on the in many ways interesting novel *The Sleepwalkers,* see my essays "Auto-renstrategie und Leser im Gedankenroman," *Zeitschrift für Literaturwissenschaft und Linguistik, Erzählforschung,* 3, ed. Wolfgang Haubrichs (Göttingen: Van-denhoeck und Ruprecht, 1978), pp. 223–55; "Hermann Broch—das autonome Ich," *Neue Rundschau* 87 (1976): 326–33; "Massenpsychologie als Metaphysik: zu Brochs Begriff eines Irdisch-Absoluten," *Musil-Forum* 3 (1977): 159–91, *Musil-Forum* 4 (1978): 60–103, 244–69. See also Wolfgang Freese and Karl Menges, *Broch-For-schung Rezeptionsproblematik* (Munich: Fink, 1977; *Musil-Studien* Beihefte 1), the excellent unpublished 1958 Freiburg dissertation of Erna Wieslawa Wolfram, "Der Stil Hermann Brochs. Eine Untersuchung zum 'Tod des Vergil,'" and Hermann Krapoth, *Dichtung und Philosophie: Eine Studie zum Werk Hermann Brochs* (Bonn: Bouvier, 1971).

2. Walter Jens, "Mathematik des Traums," in *Statt einer Literaturgeschichte*

(Pfullingen: Neske, 1957), pp. 109–31. See the discussion of Broch's application of the theory of relativity to his theory of the novel in Theodore Ziolkowski, "Hermann Broch und die Relativität im Roman," in *Perspektiven der Forschung,* ed. Manfred Durzak (Munich: Fink, 1972), pp. 313–27.

3. Broch was extremely fortunate in his translators Willa and Edwin Muir, who were both infinitely patient, especially Willa Muir, sensitive, and technically excellent; their English translation arguably improves on Broch's German.

4. Letter to Daniel Brody, Aug. 5, 1931, *Briefe,* vol. 1, pp. 150ff.

5. On the irrationalist basis of Broch's *Werttheorie* (theory of values) see Krapoth, *Dichtung und Philosophie,* pp. 39ff; Karl Menges, *Kritische Studien zur Wertphilosophie Hermann Brochs* (Tübingen: Niemeyer, 1970), pp. 108ff; see also the short comparison between Scheler and Broch in my "Massenpsychologie als Metaphysik," *Musil-Forum* 4 (1978): 71f.

6. *Briefe,* vol. 1, pp. 150ff; he had written to Willa Muir two days earlier in almost identical terms (ibid., pp. 147ff). In his essays and in the essayistic passages in the novel he deals with those questions as aspects of his theory of *Wertzerfall* (disintegration of value), of his *Erkenntnistheorie* (epistemology), his *Massenwahntheorie* (theory of crowd madness). His argumentation here is conceptually disorganized, opaque, and highly redundant (see discussion below); in his letters to his friends (including his publisher) his statements regarding the intentions and especially the achievement of his work are tempered in tone, but not in substance, by some nice self-irony and colloquial phrasing. The theoretical passages in his texts largely resist translation: claiming the authority of discourse within a tradition of European, especially German philosophy, he is frequently not familiar with the conventions of this tradition and its discourse, and instead imposes on his reader an idiosyncratic lyrically self-sufficient set of terms and concepts, *Gedankendichtung.* Paul M. Lützeler, editor of the new Broch edition with Suhrkamp and, most recently, his biographer (*Hermann Broch,* Frankfurt: Suhrkamp, 1985), has consistently attempted to argue for Broch's importance as a great novelist whose contributions to social philosophy and theory have to be taken seriously. His edition of Broch's mass psychology, *Massenwahntheorie* (Frankfurt: Suhrkamp, 1979), vol. 12, arranges the repetitive fragmentary texts, which read like first drafts, according to a table of contents left by Broch, thus suggesting a degree of coordination and completion of the project which is not born out by the texts. Very positive in his evaluation of Broch's achievement in this field of inquiry, Lützeler stresses the fact that the concept of a conversion *(Bekehrung)* of the masses is central to Broch's argument and synonymous, for him, with their "Demokratisierung." Lützeler states that Broch's approach to the question of crowd behavior, arguably one of the most important phenomena in modern history, was "philosophisch-ethisch" in direct contrast to an empirical method. He simply echoes Broch's vague idea of what constitutes a philosophical approach, and—this is even more serious in the context—he never questions the validity of such an emphatically nonempirical perspective (theory) on social-psychological phenomena (see pp. 580f).

7. Letter to Daisy Brody, July 23, 1931, *Briefe,* vol. 1, pp. 144f. Broch is referring here to part 3, *Huguenau, or The Realist,* of the trilogy.

8. *Essays,* vol. 1, pp. 197f.

9. Especially the letters he wrote while at work on the third part, *Huguenau,* are filled with speculations about reader reaction: the reader has to be moved to "swallow" (to Daisy Brody, July 23, 1931, *Briefe,* vol. 1, pp. 144f) the knowledge offered to him in Broch's theory of a disintegration of value integrated into the novel, and he should do so unaware of the "weightiness" of the offering, which, Broch is firmly convinced, constitutes "in a quasi-scientific sense (a) completely new philosophy of history" (to Daniel Brody, August 5, 1931, *Briefe,* vol. 1, pp. 150ff). Broch is understandably concerned about selling a difficult novel; *Ulysses* had impressed him

precisely because it paid no attention to its reader but gave him a slap in the face on every page, as he wrote to a friend on April 6, 1930 (*Briefe*, vol. 1, p. 84). But all these speculations and strategies ("let's hope the reader won't notice," ibid., p. 150) circle around the fact that the novel claims to be in serious ways philosophical, and they do not address any specific difficulties or problems.

10. "Das Weltbild des Romans," *Essays*, vol. 1, p. 237. The expression is also used in the 1945 essay "Die mythische Erbschaft der Dichtung," (*Essays*, vol. 1, p. 246) and in the fragment "Autobiographie als Arbeitsprogramm" which contains the most important parts of what he called his *Massenpsychologie* (*Werke*, vol. 9, p. 45).

11. See Brody to Broch, Oct. 5, 1948 (*Briefwechsel*, no. 500) and Broch's immediate answer (no. 501).

12. See Heinz D. Oesterle, "Hermann Broch: 'Die Schlafwandler' Kritik der zentralen Metapher," *Deutsche Vierteljahresschrift* 44 (1970): 229–68. Oesterle points out rightly that the sleepwalkers, notwithstanding the social implications of their metaphysical-existential status, are both put into this state and, in the end, led out of it by an external agency—the author as *deux ex machina*. There is a similar problem with the 1936 novel fragment *Bergroman* where mass seduction occurs in a rural setting among "wise" peasants who, according to their status in Broch's value system (see below, sec. 2), would not be expected to be so easily tempted by an evil charismatic figure (Hitler or Goebbels); again, they are both wise and unwise by the (arbitrary) fiat of their author, not by any human psycho-logic. See here the useful discussion of this problem in Michael Winkler, "Die Funktion der Erzählungen in Hermann Brochs 'Bergroman,'" in *Perspektiven*, pp. 251–69.

13. Broch to Einstein on his *Massenpsychologie*, Sept. 6, 1945, *Briefe*, vol. 3, pp. 16ff, and to Hermann Weyl, Dec. 20, 1949, ibid., pp. 383f.

14. Albert Einstein and Leopold Infeld, *The Evolution of Physics* (New York, 1938), pp. 125ff.

15. Letter to Wilhelm Emrich, April 10, 1951, *Briefe*, vol. 3, pp. 532f.

16. See his letters to Eugen Vietta, Aug. 25, 1933, *Briefe*, vol. 1, pp. 249f, and Nov. 30, 1948, *Briefe*, vol. 3, pp. 274ff; to Wilhelm Emrich, ibid., pp. 532f; to Daniel Brody, Sept. 10, 1948, ibid., p. 257.

17. "Autobiographie als Arbeitsprogramm," *Werke*, vol. 9, p. 45. On Broch and mathematics see my "Hermann Broch—das autonome Ich," *Neue Rundschau* 87 (1976), esp. pp. 329ff. The notes found among his papers are mainly excerpts from college level textbooks.

18. See below, sec. 2.

19. On his views of Marxism and his claims that his "new science" provides the only viable way of superseding this to his mind fascinating and dangerous dogma, see my "Massenpsychologie als Metaphysik," *Musil-Forum* 4 (1978): 76ff.

20. *Werke*, vol. 9, p. 40.

21. For a detailed critical discussion of his peculiarly opaque style, his use of verbal clues in suggesting but never delivering conceptual coherence and consistency, his uncontrolled use of repetition and tautology, see the studies listed in note 1. Hannah Arendt seems to have had a peculiar tolerance for what she calls Broch's "highly original" concept of *Wissenschaftlichkeit*, especially in his later epistemological texts where, as she sees it, he is going back, on a higher level, to logical positivism (*Essays*, vol. 1, pp. 32ff, and *Essays*, vol. 2, p. 291): see my "Massenpsychologie," *Musil-Forum* 4: 80ff. However, as she wrote to her friend Kurt Blumenfeld on July 31, 1956, her introduction to Broch's essays had been a service to the dead friend. "The thoughts I present or try to present are very alien to me. He knew that and yet relied on my loyalty" (Literaturarchiv Marbach 76.934/2; my translation).

22. See his lamentations to his publisher Brody in the forties, especially the letter of Sept. 28, 1948, *Briefwechsel*, no. 498, listing the seven major manuscripts he was

working on simultaneously. See also his letter to his wife, Sept. 14, 1948, *Briefe*, vol. 3, pp. 242ff.

23. See his letter to Friedrich Torberg, April 10, 1943, *Briefe*, vol. 2, p. 318. Broch held these views for all his adult life from the 1918 "Die Strasse" (*Werke*, vol. 10, pp. 257–60) to the essay fragments written in the forties as parts of the *Massenpsychologie:* modern man is faceless, never reaches full consciousness, never seeks, much less attains, knowledge. There is a leitmotif formula in the later essay fragments: totally disoriented urban man ("der dahindämmernde Städter") in his faceless promiscuity of knowledge ("physiognomielose Erkenntnispromiskuität") (see especially "Geschichtsgesetz und Willensfreiheit," *Werke*, vol. 9, pp. 276ff).

24. It is only the peasant who transcends this "empirische Erbärmlichkeit" (empirical wretchedness) in his occupation of the "wise ["sophrosynisch"] midpoint between god and animal, the midpoint of mankind, perhaps even the most human happiness in the earthly realm" (ibid., p. 277). Man, as the young and the old Broch declared emphatically, is an animal ("ein Viech"), to be controlled by very strict rules. In his letters to Friedrich Torberg, July, 28, 1950, *Briefe*, vol. 3, pp. 486ff, and Hans Sahl, February 28, 1945, *Briefe*, vol. 2, pp. 437ff, Broch refers to man in these terms arguing that the totalitarian aspects of Marxism respond realistically to man's "empirische Erbärmlichkeit" and that Marxism, therefore, is an admirable model for political power to be overcome only by his own political theory based on his own *Massenpsychologie* which calls for a "totalitarian democracy" ("Zur politischen Situation unserer Zeit," *Werke*, vol. 9, pp. 413ff).

25. *Sleepwalkers*, p. 20; *Die Schlafwandler* (*Werke*, vol. 2), p. 19.

26. Letter to Brody, June 7, 1930, *Briefe*, vol. 1, p. 89; letter and commentary to H. G. Meyer, April 10, 1930, *Briefe*, vol. 1, p. 87.

27. Broch brought together a number of stories written over a period of several decades in the 1950 *Die Schuldlosen* (The guiltless) in order to enable a postwar German audience to become reacquainted with him, while he was working on his mass psychological and political texts which he found impossible to complete. The original stories, skillfully narrated psychological studies, were left largely intact and held up quite well under the added "metapolitical" connections consisting of opaque ruminations about the bourgeois characters' guiltless guilt regarding the German catastrophe, that is, again, their apolitical sleepwalking and their groping for redemption. On this problem see Daniel Brody's perceptive remarks, Nov. 16, 1949, *Briefwechsel*, no. 521. In *The Sleepwalkers* the metacultural comments are too overpowering, because they have pervaded the characters from the very beginning causing them to become allegorical markers on Broch's scale of cultural disintegration. Occasionally Broch does get intrigued with the physical individuality of a character, especially if it concerns a woman. There is, in pt. 3, *Huguenau*, a convincing sketch of an upper-middle-class pretty young woman, Hanna Wendling, whom he uses to show the experience of an existential and/or cultural malaise. Broch had a good eye for the details of women's physical existence—Hanna waking up, touching her relaxed sleepy body and her confused thoughts (pt. 3, chap. 8), walking in town on a sunny spring day in a fashionably ankle-length frock, feeling at home in her healthy young body, enjoying a light flirtation (chap. 17). But the reader is told all these details just to have them disappear into long passages of comments on Hanna's typical total lack of self-knowledge and significance (the entire chap. 13; parts of chap. 17): her mood swings are "not in the least the immoderation of the Renaissance popes, but simply the inability and insignificance of an ordinary bourgeois who lacks a sense of values." (*Sleepwalkers*, pp. 385f) Finally Hanna is made to die in the influenza epidemic at the end of the war so that the author can comment on "the isolation of a highly insignificant woman" as "a metaphysical necessity" (chap. 71; *Sleepwalkers*, pp. 556f).

28. See Gisela Brude-Firnau, ed. *Materialien zu Hermann Brochs 'Die Schlaf-wandler'* (Frankfurt: Suhrkamp, 1972), p. 103.

29. See letters to Daisy Brody, March 19, 1932, *Briefwechsel*, no. 183; to Willa Muir, Aug. 3, 1931, *Briefe*, vol. I, p. 148: here he relates questions of the novel's "architectonic principles" connected with *Wertzerfall* to the voice speaking in the "Story of the Salvation Army Girl," episode 9. The voice speaking in the first person is that of Bertrand Müller who, we are told, is the author of the *Wertzerfall* passages. Dorrit Claire Cohn, *The Sleepwalkers: Elucidations of Hermann Broch's Trilogy* (The Hague: Mouton, 1966), pp. 103ff, argues that Bertrand is presented as the author of the whole trilogy—an ingenious attempt to construct a novelist within the novel, a self-conscious and controlled play with the relations between reality and fiction which, however, is not supported by the text. Brude-Firnau in her essay "Die 9. Episode der 'Geschichte des Heilsarmeemädchens,'" in *Materialien* (pp. 180–96) agrees with Cohn's suggestion to see the lyric voice of the Ahasver poem as a mythical invocation of the Bertrand figure and of Broch; she does not, however, extend this equation to the whole trilogy but analyzes Bertrand's purification in this episode in terms of a specifically Jewish religiosity which she thinks central to Broch's work. Her analysis is convincing in the context of this particular episode. But her conclusions (pp. 184ff), which could be supported by the diffuse, ambiguous religiosity to be found throughout the text (the sociopolitical world as construct of a higher being, Broch as a mouthpiece of that higher authority, chap. 72), undermine Broch's claims to the "epistemological" dimension of the *polyhistorisch* novel, which she does not question.

30. Broch uses *sachlich* idiosyncratically (see his statement to H. G. Meyer quoted above), and Huguenau's *Sachlichkeit*: a man who is "liberated from values and from style, and can be influenced only by the irrational" (chap. 88, "Disintegra-tion of Values," sec. 10, epilogue) has nothing to do with the concept of *neue Sachlichkeit* (new objectivity, matter-of-factness) as an intellectual trend during the earlier years of the Weimar Republic—see pt. 1 of this study).

31. Letter to Broch, Sept. 29, 1931, *Briefwechsel*, no. 152.

32. Robert Musil, *Gesammelte Werke in neun Bänden*, ed. Adolf Frisé (Reinbek by Hamburg: Rowohlt, 1978), vol. 7, p. 850.

33. See here Gertrude Ezorsky, "Performative Theory of Truth," *The Encyclope-dia of Philosophy* (New York: Macmillan, 1967), vol. 5, pp. 88ff.

34. See Brody to Broch, November 22, 1933, *Briefwechsel*, no. 299, in answer to Broch's letter to Daisy Brody, November 18, 1933, *Briefe*, vol. I, pp. 262f, about the question of "rational-irrational" in the context of his new religious novel which was to become the *Bergroman* and later *Der Versucher*: "I gathered from today's letter to my wife that we mean something else entirely by 'rational-irrational'; this we'll have to clear up."

35. Letter to Brody, February 6, 1932, *Briefwechsel*, no. 174, and March 17, 1932, *Briefwechsel*, no. 182, note: "In dieser Vereinigung der erkenntnismässigen mit den rein dichtungsmässigen Darstellungsmitteln bilden die 'Schlafwandler' nicht nur einen ganz neuen Typus des Romans, sie bedeuten nicht nur einen Markstein und einen Wendepunkt in der Entwicklung deutscher Erzählkunst, sondern weit darüber hinaus: in ihrem geschichtsphilosophischen Gehalt, in ihrer dichterischen Schau, in ihrer wissenschaftlichen und dichterischen Präzision erheben sie sich zu einer Höhe, die ihren Dichter zum wegweisenden Deuter dieser Zeit macht."

36. There are some exceptions: the earlier stories later collected in *Die Schuldlosen*, among the essays a long piece "Hofmannsthal and His Times." The most problematic texts in this respect are those in which Broch explicitly addresses contemporary questions from his radically conservative position.

37. A remarkably clear example of such circularity can be found in a passage in

the first chapter of "Geschichtsgesetz und Willensfreiheit" (*Werke,* vol. 9, pp. 247f).
    38. Ibid., p. 279, 245.
    39. "Politik: Ein Kondensat" Fragment, *Essays,* vol. 2, p. 209.
    40. "Die Strasse," *Rettung,* December 20, 1918 (*Werke,* vol. 10, pp. 257–60); see also Lützeler, *Hermann Broch,* pp. 73f: Broch seems to have observed the crowds demonstrating on November 12, 1918, from a considerable distance.
    41. *Politische Schriften,* ed. Paul M. Lützeler (Frankfurt: Suhrkamp, 1978), vol. 11, p. 11.
    42. *Werke,* vol. 9, p. 301.
    43. References are to Alfred Döblin, *Ausgewählte Werke in Einzelbänden,* ed. Walter Muschg and Heinz Graber (Olten and Freiburg: Walter, 1961ff) (*AW*); unless stated otherwise translations are mine. In autobiographical notes Döblin remarked repeatedly that he combined psychiatry and internal medicine because in dealing with mental illness he had found psychoanalysis an insufficient tool (*Autobiographische Schriften,* in *AW* [1980], vol. 19, p. 25).
    44. Döblin to Mauthner, October 24, 1903, *Briefe,* in *AW* (1970), vol. 13, p. 21. Nothing is known of Mauthner's reaction, but he continued to be important for Döblin who twenty years later paid hommage to the outsider philosopher in one of his pointed, often satirical commentaries on current events which he published between June 1919 and May 1921 in Fischer's respected *Neue Rundschau* under the pseudonym Linke Poot. At that time personal contact was established. These commentaries were collected in the 1921 *Der deutsche Maskenball;* Tucholsky admired them for a new kind of wit successful in dealing with extremely difficult polarized political developments. Döblin's decision to join the SPD in 1921 marks the end of his active involvement in political journalism. His tendency to say yes *and* no to the more radical utopian and authoritarian trends on the left is clear from the beginning.
    45. See his letter to the publisher Axel Juncker, April 9, 1904, *Briefe,* p. 23.
    46. See Döblin on his experiences as a young intern in *Autobiographische Schriften,* p. 26. His descriptions of severely disturbed individual and social behavior are informed by his extensive clinical experiences; see Harald Neumann, *Leben, Wissenschaftliche Studien, Krankheiten und Tod Alfred Döblins* (St. Michael: Blaeschke, 1982), pp. 58ff.
    47. "Erster Rückblick," *Autobiographische Schriften,* pp. 39ff.
    48. Klaus Schröter, *Döblin* (Reinbek by Hamburg: Rowohlt, 1978; Rowohlts Monographien), p. 7. The year of his centenary, 1978, saw many publications on Döblin, among them the excellent catalogue of the Döblin exhibition of the Marbach Deutsches Literaturarchiv, arranged and edited by Jochen Meyer and Ute Droste, *Alfred Döblin 1878–1978* (Munich: Küsel, 1978). Among the many celebratory publications Schröter's very critical analysis would be a welcome change were it not for its compulsive judgmental attitude and conceptual simple-mindedness: Döblin, for him, is the archetypical *Kleinbürger* who has retreated from (the correct) politics on the extreme left and writes from the position of a decidedly false consciousness. Winfried Georg Sebald, *Der Mythos der Zerstörung im Werk Döblins* (Stuttgart: Klett, 1980), following Schröter, accuses Döblin of having committed every imaginable intellectual crime: regression, protofascism, repression, aggressivity, all associated with the petty bourgeois. He does make some valid observations on the sometimes problematic (but not in terms of *kleinbürgerlich*) imagery. But all he has to say is entirely predictable because he does not consider narrative strategies and so misses all the more complex problems in the Berlin novel which is the only text he likes to a degree. For intelligent helpful discussions of narrative strategies see Otto Keller, *Döblins Montageroman als Epos der Moderne* (Munich: Fink, 1980).
    49. "Futuristische Worttechnik. Offener Brief an F. T. Marinetti," *Aufsätze zur Literatur,* in *AW* (1963), vol. 8, pp. 9–15.

50. "Autobiographische Skizze," *Autobiographische Schriften*, p. 20; "Arzt und Dichter," ibid., p. 26.

51. "Autobiographische Skizze," pp. 20f.

52. Ibid., p. 21.

53. "Futuristische Worttechnik," p. 15. See Judith Ryan, "From Futurism to 'Döblinism,'" *German Quarterly* 54 (1981): 415–26.

54. "Berliner Programm," *Aufsätze zur Literatur*, p. 16.

55. Ibid., pp. 17ff.

56. See his 1917 essay "Bemerkungen zum Roman," *Aufsätze zur Literatur*, pp. 19–23. This is an aspect of "Döblinism" neglected in Ryan's useful piece "From Futurism to 'Döblinism' "; her analysis of the development of perspectivist complexity in narration culminating in *Berlin Alexanderplatz* remains too narrowly technical (see pp. 419ff). In his 1928 lecture "Der Bau des epischen Werks" (*Aufsätze zur Literatur*, pp. 103–32) Döblin speaks about his marvelous, crazy, confusing discovery—he is clearly referring to the Berlin novel—of the "Ich selbst," the presence of the self of the author in the epic work, the novel: no longer distant, the author has to "jump" into the epic world and he has to participate in the chaotic lives of the characters he created (p. 114). Having taken the risk of experience he has to take the risk of creating out of this experience.

57. "Reform des Romans," *Aufsätze zur Literatur*, pp. 43f.

58. Ibid., pp. 35, 41. There are no essayistic, "philosophical" passages in *Berlin Alexanderplatz*.

59. "Der Geist des naturalistischen Zeitalters," *Aufsätze zur Literatur*, pp. 66ff.

60. Ibid., pp. 70ff; "Das Kollektivwesen Mensch stellt als Ganzes erst die überlegene Art Mensch dar" (p. 73).

61. Ibid., pp. 72ff.

62. Ibid., pp. 78f.

63. Ibid., p. 81.

64. Ibid., p. 83.

65. See his account of the experience in his *Reise in Polen* (Berlin: S. Fischer, 1926), *AW* (1968), vol. 12, pp. 239f, 247, 261; and his postwar intensely religious autobiographical text *Schicksalsreise Bericht und Bekenntnis* (Frankfurt: Josef Knecht, 1949), *AW* (1980), vol. 19, pp. 186ff ("Das Kruzifix") and pp. 244ff.

66. Döblin had not been interested in Jewish history and tradition before the midtwenties. In *Schicksalsreise* he remembers seeing his mother reading in Hebrew books, but this was the extent of his awareness. As an adolescent and young man he was mainly influenced by Kleist and Hölderlin, Dostoievski and Nietzsche. In the early twenties he took an anti-Zionist position because of the movement's racist implications. See his essay "Zion and Europa," *Der neue Merkur* 5 (August 1921): 338–42. His reservations regarding certain aspects of Zionism were not dispelled by the Polish experience: see "Wie lange noch Jüdisches Volk-Nichtvolk," in *Unser Dasein* (Berlin: Fischer, 1933), *AW* (1964), vol. 9, pp. 355–413.

67. Alfred Döblin, "Ostjüdische Erzähler," *Vossische Zeitung*, August 24, 1924; for the library receipts see *Alfred Döblin 1878–1978*, pp. 365f.

68. *Reise in Polen*, in *AW*, vol. 12, pp. 256, 326ff. Döblin collected a large number of postcards with Jewish motifs on this trip. To his son Wolfgang he sent a postcard with the picture of the famous Gothic church St. Mary's in Krakow where he had had his original conversion experience.

69. Sept. 18, 1932, *Briefe*, in *AW*, vol. 13, p. 166.

70. See Musil's sympathetic and critical review in *Berliner Tageblatt* 56, no. 271 (June 10, 1927), pp. 2f; *Alfred Döblin 1878–1978*, pp. 194ff. Musil does not accept Döblin's nebulous concept of the epic as the contemporary fictional mode, but he does point out the risks Döblin took with this enterprise and the possibly rejuvenating

power, for the contemporary novel, of his particular prose style.

71. *Der Lesezirkel,* vol. 19, no. 5 (1932): 70–71, now in Matthias Prangel, ed. *Materialien zu Alfred Döblin's 'Berlin Alexanderplatz'* (Frankfurt: Suhrkamp, 1975), pp. 43f.

72. Prangel, p. 43.

73. "Epilog" (1948), *Autobiographische Schriften,* in *AW,* vol. 19, p. 445.

74. Ibid.; approximately, "the story of one Franz Biberkopf."

75. *Alexanderplatz Berlin: The Story of Franz Biberkopf,* trans. Eugene Jolas (New York: Ungar, 1976), p. 633; references are to this edition.

76. Walter Benjamin, "Krisis des Romans Zu Döblins 'Berlin Alexanderplatz,' " *Die Gesellschaft* 7 (1930): 562–66; now in Prangel, p. 109. On the whole Benjamin's reviews, written largely to earn money, are much less opaque than what he considered his serious texts, but here he is sufficiently involved to attempt a more permanent statement and so the passages in which he compares the epic and the novel theoretically and discusses the application of such comparison to Döblin's work are quite impenetrable and very difficult to translate.

77. "Nun ist es wahr, dass selten auf diese Weise erzählt wurde, so hohe Wellen von Ereignis und Reflex haben selten die Gemütlichkeit des Lesers in Frage gestellt, so hat die Gischt der wirklichen gesprochenen Sprache ihn noch nie bis auf die Knochen durchnässt" (Prangel, p. 110). The metaphor nicely expresses Benjamin's appreciation for Döblin's skillful recording and arranging of contemporary speech. The reader's coziness was indeed disturbed: see the discussion of letters sent to the editor of *Frankfurter Zeitung* (Prangel, pp. 60f). In this context the American reviews of the excellent translation of the novel by Eugene Jolas (Viking, 1931) are instructive too: the "color, the cruelty, the breadth of the novel, its speeding, swirling creation of a chaotically moving savagery, the passionate rhythm of the underworld" are seen by some reviewers to form meaningful patterns, by others to just repeat the chaos, and they tend to be disturbed by Döblin's focus on the sordid side of humanity (Prangel, pp. 114ff).

78. *Alexanderplatz Berlin,* pp. 632f.

79. See, e.g., *Alexanderplatz Berlin,* pp. 82ff (Franz talking to the newspaper vendor about sex education), pp. 100ff (Franz getting involved in a political dispute in a bar; political affiliations are based on present and past personal experience and needs).

80. For a short introduction in English to Döblin's political attitudes and activities see Reinhard Alter, "Alfred Döblin's Republicanism 1918–1933," *German Life and Letters* 35 (1981): 47–57. Döblin, when elected to the *Sektion für Dichtung* of the *Preussische Akademie der Künste* in January 1928 with strong reservations voiced by the right, the left, and the center (Thomas Mann), took a stand against aggressive völkisch as well as Moscow-controlled Communist interests in cultural politics, and this position caused the unanimous and uniform damnation of the Berlin novel by the radical left (see the articles in *Linkskurve* 1929 and 1930; in Prangel, pp. 86ff). Communist writers had founded in October 1928 the *Bund proletarisch-revolutionärer Schriftsteller* (BPRS) after the demise of Gruppe 25 with its wide spectrum of Marxist and liberal writers like Döblin, Musil, Brecht (Brecht admired Döblin and his theory of an epic theater was influenced by the older friend), Johannes R. Becher, Ernst Bloch, Tucholsky, Max Brod, Willy Haas. The BPRS blamed the demise of Gruppe 25 on Döblin and when Döblin defended his novel against their attacks ("Katastrophe in einer Linkskurve," *Das Tagebuch,* May 3, 1930), they protested against a Moscow publisher's *(Fabrika)* plans to come out with a Russian translation of the novel: "A writer who insults German proletarian literature with such impunity is not entitled to an audience of workers of the Soviet Union" (*Linkskurve,* vol. 2, no. 10 (1930): 36). However, Gruppe 25 (as happened ten years later to the 1935 antifascist

Volksfront) had been torn by conflict from the moment of its inception: see the articles published between 1925 and 1928 in the Communist *Rote Fahne* and the leftish-liberal *Literarische Welt:* from the beginning, the radical left attacked all non-party-line literature as destructively, decadently bourgeois, claiming to be the only intellectual vanguard with a historical mission, and they did so in terms which are remarkably similar to those used by the radical right claiming a higher mission of blood and soil and the preservation of the organic whole of the *Volk.* Willy Haas in his *Literarische Welt* lamented the Communists' "proletarische Literaturdiktatur" (December 1926) but he also attacked the republic's Academy of Arts and Sciences for being too upper-middle-class censorious, calling for a third position of "bürgerlicher Radikalismus." In this article Haas recommends emphatically Döblin's academy nomination. Significantly, Thomas Mann's difficulties with Döblin had been caused by Döblin's "social person" ("seine gesellschaftliche Person"), i.e., his cultural politics on the left, not his works. Döblin had been a leader in Gruppe 25, and he assumed leadership in the academy with his taking a strong position against censorship of any kind and against falsification of cultural and political history in literary anthologies and history books across the ideological spectrum (See Inge Jens, *Dichter zwischen links und rechts. Die Geschichte der Sektion für Dichtkunst der Preussischen Akademie der Künste dargestellt nach den Dokumenten* [Munich, 1971], pp. 134, 287). He did try to steer a liberal middle course, that of "bürgerlicher Radikalismus" (in a letter to Johannes R. Becher, Sept. 10, 1956, he writes, on the occasion of Brecht's death, remembering Gruppe 25 as "eine kleine Linksradikale Gruppe," *Briefe,* in *AW,* vol. 13, p. 476). Chiding the intellectuals for their easy appropriation of *Geist* as escape mechanism, however, he is himself rather skeptical about the intellectuals' relation to power: especially that of the state. "Wir stehen der Staatsmacht gegenüber und wir stehen vor der schwierigen Frage, wieweit wollen wir auch Macht sein?"—the age-old German problem of the intellectuals' fear of contamination by power through involvement and their passivity when faced with its ascendency. Döblin makes this statement in the context of protesting strenuously Heinrich Mann's resignation, under heavy political pressure, from the academy on February 15, 1933 (Jens, p. 184).

81. See the structurally important Job scene: "That's it, Job, that's what you suffer from most. You do not like to be weak, you would like to be able to resist, or rather be full of holes, your brain gone, your thoughts gone, and then become like a beast of the field. Make a wish" (p. 186). It is the same narrating voice which speaks to Franz, and the link between Job and Franz is quite obvious. Whether or not this scene is intended to be read as a foreshadowing: Franz II in some ways answers the wish described here, because Franz I had not relinquished his pride in his strength willingly. See also Franz being prepared for rebirth by Death accompanied by the narrating voice: "(Guilty, guilty, guilty, ah, that's it, you have to be, you had to be guilty, you ought to be guilty a thousand times more!) Such a deed is punished harshly, custom, morals have this meaning, to a cell within the prison back he wandered, sadly keening. (Franz, hallelujah, you can hear it, doomed to be a thousand times more guilty, a thousand times more guilty)" (p. 560).

82. See for instance pp. 358ff: Franz observes Mieze in front of Aschinger's; this passage has frequently been pointed out as characteristic of the influence of filmic techniques on Döblin's narration. See also pp. 234ff: Franz sees Reinhold for the first time in a bar; the description of the visual-emotional impression is extraordinarily vivid.

83. Prangel, p. 114.

84. "Epilog", in *AW,* vol. 19, p. 445; Döblin wrote a radio play based on *Berlin Alexanderplatz,* broadcast Sept. 30, 1930: the title is *Die Geschichte vom Franz Biberkopf* and the actor was, as in the 1931 movie *Berlin Alexanderplatz,* the powerful

Heinrich George. The scenes reflect events important to the plot as Franz's story (Franz and Reinhold, the burglary, the escape in the car and Franz's loss of his arm, Franz and Mieze) and, in addition, the Job passages.

85. "Epilog", in *AW*, vol. 19, p. 445; the qualification (der "gute" Franz Biberkopf) is Döblin's.

86. This passage is taken from an epilogue to a 1955 edition of the novel, Prangel, p. 46.

87. Ibid., p. 47.

88. It is significant, however, that even in hindsight he stresses the silence of Franz's sacrifice: "Das Opfer ist lautlos vollzogen." This refers to Franz's working as an assistant doorman, cautiously watching life go by his door (Prangel, p. 47). The voices of Berlin, however, continue noisily and forcefully.

89. Reinhold's latent homosexuality, the source of his pathological need to prove himself as a superman by possessing all women, be it, as in Mieze's case, by murdering them, is clearly revealed only toward the end of the novel when Reinhold falls in love with a young man in prison (pp. 578ff). Franz II's testimony at the murder trial denies the complexity of their relationship; the fascination, the bondage is dissolved: they were good friends, he testifies, but Reinhold had "a terrible abnormal craving for women, that's how it came about. Whether Reinhold has predispositions to sadism, he doesn't know. He suspects that Mieze resisted Reinhold in Freienwalde, so he did it in a fit of rage" (p. 630).

90. *Alexanderplatz Berlin*, pp. 459ff.

91. Ibid., pp. 17ff.

92. Ibid., p. 549.

93. Ibid., p. 593.

94. Ibid., p. 599.

95. Ibid., pp. 609ff.

96. Ibid., p. 619.

97. Ibid., pp. 625–29.

98. Willy Haas in a long interesting review of the novel for *Neue Rundschau* 40 (1929): 835–43 (Prangel, pp. 78–86), sees the end as life affirming: it is the gigantic, measureless, howling, laughing, etc., life itself which, overcoming death, embraces Franz II. Haas stresses the novel's epic breadth and energy and its dynamic anti-intellectuality (Prangel, p. 80). True, it is only from hindsight that the march into war suggests itself so strongly, but the expectation of a violent end to Weimar cultural and political chaos during the last years of the republic was pervasive and powerful. It is interesting that Haas did not pick up certain (almost) unmistakable resonances in the novel. He also does not wish to see the diminished state of Franz II: Biberkopf "dies; and another, bright, thoughtful, social Biberkopf wakes up and goes on living" (Prangel, pp. 85f).

99. See "Mein Buch 'Berlin Alexanderplatz,'" *Der Lesezirkel:* 19 (1932): 70–71. (Prangel, pp. 43–45), where Döblin stresses his extensive and intimate experience of social life around Alexanderplatz. See also his " 'Ulysses' von Joyce," *Das deutsche Buch* 8 (1928): 84–86 (Prangel, pp. 49–52). Many of the critics had assumed a strong Joyce influence on *Berlin Alexanderplatz:* see Ingrid Schuster and Ingrid Bode, *Alfred Döblin im Spiegel der zeitgenössischen Kritik* (Bern and Munich: Francke, 1973), pp. 207ff. Döblin had, from the very beginning, rejected this assumption and had repeatedly complained that it lingered on in critics' analyses of the novel. In this context he pointed out his own 1918 novel *Wallenstein* which, if one wanted to use this term, had used Joycian techniques before Joyce. He had read *Ulysses* with admiration when it came out in German translations (Rheinverlag) in 1927 while he was working on the Berlin novel. In his review he points out certain technical aspects which are also found in *Berlin Alexanderplatz:* "impressionistic," "pointillist," the absence of larger connecting concepts *(Zielideen)* which have been replaced by associative linkage of

many different ideas and images. Döblin stresses the experimental nature of *Ulysses*, "neither a novel nor poetry"—this echoes vaguely his (vague) concept of the epic with respect to the Berlin novel. Most important, *Ulysses* is "the most energetic attempt to deal with contemporary dailiness to date." It is essentially "biological, scientific and exact." The three protagonists are a mere structuring device for the mass of information, speculation, and fantasy which constitute almost the sum of contemporary "Natur- und Geisteswissenschaft." (Here he echoes Broch's reasons for admiring Joyce.) The book, coming from the consciousness of a *(the)* contemporary intellectual ("des heutigen geistigen Menschen") seeks to pose and answer the question: how is it possible to be a creative writer today. Every serious writer has to deal with the book, but there is no need to imitate Joyce, as the road to the modern novel is not a one-way street: Joyce's surety and decisiveness in going *his* way constitutes the model to be followed by others going *their* way.

100. *Wissen und Verändern*, in *AW*, vol. 14 (1972), pp. 131ff.
101. Ibid., pp. 142, 143, 170.
102. See above n. 80.
103. *AW*, vol. 14, p. 142.
104. Ibid., p. 190.
105. Ibid., pp. 230f.
106. Ibid., p. 241.
107. Ibid., pp. 248–53.

EPILOGUE

1. Friedrich Meinecke, *The German Catastrophe: Reflections and Recollections* (Boston: Beacon Press, 1963), chap. 15: "The areas in which we must spiritually establish ourselves again are marked out for us. These areas are the religion and the culture of the German people" (p. 112). "In order to win back a spiritual contact with the other Occidental countries," Meinecke emphasizes, in 1946, when this book came out in Germany, "the cultivation of our own peculiarly individual German spiritual life" by establishing "Goethe Communities" in "every German city and larger village" (pp. 117–21).

2. Jürgen Habermas, "Student Protest in the Federal Republic of Germany," in *Toward a Rational Society* (Boston: Beacon Press, 1971), p. 25.

3. Herbert Marcuse, *Eros and Civilization: A Philosophical Inquiry into Freud* (Boston: Beacon, 1966), pp. XXV, 150.

4. *Toward a Rational Society*, p. 26.

5. Ibid., pp. 25, 26.

6. *Eros and Civilization*, especially chaps. 3, 4, 6, 7.

7. Ibid., p. 150.

8. Jürgen Habermas, "Herbert Marcuse. Einleitung zu einer Antifestschrift," *Philosophisch-politische Profile* (Frankfurt: Suhrkamp, 1971), pp. 168f.

9. *Eros and Civilization*, p. 144.

10. Ibid., p. 211.

11. Ibid., p. 143.

12. In *Eros and Civilization*, Marcuse consistently undermines the Enlightenment aspects of Freud's late texts, and it's curious to see him attack Jung (to whose position Freud is quite close in his 1918 "From the History of an Infantile Neurosis") for his elimination of the "critical insights of Freud's metapsychology" (p. 148).

13. Habermas has, on occasion, taken a stand against certain implications of certain "postmodernist" assertions: see his "Die Moderne—ein unvollendetes Projekt," *Kleine politische Schriften* (Frankfurt: Suhrkamp, 1981), pp. 444ff, and *Theorie des kommunikativen Handelns* (Frankfurt: Suhrkamp, 1981), vol. 2, pp. 583ff. But

though he has objected to the conceptual obscurantism characteristic of the modernism/postmodernism debate, he has not been sufficiently clear in his own usage of concepts like rationality in the context of his contrasting system and life-world.

14. Jürgen Habermas, ed., *Observations on "The Spiritual Situation of the Age"* (Cambridge, Mass.: MIT Press, 1984), p. 2; *Stichworte zur "Geistigen Situation der Zeit"* (Frankfurt: Suhrkamp, 1979).

15. Ibid., pp. 2f.

16. Jürgen Habermas, "The Entwinement of Myth and Enlightenment: Re-Reading *Dialectic of Enlightenment*," *New German Critique* 26 (Spring/Summer 1982): 13–30.

17. *Observations*, p. 7.

18. Ibid., p. 19.

19. Ibid.

20. Ibid., p. 24.

21. Ibid., pp. 24f.

22. Bohrer's cultural activities include the editorship of the liberal mainstream journal *Merkur* which has become more "High Culture" under his guidance.

23. Karl-Heinz Bohrer, "The Three Cultures," *Observations*, p. 136.

24. Ibid., p. 145.

25. Ibid., p. 136.

26. See my discussion of Bohrer's Jünger interpretation, chap. 5, n. 16.

INDEX

Lightning Source UK Ltd.
Milton Keynes UK

171382UK00001B/2/A